ERRATUM

On page 185, the second line of the penultimate paragraph should be the second line of the last paragraph.

THE ORGAN

THE ORGAN

Evolution, Principles of Construction and Use

BY

WILLIAM LESLIE SUMNER

Formerly organist at King's College, London;
. Fellow of the Institute of Musical Instrument Technology, London

MACDONALD : LONDON

First published April 1952
Second edition August 1955
Third edition (revised and enlarged) April 1962

Published by
Macdonald & Co. (Publishers), Ltd.
16 Maddox Street, W.1
Made and printed in Great Britain by
Purnell and Sons, Ltd.
Paulton (Somerset) and London

Dedication

To the memory of

MY MOTHER

WHO FIRST MADE ME INTERESTED IN THESE MATTERS

"The work and worry that fell to my lot through the practical interest I took in organ-building made me wish that I had never troubled myself about it, but if I did not give it up, the reason is that the struggle for the good organ is to me a part of the struggle for the truth."

ALBERT SCHWEITZER, 1930.

"The art of building organs has attained such heights from one year to the next that one may with reason be amazed at it. And Almighty God alone can never be given sufficient thanks for having granted to man in His mercy and great goodness such gifts as have enabled him to achieve such a perfect, one might almost say the most perfect, creation and instrument of music as is the organ in its arrangement and construction; and to play upon it with hands and with feet in such a manner that God in Heaven may be praised, His worship adorned, and man moved and inspired to Christian devotion."

MICHAEL PRAETORIUS, 1619.

PREFACE

It is nearly a century since Dr. E. F. Rimbault wrote the historical introduction to the notable work *The Organ, Its History and Construction*, the latter part of which was by Dr. E. J. Hopkins, organist of the Temple Church, London. Hopkins and Rimbault did a useful service in printing a number of records of organs, but they were unable to give an account of the evolution of the instrument from the tonal point of view in relation to the music which was played on it. It is only to be expected that the passage of nearly a hundred years would bring to light new evidence and materials for a historian of the organ.

For a period of twenty-five years the author has collected books, papers and notes concerning the development of the organ in Britain, Europe and America, and amongst other journeys, has several times repeated the tours of that greater musician, traveller and writer, Dr. Charles Burney, but with similar ideas in mind.

No doubt the ability to make and to control an organ in former times was often regarded as a secret not to be vulgarised. Consequently, and in view of its great antiquity, the history of the instrument has been entangled with all manner of tradition and romance from which it has been separated with difficulty.

The contents of this book have been selected from a large mass of material, and the author has kept in view the needs of the musician and musical historians, and he has tried to maintain a cosmopolitan outlook. Two other works on the organ are projected as by-products of the present volume. One already prepared for the press is a study of Victorian organ-building and is entitled: *The Life and Work of Henry Willis*, and the other: *Documents for a History of the Organ in Britain.*

The second section of the present work is designed to show the acoustical. mechanical and electrical principles which govern the working of the instrument and is not intended to be a working guide to organ-builders. There has been no attempt to mention every variety of device employed by all organ-builders, nor would this be possible. Nearly every organ-builder has his own modification of the basic principles of mechanical, pneumatic or electrical organ-action; and organ-building is one of the few trades in which traditional methods still prevail. It is fervently to be hoped that the ideals of craftsmanship and the individualities of artist-workers will still continue in organ-building. We live in an age when the electrical marvels of today are the museum-pieces of tomorrow. There are certain fundamental necessities in the mechanism of an organ if it is to be regarded as a satisfactory musical instrument; and in the apparatus which has been used to control the instrument it is necessary that mere ingenuity shall not displace engineering skill. The greatest organ-builders have always been engineers, acousticians, architects, skilled workers in wood, metal and other materials, and often good musicians.

The tonal resources and qualities of an organ are the most important aspect of it, and, strange though it may seem, this is sometimes overlooked. The most perfect mechanisms in the world, actuated from an elaborate console of advanced design, do not make an organ, which is only a machine up to its pipe-feet. The author has dealt with certain principles of tonal design and tonal quality which he believes to be fundamental to the nature of the organ as a musical instrument.

The short section on the use of the instrument is not intended to be an organ-playing primer, but it would be a soulless matter to deal with the organ merely in terms of wood, metal, ivory, wires and magnets. The instrument is not an end in itself, and even the most beautiful combinations of tones must be regarded merely as media for musical expression. The author has met many of the leading performers of the century in many lands and is grateful for their kindness and help. Organists are a patient and hospitable brotherhood.

Organ-playing is neither a lost art nor an esoteric cult. In the Christian civilisation it now has more exponents with a high level of skill than at any time in history.

It is impossible to give a complete list of those to whom I am indebted. I owe much to many librarians in various parts of Britain and Europe, to cathedral and church authorities, the heads of organ-building firms, and authorities in many parts of the world. In particular I have to express thanks to Dr. Paul Rubardt of Leipzig; Dr. M. A. Vente of Zwolle; Dr. Christhard Mahrenholz of Hanover; Dr. Norbert Dufourcq, Professor of the History of Music at the Conservatoire of Music, Paris; Henry Willis and Aubrey Thompson-Allen of the firm of Henry Willis and Sons; John Compton; C. T. L. Harrison of Durham; and G. Donald Harrison, Director of the Aeolian-Skinner Co., U.S.A. I am grateful to the Librarian of the University, Nottingham, and his staff for their patience over many years in borrowing rare books from other libraries. I have found the notes of the late Rev. Andrew Freeman on some English organs of the seventeenth and eighteenth centuries of great value. I am grateful to Mr. Reginald Whitworth, M.B.E., and my sister, Miss Grace Sumner, for some of the diagrams. Finally, I have to thank my friend, Mr. C. S. Bayes, the Sub Librarian of the University, for kindly reading the proofs.

Nottingham, December 1951 W. L. SUMNER

PREFACE TO SECOND EDITION

DURING the preparation of this new edition I have been indebted to Dr. J. Dykes Bower, Cecil Clutton, Ralph Downes, Laurence Elvin, Rev. N. Bonavia Hunt, Thomas Stevens, Rev. B. B. Edmonds, N. P. Mander, Harold Helman, John W. Wilson, William King Covell, Dr. M. Conway, R. Spurden-Rutt, W. Shewring, C. Holt, H. F. Latham, J. R. Thornton, E. J. Barton, E. R. Tomkins.

May 1955 W. L. SUMNER

PREFACE TO THIRD EDITION

It is gratifying to the author that four printings of this book have sold in less than a decade. In this short period much of interest has happened in the organ world. Two considerable shelves of books and periodicals, devoted to the instrument, have been collected from America and Europe during that time; and the additions made in the present volume are the author's attempt to summarise the new material. Inevitably, much must be omitted from a book no larger than this. Recent years have seen in Europe a re-assessment of the aesthetic of the organ and its music; but in the post-war world the most striking features of the organ have been the remarkable developments in the North American continent. Thousands of new organs of enlightened design have provided suitable media for the performance of organ works of all types, not least those indigenous in America. Here, too, the pedagogy of the organ offers facilities unmatched elsewhere.

The author is grateful to the following (in addition to those mentioned above), who have generously given him information, illustrations or criticisms towards the preparation of the present edition: John Holmes, Marilyn Mason, Wilma Jensen, Francis Jackson, A. E. Warth, Gordon Paget, Robert Noehren, Arthur Howes, Edward Flint, Franz Sauer, Karl Benesch, Karl Bormann, Stephen Dykes Bower, Gordon Phillips, Guy Oldham, Donald Shanks, Maurer Maurer, Geraint Jones, Noel Mander, K. F. Simmons, J. E. Blanton, W. Supper, Hans Klotz, Leslie Spelman, G. J. Eltringham, D. O. Jones, Max Hinrichsen, E. A. Thompson, Lady Susi Jeans, R. Yates, Hans Klotz, Stanley Godman, E. Power Biggs, Evan Rigby, H. Stubington, Roger Yates, and the Directors of the following firms of organ builders: Aeolian Skinner of Boston, U.S.A.; Schantz of Orrville, Ohio, U.S.A.; Holtkamp of Cleveland, U.S.A.; Schlicker of Buffalo, U.S.A.; Wicks of Highland, Illinois, U.S.A.; Austin of Hartford, U.S.A.; Estey of Brattleboro', U.S.A.; Möller of Hagerstown, U.S.A.; Hillgreen Lane of Alliance, Ohio; W. H. Reisner, Hagerstown, U.S.A.; Frobenius of Lyngby, Copenhagen; Laukhuff of Weikersheim; Rieger of Schwarzach, Vlbg., Austria; Flentrop of Zaandam; Marcussen of Aabenraa; Kuhn of Mannedorf; Goll of Lucerne; Klais of Bonn; Walcker of Ludwigsburg; Casavant of St. Hyacinth, Canada; Walker of Ruislip, England; Hill, Norman and Beard, London; Rushworth and Dreaper, Liverpool; Percy Daniel of Clevedon, Somerset.

January 1962 W. L. Sumner

NOTE

ORGAN pipes are divided into two classes: (*a*) *flue* (*labial*) pipes, in which the sound, originated by a stream of air blowing over a lip, is qualified by resonance in a pipe; and (*b*) *reed* (*lingual*) pipes, in which a stream of air causes vibration in a tongue, usually of metal, and the sound is qualified by a tube. The pipes stand on a "sound-board" or on top of a "wind-chest", and the valves which let air into the pipes or the channels over which pipes are standing are known as *pallets* (in all but *some* instruments made in the nineteenth and twentieth centuries).

Notation and Pitch

The frequencies of vibration given in this illustration have been used because they are convenient multiples of two (International standard pitch is a′ = 440).

Note that organ-builders sometimes use B instead of B♭ and ♮ instead of B. (Hence B. A. C. H. = B♭. A. C. B.)

Organ-builders have not yet been converted to the more convenient Helmholtz pitch-notation, but it is usually possible to find the notes which they intend by reference to the context. Organ-builders' 8-ft. C [CC], 4-ft. or tenor C [C], 2-ft. or middle C are given respectively by Helmholtz as C, c, c′ and so on. It should be pointed out that historically in England the octave often began at G, e.g. GGG was *below* CCC.

Pitch has been referred to vibration numbers (i.e. complete cycles) per second, written as c.p.s. When small relative pitches have been considered each semitone is divided into a hundred parts: each is called a *cent*.

CONTENTS

SECTION 3

LIST OF PLATES

SECTION 1

CHAPTER I

THE ORGAN OF THE ANCIENTS

It is a source of perpetual wonder that the highly complex organisms of the animal and vegetable kingdoms have grown from tiny fertilised cells. It is a far cry from the largest and most complicated of all modern musical instruments to its origin in the simple pipes of Pan made from reeds growing by the water-side.

The simple and rude ancestors of the organ were made by man before the dawn of recorded history. The syrinx and pan-pipes figure in mythology. Add a box or chest on which to plant these pipes, and sliders or other devices to control the supply of wind to each pipe, and we have the germ of the organ. Instead of human lungs to supply air to the pipe-chest, let us imagine the substitution of the skin of an animal from which air could be squeezed into the chest, and we have an instrument which contains the three essential features of the modern instrument: a wind supply; a wind-chest with holes which can be opened or closed by valves; and pipes planted over these holes. Clearly the early organ is a near relation of the bagpipes.

The word "organ" (ugab) as used in the Psalms and elsewhere in the Old Testament does not necessarily refer to an instrument which had the three distinguishing features[1] which we have just mentioned. The Greek translations and Greek usage in general apply the word indiscriminately to any instrument of music and indeed to other mechanical devices and the human voice. Plato calls the stars "the organs of time" and talks about the "sense-organs" as we do today.

[1] Ugab. Gen. iv. 21; Ps. cl; Ps. cxxxvii: "As for our *harps*, we hanged them up upon the trees that are therein." Ugab probably referred to a large syrinx.

The Vulgate ugab=organum may have been used for stringed instruments as well as for pipes. References are found in Cato, 77, 9; Lucretius, 3, 132; Firmicus, 3, 4; and St. Augustine in his Commentary on Psalm lvi, 16 (fifth century), in which he says: "All musical instruments are called *organ*. Not only that is called *organ* which is blown by bellows, but also whatever is fit for music and has a bodily form (i.e. not the human voice)."

Cassiodorus, who was consul of Rome under King Vitigas the Goth in 541, described the organ of the time as an instrument composed of divers pipes formed into a kind of tower which by means of bellows is made to produce a grand sound. (Commentary on Ps. 150.)

Until the time of Milton the English word organ was often used to denote a single pipe or other musical instrument. Shakespeare writes in *Hamlet*, III, ii, 385 (A.D. 1602):

> "Will you play upon this little Pipe,
> There is much Musicke, excellent Voice in this little Organe."

And Milton writes in *Paradise Lost*, vii, line 596:

> "The Harp, the Solemn Pipe,
> And Dulcimer, all organs of sweet stop."

The Cheng,[1] which has been used in China for more than five thousand years, shows some of the features of a primitive organ. Hollow reeds are arranged on a wind-chest in the form of a bowl. Air is drawn from or blown into this by means of a mouthpiece. A pipe will sound only when a hole at the base is stopped with the fingers.

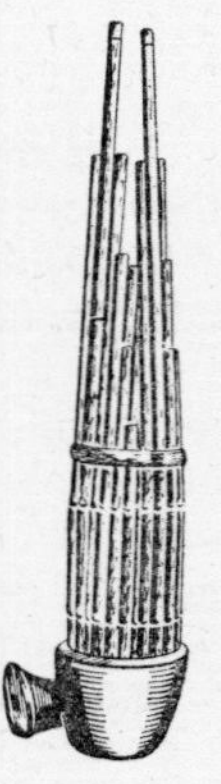

FIG. 1A. A Cheng or Sheng.

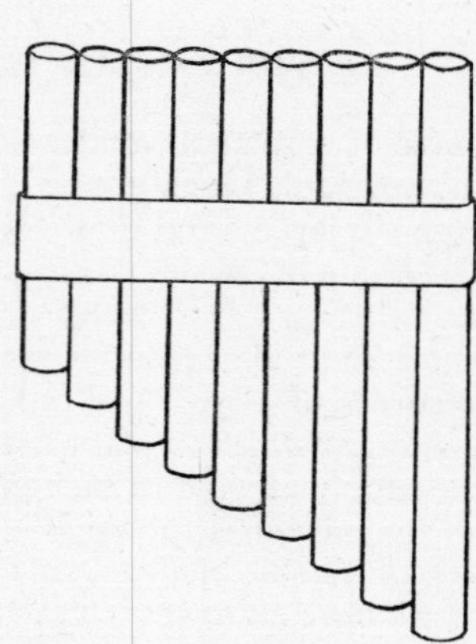

FIG. 1B. Panpipes or Syrinx.

The old Greek shepherds made pan-pipes with seven or eight strong reeds fastened together with wax or tied with thongs. Virgil describes such an instrument with twelve pipes, and Lucretius gives an account of its use in his Book V.[2]

About the year 265 B.C., in the reign of Ptolemy II Euergetes, there lived in Alexandria an engineer called Ctesibius, who invented or improved the water organ (hydraulis, hydraulus, hydraule). "And this organ is like a round altar; and they say that it was invented by Ctesibius the barber who dwelt at the time in the territory of Aspendor during the reign of Ptolemy II Euergetes. They say also that he was a very eminent man and learnt a good deal from his wife, Thaïs."[3] The Roman architect Vitruvius writes: "Ctesibius was born at Alexandria, his father being a barber. He was ingenious, and withal exceedingly industrious, and his hobby was said to be inventing."[4] Vitruvius says that Ctesibius obtained the germ of the idea for his hydraulic organ by observing a counterpoise weight for a mirror in his father's shop. The hidden weight worked up and down in a closed cylindrical tube, and so close was the fit that sometimes the air was compressed and, forcing its way past the weight,

[1] Cheng or Sheng. This was a precursor of the harmonium. Each pipe is fitted with a small brass reed. The "wind-chest" is a gourd, calabash or bowl of wood. R. Lachmann, *Musik des Orients* (1929).

[2] J. Tregenna, *The Pipes of Pan*, London (1926).

[3] Athenaeos, *Deipnosophistae*, iv, 174c. K. Schlesinger in *The Greek Aulos*, has pointed out that the aulos was usually a reed pipe and not a flute.

[4] Pliny the Elder (*c*. A.D. 79), in his *Encyclopædia of Natural History*, also mentions that Ctesibius lived in the time of Ptolemy II.

produced a clear note. "When, therefore, Ctesibius observed that sounds were generated from the effect of the hollow tube and expulsion of the air, he first made use of that principle in devising hydraulic organs."[1] Here is a translation of an account of the hydraulus given by Vitruvius in *De Architectura*, chap. xiii, Bk. 10.

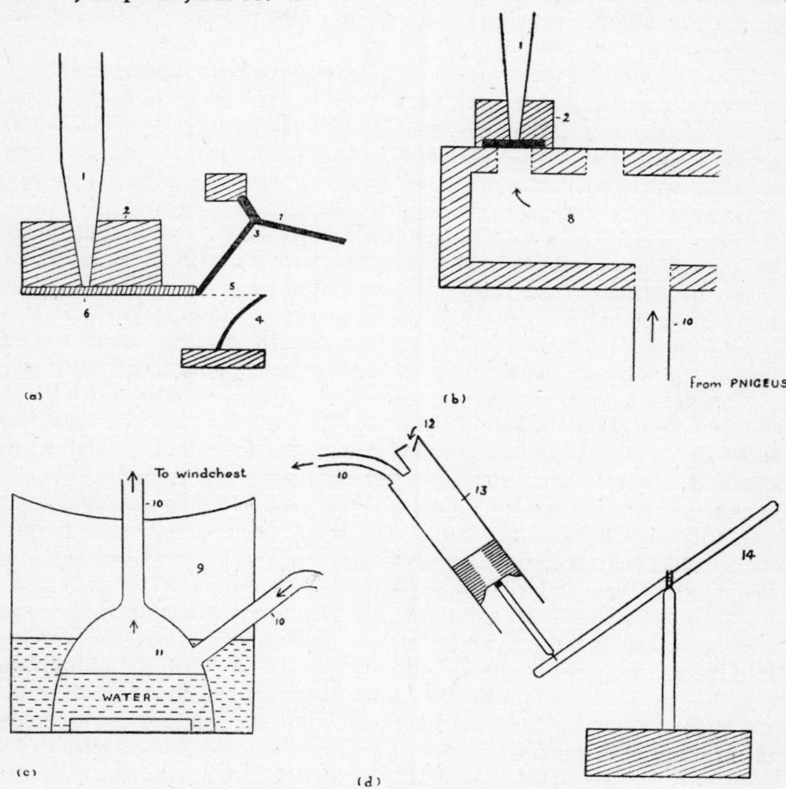

FIG. 2. A, B, C, D, Details of the Water Organ.
1. Aulos. 2. Glossokomon. 3. Ankoniskos trikolos. 4. Spathia.[2] 5. Neura. 6. Poma. 7. Perone. 8. Solen plagios. 9. Bomiskos. 10. Solen. 11. Pnigeus. 12. Platusmation. 13. Pyris. 14. Emboleus. The Slider 6 is perforated.
The wind pressure could be altered by varying the amount of water.

"I must not omit to explain as briefly and explicitly as I can the principles on which hydraulic organs are constructed. A base of wood is prepared, and on it a brazen cistern mounted. On the base to left and to right are erected uprights with ladder-like struts to hold them together. Between these are enclosed brazen cylinders, with movable pistons turned perfectly true, packed with unshorn sheepskins and having bent irons fixed to the centres, which are joined by pins to levers.

[1] Vitruvius op. cit. ix. 8. [2] A spring made of horn.

"There are also on the upper surface (of the cylinders) posts of about three inches diameter, close to which are fixed on pivots brazen dolphins with cymbals hanging by chains from their mouths below the posts in the cylinder. Within the cistern that contains water is the pnigeus[1] resembling an inverted funnel, and under it blocks about three inches high serve to keep a level distance between the lower lips of the pnigeus and the bottom of the cistern.

"Over the neck of the former a chest framed together supports the head of the instrument, which in Greek is termed the *canon musicus*,[2] and in which are longitudinal channels: four in number if the organ be tetrachordal, six if hexachordal, and eight if octochordal. In the several channels are fitted valves connected with iron winches. When the latter are turned, orifices are opened from the chest to the channel.

"The *canon* has also holes ranged transversely leading from the channels and coincident with the holes in the upper board, which in Greek is termed *pinax*. Between this board and the *canon* slides with corresponding perforations are inserted and treated with oil to ensure easy movement to and fro in closing the holes. They are called *pleuritides*, and the passing backwards and forwards of them alternately opens and shuts off communication to the pipes.

"These slides have iron springs affixed and united to keys which when touched control the motion of the slides. In the table are holes that lead direct from the channels and allow passage to the wind. To laths are cemented rings in which stand the feet of all the organ pipes. From the cylinders trunks are directly united with the neck of the *pnigeus*, and communicate with the apertures in the wind-chest. Well-turned valves fit into these trunks, and when the wind-chest is charged with compressed air close the mouth of them and will not allow the air to return.

"Thus, when the levers are raised, the pistons are drawn to the bottom of the cylinders, and the dolphins[3] rocking on their pivots lower the cymbals into them, and thus fill with air the cavities thereof. Then the pistons are raised again in the cylinders with rapid, vigorous movements, and cause the cymbal-valves to close the inlet posts. So the confined air is forced under pressure through the trunks, flows into the *pnigeus* and thence by its neck into the wind-chest. But with a more vigorous movement of the levers violently compressing the air, it rushes through the stop-apertures and fills the channels with wind.

"The keys, therefore, when touched by hand, thrust forward and draw back the registers, alternately closing and opening the holes. Thus are produced melodies of infinite variety according to the rules of the Art of Music. I have endeavoured to set forth as clearly as I could in writing an explanation of this intricate machine. But it has been no easy subject to treat of; nor, perhaps, shall I be intelligible save to those who are versed in matters of this sort. But however little some may have understood it from my description, when they see the actual instrument they will find it an ingenious piece of mechanism as a whole."

[1] The funnel- or dome-shaped air reservoir. (See figure 2c.) [2] The sound-board.
[3] Delphini—miniature "see-saws", representing dolphins sporting.

It would be difficult to construct a hydraulic organ by sole reference to the account of Vitruvius, and in particular this writer does not explain the reason for using water! (As his account was the only one which was known to Western writers on the organ, many curious theories concerning the action of this instrument have come down to us. Dom Bédos de Celles[1] in his monumental work on organ-building writes that the hydraulic organ is a mystery. Other writers have even suggested that the pipes were blown and sounded by water.)

Philon[2] describes the water organ as "the syrinx played with the hand which is called the hydraulis, the bellows forced the wind into an oven (*pnigeus*) of bronze, which was in the water". His *Pneumatics*, which has survived in the Arabic version called the *kitāb fi'l-hiyah al-rūhāniȳha*, gives accounts of the cylindrical piston for blowing and also a collapsible cylindrical bellows such as was used by the goldsmiths at an earlier date.

References[3] to the water organ are frequent in classical literature, and here are some examples:

> "Come hither, all ye drinkers of sheer wine,
> Come and within this shrine behold the rhytum,[4]
> The cup of fair Arsinoë. Zephyritis,
> The true Egyptian Besa that pours forth
> Shrill sounds, what time its stream is opened wide—
> No sound of war: but from its golden mouth
> It gives a signal for delight and feasting,
> Such as the Nile, King of flowing rivers,
> Pours as its melody from its holy shrines
> Dear to the priests of sacred mysteries.
> But honour this invention of Ctesibius,
> And come, ye swains, to fair Arsinoë's shrine."[5]

[1] *L'Art du Facteur d'Orgues* (Paris 1766–78).

[2] Carra de Vaux, *Philon de Byzance*, 223.

[3] References to the hydraulic organ in Greek and Roman literature occur in: Vitruvius: *De Architectura*, x, 13; Cicero: *Tusc. Ep.*, iii. 18; Pliny: *Nat. Hist.*, vii, 38; ix, 8 : 1; Heron: *Works*, 42; Suetonius: *Nero*, 41 and 54. Nikomachus: *Meibom*, 8; Julius: *Pollux*, iv, 70; Tertullian: *De Anima*, xiv; Athenæos: iv, 75.

Vitruvius, Philon and Hero (or Heron) all wrote about the hydraulus, and it is necessary to consider their statements in terms of their (supposed) dates. Baron Carra de Vaux, Paul Tannery and Sir Thomas L. Heath conclude that Philon lived at the end of the second century B.C., Vitruvius, first century A.D. and Heron third century A.D. Heron has sometimes been described as a pupil of Ctesibius, but in view of the possible gap of five centuries this needs qualification! Neugebauer gives Heron's date as *c.* A.D. 62 and on his evidence this seems the most likely.

It is probable that the instrument of Ctesibius was merely a single horn (rhytum) attached to the top of the pnigeus (air-pressure chamber) and sounded continuously so long as wind was supplied to it. This was the primitive machine which was carried into battle to frighten the enemy.

"The Greeks used to employ it in the wars, in order to terrify the souls of the enemy. And they stopped their own ears when they used it and played it." (*Kitāb Khwān al-Sāfa*, 1, 92; edit. *Ahmad ibn Abdallāh*, 4 vols., Bombay, 1887–9.)

[4] A large drinking horn.

[5] By Hedylus, librarian to Ptolemy Euergetes and rival of Callimachus, court poet, quoted in *Deipnosophistæ*.

"For upon the Pan-pipes played with the hands, which we call the hydraule, the type of bellows that sends wind to the reservoir in the water is of bronze" (Philon).

" . . . the dolphin, a creature fond not only of man but of the musical art, is charmed by harmonious melody, and especially the sound of the hydraulus" (Pliny, *Nat. Hist.*, ix, 8 : 8).

"Hydrauli hortabere ut audiat (amicus aegrotans) voces potius quam Platonis" (If a friend is suffering from depression will you urge him to listen to a hydraulus playing rather than to Plato discoursing.—Cicero, *Tusc. Disp.*, iii, 18 : 43).

The hydraulus was improved between the time of Ctesibius and Heron, and Heron's account, which is here given, describes an instrument with a keyboard and springs for returning the sliders which open the wind-holes (Heron, *Works*, 42):

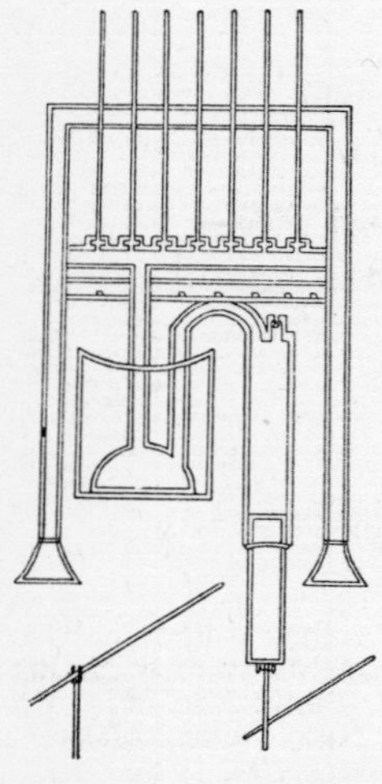

FIG. 3. The Hydraulus of Heron (Brit. Mus. MS. Harl. 5589). The seven pipes are of very small scale.

"The economy of the hydraulic organ. Let there be an altar-shaped stand of bronze containing water, and in the water a hollow hemisphere called the pnigeus, laid convexly, so as to allow the water underneath it free circulation.

"Let two pipes leading off from the top of it project above the stand, one being bent down outside the stand and communicating with the cylinder-box of the force pump that has its opening on the underside and its internal surface finished smooth and true to fit a plunger. Let the plunger fit truly into this box so as to prevent any air escaping past. To the plunger fix a very strong rod, and to this attach another rod rocking on a fulcrum-pin set in it. Let this rod swing up and down upon a firmly erected upright.

"On the inverted bottom of the box, another and smaller box opening into the larger is placed. It is also covered, and has a hole in its upper part through which the air from without may enter the larger box. Below this hole, let there be a thin plate to close it, supported by pins with heads (to prevent the plate falling off) passing through holes made in it. This plate is called *platusmation.*

"The other tube, from the top of the pnigeus, must extend to a transverse channel (in the wind-chest) through which air passes to the organ pipes planted above. These have in their extremities *glossokoma*, or key-boxes. The footholes are left open.

"Now, across these footholes work sliding lids, properly perforated, so that, on the lids being thrust home, the orifices in them coincide with the footholes of the pipes; but when drawn out they miss the others and close the air-way to the pipes. If, therefore, the blowing-lever be depressing at its extremity, the piston will be raised and compress the air in the cylinder-box. The force of this air will shut the hole in the smaller box by acting on the above-mentioned *platusmation.* The air will now pass through tube No. 1 into the pnigeus, and from here it will fill the transverse groove in the wind-chest by tube No. 2. Lastly, from this groove it will flow into the pipes whenever the holes in the pipes and in the sliding lids respectively correspond—that is, when the lids or some of them are pushed in.

"Accordingly, if we wish any pipe to sound with the holes open, or to cease sounding with the holes closed, we must set about in this wise:

"*Key Action*

"Suppose one of the key-boxes to be isolated, mouth downward. There is also to be an organ pipe projecting through, and an accurately fitting lid, with its orifice closed to the foot-hole.

"There is also a kind of three-arm crank, of which the lower arm is to be united to the slide-lid and, jointed to the key-touch arm, to turn about a pin in the centre. Now, if with the hand we depress the end of the key-arm towards the mouth of the key-box, we shall be pushing the lid inwards, and when it is in, the hole in it will coincide with that in the pipe-foot. But to ensure that when we raise the hand, of itself the lid will return and close the air duct to the pipes, the following means are employed.

"Under the key-boxes, a rail of the same length as, and parallel to, the wind-channel is laid. Into this should be fixed horn springs, resilient and curved, one of which we will imagine to be lying over against the key-box. A sinew fastened to the tip of this spring is also secured to the extremity of the lower arm of the crank, so that when the slide-lid is pushed in from without the sinew is fastened. If, therefore, we depress the end of the key-arm and thus drive inward the slide-lid, the sinew will force the horn spring upright; but if we withdraw the hand, the spring will recoil to its original position, draw away the slide-lid from the mouth of the key-box and so cut off communication to the pipes.

"These accessories are fitted to each of the key-boxes; and when we require any of the pipes to sound, we must press down with the fingers the proper key. Conversely, to silence a pipe we must raise the fingers; whereupon, the slide lid will be drawn out and the sound cease.

"Water is poured into the stand in order that an excess of air in the *pnigeus*—I mean the air that is forced out from the cylinder-box and raises the water in the stand—may be retained there, so that the pipes shall always have a supply to cause them to speak.

"The piston being raised, as described, forces the air in the cylinder-box thence into the *pnigeus.* On its downward stroke it opens the little inlet post through which the cylinder is fed with air from outside. Again, then, the piston is thrust upwards and injects air into the *pnigeus.*

"It is better that the piston-rod should work round a centre-pin where it joins the lever, and this by means of a ring in the end of the piston-rod, through which a centre-pin (viz. the tip of the lever-rod) must pass in order that the piston may not be twisted askew but rise and fall vertically."[1]

[1] This translation was made by D. Batigan-Verne.

This account does not give us the dimensions of the instrument, nor does it tell us the compass of the keyboard and the size of the pipes, but it shows how the instrument must have been improved since the time of Vitruvius. The key action with springs is particularly noteworthy.

Hero also mentions that an organ could be blown by a water-wheel or a windmill.

When the arts and sciences were kept alive and developed in Arabia after the decay of the Roman civilisation, translations of Greek and Roman works now lost were made in Arabic, and these have survived. The Muristus[1] treatise translated by H. G. Farmer describes an organ which was fully automatic.[2] Here water was not only used for stabilising the wind-pressure but for generating the wind as well. Farmer has shown that there is no reason why the Muristus treatise should not have been written originally by Ctesibius and that the first name may really be a transcription of the latter which has suffered gradual modification. Thus, the ancients must have known three types of organs: (1) the pneumatic organ with its blast bag and unsteady wind supply; (2) the hydraulus, which was blown by hand, and in which the water was used to stabilise the wind pressure; and (3) the hydraulic organ, in which the air was generated by the gravitational effect of water.

In 1885 there was discovered at Carthage a little model of the hydraulus about seven inches high and made of baked uncoloured clay. It bears the name of its maker, Possessor, a well-known potter who lived about A.D.120.[3] This was sufficient, when taken in conjunction with the descriptions of Hero and Vitruvius, to enable a model of the instrument to be made.[4] Arguments about the nature of the instrument and many centuries of mystery concerning its action were terminated when it was established, once and for all, that at the beginning of our era and probably earlier the hydraulus was provided with a

FIG. 4. A rough idea of the Greek modes, without subtleties of intonation, may be obtained by playing, upwards on the "natural" notes of the keyboard, an octave from each note as follows:

B. Mixolydian
C. Lydian
D. Phrygian
E. Dorian
F. Hypolydian
G. Hypophrygian
A. Hypodorian

[These must not be confused with those of mediaeval times. Changes and developments, bound up with the work of the Schola Cantorum in Rome and probably originating in a misinterpretation of the Greek system, resulted in a dual system of authentic and plagal modes, from the sixth to the ninth centuries.

			Dominent	*Final*
1st Mode	Dorian	D–d	a	D
	Hypodorian	A–a	F	D
2nd Mode	Phrygian	E–e	b	E
	Hypophrygian	B–b	a	E
3rd Mode	Lydian	F–f	C	F
	Hypolydian	C–c	a	F
4th Mode	Mixolydian	G–g	d	G
	Hypomixolydian	D–d	C	G

These matters are discussed at length in *Grove's Dictionary* (Blom Edition), in articles Greek Music (Ancient) and Modes.]

[1] *Muristus San'at al-urghīn al-būgī*, Brit. Mus. MS. (Or. 9649).

[2] H. G. Farmer, *The Organ of the Ancients*, chap. vi (London, 1931).

[3] H. J. Moser (*Geschichte der Deutschen Musik*, Stuttgart, 1926, p. 59) describes the finding of a mosaic at Nennig bei Sierck on the Mosel which dated from the second century. On it was depicted a hydraulus with twelve pipes.

[4] F. W. Galpin, *The Reliquary*, 1904.

balanced keyboard and stops. The late Rev. F. W. Galpin,[1] a leading English authority on old musical instruments, made a model of the hydraulus at the beginning of the present century. Mr. Galpin concluded that the tone of the hydraulus, though effective only in melodic music, was, as Optatianus tells us, "suitable for quick measures and for song" because "the slides are made to move at the slightest touch".

A number of contorniates and medallions preserved in the British Museum show the hydraulus. One depicts Laurentius, who has been victorious in the games, standing beside his hydraulus and holding a large fan (flabellum). On the other side is a representation of Nero with the letters "Imp. Nero Caesar Aug. P."[2]

Emperors improvised on the hydraulus, and Nero was an enthusiastic player on the instrument. Wealthy men employed it to produce an accompaniment to their feasts.[3] Sidonius Apollinaris praised Theoderic II for the simplicity of his meals, adding: "There is no noise of hydraulic organ, or choir with its conductor intoning a set piece."[4] The poets mentioned it in their songs. It was used on feast days, festivals and at the games. Great skill in its use was rewarded with a crown of laurels. Other specimens of models and carvings of the hydraulus have come to light since the Carthage specimen. The Roman sarcophagus of a musician in the Museum of Arles, France, shows a hydraulus with nine pipes and two blowing cylinders. (See Plate 1.) At Naples, hydraulus fragments, dating before A.D. 97, are preserved in the museum.

The older hydraulus which was carried into battle in order to demoralise the enemy seems to have had a single horn through which air was forced under the greatest pressure which could then be raised.

For a time archaeologists ascribed the invention of the hydraulus to Archimedes because of the reference by Tertullian (*De Anima*, cap. xiv). Archimedes may have known of the invention as he was a contemporary of Ctesibius. The skill of the great Syracusan engineer in hydraulics is well-known but a careful sifting of the evidence by Sir Thomas L. Heath (*The Works of Archimedes*, Cambridge, 1897) does nothing to take the honour from Ctesibius. Here is Tertullian's over-enthusiastic reference:

"Observe the extraordinary genius of Archimedes: I refer to the water organ; so many members, so many parts, so many joinings, so many roads or passages for the voices, such a compendium of sounds, such an intercourse of modes, such troops of pipes, and all composing one great whole. The spirit or air which is breathed out from this engine of water is administered through the parts, solid in substance but divided in operation."[5]

Publilius Optatianus wrote a poem about the hydraulus *in the shape of the instrument*. The pipes are represented by twenty-six lines which increase in

[1] F. W. Galpin, *The Reliquary*, 1904.

[2] B.M. No. 1844–4–25–1312. Also *Cabinet des Médailles*, Paris.

[3] Petronius, *Satyricon*; Gaius Lucilius, *Aetna*, ii; Claudian, *Epithalamium Laurentii*.

[4] Epistolae 1, 2 (*Patr. Lat.*, lviii, 449). Unfortunately the idea still persists that noisy music (though not that of the hydraulus) is an aid to ingestion and digestion in twentieth-century public eating places!

[5] Tertullian cited by Vossius, *De Poematum* (Oxford, 1673).

length each by one letter, until the last line is double the length of the first.[1] The verses are in the form of the instrument "on which one can bring forth variegated songs, and whose sounds escape from round open pipes of brass and whose length increases regularly. Below the pipes are placed the levers by which the hand of the artist, opening or closing at will the conduits of wind, gives out a well-rhythmed, agreeable melody. Water, placed beneath the pipes and agitated by air pressure, which takes the labour and efforts of several youths, gives the necessary assorted sounds to the music. At the least movement, the levers, opening the pipes, can express rapid and vigorous songs, or a calm and simple melody, or yet again, by the power of rhythm and melody, can inspire a religious terror."[2]

Claudian (Claudius), who lived in Rome in A.D. 397, wrote a poem in which a passage refers to a performance on a hydraulus: "Let there be also one who by his light touch manages the unnumbered tongues of the field of brazen tubes, can with nimble fingers cause a mighty sound: and can rouse to song the waters stirred to their depths by the massive lever".[3]

Busby (*General History of Music*, 1819, vol. i, p. 220) gives the following translation in verse:

"With flying fingers as they lightsome bound,
From brazen tubes he draws the pealing sound,
Unnumber'd notes the captive ear surprise
And swell and thunder as his art he plies,
The beamy bar he heaves ! the waters wake!
And liquid lapses liquid music make."

It is doubtful whether the translator understood the nature of the instrument and apparently he imagines that the organist had to act as his own blower !

The number of misconceptions throughout history concerning the nature of the hydraulus is quite remarkable. As we now know how the instrument worked, there is no need to multiply instances of wrong ideas. As has been hinted already, some writers imagined that the pipes were blown with water ! The following is an example taken from Dr. Powell's *Humane Industry, or a History of Most Manual Arts* (London, 1661, p. 38): "There are in sundry places of Italy and elsewhere certain *Organa Hydraulica*, that is, organs that make good Musick of themselves, only by forcing water up the pipes, and by the collision of the Ayr and Water therein: The lower part of the pipes are placed in the water . . . which water being forced up with a scrue, or such device, doth inspire the pipes, as well as the wind that is made with a bellows." It must be remembered that until the seventeenth century work of Torricelli (1643), Boyle (1660) and Von Guericke (1672), there was no adequate conception of the physical nature of air pressure; and until the three- and four-element theories of matter were finally set at rest in the following century, it was believed that liquids agitated by boiling or by mechanical means could change into air or gases.[4]

[1] Wernsdorf, *Poetae Lat. Min.*, vol. ii, p. 394.
[2] Optatian, *Patr. Lat.*, xix, 429–430.
[3] Claudian, *Epithalamium Laurentii.*
[4] Cf. Kircher's account on p. 28 and Plate 3.

On the site of the long-ruined Roman town of Aquincum, a fortress outside Budapest, the capital of Hungary, the bronze remains of a hydraulus were unearthed in 1931. The wooden parts had been destroyed by the burning of the building which had housed the organ, but much of it had been preserved by falling into a cellar. The instrument, called a "hydra", was in use in the year A.D. 226, and was buried in the ruins for more than seventeen centuries. It is of even more value than the terra-cotta models of the hydraulic organ, for many of its pipes, its sliders and other parts of the mechanism are well-preserved. It contains four ranks of leaden pipes of different tone, with thirteen pipes to each rank. The longest pipe is 16 in. high and the shortest 1.6 in. Unfortunately it is not possible to give the exact scale of the instrument by reference to the pipe lengths. The mouthpiece of the pipe is made from a piece of wood thrust into it. There are four longitudinal "blocks", each with thirteen holes and controlled by small stop-knobs at the end of each. The keys are balanced and the notes are played by small sliders, each with four holes, which are drawn forward as the keys are depressed. The touch would be no heavier than that of a piano. This survival is quite unique and serves to verify the ideas concerning the nature and action of the hydraulus which we have had by reading the accounts in classical literature and by reference to classical models. The blowing apparatus of this instrument did not survive, but in view of the name which it bears it could hardly have been otherwise than a hydraulus or hydraulic organ. The ventils used when the stops were changed were not unlike those used in more modern organs. The small sliders with punched holes resembled Meccano strips. These were worked by the keys; they would require only a light touch of a few ounces, and the "key width" was hardly greater than that of a modern instrument.[1]

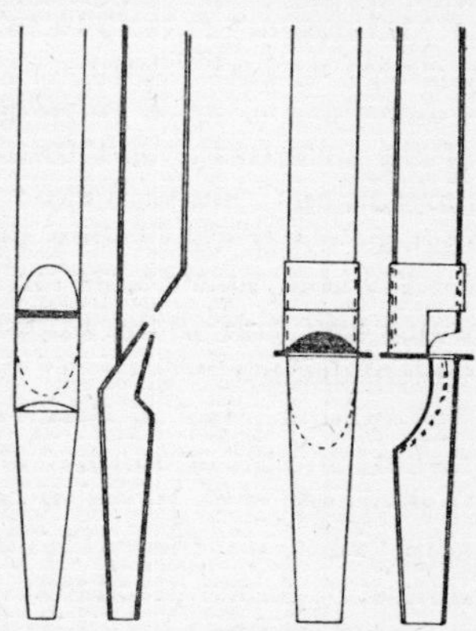

FIG. 5. Organ pipes from the Aquincum Organ, A.D. 226. Left: foot and mouth of open pipe. Right: stopped pipe.

[1] A full description of the instrument is given in Lajos Nagy, *The Organ of Aquincum* (Aquincum II Museum, Budapest, 1933) in German and Hungarian. The organ was used to accompany a singer who performed during the night to keep the firemen awake.

Further references to the Hydraulus and the Mediaeval organ:

Farmer, H. G., *A History of Arabian Music to the Thirteenth Century* (London, 1929); *Byzantine Musical Instruments in the 9th Century* (London, 1925); *The Influence of Music from Arabic Sources* (London, 1926); *The Organ of the Ancients from Eastern Sources* (London, 1931). Galpin, F. W., *Notes on a Roman Hydraulis* (The Reliquary, London, 1904). Pauly-Wissowa, article "Hydraulis" (by Tittel) in *Realenzyklopädie des klassichen Altertums*, ix (1916). Tannery, P., *L'Invention de l'hydraulus* (*Revue des études grecques*, xxi, Paris, 1908). Archimedes, *Alat al-zāmir* (Brit. Mus. MS. Or. Add. 23391). Schlesinger, K., "Researches into the Origin of the Organs of the Ancients" (in the *Sammelbände der Internationalen Musikgesellschaft*, Leipzig, 1901). Bacon, R., *Secretum secretorum*, Edit. Robert Steele, (Oxford, 1920). Bittermann, H. R., *The Organ in the Early Middle Ages*, Speculum

Isaac of Antioch, who died in 460, gives an account of the important part which the hydraulus played in the lives of the people. After this and a reference in the Talmud nothing is heard of the instrument for more than three hundred years, and then we find the Greek treatises on the sciences and arts are translated and understood by the Arabs. In spite of the fact that the hydraulus was repugnant to Judaism and Christianity, the instrument was popular until the fifth or sixth century. Farmer attributes the disuse of the hydraulus to the triumph of the barbarians, the rise of Christianity, of a puritanical Judaism and the greater simplicity in construction of the pneumatic organ. The hydraulus seemed to remind the devout Jew of the circus and the pagan orgies.[1]

A belief that organ pipes were blown by steam in early times seems to be founded on a passage written by William of Malmesbury concerning the skill of Gerbert (later Pope Sylvester II) as an organ-builder, who is said to have constructed a hydraulic organ at Rheims about the year 976, and who frequently mentions the organ in his letters. In *Gesta rerum Anglorum*[2] William of Malmesbury says: "In that church (Rheims) are still extant proofs of his science: a clock constructed on mechanical principles and a hydraulus in which the air, *aquae calefactae violentia*, by hydrostatic force, fills the cavity of the instrument and through numerous apertures the brazen pipes emit harmonious sounds." The words *calefactae violentia* have been taken to imply that the water was boiling, and by reference to a diagram of the hydraulus it is readily seen that excess air, not used by the pipes, will bubble through the water and give it the appearance of ebullition. Overblowing would cause violent disturbances of the water, and there is no need to assume that the water was boiling. The possibility cannot be excluded, in view of Heron's steam turbine and the undoubted improvements of his day in hydraulus construction, that organs were blown by steam, like the American calliopes of the Mississippi boats, but there is no evidence for it. There is no mention of a fire, and it must be remembered that if the water were boiling in a closed metal chamber it would not be seen to be in violent agitation.

We now turn to the organs of the Arabians. By the fourth century B.C. Greek science had followed the conquering Alexander the Great to Syria, Mesopotamia and Persia. The Arabian khalifs became interested in the Greek methods, and it was through the Arabs, such as Khalif Al-Mansūr (754–75), that science was developed in the Middle Ages. Translations of the Greek works were made first in Syriac and then in Arabic. Khalif Al-Ma'mūn (813–33) founded the Baghdūd College of Science, and it was here

---

iv (1929). (Corrected in small details by Laistner, vol. v.) Verne, D. B., *The Water Organ of the Ancients*, *The Organ*, vol. ii (1922).

[1] H. G. Farmer, *The Organ of the Ancients*, quotes *Al Mas'udi*, ii, 320: "In the days of the ancient Greeks, and in the first period of the Kingdom of Byzantium, Science was developed and scholars were honoured. Then came the Christian religion which became fatal to scientific knowledge. Among the noble sciences which were thrown aside with the advent of Christianity was the science of music."

[2] *Gesta rerum Anglorum* 1125 (edit. T. D. Hardy, 1840, 1: 276): also cited and misinterpreted by Dom Bédos in *L'Art du Facteur d'orgues*.

that at least one of the works on making organs by the Bānū Mūsā was produced.[1] This *Mūristus* treatise on the hydraulus may be a translation of the actual work of Ctesibius (Ktesibios).[2]

Most of the translation was the work of the ninth century, and thus the art of hydraulus-making was revived after a lapse of nearly three centuries because of these translations.

The pneumatic organ, the hydraulus in which water was used for stabilising wind pressure, and the hydraulic organ in which water was used as the source of energy for compressing the air, were all known to the Arabs. In the last, the blowing apparatus consisted of a raised reservoir from which water coming from a pipe turned a small water-wheel, which acting through reduction gears, controlled the movements of valves at the bottom of a lower cistern which governed the flow of water into two blowing chambers. As the pressure water drove air from one of the cylinders into the organ, the other was emptying itself of water. The process was continuous and automatic so long as there was water in the upper reservoir.

The organ could also be played automatically. A cylindrical drum, revolving by means of a water wheel, has projecting pieces fixed to its curved part, almost like those of more modern carillon players. When each projection comes into contact with a balanced lever a hole on a horizontal pipe is uncovered and the note sounded by this (single) pipe is changed. This device is only mentioned in reference to a single horizontal pipe, but it could also be adapted for playing all the pipes of the hydraulus.

The instrument which is described and pictured in the work of Athanasius Kircher (and by Schott[3]) appears to be an attempt on his part to delineate the Mūristus (and probably Greek or Roman) organ. It will be observed in Kircher's picture that his method of providing pressure wind would not produce a continuous supply and that soon water and not wind would be delivered to the pipes. It is probable that he found in some account, now lost, a description of the two-chambered wind-generator such as was found in the

[1] The matter is fully discussed by Farmer in *The Organ of the Ancients*. Copies of the Mūristus manuscript are possessed by the libraries of the Church of St. Sophia, Constantinople, the Catholic University and the Three Moons College, Bairūt. There are several specimens, including the best extant, in the British Museum. The first references to Mūristus are due to Ibn-al-Nadim—(d. *c.* 996), who says "Mūrtus or Mūristus." And among his books are the *Book on the Musical Instruments Called the Flue-pipe Organ, and the Reed-pipe Organ* and the *Book on the Musical Instrument Which May Be Heard Sixty Miles.* A translation of the treatises was made by Wiedemann into German, but that of H. G. Farmer from the superior copy in the British Museum is better. The organ appears to have been known to Ulayya (d. 825), the daughter of Al Mahdī, and this is earlier than one of the "brothers" Bānū Mūsā of whom Muhammed died in 873.

[2] Farmer says: "We know little of the writings of Ktesibios, since nothing has survived of them that ought not to prevent us from accepting the Arabic Mūristus treatise on the *hydraulus* (not on the pneumatic organ) as the work of Ktesibios, as there are several Greek works which have only survived in Arabic including the Pneumatics of Philon, the Mechanics of Heron, the Conic Sections (Books 5 to 7) of Apollonios and the treatises on the Automatic Wind Instrumentalist by Archimedes and Apollonios." There is also a possibility that Mūristus may have a separate existence from Ameristos, Ariston or Ktesibios.

[3] Also spelt Schotto.

Mūristus organs and tried to express it in pictorial terms. Moreover, he does not show how the water, falling under gravity through a long vertical pipe, carries down entrapped air with it. Kircher's drawing of the automatic organ is as imaginary as his attempt to reconstruct the Jewish *magrepha.*[1]

Athanasius Kircher (1601–80), a German Jesuit archaeologist, scholar and mathematician, Professor of Physics, Mathematics and Oriental Languages at Rome (and the presumed maker of the first "magic lantern") described an organ in *Musurgia Universalis* (Rome, 1650) which in principle is not unlike that described by the Bānū Mūsā. It is evident that he had access to a manuscript which may have been a Latin work or translation from an Arabian. It is clear that the organ would not work as shown in his figure, because the double air reservoir would soon fill with water. Moreover, it is evident that he added a few fanciful details. It is possible that he never made or saw an instrument such as he depicted, though there were organs in Italy of his time which were blown by water-wheels. Kircher, like the Bānū Mūsā, also mentions "figures which dance and follow this organ", and there were "figures of peacocks on the instruments which flapped their wings and danced in time with the music". Similar figures appeared on the Chinese organ presented by the Muslim Kingdoms "as an offering from the lands of the West", probably by Hūlāgu to Khubilāi (*c.* 1260–4).[2]

A. Schott in *Magiae universalis naturae et artis*, part ii Acustica (Wurzburg, 1657), unblushingly and uncritically copies Kircher's work. Here is an account of the Kircher-Schott organ given by the former:

"*How to construct an automatic hydraulic organ.*

"For an hydraulic organ three things are necessary: water, air, and a recording barrel (rota phonotactica). First of all there must be flowing water; air as wind for the organ; and a recording barrel as the instrument of automatic sound.

"You proceed in this way: An organ having been arranged for in a suitable place, in accordance with given designs, you first of all construct a wind 'feeder' (camera aeolia), as already described in Pragmatia II. So let there be a 'feeder' VXYR, five palms in height, and three and a half palms in width, with diaphragms perforated in the form of a sieve, and provided with two pipes, of which the larger, TS, will supply fresh water with a stop cock (epistomium) at T for stopping the flow when required. This pipe will be diverted within the vessel (= feeder) at R, puts in constant motion air already there, and other wind generated afresh. And the air, compelled by the density of the moisture, seeking expansion through the

[1] His drawing of this as the organ of the Jews has persisted in standard works until recently, e.g. Hopkins and Rimbault, *The Organ*; J. Stainer, *The Organ*; *Grove's Dictionary of Music*, 3rd ed., etc.

[2] Note on the Bānū Mūsā by Farmer: "The three sons of Mūsā (Bānū Mūsā) were Muhammed (d. 873) Ahmad and Al-Hasan, and they were the most celebrated Arab scientists of their day. Khalif Al-Mamūn (813–33) the great patron of learning gave them positions at the House of Wisdom (the College of Science) at Baghdād. They attracted translators from other countries and many Greek treatises were translated there which revealed the marvels of science to the Eastern world and later to the West."

perforated or carded diaphragms, and unable to find it, will escape through VZ into the 'wind-chest'.

"Further, the water, escaping with great force through the opening R, turns the water wheel (rota) MR, and will turn the cog-wheel (vertebra) L and the cylinder or recording HK. This (recording barrel) with its teeth regularly disposed on the surface in accordance with the designs given, will touch each of the levers (spatulae) working on a steel rod AB. The levers, being caught by the teeth of the recording barrel, will pull down the 'pallets' (palmulae) of the abacus claviarius or keys (tasti) EF, to which they are joined. These being pulled down open 'valves' (platismatia) or as the Italians call them, battiventi, and thus the wind, forced violently into the wind-chest through the open 'valves' will enter the organ pipes, and the desired harmony will finally be obtained. . . .

"This automatic construction can be applied not only to organs but also to stringed instruments." [See Plate 3.]

A fully automatic instrument actuated by water pressure on the principle of Apollonios was improved by the Arabs in the ninth century and was called "The Instrument which plays by itself". This "organ" had only one flute pipe, and the holes in it were opened and closed by levers actuated by projections from a revolving drum. Animal fat was used to ensure that the holes were tightly closed by the ends of the levers. The notes yielded by the pipe were:

Notes	F	G	a	b♭	b	c	d	e	f	g
Pitch in Cents	O	204	408	(498)	612	702	906	1108	1200	1404

A Byzantine organ at Constantinople is described by Ibn Rusta, an Arab Persian scholar of Isfahan (ninth–tenth century), in the following terms:[1]

"Then there is brought a thing called an organ (urganā) and it is made of a square (case of) wood in the shape of a wine press and this latter is covered with strong skin. Then there are made in it sixty pipes of brass, the heads of which, as far as the middle, project above the case. These pipes are covered with gold above the case, with the exception of a small portion in proportion to their sizes, one longer than the other.

"At the side of this square thing (the case) are holes in which are fixed the bellows which resemble the black-smith's bellows. Then there are brought three crosses; two are placed on the ends and one in the middle. Then they press the bellows with the feet, and the organist stands and plays upon these pipes, and each pipe he makes to speak in turn according to what he plays."

It is evident that the crosses refer to bars or levers used for working the bellows.

Writing about *Musical Instruments* in the middle of the tenth century, Muhammad ibn Ahmad al-Khwārizmi says: "The organ is an instrument of the Greeks and Byzantines. It is made of three large bags of buffalo skins, one being joined to another. And there is mounted upon the head of the middle-bag a large skin. Then there are mounted upon this skin (pipes) having holes upon recognised ratios from which proceed beautiful sounds, pleasing or melancholy, according to what the player desires."[2]

[1] *Bibliotheca geographorum Arabicorum*, vii, 123.

[2] Farmer, op. cit. p., 77.

A representation of an organ with diagonal bellows is seen in an obelisk at Constantinople erected by Theodosius I[1] (d. 395).

The eight pipes seem to be made from large reeds or canes. It will be noticed that there is no great difference in size between the longest and shortest pipes. This is much less than the 1 : 2 ratio necessitated by an octave relationship. Probably it is an error on the part of the sculptor, as it is unthinkable that an extreme interval of a third would be satisfactory.

FIG. 6. The obelisk of Theodosius. Constantinople (A.D. 395), (after Coussemaker: Annales Archéologiques 11.277 Paris 1845).

Byzantine organs were adapted both by the Arabs and by the Christians after the eighth century, but there is no documentary account which gives us any clue concerning the development of the instrument from the time of this obelisk for some centuries.

The picture which is now given represents a degenerate form of hydraulus.[2] It is from the ninth-century Utrecht Psalter, and a poor copy is seen in the twelfth-century Eadwine or Canterbury Psalter (*c.* 1150) in the library of Trinity College, Cambridge.[3]

[1] Maclean's assertion that the simple animal-skin blast bag did not give way to the diagonal bellows until the ninth century can therefore be discounted. C. Maclean, "The Principle of the Hydraulic Organ" in *Sammelbände der Internationalen Musikgesellschaft* (Leipzig, 1906).

[2] Hopkins and Rimbault (op. cit.) wrongly describe it as a pneumatic organ.

[3] The Cambridge Psalter in *The Western MSS*, ed. M. R. James, vol. ii (C.U.P., 1904), p. 402.

A facsimile of the Utrecht Psalter is kept in the library of Trinity College (press mark H. 16, 18). The date of this Psalter is not certain. It has been fixed as early as the sixth century, but this is almost certainly too early by two centuries.

The Cambridge Psalter was written in the mid twelfth century by Eadwine, an otherwise unknown member of his house. The pictures are at times poor copies of those in the Utrecht Psalter. This is now in the University Library of that town. It was given in 1718 by Will. de Ridder. It was at Canterbury for a long time, probably from the tenth century to the time of the Dissolution of the Monasteries and was in the Cotton collection until the late seventeenth century. It was written in the Diocese of Rheims, probably at the Abbey of Hautvillers. It is possible that the pictures are taken from earlier Greek models, for there is a Vatican Psalter (Gr. 1927) with the same archetypes; but Tikkanen thinks that it is a copy of an earlier Latin

The design is not very helpful to us, and it is certain that it contains imaginative features on the part of the artist. One of the players seems to be admonishing, with an angry fore-finger, the undernourished, kyphotic organ-blowers. The other, with acromegalic hands is apparently stopping leaks in the sound-board. The shapes and sizes of the pipes are misleading. The points of interest are the uprights and cross-pieces which may have held up a curtain or cover for the pipes and the holes which are probably intended to hold a second set of pipes. Almost the only real value of the picture is that it represents a hydraulus, and that there are two players.

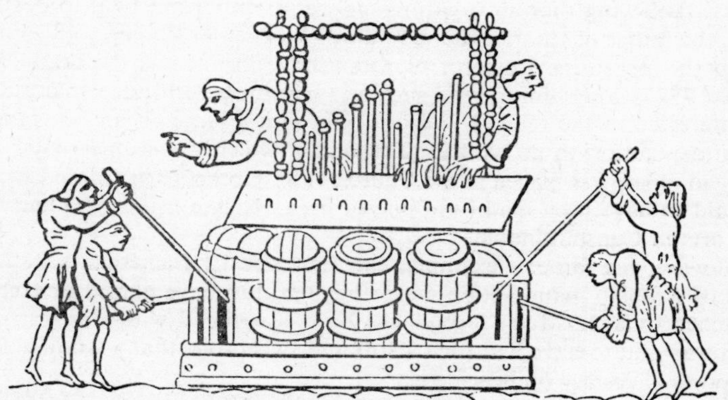

FIG. 7. The hydraulic organ of the Utrecht and Cambridge Psalters (Ps. 150).

When the Arab ambassadors visited the court of Constantine Porphyrogenitus in 946 there were wonderful organs of gold and silver. One such instrument is described by the Syrian Isho' bar Bahlul as follows: "This organ consists of two columns hollow and slender, beautifully made of marble. And these stand upright closely united in a skilful way. Below are bellows like those which a blacksmith uses, although not so large but small and elegant. The organist sits above and those who perform the song, whatever it may be, stand on the right and left. . . . They say that such an organ is in that church (St. Sophia) in Byzantium."

---

work. The interesting point about these opinions is that the organs therein depicted may be traditional drawings of the water organs of a much earlier period and may not give any clue concerning instruments of the time when the Utrecht Psalter was produced. The pictures of organs are given with Ps. lxx (the tops of eight pipes and the two blowing tanks of a water organ); Ps. cl (the well known water organ with two players and four blowers here illustrated), and Apocryphal Ps. cli (a water organ similar to the last, without blowers but with King David holding two pipes, but what is more probable, making them sound by stopping holes with his fingers).

References: Benson and Tselos, *New Light on the Origin of the Utrecht Psalter*, *Art Studies*, xiii (1931); Tikkanen, *Die Psalterillustration im Mittelalter* (1903); E. T. de Wald, *The Illustrations of the Utrecht Psalter* (Princeton, 1932).

It has been said that Pope Vitalian introduced the organ at Rome about the year 666 in order to improve the singing of the congregations, but Buhle,[1] who has carefully considered the evidence, does not support this view.

The art of organ-making and the use of the instrument were known in England at the beginning of the eighth century, and pipe decoration was practised in this country. Aldhelm (d. 709)[2] mentions the gilding of organ cases by the Anglo-Saxons: "Hearing the enormous organs with a thousand blasts, the ear is soothed by the windy bellows, while the other portions of the organ shine in golden cases."

Organ-making was started in France about the middle of the eighth century. Believing that an organ would be an important help to devotion, Pepin, the father of Charlemagne, finding no organ in France and Germany, sent to the Byzantine Emperor Constantine Copronymus the Sixth, about the year 757, asking him to send such an instrument to France. Constantine was interested in the request and not only sent a large organ but caused a special deputation to go with it. The organ, which was a pneumatic organ with lead pipes, was placed in the Church of St. Cornelius at Compiègne, and it is said to have been made and played by an Italian priest who had learnt these arts in Constantinople.

Following his father's example, the Emperor Charlemagne sent for an organ of Arabian manufacture which he is said to have placed in a church at Aachen in 812. Much legend has been associated with this instrument which was said to have had such a soft and sweet tone that a woman died in transports of ecstasy on hearing it.

According to the legendary story the organ was sent by Caliph Hārūn al-Rashid and was made by an Arabian called Ja'far. The incident was used by Madame de Genlis[3] in her historical novel *Les Chevaliers du Cygne* and thence found its way *as history* into many standard works.[4] Farmer, the leading authority on Arabian music, was inclined to reject the whole story, and in his *Organ of the Ancients* (1931) stated that he could find no evidence for it. More recently he has found a long account of this Arabian organ in a "manuscript" *Kaslif al-humūm wa-l-kurab* of the fourteenth century, preserved at Stamboul.[5] The organ is called *al-mūsīqā* (the music) and its maker is Taqī al-Din al Fārābi or al-Fāryābī. This man was brought to the notice of the Caliph al-Ma'mūn (813–33) by Ja'far and there were provided for the craftsmen "copper and smiths, wood and joiners" and so the wonderful instrument was constructed. Farmer describes it as "a mechanically contrived organ which combined the functions of a wind and a string instrument. It was rectangular in shape and resembled a pulpit, being nearly the stature of a man in height and twelve cubits in circumference." In this account there

[1] Buhle, *Die musikalischen Instrumente in den Miniaturen des frühen Mittelalters* (Leipsic, 1903).

[2] Migne, J. P., *Patr. Lat.*, lxxx, 9: 240. (*Patrologiae cursus completus*, Paris.)

[3] Genlis (Stéphanie, Comtesse de), *The Knights of the Swan, or the Court of Charlemagne*. Tr. from the French by Rev. Mr. Beresford, 3 vols. (London, 1796.)

[4] E.g. *Grove's Dictionary*, 3rd ed.; Audsley, *Art of Organ Building; La grande encyclopédie*, etc.

[5] H. G. Farmer, *Sources of Arabian Music*, p. 59.

PLATE 1.

Roman Sarcophagus of a Musician, Museum of Arles, France. Hydraulus (the case on the wall was probably intended to contain a Syrinx or Pan-pipes)

PLATE 2.

Organ and symphony, Belvoir Psalter c. 1270. (Note the method of blowing the organ, with two ropes so that the feeders work in alternate motion)

is told at length of the intrigues of the Franks to learn the secret of this instrument and of their success.

Two illustrations of the *mūsīqā* depict a rectangular instrument which is quite twice the size of a man, with four men blowing the instrument by means of what appear to be diagonal bellows. The names of the "modes" with which the organ case is decorated are certainly later than the ninth century.

The author or compiler of the Arabic Mūristus works on the hydraulus says that he constructed a water organ for the "king of the Inner Franks", and it has been suggested by Derenbourg[1] that this was King Pepin, while Wiedemann[2] also thought that it was one of the Carolingian or Saxon emperors. Farmer thinks that it is not likely that Pepin was the king. It is not improbable that Georgius Monachus, a Jerusalem monk, who was a member of Caliph Hārūn's embassy to Charlemagne in 807, was the same man as Georgius, now surnamed Veneticus, who went to the Frankish court and promised to make a hydraulus in the year 826 or 828.[3]

The pneumatic organ of the Arabs was a much simpler affair. There were as many as twelve blowers for as many pipes, and in some of the simpler instruments the air was blown in by the lungs of three "blowers". The ideas of the Greeks that the different "modes" produced different psychological reactions in the hearers were seen in the instructions given to those who worked the organ. The ears had to be stopped for certain modes, "and if you wish to perplex the listeners until their souls become flaccid and the bodies weak, then open the holes of the upper pipes of the three skins and the holes of the pipes opposite the upper pipes and they are the low (sounds) which means that the man opens the (particular) stoppers. . . . Then you will see a marvel, because this 'compound' is alien to the temperament of man, because a man does not comprehend upon hearing it what we have mentioned".[4]

The pipes were caused to sound or to become silent by means of stoppers. The document of which the above is a quotation refers to an organ much older even than that depicted on the obelisk of Theodosius.

"The pneumatic organ belongs to a period long before the fourth century B.C.,"[4] and it is probable that a pneumatic organ was known on the Mesopotamian plains before the instrument was made in Greece. No word in the Assyrian language gives any hint of an organ, and the earliest trace in the writings of the Semitic East is in later Hebrew-Aramaic sources. It is possible that the Mashroqitha mentioned in the Book of Daniel iii. 5, 7, 10, and 15 was a pneumatic organ. Kircher in his *Musurgia* has an imaginative drawing of the Magrephah, the legendary pneumatic organ of the Jews.[5] Porta, writing about the same instrument, is less confident and closes his description

[1] H. Derenbourg, *Revue Musicale VI*, p. 193.

[2] E. Wiedemann, *Archiv für die Geschichte der Naturwissenschaften und der Technik*, 155.

[3] H. G. Farmer, *The Organ of the Ancients*, p. 143.

[4] H. G. Farmer, ibid. Farmer has found no evidence for the use of the magrephah (pneumatic organ) by the Jews after the destruction of the Temple at Jerusalem in A.D. 70. Any Jewish reference to "idrablis" or "hirdaulis" is clearly a Greek derivation.

[5] This sketch, which shows two diagonal bellows which feed a wind-chest on which stand thirteen pipes actuated by *fourteen* sliding rods, is not only a bad

with the words: "If you are satisfied, then so am I. If not, then choose another opinion which may be correct."[1] The Talmud mentions a handle which may have been used for blowing, and the instrument mentioned in Tamid iii. 8 is said to have been so powerful that it could be heard in Jericho, about ten miles away.

The Emperor Julian, known as the Apostate, who died in A.D. 363, is believed to have written an enigmatical epigram in Greek which evidently refers to a pneumatic organ[2] and is here translated:

"I see a species of reeds: which have quickly sprung from another and a brazen soil. Nor are they agitated by our winds but a blast rushing forth from a cavern of bull's hide makes its way from below the root of reeds with many openings; and a highly gifted man, with nimble fingers, handles the yielding rods[3] of the pipes, while they, softly bounding, press out a sound."[4]

In a letter to Dardanus, often ascribed to Jerome (d. 420), there is mention of an organ similar to one at Jerusalem which could be heard at the Mount of Olives, a thousand paces away.[5] It was said to be made from two elephants' skins, fifteen smiths' bellows, and it had twelve pipes. The account seems to be fanciful and symbolical, for the two hides were said to represent the Old and New Testaments, the twelve pipes the apostles and the fifteen bellows the patriarchs and prophets.

---

drawing but shows the pipes as being alternately long and short. It is surprising that such a palpably imaginary and not even plausible arrangement could have been accepted as having historical value by Stainer, Hopkins and Rimbault, Grove, Audsley and many others.

[1] Abraham de Porta Leon, an Italian Jew, published this account in Hebrew at Mantua in 1612. He says that the Magrephah was like a box of wood, resembling the shovel of the baker, and it had ten pipes each with ten holes.

[2] *Anthologia Graeca* (ed. Lips, 1794), vol. iii, p. 111.

[3] This passage clearly shows that the instrument had no keyboard. Nevertheless, Burney (*History of Music*, vol. ii, p. 65), Busby (*History of Music*, vol. i, p. 263), and Wackerbarth (*Music and the Anglo-Saxons*, p. 9) deliberately mistranslate the word κανόνας (canonas) as *key* and then infer that the instrument had a keyboard !

[4] In a significant article in *Speculum*, xxiii, p. 191, "Early History of the Organ", W. Apel reminds us that, apart from any considerations of the translations of Julian's epigram, there were keyboards before this time. He believes that two-part playing was practised on organs like that at Aquincum and, moreover, interprets the poem concerning the Winchester organ to mean that each player managed his own complete melodic line, and that polyphonic playing was possible. Thus the enormous grand organs of the west-end "tribunes" stood out from the general development of keyboard playing. The grand organ of the sixteenth and seventeenth centuries was the result of rendering the large organs more tractable and combining with them (amongst other things) the resources of the small positive as a rückpositiv, as had been done for many years; and the still smaller portative or regal as brustwerk. If Apel is correct, Western polyphony developed from Byzantine organ-playing, and the year 757 becomes an important one, as it marks the introduction of Western polyphony.

Apel also quotes Hawkins, *A General History of the Science and Practice of Music* (London, 1776), ii, p. 163: "It is scarce credible that during so long a period as between 800 and 1020 during all which the world was in possession of the organ, neither curiosity nor accident should lead to the discovery of music of consonance. Is it to be supposed that this noble instrument so constructed as to produce the greatest variety of harmony and fine modulation was played by one finger only?"

See also Degering, H., *Die Orgel, ihre Erfindung und ihre Geschichte bis zur Karolingerzeit* (Munster, 1905).

[5] Migne, *Patrologiae cursus completus* (Latin series, xxx, 219).

CHAPTER II

THE MEDIAEVAL ORGAN

WE HAVE already seen how the organ reached a remarkable degree of development under the Greeks and Romans, and with the decline of these civilisations it passed to the Middle East and gradually filtered back to the West, where it was used as an aid to Christian worship. Much had to be reinvented, but in England and in Europe organ-making was actively carried on from the beginning of the eighth century. St. Maildulf or Mailduf, an Irish saint who settled in Wiltshire and founded Malmesbury Abbey (d. *c.* 675), and St. Ethelwold (d. 984) made organs, and we have already noted the interest of St. Aldhelm in the instrument in the seventh century.[1]

St. Dunstan (925–88) was a keen musician and organ-builder and played the organ, psaltery, harp and chime-bells as well as other instruments. Galpin[2] says that he was imagined to be a sorcerer because he constructed an Aeolian Harp which played when it was placed against a crevice in a wall. Dunstan built or superintended the building of several organs in England, one of which, at least, had pipes of brass. An organ in Glastonbury Abbey was built under his direction.[3] Also in the tenth century Count Elwin gave an organ to the convent of Ramsey. "The earl devoted thirty pounds to make copper pipes of organs, which, resting with their openings in thick order on the spiral winding in the inside, and being struck on feast days with a strong blast of bellows, emit a sweet melody and a far resounding peal."[4]

Organ-building made much progress in Germany in the late ninth and early tenth centuries. A number of treatises and short works which deal with the making, and in particular the lengths of organ pipes, have come down to us. Mahrenholz[5] has listed twenty-nine of them, and it is possible to give an account of the various scales then in use.[6] There are a number of references in M. Gerbert's *Scriptores ecclesiastici de musica sacra potissimum* (St. Blasien, 1784). Some of the works are anonymous, but others are due to Hucbald (*c.* 840–930), Bernelinus (*c.* 1000) and Notker Lablo[7] (d. 1022). These works referred to contemporary organs, but it is clear that the

[1] Migne, *Patrologiae cursus completus* (Latin series, xxx, 219).

[2] Galpin, *Old English Instruments of Music* (London, 1910).

[3] William of Malmesbury, op. cit.

Odo, Abbot of Cluny (d. 942), was the reputed author of a treatise on organ-building, but it is doubtful whether it was his work (M. Gerbert, *Scriptores* 1,303).

[4] *Acta Sanctorum Ordinis Benedict Saec.*, vol. v, p. 756.

[5] Ch. Mahrenholz, *Die Berechnung der Orgelpfeifen-Mensuren* (Kassel, 1938).

[6] Schmidt-Gorg, Joseph, *Ein althochdeutscher Traktat über die Mensur der Orgelpfeifen* in *Kirchenmusikalisches Jahrbuch*, xxvii (1932), p. 58.

[7] Not to be confused with Notker Balbulus who lived about a century earlier. Lablo was an instructor at St. Gall. There is also an eleventh-century tract "De organo" (Bibl. Nat. Paris Lat. 7202).

Pythagorian method of tuning was known. The divisions of the string of the monochord were taken as a guide. There were considerable differences both in the notes included in the scale and also in the pitches of the notes themselves.

A poem dedicated to Bishop Elphege by Wulstan (d. *c.* 963) gives an account of a large organ at Winchester which dates from the tenth century. (Elphege held the Bishopric from 935 to 951.) Here is a translation.[1]

"Such organs as you have built are seen nowhere, fabricated on a double ground. Twice six bellows above are ranged in a row, and fourteen lie below. These, by alternate blasts, supply an immense quantity of wind, and are worked by seventy strong men, labouring with their arms, covered with perspiration, each inciting his companions to drive the wind up with all his strength, that the full-bosomed box may speak with its four hundred pipes which the hand of the organist governs. Some when closed he opens, others when open he closes, as the individual nature of the varied sound requires. Two brethren (religious) of concordant spirit sit at the instrument, and each manages his own alphabet. There are, moreover, hidden holes in the forty tongues, and each has ten pipes in their due order. Some are conducted hither, others thither, each preserving the proper point (or situation) for its own note. They strike the seven differences of joyous sounds, adding the music of the lyric semitone. Like thunder the iron tones batter the ear, so that it may receive no sound but that alone. To such an amount does it reverberate, echoing in every direction, that everyone stops with his hand to his gaping ears, being in no wise able to draw near and bear the sound, which so many combinations produce. The music is heard throughout the town, and the flying fame thereof is gone out over the whole country."

The poem is probably an unreliable guide to the organ which it describes and the Benedictine *Acta Sanctorum*, which contains the poem, calls Wulstan "Monachus", and many subsequent translations and quotations erroneously describe him as a king. The *Saxon Chronicle* (963) says that he was a deacon, and it is reasonable to suppose that this is correct, as the monks did not succeed the secular clerics at Winchester until after the death of Wulstan. It is impossible to be certain of the type of "bellows" used in the Winchester organ. Already in the fourth century diagonal bellows had been used in the pneumatic organ, as we observe in the Byzantine organ depicted on the Theodosius obelisk.[2] The later hydraulus had been equipped with cylindrical pumps and an air-pressure stabiliser, but these improvements were lost or remained latent in the Dark Ages and gradually returned to the West through its contact with Arabian culture. It is probable that some improvements such as the perforated slider for the registers, and springs for restoring a "key" or slider to its closed position known in the classical times, had to be devised anew. Many of the early organs of Western Christendom were blown from primitive blast-bags retaining their original animal shape. The fact that the word *follis* (i.e. bellows) is found in mediaeval Latin works does

[1] *Acta Sanctorum Ordinis S. Benedicti*, vol. 7, p. 617 (Venice *c.* 1738). A fanciful translation is given in Wackerbarth's *Music and the Anglo-Saxons*.

[2] See page 30.

not imply more than such simple hide blast-bags, and these were used until the twelfth century, as we see in two Cambridge manuscripts. In the thirteenth century the diagonal bellows were generally in use and these are shown in the Belvoir Castle *Psalterium* and in the well-known Airdale Manuscript, now known to belong to the same century (see Plate 2).

As an intermediate stage between the blast-bag and the bellows, we can trace the semi-circular metal hoop to act as a former for the leather-skin, and a flat board on the top of it to protect the hide and to secure a better distribution of pressure.

It is apparent that in the Winchester organ there were forty notes and sliders and that each controlled ten pipes. In fact the whole organ was just a large mixture stop. It seems that there were three players (the chief organist and two brethren of concordant spirit). As each organist managed his own alphabet,[1] it may be supposed that each controlled eleven diatonic sounds from C to F with the addition of the lyric semitone B♭. These would be all that was required by the old chants and would account for thirty-six of the notes. The remaining notes may have been the perquisite of the chief organist and may have controlled large drone pipes, or again they may have extended the compass upwards.

It would be pleasant to assume, as several writers have done, that the *Winchester Tropary*, preserved in the Bodleian Library at Oxford, was prepared for use with this organ.[2] The Winchester Tropers are unique and important because they show, though rarely, the beginnings of contrary motion, but we must not assume that they represent instrumental music or even an instrumental line which doubles that of the voice at an interval of a fifth or a fourth. The origin of organum is uncertain and a number of views have been analysed by Gustave Reese.[3] "Gastoué[4] sees in the two primitive parts of vocal organum an imitation of two-part music played on the hydraulic or pneumatic organ and believes organum to have been named after the instrument. It has been contended that the rudimentary part-music performed on the organ or other instruments was conceived as a copy of primitive vocal part-music, and that it is from this copy that stylised vocal 'polyphony' derived its name." It must be remembered that the Latin word *organum*, besides meaning *organ*, might refer to any musical instrument or even to *organised* singing. Gastoué is contradicted by other authorities and the entire matter is one of speculation.

Hucbald[5] (*c.* 840–930) in his *De Harmonica Institutione* says:

"Consonance is the judicious and harmonious mixture of two tones, which exists only if two tones, produced from different sources, meet in one joint

[1] It will be seen that the use of lettering keys persisted until the fifteenth century and keys were called letters in England even in the sixteenth century. It is possible, though not likely, that the Winchester organ had ten keys each controlling forty pipes.

[2] E.g. A. C. Piper, "Notes on Winchester Cathedral Organs", *The Organ*, vol. i (1921).

[3] *Music in the Middle Ages* (New York, 1940), chap. ix.

[4] *Encyclopédie de la musique et dictionnaire du conservatoire* (ed. A. Lavignac and L. de la Laurencie, Paris).

[5] M. Gerbert, *Scriptores ecclesiastici de musica*, 3 vols. (St. Blasien, 1784. Facsimile ed. 1193).

sound, as happens when a boy's voice and a man's voice sing the same thing, or in that which they commonly call Organum."

The organ was by no means universally popular amongst Christians, and from time to time divines and philosophers have raised their voices against its use as an aid (or impediment) to worship.

Clement of Alexandria, who lived about 150 to 215 A.D., was interested in music and poetry, and although he allowed the lyra and cithara because King David was alleged to have used them, he would not tolerate other instruments including the organ probably because these would remind devout Christians of the pagan orgies and plays. "The one instrument of peace, the Word alone by which we honour God, is what we employ . . . no longer the ancient psaltery, the trumpet, the timbrel, and aulos, which those expert in war and contemners of the fear of God were wont to make use of also in the choruses at their festive assemblies; that by such strains they might raise their dejected minds."[1]

St. Jerome (*c.* 340–420), when advising Laeta how to rear her daughter, wrote:[2]

"Let her be deaf to the sound of the organ, and not know even the uses of the pipe, the lyre, and the cithara."

Ailred (Ethelred or Aelred), Abbot of Rievaulx (1109–66),[3] said:

"Let me speake now of those who, under the show of religion, doe obpalliate the business of pleasure . . . whence hath the Church so many organs and Musicall Instruments? To what purpose, I pray you, is that terrible noise of blowing of Belloes, expressing rather the crakes of Thunder, than the sweetnesse of a voyce."

Or again the same authority says: "Why such organs and so many cymbals in the Church? What with the sound of the bellows, the noise of the cymbals and the united strains of the organ pipes, the common folk stand with wondering faces, trembling and amazed."

Erasmus (1466–1536) (*Life and Letters of Erasmus*, ch. vii) wrote: "There was no music in St. Paul's time. . . . Words nowadays mean nothing. They are mere sounds striking upon the ear, and men are to leave their work and go to church to listen to worse noises than were ever heard in Greek or Roman theatre. Money must be raised to buy organs and train boys to squeal."[4]

Praetorius in his *Syntagma* says that the organ was introduced into the mass by Pope Vitalian in the seventh century. It is apparent that the assertion was first made by Platina in his *De Vita et Moribus Summorum Pontificum Historia* (1530), but the organ was used in Christian worship during the sixth

[1] Migne, *Series Graeca*, viii, 443, trans. from Ante-Nicene Series, ii, 249.

[2] Migne, *Series Latina*, xxii, 871, Nicene and Post-Nicene Series, 2, vi, 193.

[3] Translation by Prynne, *Histriomastix*, chap. xx (*Patr. Lat.*, cxcv, 571).

[4] Cf. G. B. Shaw: "I am as fond of fine music and handsome buildings as Milton was, or Cromwell, or Bunyan: but if I found that they were becoming the instruments of a systematic idolatry of sensuousness, I would hold it good statesmanship to blow every cathedral in the world to pieces with dynamite, organ and all, without the least heed to the screams of the art critics and cultured voluptuaries" (preface to *Plays for Puritans*). See also the section on the organ in England *c.* 1642, in the present work.

century and probably before this. The organ was used in Byzantium[1] for secular purposes, and it was only in the Western Church that its voice was heard in church services. Before the fourth century only the cithara and lyre were permitted, but the organ gradually came into its own until by the eleventh century it began to displace all others,[2] and in the fourteenth century Guillaume de Machaut[3] (*c.* 1300–77) refers to the organ as "de tous instruments le roi", an epithet which has endured.

It appears that the organ was not used in the mass until the twelfth century. Some monastic establishments such as the Benedictines at Fulda did not use the organ at their services, and the ancient customs of Monte Cassino forbade the making of organs without the express permission of the head of the chapter.[4]

The early Western organ must have been very noisy and, as it was thus unsuitable for accompanying a few voices, it would not be used in the mass. In the eleventh century, smaller organs were coming into being, and from this time until the thirteenth century the intractable sliders for letting wind into the pipes were giving way to early keyboards. Organs were sometimes used at this time in alternation with voices, a custom which has prevailed to this day in Catholic churches on the continent. Honorius of Autun, writing in the first part of the twelfth century, justifies the use of the organ by quoting from the Bible,[5] and Balderic, Archbishop of Dol, in the twelfth century said that the complaints which were made concerning the instrument because of its noisiness were not justified. The organ needed more care in its preservation and use.[6]

Johannes Aegidius says that in the thirteenth century the organ had displaced all other instruments in the music of the mass.[7] England, France, and the German countries each contributed to the development of the organ, but in spite of the fact that legendary reports said that Venice was famous for its organ-builders in the ninth century, Pope John VIII (*c.* 872) sent to Bishop Anno in Germany saying: "Send me the best organ that you can obtain, together with a player, *as we have none here*."[8]

Of the numerous accounts of the methods of making organ-pipes, which appeared in Europe after the ninth century, none is more interesting than that of Theophilus (or Ruger), which is found in a larger work dealing with the practical arts of the eleventh and twelfth centuries.

[1] Mrs. Bittermann (*Speculum*, vol. iv) points out a "tantalising" reference to Julian (later the apostate) who composed the poem given on p. 34, as he was leaving a church in Constantinople. Can it be assumed that he had been inspired by an organ in the church ? There is, however, no evidence for this and the tendency in the Eastern Church was against the use of an organ.

[2] It is difficult to know exactly what instrument is meant when "organ" is referred to in these early centuries. Jerome's translation of the Bible into Latin (Vulgate) gives *organum* for any instrument. For instance the English use of the word *organ* in Ps. cl may be read *pipes* or *instruments*.

[3] *Musikalische Werke*, ed. by Ludwig (Leipzig, 1926).

[4] Bittermann, *Speculum*, vol. iv, p. 407.

[5] "Gemmae animae," c. 77 (*Patr. Lat.*, clxxvii, 567 D).

[6] "Epistola ad Fiscamneses," c. 7 (*Patr. Lat.*, clxvi, 1177).

[7] Martin Gerbert, *Scriptores*, vol. ii, p. 388.

[8] H. G. Farmer, *The Organ of the Ancients.*

"*Theophilus's Treatise on Organ Building.*[1]

"*Chapter LXXXI. Of Organs*

"The maker of organs should first possess the knowledge of the measure, how the grave and sharp and treble pipes should be meted out; he may then make for himself a long and thick iron to the size which he wishes the pipes to possess; this must be round, filed and polished with great care, thicker at one extremity and slightly diminished, so that it can be placed in another curved iron, by which it is encompassed, after the portion of the wood in which the augur is revolved, and at the other extremity let it be slender, according to the size of the lower end of the pipe which should be placed on the bellows. Then pure and very sound copper is thinned, so that the impression of the nail may appear on the other side. When this has been marked out and cut according to the size of the iron for the longer pipes, which are called grave, an opening is made according to the precept of the lesson, into which the valve should be placed, and it is rasped round a little to the size of the pipe, and tin is anointed over it with the soldering iron, and it is rasped upon one edge of the length inside, and outside, upon the other edge, and it is tinned over very thinly. Which tinnings, before the newly made lines are scraped, are slightly anointed, the copper being warmed with resin of the fir, that the tin may the more easily adhere. Which being done this copper is folded around the iron and is strongly bound round with an iron wire moderately thick, so that the tinned lines may agree with each other. This wire should be first carried through a very small hole which is at the thin extremity of the iron, and be twisted twice round in it, and so be carried down revolving to the other extremity, and be there similarly fastened. Then with its joinings agreeing together and carefully fastened, it is placed with its ligature, as with the iron, before the furnace upon the glowing embers, and the boy sitting and slightly blowing, in the left hand is held a thin wood, at the split top of which a small cloth with resin is fixed, and in the right can be held a long piece of tin beaten thin, so that directly the pipe has become hot he can anoint the joint with the rag filled with resin, and the tin applied may liquefy, and he must carefully solder the join together. Which being done, the pipe cold, the iron is placed in the instrument prepared like that of a turner, and the curved iron being placed on, and wire loosened, one can revolve the curved iron, the other, both hands being provided with gloves, can hold the pipe firmly, so that the iron may be carried round and the pipe remain still, until it appear elegant to the eyes as if turned. The iron then being taken out, the pipe is struck slightly with the hammer near the opening, above and below, so that this round shape may depress almost to the centre for a space of two fingers; the languid may be made from copper somewhat thicker, like a half wheel, and be soldered over about the round part, as the pipe above, and be so

[1] Theophili et Rugeri, *Presbyteri et Monachi Libri III de Diversis Artibus*, Harleian MS., Brit. Mus. 3915. There are other copies at Wolfenbuttel, Vienna and at Cambridge. The work was translated by Robert Hendrie in 1847 (London, John Murray). Theophilus refers to the eleventh-century practice of organ-building. A new translation has been made by the author. See Johnson, R. P., *Speculum*, vol. xiii, p. 90. There is evidence that many of the practical arts described by Theophilus were inspired by Byzantine culture.

placed in the lower part of the opening that it may stand equally under its edge, nor protrude below or above. He can have also a soldering iron of the same breadth and roundness as the languid. With this heated he can place small particles of tin upon the languid and a little resin, and can carefully pass over the hot iron, that he may not move the languid, but that the tin being melted it may so adhere that no wind can come out in its circumference, unless only into the upper opening. Which being done, he can bring it to his mouth and blow at first slightly, then more, and then strongly; and, according to what he discerns by hearing, he can arrange the sound, so that if he wish it strong the opening is made wider; if slighter, however, it is made narrower. In this order all the pipes are made. He can make the measure of each, from the languid upwards, according to the rule inculcated, but from the languid below, all will be of one measure and of the same thickness.

"*Chapter LXXXII. Of the Organ Erection*

"In the manufacture of the structure, upon which the pipes are to stand, see whether you intend to have it of wood or copper. If of wood, procure for yourself two pieces of wood of the plane tree, very dry, two feet and a half in length, and in breadth rather more than one: one four, the other two fingers thick, which must not be knotty, but without blemish. Which being carefully joined together, in the lower part of the thicker wood a square hole must be made in the centre, four fingers in breadth, and about which a border must be left of the same wood of one finger in breadth and height, in which the bellows can be placed. In the upper part of the side, however, small hollows are made, through which the wind can arrive at the pipes. But the other part of the wood, which should also be uppermost, is measured out inside equally, where seven or eight small openings are disposed, in which the sliders are carefully joined, so that they may have an easy means of being drawn out and restored, so, however, that no air can come out between the joints.

"In the upper part, however, cut small openings opposite the lower ones, which are to be rather wider, in which may be joined so many pieces of wood, so that between these and the larger the openings of the wood may remain empty, through which the wind can mount to the pipes; for in these same pieces of wood openings should be made in which the pipes are to be made fast. The openings in which the sliders are fitted in the front part should proceed, like slanting windows, through which these sliders are introduced and removed.

"In the hinder part, under the end of these sliders, holes are made equally wide and long, of the size of two fingers, through which the wind can ascend from the lower to the upper parts, so that when the sliders are placed upon them these holes may be stopped by them; when, however, they are withdrawn, they may again lie open. In those pieces of wood which are joined upon the sliders, openings are made, carefully and in order, according to the number of the pipes of every tone, in which these pipes are placed, so that they may stand firmly and receive the wind from the lower parts. But in the handles of the sliders letters[1] are marked, according to the rise and fall of the sound, by which it can be known which tone it may be. In each one of these

[1] As late as the sixteenth century organ-keys were so marked and were called letters.

sliders single slender holes are made, half of the little finger in length, in the front part, near the handles, lengthwise, in which single copper-headed nails may be placed, which may pass through the small windows in the middle, by means of which these sliders are drawn from the upper side of the structure down to the lower, and the heads of the nails appear above, so that when the sliders are withdrawn from the sounding instruments, they cannot be quite extracted. These things being thus arranged, these two pieces of wood, which perfect the organ-house, are joined together with cheese-glue; then those parts which are joined over the sliders, in which the holes exist, are also pared round carefully, and scraped.

"*Chapter LXXXIII. Of the Bellows*

"In making the wind-chamber, join together two pieces of wood of the plane tree, in the above mode, of one foot in length, one of which may be a palm thick, the other three fingers, and let them be round at one end like a shield and there a foot and a half wide, at the other end blunt, a palm in breadth. When these have been carefully fitted together, cut, in the round front in the thicker wood, the openings which you wish, according to the number of the bellows, and in the blunt end one, which must be larger. Then cut, from each opening, a hollow leading to the larger opening, through which the wind may have way to the working bellows; and you will thus glue these woods together with the cheese-glue,[1] and you will bind them round with a linen cloth, new and strong, which you anoint with the same cheese-glue that it may adhere: you also make strong iron bindings tinned over within and without, that they may not become disunited from the woodwork, these you will fix on with long nails, headed and tinned, so that between the two openings a binding may exist, which may include each wood from the upper to the lower side. Then procure for yourself a curved piece of oak wood, sound and strong, which must have at one end, from the curve, the length of one foot, in the other of two, which you will pierce in each end with a large auger, with which the middle portions are pierced in the wheels of ploughs. But because the openings cannot meet together, on account of the curve, make for yourself an iron which may have a round head, like an egg, and a long thin stem, which is fitted with a handle, and let it be slightly curved, near the head, with which, made hot, you burn the holes curved inside, until they meet together in an even manner. Which being done, cut this wood in a square manner, set so that it be one palm wide in each side, to the size of the wind-chamber in the blunt part. After these things join this wood on the longer part, to the lower opening of the organ structure (building frame), so that a projection may be cut to the same wood a thumb in length, which can be placed, or forced into this opening, and that the joint be so subtle that no wind can escape from it. You join on in the same manner the other wood with cheese-glue, and will wrap round the whole wood, with the join, with cloth, to which you also fix a wide piece of copper which may also compass the edge of each wood. These things being thus completed, should you wish to establish the organ beyond the masonry of the wall, so that nothing may appear within the

[1] In chapter xvii of his book Theophilus explains how to make casein glue by boiling cheese with water and adding lime.

cloister, unless the erection alone with the pipes, and that the bellows may lie on the other side, you must so turn the structure that the sliders may be drawn out towards the bellows, and an arch may be made in the wall itself in which the chanter (i.e. performer) can sit, whose seat is so adapted that he can keep his feet above the bellows. There is also a square opening in the middle of the arch through the masonry, through which the structure with the pipes is exposed to view; and upon the neck of the bellows, which is in the wall beneath, the opening is made firm with stones, it is supported at its junction, and is rested upon two long iron nails evenly fixed in the wall; to this opening a wooden window hangs, which, when shut, is defended by a lock and key, that no stranger coming unaware be able to learn what may be contained in it. Outside, also, above the organ, a thick drapery, extended inside with wood like a dome, for warding off the dust, can hang by a rope from the ceiling, which rope, arranged with art around a wheel above the ceiling itself, is drawn whilst the organ is sounding, and thus raises the roof, and the chant being finished, it is lowered upon the organ. This dome also has a spire, made from the same cloth, extended by four pieces of wood in shape of a triangle, at the top of which a small wooden ball can stand, to which the rope cleaves. The bellows, and the instrument upon which they may lie, arrange at your pleasure according to the situation of the spot.

"*Chapter LXXXIV. Of the Copper Construction and Its Bellows.*

"Dispose the length and width of the case according to the number of the pipes, and make a mould in beaten clay, and, being dry, cut it to whatever size you may wish, and cover with wax carefully thinned, between two rods equally thick, with the round wood. Then cut the openings of the sliders in this wax, and the hole below through which the wind can enter; the air-holes with the funnel being added, cover altogether with the same clay, and again, and a third time. And when the mould has become dry, cast in the same manner as the form of the censer above mentioned. You will also fashion the bellows in clay, the wind-issues proceeding everywhere below in the similitude of the roots of a tree, and meeting at the top in one opening. Which, when disposed in rule you have cut with a knife, cover with wax and act as above. And when you have cast the case, you join, inside, at the height of one finger from the bottom, a beaten copper plate, in an even manner under the openings of the stops, that these stops may rest upon it, so that they can be smoothly drawn forth and return; and lining these stops with thin clay, you pour over the rest of the case some melted lead everywhere, over these stops up to the top. This being done, you cast out this lead and will carefully mark the openings of the pipes in the stops; then you will most carefully perforate in this lead with a thin iron or with a bore. Then you make the channels for the wind under the sliders; you introduce these sliders singly in their places, and you replace the lead, and you fit them to the organ frame by beating with the hammer, so that no wind can issue, unless through the openings in which the pipes are placed. When the wind-case has been cast and filed, and the pipe of each air-hole fitted to its wind-channel, it should be joined together and firmly soldered below to the organ structure, so that the wind may find its access freely, and can in nowise issue through the other joints. This also is to be carefully provided, that a thin piece of copper may hang down before the opening of its pipe, which can close the access of the air-hole, so that when by the breathing of the bellows this copper is displaced, it may rise, and the wind may freely issue: and when the bellows is raised, so that it may recover air through its own ventilator, this copper can quite close its mouth and not permit the wind which it emitted to return." (The copper plate is to act as a valve.)

Until the eleventh century flue pipes were either of "diapason" quality or of "stopped" tone. A whole rank of pipes irrespective of length would be made on the same mandril and thus be of a common diameter. Accordingly the pipes of lower tone would yield a thin, bright tone and those of higher tone would give a dull tone of flute quality. Pipes were made of copper,[1] brass or wood. Theophilus indicated that different methods of finishing pipes would produce different qualities of tone, but at a much earlier date Theodoret noted that a change in pipe materials produced a modification of tone quality.[2]

At this time various methods of playing were in use, including the pressing of levers.

We get glimpses of large and rather intractable organs from the tenth to the twelfth centuries, not unlike those at Winchester, Rheims, Erfurt, the abbeys of Limoges and Fécamp. The compass was from sixteen to twenty notes, each one controlling a considerable number of pipes, so that the entire instrument contained some hundreds. Octave and fifth speaking ranks were there in abundance, and the parallel motion of the vocal organum was in the instrument itself. Reeds and stopped pipes were also known. When sliders were displaced by keys in the thirteenth and fourteenth centuries these were of considerable size and needed the whole hand to press or strike them, and the organist who played these unwieldy instruments was known as "pulsator organorum". The keys were 3 in. to 5 in. wide, 2 in. thick and upwards of 1 ft. in length. The "depth of touch" was often 1 ft. The mechanism of the little hydraulus of Aquincum had to be reinvented in Christendom. The Winchester organ and the large instruments which existed until the end of the Gothic period were simply huge mixtures, and when organ-stops were reinvented their purpose was *to shut off* parts of the instrument.

From the eleventh to the thirteenth century three types of organs were developed: the large and cumbrous instrument which was built in the tribunes, pulpita and galleries of the abbeys and cathedrals in Europe and England; the positive organ, so called because it was used in one place at a time and was not carried during performance. It was transportable rather than portable Then there was the tiny portative organ, which could be carried by a strap or band round the neck of the performer. Its small bellows were worked by the left hand and it was played with the right hand, and, like the positive, was capable of harmony. Small portative organs with reeds instead of flue pipes were known as *regals*.

[1] *Vita S. Oswaldi Archiepiscopi Eboracensis*, xxvii, 66.
[2] *De Providentia Oratio iii* in *Patri. Graec.*, lxxxiii, 590A.

The Large Organ Until the End of the Gothic Period

Although there is a possibility that other cathedrals and abbeys in England had instruments like that at Winchester, it is clear that large organs such as this were not typical. Positive and portative organs were much more common. In France and Germany such instruments were more numerous. Here is one of he earliest references to an English cathedral instrument which was clearly a large positive organ:

Ripon Cathedral[1]

A.D. 1399:

The Fabric Rolls record that in 1399 several sums of money were paid for materials for the repair of the organs.

Two horses' skins for two pairs of new bellows	2*s*. 8*d*.
Two calves' skins and two sheeps' skins for same	1*s*. 6*d*.
Half a thousand small nails for same	8*d*.
Pack thread	3*d*.
One man working on the aforesaid organs, by agreement	3*s*. 4*d*.
Drink given to the said man	2*d*.

A.D. 1408:

A piece of timber was purchased at a cost of 1*s*. 6*d*. for the foundation of the "purpytyl" (choir-screen).

A.D. 1453:

20*s*. was paid for mending the organs and 4*s*. 2*d*. was paid to Robert Wright for work upon the purpetyle of the said organ, and to William Wright for working six days upon the same, 2*s*. 6*d*. Richard Carver received 6*d*. for "gropying mensal" (probably the "keyboard") of the said purpetyle.

Ely Cathedral

An interesting price list of the materials necessary for making an organ is found in the precentor's account of Ely Cathedral for the year 1407 as follows:

20 stones of lead	16*s*. 9*d*.
4 white horses' hides for 4 pair of bellows	7*s*. 8*d*.
Ashen hoops for the bellows	4*d*.
10 pairs of hinges	1*s*. 10*d*.
The carpenter, eight days making the bellows	2*s*. 8*d*.
12 springs	3*d*.
1 pound of glue	1*d*.
1 pound of tin	3*d*.
6 calf skins	2*s*. 6*d*.
12 sheep skins	2*s*. 4*d*.
2 pounds of quicksilver	2*s*. 0*d*.
Wire, nails, cloths, hoops and staples	1*s*. 0*d*.
Fetching the organ-builder and his board thirteen weeks	40*s*. 0*d*.
	£3 17*s*. 8*d*.

[1] *Records in Ripon Cathedral.*

The pipes were made of lead, and as there was twenty stones of it and only twelve notes there might have been two, three or four pipes for each note, although it is possible that there were only twelve pipes of good substance. The mercury and tin were mixed with lead to make solder according to a process which is given by Henri Arnaut and is described later.[1] The instrument was in no sense a "grand organ". In the middle of the fifteenth century Abbot Whithamstead of St. Albans Abbey spent £50 on an organ and such a sum must have purchased an instrument of considerable size. (Until the time of Whithamstead the organs had been cheap and music had been neglected to such an extent that in 1421 one of the monks deserted to Canterbury in order better to study the art.) Wheathampstede's (Whithamstead's) Registrum gives an account of this organ.[2] "That young men and maidens, and old people besides, should be able to praise the Lord of Heaven, and extol Him in the highest, not indeed, with the drum and the dance, but with stringed instruments and the organ and its pipes, and a sound as of sweet voiced cymbals, he (the abbot) caused to be made a pair of organs than which there was not to be readily found, as was believed, an instrument more beautiful to look upon or more sweet to hear, or more elaborate in workmanship in any monastery, throughout the whole kingdom. As to its cost, in the making and fixing it in position more than fifty pounds was spent."[3]

Two stipendiary organists were maintained for playing this instrument.

[1] See p. 49.
[2] *Chron. Whithamstead*: ed. Hearne, vol. ii, p. 539.
[3] *Translated by the late Dean Lawrence* in *The Musical Times* (1909).

CHAPTER III

FROM GOTHIC TO RENAISSANCE ORGAN

WE HAVE no comprehensive report or treatise on organ-building in England from the time of the Winchester organ. We can only reconstruct a picture of the instrument and gain an idea of the varying esteem in which it was held in the religious changes in the country from the numerous references to payments for materials used and work in making these instruments. There are several German works on organs of which the most notable is that of Praetorius[1] (1619). Praetorius is not always reliable as a historian in his statements about instruments of the early times, but he gives an excellent picture of the sixteenth-century organs and glimpses of those of the Gothic period. Thus we can trace the history of the German instrument through the Gothic and Renaissance periods to the early Baroque.

Setting aside for the present the magnificent eighteenth-century French volumes of Dom Bédos, with which we shall deal later, we find that the works of Henri Arnaut of Zwolle, the fifteenth-century astrologer to the Duke of Bourgogne (Burgundy), give us a picture of fourteenth- and fifteenth-century organs of France and the Low Countries.[2]

Burney, in the eighteenth century, remarked that large organs seemed to be a natural growth in Germany,[3] and from the twelfth century there were large instruments in that country.

But Germany was not alone, for large organs were found in France, Spain and the Low Countries. England and Italy developed a smaller type of instrument which was easy to play, readily portable, would permit rapid execution of contrapuntal music, and would sustain harmonies. No English organ until the Reformation is known to have had more than one manual and half a dozen stops and there were no pedals. As we shall see, these were unknown in Britain until the eighteenth century.

We will now deal with the development of the organ in France and the Low Countries. The positive organ had developed in the thirteenth century and organ-builders knew how to make a wind-chest with as many as thirty-two to thirty-six notes of "four feet" pitch and with from five to eight pipes for each note. The well-known Van Eyck panel (Plate 8) in Ghent Cathedral, which shows an angel playing a positive organ, clearly depicts a separate bottom note which can be held down when necessary by a latch. The effect of

[1] Michael Praetorius, *De Organographia*, vol. ii of *Syntagma Musicum* (Wolfenbüttel, 1619. Facsimile ed. Kassel, 1929).

[2] *Les Traités d'Henri Arnaut de Zwolle et de divers Anonymes* (d'après le MS. Latin 7295 de la Bibl. Nat. Paris), edited by G. le Cerf and E. B. Labande (Paris, Picard, 1932).

[3] C. Burney, *Tour Through Germany and the Netherlands* (London, 1773), vol. ii, p. 275.

a drone, or, as it would be called at a later date, a pedal-point, was appreciated. Thus, when the problem of extending the smaller organs presented itself to the old organ-builders it could be met by adding large pipes to the bass and high-pitched pipes to the trebles. It was easy to make a keyboard which would actuate small pipes of small diameter, but no mechanism was yet known for playing a pipe which was not planted above the key controlling it. The *roller-board*, which transmitted the movement of a key to a position lateral to it, had not yet been invented. The bass "drone" pipes, about ten in number, the longest of which might be 12 ft. in length, were played from a second keyboard and were known as bourdons. In order to restore the balance between bass and treble another keyboard controlling high-pitched pipes was also employed. This was known as the descant[1] manual and was, in fact, a large mixture stop. There were no stops to shut off some of the pipes from any of the manuals. The invention of pedals will be discussed at a later stage, but it is easy to imagine that they originated in the means employed to pull down the keys of the "tenor[2] keyboard" which controlled the large pipes by means of cords and wooden levers for the feet. The large pipes of the tenor or contra-tenor clavier could be arranged in the case of the instrument, in towers at each side, and thus designers of organ cases could plan for more imposing structures. The large pipes in the case-work were called "trompes"[3] and an example of an enlarged organ-case on these lines was made in Rouen Cathedral in 1386. The pipes of the descant or small organ would be placed on a gallery at the base of the main woodwork in a small, separate case, often placed at the back of the player (positif de dos). (This was the equivalent of the English Chair Organ of a later date.) Such a little "positif de dos" of the fifteenth century mentioned by Henri Arnaut contained 195 pipes, and he mentions other instruments in which the main-organ, "les grandes orgues", contained 495, 579, 660, 768, and 636 respectively, without counting the tenor pipes and reeds. Antoine Artesan records that there were 1,400 pipes in the organ at the Château de Blois in 1451, and records of Amiens Cathedral show that the organ contained 2,500 in 1429.[4]

Wood was not used in the making of pipes in France, the Low Countries and North Germany at this period. However, we hear of its use in Bavaria for this purpose in the fifteenth century.[5] In France almost pure tin (étain de glace), brought from Cornwall as early as 1386, a mixture of tin and lead

[1] Descant = old French *deschant* from the Latin *dis* (away) and *cantus* (song), i.e. a song away or different from the tenor.

[2] The word "tenor" (= old French *tenour*, Latin *tenere*, to hold) was used because in early times the chief melody was sustained by an adult male voice.

[3] Not to be confused with trumpets. It is also necessary to point out that the bourdons were open pipes and bore no relation to the pipes of the modern stop of that name. (Hopkins and Rimbault wrongly presumed that they were stopped pipes.)

[4] N. Dufourcq, *Esquisse d'une Histoire de l'Orgue en France* (*XIIIe–XVIIIe Siècles*) (Paris, 1935).

[5] Wood has never been popular as an organ-pipe material in France, the Low Countries and North Germany. The great Haarlem organ (q.v.), 1735–9, did not contain a single wooden pipe originally—a fact ascribed by Leopold, the father of W. A. Mozart, to the difficulties arising from a wooden construction in a damp climate. (Letter 16.5.1766 from Paris to Lorenz Hagenauer.)

(known as l'étoffe in France and, later, "metal" in England), and lead were used. The tin favoured a bright tone whereas lead tended to produce a duller quality lacking in harmonic development. Jean Piaz of Meaux, who built the organ for the Sainte-Chapelle at Chambéry in 1472, has left a document describing the making of organ pipes, a process which has changed remarkably little throughout the years.

"Après avoir tenu et gouverné les plates d'étain sur l'encleume, il faut les dresser et redoucer, car toutes sont ployez par la bateure."[1] The sheets were cast by filling a wooden box, which had a horizontal slit at the bottom of one side, with the molten metal and then pushing the box over a smooth surface so that a flat stream of metal ran out and solidified to form a sheet. The sheets were held on an anvil and beaten with a hammer and then it was necessary to straighten them and smooth them out. They were then cut up with shears and scraped with a "*parouer*". The dimensions of the pieces were marked out with dividers, and by means of a mould or mandril the pieces were shaped and soldered up. Pipes frequently sagged into their feet and the same moulds and mandrils were used for straightening the pipes. Sometimes the pipes had to be taken to pieces, rebeaten, and after coating them inside and out with vernis blanc (white varnish) they were soldered up again.

Arnaut gives the method of soldering, and an earlier method has been described in the Treatise of Theophilus the Monk. One part of lead to two parts of Cornish tin were melted together, and when a bluish tinge appeared on the surface of the alloy one ounce of mercury was to be added.[2]

Tin pipes were used for the show pipes in the case of the organ: the *montres* and the *prestants*; they were burnished with a *brunyssouer*, but lead pipes, which are recorded as early as 1372 in the organ of the Grey Friars at Avignon, were used for those that stood inside the organ and where duller, unassertive tones were required. It is interesting to note that the words *montre* (a show pipe) and *prestant* (praestans, i.e. standing in front) are still retained as organ-stop names for open metal flue pipes. The nearest equivalent in the English organ would be *open diapason* and *principal* respectively. Henri Arnaut divides his sets of pipes into three pitches: barduni (bourdons), naturales and supernaturales. The natural or normal pitch was equivalent to our 4-ft. pitch; that is to say, on modern reckoning, the speaking length of an *open* pipe giving CC two octaves below "middle C" would approximate to 4 ft. The bourdons would be an octave lower. Arnaut tells us that the old organ at Notre Dame, Dijon, reached up from BBB (below present 8-ft. CC). Niccolo d'Este, Marquis of Ferrara, visited the Cathedral of Notre Dame, Paris, in 1414 and saw "two very large organs, one of which had sixteen bellows, and the scale of 9 ft.".[3]

The buzzing *open* flue drone pipes only numbered three or four, but were afterwards increased to nine or ten. They must have produced powerful

[1] Chambéry, Duffour et Rabut, *Les Musiciens, la Musique et les Instruments de Musique du XIIe au XIXe Siècle* (1878).

[2] Prévost, *Instruments de Musique usités dans nos Églises depuis le XIIIe Siècle* (1904). Record of S. Pierre de Troye, 1381.

[3] L. Mirot, "Autour de la Paix d'Arras", in *Bibl. de l'École des Chartes* (1914), pp. 261 and 305.

sounds, for in 1382 at Rouen Cathedral the organ-builder was asked to remove these pipes because the tenor overweighted the smaller stops. The bourdons were usually regarded as an optional addition, but in 1421, in the organ at Ste. Marie-de-la-Mer, it is specified that the instrument shall have "per nombre ab los bordons XXXV" (thirty-five notes including the bourdons).

As regards the high-pitched *supernaturales*, the top pipe was of 1½ in. speaking length.

Little is known of the method of voicing the pipes mentioned by Arnaut. The circumference of the pipes was a sixth or seventh (and occasionally a fifth) of the length of the pipe at 4-ft. C and the width of the mouth was a quarter of the circumference of the pipe. Dufourcq is of the opinion that various scales were employed in the different pipe ranks and that advantage was taken of the fact that a small $\frac{\text{circumference}}{\text{length}}$ ratio gives a stringy, bright tone, and a large ratio a dull tone.[1] We do not know other important matters such as the relative heights of the pipe mouths and the pressure of wind employed.

The fifteenth-century organ grew to a considerable size, and the organ-builders must have seen its potentialities for power and tonal variety. At first it spoke as an enormous mixture stop with its montres or principals of 16, 8, 4, 2, 1 ft. and its cymbales and fournitures.

Arnaut carefully lists the different families of stops, namely, the 8-ft. stops, the 4-ft., the quints, the fournitures and cymbales, the reeds. Stops were invented for shutting off parts of the organ. The smaller organs must have possessed means of bringing on and taking off the tone of pipe-ranks, for Arnaut states that the organ used for "the Mass of Monseigneur, the Duke of Burgundy, possessed five registers: a principal (montre), divided by stop action into two, a quint (fifth), an octave and a twelfth". Undoubtedly this was a 4-ft. organ and the pitches of the stops would be 4 ft. (divided), nazard 2⅔ ft., doublette 2 ft., and larigot 1⅓ ft.

The European organ of the fourteenth and fifteenth centuries had a powerful principal, a stop whose lowest note was of 8-ft. or 6-ft. pitch, with quints and octaves. The fourniture was another principal, with its own series of quints and octaves. Sometimes this was not separated from the main principal, and the whole would form a brilliant *organum plenum.* The organ described by Henri Arnaut contained no other type of foundation stop than the principal and thus such ranks were often duplicated. The principal or montre in the case of the organ was made of tin, but the other principal inside the instrument was of plain metal or lead, and ultimately gave place to the stopped flute or bourdon. The lowest note of the principal varied from organ to organ, but it was on the 4-ft. note that the builder constructed his tonal superstructure. The "choirs" or "choruses" of principals, that is, the open flue chorus, consisted of open pipes of 8 ft. (or 6 ft.), 4 ft. (or 3 ft.), 2 ft. (or 18 in.), 1 ft. (or 9 in.).

[1] MM. le Cerf and Labande (op. cit.) have compared Arnaut's scalings with those of Mersennus, Praetorius and Dom Bédos.

The fourniture[1] was not used to make the principal tone more shrill or piercing but to broaden and enrich the tone. The number of ranks of the fourniture increased as the scale ascended. Great skill on the part of the organ-builder was necessary in order to arrange the breaks in the mixture so that as soon as a pipe-length reached 3 in. it doubled back to a length of 6 in. for the next pipe. The fourniture was made of octave and fifth sounding pipes, but rarely included the twelfth of 2⅔ ft. At a slightly later date the cymbale stop was introduced.

Reed pipes were in use after the fourteenth century. The regals or reed-portatifs had a single set of reed pipes of short length with reeds and shallots. According to Arnaut the reed stop on large organs began with the note F of 6-ft. pitch.

By the end of the fourteenth century a second set of keys had been added to the larger organs. Reports show that the Rouen Cathedral organ of 1386, and those at Troyes Cathedral in 1422 and Argentan in 1462, were thus equipped. It is probable that the "dui organi grandissimi" mentioned by Niccolo d'Este at Paris in 1414 was a great organ and its positif, but the term "pair of organs"[2] does not usually refer to a two-manual instrument.

The compass of the keyboards varied between two and a half and four octaves. The organ at Ste. Marie-de-la-Mer, built by Graynena in 1421, had thirty-five keys "ab los semitons y ab los bordons" (including the semitones and the bourdons). Henri Arnaut describes instruments with 31, 36, 43 and 47. Some instruments began with the note of 3-ft. pitch, others with the B below 4-ft. pitch, the F of 6-ft. or the B below 8-ft. pitch. The compass of the second keyboard was shorter. The "teneure" keyboard of St. Cyr at Nevers had twelve notes, that at the Franciscan Grey Friars' Church had ten, and at Rouen Cathedral sixteen notes. Although the length of the clavier on the organ of St. Cyr at Nevers was known to be 22½ in. long, we do not know how many notes it possessed, and thus it is impossible to give the extent of an octave.

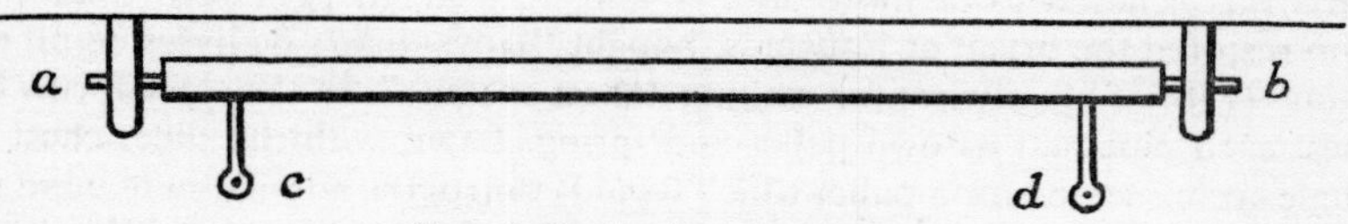

FIG. 8. Roller in roller-board.

Roller-boards were already in use in the fourteenth century, and this enabled the pipes to be planted above and laterally displaced from their respective keys. All we know of these roller-boards is that they were in frequent need of repair. At the beginning of the fifteenth century we find frequent requests made to organ-builders for them to regulate and "ease" the

[1] The word "fourniture" from the old French *fournir*—to supply—infers that the stop supplied power and brilliance. The word bourdon (French drone or buzz) may also be related to "burden", the tenor theme of a song.

[2] The word "pair" is used in the same sense as a "pair of bellows" or "a pair of stairs".

key action. In spite of the fact that the coupling of the keyboards together served to make the playing of the instrument more difficult, it was known and used in the late fourteenth century. In the records of Rouen Cathedral (1386) we read that the second keyboard of sixteen notes would sound and play alone when one wished, and the grand organ alone, and as a whole, coupled together, when one so wished. Later on in the manuscript this facility is described as a novelty. Arnaut tells us how this coupling was carried out, in his description of the Grey Friars' organ. Into the end parts of the lower keyboard a number of small wooden plugs were fitted. When the coupler was in use these plugs were brought into a vertical position and the plug rising from the lower key fitted under the upper key, set a little further back. As the keys were hinged at their ends and not balanced, the depression of the top key would take down the lower. The first record of a pedal in a French organ was that at Troyes in 1432. It is impossible to say what was the exact nature of this pedal, but it is probable that these early pedals were "pull-downs" and were connected to the manual keys.

The wind-chest of the organ at Ste. Marie-de-la-Mer in 1421 was made of hard oak, known as *bois de Flandres*. Arnaut gives the following dimensions for the chest at St. Cyr. It was nearly 22 in. broad, 3¼ in. high and rather more than 30 in. long in a "four-feet" organ. The chests were in frequent need of repair and were made windtight with codfish glue, red leather and nails.[1] We read in the account of the Rouen organ the use of twenty-seven skins of lamb, one hind-skin covered with alum and eight cow skins.

The chests were covered inside and outside with leather, but even this did not render them quite airtight. In the Ste. Marie-de-la-Mer organ (1421) it is specified that "the wind-chest shall be airtight without the use of glue and should be so made that it could be opened and closed at will by means of studs (boutons)".

There is frequent reference in the accounts which we have mentioned above to the "regeteurs" or pallet springs. These frequently broke, and brass from Paris was believed to be more durable and flexible. In 1474 Jean Challays, who restored the organ at Fougères, bought "troys quarts de livres de fill de leton" (¾ lb. of brass wire) for making "chest-springs". In the early forms of chest each pipe had its own pallet and spring. Later, with the slider-chest a single spring served for a pallet which would control the admission of wind to all the pipes playable from a single note. The chest belonging to the main keyboard was about a yard above the keyboard. When Godefroy de Furnes in 1386 added a "support" of sixteen keys to the Rouen organ, he placed his second wind-chest above the other. In the case of the ten or twelve large pipes of the lower "teneure" keyboard these were divided into two groups of five or six pipes each and placed in the case-work at the sides.

On 23rd February 1361, Nicholas Faber completed an organ at Halberstadt Cathedral, an instrument which was renovated in 1495 by Gregory Kleng. Praetorius[2] gives us a description of this instrument and illustrates its key-

[1] At Rouen, in 1386, G. de Furnes supplied "la colle de morue et cuir rouge mis en oeuvre à recoller entour le sommier des orgues".

[2] Praetorius, op. cit. [See Plates 4a, b, c.]

boards. Its compass was twenty-two notes, with fourteen "naturals" and eight sharps, from B♮ (H in German) to A, and it was blown by twenty bellows worked by ten men. The lowest B♮ pipe was 31 Brunswick ft. in length and about 14 in. in diameter. It gave the note below the lowest of a 32-ft. rank, but in view of the higher pitch of this old organ, the note which it spoke would be about a semitone above the present CCC 32-ft. pipe. The Halberstadt organ had three manual claviers and pedals. The top keyboard or first descant manual controlled the full chorus of unison, quint, octave, octave quint-super-octave, mixtures and cymbals; the next keyboard controlled the principal alone; the lowest keyboard, which Praetorius suggests might have been played by the knees as well as by the hands, controlled an octave of the lowest pipes. The compass of the two descant manuals was two octaves, less one key—H (B♮) to A with all semitones. The first descant manual controlled the Praestant ("open diapason") and the Hintersatz, which was a mixture of thirty-two to fifty-six ranks of pipes. The Hintersatz was so-called because of its position in the organ. The bass or pedal-pipes at the sides were sometimes called Seitenwerk(e).

The lowest or bass manual had a compass of one octave and a semitone (B♮ to C) and the longest pipes were in the large side towers of the case. It is surprising that the lyric semitone (B♭) was not supplied. The pedal of an octave compass controlled a principal and a Hintersatz with sixteen to twenty-four ranks of mixture, but, in the words of Praetorius, "all was of coarse mixture. This is evident from the size of the prestant pipes, and from the small compass of their clavier, which did not extend high enough for beauty, but produced a deep, coarse roar and fearful growling, to which the mixture pipes added an extremely loud noise, a terrible scream. . . ."[1]

It is recorded that in 1350 a monk at Torun (Thorn) in Poland built an organ with twenty-two keys.[2]

Large instruments built in fine cases were found in many parts of Europe in the fifteenth century. They were intractable to play, capable of sustaining only the crudest counterpoint and sometimes only single-line melodies played with mixtures containing repeated octaves and fifth-sounding ranks, with an occasional change to other brilliant mixtures and, less frequently, a single loud 8-ft. stop. When the tone was mollified by the reverberation of a vast Gothic cathedral there can be no doubt that its powerful diapason chorus would have considerable emotional effect. At St. Laurence, Nuremberg, in the instrument built by Leonard Marca in 1479,[3] there were 1,100 pipes on

[1] The great mixtures of the Gothic periods would probably have ranks of the order of the following. The pitches of the ranks are given:

16 8 8 5⅓ 4 4 4 4 2⅔ 2⅔ 2⅔ 2⅔ 2⅔ 2 2 2 2 2 2
1⅓ 1⅓ 1⅓ 1⅓ 1⅓ 1⅓ 1 1 1 1 1 1 1 1 ⅔ ⅔ ⅔ ⅔ ⅔ ⅔ ⅔ ⅔ ⅔ ⅔

The Winchester mixture would probably be

8 4 4 2⅔ 2⅔ 2 2 1⅓ 1⅓ 1

There is no evidence for the use of tierce or third sounding ranks at this time.

[2] Praetorius, op. cit.

[3] Sponsel, *Orgelhistorie* (Nuremberg, 1771); and Dietz, *Lorenzer Orgelbüchlein* (Kassel, 1937).

the great organ and "454 on the positive". The largest pipe including the foot was 39 ft. long.[1] The organ built by Heinrich Traxdorf for St. Sebald's Church in the same city in 1444 was a large instrument which cost 1,150 florins. The wealthy merchants of the Hanseatic cities of Lübeck and Hamburg equipped their churches with great organs. We have already noted that at Amiens in France the organ had 2,500 pipes in 1429. The organ at Rheims Cathedral by the great builder Oudin Hestre had pipes 27 ft. long and a case 54 ft. high, in 1487. These represented the Gothic organ at its apogee. In England we get no hint of even a moderate-sized organ after that given to St. Alban's Abbey in 1450, and for which £50 was paid by Abbot Whithamstead.

We will now turn aside from the "grand" organ in the West-end "tribune" of the European cathedrals and discuss the two smaller instruments, the portative and positive organs which developed at the same time.

The portative organ (nimphale), which could be carried in the hands or suspended from the neck and shoulder by a band or belt, was first heard of in England in the twelfth century and it flourished both there and on the Continent in the following three centuries. We find so many representations of it—in church windows, wood and stone carvings, in paintings, in psalters, and other illuminated works—that it is easy to trace its growth and describe its action. After the sixteenth century less is heard of it. It was played with the right hand and blown with the left, and thus we can see it in the eighth panel of the Minstrel's Gallery at Exeter Cathedral (fourteenth century). In common with the lute, the clavecin and the clavichord it was a harmonic instrument and two or three parts could be played on it simultaneously in the type of polyphonic music composed by Léonin or Pérotin in the thirteenth century. It was carried in processions within and without the churches. It was found in the houses of merchants, in the private chapels of the nobility. It was used instead of the flute or chalumeau; it could replace voices or it could assist them. It was used for giving the note to the "schola" and for sustaining the plainsong melody. It was used at the portals of the cathedrals for accompanying the Miracle and Mystery plays. Both "infernal" and "heavenly" music were played on it.[2]

The positif organ was of two kinds—the small positive which stood on a table and the larger type which stood on the floor (*positif de table* and *positif à pied*. Plates 5 and 6).

They are first recorded in the late tenth century as was the portative also. The positive was found in houses as well as in churches. Like its smaller brother, the positive was also used in Mystery plays "pour accompagner les Voix du Ciel ou les Diablotins descendus sur terre". It was a favourite instrument of both nobles and bourgeois. It was played by both men and women. After the passing of the large Gothic organ in England, the organs were either positive or portative until the sixteenth and early seventeenth centuries, and even then the size of the large instruments in this country was modest compared with the European "grand" organs.

[1] Longer than any organ pipe in England today.
[2] Hans Hickman, *Das Portativ* (Kassel, 1937).

In France, Italy, Germany and the Low Countries the table positive was favoured by all fourteenth-century society. The positive could usually be carried short distances by two horizontal poles, and this required a minimum of four men. Two hands were used for playing the positive and one or two

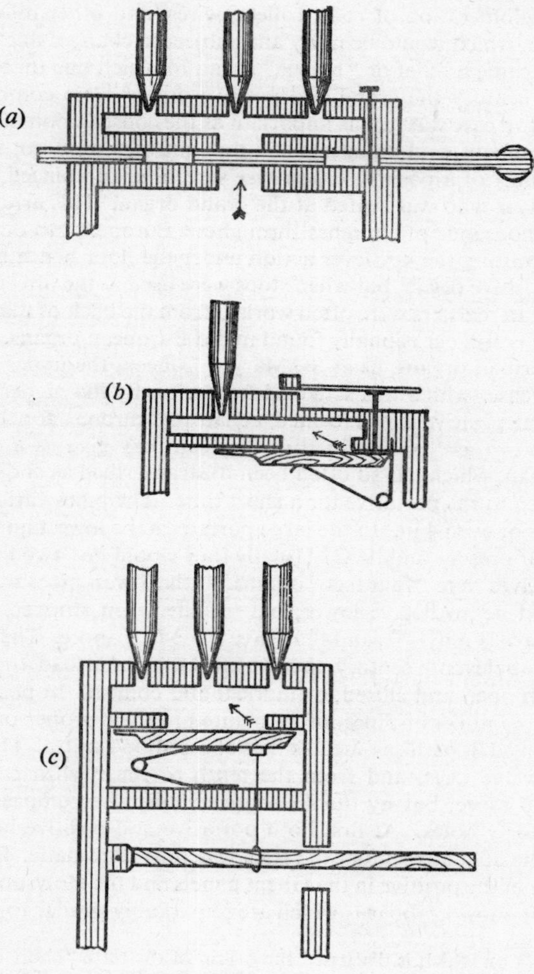

FIG. 9.

(*a*) Slider action (twelfth century). This was used for both small and large organs, though sometimes the former were played by stopping holes with the fingers. (*b*) Pin action for small organs (thirteenth century). (*c*) Tracker action (fourteenth century). Although these actions were common at these dates, keyboards were in use earlier than the twelfth century.

blowers were required for working the diagonal bellows which were placed at the back and outside the organ case. The portative disappeared in the seventeenth century, but the positive survived. It had been placed on the screen (pulpitum) or in the tribune side by side with the great organ. It would be turned to with relief by the "pulsator organorum" struggling with the intractable conglomeration of rods, rollers, wires, and other movements of his grand organ, which would be noisy and subject to changes due to climate. The positive became a relief or "helper" organ to which one turned.[1] From the fourteenth century the grand and positive organs were combined. The design of an organ case was just as important as the construction of the sound-producing instrument, and architects and draughtsmen were not slow to see the beautiful effect of a positive organ case screening and placed behind the back of the player who was seated at the grand organ. This arrangement is still found in thousands of churches throughout Europe.[2] No difficulty was found in transmitting the key lever action under the floor beneath the organ pedals to the positive organ, but when stops were used in the fifteenth century the positive organ registers were often worked from the back of the organist—a system which is still occasionally found in old European organs.

In North German organs, as at St. Mary's, Lübeck, the upper part of the positive organ case (which was screened from view by the higher pipe-work and casing of the positive front) formed a chair or "throne" for the organist. It was then known as "positiv in stuhl", which may give us a clue to the name chair organ, which has so often been mistranscribed as choir organ.[3]

We will return to the portative for a short time. The pipes varied in length from 24 in. to 8 or even 4 in. In the large portatives the lowest note would be not far from our present middle C. Usually they would be "two feet" organs just as the positives were "four feet" organs. If the lowest pipes were stopped the pitch would be an octave lower, but usually when stopped pipes were used the longest was only 1 ft. and thus gave the 2-ft. C. note. The pipes were made of tin in the eleventh century, then an alloy of tin and lead, then of wood. They were both open and closed, cylindrical and conical. In positives there were two or three ranks of pipes, often planted in their proper order. Later they were arranged in patterns such as that of a bishop's mitre. The portative had nine to twelve keys, and from the tenth to the twelfth centuries the positive had no more, but by the sixteenth century the compass was from thirty-four to forty notes. At first both portative and positive had diatonic scales, but by the fifteenth century the scale was fully chromatic. The detailed representations of the positive in the Ghent panels and the Holyrood paintings (Plates 8 and 7) show keyboards which are remarkably similar to our present

[1] See pp. 161–3 on which is discussed the origin of the term "choir organ". The misused word "choir" may have come from chor, chair (O.E.) or Kehr (Germ.)—a helper.

[2] In England it is not often found, and where it does exist it is usually for the sake of appearance only, e.g. at St. Paul's Cathedral the organist now sits in the original "chair organ" case and another case on the opposite side has been made to contain the "chair" organ. Originally there was only one chair organ case, the organ stood on a screen and the case faced west.

[3] See page 161, and Appendix Specification No. 1.

type, though the keys are shorter in length. It will be observed that sometimes one or more large pipes were planted out of order. In the Van Eyck panel at Ghent a key which can be held down by a latch is clearly seen on the extreme left. These pipes were drones and their sustained bass notes would be the origin of the pedal point or "pedal" of later organ music, a harmonic device which is still in use today.

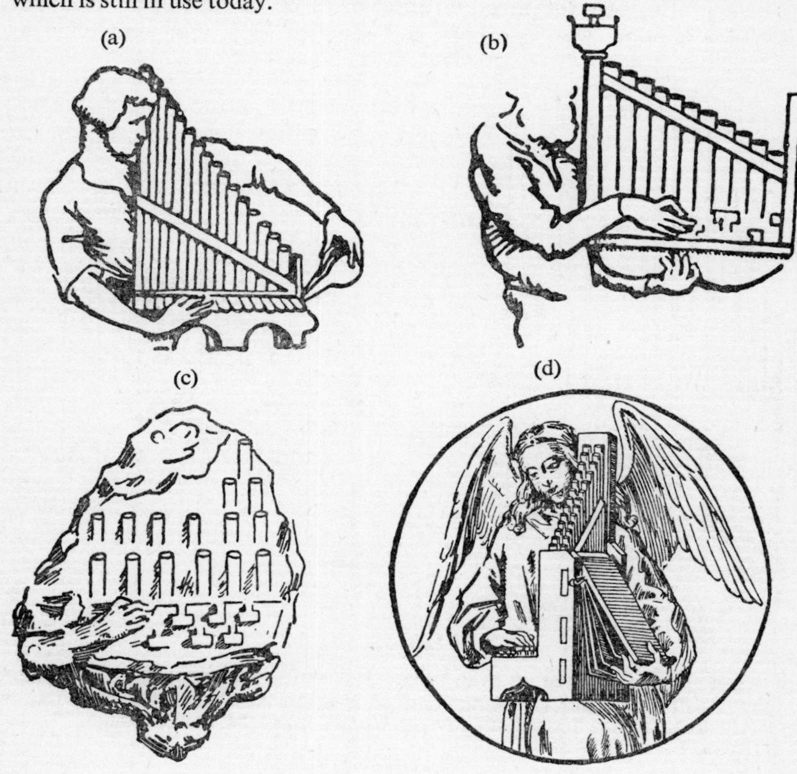

FIG. 10.

(a) Portative organ—St. Savin (Hautes Pyrénées) fresco under the altar canopy (XIV c).
(b) Portative organ—Window in the Chapel of the Virgin in Rouen Cathedral.
(c) Fourteenth-century remains of a stone carving from Nonancourt (Eure) showing a portative organ with keys of "type-writer" pattern.
(d) Angel with portative organ depicted by Memling, shrine of Ste. Ursula in the Hospital Saint-Jean at Bruges (fifteenth century).

The portative had a single bellows, but there were two or three to supply wind to the positives. These were made in triangular, semi-circular, pear-shaped or rectangular form and could be worked either by hand or feet.

At first the keys were simple flat levers, the ends of which were placed between the ends of the pipes and the wind-chest. Later keys which resembled large typewriter keys were affixed to these levers (see Fig. 10). The pallet or wooden lever-valve (see Fig. 9) was invented in the fourteenth century and is still in use in thousands of organs. The modern keyboard evolved from the round or square keys. There was an upper range of ebony or ivory "touch-buttons" and a lower one for the diatonic notes.

The portative was the favourite instrument of the important musician Francesco Landini, who was born in Fiesole in 1325, and went blind in

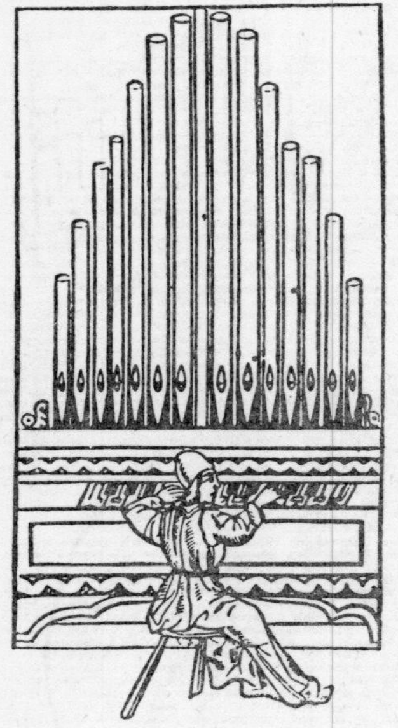

FIG. 11.

An organ (left) illustrated in Franchinus Gaffurius' "Theorica Musica" (Milan 1492). (This was purely diagrammatic to illustrate certain acoustical points.)

A small organ of the fourteenth century (right) from the Peterborough Psalter (Royal Library, Brussels).

childhood, apparently from smallpox. He was an excellent player on several instruments, but he preferred the portative or organetto. His playing, poetry, and music, of which last 150 works remain, were admired by Petrarch and by Peter the Great, King of Cyprus.

In a Romanzo written in 1389 by Giovanni da Patro[1]—*Il Paradiso degli Alberi*—Landini is mentioned: "No one had ever heard such beautiful harmonies, and their hearts almost burst from their bosoms." When a thousand birds were singing Landini was asked to play his organetto to see what effect it would have. At first the birds hushed their singing to listen to his music and then sang more lustily, while a nightingale flew down and perched on a branch above the musician's head. Landini died on 2nd

[1] L. Ellinwood, "Francesco Landini and his Music"—*Musical Quarterly*, vol. xxii (1936), p. 190.

September 1397 and was buried in Florence. The blind musician holding his organetto is shown on his tombstone.

An account of the early sixteenth-century positive organ and how it was used are set down for us in *Spiegel der Orgelmacher und Organisten*, by Arnold Schlick, a blind organist, lutenist and composer, who published this work in Mainz in 1511.[1] The title page, reproduced in Plate 9, gives an idea of the German positive organ of the time. After a statement of "privilege" from *Römischer Kaiserlicher Majestät* (the Elector Palatine) to print the book, and a brief account of the uses of the organ in the services of the church, ten short chapters are devoted to the construction of the instrument and the use of the stops. Schlick supplies precise dimensions of the various parts of the organ by the simple expedient of drawing lines which are a stated fraction of the original in length. The length of the body of the largest manual pipe is 7 ft., which is not far short of that of the present 8-ft. diapason. There are two scales in use and this pipe would speak to F on one scale and C on another.[2]

In Schlick's organ the length of the manual semitones was 2·6 in., that of the naturals 4·35 in., the length of an octave 8 in. (Strange though it may seem, there is now no generally accepted standard for organ-key dimensions and claviers by different makers differ by as much as a white key width in length !) We give the corresponding standard pianoforte key dimensions respectively as 3·45 in., 6 in., 7·4 in. (to extreme sides of keys). Organ keys are usually shorter from back to front.

By making various assumptions concerning the shape and end-corrections of the bass 7-ft. pipes, Ellis in his *History of Musical Pitch* (London, 1881)

[1] Only two copies of this important work are known and one is in the Paul Hirsch collection (Brit. Mus.). It was discovered by a schoolmaster behind the "chimney-piece" of an old house in Saxony. An edition in modern German was printed in 1932 by Rheingold Verlag, Mainz, and a reprint of the book has been produced by the same press. A second copy has been discovered in Halle in recent years. Arnold Schlick (*c.* 1445–1516) was an important figure in the history of organ music. His later work, *Tabulaturen etlicher Lobgesang*, is dated 1512.

[2] "The necessity of the transposition of the plainsong to accommodate voices, for which we have the authority of Arnold Schlick, had brought about the intercalation of the chromatic keys or 'ficta' (feigned notes) and consequently the restricted compass of the Halberstadt organ originally chromatic."

A. J. Hipkins, *Third Cantor Lecture* (Society of Arts, London, 1891). In addition to this the drone bass pipe of the fifteenth century organ and the use of pedals had tended to kill the "scholastic tetrachordal" idea of the scale.

The C and F pitches were used as follows:
1st tone (dorian mode): c, d, e♭, f, g, a, b, c.
7th tone (mixolydian mode): c, d, e, f, g, a, b♭, c.
1st tone: d, e, f, g, a, b, c, d.
7th tone: d, e, f♯, g, a, b, c, d.

On the F and C compasses the tones worked out as follows:

	F	C
Tone 1 (dorian):	g, a, b♭, c, d, e, f, g.	d, e, f, g, a, b, c, d.
,, 7 (myxolydian):	g, a, b, c, d, e, f, g.	c, d, e, f, g, a, b♭, c.
,, 3 (phrygian):	a, b♭, c, d, e, f, g, a.	f♯, g, a, b, c♯, d, e, f♯.
,, 5 (lydian):	f, g, a, b, c, d, e, f.	
,, 6 (hypolydian):	b♭, c, d, e♭, f, g, a, b♭.	

Note that these are given in English notation. In German h = b♮, b = b♭.

gives A = 377 vibrations per sec. for his lower pitch and 504 for his high pitch.

The length of the pedal-keys was 17·5 in. and an interval of a third on the pedals was 7·4 in. The height of the (lower) manual keyboard above the pedal-board was 36 in. and the height of the seat above the pedal-board surface was 26 in. Schlick says that the organ should be near the choir so that the organist can hear the priest at the altar and that the choir should be able to hear one stop. The place where the organ stands should be free from damp and be placed so that the roof will not fall on it. The bellows should be placed in a special chamber and should not be exposed to the sun or they will become hard and crack. Plainsong should be played in the keys C, D, E, F. In harmony the semitones should be avoided as much as possible because of the unequal temperament of the tuning, but in a single line of melody such tuning gives no offence. The trumpet and other reeds are usually either sharp or flat to the rest of the (flue) pipe-work. Schlick mentions a transposing keyboard, "a rare thing but one that I use daily". The compass of the manuals was three octaves and a third (F to a). The keys "should not be as wide as the old, or as narrow as the new, which latter are only fit for children. It should be possible to hold an octave comfortably". (Each key with its "space" was just an inch in breadth.) The keys should be easy to press down and the semitones should not be so thin and so low that they come to rest below the surface of the naturals. Schlick discusses the compromise between deep and light touch and a shallower, heavier touch. He considers various problems of tuning and refers to an organ with double semitones a century before.[1]

He deals with a considerable variety of organ stops and mentions the principale, octav, superoctav, various mixtures including the high pitched zimbel, the rauschpfeife, the schalmei, zink (a quiet reed), the schwegel (a flute), the trompete and posaune. He also mentions a "holzerne gelachter",[2] which is a mystery.[3] [See the specification on p. 66.]

[1] Cf. p. 267.

[2] It has been said that this was a tremulant with a wooden box. Mahrenholz (*Orgelregister*, p. 246) believes that it was a compound stop of flute type. It is probable that it was a percussion stop with wooden bars (i.e. a xylophone).

[3] Schlick says: "The organ must be an ornament to the church and a help to godly singers. It must have suitable figures upon it, not trivial and ridiculous tricks, such as was made a few years ago in a Capuchin monastery, in which a large figure of a monk looked out of a window, rising as far as his girdle, and then suddenly disappeared, so that the young and old, man and women, were startled, and some began to laugh, others to curse. Monkey faces and priests with monkey faces, with wide mouths, which open and shut, and with long beards, and that rattle money in their pockets, are things to be avoided."

The same bizarre ingenuity which went into clock-making in Germany did not leave the organ untouched, and such "grotesques" persisted until the end of the eighteenth century. The fox-tail stop was quite popular; in an Erfurt example "a fox's tail brushed the face of any curious person who drew the stop." Adlung tells us that at the Garrison Church organ at Berlin there were two Suns, towards which two eagles flew; and two angels which flew upwards and placed trumpets to their lips during the flight, and put down the trumpets during their descent, while other angels played the drums. . . .

A book by Sebastian Virdung, which appeared in Basle at about the same time as

Praetorius says Heinrich Traxdorf of Nuremberg constructed an organ in 1460 which gave a sound "like that of a shawm" and the voix humaine or regal made its first appearance in France during the same century. This was probably the beginning of reed pipes in the Christian era, though it must be recalled that the organs of the ancients may have contained reed pipes, and even in the Winchester organ the word *musae* is used for organ pipes. These may really have been musette or "bagpipe" tones, but it may be that the poet found that the more usual word for an organ-pipe *fistula* would not fit his metre.

The regal was a small positive or, more rarely, a portative organ in which small reeds replaced the flue pipes. The pitch of each note was dependent to a great extent on the tongue, and the regal would keep pitch far better than the small flue organs when subjected to fluctuations of wind pressure inevitable in these old instruments. Galpin[1] has discussed the origin of the word *regal*. The most usual explanation is that it was first made as a present to a king. Again, the word has been regarded as a corruption of Rigabello, an instrument formerly used in Italian churches before the introduction of the organ. Or it may have been a contraction of the Latin *regula* and it appeared as rigol or regol, an instrument for keeping the "rule" or "order" of the plainsong.

About 1550 an ingenious Nuremburg instrument-maker, George Voll, made a regal in the shape of a large book, so that the keyboard, reeds and bellows which were formed by the covers or boards of the book could be closed up after use. Thus was invented the Bible regal which was used to accompany small choirs in Germany until the nineteenth century, and even today is used for giving the pitch for "a cappella" singing. Such regals were the precursors of the harmonium, but owing to the fact that the reeds had negligible resonators the tone was not so satisfying as that of the larger positive regals.

In the early years of the sixteenth century the word regal was often given to any small organ, even though it did not consist entirely of reed pipes. In the inventory of the Musical Instruments of King Henry VIII,[2] a number of single and double regals are described. One of the single regals had three stops, " one (flue) stoppe pipe of tinne, one regale of tinne and a cimball." The tubes of the pipes were of "papiri". The cimball (cymbale or German zimbel) was a small mixture stop, and it is interesting that here in miniature was a combination which has delighted the ears of organists ever since, that of reeds and mixtures sounded together.

A novelty, sometimes found in regals as well as in larger organs, was the

---

Schlick's *Spiegel* in Mainz (1511), was entitled *Musica getutscht und auszgezogen durch Sebastianum Virdung Priesters von Amburg und alles gesang ausz den noten in die tabulaturen diser benanten dryer Instrumentem ten der Orgeln. . . .* The book deals with all musical instruments then known, but is not as helpful as that of Schlick where the organ is concerned. Nevertheless, it corroborates that there were: organs with three "divisions", positive and chamber organs, portative organs, regals (or small reed organs). Virdung specialises in stringed instruments of all kinds and is more useful in this connection.

[1] F. W. Galpin, *Old English Instruments of Music* (London, 1910).

[2] *Inventory of the Guarderobes*, 1547. (Brit. Mus., Harl. 1419.)

nightingale pipe "which containeth water,"[1] or the small-scaled flue pipe bent over into a small vessel full of water. The air bubbling through the water produced in the pipe an intermittent note of varying pitch. The device still remained in many German organs in the post-Bach period.

Many references to regals are found in the accounts of the expenses of the English royalty and nobility in the sixteenth century. The regal was also used to accompany the mystery plays, and accounts of its use at Coventry between 1530 and 1565[2] carefully distinguish it from the organ.

A large positive regal made by John Loosemore (q.v.) of Exeter in 1650 is preserved in Blair Atholl Castle, Scotland. It stands on a frame with four legs, it has two diagonal bellows, a four-octave keyboard with short octave, white naturals and black sharps, and the following stops drawing in halves: stop diapason, principal, twelfth, fifteenth, and trumpet, which was the improved regal stop.[3]

The words *single* and *double* as applied to sixteenth-century organs and regals have been the subject of much discussion. Rimbault suggested that single regals had one row of pipes and double regals two, but as some of Henry VIII's single regals had three and four whole stops and another had seven half-stops, Rimbault's suggestion cannot be entertained. Sir George Grove and A. J. Hipkins maintained that single regals had one manual and double regals had two, but again no example of such double regals has ever been recorded. King Henry VIII in 1547 left five double regals, and two of them only possessed two stops each! Clearly these were single-manual instruments.

The first use of the term "double organ" for an instrument with two manuals was in reference to the organ built by Thomas Dallam for Worcester Cathedral in 1613. Various compositions written after this date call for a double organ. For instance, Matthew Locke in *Melothesia* (1673) has a movement for a double organ, that is a "Chaire organ and Greate organ". The compositions of Purcell and Blow for double organ are now available in modern editions.

Canon Galpin[4] has shown that during the sixteenth century the word "double" or "single" regal or organ denotes the pitch and depth of tone of the instruments. In Anthony Duddington's contract for the organ in the

[1] Francis Bacon, *Sylva Sylvarum* (Brit. Mus., Harl. 4160), "the way of making an artificial nightingale as it is in waterworks with pipes of metal or wood like a flagellat".

[2] Galpin, op. cit.

[3] Galpin says: "The name regal for any reed organ survived many years after the original instrument had disappeared; in 1684 we find Henry Purcell appointed to the office of keeper, maker, repairer, mender and tuner of the 'King's Regalls, Virginalls and Organs'. He was succeeded by Dr. John Blow and Father Bernard Smith. Here follow some references to regals in the time of Henry VIII: (on p. 79a.)
Jan. 1537: Gevene to Heywood's servante for bringing of my Lady Grace's Regalles from London to Grenewiche.................................xxd.
May 1538: Paid for a payre of Regalls.........................IV l. Xs.
Jan. 1543: Paid to Betyne's servante for mending the Regalles........VIIs. VId."
from the Privy Purse Expenses of Princess Mary, quoted by Galpin, *Old English Instruments of Music*.

[4] Galpin, op. cit.

Church of All Hallows, Barking (by the Tower), the compass of the instrument descends to "double Ce fa ut", that is, to CC. In a similar way the single regal descended only to C (i.e. tenor C, the octave below middle C) whereas double regals extended to double C or double G. Galpin remarks: "We have an interesting corroboration of this meaning of the words by Praetorius, for he informs us that in England the Fagotto (Bassoon) descending to single G was called the Single Courtal and that reaching double C the Double Courtal."

Magnificent advances in organ construction were made throughout Europe in the late Gothic and early Renaissance periods.[1] In Germany, Burgundy and Flanders in the late fifteenth century, and in Normandy, Castile, the plains of the Po, in the Austrian lowlands, human mechanical ingenuity, interest and wealth contributed to the fullest to develop the organ. The pedal with separate pipes, couplers between manuals and between manual and pedal, stops of all pitches with great varieties of tone-colour, were developed and were exploited by players and composers.[2]

[1] We may summarise the dates of the various epochs of organ construction as follows:

Early Gothic	:	1250–1400
High Gothic	:	1400–1470
Later Gothic	:	1470–1540
Renaissance	:	1540–1600
Early Baroque	:	1600–1650

but these are only approximate: each merged imperceptibly into the next.

[2] The earliest known examples of organ music (*c.* 1325) are intabulations and estampies in the Robertsbridge manuscript (Brit. Mus., Ms. Add. 28550). This is of either English or Italian origin and has been transcribed by H. E. Wooldridge, *Early English Harmony*, vol. i (1897). German tablatures of the fifteenth century are described by L. Shrade, *Die altesten Denkmaler der Orgelmusik* (1927).

Of particular importance are:

(*a*) The tablature of the monk Adam Ileborgh (1448) with its use of the pedal and its free preludes and rambling style (Davison and Apel, *Historical Anthology*, Harvard, 1947).

(*b*) The *Fundamentum organisandi* of Paumann (1452), a blind musician serving in the Bavarian Court, in which German songs are developed on instrumental lines. Paumann taught his pupils to improvise on liturgical themes and to transcribe vocal music for the organ. (Davison and Apel, *Historical Anthology*, Harvard, 1947.)

(*c*) The Buxheim book of *c.* 1470 with its use of Burgundian songs. The compiler of this is unknown, but the works of Paumann were given an honoured place and there were transcriptions of the best songs and motets of Dunstable, Binchois and Dufay (Munich, Staatsbibliothek, Mus. MS. 3725. A new edition has been published by Hinrichsen, 1960).

Organ music at the end of the fifteenth century was marked by three important names: Henrich Isaak, A. Schlick and Paul Hofhaimer. The works of the first have not survived, but various transcriptions made by his pupils serve to show his qualities in decorating and developing a theme. Schlick developed the method of playing the plainsong theme in long notes in the pedal bass against three-part counterpoint on the manual, a method which continued for two and a half centuries as a standard practice and is even used today in organ composition and extemporisation. Paul Hofhaimer (1459–1537), known as "the prince of the organ", was in the service of the Archduke Sigmund at Innsbruck and later with the Emperor Maximilien. He was the first great master of the instrumental art with an international reputation. Hofhaimer's tradition was continued by his pupils Kotter, Sicher, Buchner and Kleber, and by Ammerbach and B. Schmid. This tradition was further continued in some Polish tablatures of the middle of the sixteenth century and these show the

The Renaissance organ was a transition instrument between the mixture organ of the Gothic period and the baroque instrument with its variety of separate stops and its possibilities of synthetic tone-building.

In the fifteenth century registers were used to isolate families of stops. The "spring" wind-chest (springlade) was then in vogue and, as will be appreciated from Fig. 12, was better adapted for the isolation of groups of

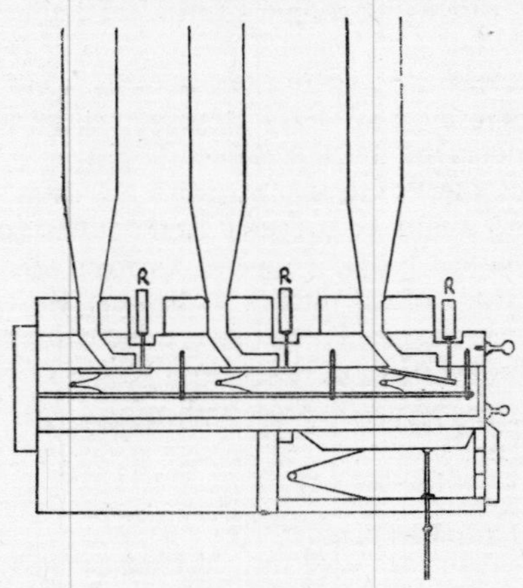

FIG. 12. An old "spring-chest".

The pipes sound when the key pallet is opened and when the small pallets of the register are opened by pressing down the rods R. Praetorius says that such a chest was first made by Timotheus for the monastery of the Bishop's palace at Wurzburg.

---

influence of Buchner in particular. (H. J. Moser, *Frühmeister des deutschen Orgelspiels*, 1930.)

Another pupil of Hofhaimer, O. Nachtigall, who was the organist of St. Thomas's Church, Strasbourg, and Kleber (d. 1556), organist at Pforzheim, left rich tablatures for the organ in which the pedal is generally used and the device of an echo between two parts. H. Kotter (d. towards 1542), who was organist at Fribourg in Switzerland, adapted Latin motets, German, Italian and French songs, or even dances. He loved to disarticulate the rhythm and decorate the subjects until they were difficult of recognition.

In the work of these three we see the origins of another style in which the first signs of harmony and the sounds of chords were growing from the counterpoint.

The end of the fifteenth century was as rich in France as in Germany, but the organ works of the former were those of anonymous composers.

In the first thirty years of the sixteenth century Pierre Attaingnant collected their works in the form of ornamented transcriptions of polyphonic motets (Févin, Obrecht, Compère, Brumel), and versets for the Mass.

Two important Italian composers of the early sixteenth century mark the distinction, not entirely evident previously, between the vocal and instrumental arts.

The earliest printed Italian organ music which has survived is in two collections: Marc Antonio Cavazzoni da Bologna's *Recerchari*, *Motetti*, *Canzoni*, *Libro Primo* (Venice, 1523), and Andrea Antico da Montona's *Frottole Intabulate da Sonare Organi* (Rome, 1517). The only copy of Cavazzoni's book is in the British Museum. Antico's work was found in 1939. Jeppesen found a copy in the library of the Marchese Polesini at Parenzo. If Petrucci ever made use of the privilege to print *intavolature d'organo* obtained in 1498, the works themselves are now lost. (Knud Jeppesen, *Die italienische Orgelmusik am Anfang des Cinquecento*, Copenhagen, 1943.)

PLATE 3.

Kircher's Automatic Hydraulic Organ. It is probable that Kircher never made one like this. The blowing chamber would either soon deliver water to the pipes or would fail to deliver wind. Kircher does not show or explain how the air is produced in the blowing chamber. The mystery is solved by reference to the methods formerly in use in Europe for producing blasts of air for smelting purposes. In the section on smelting metals in Diderot's *Encyclopédie* two arrangements are depicted. The devices are known as "trompes". Water flowing into long vertical tubes from their tops carries air down with it. Air under pressure and water are separated in a chamber at the bottom. The device in the top left-hand corner shows how the triangular harp may be played automatically by the projections on the vertical rods fixed in a frame which slowly descends

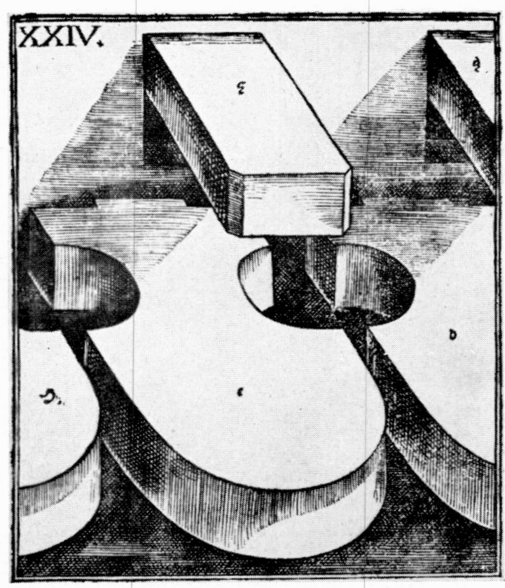

PLATE 4a.

Old keyboard in Halberstadt Cathedral organ (Faber 1361). Plate 24 in Praetorius's Syntagma Vol. II

PLATE 4b.

Keyboard of Rückpositif at Aegidienkirche at Brunswick (1456) (from Praetorius Plate 28)

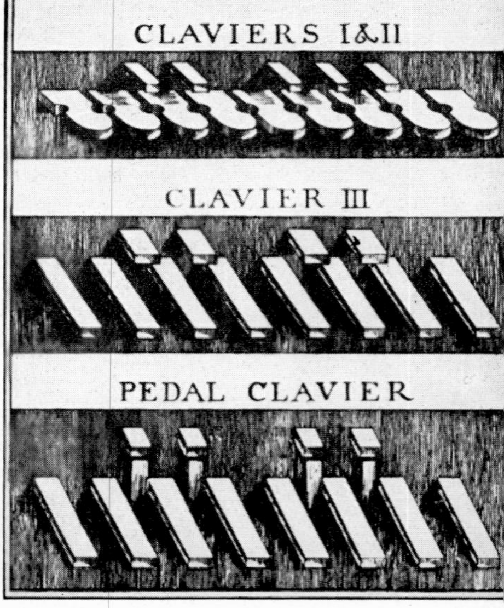

PLATE 4c.

The Halberstadt Cathedral keyboards 14th century (from Praetorius Plate 25)

14th CENTURY POSITIVE ORGANS.

PLATE 5a.
Brit. Mus. Add. ms. 29902 fo. 6

PLATE 5b.
Bibl. Nat. ms. fr. 13096 fo. 46

PLATE 5c.
Brit. Mus. Add. ms. 27695 fo. 13

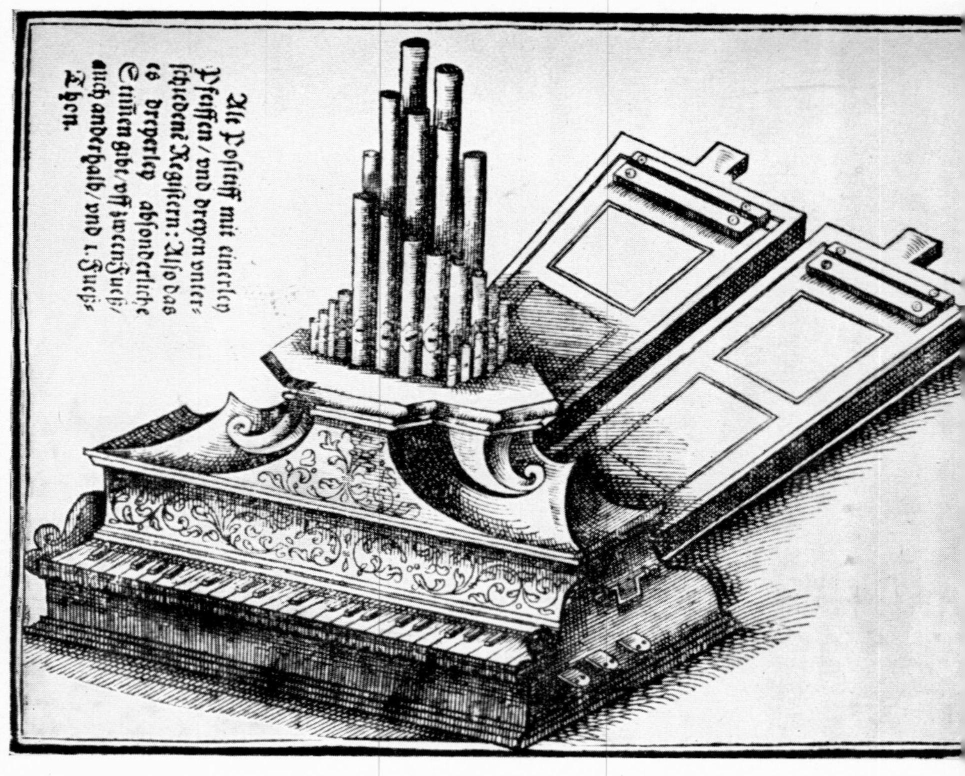

PLATE 6.
A table positive organ, 16th century (from Praetorius Plate I.)

stops than for the separate ranks of large organs. In the sixteenth century the slider-chest was rediscovered (Fig. 22). Here a separate flat length of wood with holes corresponding to the pipe-feet of the rank was used. This could be drawn in and out so that the passage of wind was allowed or prevented. Sometimes, as in the Old Radnor, Wales, organ (one of the few survivals, as far as an organ case is concerned, of a pre-revolution instrument), the sliders were worked by levers at the ends of the wind-chest and at the side of the instrument; but later a trundle action was devised so that by a system of moving levers the organist could control the stops without moving from his seat, though often he had to stand up or go to the sides of the keyboards to reach them, a practice which is not unknown in many European organs to this day. With the slider-chest new types of organ stop appeared in great profusion. Flue stops of various widths,—open, closed and "half" closed, made in cylindrical shape or with "tapering-in" or "tapering-out" form, flute stops of divers patterns, recorders, schwiegels, bourdons, gemshorns, spitzflöten, made their appearance. It should be added that the mixture stops were composed of the ranks which it was not worth while to separate.

The early reed stop, the regal, developed along two lines. The tones of the vibrating tongues were qualified either by short resonators or by long, horn-shaped or conical brass or tin tubes. The former types of reeds which included the old regal, vox-humana and musette, were called "schnarrwerk" and the latter were the trumpet, posaune and bombarde or the fagotto (bassoon) if the tube was thin and almost cylindrical. The difference in power between the reeds and the flue stops was not as marked as it is today.The "schnarrwerk" could be used for solo purposes with the help of a light flue stop known as *koppel* (a tone to which another is added or coupled). There were many types of regals and they were often described in terms of the shape of the short resonator attached to the reed and its frame, tube or shallot. Knopregals, apfel-regals, trichterregals (funnel-regals) and other shapes, more ingenious than useful, were invented. The vox humana was a type of regal and its resonators were modified in an endeavour to produce various vowel sounds. Also in this class of stop were found the "bearpipes" (bärpfeifen), so-called because they produced a growling sound.[1] As can be imagined, the stops of the regal class were difficult to keep in tune; and apart from the vox humana and musette they tended to disappear before the nineteenth century.

The majestic Gothic organ had been constructed in a case which was intended to be viewed as a whole at a distance, but in the Renaissance organ there was much rich ornamentation and the details were such that only examination at close quarters would reveal the beauties of the scheme. In the Gothic organ decorations had appeared on the pipes, but the woodwork itself was simple. In the Renaissance period many organs had large wings at the sides which could be opened by the organist. These bore large paintings and other decorations. The sixteenth-century organ, particularly in central and southern Europe, was well decorated. The pipes were silvered or gilded,

[1] The Baarpijp is also a common stop in old Dutch organs (e.g. at Haarlem, Specification No. 17), but in Holland it is a flue stop.

and the case was rich with gold, azure and vermilion, and the appearance must have been sumptuous. There were German organs with three or four keyboards before the Renaissance period and some Netherlands organs were surprisingly large. The Brustwerk (Breast-work), a smaller and quieter set of stops played from a separate manual, with a sound-board placed between the console and the great organ, had existed in Germany since the end of the fifteenth century, and the Oberwerk (with pipework above that of the great organ) or Récit at the end of the sixteenth century.[1] The Oberwerk appeared in the Netherlands as early as 1500. It later contained conical reed-stops, mutations such as the nasard ($2\frac{2}{3}$ ft.), flue registers of 8-ft. and 4-ft. pitch, and zimbel (cymbal). The Oberwerk was the origin of the later solo and echo organs. During the sixteenth century the pedal organ had developed in Germany and its selection of stops was often greater than that of the manual divisions. The French pedal organ did not develop greatly during this period. The type of organ common in Italy at this time contained only one manual and short pedal "pull-downs" of the French type. The Italian organ was a single "plein-jeu" of fairly small-scale stops[2] and each stop in the harmonic scheme was capable of isolation. Often there was a single flute stop in addition to this. The ensemble was the *ripieno*. The Spanish organ was rich and progressive at this time, and a number of composers of significant organ works produced music for it. It was characterised by claviers of four octaves with deeper notes than the contemporary instruments of France, and large families of trumpet stops, for which the Spanish organ has been notable ever since. The English organ of the sixteenth century had one clavier, several stops and no pedal-board. We shall deal later with the varieties of the organ art in different countries.

The transition from the mixture organ to the type of instrument with separate stops can be traced in the following specifications:

Fr. Krebs, St. George, Hagenau, 1491.

Positiv

Zwifach (two ranks).

Manual

Dreifach fleiten (three ranks of principal type 8, 4, 2).
Das werk (many-rank mixture)
Ein zymmet (Zimbel—high-pitched mixture).

Here is a specification given by

Arnold Schlick in Spiegel der Orgelmacher und Organisten, 1511.

Positiv

Principaln 4 höltzen ode zynnen (wood or metal)
Gemshlein (small gemshorn)
Zymmelein (small cymbal)
Hindersetzlein (mixture).

[1] Often the brustwerk was enclosed by "cupboard" doors which could be opened or closed by the organist without leaving his seat. Clearly this was a precursor of the swell organ.

[2] The large-scale Italian "diapasons", sometimes spoken of, are not earlier than the eighteenth century.

Manual

Principaln 8 (Two ranks: narrow and wide)
Octaff 4
Gemser hörner 4 (open flute)
Zymmel (cymbale)
Hindersetz (a mixture of 16–18 ranks)
Raus pfeiffen (Rauschpfeife) (2 + 2⅔)
Oder uff schallmeyen art (or a schalmei reed)
Hultze glechter (a xylophone?) (see footnote p. 60)
Zink (reed)
(Schweigeln=schwegel, a flute)
(Regall oder super regall)

Pedal

Principaln 16
Octaff 8
Hindersetz (mixture)
Trommettan oder basaun (trumpet or bassoon).

A minor revolution was taking place at the end of the fifteenth century through the influence of the three great master players: Isaak, Schlick and Hofhaimer. A careful study of the Krebs specification (Hagenau, 1491) will show that there are fundamental differences from that of Schlick (1511) particularly in the manner in which it is set out. The first is purely a number of mixtures, whereas the second offers analytic and stop selection possibilities. We have found many details of materials and costs of the organs of European countries, including England, in the fourteenth and fifteenth centuries, and it is not difficult to reconstruct an accurate picture of the actual instruments. We even know exactly the number of pipes, their lengths and how they were made, in these organs. Surprise has often been expressed that we have not found specifications or stop lists set out in more modern form. The reason for this should be evident. The mediaeval organ was a unified instrument in the form of a large mixture. It grew by the addition of a positiv as a separate section, a pedal organ, and later a separation of the upper part of the mixture (werk or hintersatz) from the rest of the chorus by a device for cutting off its wind. Stops were not reinvented in late mediaeval times as a means of piling tone on tone, but for removing blocks of tone, in the form of large mixtures, from the rest of the organ. Where there was no need for separate stops, there was no need for separate stop names. In the specification of the Schlick organ, here given, the beginnings of the need for stops for the composition of complex tones is seen in embryo. Progress was rapid in the sixteenth century. Mechanical and scientific improvements in France and Germany, and the development of new reed tones, attempts at the imitation of orchestral instruments, and experiments in the development of thin or male (mannlich) and wide or female (weiblich) flue pipes of individual tone culminated in the fine late Renaissance and early Baroque instruments described by M. Praetorius (*c.* 1619), in which the separate ranks of many of the stops were named and under the control of the organist through stop-knobs or levers. The large mixtures of a dozen or more ranks were not separated into their constituent pitches. Thus the "werk-orgel" gave place to the Renaissance and early Baroque instruments.

A similar transformation in the conception of the tonal nature of the organ took place in Holland at the same time. The great players and composers of the Netherlands, Obrecht (1430–1505), Isaac (1450–1517) and Willaert (1485–1562), were paving the way for a more poetical use of the instrument. The blokwerk was analysed to its component parts to some extent. The great humanist, Rudolf Agricola, began the reconstruction of the organ in St. Martin's Church, Groningen, in 1479. In the Rugwerk (Positiv) were found quintaden[1] 16 ft., Wijdgedekt 8 ft., Holfluit 2 ft., but this was not typical. In 1480 the well-documented organ in St. Nicolai, Utrecht, had an echo division composed of open flue ranks, and in 1500 the organs at Arnhem and Nijmegen had borstwerk, "breast-work" (a minor chorus in the front of the organ). The Utrecht organ had a mixture (or rather one of its divisions was a mixture) of eleven to nineteen ranks founded on a Praestant 16 ft., Octaaf 8 ft., and Octaaf 4 ft. It was in the echo (boven) division that the first attempts to split the large mixtures were noticed.

On a spring-chest were the following stops: Roerfluit 8 ft., Praestant 4 ft., Nachthorn 4 ft., Roerquint $2\frac{2}{3}$ ft., Nachthorn 2 ft., and Nachthorn 1 ft.

Here is the specification of a small Dutch organ built in 1521 at the Hervormde Kerk, Oosthuizen (N.H.). It has pedal pull-downs and a "short" clavier.

Bourdon 16 (originally 8 ft.)
Praestant 8
Octaaf 4 (doubled pipes above a′)
Quint $2\frac{2}{3}$
Woudfluit 2
Mixtuur, two to three ranks
Sesquiltera $2\frac{2}{3}$ ($+ 1\frac{1}{2}$), two ranks
Built by Jan van Kovelen.

The organ in the Choir at the Groote Kerk, Alkmaar, built in 1511 by Jan van Kovelen of Amsterdam, has the following Stops:[2]

Manuaal I (Borstwerk)

Holpifpe 8
Fluijte 4
Octaaf 2
Schivelet 1 (= Nachthoorn)
Sexquialtera (2 ranks)

Pedaal

Trompet 8

Manuals
F. G. A. . . . g^2a^2
Pedaal
F.G.A. . . . to c^1

Manuaal II (Hoofdwerk)
i.e. "Great Organ"

Doeff 8 (= Praestant)
Holfluite 8 (Rohrflute)
Coppeldoeff 4 (= Octaaf)
Baertfluijte 4 (="Bear pipe")
Gemsenhoern 2
Micxtuijre 2 (two, three, four ranks)
Scerp 1 (sharp mixture three to four ranks)
Trompet 8

[1] An overblown stopped pipe speaking the twelfth as well as the ground-tone.
[2] These organs are still in their "original" condition.

This is quite a remarkable instrument for the date. It is evident that Dutch composers were expecting more flexibility from their instruments, were exploring to the full everything that organ-builders could give them, and were seeking to use the organ in a more restrained and artistic manner. Organ-builders were assimilating the ideas of those in neighbouring countries and were making innovations. Here was a real step forward in which organ-building, playing and the composition of organ pieces were going hand in hand.

The trumpet on the pedals had a melodic function and was not to be thought of as a bass to the manuals. It would be used for sustaining a strong line of "choral" melody with counterpoint on the manuals above. The specification of this two-manual organ anticipates many future developments in tonal design. It would give a much better rendering of Bach's music, composed two centuries after it was built, than many English organs of the twentieth century.

Here is the specification of the grand organ in the Cathedral at Toulouse, France,[1] in the years 1530–1.

Grand Orgue

Et premièrement grand jeulx (large mixture)
le jeu de papegayl (bird song ?)
le jeu de chantres (regal)[2]
le jeu des fleustes d'allemans (German flute)
le jeu de pifres (piccolo).
le jeu court (stopped flute ?)
le jeu de nazars petits et grands (Nasard $5\frac{1}{3}$ and $2\frac{2}{3}$)
le jeu de cornes (cornet or trumpet)
le jeu de simbales (sharp mixture)
le jeu de fleustes (open flute)
le jeu de carillon (small bells or carillon flue mixture).

Clavier de Positif

le jeux de petites orgues (mixture)
le jeux de orgues enfleustes (open metal flute)
et sic de aliis (various high-pitched ranks)
le tabourin (tambourine ?, i.e. small drum)
un jeu de regalles (reed stop).

The first stop on each manual would represent a complete open flue chorus. The transition from the old mixture or werk organ to an instrument capable of giving solo and imitative effects obviously took place in France at about the same time that it did in Germany. The absence of a separate pédale on the French organ is noteworthy, but it is probable that there were pedal pull-downs playing the lower keys of the grand orgue.

The Introduction and Early Development of the Pedal

Curious traditions have existed concerning the introduction of the pedal clavier, and the evidence concerning this has been carefully sifted by the author.

[1] Given in the Tabulatur book of Pierre Attaingnant, 1530–1 (edited by Y. Rokseth: *Deux livres d'orgues*, Paris, 1925).

[2] The regal was used to accompany the singers in the Mass.

R. Schlecte (*Geschichte der Kirchen Musik*, Leipzig, 1871) quoted a passage from a Flemish chronicle of A.D. 1319 to 1350 at Antwerp, which related to Ludwig van Vaelbeke of Brabant, who died in A.D. 1312. "Van Vaelbeke in Brabant. Hy was d'eerste die wa, van stampen die manieren die men noch hoet antieren" ("He was the first who mentions treading in the manner that men nowadays practise"). It is well-known that carillons were played with the feet as well as with the hands in the Netherlands in the middle of the fourteenth century and in view of the fact that the methods of working both organ and carillon were not unlike we may assume that an equipment of the one would be adapted to the other. This document, by an Abbé de Geus-quière, was transcribed by F. J. Fétis (1784–1871) in his *Histoire Générale de la Musique*. Although this contains some errors and prejudices, there is no reason to doubt the truth of the passage. Undoubtedly the reference is to the carillon at St. Nicholas' Church at Brussels.

In the Halberstadt organ, built by Faber in 1361, which we have already described, an octave of pedal keys was provided and it is unlikely that this was a unique instrument, for the use of the foot would be an easier means of controlling the wind supply to the large pipes of 32 ft. in length and their dozens of mixture ranks than even the muscular force of the whole arm.[1] The first mention of a pedal in France was at Troyes Cathedral in 1432,[2] and then with only eight keys, a number increased to seventeen by the end of the sixteenth century and to twenty-four by the year 1640. The large Gothic organ had pedals which had separate pipes and also those which acted through "pull downs" on the lower set of manual keys. In 1551 Josse le Bel, repairing the organ at Saint-Germain-l'Auxérrois, Paris, added a principal of 12-ft. pitch, the bass of which could be "played without pedals and with pedals".[3] The method of holding drone notes with a latch or other device which preceded the use of pedals must have suggested a development towards the use of more than one drone and a better method of control which the pedal would give. The step forward from the "drone" to the simple slow cantus firmus of the plain-song with contrapuntal decorations on the manuals is not difficult to imagine. Praetorius remarks that the pedal organ was neglected in Italy and England. Nevertheless, it was known in the former country in the fifteenth century, if not before this, but in the latter there is no evidence either in documents or by reference to organ music until the year 1720–1, and many historians have erroneously given the end of the eighteenth century as the date of the first use of the pedal in England.[4] Praetorius says that Bernhard (organist to the Doge of Venice in 1471) invented the pedal keys, but he is not consistent, and it is certain that pedals were in use before this, and thus

[1] There is no need to assume, as some writers have done, that the pedals were added in 1495 by Kleng, who repaired the organ.

[2] D'Arbois de Jubainville, *Notice sur la construction des orgues de la Cathédrale de Troyes* (Troyes, 1872).

[3] N. Dufourcq, op. cit.

[4] In *The Musical Times* for 1960 attempts were made to show that the pedal was used in England before the Commonwealth. No direct evidence was brought forward. The best argument in favour of the early pedal key-board arises from some late sixteenth- and seventeenth-century music, in which some bass passages could be played more conveniently by using pedals.

Bernhard must have improved the pedal action. "In the year 1818 a new organ was erected in the church of Beeskow, five miles from Frankfort on the Oder, on which occasion the organ-builder, Marx senior, took some pains to ascertain the age of the old organ which he had to remove. On a careful investigation it appeared that the old organ had been built just four hundred years before, the date MCCCCXVIII being engraved on the upper part of the two largest principal pipes, for that these pipes did belong to the pedal was clear from their measurement."[1]

An account by a Dutch writer, Lootens, who claimed that a wind-chest for pedal pipes bearing the date 1120 had been found in the Minster Church in Zierikzee (Holland), has appeared in a number of historical accounts of the development of the organ. There is no truth in this. It is extraordinary how often this story has been repeated. The present author has been able to trace its origin. On the occasion of the opening of a new organ in the Groote Kerk of Zierikzee, built by Johan Heinrich Hartman Bätz in 1770, a booklet was written bearing the title "Description of the old and new organ in the Great or St. Leivens Minster Church of the City of Zierikzee. In addition some short notices about the old organs until the present time by William Lootens, Organist and Carillonist of the City of Middelburg in the province of Zeeland. Printed for J. P. Lootens, Organist and Carillonist of the City of Zierikzee, 1771." In this booklet Albertus van Os, living in Flushing, is stated to have told the author that about forty years before, with a Utrecht organ-builder, Master Van Limburg, he had found the date 1120 on the chest of a great mixture which could only have been played by the feet, in the organ of St. Nicholas, Utrecht. Fortunately the records of this church are preserved. The organ was built by Peter Geerts of Utrecht in the year 1477–8 and enlarged in successive years until, in 1580, a pedal trumpet was added. In 1580 this organ had three manuals: the first was for the rugpositief (with slider-chest), the second was for the great mixture about which Van Os was speaking, the third was for the upper work with its large flue stops and with a spring-chest. The pedal was coupled to the second manual before 1580 and after this date it had its own pedal trumpet. There are records in the church that Limburg did tunings from 1709 until 1737 and that the instrument was restored by Christiaan Müller (who built the great Haarlem organ) in 1733. Several repairs were effected in 1620 and it must have been this date which Van Os saw and mistook for the earlier one. (The case and front pipes of this old organ are preserved in the National Museum at Amsterdam.)

The first real evidence of the use of the pedal in organ music is the preludes of the brother (the monk), Adam Ileborgh, the rector of Stendal in 1448. In addition to these there are long improvisations with "interminable sequences, repetitions and rosalias". The Ileborgh tablatures are important in the history of organ music, and show the use of double pedalling.

The development of the pedal organ will be evident when we consider the composition of the Renaissance and Baroque organs. The late introduction of the pedal into English organs and the subsequent tardy realisation of its value will be discussed later.

[1] *Allgem. Mus. Zeitung* (Leipzig, 1836).

The development of polyphonic singing made the single melodic mixture line of the mediaeval organ sound unsatisfactory. In the northern provinces of Europe, particularly in the Hanseatic ports, singing did not develop as it did elsewhere, and it was here that large and powerful organs were built. It is significant, too, that it was in this region that there was considerable scientific and technical advancement, great wealth and interest in these large structural projects.

It was in the smaller organs such as the positive of the van Eyck panel and the portative that a convenient keyboard, wherewith chords could be played by the fingers, developed. Considerable physical force was necessary in order to actuate the cumbrous mechanism of the large west-end German organs and the keys had to be grasped with the hand and forced down or struck with the whole of the hand. Thus the organist was sometimes referred to as the "pulsator organorum". No doubt the heavy "touch" of the manual keys was an incentive to develop a pedal action for pulling down the keys.

In the fifteenth century the spring-chest enabled certain families of stops, and even separate stops, to be added to or subtracted from the tone mass; but only with the invention of the slider-chest, about the beginning of the sixteenth century, could separate ranks of pipes be isolated and combined together easily to suit the fancy of the player, in the manner mentioned by Schlick.[1] At this early date in the sixteenth century, sharply contrasted, bright and even cutting tones ("scharf schneidend"), of various types of flue and reed, were in vogue on the organs which he describes. Manual and pedal technique improved, and, although the thumbs were hardly ever or never used on the manuals, Schlick mentions the possibility of three-part playing on the pedals.[2]

An interesting manifestation of the late-Gothic and early Renaissance organ appeared in central Europe, particularly in Austria, in the form of Hornwork. Originally, this was a mixture organ whose tone was probably designed to imitate that of the Alpine horns. The tone of the Hornwork was different from that of the mixture Blockwork of the church organ. The Hornwork organ projected its tones to the open air from a tower or other high building. Originally, the Hornwork organs produced only a few notes of powerful compound tone, which would be heard over a wide area. Later, the scope of some of these instruments was enlarged so that tunes could be played on them by means of a barrel. Two examples, which are well-known to tourists, are the "bull organ" which projects its tones from the Archbishop's castle high above the city of Salzburg and that at the summer residence at Hellbrunn on the outskirts of the same city. The latter accompanies a remarkable open-air theatre of moving figures all actuated by water power, which is also used for blowing the organ. The Salzburg organ was called the *Stierorgel* (bull organ) even in the time of Leopold Mozart, probably because the noise of many of its pipes sounding together at the end of a

[1] Even today (1959) spring-chests still function in the Schnitger organ in the church of St. Cosmae, Stade (N. Germany).

[2] Kastner has published (Hommage à Charles V; Boileau, Barcelona) a ten-part study by Schlick with four parts on the pedals.

rotation of a barrel was supposed to resemble the roar of a bull. The organ, built in 1502, has 200 pipes (not 200 stops as reported in Batsford's guidebook) and still plays, three times a day, tunes by Joseph Haydn, the Mozarts (father and son), Eberlin, Paul Hofhaimer, who seems to have shown great interest in open-air organs, and Michael Haydn.

The North Brabant School of Organ-builders

We owe much of our knowledge of the Netherland School of organ-builders to the magnificent researches of Dr. M. A. Vente, who believes that Hendrik and Nicolaas Niehoff are among the most important organ-builders in the whole history of the organ, if not the most important. "If Bach is the end of the road which Sweelinck opened, then Schnitger is the end of the road which Niehoff opened." They made great organs with magnificent organo-pleno, Bovenwerk with large-scale flutes, prestants, tierce-cymbels of very high pitch and new forms of reeds. They invented full-length reeds and thus they had to make larger chests for them. The wonderful quality of their pipe-work is evident from the fragments which survive at Leiden, Schiedam, 's-Hertogenbosch, etc.

Niehoff (Neuhoff, Nyhoff, Nieuwenhuys)

In Cologne in the middle of the fifteenth century there lived the organ-builder Levinus Sweyss (Lieven Zwits, Lieven van Colne, etc.). His chief works were:

Frankfurt-on-Main, cathedral, repairs, 1440.
Koblenz, St. Kastor, repairs, 1448.
Brussels, St. Nicolaas, repairs, 1449.
Cologne, St. Lorenz, new organ, 1445.
Cleve, Parish Church, repairs, 1453.
Delft, Nieuwe Kerk, new organ, 1459.
Utrecht Cathedral, inspection, 1467.
Delft, Nieuwe Kerk, new organ, 1479.
Antwerp, "Our Lady", repairs, 1469.

Of the same family is Hans Zwits (Hans Suys, Suess, Zuesz) of Cologne, also called Hanske van Keulen:

Liège, St. Michel, new organ, 1500.
Antwerp, "Our Lady", finishing a new organ, 1509.
Haguenau (Alsace), 1511.
Brussels. A clavecimbel delivered to Eleonora of Austria (sister of Charles V), 1512.
Besançon, St. Étienne, repairs, 1512 and 1517.
Cologne, St. Kunibert, new organ, 1514.
Kalkar and Strassburg, 1516.
Xanten Cathedral, 1518.
Amsterdam, Oude Kerk, new organ, 1539.

He died before 1544. In Amsterdam he was known as Jan Bestevaer, which name indicates that he was very old at that time. He was associated with

Hendrik and Herman Niehoff in the same city. Hendrik learned his art with Jan van Covelen (Johannes Confluentius) of Koblenz. He was also called Jan Cornelis and Jan Frankens and he died in 1532. His wife was called Sophie or Fie, and they had a son, Doof Otto, who was not an organ-builder.

Jan van Covelen's chief works were:

Alkmaar, St. Laurens, small organ, still in use, 1511.
Hasselt, St. Steven, 1515.
Delft, Oude and Nieuwe Kerk, 1518 and 1519.
Utrecht, Oudmunster, new organ and repairs, 1522, 1525, 1526, 1527.
Haarlem, St. Bavo, new small organ 1523; repairs 1535.
Hoorn, Grote Kerk ? 1523.
Kampas, St. Nicolaas, new organ, pipes still existing, 1523.
Utrecht, St. Maria, new oberwerk and regal, 1525.
Franeker, St. Maarten, new organ, pipes still in use, 1528.
Oosthuizen ?? *c.* 1530.

From 1525 Hendrik Niehoff worked with Jan van Covelen as his foreman. Thereafter he lived at Amsterdam and died at 's-Hertogenbosch in 1561. His son, Nicolaas, was an organ-builder and a considerable "school" of organ-builders continued his work. These organs were found in North Germany, Cologne, and the Rhenish towns as well as in the Netherlands. The fame of the pupils, Floris, Lampeler van Mill, Maass and the Hocquet family, spread through many of the north and western parts of Germany.

Hendrik Niehoff's chief organs were made for:

Maastricht, St. Servaas, new organ, 1525.
Kampen, St. Nicolaas, as worker of Jan van Covelen 1527; again 1540.
's-Hertogenbosch, St. Jan, repairs, 1532–4.
Utrecht, St. Marie, repairs, 1533.
's-Hertogenbosch, repairs, 1536.
Gouda, St. Jan, repairs, 1536 idem 1548.
Franeker, repairs, 1534.
Sent to Liège by the Our Lady's Brotherhood at 's-Hertogenbosch in order to study new organs at Liège and at Maastricht, 1537–8.
's-Hertogenbosch, St. Jan, Our Lady's organ enlarged with Ruckpositiv and pedal 1538–9; repairs, 1559.
Naaldwijk, new organ, before 1540.
Schoonhoven, new organ, before 1540.
Amsterdam, Old Church, new main organ (Sweelinck), 1539–42.
Monastery Baseldonk near 's-Hertogenbosch, new organ, before 1542.
Delft, Old Church, new organ, 1545.
Delft, New Church, new organ, repairs in the Old Church, 1548.
Zierikzee, new organ, 1548.
Hamburg, St. Peter's, enlargement and modernisation (Praetorius), 1548–50.
Utrecht, Oudmunster, enlargement, 1545.
Lüneburg, St. Johannes (Praetorius), 1551–2.
Hamburg, St. Katharinen, repairs, 1551–2.
Gouda, St. Jan, new organ, 1555–6.

Veere, repairs, 1551.
Tongerloo, Abbey, new organ, 1543.
Schiedam, new organ or big repairs, before 1553.
Amsterdam, Old Church, small organ (Sweelinck), new, 1544–5.
Woerden, probably new organ, 1554–5.
Bergen op Zoom, new organ, 1555.[1]

Some important Gothic organ cases survived until 1942 and most of them are still well preserved. The Lübeck and Dortmund cases were destroyed, but photographs and drawings are still available.

Sitten (Sion), Valais, Switzerland (*c.* 1400).
Kiedrich, S. Valentine, second third of the fifteenth century, restored in the nineteenth.
Strassburg, Minster, 1489–91.
Lübeck, St. Mary, organ in the Totentanz Chapel, end of the fifteenth century (except for the Rückpositive).
Lübeck, St. James, small organ about 1500 (except for the Rückpositive).
Garding (Schleswig), 1512 (except for the Rückpositiv and Pedal).
Rysum (East Friesland), 1513.
Lübeck, St. Mary, large organ, 1516–18.
Dortmund, St. Mary, *c.* 1530.

Outside Germany, these Gothic organs in the Netherlands show the strongest interest:

Alkmaar, St. Lawrence, small organ, 1511 (by Johann van Koblenz).
Utrecht, St. Nicholas, 1477 (1480?) (Master Peter). Long time in the Rijksmuseum, Amsterdam, now in Middelburg.
Jutfaas, Catholic Church, *c.* 1500. Originally in the Nieuwe Zijdskapel, Amsterdam.
Harenkaspel, first half of the sixteenth century, now in the Rijksmuseum, Amsterdam.
Scheemda, 1526 (by Johann von Emden). Now in the Rijksmuseum, Amsterdam.
Monnikendam, *c.* 1530.[1]

[1] A detailed account of the important school of Brabant Organ-builders is given in Dr. M. A. Vente's book *Die Brabanter Orgel*, Amsterdam, 1958.

CHAPTER IV

THE BAROQUE ORGAN IN EUROPE AND THE ORGAN OF BACH

THE BAROQUE period may be divided into two parts: early Baroque (1600–50) and high Baroque (1650–1720).

In Germany the Thirty Years War (1618–48) was disastrous to the development of the organ and inflicted "on organ-building the most grievous wounds",[1] but in France and the Low Countries there was continuous progress. What happened in England as regards the art of the organ will be considered in the next chapter. Praetorius, whose book we have noticed in the last section, gives an excellent picture of the instrument and its structure, particularly in north Germany, where it had developed both in size and in scope to a greater extent than elsewhere. The Hanseatic towns of Germany and north Holland had a strongly developed civic sense, and the possession of good organs and skilful players who were patronised by the wealthy merchants was a matter of friendly rivalry between them. The organs at Hamburg and Lübeck, the capital city of the old Hanse, were particularly noteworthy both in number and in size. The young J. S. Bach came to both of these to hear the masters Reinken and Buxtehude display their great skill as players, at a time when the Baroque organ was approaching its apogee. So resourceful had the instrument become that, for instance, the design of its pedal section was such that it was difficult to find its match in any British organ two hundred years later, and even today we rarely find in England so comprehensive a system of mutation and compound stops for enriching the true organ tone.

Mersenne (Marin Mersennus, 1588–1648), a leading scientist of his day and a man of great versatility, published in 1635 his best-known work, *Harmonie Universelle*,[2] in which he dealt with many aspects of the theory of music and acoustics. He included descriptions of all European musical instruments in use at the beginning of the seventeenth century, with accounts of their manufacture. His work is the French counterpart of the *Syntagma* of Praetorius. The French organ was not so well constituted as the larger instruments of the northern provinces; in particular, the pedal organ, used so early in France, had not developed much in that country. Nevertheless the grand orgue was the major part of the instrument and contained "fat" and "thin" choruses with better reeds than were usual in Germany. The pedal organ, with flue and reed stops of 4-ft. pitch, was intended for melodic or solo purposes, particularly for sustaining a cantus firmus or slow choral melody. In larger instruments a small positif organ played from a second

[1] Ernst Flade, *Gottfried Silbermann* (Leipzig, 1926).

[2] A copy of the Latin edition (1636) is in the library of Aberdeen University.

manual would be found. This was the type of organ known to the composers and organists Jean Titelouze (1563–1633) of Rouen,[1] Nicolas Gigault (1624–1707) of Paris, Nicolas de Grigny (d. 1703) of Paris, and (with certain improvements) to the eldest François Couperin (1631–1703), also of Paris.

Mersenne described the quintaton type of stop which gives two notes to each pipe, the various tapered pipes, the bear pipes and "schnarrwerk", which are described by Praetorius. He dealt thoroughly with the problems of obtaining vowel sounds from vox humana and regal stops. Mersenne had a knowledge of synthetic tone-building, and to some measure anticipated the acoustical work of H. Helmholtz[2] two and a quarter centuries later.

Mersenne described the tonal combinations, then very popular, which contain a strong nazard (twelfth) flavour. A musette tone, he says, could be made by adding the cromorne to a soft nazard.

Here is the list of stops given by Mersenne. (In the 1636 edition of his work each name is translated into Latin with ungracious results.)

A two-manual organ specification given by Mersenne:

Grand Orgue

Montre	Bourdon 16	Trompette 8
Montre	Flûte allemande 4	Clarion 4
Prestant	Flageolet 1	Cromorne 8
Doublette	Nazard $5\frac{1}{3}$	Voix humaine 8
Fourniture 2, $1\frac{1}{3}$, 1, $\frac{2}{3}$, $\frac{1}{2}$, $\frac{1}{3}$	Nazard $2\frac{2}{3}$	
Cymbale 1, $\frac{2}{3}$, $\frac{1}{2}$	Tierce $1\frac{3}{5}$	
Cymbale 2, $\frac{1}{3}$ [*sic !* $\frac{1}{2}$, $\frac{1}{3}$?]	Larigot $1\frac{1}{3}$	
	Cornet 8, 4, $2\frac{2}{3}$, 2, $1\frac{3}{5}$	

Positif

Montre 8	Bourdon 8	Cromorne 4
Prestant 4	Flûte allemande 4	
Doublette 2	Flageolet 1	
Fourniture 1, $\frac{2}{3}$, $\frac{1}{2}$	Nazard $2\frac{2}{3}$	The division of the flue stops into narrow- and wide-scale groups is noteworthy.
Cymbale $\frac{1}{2}$, $\frac{1}{3}$	Larigot $1\frac{1}{3}$	
	Tierce $\frac{4}{5}$	

Pédale

Pédale de flûte 16	These stops may be given as 8.4.4. ft. pitches respectively according to the method of regarding the pedal compass which did not start at cc.
Pédale de flûte 8	
Pédale d'anche 8	

Mersenne gives a number of "stock" combinations of organ stops:

Plein jeu consists of the full narrow-scale flue work and pedal with reeds.

Jeu musical:			
	Montre 8	or	Montre 8
	Bourdon 8		Bourdon 8
			Prestant 4

[1] W. L. Sumner, Preface to Titelouze, *Pange Lingua* (Peters ed., 1957).

[2] *Die Lehre von den Tonempfindungen, als physiologische Grundlage für die Theorie der Musik* (1863). Translated by A. J. Ellis, *On the Sensations of Tone* (1872).

Pédale—cont.

Jeu fort harmonieux :	Montre 16	or	Montre 8	
	Montre 8		Prestant 4	
			Flûte à cheminée 4	
Jeu doux harmonieux :	Bourdon 16			
	Bourdon 8			
	Flute 4			
Jeu fort aigu :	Montre 16			
	Montre 8			
	Prestant 4			
	Doublette 2			
	Flageolet 1			

Combinations containing strong nazard (twelfth) harmonics, tierces and cornets were evidently much in use, e.g.

Nazard :	Bourdon 16		Montre 8
	Montre 8	or	Prestant 4
	Prestant 4		Doublette 2
	Nazard $5\frac{1}{3}$		Nazard $2\frac{2}{3}$
			Flageolet 1
			(with tremulant)

Le Cornet :	Bourdon	16
	Montre	8
	Prestant	4
	Doublette	2
	Nazard	$2\frac{2}{3}$
	Tierce	$1\frac{3}{5}$
Le Larigot :	Bourdon	16
	Montre	8
	Larigot	$1\frac{1}{3}$
Nazard très fort :	Bourdon	16
	Montre	8
	Prestant	4
	Doublette	2
	Nazard	$2\frac{2}{3}$
	Larigot	$1\frac{1}{3}$
Cornet entier :	Bourdon	16
	Montre	8
	Prestant	4
	Doublette	2
	Nazard	$2\frac{2}{3}$
	Tierce	$1\frac{3}{5}$
	Larigot	$1\frac{1}{3}$
La Trompette :	Montre	16
	Montre	8
	Prestant	4
	Trompette	8

Le Cromorne:	Bourdon	16
	Montre	8
	Prestant	4
	Cromorne	8
Le Clarion:	Bourdon	16
	Montre	8
	Prestant	4
	Nazard	$2\frac{2}{3}$
	Trompette	4
	(with tremulant)	
Le Flageolet:	Bourdon	16
	Montre	8
	Flageolet	1

Dufourcq[1] gives the following dates for the introduction of (or earliest-known references to) various sections of the organ in France.

Grand orgue: end of thirteenth century (38–41 keys, 1475) to beginning of fourteenth century (45 keys, 1475–1580).
Positif: Rouen, 1386 (45–48 keys, 1580–1660; 50–52 keys, 1660–1790).
Echo: Chartres, 1647 (25–39 keys, 1650–1790).
Récit: Paris, 1660–70 (25–34 keys, 1670–1700).
Bombarde: Paris (Notre Dame), 1730.
Pédale: Troyes, 1432 (8 keys fifteenth century; 8–17 keys, 1475–1580; 17–24 keys, 1580–1640; 24–35 keys, 1660–1790).
Montre: 32–24 ft.: Normandy, 1450–1550; Burgundy, 1730–80.
Montre: 16–12 ft.: Chartres, 1475.

The great French organ-builders of the fifteenth and sixteenth centuries were Oudin-Hestre, Nicolas Petit, Jousseline and François des Oliviers. These men were great creators and artists, giving attention both to sound design and to detail. They were followed in the seventeenth century by Nicolas Barbier, Crespin Carlier, G. Lesselier,[2] R. Gouet, Cl. de Villers, Cl. et Ch. Lefebvre, R. Ingout (Normandy), d'Argillières, Langueudeul, Le Pescheur, P. Maillard, de Heman, Thierry, Du Castel, Clicquot, De Joyeuse,[3] Lesclop (Ile de France), Le Bé (Champagne), P. Marchand and Ch. Boisselier (Provence). Many of these established families which built organs for a number of generations.

Rouen Cathedral: 1657. Organ by Pierre Thierry and Pierre Desenclos

Grande Orgue			*Positif*		*Echo*
			Montre	8	Fourniture 3 ranks
Montre	16	Fourniture	Bourdon	8	Cornet 5 ranks
Bourdon	16	Cymbale	Prestant	4	Voix humaine

[1] *Esquisse d'une Histoire de l'orgue en France* (Paris, 1936).
[2] William Leslie, who in common with other Scots settled in France at this time.
[3] De Joyeuse did much to take the Parisian organ art to the Midi. His masterpiece was an organ of 4 manuals and 28 speaking stops at Auch.

Grande Orgue—cont.			*Postif—cont.*		*Pédale*	
Montre	8	Flageolet	Doublette	2		
Prestant	4	Quarte de nazard	Fourniture 4 ranks		Open pipes	8
Doublette	2	Trompette	Cymbale 4 ranks		Open pipes	4
Flûte		Clairon	Flûte	4	Trompette	8
Cornet		Clairon	Nazard			
Nazard		Voix humaine	Quarte de nazard			
Grosse tierce		Cromorne	Tierce			
Larigot			Larigot			
Petit nazard			Cromorne			

The supremacy of the grand orgue will be noted. The echo mixtures of soft intonation must have been very beautiful. The pedal still had a melodic function. The grand-orgue was scaled in 16 ft.; the positif an octave higher.

By contrast, the Italian organs were quite small instruments, with very few exceptions, until the end of the sixteenth century. The specifications were of a uniform type. There was one manual and sometimes an octave of pedal pull-downs, and this controlled a very light pressure flue chorus of small-scaled stops, with a flute stop or two. No third-sounding ranks were introduced into the chorus, which was kept as clear in tone as possible. A five-stop instrument built at Lucca in 1495 contained Tenore (probably 8 ft.), Ottava (4 ft.), Quintadecima (2 ft.), Vigesimaseconda (1 ft.) and Flauti (probably 4 ft.). Larger instruments would have further octave and fifth ranks as far as Trigesimasesta ($\frac{1}{2}$ ft.), though the Duodecima ($2\frac{2}{3}$ ft.) was rarely found. At the end of the sixteenth century a regal (regale or vox humana) was added to the flue chorus. The tuning was to mean-tone temperament, and the thirds were kept pure.[1]

The most illustrious organ-builders in Italy during the fifteenth and sixteenth centuries were the members of the Antegnati family. Bartholemeo Antegnati constructed the organs in the cathedrals of Milan, Como, Bergamo, Brescia, Cremona and Mantua. Graziadio Antegnati, his son, was probably the most capable artist of the family, but his son, Costanzo, was more versatile, for, besides making organs, he also played them and composed both sacred and secular music for the instrument. He wrote *L'Arte organica*,[2] which appeared in Brescia in 1608. In this he gives a list of the organs built by the family, and by the latter part of the sixteenth century there were more than four hundred instruments in various parts of Italy. Antegnati gives the specifications of several of these organs, which were almost uniform in style.

[1] Knud Jeppesen *Die italienische Orgelmusik am Anfang des Cinquecento* (Copenhagen: Munksgaard, 1943).

[2] A facsimile of this very rare work was printed by the *Rheingold Verlag* (Mainz, 1938). Another work "Il Transilvano" by Girolamo Diruta appeared in 1609, and in it the methods of combining the stops in the type of organ given by Antegnati are also mentioned. In particular he gives the registration for the grave and gay moods of the twelve ecclesiastical tones. A MS. in the library of the Academy of Music at Bologna by Antonio Barcotto de Montagnano of Padua (1652) deals in eighteen short chapters with the construction of organs, but it does not tell us anything new. This has been reprinted by R. Lunelli (Florence, 1953). See also "Notes on the Organ in Italy," by Walter Shewring, in *The Organ* Nos. 117, 119, 124, 140, 141 and Renato Lunelli: *Der Orgelbau in Italien*, Mainz 1956.

They consisted of an open flue chorus of principal scale and a few flutes of wider scale. Many of these one-manual organs had pedal pull-downs. Such was the instrument on which Frescobaldi (1583–1643) played his toccatas.

1. Principale
2. Principale soprano e pedale
3. Ottava
4. Decimaquinta
5. Decimanona
6. Vigesimaseconda
7. Vigesimasesta
8. Vigesimanona
9. Trigesimaterza
10. Altra vigesima seconda (larga)
11. Flauto in decimaquinta
12. Flauto in ottava Tremolante

In the later part of the work Antegnati shows how the stops may be combined to give compounds of various qualities and degrees of brilliance.

We owe much of our knowledge of the late Renaissance and early Baroque German organs to Praetorius.[1] In his scheme of reed and flue organ pipes, here set forth, we see the remarkable number of different types of organ tone which were then available.

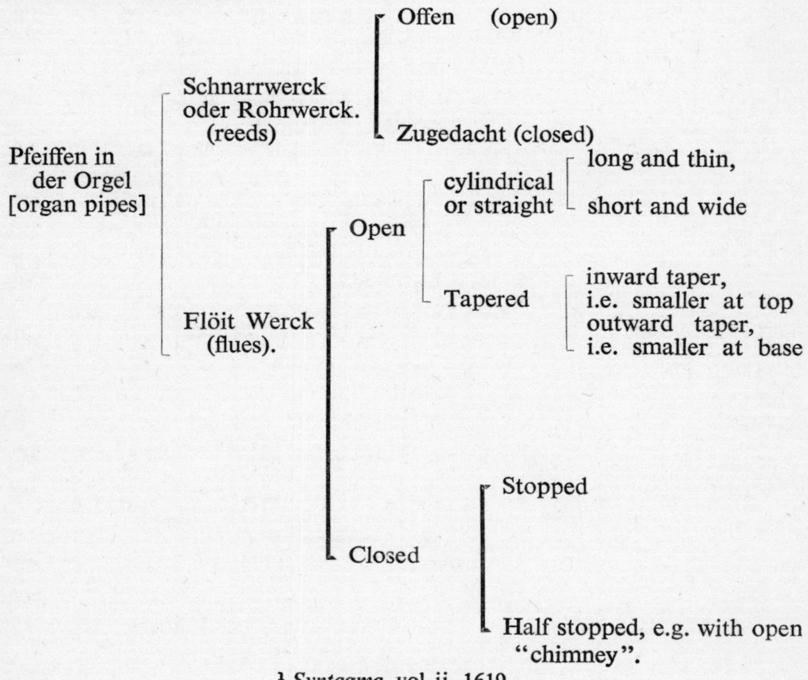

[1] *Syntagma*, vol. ii, 1619.

M = in manual; P = in pedal.

			feet
Schnarrwerck or Röhrwerck [i.e. reeds]	Open	P Posaunen Bass	16
		M Trommeten	8
		P Trommeten Bass	8
		MP Schallmeyen	8
		P Klein Schallmeyen	4
		P Gross Krumbhorn Bass	16
		MP Krumbhorner	8
		P Klein Krumbhorn Bass	4
		M Gross Regal	8
		MP Kleingeigend or Jungfrau Regal	4
		M Zimbel Regal	1
		M Zincken Discant	8
		P Cornett Bass	4 / 2
	"closed"	MP Sorduen	16
		MP Gross Rancket	16
		MP Rancket	8
		P Gross Baerpipen	16
		MP Baerpipen	8
		MP Gross Bombart	16
		MP Bombart	8
		M Fagott	8
		P Dulcian Bass	8
		M Apffel or Knopff Regal[1]	8
		M Kopfflin Regal	4
"Long and narrow"	Principaln	P Gross Sub Princip. Bass	32
		M Gross Principal	16
		P G. Pri or Principal Untersatz	16
		MP Princ. or Prestant	8
		MP Klein Principal	4
		M Klein Princ. Discant	4
	Octaven	MP Gross Octava	8
		MP Octava	4
		MP Klein Octava	2
		M Super Octavlin Sedetz	1
	Quinten	MP Gross Quinta	$5\frac{1}{3}$
		MP Quinta	$2\frac{2}{3}$
		M Klein Quinta	$1\frac{1}{3}$
		Rauschpfeiff or Rausch Quint.	3 and 2
	Schweitzer Pfeiffen	MP Gross Schweitz Pfeiffe	8
		M Klein Schweitzer Pfeiffe	4
		M Klein Schw. Pfei. Disc.	4
		P Klein Schw. Pf. Bass	1
	Mixturen	MP Grosse Mixtur	1
		MP Mixtur 2 or 1 [*sic.*] ranks	
		MP K. Mixtur or Scharp	

[1] Apple or knob (head) Regal, so called from the shape of the tubes.

			feet
Zimbeln		MP Grosser Zimbel	
		MP Klingend Zimbel	
		MP Zimbel	
		M Kleiner Zimbel	
		M Repetirende Zimbel	
		P Zimbel Bass	
Holfloiten ("Short and wide")		MP Gross Holfloiten	8
		MP Holfloiten	4
		M Holpfleiffen Discant	4
		MP Holquint	3
		MP Kleine Holfloit	2
		M K. Hol. Qu(int) or Qu. Floit.	1½
		M Suiffloitlin or Stefflit	1
		M Wald floitlin	2
		P Klein floitlin Bass	1
		MP Gross Schwiegel	8
		MP Klein Schwiegel	4
Wide at bottom; thin at the top.	Gemshorner or Spillfloiten	MP Gros Gembshorn	16
		MP Gembshorn	8
		MP Octaven Gembshorn	4
		MP Gembs. Quinta.	3
		MP Kleine oder Super Gembshornlein	2
		M Klein Gembs. Quinta. Nasat.	1½
		Spillfloiten	4
	Spitzfloiten	M Spitzfloit	4
		MP Klein Spitzfloit	2
		M Spitz Quintlein	1½
		Blockfloiten or Plockpfeiffen	4
	Flachfloiten	MP Grosse Flachfloit	8
		MP Flachfloiten	4
		MP Klein Flachfloit	2
		M Klein Flachfloit Discant	2
Thin at bottom; wide at top		Dulzaen	8
Quintadeen Scale	Quintadeen	MP Gross Quintadeen	16
		MP Quintadeen	8
		MP Klein Quintadeen	4
	Nachthorn	MP Nachthorn	4
		P Klein Nachthorn Bass	2
	Querfloit	MP Gross Querfloit	8
		MP Querfloit	4
	Gedacten	P Gross Gedacter Sub. Bass	32
		M Gross Gedact	16
		PG Gedact Bass or Gedact Untersatz	16
		MP Gedact	8
		MP Klein Gedact	4
		M Gedacte [*sic.*] Quinta	3
		M Super Gedactlin	2
		P Bawerflöte Bass	1
Rohrfloiten ("closed", with open chimney)		MP Grosse Rohrfloiten	16
		MP Rohrfloiten	8
		MP Kleine Rohrfloite	4
		M Super Rohrfloitlin	2
		P Bawer Rohrfloitlin Bass or Rohrschell	1

Compenius, Fritsche, and the Scherer family were amongst the most distinguished north German organ builders of the late Renaissance and early Baroque periods. Some specifications of organs built by them are now given.

The organ in the Church of *St. Petri, Hamburg*, reconstructed in 1603–4 by Hans Scherer.

Hauptwerk F-a_2 Middle Clavier

Prinzipal	16
Oktave	8
Mixtur	
Scharf	
Quintadena	16
Gedackt	8
Rohrflöte	4
Rauschpfeife	$2\frac{2}{3}$
Zimbel	

Oberwerk C-a_2 Upper Clavier

Rohrflöte	8
Rohrflöte	4
Nasat	$2\frac{2}{3}$
Nachthorn	2
Sifflöte	$1\frac{1}{3}$
Trompete	8
Regal	8
Zink	8 (Diskant)
Krummhornregal	8
Prinzipal	8
Zimbel	3 ranks

Rückpositiv C-a_2 Lower Clavier

Prinzipal	8
Oktave	4
Mixture	
Scharf	
Gedackt	8
Quintadena	8
Rohrflöte	4
Nasat	$2\frac{2}{3}$
Bärpfeife	8
Regal	8
Krummhorn	8

Pedal
(from C)

Prinzipal	32 (from F)
Oktave	16
Oktave	8
Mixtur	
Subbass	16
Posaune	16
Krummhorn	16
Trompete	8
Kornett	2
Nachthorn	2

Tremulant.

Schlosskirche Dresden, organ built in 1614 by Gottfried Fritsche.

Hauptwerk: Upper Manual CDEFGABHC-d_3
"für alle es/dis und as/gis Sonderkanzellen, 53 Tasten."

Prinzipal	8 (fine tin)
Oktave	4 (fine tin)
Quinte	$2\frac{2}{3}$
Oktave	2
Mixtur	4 ranks
Quintadena	16
Quintadena	8
Spitzgedackt	$5\frac{1}{3}$
Koppelflöte	4 (fine tin)
Quintadena	4 (fine tin)
Gedacktnasat	$2\frac{2}{3}$

Seitenwerk
(This section was at the side of the main organ) (C-d_3.)

Prinzipal	4 (fine tin)
Oktave	2 (fine tin)
Mixtur	2 ranks
Gedackt	8
Spitzgedackt	4
Nasat	$2\frac{2}{3}$
Krummhorn	8

Spitzgedackt	2 (fine tin)	*Pedal*	
Sifflöte	$1\frac{1}{3}$	(from C)	
Schwegel	1 (fine tin)	Prinzipal	16 (wood)
Trompete	8	Oktave	8
Regal	4	Sub-bass	16
Schwebungs-prinzipal	8	Quintadena	16
(Wood, thin scale, sweet tone)		Posaune	16
(Tuned to make céleste effects)		Kornett	2
		Querflöte	1
Zimbel	2 ranks	Klingende Zimbel	

Couplers: upper to lower manual; lower manual to pedal; drums, cymbalstar, tremulants to manual divisions.

An excellent example of the early Baroque northern organ of the time of Praetorius and Scheidt is the instrument built about 1610 and re-erected by Esajas Compenius in the Castle at Frederiksborg, near Copenhagen, in 1616. Happily, the instrument is still in excellent condition. Its specification is worth careful study:[1]

Hauptwerk		*Unterwerk*		*Pedal*	
Prinzipal	8	Quintade	8	Sub-bass	16
Gedackt	8	Kleingedackt	4	Gemshorn	8
Prinzipal	4	Prinzipal	4	Quintade	8
Nachthorn	4	Blockflöte	4	Querflöte	4
Blockflöte	4	Gemshorn	2	Nachthorn	2
Gemshorn (or little viol)	4	Nasat	$1\frac{1}{3}$	Bauernflöte	1
Supergedackt	2	Zimbel (1 rank)	$\frac{1}{4}$	Sordun Bass	16
Gedacktquinte	$2\frac{2}{3}$	Krummhorn	8	Dulzian	8
Rankett	16	Geigend Regal	4	Jungfern Regal	4

On both manual and pedal the 16-ft. reed takes precedence. Synthetic tone-building on the pedal was as important as on the manuals. The pedal of these organs not infrequently controlled more stops than any of the manuals. At this period and in the later Baroque days the pedal had a versatility which it soon was to lose. It offered a wealth of solo effects which few of our cathedral organs can approach; it made a suitable bass for the manuals; it could sustain a melodic line with a variety of definite tone-colours and dynamics, and the great-to-pedal coupler was unnecessary. Usually the positif-to-pedal coupler was the first pedal coupler to be supplied, as it enhanced the melodic effects obtainable from the pedal.

The stops could be divided into two groups on each division of the organ. These were known as the male and female, or the narrow and wide groups. The stops of bright "open" tone, including small-scaled reeds and fifth-sounding mutations, were of the first class, while flutes, quintatons, regals and bear pipes (and at a later date tierces and third-sounding mutations) were of the second class. It was not permitted in the late sixteenth and early seventeenth

[1] The instrument was constructed originally in 1609–10 as a house organ.

centuries to add the thick tone of a female-class stop to the transparent bright choruses of the male-class stops. Thus, an open flue chorus with a quiet 16-ft. stop of trumpet tone would be admirable for playing contrapuntal music at *mf*.

St. Mary's, Bernau, organ built by Hans Scherer the elder, 1572–73.

Hauptwerk (*Upper Manual*)
(C.D. – C_3, 48 notes)

Stop	
Prinzipal	16
Oktave	8
Oktave	4
Oktave	2
Mixtur	12 ranks
Scharf	3 ranks
Gedackt	8
Quintadena	8
Quinte	$5\frac{1}{3}$
Rohrflöte	4
Quintadena	4
Nasat	$2\frac{2}{3}$
Blockflöte	2
Sifflöte	$1\frac{1}{3}$
Bärpfeife	8

Rückpositiv (*Lower Manual*)
(C.D. – C_3, 48 notes)

Stop	
Prinzipal	8
Oktave	4
Oktave	2
Rohrflöte	8
Spillflöte	4
Rohrnasat	$2\frac{2}{3}$
Nachthorn	2
Sifflöte	$1\frac{1}{3}$
Klingende Zimbel	3 ranks
Trompete	8
Singend Regal	4

(Koppel: lower to upper manual.
Koppel: Rückpositiv to pedal tremulant.)

Pedal

Stop	
Prinzipal	16
Posaune	16
Bauernflöte	1

Another fine example of a late Renaissance organ, given by Praetorius, is that at *St. Mary's Church, Danzig*, built in 1585 by Julio Antonio.

Oberwerck
(13 stimmen)

	Stop	
These stops have 48 pipes (each)	Principal	16
	Holfloite	16
	Quintadehna	16
	Spillpfeiffe	8
	Octava	8
	Quintadehna	8
	Offenfloite or Viol	3
	Spillpfeiffe }	4
	Viol }	
	Sedecima	
	Rauschquint	

144 pipes. Zimbel 3 ranks
1,152 pipes. Mixtur 24 ranks

Im Rückpositiff
(18 stimmen)

Stop	
Principal	
Holfloit or Holpfeiff }	8
Spillpfeiff or Blockfl. }	
Octav }	4
Offenfloit or Viol. }	
Kleine Blockfluit }	
Gemshorn	
Sedecima	
Floit	
Waldfloit	
Rauschquint	
Nasatt	
Zimbel of 144 Pfeiffen	
Mixtur of 220 Pfeiffen	
Trommet }	8
Krumbhorn }	
Zincken }	4
Schallmeyen }	

In der Brust or Positiff
(8 stimmen)

Gedacte Stimm	8
Gedact	4
Principal	4
Quintadehna	4
Zimbel	
Dunceten	2
Regal Singend	8
Zincken	4

In the Oberwerke Pedal
(4 stimmen) (43 pipes each)

Gross unter Bass	32
Unter Bass	16
Posaunen Bass	16
Trommete	8

In Pedal at each side
(12 stimmen)

Floiten or Octava	8
Gedact	8
Quintadehna	4
Superoctav	2
Nachthorn	2
Rauschquint	$2, 2\frac{2}{3}$
Bawerpfeiff	1 (?)
Zimbel of 144 pipes	
Mixtur of 220 pipes	
Spitz or Cornett	
Trommeten or Schallmeyen	
Krumbhorner	
Tremulants	
Bass Drums	

The most important organ-builders in Germany, and probably also in Europe, during the middle and later Baroque periods were Arp Schnitger, the Silbermann brothers and Joachim Wagner.

Arp Schnitger

Arp Schnitger, the greatest German organ-builder of the high Baroque period, may be regarded as the successor of the Scherer family who represented the great tradition of organ-building in north Germany in the sixteenth century. As their work is faithfully recorded by Praetorius and we have given specifications of their organs, a short statement of their chief works will suffice.

(1) Jacob Scherer was at work between 1545 and 1565, and his chief instruments were:

1547	Lübeck, St. Marien: "Totentanzorgel",[1] new Rückpositiv.
1549	Lübeck, St. Marien: repairs to the chief organ.
1557	Stargard: work on the organs at St. Jacob's and St. Marien.
1557	Alten-Brandenburg, St. Gotthardt.
1557–8	Lübeck, St. Marien: new stops for the Totentanzorgel.
1557	Stettin, St. Marien.
1559	Hamburg: new stops for the organ of St. Catherine's Church.
1560–61	Lübeck, St. Marien: new stops for the main organ.
1570	Ratzeburg: rebuilt cathedral organ.

(2) Hans Scherer the older (at work 1570–1611) built and repaired organs at Bernau, Stendal, St. Nicholas; Stade, St. Jacobi and St. Catherine; Hamburg, St. Cosmae; Stade, Bergedorf, St. Petri and St. Jacobi; Hamburg, the Castle at Rotenburg, St. Martin, Kassel, St. Lamberti Lüneburg (?).

(3) Hans Scherer the younger (at work between 1590–1630). Organs at Hamburg, Lübeck, Bergedorf and Stade.

[1] The organ in the Chapel of the Dance of Death was destroyed in an air raid during the night of Palm Sunday, 1942.

(4) Fritz Scherer, the brother of the above (1603–4) repairs to the St. Petri and St. Jacobi organs at Hamburg.

Michael Praetorius published his *Syntagma* (vol. ii, "De Organographia") in 1619 and devoted considerable space to detailed descriptions of the large organs of his time. There were organs of sixty speaking stops with 32-ft. manual stops at Lübeck, the old Hanseatic capital, pedal organs of twelve stops or more complete from 32 ft. to mixtures and many varieties of flue and reed stops. Praetorius's systematic analysis of pipe types has been reproduced earlier in this chapter. A remarkable group of organ-players and composers was flourishing in the Hanseatic towns at the time.[1] J. P. Sweelinck, the organist of the Old Church at Amsterdam, had shown how to treat the organ in a lighter poetic manner. He died in 1621, two years after Praetorius's book had appeared. This was the "Stadtisch bürgerlichen" period, and each large town took a pride in trying to rival the others in the quality and size of its organs and the skill of its organists, but before Praetorius's book had been published the Thirty Years War started. Little organ-building was done during this long period and many fine instruments were ruined. In the second half of the century many new organs were called for and there was much repair work.

Arp Schnitger[2] was born on 9th July 1648 at Schmalenfleth, near Golz-

---

[1] The chief composers of organ music at this period were: Michael Praetorius (1571–1621), Wolfenbüttel; Jan Pieterzoon Sweelinck (1562–1621), Amsterdam; Samuel Scheidt (1587–1654), Halle; Girolamo Frescobaldi (1583–1643), Rome; Heinrich Scheidemann (1595–1663), Hamburg; Matthias Weckmann (1621–74), Hamburg; Johann Adam Reinken (1623–1722), Hamburg; Franz Tunder (1614–67), Lübeck; Dietrich Buxtehude (1637–1707), Lübeck; Nikolaus Bruhns (1665–97), Lübeck; Joh. Jakob Froberger (1616–67), Vienna; Joh. Kasper Kerll (1627–93), Munich; Georg Muffat (1645–1704), Passau; Johann Pachelbel (1653–1706), Nuremberg and Erfurt; Joh. Christopher Bach (1642–1703), Eisenach; Jean Titelouze (1563–1633), Rouen; Nicolas Gigault (1625–1707), Paris; André Raison (d. *c.* 1700), Paris; Nicolas de Grigny (d. *c.* 1703), Paris; François Couperin (1631–1703), Paris; Bernardo Pasquini (1637–1710), Rome.

Contemporaries of J. S. Bach.

G. F. Handel (1685–1759), London; Vincent Lübeck (1654–1740), Hamburg; Georg Böhm (1661–1733), Lüneburg; Joh. Gottfried Walther (1684–1748), Weimar; Joh. Kasper Ferd. Fischer (d. 1746), Rastatt; Geog Phil. Telemann (1681–1767), Hamburg; Claude d'Aquin (Daquin) (1694–1772), Paris; Jean François Dandrieu (1684–1740), Paris.

Collections of their works may be found in: Karl Straube, *Choralvorspiele alte Meister* (Peters, 1912); Karl Straube, *Alte Meister des Orgelspiels* (Peters, 1927); Karl Straube, *Alter Meister des Orgelspiels* (Neue Folge I, II); "Organum", *Sammlung alter Musik*, collected by Max Seiffert (Kistner und Siegel, 1926); Jan Peterszoon Sweelinck (1562–1621), Organ works (Breitkopf & Härtel); Samuel Scheidt (1587–1654) *Tabulatura Nova* (Breitkopf & Härtel); Jean Titelouze (1563–1633) *Hymnes d'Eglise* (in Guilmant's "Archives"), Schott. (Mainz); Girolamo Frescobaldi (1583–1643), Works (Breitkopf & Härtel); Hans Leo Hassler (1564–1612), *Denkmäler der Tonkunst in Bayern*, Jahrgang IV Band 2; Christian Erbach (1570–1635), ibid; Ulrich Steigleder (1593–1635), *Vier Ricercare* (Bärenreiter); Michael Praetorius (1571–1621), Collected organ works, ed. by Gurlitt (pub. Kallmeyer Wolfenbüttel).

[2] Hopkins and Rimbault (op. cit.) speak of him as the Abbé Schnitger, but this is a misreading of his Christian name. Schnitger, by heredity and environment, showed affinities both to Holland and Germany. He has been acclaimed both Dutch

warden, in Oldenburg. His father was an expert joiner and carver, and, as the name suggests, this was the family tradition.

At the age of eighteen, Schnitger was apprenticed to his cousin, Barendt Huss (Berend Huess), an organ-builder in a small way, and remained with him for four years. Huss has built organs in the district north of Hanover. In 1676 Huss died, and three years later Schnitger settled in Neuenfelde in the house which was known in recent times as Orgelbauerhoff. (There are three places called Neuenfelde at the south of Hamburg. Schnitger's workshop was in that between Buxtehude and Harburg in the district known as Altes Lande.) Schnitger is buried in the church there. The west-end organ, with characteristic case, was given by him, and above the altar is his coat of arms carved in oak.[1] He founded a guild of master craftsmen and the design bore acorns, ears of wheat, a pair of dividers, and other symbols of the wood-carver's craft. Schnitger found inspiration in the work of the Scherer family and jealously conserved anything that was still usable when he rebuilt their organs. Schnitger regarded his work as his prayer and a hundred and fifty organs, many of them of three- and four-manuals, with pedal organs of a dozen stops or more, are known to have been built by him. Schnitger was twice married. His first wife, Gardrudt Ottens, bore him six children. Two of the boys died during his lifetime and two more were destined to become great organ-builders. Schnitger died on 24th or 25th July 1719 at the age of seventy-one, and his second wife married Burgomaster Gerels of Oldenburg.[2]

The Characteristics of Schnitger's Organs

In view of the fact that Schnitger is a more important and characteristic builder of the Baroque period than the Silbermanns, it will be worth while to dwell a little on the essential features of this important school of organ-building, which is made more important by the fact that it was this type of instrument which Bach had in mind as an organ composer. The finest organ on which Bach ever played was the Schnitger instrument in the St. Jakobi Church, Hamburg. Bach coveted the post of organist here, but it was given to a clerical amateur who paid a premium[3] and "could prelude better with thalers than with his fingers".

Schnitger's organs were always provided generously with apparatus for raising the wind.

The following are examples of his bellows:

Organ at St. Nicholas, Hamburg:	67 stops,	16 bellows.	10 ft. × 5 ft.
Organ at St. Nicholas, Berlin:	40 stops,	8 bellows.	9½ ft. × 5 ft.
Organ at Buxtehude Church:	35 stops,	6 bellows.	8 ft. × 4 ft.
Organ at Moorburg Church:	14 stops,	3 bellows.	6 ft. × 3 ft.

and German. The art (and people) of the Friesian Islands, the provinces of Groningen, Friesland and Oldenburg, have many points of similarity. Here are to be found many Schnitger organs. The name is sometimes spelt Schnittker, which is the form he often used when writing in Dutch. Burney's spelling (Splitger) is obviously wide of the mark.

[1] The organ is still (1948) in perfect condition.

[2] W. L. Sumner, "Arp Schnitger and His Organs" *The Organ*, vol. xvii, pp. 139, 193.

[3] See Spitta, *Life of Bach*, vol. ii, pp. 18–21.

The wind pressures varied between 3 in. and 3·6 inches. (Schnitger measured wind pressure in terms of the Grad, which is about ·083 in.)

The naturals of the keys were covered with ebony or beech or strips of glazed pottery, and the sharps with ivory or bone. The length of a manual keyboard of forty-five notes was 26·5 in., that of a "sharp" key 2·6 in. and a "natural" key 4·2 in. The depth of touch of the different manuals varied between ¾ in. and ⅓ in. and for the chief manual (Hauptwerk) was often so great as to be uncomfortable for modern methods of playing. The bottom C♯ key and sometimes D♯ and G♯ were omitted from Schnitger's manual keyboards, as they were not usually required when playing with the restricted keys dictated by mean-tone temperament. The pedal claviers usually had twenty-six or twenty-seven keys and the lengths of the claviers varied from 43½ in. to 46 in.

The majority of the Schnitger organs contain no wooden pipes. It is easier to make and voice metal pipes than those of wood; and the lead-tin alloy is better than glue-joined wood in the damp climate of the north German and Dutch districts. English tin of 95 per cent purity was used for the show pipes; and for the principal-toned stops inside the instrument a lead-tin alloy of the proportion 10:3. The flutes and cornets were made of a metal containing an even larger proportion of lead. Brass was often used for the tubes of the smaller reeds. Although excellent light-winded flute and "gedeckt" pipes of the baroque type can be made of copper, there is no evidence that Schnitger used this metal, but it has become popular in the twentieth century for the pipe-work of neo-baroque organs.

The pitch of Schnitger's organs was about three-quarters of a tone higher than that at present (A=440). The organs were tuned to mean-tone temperament, in which the octaves and ascending thirds were tuned true, and the fifths were narrowed. Modulation into remote flat and sharp keys was impossible with such tuning, but in a few major keys the effect of the pure thirds must have been very satisfactory. Towards the end of the seventeenth century and early in the eighteenth the influence of Bach and Werckmeister was being felt and many organs were then tuned in equal temperament, or something approaching it.

Schnitger brought the Praetorius organ to its logical conclusion. He represented the German democratic Lutheran tradition and he only felt the Latin influence to the trifling extent of adding a few of the Italian stops towards the end of his life. The Silbermann organs, on the other hand, are more sophisticated and show southern characteristics.

Schnitger always had a sure touch with his pedal organs; on his larger instruments he developed the flue tone from 32 ft. to a choice of mixtures and the reeds from 32 ft. to 2 ft. It is noteworthy that he knew how to make a 16-ft. manual stop playable on the pedals, but he rarely used the device. Everything had to be independent. He did not make the mistake of later times of multiplying unison tone at the expense of proper harmonic ranks. To a modern organist it might appear at first sight that there was often a poor choice of 16-ft. tone on the pedal, and 8-ft. on the manual. In practice this was not so, for a considerable portion of the upper work was so quiet that its main purpose was to strengthen and qualify the unison tone without adding much brightness to it. Schnitger knew a great deal about synthetic tone-building a century and a half before Helmholtz.[1] He almost certainly sensed something which Helmholtz never discovered, namely, that the synthesis of tone from true harmonics has its limitations. Schnitger thus found that the rather insignificant buzzing tones of his baerpfeifen gave a richness to his ensemble flue tone which no mixture or mutation scheme could achieve. The reeds of the Baroque organ had no climactic effect and their tones were absorbed by that of the full flue-work. Only the pedal reed in the southern German and French organ was loud enough to penetrate the flue-work of the manual. As the soft reed Schnarrwerk had very small resonators of curious shapes, it was only in tune on favourable occasions, as is shown by the following quotation from Werckmeister.[2]

"Schnarrwerk, ist unterweilen Narrwerck
Ist est aber rein and guth so er frischtes Herz und Muth"
("Schnarrwerk is often the work of fools, but when it is pure and good, it rejoices heart and mind.")

The division of the stops into thin and wide groups (male and female stops) which grew up in the Renaissance continued in the Baroque period. The thin group consisted of a bright-toned principal chorus with trompete and the whole was of moderate power. This was contrapuntal tone par excellence. The 8-ft. rank was of quiet, bright tone and was not too loud to give an accompaniment to a solo played on the rückpositiv. Third-ranks such as the tierce, which give a reedy or growling quality to the tone, were excluded from the narrow group: they appeared in Germany after 1620.

The following example from the Hauptwerk of Schnitger's organ at Norden, built in 1686, illustrates this:

Group I (Narrow scale)		*Group II* (Wide scale)	
Trompete	16	Quintadena	16
Principal	8	Rohrflöte	8
Oktav	4	Spitzflöte	4
Quinte	$2\frac{2}{3}$	Nasat	$2\frac{2}{3}$
Oktav	2	Gemshorn	2
Mixtur	8 ranks		

The true German organ reached the peak of its development about 1700 and after this other influences were apparent. Towards the end of his life Schnitger occasionally felt the Latin influence which was so apparent in the work of Silbermann. His instrument, built between 1715 and 1718, for the church of St. Marien, Frankfurt-on-Oder, is typical of his later work. There was comparatively little difference in power between one stop and another, and the enormous difference in output between a soft gedackt and a trumpet on a modern organ was a thing unknown. Praetorius gave explicit instructions

[1] H. von Helmholtz, *Tonempfindungen* (Berlin, 1863).
[2] A. Werckmeister, *Orgelprobe* (Quedlinburg, 1698) p. 48.

concerning the use of the stops in groups and it was forbidden to destroy the clarity of a narrow-scaled chorus by the addition of certain of the wide-scale stops. As Adlung[1] points out, the rules were often broken at the end of the seventeenth century, and Forkel[2] tells us that Bach was to the fore in finding new ways of combining the stops and set aside all rules.

In the large baroque organs the principal pitch of each manual often differed by an octave from the last one.

The large pedal divisions were scaled in 32-ft. pitch, the Hauptwerk divisions scaled in 16-ft., the Rückpositiv in 8 ft., the Brustwerk in 4-ft., and the Oberwerk in 2 ft.; or in smaller organs the pedal was in 16-ft., the Hauptwerk in 8-ft. and the Rückpositiv in 4-ft. In French organs there was no great development of the pedal organ at this period and the grand orgue of a large instrument would be developed from the 16-ft. ranks, while the pedal often remained as a solo flute and reed organ of 8-ft. pitch.

The specification of the Schnitger organ at Frankfurt-on-Oder.

	Hauptwerk		*Rückpositiv*		*Oberwerk*	
Group I, narrow scale	Prinzipal	8	Quintadena	8	Oboe	8
	Oktav	4	Prinzipal	4	Prestant	4
	Traversflöte	4	Superoktav	2	Quinte	$2\frac{2}{3}$
	Superoktav	2	Scharf	4 ranks	Superoktav	2
	Mixtur	5–6 ranks			Superoktav	1
Group II, wide scale	Quintadena	16	Grobgedackt	8	Gedacktflöte	8
	Gemshorn	8	Flöt douce	4	Kleingedackt	4
	Rohrflöte	4	Quinta	$2\frac{2}{3}$	Flageolett	2
	Quinta	$2\frac{2}{3}$	Sesquialtera	2 ranks	Superquinte	$1\frac{1}{3}$
	Scharf	4 ranks (used with both groups)				
Group III			Gamba	8	Vox humana	8
	Salizional	8	Trompete	8		
	Cornettin		Singend röhrwerk	4		

Pedal

Prinzipal	16
Violon	8
Oktav	4
Oktav	2
Mixtur	6 ranks
Trombone	16
Trompete	8
Schalmei	4
Cornett	2
Subbass	16
Gedackt	8

(This organ was built just before his death and certain southern influences are already at work, e.g. the Salizional on the Hauptwerk.)

[1] J. Adlung, *Musica Mechanica Organoedi* (Berlin, 1768).
[2] J. N. Forkel, *Life of Bach*, ch. v, 1802.

The scales of Schnitger's pipe-work in a moderate-sized organ are as follows (organ at Mittelnkirchen, 1688):

Diameters of Pipe Tubes in Inches

	CC	C	mid. c	c′	c″
Principal 8	5·4	3·25	2·4	1·5	1
Oktav 4	3·28	1·77	1·0	·60	·36
Superoktav 2	1·76	1·08	·56	·36	·25
Gedackt 8	3·5	2	1·2	·9	·64
Tierce 1⅗	1·72	1·04	·6	·44	·28

The Silbermann Brothers

The Silbermann brothers have been famed for their fine organs in Alsace, in Saxony and in the Dresden districts. It need not detract from the just esteem with which they are regarded as amongst the first dozen of their profession in the last five centuries, to say that they were particularly fortunate in that many of their instruments were found in centres of culture, and Gottfried received royal patronage and was associated with J. S. Bach. Nevertheless, the organ music of Bach and the great northern school of organists such as Buxtehude, Reinken, Lübeck and Böhm speaks more fittingly through the Schnitger organs. The Silbermann instruments derive from the Latin countries, they reveal the Roman Catholic influence and show a sophistication and objectivism which is not found in the more contemplative Schnitger instruments. If the Silbermann instrument is a very good medium for the toccatas, fantasias, and fugues of Bach, the Schnitger instrument is even finer when the subtleties of the chorale preludes are considered. Andreas Silbermann, with whom his younger brother worked for a time, was influenced by the elder Casparini. Eugen Casparini was a German, born under the name of Caspar[1], in Sorau, in 1624. At the age of seventeen he left home and worked for three years in Bavaria. After this he worked for a considerable time in Padua, Italy, and adopted the Italian form of his name. He built a number of instruments in Venice as well as in the Austrian Tyrol, but he is remembered for a large organ of excellent qualities in the new church of SS. Peter and Paul at Goerlitz, Germany. Assisted by his son, Adam-Horace and Andreas Silbermann, he took six years to build this fine instrument and completed it in 1703 in his eightieth year (specification, No. 10).

The father of the two brother organ-builders, Veit Silbermann, a shoeing smith and justice of the peace, was born in Kleinbobritzsch, near Frauenstein, in Saxony in 1620. He had six sons, of whom Andreas was born on 16th May 1678 and Gottfried on 14th January 1683. Andreas, who settled in Strassburg, had four sons, three of whom became organ-builders, but Gottfried never married. Andreas worked with Casparini until 1701 and learned much from him. Andreas was also in touch with Thierry and other leading French organ-builders. Casparini's ideas, which were developed by the Silbermanns, showed themselves in the following ways:

The careful grouping of stops into narrow and wide scales was abandoned and many varieties of scales were employed.

[1] Or Gaspar.

Wood pipes were used for many of the pipe ranks and the lowest notes of the 32-ft. and 16-ft. ranks on the pedal organ were made of this material.

Larger proportions of tin were used in the pipe metal than was common in the Schnitger organs, and the tone of the pipes was thus brighter.

String tone and undulating stops became a feature of the instrument and paved the way for the later romantic movement in organ building.

The cornets made from ranks of pipes in harmonic series gave a striking imitation of reed tone.

The general treatment of the tone mass was more powerful and smooth than that of Schnitger's organs. The organ tended to integration.

Many Andreas Silbermann instruments are still in existence in Alsace, though some have been rebuilt beyond recognition. The Dresden instruments of Gottfried, and of Jehmlich who built in his style, suffered badly in the war. Those at Freiberg in Saxony and at Rötha near Leipzig are still in a good state of preservation. Gottfried died at Dresden on August 4th, 1753.[1]

Joachim Wagner

Wagner, who felt certain foreign influences, was at work between 1720 and 1750 in Berlin. Organs are known to have been built by him at:[2]

1. Berlin Marienkirche, 1721
2. Berlin Garnisonkirche, 1725
3. Berlin Parochialkirche, 1730
4. Berlin Alte Jerusalemkirche, 1723
5. Berlin Französische Klosterkirche
6. Berlin Friedrich-Wilhelms Hospital
7. Berlin Alte Georgenkirche
8. Berlin Friedrich Werderschekirche
9. Potsdam Garnisonkirche, 1732
10. Brandenburg Dom, 1725
11. Brandenburg Katharinenkirche, 1726
12. Brandenburg Gotthardkirche, 1745
13. Königsberg (Neumark) Marienkirche
14. Angermünde Stadtkirche, 1742
15. Gransee Marienkirche, 1744
16. Treuenbrietzen Marienkirche
17. Jüterbog. Nikolaikirche, 1737
18. Jüterbog Marienkirche, 1737
19. Königswusterhausen Stadtkirche, 1730
20. Magdeburg Heilige-Geistkirche, 1739
21. Werben (Elbe) Johanniskirche 1747
22. Barnewitz
23. Plötzin
24. Roskow
25. Buch, 1736
26. Blumberg

[1] W. L. Sumner, "The Silbermanns and Their Organs", *The Organ*, vol. xviii pp. 129–39, 221–30.

It is remarkable that the Silbermanns have had a number of books devoted to them whereas the greater figure of Arp Schnitger has been given comparatively little attention. L. Moser, *Gottfried Silbermann, der Orgelbauer: ein historisches Lebensbild* (1857). G. Zschaler, *Gottfried Silbermann, Hof-und Land-Orgelbauer von Sachsen* (1858). L Moser, *Das Brüderpaar, die Orgelbaumeister Andreas and Gottfried Silbermann: historische Skizze . . .* (1861). E. Flade, *Der Orgelbauer Gottfried Silbermann* (1926). E. Gessner, *Zur elsässisch-neudeutschen Orgelreform* (1913). R. Pugh (Thesis for Ph.D.), *Les Silbermann, leur Vie, leur Oeuvre dans la Région Alsacienne* (University of Strassburg, 1932).

[2] Gerber's "*Lexicon der Tonkünstler*" and *Sammlung einiger Nachrichten von berühmten Orgelwerken* (Breslau 1757).

Nos. 1, 2, 3, 9, 10, 11, 12, 13, 17 and 20 were large instruments of thirty stops or more built on a grand style. Many of the Wagner organs had very ornate cases and some had fanciful decorations, e.g. carved birds which moved when the wind was in the organ, figures beating drums, etc.

"At Garrison Church, Berlin, the ornaments and machinery of the case, which are in the old Teutonic taste, are extremely curious.

"At each wing is a kettle-drum, which is beat by an Angel placed behind it, whose motion the organist regulates by a pedal; at the top of the pyramid, or middle column of pipes, there are two figures, representing Fame, spreading their wings, when the drums are beat, and raising them as high as the top of the pyramid; each of these figures [*sic*] sounds a trumpet, and then takes its flight.

"There are likewise two suns, which move to the sound of cymbals, and the wind obliges them to cross the clouds; during which time, two eagles take their flight, as naturally as if they were alive."[1]

Here is the specification of a typical Wagner organ, that at the Marienkirche in Berlin.[2] It had forty stops with sixty-one ranks of pipes.

Hauptwerk (Middle keyboard)		*Oberwerk* (Top keyboard)		*Unterwerk* (Lowest keyboard)	
Prinzipal (front pipes)	8	Prinzipal (front pipes)	8	Prinzipal	4
Bordun	16	Quintaton	16	Gedackt	8
Gambe	8	Gedackt	8	Quintaton	8
Rohrflöte	8	Oktave	4	Fugara	4
Oktave	4	Rohrflöte	4	Nasat	$2\frac{2}{3}$
Spitzflöte	4	Nasat	$2\frac{2}{3}$	Waldflöte	2
Quinte	$2\frac{2}{3}$	Vox Humana	8	Zimbel	3 ranks
Oktave	2	Oktave	2	Echokornett	5 ranks
Kornett	5 ranks	Terz	$1\frac{3}{5}$		
Scharff	5 ranks	Sifflöte	1		
Zimbel	3 ranks				
Trompete	8				

Pedal

Prinzipal	16 (front pipes)
Violin	16
Gemshorn	8
Bassflöte	8
Quinte	$5\frac{1}{3}$
Oktave	4
Mixtur	6 ranks
Posaune	16
Trompete	8

(The almost complete absence of reeds on the manual divisions is noteworthy. Wagner thought in terms of varieties of "organo pleno" with reed-work on the pedals only. Many quasi-reed tones could be synthesised by using the quiet mutations and compound stops. Even the vox humana was sometimes made as a flue stop.)

[1] C. Burney, *Tour through Germany and the Netherlands*, vol. ii, p. 104.
[2] Heinrich Scholz, *Geschichte der Orgel der Marienkirche in Berlin* (Berlin, 1909).

The organ of the high Baroque period was the instrument of John Sebastian Bach, and it is therefore worthy of careful study.

The Schnitger organs were more thoroughly German than those of the Silbermanns. André Silbermann had felt the Latin influence in his work in Alsace, and Gottfried by his contact with Casparini, who had worked for many years in Italy and in his old age had built the great organ in the Church of SS. Peter and Paul at Goerlitz. The work of Wagner, the Berlin organ-builder, with which Bach had little or no contact, and of Scheibe, the Leipzig builder, whose instruments Bach played (and who was the father of one of Bach's critics), and others, such as Trost and Wender, also showed the Latin influence. The method of building tonal pyramids with mutation and mixture stops, of making choruses by adding harmonics of flue pipes, and finally, rich, quiet reeds, was giving way to the use of highly spiced tones such as the viol di gamba. Thus the Thuringian and Saxony organs which Bach knew received influences from both north and south. After 1720 the German organ declined. It lost its identity and sense of purpose, and in the later eighteenth century size, ornament, rococo and romantic tendencies brought in a period outwardly rich, attractive and progressive, but inwardly sterile and soulless. The art of music had other attractions, and the mature Mozart, Haydn and, later, Beethoven sought other media. Moreover, even the generation following Bach evolved new forms of expression and new techniques, and shelved his work and made latent his influence. It is true that the swell pedal was unknown to Bach (or was heard of as an English curiosity) and that all his organs had tracker action, but it must be pointed out that the "block dynamic" of the Baroque organ did not need the swell pedal, which might be fatal to good contrapuntal playing, and that no electric or pneumatic action, however well made, can rival tracker action, applied to organs of moderate size working on low pressures, for allowing subtleties of touch and phrasing.[1]

The proving and testing of organs was quite a feature of church life during the Baroque period. The erection of a new instrument was a matter of great interest and pride in any German or Dutch town. Experts from distant places were paid to come from distant towns to test every small part of an organ, and the process sometimes took a week. J. S. Bach was himself in great demand as an organ-prover. Andreas Werckmeister wrote a little work, *Orgelprobe* (Quedlinburg und Aschersleben, 1698. Facsimile Kassel, 1932), which had considerable popularity, and the same author in another booklet, *Organum Gruningense redivivum* (Quedlinburg und Aschersleben, 1705)[2] describes the "proving" of the organ in the Castle Church at Gruningen in Germany by fifty-three experts, including Praetorius and Compenius, and others from every part of Germany. The bill for "Dranckgeld" was 3,000 thalers. It is a pity that many modern organs are not inspected by experts who are competent as builders, engineers and acousticians as well as organists. The custom continued abroad until the nineteenth century and many of Cavaillé-Coll's organs were subjected to similar tests.

[1] See specifications Nos. 11–16 and the section on organ-playing.
[2] Reprinted by the *Rheingold Verlag*. (*Mainz* 1932).

PLATE 7.

A 15th century positive organ (Hugo van der Goes, 1476. Holyrood Palace). The keyboard, apart from the shorter keys, is remarkably similar to that in use at present. (By gracious permission of Her Majesty the Queen)

PLATE 8.

A drawing of the Van Eyck panel, 1425, at Ghent. The latch on the left of the key-board is to hold down the lowest key which caused a drone pipe to sound

Spiegel der Orgelmacher vñ Organisten allen Stifften vñ kirchē
so Orgel haltē oder machē lassen hochnützlich. durch den hochberüm
ptē vñ künstreichen Meyster Arnolt Schlicken Pfalzgrauischen
Organistē artlich verfaßt. vñ vß Römischer Kaißerlicher maiestat
sonder löblicher befreyhūg vñ begnadūg außgericht vñ außgangē.

PLATE 9.
The title page of Arnold Schlick's "Spiegel", 1511, showing a positive organ of the early 16th century

PLATE 10, a and b.

Two old Spanish organ cases; Tarragona (1563) and Zaragoza (c. 1413) Cathedrals (after A. G. Hill)

A document[1] preserved in the archives of the Franciscan Monastery of Saint Bonaventura in Seville throws an interesting light on the early eighteenth-century organs of Spain. The description, dated 1721, concerns an organ built early in the century.

"The organ case is 49 feet high and 22 ft. broad. There are five 'towers', 3 in the front and 2 in the side, together with 6 pipe-flats in the front, in the middle tower are 5 large pipes of the Flautado [open flute] of 26 [ft.]. Under these show pipes are a battery of 4 'prospect' trumpet stops: Trompeta de Batalla (8), Clairon (4), Clairons (4 and 8) and Trompeta magna (8 and 16)."[2]

Then follows a description of the mixture and cymbals, of which one has sixteen ranks. The second manual is a "Rückpositiv", with its pipes in a case under and behind the organist's seat. It had a Principal 8 ft. "in prospect", Bordon 8 ft., Octave 4 ft., Octave 2 ft., Quint, Mixtur, Cymbel; and a "small English Cornet" Manual III is a *swell-organ* with the following nine stops: Bordun 8 ft., Octave 4 ft., Tapadillo 4 ft., Quint $2\frac{2}{3}$ ft., Tierce $1\frac{1}{3}$ ft., Octave 2 ft., Corneta real 6 ranks, Trompeta 8 ft., Clarines 4 ft. (The names have been translated where it is thought necessary.)

Here follows the specification of a large Spanish organ, *Seville Cathedral* (1673), half a century earlier.

I Positiv	
Flautado de	13
Flauta in octava	4
Quincena	2
Corneta Tolosana	
Trompeta real	8
Bajoncillo y Clarin 8 + 4	

IV Positiv	
Flautado de Violón de	13
Flauta tapada	8
Octava	4
Quincena	2
Nasardos de 4 hileros	
Voz	16
Regalia	8
Voz	4

II Hauptwerk (great organ)	
Bordun de	26
Flautado de	13
Violón	8
Octava	4
Tapadillo	4
Flauta chica	2
Lleno de 8 hileras	
Nasardos de 5 hileras	
Trompeta imperial	32
Trompeta magna	16
Trompeta de batalla	8
Clarin brillante	4
Trompeta en quinta (added 1703)	$5\frac{1}{3}$

Pedal	
Contras profundas de	32
Contras de	26
Contras de	13
Violón en octava	4
Violón en quincena	2
Contras de Bombardas	32
Contras de Fagót	16
Contras de clarines	8
Quinta subgravis	($21\frac{1}{3}$)
Quinta gravis	($10\frac{2}{3}$)
Quinta	($5\frac{1}{3}$)
Trompeta en quinta (added 1703)	($5\frac{1}{3}$)

III Oberwerk (enclosed in swell-box 1703)	
Contrabajo de	26
Flautado de	13
Violón	8
Fagót	16
Trompeta real	8
Chirimia	8

IV Echo (1703)	
Bajón	16

[1] *Breve resumen de las diferencias de este Zelebre órgano del combento casa Grande de N.P. San Francisco de Sevilla, ideado y echo de fr. Domingo de Aguirre acovose año de* 1721.

[2] That is, large reeds arranged to lie horizontally "in chamade".

III Oberwerk—cont.

Voz	8	Octava	4	Orlos	8
Trompeta de ecos	8	Flautadito	4	Clarin brillante	4
		Flautin	2		
				Docena y quincenas ($2\frac{2}{3}$ + 2)	
				Corneta clara de 5 hileras	

[Flautado de 13 = 8 ft. open diapason
Quincena 2 = piccolo
Bajoncillo = fagotto or bassoon
Voz = vox humana or regal
Regalia = regal
Tapadillo = small stopped flute
Lleno = mixture
Orlos = A regal or vox humana
Trompeta real = royal trumpet
Docena y quincena = quartane (rauschpfeife) $2\frac{2}{3}$ + 2]

(The pipe lengths are given in palmas = palms, 13 palms = 8 ft.)

This remarkable "Epistle" organ was the first four-manual organ in Spain.[1] It was not the only organ in the cathedral, for another stood on the opposite side on the chancel. The 32 ft. reeds in the great and pedal were the first reeds of this pitch which were to be found in Spanish organs. The possibility of obtaining a 64-ft. acoustic bass on the pedals by the combination of the 32-ft. flue rank and the $21\frac{1}{3}$ quinta subgravis will be noted.

The organ, originally built in 1668–73, by a Portuguese master, Antonio Pedro Faleiro, was improved in 1703 by a compatriot, Faustino Carvalho. In particular, the pipes of Manual III, a large section of thirteen stops and eighteen ranks, were enclosed in a swell-box. A small echo organ placed at a height of nearly 140 ft. above the floor of the cathedral and played by means of trackers 180 ft. long was also a feature of this remarkable instrument. The compass of this little organ of three reed stops was three octaves. The quinttrompete $5\frac{1}{3}$ ft., which even now is of rare occurrence, is worth noting.[2] The swell-box, though it was a natural step from a boxed-up echo, soon became popular in Spain. The specification of the swell organ with its

[1] Gonzalo Silva y Ramón, *Die Orgelwerke der Kathedrale zu Sevilla* (Mainz, 1939).

[2] There are examples of Quint reeds in Johannesburg Town Hall Organ, designed by Hollins (1916) and built by Norman & Beard, England, and occasionally in large American and English organs of more recent date.

The most illustrious of the historic Spanish composers was Antonio de Cabézon (1510–66), but others may be noted:

Pedro de Soto (*c.* 1550); Tomás de Santa Maria (d. 1570); Pere Alberch Vila (1517–82); Francisco Peraza (1564–98); Sebastián Aguiléra de Herédia (1570–16—); Eznarriága (*c.* 1650); Joan Cabanílles (1644–1712); Miquel Lopez (1669–1723); Franciso Fernandez Paléra (*c.* 1550); Diego de Torrijos (1640–91); Cándido Juan Moreno (16—1776); Gabriel Menalt (d. 1687); Joseph Elias (1675–1749); Pau Bruna (*c.* 1650); Francesc Llusá (*c.* 1700); Joaquin Oxinagas (*c.* 1750); Anselm Viola (1739–98); Narcís Casanovas (1747–99). These may be studied in the editions of Prof. Kastner. See also articles by Vente and Kok in *The Organ*, vols. xxxiv and xxxv (1955, 1956) and Donald Shanks, *Dissertation for D. Phil* (Oxford, 1959).

battery of reeds and mixtures was uncommonly like those developed by Henry Willis in large English organs more than a century and a half later. The characteristic of the Spanish organ was its reediness, a quality which benefits by the application of a swell-box more than the gentle flute, principal and diapason tones. The manual compasses were divided in a way which must have "inspired" the nineteenth-century harmonium. It was this diversity of reed tone which inspired the youthful Aristide Cavaillé-Coll, who worked on the northern Spanish organs in his boyhood. Thus this influence passed indirectly to the first Henry Willis, who in his early years as an organ-builder knew Cavaillé-Coll. The "symphonic" organs of Cavaillé-Coll in France and those of Henry Willis in England owe much to the remarkable Spanish innovations in organ-building. Abraham Jordan's independently invented swell of a few stops in the year 1712 seems a very puny thing by comparison with these Spanish examples of an earlier date. Moreover, improvement in England was slow; and small, short-compass swell organs of four or five stops persisted until in *c.* 1850 Willis produced finer full-compass swell divisions in his large organs. In France the English builder, Abbey, introduced small swell organs of the type he knew so well, from the year 1826, but in 1841 Cavaillé-Coll had produced a better example in the large organ at St. Denis Abbey. Even so, many of the French "Récit-Expressif" divisions were ill-equipped compared with the larger grand and positif sections of the instrument, until the twentieth century. Only in England did the swell organ develop to a section of equal or superior importance to the great organ. It is perhaps necessary to notice that really such a development was out of keeping with the true tradition of organ music and organ playing, in spite of the inspiring and thrilling use to which such a swell organ could be put. For it could not displace properly equipped great and positive organs for the playing of the great organ music, and it had limitations in accompanying voices. It was carried forward on a great interest in symphonic and orchestral treatment of the instrument, foreign to the simple clear contrasts of the "block-dynamic" of the Baroque period. Thus we can understand the fact that the swell organ made so little headway in the eighteenth- and early nineteenth-century Germany where there was no lack of progressive and ingenious organ-builders. The artificial crescendo of the swell was foreign to their organ art; it was not required by any of their organ music; it would tend to obscure the clarity of their choruses in which reeds played a subsidiary part; and its effects were disturbing both to the pitch and tone quality of the pipes affected by it. Its results were not to be compared with the increase in intensity and character which mark a crescendo on a real orchestral horn. It is not to despise the boon conferred on organ-building by the invention of the swell-box to say that the neglect of this device by the Germans was far less serious to the art of organ-playing than the British neglect of the pedal organ and its possibilities. In the earlier Baroque organ significant use was made of the disposition of the various sections of the organ in space, of the different radiating areas of each "werk" from the large "backcloth" of the Hauptwerk to the smaller Ruckpositiv and the still smaller Brustwerk, and of the principal pitches, differing by an octave in each division.

It is necessary to emphasise the great tonal differences which existed between French and German organs of the high Baroque period: the French with its "montreflutes" and acid-keen narrow-shalloted reeds on the one hand, and the German organ with its keen-toned principal chorus and restrained, relatively smooth, wide-shalloted reeds on the other. In the Renaissance and early Baroque periods the Dutch and German builders employed low pressures (generally around 2 in.) and big foot-holes, relying on mouth-treatment for regulation. Towards the end of the seventeenth century wind pressures rose by about 50 per cent, and power regulation was primarily effected at the foot-hole. Pipes were not "nicked" until the end of the eighteenth century and spoke with natural initiation characteristics.

CHAPTER V

THE ORGAN IN BRITAIN UNTIL THE NINETEENTH CENTURY

"*His voys was murier than the murie orgon.*
On Messedays that in the churche gon."
Chaucer, c. 1388
Nun's Priest's Tale.

"*The Swete Orgayne pipis comforteth a stedfaste mynde.*
Wrong handlynge of the stoppis may cause them sypher from their kynde.
But he that playethe of pipis, wher so grete nowmber is
Must handill the keyes all lyke that by mysgovernance they Sownde (not) amyss."
Leckingfield Proverb, c. 1520.

IT WILL be convenient to deal with the development of the organ in Britain separately, as it did not follow the lines of the progress of the instrument on the continent. English cathedrals and churches were not so well adapted as those abroad for the erection of large organs on galleries and tribunes at the west end of the buildings. Moreover, English church musicians showed more interest in singing than in the manipulation of large instruments. Accordingly, quite small organs of the positive or portative type would suffice. After the Dissolution of the Monasteries in 1536 the organ was often identified with Roman Catholicism to such an extent that it had a very chequered history until it was completely disposed of by Cromwell in 1642, as far as its use in Christian worship was concerned, for a period of eighteen years. But for a hundred years before this, waves of "Puritanism" had gone far to cause the neglect or destruction of many instruments, notably in the London district during the reign of Elizabeth.

No English organ up to the time of the Reformation is known to have had more than one manual and half a dozen stops. There is evidence to show that organ cases were more imposing than their modest contents may have led one to suppose, and their decoration was often both rich and artistic. In the early sixteenth century, there must have been some hundreds of these small organs in the country and we have many records of organ-builders who were doing what by continental standards was very modest work. Sometimes the organ-builder was a priest, sometimes he was a carpenter or bellows-maker, and often he was also an organ-player. Organ-blowing was a separate and comparatively well-paid job, and, as it was often accomplished by pulling on a rope, it was spoken of as "drawing the organs". The phrase "a pair of organs" does not mean that there were two, or that the instrument had two manuals: the words were used in the same way as "a pair of bellows" or "a pair of stairs". The bellows of these old organs were not contained in the cases, which could then be designed to have the pleasant appearance of the overhang of the pipe-rack above a more slender wooden case. The instrument was often provided with folding doors which were well decorated with religious pictures and symbols. In Hollar's[1] engraving of the Chancel of "Old St. Paul's", London, an organ with such painted doors, of no great size, is seen in one of the north bays of the chancel.

In the records of British organ-builders or organ-makers we can see the tools and materials which they used, and in consideration of the expense and quantities employed it will be apparent that their works, though durable in many cases, were not grand organs of the type which were being erected by their contemporaries in many churches abroad.

Records of English Organ-builders

St. Dunstan, who died in 988. Osbern (*Vita St. Dunstan*) says that he was taught the craft by the Irish masters in the Abbey at Glastonbury. Dunstan made organs in the West of England.

St. Aethelwold, who was Abbot of Abingdon in 955 and built an organ there. He became Bishop of Winchester in 963.[2]

Hugh le organer. No records of his achievements remain. He is the first lay organ-builder on record. The Calendar of Patent Rolls records that he was granted a pardon on 10th November 1303 for causing the death of William, son of William de Gunewardly.

Robert organer, who lived at Spalding. The Calendar of Patent Rolls, 3rd December 1308, records that he was relieved from paying tolls at the request of Isabel, Queen of England.

Peter organer (also "organistre"). The Calendar of Patent Rolls, 14th June 1310, records that he was pardoned for entering the close of Thomas de Tydenton. (Among other delinquents was John de Derby, Dean of St. Chad's, Lichfield.)

Thomas de Ledenham. A reference in Lincoln Cathedral says that in 1311 a fee of 20*s*. was paid to this vicar for taking care of the organs, blowing [*sic*] and cleaning them.

Walter the organer.[3] There is no record of any organ work by him, but he made or repaired a clock at St. Paul's Cathedral, 1344.

John the organer.[4] He repaired the organ which King John of France, while an English prisoner, took with him to Somerton Castle in 1359.

John of Gloucester repaired the organ at Wells in 1414, for which he received 6*s*. 8*d*. in part payment.

John Couper, who constructed two pairs of bellows for the organ in York Minster in 1419.

Thomas Seyntjohn of London, who was granted a pardon for an offence which was not stated, in 1430.

[1] In Sir Wm. Dugdale's *The History of St. Paul's Cathedral*, 2nd ed. (London, 1716). This case, in spite of the later date (*c*. 1650) is in simple Renaissance style and is quite small in comparison with the continental early Baroque examples.

[2] J. Townsend, *History of Abingdon Abbey* (Oxford).

[3] Andrew Freeman, *Dictionary of Organs and Organists* (1921).

[4] Andrew Freeman, *ibid.*

William Barbour, of Brussels and Westminster, and *Lawrence*, of Nymmagen and London (organ-makers), were granted letters on 8th April 1436 "to inhabit the realm peaceably and enjoy his goods".

John Hemden. The Calendar of Patent Rolls, 5th July 1440, mentions a debt of £10 to this man, "citizen and organ-maker of London".

Arnald organer of Norwich. In September 1442 he agreed to set up a new organ in the quire of Lincoln Cathedral at a cost of 5 marks. The freedom of Norwich was given to Arnald Mynhamber and John Ashwell in 1446. It is probable that the former is identical with Arnald organer.

Sir John, a priest, received "12*d*." in 1444 "for the amendyng of the organs" at St. Mary's, Sandwich.

Nicholas Rawnce received 66*s*. 5½*d*. for making one pair of organs for Canterbury Cathedral in 1447.[1]

John Hudene, who built an organ at Saffron Walden in 1451.[2]

John Roose (or *Rouse*), a Dominican friar, who built organs at Kilkenny and York in 1450–69.

Will the organ-maker was paid 20*s*. in 1453 for mending the organs at Ripon Minster. There is also a reference to Will the organ-maker at St. Margaret's, Westminster, in 1460–1.

Robert Harpmaker[3] was paid 2*d*. for repairs to the organ in St. Augustine's Church, Hedon, Yorks, in 1453.

Arnald Johnson of Gorleston is mentioned in Yarmouth Corporation Records of 1462–3 as an orgglmaker [*sic*].

John Dyer of Oxford. In 1469 the churchwardens of St. Mary's, Thame, "payd Jhon Dyer organt-maker of Oxford for mending of the organts and makyng the belyis for owr part vs vjd".

George the organ-maker set up new organs in 1470 in St. John's Church, Glastonbury, and Stephen the carver helped him and also made a canopy of wenscott over the altar.

George Gaunte and *Richard Sowerby* are mentioned as organ-makers in the Fabric Rolls of York Minster in 1470 and 1473 respectively.

Records of Andover Parish Church record, in 1472, "To William Plomer and William Sadeler for amendyng of the wyndbagge of the organys 6*d*. For a skynne to the same 3*d*.". There are later references to Plomer's work and the purchase of "sowdyr" (solder).

William Bell and *John Gibbes* did organ-work at St. Edmund's, Salisbury, from 1475 to 1477.

Myghell Glaucets built an organ in the "Rodelofte" at St. Michael's, Cornhill, in 1475 for "9 *l*" and the old organ. Successor to John of Gloucester.

Mighaell Glocetir, who is evidently identical with the above worker, was paid "viij *d*" for "mendynge" the organ in St. Mary-at-Hill, London, in 1477–9.

[1] Woodruff and Danks, *Memorials of the Cathedral and Priory Church of Christ in Canterbury*.

[2] R. Griffin, *History of Audley End* (1836).

[3] J. R. Boyle, *History of Hedon*.

John Lawless the organ-maker constructed a number of organs about the year 1476.[1]

John organ-maker and his partner, *Edward Johnson*, made a new organ for Thame Church in 1477–80.

John London is recorded in the Churchwardens' Accounts at Hythe Church to have been paid 10*s*. 2*d*. in 1480 for mending the organs.

Robert Borton of Stowmarket was paid "vij *s*" "for mendyng of organys" (*Household Book of Duke of Norfolk*, 1480).

William Wotton[2] made an agreement in 1487 with R. Fitzjames, warden of Merton College, Oxford, for "a pair of organs" (i.e. an organ) like the organs in the chapel of St. Mary Magdalen College, against the vigil of Whit Sunday, 1489, for the price of £28. (Records in Magdalen College show that in 1486–7 Wotton had been paid £13 in part for one pair of organs.)

There are many references to organs and organ-makers in East Anglia at this time. The Yarmouth Corporation Records of 1486–7 refer to *John* an organ-maker; and in 1493 *Robert* of Norwich was fined for selling beer in Yarmouth "contrary to the assize". *John Hayne* of Norwich, an organ-maker, died in 1496.

Richard Gilbert and *John Harris* of Christchurch repaired the organ in Wimborne Minster in 1495.

The Churchwardens' Accounts of St. Ewen's, Bristol, record: "1496–7 Item to *John Cockes* for lether and glewe and for his laboure to mend the organ belowes vjs."

The records of Winchester College record in 1498: "For the commons of *Walter* the organ-builder and his men in repairing two pairs of organs with four sets of bellows over eight weeks, together with 20d for faggots and fuel and 12d for candles 19s 8d."

Richard Sawtry was paid 4*d*. for repairing the organ in St. George's Church, Oxford, in 1500.

The Calendar of Patent Rolls mentions *William and Nicholas Stroke*, organ-makers of "Wyrkesworth", Derbyshire, in 1503, but no account of their work has been found.

John Chamberleyne provided Magdalen College, Oxford, with an organ for £8 in 1508.[3]

Thomas Browne (or *Broune*) was at work in Canterbury between 1504 and 1515 making organs. In 1508 Browne received 33*s*. 4*d*. in part payment of £8 for making "great organs" in the chapel of King's College, Cambridge. In 1521 he did work in Henley Parish Church; and in 1554 and 1559 he

[1] Gratton Flood, "Irish organ-builders from the eighth to the close of the eighteenth century", *Journal of the Royal Society of Antiquaries of Ireland*, vol. xi (1910).

[2] Anthony Wood in his *Annals* (1486) says that the "pretender", Lambert Symnell, was really the son of this Wotton, "an organ-maker of the University of Oxford".

[3] In 1500 £13 6*s*. 8*d*. was paid for a "pair of Flemish organs" to be placed on the rood-loft at Louth Parish Church, Lincolnshire. This looks like an example of an occasional importation. *Archeologia*, vol. x, p. 91.

received small amounts for the repair of the organ. He repaired the organ in Magdalen College, Oxford, in 1554 and 1559.

A legal dispute between Browne, who supplied the knowledge and skill as an organ-builder, and Colyns, who supplied the goods, is interesting because the report gives an inventory of the stock-in-trade and tools of an organ-builder *c.* 1515:[1]

"Imprimus ij grete organ cacez with carven worke.
Itm. ij cobbordes for to ley in the belowes in the same casez.
Itm. ij smaller casez with carved worke and the song-bordes redy wrought to set in pypes.
Itm. xxviij of fyne tynne in plate redy wrought.
Itm. in ley metall xiij lb. weight.
Itm. in lede iiij lb. weight.
Itm. a pytt of erthe to melte tyn inn.
Itm. iijxx pypes of tymber, the most part redy-made.
Itm. a stoke and a grete hammer for the same.
Itm. a longe planke for to plane metall uppon.
Itm. an organ case peynted grene with keys and a song-borde redy made to set in pypes, with a case of white tymber therefor, redy made.
Itm. ij planes for to plane metall with, and the irons to the same.
Itm. iiij planes with irons to the same.
Itm. iij hollow planes.
Itm. v gowges and formes and metal coffyns.
Itm. ij irons for to shave metall bright in square.
Itm. iij mawndrells.
Itm. a grete knyff for to cutt lede with.
Itm. iiij rowndes for to tune pypes with.
Itm. iiij peces for to caste with metall.
Itm. ij swages with branches and byrdes."

William Lewkenore was paid "for the orgens ye hole yere", in 1501–2, at St. Mary the Virgin, Thame. There is nothing to show whether he was performer or repairer.

Sir William Bryse, a priest, repaired the organs at St. Mary-at-Hill, London, during 1509–10.

Thomas Sexton mended the organs in the Parish Church of Kingston-on-Thames in 1509.

Robert Barkby. The Churchwardens' Accounts of St. Lawrence's, Reading, contain many items relating to the organ. (The histories of the church and organ are well documented.)

1510. "It payd to Backebye vppon a bargen of a peyr of orgaunce at the instaunce of the pisshe [parish] at ij tymes iiij li."

William Lewes was "keeper and tuner of the King's instruments in 1514 at 100 shillings per annum".

[1] Given by Andrew Freeman in *Dictionary of Organs and Organists* (1921).

Sir Thomas Cobbe, a priest, either made or supplied an organ for the Church of All Hallows, London Wall, in 1515.

James Dempsey (or *Demssey*), organ-maker to the Earl of Kildare in 1515, settled in England and was buried on 27th July 1567 in Doncaster. He made organs of Ripon Minster and Doncaster Parish Church.

Joyce between 1517 and 1518 made "portatyfes" for the quire at St. Andrew's Church, Canterbury. (A larger instrument built in 1512–13, at a cost "xiij li" brought by "water and by lande", stood in the rood-loft guarded by a new door.)

John orgaynmaker of Leicester held tenements there (*c.* 1518) (Chamberlain's *Accounts of the Borough of Leicester*).

Sir William Argall, a priest, made organs in Lambeth between 1515 and 1521.

William Beton or *Bylton* of King's Lynn. He also appears as Byttn, Bytt, Betton, Betyne, Beyton, Boton. (The Calendar of the Freemen of Lynn, 1292–1836.) Beton, who had three assistants, did work at Christ's College Chapel, Cambridge, Ely Cathedral, at Louth Parish Church, where he built a new organ which gave great satisfaction and cost £xxij, at St. Margaret's, King's Lynn ("mending the Regalls"), and probably at "old" St. Paul's, London.

Simon the organ-maker did work at St. Peter-in-the-East, Oxford, in 1519.

Anthony Duddyngton was an important figure at this time. He did work at St. Andrew's, Canterbury, in 1520–1, at St. Margaret Pattens, Rood Lane, London, in 1523, and at All Hallow's Barking (by the Tower), London. A contract is still extant which records the agreement between the churchwardens of "Allhallows, Barking," and Anthony Duddyngton, for the organs, A.D. 1519. The organ was to have three stops, namely, a "Diapason" containing a length of "x foot" or more and "dowble principalls throweout", to contain the length of "v foote". The compass was to be "dowble Ce–fa–ut" and comprise "xxvij playne keys", which would doubtless be the old four-octave short-octave range in which the apparent EE key sounded CC, and so on, up to C in alt. Further, it was specified that "the pyppes w^t inforth shall be as fyne metall and stuff as the utter parts, that is to say of pure Tyn, wt as fewe stops as may be convenient", and the cost was to be "fyfty poundes sterlinge". It was also stipulated that the organ-maker should convey the "belowes in the loft abowf, w^t a pipe to the sounde boarde". It is evident that the English builder had made himself acquainted with stops and sound-boards reinvented abroad some years previously.

This is the first-known specification of an English organ (and obviously it would not be possible to have a specification in the form of a list of separate stops, until stops could be used separately).

Dr. E. J. Hopkins[1] was probably correct in his inference that the "xxvij playne keyes" refer to the naturals and that the requisite number of sharps was understood. "This," he says, "would give the compass, if the scale were unbroken, as from CC to A in alt.; and, if broken (that is to say, having the CC pipe planted on the apparently EE key) a range corresponding exactly with the octave CC four octave compass, still occasionally to be met in some

[1] Hopkins and Rimbault, op. cit., p. 57.

of the old German organs." This seems reasonable enough, though the only certainty is that the lowest note was called CC. Hopkins also conjectured that the pipe lengths mentioned included the length of the pipe feet, since "v foot" for the "pryncipale" and "x foot or more" for the diapason would allow for 1 ft. and 2 ft. respectively for their pipe feet. This seems reasonable, but it is quite possible that the pitch of the organ was so low as to call for a 10-ft. speaking length at CC.

Hopkins also surmised that the stops were three in number: an open diapason and two principals; but it is at least credible that the doubling of the principal refers to its length and not to its duplication, and that the diapason was merely a bass stop with one octave of pipes. Thus the named stops would then be a *double principal* of 8-ft. tone, stopping at tenor C with an *open diapason* bass, completing its compass to CC.

There would be other registers of more acute pitch, "as fewe stops as may be convenient", but these it was not considered necessary to specify.[1]

The reference to the bellows is very interesting. As is well known, the bellows of most organs, down to the beginning of the eighteenth century, stood outside the case. At All Hallows (which was not a large church) the authorities were clearly reluctant to spare the necessary room for them (there would be at least two diagonal bellows in order to secure a constant supply of wind) and for the man who worked them. Possibly, also, they did not consider bellows-blowing an edifying spectacle. So it was arranged that the bellows should be placed "in the loft abowf the said Quere" (probably the rood-loft), whence the wind was to be conveyed to the sound-board by means of a conveyance. From the fact that Duddyngton was to be paid two pounds for this part of the work, irrespective of the success of the rest of the instrument (which was to be removed without compensation if not approved), we may perhaps infer that the bellows were already there and that they belonged to a previous organ.[2]

Although this agreement contains an early use of the word " stops", an earlier English reference is found in the records of the Church of St. Lawrence, Reading, in connection with a not very successful organ made by Robert Barkby in 1510. Here in 1513 "xjd" was paid for "ij lokks . . . one for the stopps and the other for the keyes".

William, "orgayn maker", was at work in 1521–2 at St. Andrew's, Canterbury. *Danyell Lokyar* was paid "xijd" for "the making of iij stoppys of iron for the same organes".

Winsborough, a monk, did work at St. Mary's, Sandwich (1521) and *Segemond* (or *Segesmond*) used 211 lb. of lead and other materials to make new pipe-work for the organ at St. Lawrence's, Reading (1519–20).

About this time there are references to:

Robert at St. Edmund's, Salisbury, 1523–4.

John Smythe at St. Peter's West Cheap, London, 1524.

[1] We have already noticed that mixtures were the parts of the tonal equipment of the organ which it was not worth while to separate as independent ranks, after the organ had ceased to be one or more large mixtures.

[2] Andrew Freeman, *The Organ*, vol. viii, pp. 87–8.

John Northfolke at St. Mary-at-Hill, London, 1524.

Sir Richard Baynton, a priest at Henley on Thames, 1524.

Richard Bodye at St. Lawrence's, Reading, 1524.

John de John, mentioned in King Henry VIII's Household Accounts.

Mighel Mercator also did work for the King, 1529–34, and received £22 10*s.* a year.

Halyar of Bristol brought organs to Yatton Parish Church, 1527–8.

John Hanson repaired the small organs at Magdalen College, 1529.

John Scute repaired the organs in the choir here during the same year.

John Badcokk repaired the organ at Wye in Kent, 1530. (The pipes of this organ were sold as old metal in 1571 for 45*s.* 4*d.*).

John Wenscott was paid "vli xiijs iiijd" for making an organ in Exeter (Exeter Receiver's Rolls, 1530).

The Chappington family from Devonshire were important as organ-makers at the middle of the sixteenth century. There were four: *Richard, Hugh, John* and *Ralph.*

Richard[1] built organs at St. Olave's, Exeter, 1536 and at Woodbury, Devon, 1538–9; Hugh built an organ for Exeter Cathedral, 1554, for Woodbury, 1560, and for St. Edmund's, Salisbury, 1567. He also made organs for St. Brannocks, Braunton, 1569 and for St. Brannock's Church, and for that of St. John and St. George at Store.

John Chappington went further afield. He made organs for St. Thomas's and for St. Edmund's Churches at Salisbury, for churches at Ashburton and Mere. He built organs in Westminster Abbey, 1596, St. Margaret's, Westminster, 1598, Magdalen College, Oxford, 1597 (the case of which may have been used with Dallam's organ now at Tewkesbury Abbey), and Winchester College Chapel, 1603–4.

Richard, the brother of Ralph, who died at Netherbury, Dorset, in 1619, did work at St. Thomas's, St. Edmund's, St. Martin's, Our Lady's Churches

[1] Here is an example of an organ-builder's agreement of the time.

(Deeds deposited with the Exeter City Library, July 25 1938.)
"D.D. 23141

Dated August 10th 28 Hen 8 (1536.)

Bond of Richard Charpyngton of South Molton, organ maker to Thomas Walys, clerk, John Peryam, Richard Swete, John Paramore, John Whiddon, Richard Bery, Robert Hyll, Henry Byllynger, William Cosyn, Robert Luxston, Lewis Saige, Robert Widderich in £5 dated 28 Hen 8.

Condition that whereas the above named Thomas Walys etc. of late have bought of abovbound Richard, a new pair of portavy's which now stand in the parish church of St. Olav in the city of Exeter, if the abovebound Richard from henceforth as often as need shall require without any delay at his own proper costs & charges during the life of the said Richard, do repair, sustain, maintain and amend and keep in tune as well the pipes of the said portatyves as the bellows and all other instraments now being in the said portatyves except the stop off Regals in the same instrament which must be tuned by the player thereof, within ten days next after the said Richard shall be thereof monssed and wanyd by one of the above named persons or their assured letters, that then this present obligation to be utterly void, by me Richard Charpyngton.

Seal (Latin) Endorsed.

Charpyngton's Bond to the parish to repair the organes."

in Salisbury, St. Augustine's, Bristol, and at Wedmore, Somerset, and Bridgwater Church.

John or ("Father") Howe was the most notable English organ-builder at the beginning of the sixteenth century. Howe's father, who was also an organ-maker, lived in the parish of St. Stephen, Walbrook, London, where he was churchwarden in 1519. After a period of pupilage with his father, John took over the business and took into partnership John Clymmowe, one of his father's workmen.

In the year 1526 Howe and Clymmowe contracted for an organ at Holy Trinity, Coventry, for the sum of £20. The earliest mention of an organ in the records is in 1526: "Peir of organs with vii stops and xxvii pleyn keyes, with the image of the Trinite on the topp of the sayed organs", built by John Howe and his partner, John Clymmowe, citizens and organ-makers of London, at a cost of £30. In 1570, parts of the organ were sold, and the church was afterwards without an organ for nearly sixty years.

In 1531–2 "John Clymmowe and his brother" provided a new organ for Eton College, which cost £4 14*s*. and the old organ. (The reference to "his brother" seems to suggest that one of the partners had married the sister of the other.) We last find a reference to Clymmowe in 1534–5 as churchwarden at St. Stephen's, Walbrook, in which office he had succeeded the elder Howe.

It is evident that John Howe had the most extensive business of any organ-builder before the Commonwealth.

Twenty-six organs are known to have been built or renewed by him, and there may have been others of which there is now no record. Nineteen were in the Cities of London and Westminster, two (in Lambeth and Wandsworth) in the "Suburbs" and one each in Bletchingley, Eton, Coventry, Sheffield and York.

In 1548 Howe was assisted in his work by his son, Thomas, who five years later became apprenticed to John Hallywell, a citizen, and Skinner, of London. Nevertheless, the son is mentioned in connection with organ work in 1554, and in 1561, when he was brought before the Lord Mayor on a charge of recusancy as an "organ maker, and servante wh doctor ffreer Doctor in phisych".[1] "Father" Howe, as he was called in various church records after 1558, lived in Walbrook at "the Sign of the Organe Pype." He was a member of the Skinners' Company, which would be appropriate for an organ-builder using the hides of animals.[2]

During the reign of Elizabeth Puritan tendencies were at work, and antipathy to organs showed itself in a marked way, particularly in London. The old organ-builder saw his finest instruments removed from the churches or suffered to fall into decay. Howe lived on in straitened circumstances, though

[1] Calendar of State Papers Domestic, p. 174, April 23, 1561.

"Examination of Thomas How, organ maker and servant to Dr. Freer . . ., neither himself nor his master, to his knowledge, have received the Communion since the Queen's accession."

[2] There is no evidence to show that Howe was ever a monk. The title "Father" appears to have been one of respect and endearment. The burial registers of St. Stephen's (vol. xlix of the Harleian Society's publications) have an entry: "1571 Mar. 20. John Low [*sic*] orgin-maker".

it is recorded that one church, that of St. Alphage, London Wall, continued to pay him his fee for organ maintenance during the last six years of his life (he being "a very poremane"), even after the church had ceased to use its organ.

The references to Howe and his instruments are of very common occurrence in the records of the London churches. Some of the more interesting of those in respect of his work at the Church of St. Mary Woolnoth, Lombard Street, are here reproduced.

In the year 1553 this church had two organs, one in the Quire and the other in the Rood Loft. The pipes of the second "pair" were sold in 1562 as old lead, 102 [cij] lb., "wayed by the prson [parson] and me" at "ijd" the pound, fetching in all "xviijs." Between 1539 and 1571 there are no less than fifty references to Howe in the records of St. Mary's Church. At first his fee was only "iiijd" a year, but from 1555 to 1556 it was raised to "xij" for tuning. Constant repairs, particularly to the bellows, were required. The organ was kept in tune during the short reign of Edward VI, but when Mary came to the throne a larger sum was expended. In later years Howe and his family were suspected of adhering too closely to the faith of the early sixteenth century, and this may cause us no wonder, for the reformed Church did not take so kindly to his organs.

Here follow some extracts from the account-books of the church of St. Mary Woolnoth, Lombard Street, London.

> 1552–3: "Item payd to Gregorie the clerk for playing at thorganes one holle yere liijs iiijd. Payd to Howe thorgan maker for mending of thorganes viijs ijd."
>
> 1553–4: "Item paied to Robert ffryer for two antiphons, ij grailes, i masse books, one Legend, one manuell, one venite book, iij processyons, and one derige book xli xvjs viijd."
>
> 1554–5: "Item paied to howe for mendinge of the springes of the bases of the Organs xijd. Item paied to howe for mendinge of ye bellowes of ye organs, xijd. Item paied for a case for the keys of the organs viijd. Item paied to howe for mendinge of the organs, sounding of the Condytes and new clensynge of all the pipes against witsontyde vjs."

Numerous small items appear after this and only a few of the more interesting are reproduced here.

> 1557: "ij cords for the organs ij d."
>
> 1558: "a hole newe rope for the orgaynes."

(The references to ropes and cords are indicative of the way the organ was blown by pulling ropes attached to the bellows either directly or over a pulley or smooth piece of wood. Numerous fourteenth, fifteenth and sixteenth-century references to fees "for pulling the organs" are found in cathedral and church records.)

> 1557–8: "Wyer and soder and other things layed owte about the mendinge of the orgaines, ijs."
>
> 1559–60: "Item payed to howe the orgenmaker the iiijth of Aprill for mending and sawdering the Organ pipes and Letters (keys) xvjd. Item

payed to howe the orgenmaker the xvjth daye of September 1560 for viij springes for the basys viijd."

1560–1: "Item payed to John Whytrydye the Organ player for hys wages for a quarter and a half, xxvjs viijd."

1561–2: "Item paid to John Howe organ maker for skoring[1] of the organ pypes and mending some of them iijs. Item paid to John Howe organ maker the xxiij day of June A° 1562 for foure springe of Laten for the Organs and his labor for putting them to, xd."

1563–4: "Item paid to goodman howe the Organ maker the last day of January 1563 for ij sprynges for the base pypes of the organs, vjd."

1570–1: "Item paide to John Howe Organ maker for his fee for one hole yere for lookinge to the Orgaynes endinge at the feast of Sainte Michell tharchèll laste paste 1571, xijd."

And finally:

1573–4: "Item paide the vth day of ffebruarye 1573 for v of sixepeny nayles for the pewe made where thorgaynes did stand."

A number of churches allowed Howe to continue to tune their organs until his death in 1571. Immediately after this, most of them allowed their organs to remain untuned until finally they were sold for the price of scrap metal, as can be imagined from the last reference given above. Thus ended a chapter of the story of English organ-building and playing.[2]

Historians who have stressed the severe measures taken with organs at the beginning of the Commonwealth period have overlooked the effect of the gradual increase of Puritanism and the general lack of interest in church organs which marked the end of the sixteenth century. Indeed, by the time of the Commonwealth few of the London churches had an organ in playing condition and some had sold their instruments during the previous half-century. In the reign of Mary there was a revival of interest and money was spent on organs, organists and players, but this did not last long and the splendid musical activities in the reign of Elizabeth did not manifest themselves in the form of organ-playing in churches. Poor Howe, in his later years, had the bitter experience of seeing the fine organs of his earlier life sold as "scrap" or allowed to decay where they stood. Even such remarkable organists and composers as John Redford (1485–1545), organist of St. Paul's Cathedral, were so thoroughly forgotten that it was left to the present generation to show that in some ways they produced organ work which was

[1] This word means "scouring" and not "flowring" (i.e. decorating) as it has previously been transcribed. Laten = brass.

[2] Over two hundred references to the Howes have been found in Church records in connection with new or repaired organs: York Minster, 1485, 1531, 1536; St. Mary at Hill, London, 1500–59; St. Stephen, Walbrook, 1507–48; Holy Trinity, Coventry, 1526; St. Martin-in-the-Fields, London, 1542–69; Bletchingley Church, Surrey, 1545; Wandsworth Parish Church, 1549–65; St. Michael, Cornhill, London, 1548–60; St. Peter, Cornhill, London, 1548; St. Dionis Backchurch, London, 1551, St. Mary Woolnoth, London, 1553–62; St. Peter's, West Cheap, London, 1555–6; Westminster Abbey, London, 1558; Sheffield Parish Church, 1560; St. Helen's, Bishopsgate, London, 1564; Lambeth Parish Church, 1567; St. Andrew, Hubbard, London, 1568; St. Mary, Aldermanbury, London, 1570.

superior to that of the "virginalists" (e.g. Byrd and Bull) a century afterwards.[1]

Thomas Fountayne, St. Thomas Parish Church, Portsmouth, 1539.

William Treasorer, Regall Maker to Queen Elizabeth and Edward VI.

Betts of Wetherden did work at Boxford Church, Suffolk, 1541, 1548 and 1564.

Whyte or *White*, Magdalen College, Oxford, 1532–45, St. Andrew, Holborn, 1553, St. Michael, Bishop's Stortford, 1532. Father of Robert White, of Westminster, the composer.

John Vaucks, at Wimborne, 1531.

Sir Thomas Brabant (a priest), Wing Church, Bucks.

Edmund Popinjay, repaired the Winchester College organ, 1542.

Butson, at Magdalen, Oxford, 1543.

Fortescewe, at St. Martin-in-the-Fields, London, 1544–6.

Sir William Corvehill, at Much Wenlock, 1544.

Sir Rafe (a priest), at St. Michael's, Bishop's Stortford, 1547.

John Bosten, who was also co-organist at Waltham Abbey with Thomas Tallis.

Hamme, at St. Thomas' Church and St. Edmund's, Salisbury, 1548–53.

Robartt of Crewkerne, 1551.[2]

James Hewet, regal maker at Coventry, 1554.

Tucker, at St. Edmund's, Salisbury, 1557–8.

Jasper Blankard, at London and Canterbury, 1578.

Wyllyam Squyer, at Salisbury, 1564.

Cuthbert Swynbanke, at Chichester, 1558.

Thomas Totyll, at Worksop, 1568.

John Tysdale, at Sheffield, and Ecclesfield, 1570–2.

Lodowicus Theewes made an organ in 1579, a part of which is preserved in the Victoria and Albert Museum.

"*Robert*", at St. Margaret's Church, Westminster, 1583.

Edmond Schetz, maker and repairer to Queen Elizabeth and James I, 1587–8, 1600–1.

Andrew the organ-maker, at Yarmouth, 1588.

Broughe, at St. Margaret's, Westminster, 1589–90.

William Smythe, at Durham, 1594–9.

(Minor Canon, organ-repairer and organist.)

John Sylfester, at Salisbury, 1590–1.

E. Hoffheimer made an organ, now in Carisbrooke Castle, for the Earl of Montrose with stopped diapason, flute, regal and tremolo (1602).

Hugh Rose extensively repaired the organ at Trinity College, Cambridge, 1593–4.

Henry Nugent was at work in Dublin[3] in 1595.

[1] C. Pfatteicher, *John Redford* (Kassel, 1934). The Mulliner collection of keyboard pieces is now available (Stainer and Bell). Thomas Mulliner, who followed Redford, left a collection of organ pieces used in the cathedral (Brit. Mus. Add. 30513).

[2] In 1555 there was an organ-maker living in Nottingham, for at the January sessions is recorded: "the organ-makar wyffe for cowlynge with hyre nebours".

[3] Gratton Flood: op. cit.

Christofer Cartell, was paid xijs. in 1596 at Worksop Priory for "sope to skoure pipes, quicke silver, sowther, glewe and birrages".

Stephen Bretton of Norwich (*c.* 1598). [Probably the same as *Brittaine*.]

Edmund Hooper, who came to Westminster as the first regular abbey organist in 1588 and repaired the organs in 1603. He died on 14th July 1621.

William Maye, a carpenter and amateur musician who did work at Hartland Parish Church at the beginning of the seventeenth century.

George Pendleton was paid in 1605 "For for pounds of tynne to foot ye great bass pipe." A further item is "To a porter to help carry the pipe to my house and back again after it was new footed", at Westminster Abbey.

Andrea Bassano, Robert Henlake, Edward Norgate, were appointed makers, repairers and tuners of the Court organs and other instruments in 1606.[1]

John Yorke, in 1610, provided a "newe chaire orgaine" for Hugh Rose's instrument at Trinity College, Cambridge. He did work at Magdalen College, Oxford, until 1641.

Thomas Hamlyn was paid £60 in July 1613 for enlarging with three sets of pipes the organ at St. James's Palace, London and for making the same one note deeper.[2]

Stephen Brittaine, at Trinity College, Cambridge, 1615 and 1621.

William Ward, 1615, "tuning and mending His Magistes Organes". He also did work on the Rochester Cathedral organ in 1631.

Gibbs, of St. Paul's Churchyard, may only have been a music dealer, but he appears in connection with the Dulwich College Chapel organ in 1618.

John Burward, Burrard or *Burrett* built the organ in Dulwich College Chapel (1618–1620) and rebuilt the organ in Westminster Abbey about the year 1625 and repaired the Winchester School organ in 1637–8.

A document[3] preserved in Chirke Castle relates to an organ for the Castle Chapel in the years 1631–2. The purchaser of the instrument was Sir Thomas Middleton "of Chirke Castle in County of Denbye, in consideracion of the somme of one hundred and fiftie poundes of lawfull money of England—trulie and sufficientlie make furnish and fynish for the said Sir Thomas Middleton one good and perfect Organ of such proporcion trymming and scantling as is hereafter mencioned. That is to say The case of the said organ to be in height twelve foote and a half. In breadth nyne foote and in thicknes sixe foote and a halfe having nyne Towers vizt att each end one round Tower One Square Tower in the middle one half round on each side of the said square Tower and fower flatt Towers according to a moddell or draught now shewed forth by the said John Burward—with decent and fitting carved worke pendentes fynishinges guildinges and payntinges and all other things fitting for the same."

"Item the said John Burward is to place . . . within the case of the foresaid Organ two settes of keyes and two sound-boordes and tenne stoppes all of good metall pipes namelie to the upper sett of keyes to be fitted one stopt diapason one open diapason from gamut upwards one principall for the fore-

[1] Audit Office, Declared Accounts, Bundle 37, No. 40.

[2] E. Sheppard, *Memorials of St. James's Palace*, vol. ii.

[3] A facsimile of the original was printed in the *Musical Times*, No. 503 (1904).

front paynted, and guilded workmanlike, and inwardlie a Recorder, a small principale, a fifteenth and a two and twentieth: for the lower sett of keyes three more of metall, one diapason, a principall and a small principall and that the said organ shall have three bellowes with two sound boordes conveyannces, Conduittes Ironworke and all other thinges fitting for such an Organ well and workmanlike wrought and performed."

Emanuel Craswell, built an organ in Ludlow Parish Church in 1619.

Hamden, was paid 15*s*. in 1622 "for mending ye organies at Dulwich College Chapel". This included "making 3 or 4 newe pipes for a dyapason."

John Raper, was recommended by the Archbishop of York in 1622 to "loving friends" in Kingston-upon-Hull, but the projected organ for Holy Trinity, Hull, did not materialise owing to lack of funds.

Thomas Coats of Stamford repaired the Lincoln Cathedral organ from 1635.

Harris, grandfather of Renatus Harris, was said to have built a new organ for Magdalen College, Oxford, in 1637. He received £40, but the organ was not built for this sum. (See also p. 150.)

The specification of the Magdalen Organ was

Great Organ	*Chair Organ*
Two (open) diapasons	Stopped diapason
Two principals	Two principals
Two fifteenths	Recorder
Two two-and-twentieths	Fifteenth
(8 stops)	(5 stops)

Henry Jennings, repaired the organs in Jesus College and King's College, Cambridge, in 1640.[1]

William Leslie, a Scot, built the organ at St. Godard's Church, Rouen, in 1640 (see p. 79).

Thomas Dallam

Thomas Dallam was born in the small village of Dalton near Wigan in Lancashire, about the year 1570, and when he went to London he was apprenticed to a member of the Blacksmith's Company of which he eventually became a liveryman.[2]

At the end of the sixteenth century the newly formed Levant Company wished to obtain the favour of Sultan Mohamed III in order to develop

[1] These notes on organ-builders have been put together (*a*) from notes made by the late Andrew Freeman, of his transcriptions of church accounts; (*b*) from similar notes collected by the author in cathedrals, parish and collegiate churches and colleges; and (*c*) from special sources given in their respective references. The list of organ-makers is not exhaustive, but in view of the number of visits which have been made over a period of nearly thirty years, and appeals made to clergy and other authorities by the good offices of the editor of *The Church Times*, it is doubtful whether many other names will come to light.

[2] Dallam was fined £10 for failing to act as a steward at a Lord Mayor's Day Banquet, 1626. Dallam's signature to an agreement to pay his fine with £5 down and the rest spread over three years is found in the Minute Book of the company. This entry is interesting, as it fixes the spelling of his name, which was sometimes given as Dallans, Dallow and Dallams.

trade. Queen Elizabeth was only too willing to help them as she wished to have friendly powers near the Mediterranean, in order to neutralise the power of Spain and the Catholic nations. In the State Papers, dated 31st January 1599, we read that "A Great and Curious present is going to the Grand Turk, which will scandalise other nations, especially the Germans". Dallam, who must have been the most ingenious organ-builder of the time and also a man of good presence and culture, was selected to make this present in the form of an organ and to take it out to the Sultan, erect it, and give instructions concerning its use. The instrument, which would play automatically, was set up in Whitehall and approved by the Queen before it was taken to pieces and packed for transport.

Dallam had many adventures before he returned to England in 1600 after an absence of fifteen months, and his diary gives a graphic account of life at sea in the days of Drake and Raleigh.[1]

Fortunately a drawing and description of the instrument remain to us.[2] The merchants desired to have "a new instrument of extraordinary kind, and endowed with various motions, both musical and of other special use. Such as for the rarity and art therein used may render it fit to be sent from her Majesty to any Prince or Potentate whatever". The instrument which was planned by Randolph Bull, the goldsmith, was about 12½ ft. high, 5½ ft. broad and 4½ ft. deep, and the whole was raised from the ground and supported by five small brazen lions. There was a twenty-four-hour clock in front of a "flat" of pipes and above there was a figure of the Queen, set out in real diamonds, emeralds and rubies to the number of forty-five. There were eight figures round Her Majesty which were all capable of movement. In addition there were the Royal Arms, a head which moved to announce the hour, and the whole was surrounded by a Golden Cock.

The document goes on to state:

> "There shall be placed in the lower part of the instrument three several strong, forcible and artificial bellows, with a very strong, sufficient motion of wheels and pinions, very well wrought, and sufficient to drive and move the bellows at all times from time to time, for the space of six hours together, whensoever the wheels and pinions shall be applied to such purpose; and that there shall be contained within the said instrument a board called a sound-board, with certain instruments or engines called his barrels and keys, and five whole stops of pipes, viz. one open principal, unison recorder, octavo principal, and a flute, besides a shaking stop,[3] a drum, and a nightingale."[4]

[1] *Early Voyages and Travels in the Levant* (No. lxxxvii), the Diary of Thomas Dallam (1599–1600). Published by the Hakluyt Society in 1893 from the manuscript in the British Museum (Additional MS. 17,480). See also Stanley Mayes, *An Organ for the Sultan*, London, 1956.

[2] The late Andrew Freeman and I have searched without success for this in many libraries and museums. The description given above is taken from *The Illustrated London News* of 20th October 1860 by an anonymous writer who obviously had access to the manuscript. This writer does not realise that he is referring to Dallam's organ, but there is ample internal evidence that it is no other.

[3] A tremulant.

[4] The nightingale was usually made by bending over a small organ pipe so that its end dipped into water in a small cup.

By means of the bellows, the barrel, keys and other "engines" moving the said bellows, the pipes are to sound forth musically four or five songs without the hand of any person on the keys, and are to continue playing for six hours "without any intermission, or ceasing, or discord", at the pleasure of the person directing the instrument; "and shall in the same way sound the shaking stop, the drum, and the nightingale, and every one of them severally, for six hours together, at the will of the director". Unfortunately, there is no account of the tunes played by the barrels. The other movements are described as follows:

> "Within the middle part of the instrument, and behind the dial and pipes, shall be placed and contained nine several motions, very strong and artificially wrought, which shall perform from time to time, the several actions and gestures following, viz.: The first motion, being a clock, shall drive, make to go and move the true course of the sun and of the moon, and shall show the age of the moon truly every day, with her increasing and decreasing; and it shall also show the reigning planets every day very truly. The second motion shall move an armed man in another of the towers, and shall strike the quarter of the hour upon a fine, loud, and sounding bell. The third motion shall move an armed man in another of the towers, and shall strike the twelve hours of the day in their time upon a greater bell, very loud. The fourth motion shall make the cock to crow very loud every hour, and as often as the director of the said instrument shall appoint; and the same cock shall be made strong, of metal, and shall be very artificially wrought, and made to flutter with his wings. The fifth motion shall be in the lower part of the instrument, and shall be a great barrel with a chime of very tunable bells, and shall be made to set to play a chime at any hour, as the person directing the instrument shall dispose. The sixth motion shall make all the persons (that is, the eight figures above described) to go in the presence and make their obeisance to the Queen's Majesty's image, and her personage to move her hand with her sceptre to every one of them as they pass before her. The seventh motion shall make the two trumpeters to lift up the trumpets to their mouths and to sound, as often as the director shall set the time. The eighth motion shall move and open the mouth of the great head, and make the eyes thereof to move and turn every hour at the striking of the clock. The ninth motion shall move or turn an hour-glass which an angel shall hold in his hand, and turn it every hour."

The machine cost £550 (at least £10,000–£15,000 in present-day money), and 300 ounces of pure silver had to be used in decorating it.

Thomas built an organ for Eton College in 1613–14 at a cost of almost £112.

> "Expense for the organ contayning fyve stopps.
>
> 1. a diapason of tynn fyve foote longe stopped xiiij *l.*
> 2. a principall of tynn a open stopp fyve foote longe x *l.*
> 3. a fflute unison the principall fyve foote long of tynn v *l.*

4. an octavo to the principall of Tynne v^{s}.
5. a ffyftenth of tynne v *l*.

Item the Sondeborde bellows and other necessaries excepting the case xxvj *l*."

There follows a list of expenses for the organ case, preparing the site of the organ, which together accounts for about £40 of the above sum. This includes "It. to Mr. Dallam for blewe painted paper v *s*."

In 1626–7 "one that mended the shakeinge stop" received xij *s* (Robert Dallam).

Thomas seems to have had the best work in the kingdom in his day: he built the organ in the Chapel at Windsor Castle. He did work at King's College, Cambridge, from 1605–6. It is listed on four foolscap sheets. Some of the prices of materials are interesting: 16 cwt. of tin cost £57; ebony for keys, 3*s*. 4*d*. and the total expenditure was £371 17*s*. 1*d*.

We now give an account of Thomas Dallam's Organ at Worcester Cathedral (from a document preserved in Worcester Library, Treasurer's Accounts d. 248).

The organ was built to the design of Thomas Tomkins. The pitch seems to have been very high.

"Anno Dom 1613

All the materialls and workmanshipp of the newe double organs in the Cathedrall Church of Worcester to Thomas Dallam organ maker came to	210	00	00
The Case and Joyners' worke about the loft to Robert Kettle	68	14	8
The floore and loft in Carpenters' work about	13	00	00
The guilding and painting to Willm. Peacy	77	8	0
ffor painting the Escutchions about the loft to Jo^{n} Davis of Worcester	11	00	00
	381	2	8

The particulars of the great organ.
Two open diapasons of metall.
CC fa ut a pipe of 10 foot long.
Two principals of metal.
Two small principals or 15^{ths} of metal.
One twelfth of mettall.
One recorder of mettal, a stopt pipe.

In the Chaire Organ

One principal of mettal.
One diapason of wood.
One flute of wood.
One small principal or fifteenth of mettal.
One two & Twentieth of mettal."

At this point is inserted, in a later hand: "July 2nd, 1666, add in ye new organ An open Diapason of wood leaving out nine of ye Basses."[1]

Dallam also built a "fair, large and very serviceable double organ", costing £300, for the Chapel Royal, Holyrood, Edinburgh. The case was designed by Inigo Jones in 1617 and "twenty angels" formed a part of it.

Here is an account of the work of a son, Robert, at York Minster in 1632:

Articles of Agreement between Dean and Chapter on the one hand and Robert Dallam, citizen and blacksmith, of London, on the other, touching the making of a great organ for the church, for the sum of £297 with £5 more for his journey to York.

The agreement, signed on 21st March, specifies the name and cost of each stop and of the various mechanical components. We may reasonably assume that the compass was from CC to D, 51 notes.

The case was made by a Durham workman, who was paid 20*s*. a week for a year.

"The names and number of the stoppes or setts of pipes for the said great organ to be new made; every stopp containeinge fiftie-one pipes; the said great organ containing eight [nine ?] stoppes.

Imprimis two open diapasons of tynn, to stand in sight, many of them to be chased	lxxx li.
Item one diapason stop of wood	x li.
Item two principals of tynn	xxiiij li.
Itm. one twelft to the diapason	viij li.
Itm. one small principall of tynn	vj li.
Itm. one recorder unison to the said principall	vj li.
Itm. one two and twentieth	v li.
Itm. the great sound-board with conveyances, wind-chestes, cariyages, and conduits of lead	xl li.
Itm. the rowler board, carriages, and keys	xx li.

The names and number of stoppes of pipes for the chaire organ, every stopp containeinge fifty-one pipes, the said chaire organ containeinge five stoppes.

Imprimis one diapason of wood	x li.
Itm. one principal of tynn, to stand in sight, many of them to be chased	xij li.
Itm. one flute of wood	viij li.
Itm. one small principall of tynn	v li.
Itm. one recorder of tynn, unison to the voice	viij li.
Itm. the sound bord, wind-chest, drawinge stoppes, conveyances and conduits	xxx li.
Itm. the rowler board, carriages, and keys	x li.
Itm. the three bellowes with winde truncks, and iron workes and other thinges thereto	x li.

Sume total cclxxxxvij li."

[1] A longer account of this organ appears in a letter from Nathaniel Tomkins to John Sayer in May 1665 (Bod. Lib. Add. C 304ff141).

(The builder's arithmetic is at fault to the extent of £5 in his favour, but if the recorder of the chaire organ was really "unison to the voice" it might well have cost "xiij li" and not "viij li".)

This instrument of two manuals, and fourteen stops was one of the organs that survived the Civil War. What remained of it, after sundry rebuildings, was burnt during the night of 1st February 1829.

In 1634 "Robert Dallam of the Citty of Westminster contracted for a new organ for the fellows and scholars of St. John's College, Cambridge.

". . . one payre of organs, or Instrumentes, to conteyne six several stoppes of pipes, every stoppe conteyning forty nine pipes (viz) one diapason most part to stand in sight, one Principall of Tynne, one Recorder of Wood, one small Principal of Tynne, one, two and twentieth of Tynne, with Sound boords, Conveyances, Conducts, Roller boord, Carriages and Keyes, two bellows and wind trunkes, with the case and carving onely, with all other necessaries thereunto belonging, finding all manner of stuffe, both of yron, brasse, tynne, timber and wainscoate incident to the making and finishing of the said Instrumente." The cost of the organ was £185; from the list given above the twelfth seems to have been omitted; the small principal was a fifteenth. When the new chapel was built in 1864–9 the original case went to St. Mark's Church, Old Bilton, Warwickshire, and some of the Dallam pipes to Christ Church, Cambridge.

Robert Dallam, the son of Thomas Dallam, died at Oxford on 31st May 1665, in his sixty-third year, and was buried near the west door of New College Chapel. Like his father, Robert was a member of the Blacksmiths' Company. He is usually described as "of Covent Garden and Cittie of Westminster". The organs made or repaired by him include:

Oxford, Magdalen College Chapel, 1632 and 1661. Repairs only.

Cambridge, Jesus College Chapel, 1634. Cost £200. Robert added pedals (probably shifting movements)[1] in 1635. Taken down in 1642 and set up again at the Restoration. Rebuilt (or superseded) in 1688. (See also under Renatus Harris).

Cambridge, St. John's College Chapel, 1635. One manual, six stops. Cost £185. (See above.)

London, Lambeth Palace Chapel, 1635. Repaired at a cost of £13. The bill is preserved in the Public Record Office.

Canterbury Cathedral, 1635. A new organ is said to have been made, but the Canterbury records make no mention of either instrument or builder about this time.

Lichfield Cathedral, 1636. New organ, cost £315. Destroyed by the Puritans.

Cambridge, Trinity College Chapel, 1637. Repaired at a cost of £20.

Cambridge, King's College Chapel, 1638. Repairs only, at a cost of £28.

Gloucester Cathedral, 1640. A new organ: seems to have survived the Civil Wars. (See below under Taunton and Thomas Harris.)

[1] An early form of stop control, which shut off part of the pipes without moving the separate sliders.

Oxford, New College Chapel, 1663. Cost £420. Subsequently enlarged by Green (q.v.). A few of the original pipes remain in the present instrument.

Oxford, Music School. Also ascribed (by Anthony Wood) to *Ralph* Dallam. Originally contained four stops, afterwards increased to six. In 1913 this instrument was removed to a private house in Bridgport. (See also under Green.)

Wells Cathedral. £206 paid to Mr. Dallam as part of a total cost of £398 spent on the organ.

London, St. Mary Woolnoth. Damaged in the Great Fire of 1666. Father Smith used some of the old pipes in his instrument of 1681. The present case is almost certainly by Dallam and not by Smith.

London, Old St. Paul's.

Durham Cathedral. The authority for these last two statements (Rimbault, quoting Saunderson's MS., collections for a history of Durham)[1] is not convincing:

"Tere was 3 paire of organs belonginge to the said quire for the maintenance of god's service and the better selebrating thereof one of the fairest paire of the 3 did stand over the quire dore only opened and played uppon at principall feastes, the pipes beinge all of most fine wood, and the workmanshippe verye faire partly gilted uppon the inside and the outside of the leaves and covers up to the topp with branches and flowers finely gilted with the name of Jesus gilted with gold there was but 2 paire more of them in England of the same makinge, one paire in York and another in Paules [i.e., St. Paul's Cathedral, London].

"The second paire stood on the north side of the quire being never played uppon but when the 4 doctors of the church was read,—viz, Augustine Ambrose Gregorye and Jerome beinge a faire paire of large organs called the cryers. The third paire was dayly used at ordinary services".

Robert Dallam[2] left England in 1642 and settled with his family in the old Breton city of Quimper. Thomas, who had made the remarkable organ for the Turkish Palace, had three sons and a daughter. The last had married Thomas Harris (or Harrison) and became the mother of Renatus (or René) Harris, the well-known Restoration organ-builder. The last pre-Commonwealth organ made by Robert, the eldest son, was the new instrument which he set up in Gloucester Cathedral in 1640–1. Robert had married Isabella Turpin before he left for France. Soon after his arrival, he was appointed organist of Saint Corentin, and gave himself the title of "organist to the Queen of England".[3] No account from the English side of this honour is recorded and

[1] Rimbault's statement seems to have been made by a faulty interpretation of a passage in *The Rites of Durham* (*c.* 1593), which from its date cannot possibly refer to an organ made by this Dallam. (The records of organs in Durham Cathedral go back to the year 1264: "Hugo Darlington, the fourteenth Prior of Durham, built a great belfry and larger organs.")

[2] Huskisson Stubington, "The Dallams in Brittany", *The Organ*, vol. xix, pp. 81, 118. Georges Servières, *La Décoration artistique des Buffets d'Orgues* (Paris, 1928).

[3] Le Men, *Monographie de la Cathédrale de Quimper.*

it may be that he was organist to Henrietta Maria; and if this were so the "Popish rite" which she used would be the reason for the secrecy in England and there would be no need for this in Brittany.

Dallam built three organs, which he finished in 1643 at Quimper. One of these is the basis of the fine grand organ which is found today. After three years in Quimper he moved to Villeneuve in the parish of Plougastel-Daoulas.

An interesting contract dated 16th August 1654 gives details of a new organ which he made for the Priory of Lesneven. Here is the specification:

"Devis le 1er jeu, pavement de 18 pieds
le 2me un cornet de 5 tuyaux
le 3me un bourdon de 8 pieds
le 4me un prestant de 4 pieds
le 5me une flûte de 4 douce
le 6 me un nazard de 2 pieds $\frac{2}{3}$
le 7 me une doublette [2-ft. pitch
le 8me une quart de nazard [2-ft. pitch]
le 9me une tierce du quart [1$\frac{3}{5}$-ft. pitch]
le 10me une petite quinte [1$\frac{1}{3}$-ft. pitch]
le 11me un flageollet
le 12me une fourniture de 3 tuyaux
le 13 me une symballe de 2 tuyaux
le 14me une trompette
le 15me une voix humaine
le 16me un bigearre [a reed]
le 17me un petit cromorne."

Later Dallam became organist of the Cathedral of Saint Pol de Léon. On 29th January 1660 he sold his interest in the business for 2,400 livres and in 1661 he was back in England at work on the new organ for New College, Oxford. He left his sons, Thomas and Toussaint, in Brittany, where they prospered in their father's trade, but Toussaint Dallam repaired the Dulwich College organ in 1668.[1]

Robert Hayward (*or Haywood, Heywood, Heyward*)

There were probably two makers named Hayward (or Haywood), both of Bath. The younger one (if there were two) was an alderman of that city. Between them they were responsible for the following:

[1] Servières mentions other English organ-builders who did work in France: Arnoul de Sand, who in 1585 repaired the organ at Saint-Melaine at Morlaix; Thomas Harrison [*sic*] (the father of Renatus Harris), who built a new organ in 1656 in the Church of Notre-Dame du Mur (now demolished). Many authorities hold the famous organ of Saint-Brieuc Cathedral to be of English origin.

The Dallam family did work on organs at the following places in France: Quimper Cathedral (three organs) (1642); Brassparts (1648); Saint-Jean-du-Doigt (1652); Lesneven (1654); Landerneau; Saint Houardon (1656); Cathedral of Saint-Pol de Léon (1656–60); Locronan (1672); Pont-Croix (1675); Guimiliau (1675); Ploujeau (1675); Morlaix; Saint Melaine (1682); Pleyben (1688); Sizun (1688); Saint-Renan (1689); Landerneau; Saint Thomas (1690); La Martyre (1693); Rumengol (1699); undated Goulven, Ergué-Armel, Daoulas.

Coventry, Holy Trinity Church, 1632. Repaired, and probably built, by *Haywood.* Taken down in 1641 and sold the following year.

Salisbury, St. Martin's Church, 1637. Repaired.

Somerton Church, 1641. Organ made "musicall".

Wells Cathedral, 1663. Repaired.

Wimborne Minster, 1664. New organ, cost £180. Repaired in 1670. Some portions of Hayward's instrument are said to be still in use.

Coventry, Holy Trinity Church, 1684. New organ, cost £98, exclusive of painting and gilding. Taken by Schwarbrick in part payment of his new instrument of 1732.

John Loosemore

He was born (at Bishops Nympton?) in 1613 or 1614; son of Samuel Loosemore who was also an organ-builder and who had probably learnt his business from John Chappington, of South Molton, hard by. In 1674 John handed on his business to his son-in-law, John Shearne, but lived till 1681, dying on 18th April of the latter year. He was buried in Exeter Cathedral, where his epitaph may still be read. A harpsichord of his make, dated 1655, can be seen in the Victoria and Albert Museum, South Kensington.

Hartland Church, 1635–6. John Loosemore had charge of this organ in this year. In 1637–8 he was paid £4 for "setting of ye organs upon ye roudeloft". He also did work to the pulpit, seats, etc., and occasionally played the organ here.

Blair Atholl Castle, N.B., 1650. A small positive organ-cum-regal with ten half stops; still in existence, though some of the carving has disappeared.

Exeter Cathedral, 1660. Apparently a temporary organ, unless the old pre-Restoration instrument was patched up and used. Removed in 1665.

Exeter Cathedral, 1665. Loosemore's masterpiece. Cost £677 7*s*. 10*d*. Contained fifteen stops, including a double diapason (fourteen pipes), of which the largest pipe was 20 ft. 6 in. The case on which the date appears still remains *in situ*, but two detached side-towers, which contained the largest pipes in England at the time, were unfortunately destroyed in 1875. The fourteen pipes of the double diapason in Exeter Cathedral were grouped in two sets of seven each against the columns at the south entrance of the choir and thus at some distance from the main body of the organ, and were actuated by a separate set of pallets.

The largest pipe was GGGG. Its dimensions were:

Speaking part	20 ft. 6 in. long
Nose	4 ft. 0 in.
Circumference	3 ft. 11 in.
Diameter	1 ft. 3 in.

Contents of the speaking part, 3 hogs, 8 gal.
Weight 360 lb.

The Honourable Roger North, an acoustician known to Sir Isaac Newton, said of them: "I could not be so happy to perceive that in the musick they signified anything at all," but, as is expected from such pipes, they were useful when combined with stops of higher pitch, for another writer says: "They have no effect alone, but are very fine with the diapasons and principal."[1]

Here is an account of an organ built by Loosemore for a private house:

"February the 1st. 1665. Then made a bargain wth Sr. Geo. Trevilyan for an organ wth these stops in it as follows:

One diapason
One flute
One recorde
One fifteenth
One principall
One flagilett
One trumpett
One shaking stopp.

And for this organ I am to have one hundred pound, 20 *l* whereof at the 25th day of March next and four-score residue thereof when the work is finished.

John Loosemore."

This organ stands in Nettlecombe Court in the Minstrels' Gallery of the Great Hall. The document transcribed above is preserved in the Muniment Room.

Here was an early attempt to produce a house organ with a variety of instrumental tones, particularly those of various types of flutes, including the recorder and the flageolot. When the bellows are used, two gilts tars revolve in the front of the case. This enabled the player to see that the blower was doing his work properly. Even before this time some of the German organs had this device augmented with small bells at the points of the star. Often a stop was used to control it. The "Cymbelstern" was a source of amusement and distraction to the worshippers by its visible appearance if not by anything else.[2]

Thomas Thamar

Thamar is generally considered to have resided at Petersborough; but, curiously enough, in the agreement between him and the Dean and Chapter of that city, he is referred to as "of London", while in the agreement between

[1] Roger North, *The Lives of the Norths*, Vol. 1, p. 154.

[2] Samuel and John Loosemore. The Loosemores were a well-known Devonshire family. (In the *Dom. State Papers*, John Loosemore, mariner, of Tiverton is reported to have returned from Vigo in Spain with important information about Spanish garrisons.) It is probable that they learnt organ-building from Chappington, who lived near (at Bishops Nympton and South Molton). When John Loosemore was engaged to build the organ in Exeter Cathedral he made a special journey into Cornwall "to make a choice of Tyn" and another to Salisbury "to see the organ there, the better to inform himself to make the new organ in this Church".

him and the Dean and Chapter of Winchester he is described as "of the Univery. of Cambridge". Seeing that he had such a large connection in the University town and that he had a son in the choir of Trinity College Chapel,[1] it is more than probable that he was resident in Cambridge for the greater part of the period 1660–85. He seems to have either died or retired from business in 1685, more likely the former.

Cambridge, Christ's College Chapel, 1658. This was one of the organs which escaped destruction during the Great Rebellion. It seems to have been taken down and stored, but in 1658 it was set up by Thamar in the Combination Room. Thamar had the pleasure of re-erecting it in the chapel in May or June 1660; he also had charge of it till 1684.[2]

Cambridge, The Master's Parlour, Christ's College, 1658. Either this or the chapel organ was in all probability the one made by William Beton, or Bylton, in 1532. Thamar's connection with it, as with the other, was limited to removal and repair. At the Restoration it was set up in the Combination Room, where it was repaired as late as 1733. It was lost sight of subsequently.[3]

Cambridge, Trinity College Chapel, 1662–3. The pre-Restoration organ seems to have been set up again in 1660, but Thamar either rebuilt it or made a new one, in 1662–3, for which he received £110. He had the oversight of it till Lady Day, 1685.[4]

Cambridge, St. John's College Chapel, 1663. Robert Dallam's organ of 1635 was re-erected in 1661: probably by Thamar, since the latter had charge of it from 1663 to 1684. The main case is now at Old Bilton Church. The chair organ case added by Thamar is now in Brownsover Church.

Winchester Cathedral, 1665–6. This was an entirely new instrument—"a faire, substantial, good and perfect double organ"—and it was placed on the north side of the quire in the place where its predecessor and its successors have always stood. The pitch was to be "gamut in D sol re", so that the compass would normally have been just over four octaves.

Since, however, the largest pipe of the open diapason was to be 13ft. in length, the compass would be quite extraordinary. Unless the lowest octave was very incomplete, the upward range would be extremely limited. In any event, a 13-ft. D would give very high pitch. The organ was superseded in 1693, but the cases were utilised for the new instrument and lasted till 1825. (See below under Renatus Harris.)

Cambridge, Jesus College Chapel, 1669. Robert Dallam's organ of 1635 was taken down in 1641–2, "discovered" in 1652–3 and set up at the Restoration. Thamar's name occurs twice in connection with it, namely,

[1] G. F. Cobb, *History of the Organ in Trinity College Chapel, Cambridge*, ed. Dr. Alan Gray.

[2] and [3] Willis and Clark's *Architectural History of Cambridge*, vol. ii, pp. 205–14, and John Gay's article on the organs at Christ's in the *College Magazine* (1893–4).

[4] Willis and Clark, ibid., vol. ii, pp. 572–81, and Dr. Gray's booklet.

in 1669 (tuning) and in 1670 (mending).[1] (See above under Robert Dallam, and below under Renatus Harris.)

Cambridge, King's College Chapel, 1673. Though Thomas Dallam's organ of 1606 was taken down and stored during the wars, it was probably somewhat severely damaged. When the choral services were resumed, a small organ belonging to the organist, Henry Loosemore, was used, and in 1661 Lancelot Pease (q.v. below) was paid £200 for a new chaire organ. In 1673–4 Thamar received £32 10*s*. (in part payment of £130) for setting up the loftier organ (erectionem altioris organi),[2] that is a great organ. Both Pease and Thamar seem to have fitted their organs into the old cases. This method of building an organ in sections—chaire first, great afterwards—was not at all uncommon at this time.

Cambridge, Pembroke College Chapel. A new organ by Thamar (made, according to Dr. A. G. Hill,[3] in 1674), but the case almost certainly belonged to an earlier instrument and may be dated *c*. 1580. Thamar's organ consisted of one manual, GG to D, with the following stops:[4]

Open diapason	Fifteenth
Stop diapason	Sesquialtera
Principal	Cornet
Twelfth	Trumpet.

When the present organ at Pembroke College was built, in 1708, Charles Quarles, who contracted for it, engaged to remove the old one to Framlingham Church, Suffolk, and here it has been ever since. There have been some additions (pedals and a small swell) and also a few substitutions, but much of the old work still remains, including the very beautiful case. The quality of the interior metal pipes is very high. The front pipes have rounded lips, elongated and raised considerably above the bodies. They are also elaborately decorated: the painting is said to be original.

Cambridge, Queen's College Chapel, 1678–9. Repairs only. There was a new organ (by an unknown maker) in 1710.[5]

Peterborough Cathedral, 1680. This was a new organ. It cost £115 and seems to have lasted till 1809.[6]

Ralph Dallam, James White

Apart from the scanty records of their handiwork, all that we know about these two men is contained in the inscription on the mural tablet, now destroyed, which White erected to the memory of his partner in the old church of St. Alfege, Greenwich. This was as follows:

[1] Willis and Clark, ibid., vol. ii, pp. 141–4.
[2] Willis and Clark, ibid., vol. i, pp. 519–21.
[3] *Organ Cases and Organs of the Middle Ages* (London), vol. ii, p. 8.
[4] *Musical Standard*, 30th November 1889.
[5] Willis and Clark, op. cit., vol. ii, pp. 40–3.
[6] *Musical Times* (1904), p. 571.

"Near unto this place resteth after long travail thro' many countries the body of Mr. Ralph Dallans, organ maker, while he was making this organ at the sole charge of several well-disposed parishioners, which was begun by him in February, 1672. Thomas Plume, D.D., vicar, Tho. Pattyson, Tho. Mallyn, churchwardens. James White, his partner, finished ye organ and erected this stone. Tho. Molyn, Jo. Wilton, churchwardens."[1]

Ralph is usually considered to have been a son of Thomas and brother to Robert and George. It is interesting to note his roving proclivities in connection with Thomas Dallam's memorable voyage to Turkey with which we have dealt earlier.

Windsor, St. George's Chapel Royal, 1660. There are three entries in the Windsor Chapter Acts relating to this organ. They are here quoted from Mr. W. St. John Hope's *History of Windsor Castle*:

"1660, 22nd October. Mr. Dallame to make an organ for the Church and to have 600 *li.* for it. One Hundred whereof he must have at London when Dr. Browne comes to towne.

"1661, 29th November. The Organ to be guilt. Mr. Doggerell is to guild the Organ and ye Organ case. He is first to begin with the Cheire Organ and if his workmanshipp in that be approved of, then he is to proceed on the great Organ, if not he is to loose all his labour and charges; but if he finish the whole (upon approbacon of his guilding the Cheire Organ) he is to have for all 120 *li.* if men judicious in ye art shall judg yt he deserves it.

"1662, 15th November. Ordered that whereas there remaines due fifty shillings to Mr. Doggerell of the residue of his bargaine for guilding the Organ it shal be mad up five pounds for his guilding the Angells."

According to the late Dr. Hopkins,[2] the contents of this organ were as follows:

Great Organ, GG (short) to D in alt. 52 notes

	Pipes
Open Diapason (to CC then stopped and octave pipes)	54
Stopped diapason	52
Principal	52
Twelfth	52
Fifteenth	52
Cornet, treble	III 78
Sesquialtera, bass	III 78
Trumpet, treble	26
Trumpet, bass	26

Two shifting movements (pedals), one reducing the full organ to the diapasons and principal, the other to the diapasons alone. (These pedals affect the sliders, not the stop handles.)

[1] Brit. Mus. Lansdowne MS. 938, quoted in Mr. J. E. G. De Montmorency's booklet on Greenwich church and organ.

[2] *Grove's Dictionary of Music*, vol. iii, p. 532 (1922).

If we can accept Dr. Hopkins's specification as authentic, we have sufficient evidence to show that this organ found its way to St. Martin-in-the-Fields, London, about 1674, and to St. Peter's Church, St. Albans, in 1725. Portions of this organ are still in use in the latter church. The absence of a chaire organ from Dr. Hopkins's account (again assuming it to be reliable) is capable of explanation. For it seems possible that great and chaire organs at Windsor, both on the quire screen, and facing west and east respectively, were quite separate and distinct instruments even at this comparatively late date. (There will be occasion to refer to the Dallam instrument when we deal with Father Smith.)

Norton-by-Galby Church, Leicestershire, 1664. This organ was enlarged by Father Smith in 1701, and sold to Rugby Church in 1792. The old case, widened in 1841, was dispensed with in 1877, but a few of the original pipes are still in use. (See later, under Father Smith.)[1]

Hackney, Old Parish Church, 1665. This organ, so much admired by Pepys[2] when he visited the church on 21st April 1667, was removed to Newport Pagnell Church in 1738. Since 1869 the organ part has been in Haversham Church, Bucks., and the case was in the possession of Mr. T. Atterton, organ-builder, of Leighton Buzzard.

Cambridge, A College. An organ formerly in "one of the Cambridge Colleges" partly by Ralph Dallam and partly by an older maker, was set up in the church of St. Margaret at King's Lynn in 1676. It was superseded in 1754. A fuller description of this instrument will be given under Christian Smith, as that builder repaired it in 1697. The Cambridge College has not yet been identified.

Oxford, Music School. Probably by *Robert* Dallam (q.v.).

George Dallam, Jane Dallam

George was probably a brother of Robert and Ralph and a younger son of old Thomas Dallam, but the actual relationship has not yet been established. He was at work on his own account almost immediately after the Restoration. Then, or soon after, he was living in the Parish of "St. Andrew in the Wardrobe"; but some years later, as shown by the following advertisement at the end of the 1672 edition of Playford's *Introduction to the Skill of Musick*, he moved further afield: "Mr. George Dalham, that excellent organ-maker, dwelleth now in Purple Lane, next door to the Crooked Billet where such as desire to have new organs, or old organs mended, may be well accommodated." (Purple Lane, now Portpool Lane, is a turning leading from Gray's Inn Road to Leather Lane.) The approximate date of his death is established by an entry in the account books of St. Martin-in-the-Fields. This records that on 22nd February 1685 Jane Dallam was paid "Tenn shillings in full of a quarters salary due to her Husband lately decd. at Christmas last for cleaning and tuning the Organs", and shows that he died either at the end of 1684 or at the beginning of 1685. Since his widow was paid £2 a year for tuning this organ right up to the end of 1693–4, it looks

[1] Information from Mr. C. F. Harris, of Rugby.
[2] S. Pepys, *Diary* (1667).

as if she kept the business going as well as she could after his death. Possibly, however, she sub-let her contracts, in which event Renatus Harris probably undertook most of the work, for he was the next to be employed at St. Martin's, and was, moreover, her grandson.[1]

The organs made or repaired by George Dallam included the following:

London, Westminster Abbey, 1660–1. Tuning only, for which he received 5*s*. in this year.[2]

Durham Cathedral, 1662. The agreement for "one fare double organ" to cost £550 was drawn up between the Dean and Chapter of Durham and George Dallam "of the Parish of St. Andrew Wardrobe London Organ Maker" on 5th October 1661. Though finished by Christmas 1662, this instrument was not used on Christmas Day but "a pair of little organs that cost towards 80 pound that came from London" in June 1661 was used instead; whereupon Dean Sudbury "was angry, but after, on St. Stephen's Day the said Great Organs were first played on by Mr. John Forster Organist and so continued to be played on".[3] When Father Smith built a new organ for the cathedral, in 1683–4, he took Dallam's organ in part payment. The chaire organ, with four new stops, he sold to the "Popish Chapel" at York, whence it was subsequently removed to St. Michael-le-Belfry in the same city. Here it remained till 1885, when it was sold to Mr. Bell, organ-builder, of York. The late Dr. Alan Gray had the stopped diapason from this organ, but whether it was by Dallam or Smith does not appear.[4] The fate of the great organ is not known. Smith was willing to sell it "at any rate as it is, for to mak it a good organ will cost monnes".

Robert Taunton

According to John Latimer's *Annals of Bristol in the Seventeenth Century* (1900) Taunton "petitioned the council for the freedom in May, 1662, and on the ground that there was no similar 'artist' in the city, he was admitted at the low fine of £5".

Bristol Cathedral. In a letter to the late Mr. George F. Smith, organist of St. Magnus, London Bridge, Dr. Hubert Hunt, the late cathedral organist, quotes the following from a newspaper cutting in the Brackenbridge Collection (now in the Bristol Central Library): "The college organ was built by Renatus Harris. The chaire organ was built before by one Mr. Taunton of this city."

Gloucester Cathedral. The pre-Restoration instrument (built by Robert Dallam in 1640, sold to Yate, the sheriff, and bought back at the Restoration for £80) was set up and tuned, at a cost of £10, by Taunton. This

[1] A letter from Wigorn, Bishop of Worcester, to Archbishop Sheldon, dated 5th August 1665, and quoted in full in Hopkins and Rimbault, op. cit., pp. 120–1, says that Thomas Harris (there rendered Harrison) "was old [George] Dallow's [i.e. Dallam's] servant and married his daughter".

[2] *Musical Times* (1905), p. 518.

[3] Ibid., p. 302.

[4] *Dictionary of National Biography* and letter from Dr. Gray.

PLATE 11.

Siena, Italy: S. Maria della Scala Renaissance case by B. Peruzzi (1485—c. 1536). Photograph by Grassi

PLATE 12.

The organ in St. John's Church, Lüneburg, 1551, by Hinrich Niehoff. Towers of Pedal Pipes, 1715, by Matthias Dropa

PLATE 13.
The organ case in Stanford-on-Avon Church, Northamptonshire, c. 1580.
Photograph by Roger Yates

PLATE 14a.

The organ in King's College Chapel, Cambridge. East Case 1605. One of the few pre-Restoration English organ cases

PLATE 14b.

The organ in the Church of St. Bavon, Haarlem, Holland by Christian Muller, 1735–9

was towards the end of 1661. A little later, in 1664, Mr. Dean, organist of Bristol Cathedral, bought the organ for £65, but whether for the cathedral or for his own private use does not appear. It is said that this organ afterwards found its way to Chepstow Parish Church, and that parts of it are incorporated in the present instrument.[1]

Wells Cathedral, 1662. The contract for this "fair, well-tuned, usefull and beautifull double organ" (which was to cost £800 or less, according to the award of the surveyor when the work was finished) is preserved in the Cathedral library at Wells:

" *The Forme of the New Organs*

The organs are to have two fronts, the one towards the quire, the other towards the body.

The Hight of the Organ

The Hight of the Organ must be Thirty foot.
The breadth of the same must be fifteene foot.

The Names of the Stopps

Two open diapasons of metall, the longest pipe of each Twelve foot and a halfe.
One stopp Diapason of tymber unison with the open diapason.
One twelfe of mettall.
Two principalls of metall, six foot longe the longest pipe.
One Recorder of metall.
One two and twentieth of mettall.

In the Chaire Organ

One stopp diapason of tymber.
One flute of tymber
One principall of mettall six foot long
Two fifteenths one of mettall, the other of tymber.
One two and twentieth of mettall.

And also the guilding of both the organs, both pipes and cases."

(In 1706 Renatus Harris added an "echo stop" to the great organ, and in 1728 Thomas Swarbrick carried out a restoration. In 1786 Samuel Green completely rebuilt the organ at a cost of £420.)

William Preston

Renatus Harris's opinion of the workmanship of this builder, usually known as "Preston of York", was not very flattering, for in his proposal for the repair and alteration of the organ at Magdalen College Chapel, Oxford (now at Tewkesbury), he declares that Preston had spoiled one stop and several pipes belonging to another.[2] Curiously enough, Preston was called in by the Dean and Chapter of Ely to report on the work done by Gerard Smith to their cathedral in 1689. "I doe declare," he writes, "that ye work is as

[1] Dr. Hill's *Organs and Organ Cases*, and Dr. Gee's booklet on the Gloucester organs.
[2] Hopkins and Rimbault, op. cit. p. 123.

yet very imperfect, and that 4 score pound is not only a sufficient but a liberall reward for ye said work" (Smith had sent in a bill for £130). Quite possibly there was a little professional animosity in the verdict in each instance. Preston must have done quite a lot of work, since his activities extended over a considerable period, but only two records of his handiwork seem to have come to light:

Ripon Cathedral, 4th February 1667. "Agreed by the reverend the Deane and Chapter above sd to give unto Mr. Willm Preston Organ Maker the sume of Tenne pounds, for making the Organ in the sd Collegiate Church, to have five stops such as shall be approved by Mr. Brownhill or Mr. Sorrell (the newly appointed organist) to be good and sufficient and to uphold maintain and keep the same Organ in good and sufficient Condition for the space of Three years next after it shall be approved as above allowing the said Mr. Preston Five Shillings for each time he shall be sent for by the said Deane and Chapter for his charges."[1] If we may assume Thomas Preston, organist of Ripon from 1690 to 1730, to be a son of William, we can the more easily account for the organist's ability to repair the damage caused "by the fall of the Trumpett Stop amongst the other small pipes". This was in 1708. For his skill and pains the Chapter voted Thomas the sum of £10.[2]

Oxford, Magdalen College Chapel. Repairs only, in 1680, at a cost of £23 8*s*. In 1681 he was paid 6*s*. 8*d*.[3]

William Hathaway

If, as seems likely, the same maker was responsible for the two organs next mentioned, then we have another name to add to the small list of English organ-builders who celebrated the Restoration of the Monarchy by resuming their former craft.

London, St. Martin-in-the-Fields, 1637. Since Hathaway's organ contained "Nine Rods of Iron with stubbs [i.e. studds] fastened in them" and also "nine handles to pull them rods with, filed bright", it would appear to have contained nine registers. The builder was paid £13 13*s* "for casting of new pipes and fitting all things necessary concerning the Organs and for making A new sounding board and for three pairs of bellowes thereunto belonging"—this in addition to the cost of metal and other materials. The case of the old organ, almost certainly the work of John Howe (*c*. 1544), was utilised after it had been renovated and embellished by Jeremy Kellat the joiner, Zachary Taylor the carver, and George Portmann the painter. Thereafter we find the new instrument referred to in inventories of the period as "one fair Organ gylt standing upon A fframe of Timber upon the North side of the middle Ile betwixt the pullpit and the chauncell finished in and upon the feast day of the nativity of our

[1] *Registrum A* of Ripon, quoted in *Musical Times* (1902), p. 318.
[2] Dr. C. H. Moody's booklet on the Ripon organ (Ripon, 1913).
[3] Registers of St. Mary-Magdalen College, Oxford, by John Rouse Bloxam, vol. ii, p. cxxvii.

Lord and Saviour Jesus Christ 1637". £2 per annum was paid to Hathaway for its upkeep till 1640, and perhaps a year or two later. A reference, under date 18th September 1644, to "the gallery where the Organs lately stood", is suggestive of an untimely and regrettable fate.[1]

Worcester Cathedral. On July 26th 1663, Hathaway was paid £5 for visiting Worcester and advising the Dean and Chapter concerning a new organ. (Thomas Harris had made similar proposals in 1662). Later in the same year Hathaway was paid £30 towards the new organ. He seems to have constructed a chair organ and believed that he had obtained the contract for the new great organ. When the Dean and Chapter failed to let him proceed he petitioned the Archbishop of Canterbury. A letter written to Archbishop Sheldon by Bishop Robert Skinner deals with this.[2]

The Calendar of State Papers (Domestic) contain the following references to pre-Commonwealth organ-builders:

"Grant to Thos. Cradock, his Majesty's organ-maker, of £20 per annum for the oversight and tuning of H.M. Organs at St. James's and in the Privy Lodgings at Whitehall." May 8, 1626.

"To Adam Torless £140 for a new organ to be erected in the King's private chapel in the Castle of Windsor." November 29, 1628.

". . . to the King's servant Edward Norgate £140 to be employed in altering the organ in the Chapel at Hampton Court, and for making a new chaire organ there, comformable to those already made in the Royal Chapels at Whitehall and Greenwich." February 14, 1636–7.

Lancelot Pease

In the agreement between him and the Dean and Chapter of Canterbury, Pease is described as "of Cambridge, organ maker". He seems to have been established in business in the university town within a very few weeks of the accession of Charles II, and here he was fortunate enough to get the order for a chaire organ for King's College Chapel, a job which should have led to many others in the immediate neighbourhood. It probably did, but of these we have as yet no records. Repairs to a small organ at Norwich Cathedral and the order for an important new instrument at Canterbury came his way, so that by 1662 he would seem to have achieved some fame and reputation. A few years later, however (in 1667, if not before), we find him settled in Dublin, where he had obtained the position of a lay vicar-choral and thenceforward he combined the duties of a singer in the choir with those of a maker and repairer of organs. Though we do not know which came first, the order for the addition to the Christ Church organ or the lay clerkship, we shall probably be right in concluding that he was helped in his decision to make the Irish capital his future home by the pressure of competition in England. For it must have made a considerable difference to his prospects at Cambridge when, about 1662, Thomas Thamar migrated thither from Peterborough; more especially so, since history shows that Thamar was

[1] For fuller extracts and further information, see *The Organ*, No. 1, pp. 3–6.
[2] Bodleian MS., Tanner 45, fol. 19.

not only an energetic and resourceful man of business but in all probability the cleverer and more trustworthy of the two at their common trade.

Lancelot was alive and at work in Dublin as late as 1681, while a relation (probably a son) named John Pease, who seems to have succeeded to his English connection, was engaged in repairs to two Canterbury organs between the years 1673 and 1687.

Cambridge, King's College Chapel, 1660–1. Though the cases of Thomas Dallam's organ of 1605 survived the Civil War, there can have been little else, save perhaps the sound-boards and framework, which was capable of being used. Indeed the college authorities did not wait till they could get a new organ built or the old one repaired, but made shift with one lent them by their organist, Mr. Loosemore. For removing this instrument, which must have been quite a small one, from Loosemore's lodgings to the chapel and setting it up there Lancelot Pease was paid £1 15*s*. A few months later, when he had completed a chaire organ for the chapel, he received the same amount for taking it back to its owner.[1] There can be little doubt that this chaire organ, which cost £200, was the first instalment of a new two-manual organ, and that it was not, as usually stated, an addition to the one already existing. The great organ came later, and was the work, not of Pease, but of Thamar.

Norwich Cathedral, 1661. Mr. Richard Plumm, of Bury, sold an organ to the cathedral in 1661 for £45, and in the same year £18 was paid "to Mr. Pease for a new sett of pipes". The cost of "taking down ye organ, packing it, carriage &c." was £5, and the charge for gilding the front pipes a further £2.[2] It is possible that portions of this organ remained through successive rebuilds, at least as late as 1899.

Canterbury Cathedral, 1662. The organs at Canterbury were hacked about by the troopers of Colonel Sandys quite early in the Civil War, but they were not damaged beyond possibility of repair. At any rate, the old instrument was made playable at the Restoration and used until a new one was ready to be set up in its place. In his contract for this new double organ, drawn up and signed on 17th July 1662, Pease agreed to make the great organ "in length sixteene foot, and in height to the upper part of the Cornish three and twenty foot . . . and the chaire organ . . . seven foot in length, nine foot in height, and three foot wide". He also undertook that the said double organ should be "so painted at his own charges, as to the said Deane and Chapter by and with the advice of Artists . . . shall seeme most convenient". The chaire organ was to be set up and made "fitt for the churches use and service" by Christmas 1662, and the great organ "by or before the like ffeast then next following".

On their part the Dean and Chapter promised to find "a convenient roome or place within their p'cinct for him the said Lancelott Pease and his servants or workmen to make and frame the said Double organ and fitt it

[1] Willis and Clarke, op. cit., vol. i, p. 519.
[2] *The Musical Times* (1904), 704.

for the Quire", and to pay him, besides the old organ, the sum of £600 in certain agreed-upon instalments, as well as a further sum "not exceeding ffiftie pounds, as they with the advice of Artists and men of judgement in such matters shall deem answerable to his deservings in this affair".

The specification of this very interesting instrument was as follows:

"*Great Organ*, 13 *stops*

One diapason of mettall
one diapason stopt of wood
two principalls of mettall
two fifteenthes of mettall
a small and great twelft of mettall
two two and twentieths of mettall
a flute of mettall
a recorder of wood
a tierce of mettal.

Chaire Organ, 6 *stops*

two stopt diapasons of wood
one principall of mettall in the front
one fifteenth of mettall
one fifteenth of wood
one flute of wood."

Nothing is said as to the compass of this organ, but the original designs for the two cases are still in existence.[1] These show that the great case was to consist of five towers, and the chaire of three; but the paintings and prints of this organ *in situ* rather lead one to suppose that the designs were somewhat modified in execution. All, however, portray a well-proportioned case, richly carved and otherwise ornamented, that was fully worthy of its prominent position on the north side of the quire of this famous church. The case lasted till 1784, but the organ required reconstruction before a quarter of a century had elapsed. (See later, under Father Smith.)

Dublin, Christ Church Cathedral, 1667. In *The Musical Antiquary* for January 1913 Dr. W. H. Grattan Flood states that Lancelot Pease, lay vicar-choral of Christ Church Cathedral, supplied a chaire organ with five stops at a cost of £80. "The Sound board and Roller board to be good and well seasoned oak, with a set of keys suitable to the Great Organ." The suggestion here is that the chaire organ was an addition or a substitution, and not the first instalment of a double organ.

Dublin, St. Audoen's Church, 1681. Dr. Flood is again the authority for the statement that Pease was paid £110 for building a new organ for this church in 1681.[2] A further sum of £40 was paid to a Mr. Wiseman for "gilding and beautifying" this instrument.

[1] Reproductions of both will be found in Mr. S. W. Harvey's booklet on Canterbury Cathedral organs and in Rev. Andrew Freeman's *English Organ Cases*.
[2] *Journal of the Royal Society of Antiquaries of Ireland*, vol. xl.

A few years before the Commonwealth we get a parting glimpse of some of the larger English organs in an interesting account of a journey through England in 1634,[1] from which the following extracts are taken:

"*York.* There we saw and heard a faire, large, high organ, newly built richly gilt, carv'd and painted; and deep and sweet snowy row of quiristers.[2]

"*Durham.* Away then wee were call'd to prayers, where wee were wrapt with the sweet sound and richnesse of a fayre organ, which cost £1000; and the orderly, devout, and melodious harmony of the quiristers.

"*Carlisle.* The organs and voices did well agree, the one being like a shrill bagpipe, the other like the Scottish tone.

"*Lichfield.* And no sooner were we lighted, but the Cathedral knell call'd us away to prayers: there we entred a stately, neat fabricke; the organs and voyces were deep and sweet, their anthems we were much delighted with, and of the voyces, 2 trebles, 2 counter-tennors, and 2 bases, that equally on each side of the quire most melodiously acted and performed their parts.

"*Hereford.* There we heard a most sweet organ, and voyces of all parts, tenor, counter-tenor, treble, and base; and amongst that orderly, snowy crew of quiristers, our landlord guide did act his part in a deep and sweet diapason.

"*Exeter.* The organ here is rich, delicate, and lofty, and has more additions than any other; and large pipes of an extraordinary length.

"*Gloucester.* Here were wee admiring and whispering till the Cathedral, voyces whisper'd us away to prayers, and so soon as wee heard those voyces and organs, and had view'd their fayrely glass'd and carv'd work cloyster, wee hasted away.

"*Bristol.* In her wee found (besides that fayre and strong fabricke of the Cathedrall, which was newly finish'd) 18 churches, which all are fayrely beautify'd, richly adorn'd, and sweetly kept; and in the major part of them are neat, rich, and melodious organs, that are constantly play'd on. In her [the Cathedrall] are rich organs, lately beautify'd, and indifferent good quiristers.

"*Wells.* The Cathedrall was beautify'd with ancient monuments and rich organs."

A further interesting reference to the use of the organ in York Minster (during the Civil War) is given by Thos. Mace in *Musick's Monument* (1676),

[1] "A relation of a Short Survey of Twenty-six Counties, briefly describing the Cities and their Scytuations, and the Corporate Townes and Castles therein: observed in a Seaven Weekes' Journey begun at the City of Norwich, and from thence into the North,—on Monday, August 11th, 1634, and ending at the same Place. By a Captaine, a Lieutenant, and an Ancient (Ensign): all three of the Military Company of Norwich" (Brit. Mus. Lansdowne MSS., No. 213, folios 317–48).

[2] They report that at York there was only one organ in addition to that at the cathedral.

when he gives his impression of the services held during the siege of York in 1644.

"Now here you must take notice that they had then a Custom in that Church (which I hear not of in any other Cathedral, which was) that always before the Sermon, the whole Congregation sang a Psalm, together with the Quire and the Organ; And you must also know, that there was then a most Excellent—large—plump—lusty—full-speaking—Organ, which cost (as I am credibly informed) a Thousand Pounds. This Organ I say (when the Psalm was set before the Sermon) being let out, into all its Fulness of Stops, together with the Quire began the Psalm. But when That vast-concording-unity of the whole Congregational Chorus, came (as I may say) Thundering in, even so, as it made the very Ground shake under us: (oh, the unutterable ravishing Soul's delight!) in which I was so transported, and wrapt up into High contemplations that there was no room left in my whole man, viz, Body, Soul and Spirit, for any thing below Divine and Heavenly Raptures."

The Commonwealth

Objections to the use of the organs in divine worship were no new thing. The argument against them was that they detracted from the true worship of God in its purest spiritual form. Some instances have been given on page 38.

In 1552 the organ at St. Paul's Cathedral was not used and it was only restored when Mary came to the throne in 1553, and in 1536 the Lower House of Convocation included organ-playing amongst the "84 Faults and Abuses of Religion".[1]

In 1550 many organs were removed. An injunction (4 Ed., vi, 26th October 1550) made to guard the interests of two organists of St. George's Chapel, Windsor Castle, decreed "that they should receive their salaries during their lyves, if they continue in that Colledge, in as large and ample a manner as if organ playing had still continued in the Church".

During the reign of Queen Elizabeth, in 1563 (13th February), a resolution before the Lower House of Convocation calling for the removal of all organs from places of worship was lost by a single vote.

A document of about 1567, entitled, *The Praise of Music* (Brit. Mus., Royal MSS. 136), states: "Not so few as one hundred organs were taken down and the pipes sold to make pewter dishes."[2]

In 1644 organ-playing was prohibited in church services by an ordinance of the Lords and Commons "for the speedy demolishing of all organs, images and all matters of superstitious monuments in all Cathedralls, and Collegiate or Parish-Churches and Chapels, throughout the kingdom of England and the Dominion of Wales, the better to accomplish the blessed reformation so happily begun and to remove offences and things illegal in the worship of God".

[1] P. Scholes, *The Puritans and Music* (Oxford, 1934).
[2] The same type of attitude towards organs was found in Switzerland, and many instruments were destroyed.

By this date most of the damage had been done, and not only by the uncouth soldiery of the years immediately before this, but by reason of nearly a century of antagonisms towards the organ, with only occasional patches of enthusiasm and toleration.

Many reports of the destruction of church organs, monuments and stained glass at the time of the Commonwealth are still available, and it must be remembered that most of them were written by zealous anti-Puritans. The following extracts, taken from *Mercurius Rusticus; the Country's Complaint recounting the Sad Events of this Unparraleld Warr*, 12*mo*. 1647[1] are examples of many such references.

(The soldiers must have done their work of spoliation at Canterbury in a perfunctory manner because Culmer, in *Cathedral News from Canterbury*, in 1644, says that the troopers "began to play the tune of Zealous Soldier on the organ, or case of whistles, *which never was in tune since*.")

"*Westminster*. The soldiers of Westborne and Caewoods' Companies were quartered in the Abbey Church, where they brake down the rayl about the Altar, and burnt it in the place where it stood: they brake downe the Organs, and pawned the pipes at severall ale-houses for pots of ale. They put on some of the Singing-men's surplices, and, in contempt of that canonicall habite, ran up and down the Church; he that wore the surplice was the hare, the rest were the hounds.

"*Exeter*. They brake downe the organs, and taking two or three hundred pipes with them in a most scorneful and contemptuous manner, went up and downe the streets piping with them; and meeting with some of the Choristers of the Church, whose surplices they had stolne before, and imployed them to base servill offices, scoffingly told them 'Boyes, we have spoyled your trade, you must goe and sing hot pudding pyes.'

"*Peterborough*. When their unhallowed toylings had made them out of wind, they took breath afresh on two pair of organs.

"*Canterbury*. They violated the monuments of the dead, and spoyled the organs.

"*Chichester*. They leave the destructive and spoyling part to be finished by the common soldiers; break down the organs, and, dashing the pipes with their pole-axes, scoffingly said, 'Harke how the organs goe.'

"*Winchester*. They entered the Church with colours flying, and drums beating: they rode up through the body of the Church and Quire, until they came to the altar, there they rudely pluck downe the table and brake the rayle, and afterwards carrying it to an ale-house, they set it on fire, and in that fire burnt the Books of Common Prayer, and all the Singing books belonging to the Quire: they threw downe the organs, and brake the Stories of the Old and New Testament, curiously cut out of carved work."

"*Wells*. May 1643. Mr. Alexander Pophams souldiers after dynner rusht into the church, broke down the windows, organs, fonte, seates, in the quere the busshops see besides many other villaines."

[1] Edited by Dr. Bruno Ryves, later Dean of Windsor, *Mercurius Rusticus* was originally published in numbers, and in its collected form it went through several editions. See also P. Scholes, *The Puritans and Music* (Oxford, 1934).

Other organs were suffered to decay, and those built by "Father" Howe are typical in this matter. By the time of his death he had lived to see most of his works neglected, decayed or sold for scrap.

There are few survivals of organ cases from pre-Revolution times, and little evidence of pipework.[1] Only two cases are in their original homes: those at Old Radnor, then an obscure little town, and King's College, Cambridge. Of the rest, the "Milton" organ at Tewkesbury Abbey is covered by a case which dates from 1597, that at Stanford-on-Avon (Northamptonshire) from 1580 and does not contain any usable pipework. There is a Flemish organ case at Hatfield House dating from 1609; a small case at Appleby, possibly made before 1571; an excellent case at Framlingham, Suffolk, *c.* 1570; the Choir organ case of Gloucester Cathedral, 1579; an organ case formerly in the old Chapel, St. John's College, Cambridge, 1635 and a few others in museums, etc. These modest remains stand in poor contrast with the fine structures, which, in spite of the passage of time, neglect, vandalism, and war damage, are frequent in many parts of Europe.

Scholes[2] has pointed out that the greatest destruction of organs was done before the organisation of the well-disciplined New Model Army (1644) and the official order of the same year. The spirit of rowdyism rather than of religious zeal prevailed. The Puritans did not object to music and organs as such, but rather to their use in worship. There was no mention of the use of organs in the New Testament and therefore they led to idolatry and were displeasing to God!

Not all organs were destroyed, and some were allowed to remain. Those in St. Paul's Cathedral, York and Lincoln Cathedrals, Christ's College, and probably also King's College, Cambridge, remained in place.

Evelyn notes in his Diary for 12th July 1654, ten years after the Parliament order to destroy all church organs: "Next we walked to Magdalen College, where we saw the library and chapel, which was likewise in pontifical order, the altar only I think turned tablewise, and there was still the double organ, which abominations (as now esteemed) were almost universally demolished; Mr. Gibbon, that famous musician, giving us a taste of his skill and talents on that instrument."

The Magdalen organ was removed by Cromwell for use at Hampton Court by arrangement with the fellows, and the college books record that in 1660 £16 10*s.* was paid to have the organ taken back to the college.[3]

Although it is evident that the Commonwealth was not a time of prosperity for organ-builders, organ-playing still continued to a limited extent in churches but not during divine service, in private houses, and probably in inns and other public places.

Southey, in *The Doctor*, quotes "a writer of that age" in the following words: "That nothing may be wanting to the height of luxury and unpiety of this abomination, they have translated them out of the churches to set them up in

[1] Still in use.

[2] P. Scholes, *The Puritans and Music.*

[3] A further entry shows that when a certain Dr. Clarke was running for vice-president of the college, one Fellow objected to vote for him because he consented to the giving away of the college organs to Cromwell.

taverns chanting their dithyrambics and bestial bacchanalias to the tune of those instruments which were wont to assist them in the celebration of God's praise and regulate the voices of the worst singers of the world—which are the English in their churches at present."

Ward, in the *London Spy* (1698–1709), refers to a music house in a tavern called the Mitre at Wapping (London), which had an organ.

Robert Hooke the great natural philosopher who later advanced the science of physics, "learned to play twenty lessons on the organ" when he was at Westminster School during the Commonwealth.[1] Scholes has shown that to a certain extent organ-playing and learning to play the instrument continued during the Commonwealth.[2] At times the attitude of senior army officers was to preserve the organs and not to permit the soldiery to indulge in wanton destruction. In 1641, a Scottish officer intervened to save two cathedral organs at Durham,[3] and at Worcester the commanding officer Essex "proclaimed that no soldier should plunder either church or private house, upon pain of death".

A soldier's letter written at this time reports that "Sabbath day about the time of morning prayer we went to the Minster, where the pipes played and the puppets sang so sweetely, that some of our soldiers could not forbeare dauncynge in the holie quire, whereat the Baalists were sore displeased".[4]

Milton had an organ, though not that which bears his name at Tewkesbury Abbey. Hingeston, Cromwell's private organist, had one in his own house, as the Roundhead captain, Silas Taylor, did also.[5]

In Scotland a similar anti-organ movement had been established for many years. In 1573 the Privy Council had decreed concerning Aberdeen: "The organis, with all expeditioum, be removed the kirk, and maid proffite of, to the use and Support of the poor"; and in 1633 the Kirk Session at Holyrood reported that the organ there remained in "the yle, idle, mothing and consuming" and might be "sold for a tolerable pryce, and the money given into the poore".[6] Scotland did not reintroduce organs until the nineteenth century; the official authorisation of organs was dated as follows: the Established Church, 1866; United Presbyterian Church, 1872; the Free Church, 1883.

In 1660 came the Restoration of the Monarchy and organs were hastily repaired and again used in church services.

[1] *Dictionary of National Biography*.
[2] P. Scholes, *The Puritans and Music*.
[3] *Musical Times* (February 1900).
[4] Letter of Sergeant Nehemiah Wharton, *Archaeologia*, vol. xxv.
[5] Cavalier poets and dramatists loved to poke fun at the Puritans for their hatred of organs in divine worship. Overbury in his *Characters* (1614) says concerning a Puritan: "a paire of organs blow him out o' th' parish." Middleton in *The Family of Love* (Act iii, Scene 2) makes Mistress Page express horror at the idea of organs: "She hopes her body has none." In Marmion's *A Fine Companion* there is a Puritan who is out of love with his own members because they are called organs.
[6] Dalzell, *Musical Memories of Scotland*, pp. 126, 129.

Pepys recorded a few cases of the return of the use of organs in the churches of the London district:

"July 8, 1660 (Lord's day). To White-Hall Chapel, where I got in with ease, by going before the Lord Chancellor with Mr. Kipps. Here I heard very good musique, the first time that ever I remember to have heard the organs, and singing-men in surplices, in my life."

"April 5, 1667. To Hackney, where good neat's tongue, and things to eat and drink, and very merry, the weather being mighty pleasant; and here I was told, that at their church they have a fair pair of Organs, which play while the people sing, which I am mighty glad of, wishing the like at our church at London, and would give £50 towards it."

"April 21, 1667. To Hackney Church, where very full, and found much difficulty to get pews, I offering the sexton money, and he could not help me. . . . That which I went chiefly to see was the young ladies of the school, whereof there is great store, very pretty; and also the organ, which is handsome and tunes the psalms, and plays with the people; which is mighty pretty, and makes me mighty earnest to have a pair at our church; I having almost a mind to give them a pair, if they would settle a maintenance on them for it."

At this time there was considerable difficulty in procuring organs or finding sufficient skilled workers to make them. It was not until the lapse of more than half a century after the Restoration that our parish churches began commonly to be supplied with organs. In 1708, when Hatton published his *New View of London*, a very large number of our places of public worship were without them.[1] Drake in his *Eboracum*, p. 338 (York, 1733), says: "There is now only one parish church in the whole city of York that possesses an organ; and that came from the Popish Chapel, the curators of which purchased it from Durham Cathedral."

Burney[2] says: "After the suppression of the Cathedral Service and prohibition of the Liturgy, some of the ecclesiastical instruments had been sold to private persons, and others but partially destroyed; these, being produced, were hastily repaired, and erected for present use. A sufficient number of workmen for the immediate supply of cathedrals and parish churches with organs not being found in our own country, it was thought expedient to invite foreign builders of known abilities to settle among us; and the premiums offered on this occasion brought over the two celebrated workmen, Smith and Harris."

The Restoration and After

The Restoration Period in England: the Work of "Father" Bernard Smith and Renatus Harris.

"Father" Bernard Smith

For eighteen years our native craftsmen had no opportunity to build new organs, or even to keep old instruments in good trim, apart from an occasional

[1] Hopkins and Rimbault, *The Organ*, 3rd Ed. (London, 1877).
[2] *History of Music*. Vol. iii, p. 235.

small house organ. As we have already seen, before 1642, and in fact from the beginning of Elizabeth's reign, periods of Puritanism had affected adversely the art of organ-building in England. New ideas were urgently required. The builders who were still at work in 1660 were soon outclassed by two young men, both of whom had served their pupilage in continental workshops. One, Bernard Smith, was a German, and the other, Renatus (or René) Harris, was the French-born son of an Englishman.

A search for many years in England and Germany has failed to yield any clue concerning the origin of Smith. Within a few months of the return of Charles II he came to England and (according to Burney[1] and Hawkins[2]) he was accompanied by his nephews, Gerard and Bernard.

"Bernard may have been a mistake for Christian, for nothing is heard of a second builder so named. On the other hand the contemporary State Papers, Domestic Series, contain many references to a Lieutenant Bernard Smith, an officer in his Majesty's Army, and to his widow, so that it is quite possible that the historians are correct, and that Christian came over to take Bernard's place when Bernard took to soldiering."[3]

There is no reason to doubt Burney's[4] statement that Smith's first organ was for the Chapel Royal, Whitehall; but if so, this was not the one referred to by Samuel Pepys[5] as having been played at the service on 8th July 1660 (the first he had ever heard), three months after the proclamation of Charles II. This was not a new instrument, but the old one which had been taken down and "embezled" during the Commonwealth, recovered through the efforts of John Playford, and set up in its old place a few weeks after the Restoration. Nor was it as is so often stated, the fine instrument which stood in the Banqueting Hall, whose case now adorns the Chapel of St. Peter ad Vincula in the Tower of London, for this organ was not built till the hall had been turned into a chapel, namely in 1699. It was neither of these but the "fair doble organ", built under the supervision of John Hingeston at a total cost of £959 18*s*. 10*d*. and completed, it appears, in October 1662. Nothing is known of its contents, but Burney says that it was put together in such haste that it "did not justify the expectations of those who were able to judge of its excellence". Smith learnt a lesson that he never forgot, and ever afterwards he refused to be hurried over his work, even if it meant the loss of a patron. Unfortunately this first specimen of the great builder's handiwork perished, together with the chapel and almost the entire palace, in a fire which broke out on 4th January 1697.

Smith's employment at the Royal Court was of great help in establishing his position and making him known. Curiously enough, though he is spoken

[1] C. Burney, *History of Music*, vol. iii, p. 236. Bernard Smith and Renatus Harris both gave evidence at a lawsuit in September 1703. The former was "then about seventy-four" and the latter "about fifty-one".

[2] Sir John Hawkins, *History of Music*, vol. iii, p. 430.

[3] A. Freeman, *Father Smith* (London, 1930). Against this suggestion must be set the fact that Burney hardly ever got right the names of organ-builders mentioned by him in his works.

[4] C. Burney, *History of Music*, vol. iii, p. 236.

[5] S. Pepys, *Diary* (1660).

of as the King's Organ Maker as far back as 1671, he was not given the appointment until 30th May 1681, when he succeeded James Farr, whose work he had probably done, or helped to do, for nearly twenty years. Hingeston was officially regarded as the chief organ-builder, with the official title of "keeper and Repairer of His Majesty's Organs and other Instruments", and it was under his direction that Smith worked till Hingeston's death in 1683. Smith was friendly with Dr. Blow and Henry Purcell, who supported him, and the three were often in close consultation over matters connected with the court organs.

Smith's workmanship was sound, though sometimes rough, and his materials were always of first-rate quality. Someone who knew Smith reported to Burney that the organ-builder was particularly careful in the choice of his wood. He was said to be careless or even scornful of the niceties of extreme finish, and when comments were made on the rough appearance of a pipe he was about to voice, his reply was that, though the pipe looked like the devil, he would make it speak like an angel. It is probable that Harris was inferior to Smith in tonal matters, but in those of mechanism he was superior to his German rival.

Sir John Sutton[1] who knew several of Smith's organs, which had not been greatly altered although at the time (1847) they were about a century and a half old, says the great beauty of Smith's organs consisted in the sweetness and brilliance of the wooden pipes. His mixtures also were very fine and brilliant without the shrillness introduced by Snetzler. His bass was very firm and decided, and the tone of his stops was even throughout their compass. The touch was the worst feature of his instruments—"very disagreeable to those unaccustomed to play on them, feeling as though cotton wool was placed under each key. . . . The bellows in common with all organs built anterior to the present century, supplied the wind-chest in a very irregular manner, and caused the organ to sound tremulous: there were generally two single bellows, as his organs were seldom large enough to require more."

Many stories concerning Smith have been handed down and were only recorded by Sutton in 1847.[2] Sutton states that nearly all old and worthy organs were ascribed to Smith by those who did not trouble to determine the true facts. Smith was said to have been attracted to work in England by the offer of premiums to encourage the resuscitation of the organ-building art after the Restoration. Smith was said to have been a pupil of Christian Förmer (or Förner). This may well have been true, for there was no better instructor in the art of organ-building in Germany at the time. Our knowledge of Förmer comes from the *Almanache* of J. N. Forkel (1749–1818), the biographer of J. S. Bach. Förmer was born in 1610 at Wettin, Germany, where his father was burgomaster and a master-carpenter. His brother-in-law, John William Stegmann, burgomaster, organist and organ-builder, taught him mathematics, physics and organ-building. The invention of the

[1] Sir J. Sutton, *Short of Account Organs* (London, 1847).

[2] Ibid. Smith lived "over again the Cock, in Suffolk Street near Charing Crosse" between 1694 and 1697 (document in library of St. Paul's Cathedral).

water-manometer or water-gauge for measuring the pressure of wind in organs and some improvements in the bellows system are ascribed to him. His chief organs were the instruments at St. Ulrich at Halle and the Auguste Castle at Weissenfels, of thirty-three stops, two manuals and pedals. He died in 1677 at the age of sixty-seven.[1]

Smith was a member of a small and highly select London club founded by Richard Bentley, the great classical scholar, in 1697, when he was Royal Librarian and Chaplain in Ordinary to the King, as well as Doctor of Divinity and Fellow of the Royal Society. It consisted of a small group of intimate friends who met once or twice a week in his apartments at St. James's. The original members were Richard Bentley, John Evelyn, John Locke, Isaac Newton, Christopher Wren, "names sufficient in themselves to render illustrious the age in which they lived, and the country which gave them birth".[2]

Into this select society of "friends who happened to be among the greatest intellectual characters that the history of mankind can produce" the German organ-builder, who could not write English correctly (and probably could not speak it), was admitted. The only known portrait of Smith hangs in the Examination Schools, Oxford.

Smith was a capable organist and acted in this capacity at St. Margaret's, Westminster, from 1675 until his death. His salary was £20 a year.

Smith was twice married. His first wife, Anne, sometimes went into the country to collect payments due to him. Thus she was at Worcester in 1686. There was at least one child of this union, a daughter, who married Christopher Shrider, her father's foreman and successor: but she must have died before her father, for less than two months after the old man's death Shrider remarried in Westminster Abbey. Anne died on 9th September 1689, at the age of sixty-three, and was buried at Upham, Hants. The inscription on her tomb described her as "wife of Mr. Bernard Smith, of London, one of His Majesty's servants, and chief of all that this nation has known in the art of making organs".

His second wife was Elizabeth Houghton, daughter of Humphrey Houghton. The making of a fresh will in 1699 suggests that the wedding took place in that year. In this will Smith bequeaths to all his brothers and sisters "and unto all and everyone of their children, the sume of one shilling a peece". Everything else, "all and singular, my ready money, plate, Rings, Jewells, Household Goods, Bills, Bonds, and Estate of what nature or kind soever it doth consist" he left unto his loving wife Elizabeth, whom he appointed sole executrix.

Smith died in February 1708 and was buried on the 20th of that month in St. Margaret's churchyard on the south side of the church. His widow proved

[1] Forkel says that in 1684 a work on organ-building by him was published posthumously: *Vollkommener Bericht wie eine aus wahrem Gründe der Natur in allen ihren Stück en nach Anweisung der mathematischen Wissenschaften solle gemacht, probirt und gebraucht werden, und wie man Glocken nach dem Monochordo mensuriren und giessen.* (A work on the vibration numbers of various bells and strings.)

[2] Bishop Monk in his *Life of Richard Bentley.*

the will on 17th March and not long afterwards took another husband, John Stockwell, whose interest in organs was confined to collecting debts due to his wife. Anyhow, the Stockwells lived in Bond Street and ignored the organ-building business which was taken over by Christopher Shrider. Smith's last organ was disposed of in 1711, being advertised "to be sold a great penny-worth".[1]

Smith's two nephews, after working with their uncle for a number of years, eventually started each of them on his own, Gerard before 1689 and Christian (probably) about 1690.

Why did Smith attain and hold so lofty a place in the esteem of his contemporaries and successors?

> "His organs were by no means mechanically perfect; indeed, in this respect they were probably surpassed by those of his clever and versatile rival, Renatus Harris. Smith was certainly a great artist as a voicer; though here again, Harris was a close second, and in regard to reed stops quite possibly his equal.
>
> "I believe it was because his early instruments were a revelation in ensemble to our island craftsmen. From the first he set a standard that they attempted, not altogether unsuccessfully, to reach. Thus, a Father Smith organ became an ideal and eventually a tradition which have never been lost to sight. It will be remembered that Smith came from a land where there were large and powerful organs with a considerable variety of dynamic and tonal resources. He found, on his arrival here, that the largest instruments were of modest proportions, and tonally exceedingly limited. They consisted of one or, at most, two keyboards. On the chief manual, over a foundation of two (occasionally three) 8-ft. stops—one open, the other stopped—was built up a superstructure of 4-ft., 2-ft. and 1-ft. stops (sometimes duplicated) with (very occasionally) a twelfth (the last named a somewhat late innovation). Such an organ must have been thoroughly well-made to have satisfied our church musicians, and to have won praise from such a man as John Milton. But it would sound crude to our ears; and it probably sounded crude to those brought up to admire it, after they had had an opportunity of comparing it with one of similar size made by Bernard Smith. For Smith, finding he was expected to provide organs of about the same dimensions and disposition, like a wise man, made no fuss about it, but readily complied. Probably he recognised its artistic possibilities. Anyhow, after slightly modifying the scheme to include mixture work, he directed all his genius towards making it a thing of beauty and delight. The curious thing is that, after he had taken in hand and transformed the old English organ, the result was still quite as distinctly national as ever. On foundations carefully laid by the Howes, the Chappingtons, the Dallams, and other worthy masters of the craft, Smith raised a superstructure that has resisted all attempts at demolition. There have been additions, extensions and modifications but such of these as have endured are all in accord with the original nucleus."[2]

[1] Mackenzie Walcot, *Memories of Westminster* (1849).
[2] Andrew Freeman, *The Organ*, vol. v, p. 134.

A List of Father Smith's Organs

Auckland Castle: Bishop of Durham's private chapel, 1688. Organ (enlarged) and case remain.

Bishop's Waltham Church, Hants: Now at Cheltenham. (Doubtful.)

Bridgetown (Barbados): St. Michael's Church, 1697. Destroyed.

Cambridge:

Christ's College Chapel, 1705. Case and some pipes remain.

Emmanuel College Chapel, 1686. Case remains.

Pembroke College Chapel, 1708. Cost, £210. Case and some pipes remain.

St. Mary-the-Great, 1697. Case remains *in situ*.

Trinity College Chapel.[1] Repairs to Thamar's organ in 1686. New organ (cost, £160) in 1694, and a second instrument in 1708 (his last organ). Enlarged case and many old pipes incorporated in present organ.

Canterbury Cathedral, 1684*:* A new organ in Pease's old case. Cost, £376 8*s*. 6*d*.

Carlisle Cathedral, 1683 (?)*:* Superseded in 1806.

Chester Cathedral: Now at St. Paul's Cathedral, Valetta, Malta.

Chollerton, near Newcastle: Given in 1850 by Sir J. Sutton.

Cirencester: Parish Church. 1683. Traditional.

Coventry: Holy Trinity Church, 1696. Repairs to Hayward's organ, costing £30.

Donyland Hall (near Colchester)*:* Case now at Hadleigh Church, Suffolk.

Durham Cathedral, 1684–5*:* Cost, £700 and old organ. Choir case now in University College Chapel, Durham. (Some of original stops incorporated in present Harrison organ.) Main case and front pipes erected on wall of south aisle of cathedral.

Eton College: Chapel, 1700–1. Case now at Dominican Church, Rugeley.

Gloucester Cathedral, 1687*:* Substantial repairs at cost of £150.

Hampton Court: Chapel Royal, 1690. Warrant issued to Smith, but the organ was burnt before erection. The present instrument was built by Shrider in 1712.

Highclere Castle, Hants (uncertain)*:* Removed to St. Maurice Church, Winchester, in 1756.

Hounslow Heath: King James's Travelling Organ; afterwards at Winchenden and Stow House. Now in U.S.A.

[1] Dr. Richard Bentley (Master of Trinity College from 1700 till his death in 1742) was a brilliant scholar and a far-sighted reformer, but rather overmasterful. His scheme for the renovation of the chapel and the provision of a new organ was carried through in the teeth of a vigorous and bitter opposition. Some of his opponents even accused him of spending money on the chapel in order to fit it for the reception of the new and unnecessary instrument. One fellow of the college (a Mr. Miller) in *Some Remarks upon a Letter entitled the Present State of Trinity College in Cambridge* published in 1710, said that Bentley "had promised the old organist, one of his club, whom he called Father Smith, that he should make the College an organ, soon after he was master. The old man continually dunn'd him for his promise and at last told him he had near made it, the price, I think, was about £1,500, which made it almost necessary to beautify the Chapel for the reception of this costly instrument".

Many of the members of Bentley's club, including Isaac Newton, were interested in acoustics, in particular, in its mathematical aspects.

Hull: Holy Trinity. A few pipes are in the present organ.
Isleworth: All Saints' Church. Replaced 1790.
Kendal Parish Church, 1702: Now in St. Cuthbert's Church, Darwen.
Leicester: St. Margaret's Church. Case now in Bishop St. Chapel, Leicester. Some ranks of Smith pipes in use in present Nicholson organ at St. Margaret's.
Liverpool:
St. Nicholas (the "Old" Church), 1684.
St. Peter's (the "New" Church).
London:
Banqueting House Chapel, 1699. Case now at St. Peter-ad-Vincula, Tower of London.
Danish Church, Wellclose Square, 1696.
Dulwich College Chapel, *c.* 1669.
St. Anne, Soho, 1699. Harris's organ was removed from Queen's Chapel, St. James's Palace, repaired by Smith in 1703. (Church and rebuilt organ destroyed 1940.)
St. Clement Danes, Strand, *c.* 1690. Case and some remaining stops destroyed (with the church) in 1941.
St. Dunstan-in-the-East. Some pipework formerly at Bradfield Church, Essex.
St. Giles, Cripplegate, 1688. Minor repairs.
St. Giles-in-the-Fields, 1671. Present case may be Father Smith's.
St. James', Garlickhithe, 1697. Case (somewhat altered) and some stops remain.
St. James, Piccadilly, 1691. Repairs after removal from Queen's Chapel, Whitehall.
St. Katherine Cree, 1686. Case remains.
St. Luke, Chelsea (old church).
St. Margaret, Westminster, 1675. Cost, £200.
St. Martin-in-the-Fields, 1674. Doubtful.
St. Martin, Ludgate, *c.* 1684. Destroyed.
St. Mary-at-Hill, 1692–3. Destroyed.
St. Mary-Woolnoth, 1681. Case (probably by Robert Dallam) and some pipes still in use.
St. Nicholas, Deptford, 1697.
St. Olave, Southwark. Traditional. Destroyed.
St. Paul's Cathedral, 1695–6. Case and some pipes still in use. (Small open diapason and violone, etc.)
St. Peter, Cornhill, 1681. Case and some pipes remain.
Temple Church, 1683–7. Much pipework in use until its destruction in 1941.
Westminster Abbey. Repairs and additions in 1666 and 1694.
Whitehall Palace, Old Chapel Royal, 1662. His first organ.
Maidstone: Eccles Church. Formerly in New College, Oxford; rebuilt 1953 by Norman and Beard.
Manchester Cathedral, 1684: Existed, almost as built, until its destruction in 1940.

Northampton: All Saints' Church (formerly in the gallery). A two-manual chamber organ, then belonging to Canon Sutton, Earl's Colne, Essex. Now at Compton Wynyates.

Northiam, near Rye: Brickwell House. Another chamber organ with pipes entirely of wood.

Norton-by-Galby, 1701: Ralph Dallam's organ enlarged; afterwards at Rugby Church, but since destroyed.

Oxford:

Christchurch Cathedral, 1680 (or 1685). Case intact.

St. Mary-the-Virgin, 1675–6. Cost, with additions, £361 17*s.* 6*d.* Case and some pipework in use until fire in 1948. A little pipework and casework salvaged and used in present Walker organ.

Sheldonian Theatre, 1671. New organ; cost, £126. Some pipes now at Paignton Church; part of case at Pembroke College Chapel, Oxford.

Petersfield: Formerly belonging to Mr. Seymour Powell. A chamber organ with wooden pipes.

Rochester Cathedral: Repairs and additions in 1668 and 1677.

Rougham Hall, Norfolk: A chamber organ with wooden pipes, afterwards removed to Dereham Church.

St. Asaph's Cathedral, 1685: Repairs only.

St. David's Cathedral, c. 1704: Cost, £290.

Saltwood Rectory, near Hythe: A chamber organ with all its pipes of wood, now in Canterbury Cathedral.

Southwell Cathedral: Traditional.

Sproatley: St. Swithun's (?).

Staunton Harold, Leics.: Private Chapel of Earl Ferrers. Still in "original" condition. (Doubtful; may be by Smith's uncle, restored by Mander 1955.)

Walsall Parish Church: Afterwards at Stowmarket Church, but now destroyed.

Wells Cathedral, 1664: Doubtful.

West Walton Church, Norfolk: Destroyed.

Wigan Parish Church, 1708.

Windsor:

King's Private Chapel, 1673. Later at St. Mary, Walton-on-Thames (?).

St. George's Chapel Royal, 1681. Repairs only.

Worcester Cathedral, 1686: Repairs only. A six-stop chamber organ in south choir aisle, repaired by Green & Nicholson, said to be once the property of Handel.

York: "Popish Chapel-in-the-Manor", 1685. Part of George Dallam's Durham organ rebuilt. Afterwards at St. Michael-le-Belfry, York; broken up in 1885.[1]

[1] This list has been prepared from notes supplied by the late Rev. Andrew Freeman, with additions made by the author. There is a chamber organ in a private collection (J. W. Lane) by Christian Smith, 1643, probably an uncle or older brother. A small organ at Lichfield Cathedral is probably by Father Smith.

Renatus Harris

About the year 1642 Thomas Harris, then a middle-aged organ-builder, left for France to continue his trade which for eighteen years was suppressed in England. His wife was the daughter of "Old Dallow" (almost certainly Thomas Dallam). Their child, Renatus or René, was born in France about the year 1652. No record of Thomas as a master organ-builder in France has been found; he may have worked for his brother-in-law, Robert. The boy Renatus was nurtured amongst the fine, large French organs of the time of Louis XIV. Burney says that the Harris family returned to England "not many months" after Bernard Smith had arrived from Germany.[1]

It is possible that the Harris family first settled at Salisbury, for in the Articles of Agreement drawn up in 1666 between the elder man and the Dean and Chapter of Worcester he is described as Thomas Harris of New Sarum. Certainly the first recorded work of Thomas was the setting up in Salisbury Cathedral of the old pre-Restoration organ, which had been taken down at the outbreak of the Civil War. Curious to relate, father and son each built a new instrument for this cathedral: Thomas, a small organ of five stops in 1669; and Renatus in 1710, when he was quite an old man, a real masterpiece, the first organ in England to contain four manuals.

For the first fifteen years all agreements were made with Thomas Harris; thereafter for a short period the business was run jointly by father and son. The last-known reference to Thomas is found in a letter written by Renatus to the Dean of Durham, dated from Snow Hill,[2] London, 30th August 1683. In it the writer speaks of his "poore aged father". The occasion of the letter was to importune the Dean on their behalf in the matter of the proposed new organ for Durham Cathedral. They feared that the order might be given to Bernard Smith, as indeed it had already been that very month.[3]

The Durham disappointment came soon after the competition with Smith at the Temple Church had begun in earnest. Usually referred to as "The Battle of the Organs", this would be more correctly described as a Four Years' Campaign. Both builders must have had great difficulty to keep solvent and to attend to other orders during its continuance; but when the end came, Harris had been so narrowly defeated that he retired from the conflict with no loss of prestige. Smith got £1,000 for his instrument, but Harris eventually made two instruments out of the one that had been rejected. He seems to have kept it in his factory for many years, so that all interested might see for themselves what a fine piece of work it was. Then, in 1697 and 1699, he used it up with further material in new instruments he was commissioned to build for Christ Church Cathedral, Dublin, and the Church of St. Andrew, Holborn,[4] respectively. He must have derived some satisfaction in sending part of the Temple organ to Dublin, for the order for the instrument there had been given to Smith in 1694. Smith was too busy to carry out the contract within a reasonable time, whereupon the Dean and Chapter made a fresh

[1] *History of Music*, vol. iii, p. 437.
[2] Near the present Holborn Viaduct.
[3] The letter is printed in full in *The Organ*, vol. vi, p. 161.
[4] Destroyed in 1940.

agreement with Renatus, giving him a letter of attorney to recover £100, which they advanced to his rival.

The two men were in competition for the building of the organ at St. Lawrence Jewry,[1] London. A vestry minute (14th March 1683–4) reads: " . . . the Committee having seene the draughts and proposals of Mr. Harris and Mr. Smith for the Organ and how it should be made, and being satisfied that they are both good workmen. It was put to the vestrey whether of them should make the Organ, and it was cleerely carried that Mr. Harris should make the same wch is ordered to be done by Mr. Harris accordingly."

Burney[2] says that the Harrises "met with but little encouragement at first, as Dallams [*sic*] and Smith had the chief business of the kingdom; but upon the decease of Dallams, who died while he was building an organ for the old church at Greenwich in 1672 and of the elder Harris, who did not long survive him, the younger became a formidable rival to Smith". This is not accurate: there were three builders named Dallam at work in the early years of the Restoration period: Robert, Ralph and George, who died respectively in 1665, 1672 and *c.*1684, whilst Thomas was alive in 1684. As the Dallams died, more work was available for Harris, but the records of his own and his father's work show that they met with a great deal of encouragement from the first and some of their earlier commissions were for organs in important churches. As a matter of fact the other old English organ-builders, Robert Hayward, John Loosemore, Thomas Thamar, Robert Taunton and Lancelot Pease each had a connection of his own, and when these had closed their earthly accounts Smith and Harris between them made a fairly equal division of the spoils. There were other builders at work but no serious rivals until the opening years of the eighteenth century.

In the autumn of 1677 Renatus married Joan Hiett,[3] by whom he had at least three children: Renatus, John, and a daughter whose name is unknown. Of the younger Renatus we know practically nothing. Dr. Rimbault discovered his existence from an inscription in an old MS. collection of voluntaries for the organ. "John Harris given me by my brother Renatus."[4] This rather suggests that this Renatus and not his father was responsible for the song referred to by Sir John Hawkins[5] as having been set "by René Harris" and published in the *Mercurius Musicus* for September and October 1700. He was the first organist of All Hallows, Lombard Street, playing on the organ made by his father in 1703. His stipend was £22 per annum. It would appear than the younger Renatus died at an early age, for John Harris succeeded to his father's business, carrying on in partnership with John Byfield, senior, who had married the daughter of the older Renatus.

There was a period of nearly half a century between the marriage of Renatus

[1] Destroyed in 1940.
[2] *History of Music*, vol. iii, p. 437.
[3] The licence was granted in the Faculty office to "Rene Harris and Joane Hiett" in September 1677.
[4] Hopkins and Rimbault, op. cit., p. 133. Rimbault attributed the organ at St. Dionis Backchurch to the younger Renatus.
[5] *History of Music*, vol. iv, p. 356.

and his death, and in between the two events were made some of his finest organs. These included the instruments in the Cathedrals at Chichester (1677), Bristol (1685), Norwich (1689), Winchester (1693), St. Patrick's, Dublin (1696), Christ Church, Dublin (1697), Salisbury (1710), and Cork, five in collegiate buildings (among them King's College, Cambridge) and over a score in city and suburban churches. He is also said to have built the organ at Hereford Cathedral in 1686.

Rimbault[1] speaks of Renatus as having died in or about the year 1715, but with the discovery that Letters of Administration of his estate were taken out by his two sons, John and Renatus, on 11th February 1725, it may be put with some confidence that it occurred in August or September 1724. For on 26th July of that year he himself received payment for work done to the organ at Lambeth Church; whilst the next and subsequent payments were made to his son and successor, John, the first being on 29th September.

Sir John Hawkins was probably correct in stating that Renatus retired to Bristol towards the end of his life for the agreement for the organ at St. Dionis Backchurch, London, signed on 15th December 1722, describes him as Renatus Harris of Bristol. The instrument was approved on 25th June 1724 by Dr. Croft, Raphael Courteville and John Loeillet.

Upon John Harris's death towards the end of 1743, Byfield continued until he, too, passed away in 1757. Next came John Byfield, junior, who was subsequently joined by Samuel Green, these two dying in 1774 and 1796, respectively; but the line was even then not quite extinct. For another John Byfield was tuning and repairing organs at least as late as 1803 when he lost two of his jobs, at Lambeth and St. Andrew Undershaft, apparently through neglect. (A John Byfield who was organist of Newbury Parish Church from 1812 till his death in 1833 may have been the same tuner and repairer.)

The Dallam-Harris-Byfield family may be set in genealogical form like this:

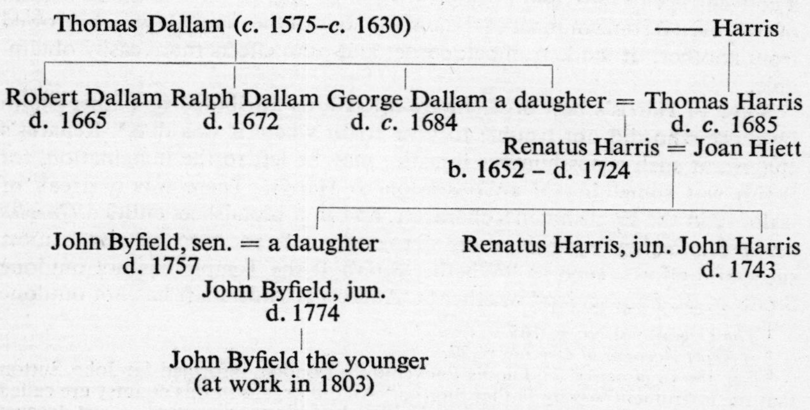

[1] Hopkins and Rimbault, op. cit.

"Grandfather" Harris is generally supposed to have been an organ-builder and to have constructed the organ at Magdalen College Chapel, Oxford, which had been at Tewkesbury Abbey since 1737. The evidence for this is that Renatus said this instrument had been made by his grandfather, together with the fact that there is an entry in the Magdalen accounts for 1637 that £40 was paid to someone named Harris *pro ecclesia*, not, be it noted, *pro organis*. £40 would scarcely buy an organ, richly encased, in 1637, and, moreover, the date 1637 is rather over-late for a grandfather of Renatus to be at work. The late Rev. Andrew Freeman, the leading authority on these matters, believed that the grandfather who made it was Thomas Dallam.[1]

In matters of mechanism and the finish of his metal pipework, it is probable that Renatus reached a higher standard than Smith. At any rate, the touch of his organs was better than Smith's, for Sir John Sutton (who placed Smith above his rival in most things) could not pass over the unpleasantness of the touch of his hero's organs. It felt, he said, "as though cotton wool was placed under each key".[2] Writing in 1847, Sutton said of such of Harris's work which remained: "His organs are certainly only second in excellence to those of Schmidt. His diapasons are both sweet and rich, and his chorus is vivacious and ringing, even more so than Schmidt's; and his reed stops, though far inferior to those made at present, are also superior to his. In many respects, there is a resemblance between the organs of these two workmen; and though Harris's wooden pipes are excellent, they never possess that peculiar reedy and brilliant tone which is so charming in all Schmidt's. Harris seemed to have been as ambitious of excelling in the manufacture of metal pipes as Schmidt was in those of wood, often using that metal for his stop diapasons."

Amongst other ingenuities of mechanism introduced by Renatus was the borrowing of stops from one manual to another "by communication" as he described it. In the days when aids to stop control were scarce, it was certainly a convenience to have two manuals instead of one, or three manuals instead of two, even if some or most of the stops on one of the manuals were borrowed from another. It made trumpet, cornet and echo effects more easily obtainable.

Some of Harris's best organs were afterwards attributed to Father Smith by those who did not trouble to give credit where it was due.[3] Renatus's chagrin at such a posthumous injustice may be left to the imagination, for Smith was something of an obsession to Harris. There was a streak of jealousy in the Englishman's character, and in a broadsheet entitled *Queries about St. Paul's Organ* there are derogatory references to his rival's most successful efforts, such as "Whether Smith at the Temple has not outdone Smith of St. Paul's? And whether St. Andrew's Undershaft has not outdone

[1] *The Organ*, vol. vi, p. 165.

[2] *A Short Account of Organs*, p. 27.

[3] E.g. the organist of St. Dionis Backchurch, London, informed Sir John Sutton that the instrument was by Father Smith. "All old organs in this country are called Father Schmidt's by those unacquainted with Schmidt's peculiarities." *Short Account of Organs*, p. 61.

them both?" Disputes with some of his clients show him in a not very favourable light; for instance, his making the organs unplayable at Christ's Hospital[1] and at St. Clement's, Eastcheap. At the latter Christopher Smith was called in to remove "the Cheat Mr. Harris putt into the Organ in order to putt the Organ out of order". And it was Harris's friends who went to the lengths of cutting the bellows of Smith's organ at the Temple Church on the eve of one of the trials.

Smith's quarter notes at the Temple, which helped to get him the favourable decision, seemed to have stung Harris into making his own experiments along the same lines, as the following shows:

"Whereas the Division of half a note (upon an organ) into 50 Gradual and distinguishable parts has been declar'd by Mr. Smith, as also by the Generality of Masters, to be impracticable: All Organists Masters, and Artists of the Faculty, are, together, with the said Mr. Smith, invited to Mr. Harris's house in Wine-Office Court, Fleetstreet, on Easter Monday next (at Two of the Clocke in the Afternoon), to hear and see the same demonstrated."[2]

Clearly Smith's organ, at St. Paul's Cathedral, could not produce the grand effect, both to ear and eye, of the large west-end European organs which must have been known to both builders. As soon as Smith was dead, Harris tried to persuade the cathedral authorities to commission him to build a large west-end organ. There can be no doubt that Harris had the requisite skill to carry out such a project had it been permitted him. Harris produced a three-page pamphlet with which he importuned prominent people. Here are some extracts from it:[3]

"This organ shall contain a double double Diapason of Profundity of which shall comprehend the utmost notes of Sound. In this stop shall be pipes forty foot long, and above two foot diameter; which will render this Organ vastly superior in worth and value to any other Diapason organs; and that the rest of the work may bear a due Proportion, it shall consist of six entire sets of keys for the hands, besides Pedals for the Feet.

"The first Set, to be wholly appropriated for a grand chorus, intended to be the most strong and firm that ever has yet been made.

"The second and third Sets to answer all Sorts and Varieties of Stops and to represent all Musical Instruments.

"The fourth to express the Ecchos.

"The fifth to be a Choir or Small Organ, yet to contain more pipes and a greater Number of Stops, than the biggest Organ in England has at present.

"The sixth to be adapted for the emitting of Sounds to express Passion by swelling any Note, as if inspir'd by Human Breath; which is the greatest improvement an organ is capable of except it had Articulation. On this set

[1] E. H. Pearce, *Annals of Christ's Hospital*, p. 143.

[2] *The Post Boy*, April 12th and 30th, 1698.

[3] The only known copy is preserved in the library of St. Paul's. It is not quite complete as the first two or three lines and the imprint have been cut off, but the date can be established by the mention of Harris's Salisbury organ of 1710, and the fact that Addison refers to the tract in the *Spectator* of 3rd December, 1712 as having "been frequently inclosed" to him. It is printed in full in ***The Organs of St. Paul's Cathedral*** by the present author (London, 1930).

of keys, the notes will be loud or soft, by swelling on a long Note or Shake, at the organist's pleasure. Sounds will come surprising and harmoniously, as from the clouds, or distant Parts, pass, and return again, as quick or slow as Fancy can suggest; and be in tune in all Degrees of Loudness and Softness.

"By means of the Pedals, the Organist may carry on three Fugues at once, and be able to do as much as if he had four hands, for the Feet would act upon the Pedal-Keys, when the hands were employ'd above, and the Sound would be proportionately strong; which in the grand Chorus in so vast a Church, ought to be as strong and bold as possible; and therefore Pedals are us'd in all the great Organs beyond the seas.

"If at the charge of the Publick, such an Organ were built in the Place propos'd, which is the most proper to give the design its full and desir'd advantage, such an Instrument, containing more Beauties and Variety than all the most celebrated Organs, as it would be by far the completest in its kind, so it would be suitable to the Grandeur of so stately a Fabricke.

"Sir, The inclos'd Proposal takes its rise from the organ I set up in Salisbury Cathedral in 1710, which was begun some years since for a Church in London, as a Master-piece of great value to have been paid for a Subscription and was made capable of emitting Sounds to express Passion by Swelling any Note, as if inspir'd by Human Breath . . .

"This instrument will be of such Reputation to the Kingdom as will far surmount the Expence of it, which will be easy whenever her Majesty and the Parliament shall further think fit to enlarge their Bounty to St. Paul's Church, by appointing a sum out of the same Revenue which built it, or any other way, as they in their great wisdom shall judge proper for the ornament and Grandeur of the State Church of the City, which is the chief of her Majesty's extensive Dominions".

Salisbury Cathedral.[1] Renatus Harris, 1710. This instrument was remarkable as an early eighteenth-century attempt at "stop control" by the multiplication of manuals and stop handles. It was an early use of "duplexing", or bringing stops or portions of stops from one manual to another by communication or "borrowing".[2]

"Four setts of keys; fifty stops, and eleven stops of Echoes. The compass was from GG (short octaves) up to C. The Echo from Middle C to C, two octaves."

Great (16 *stops*)	pipes	*Echo* (11 *stops*)	pipes
Open diapason (No. 1)	50	Open diapason	25
Open diapason (No. 2)	50	Stopped diapason	25

[1] In the Rev. Peter Hall's *Picturesque Memorials of Salisbury* (plate vi) is a full-page view of the nave of the cathedral looking east, engraved by J. S. Muller in 1754 from a drawing by James Biddlecombe. The west front of the organ has a well-proportioned classical design, out of keeping with early English architecture of the cathedral.

[2] At this time "borrowing" was effected by grooving in or conveyancing to the upper boards of the sound-board. It was necessary to fit leather "flap-valves" to appropriate orifices to prevent wind from flowing into unwanted pipes.

Great—cont.	pipes	*Echo—cont.*	pipes
Stopped diapason	50	Principal	25
Principal	50	Flute	25
Flute	50	Twelfth	25
Twelfth	50	Fifteenth	25
Fifteenth	50	Tierce	25
Tierce	50	Larigot	25
Larigot	50	Trumpet	25
Sesquialtera, 4 ranks	200	Vox humana	25
Cornet, 5 ranks (from C)	125	Cromhorn	25
Trumpet	50		
Clarion	50		
Cromhorn	50		
Vox humana	50		
Spare stop			

Borrowed Great (14 *stops*)	*Chair* (8 *stops*)	pipes
Open diapason	Open diapason (from Gamut G)	42
Stopped diapason	Stopped diapason	50
Principal	Principal	50
Flute	Flute	50
Twelfth	Twelfth	50
Fifteenth	Fifteenth	50
Tierce	Bassoon	50
Larigot	Spare stop	
Sesquialtera, 4 ranks	Drum pedal (tuned to CC)	
Trumpet		
Clarion		
Cromhorn		
Vox humana		
Spare stop		

A further comment by Charles Burney on the work of the two builders is now given:

"In consequence of the reputation which Father Smith had acquired by every piece of work he had put out of his hands, since the organ at Windsor, he was employed to build an instrument for the cathedral of St. Paul; which is generally allowed to have the sweetest tone (except that at the Temple), the most noble chorus, and a swell which produces the finest effects of any in the kingdom. In short, it is an instrument in every respect worthy of that beautiful and stupendous structure (2nd Dec. 1697). It seems as if Harris had been a candidate for building St. Paul's organ, as well as that at the Temple; for in the Spectator No. 552 for December 3rd,

1712, a proposal of Mr. Renatus Harris is recommended in the following words: 'The ambition of this artificer is to erect an organ in St. Paul's cathedral, over the west door, at the entrance into the body of the church, which in art and magnificence shall transcend any work of that kind ever before invented. The proposal in perspicuous language sets forth the honour and advantage such a performance would be to the British name, as well as that it would apply the power of sounds in a manner more amazingly forcible, than perhaps has yet been known, and I am sure to an end much more worthy. Had the vast sums which have been laid out upon operas without skill or conduct, and to no other purpose but to suspend or vitiate our understandings, been disposed this way, we should now perhaps have an engine so formed, as to strike the minds of half a people at once, in a place of worship, with a forgetfulness of present care and calamity, and a hope of endless rapture, joy and hallelujah hereafter.' "

(This was one of Steele's papers: Burney says that he was partial to Harris, who had probably built or lent him an instrument for his concert rooms in York Buildings.)

Burney's footnote to this. "It is not easy to discover what is meant by a late writer when he says that 'the organs made by Smith, though, in respect of the workmanship, they are far short of those of Harris, and even of Dallans, are justly admired'. If the utmost care in the choice of wood and composition of the metal; the neatest and most happy manner possible of forming and voicing them; together with the most grateful sweetness, and durability of his pipes, may be called good workmanship, surely Father Smith cannot, without injustice, be denied that praise in its fullest extent. That part of the organ which was originally built for the Temple Church by Harris, and sent to Dublin, was sold after the death of the elder Byfield, by his widow, Harris's daughter, to Wolverhampton for £500. It still stands in the church of that town, and is thought a very good instrument. The number of organs built and enriched with new stops by Father Smith is prodigious, and their fame equal to that of the pictures or single figures of Raphael. A single stop known to be of his workmanship is still invaluable. The touch and general mechanism of modern instruments are certainly superior to those of Smith; but, for sweetness of tone, I have never met with any pipes that have equalled his in any part of Europe."[1]

List of Organs built by Thomas and Renatus Harris

Bideford: Parish Church, 1671. Case is now in Holsworthy Church, Devon.
Bristol:

- Cathedral, 1685. The rearranged cases and some pipes remain.
- Christ Church. Harris added two stops in 1709 and was probably the original builder.
- St. James, 1718–19. Nothing remains.

[1] C. Burney, *A General History of Music* (1789), vol. iii, p. 263.

Cambridge:

Christ's College Chapel. The pre-Restoration organ tuned and repaired.

Jesus College Chapel, 1688. Possibly only repaired; subsequently in *old* All Saint's Church, since destroyed.

King's College Chapel. New organ in Dallam's (1606) case; additions in 1688, 1695 and 1710.

Chichester: Cathedral, 1677–8. Case destroyed in 1859 except for a few fragments.

Cork: Cathedral.

Dublin:

Christ Church Cathedral, 1697. Cost, £800; believed to have contained portions of Harris's Temple Church organ; removed in 1750 and afterwards set up in St. John's, Wolverhampton, where it still is.

St. Patrick's Cathedral, 1696–7. Cost, £505 and the old organ; when finished, £350 was paid for additional stops.

St. Mary's Church. Two stops in the present organ.

Gloucester: Cathedral, 1663–5. Cost, £400. The fine case and a few old pipes remain.

Hereford: Cathedral, 1686. Not authenticated as a Harris organ, but repaired by him in 1707.

Ipswich: St. Mary's Church, 1690.

Little Bardfield, Essex: Traditionally by Harris, said to have come from Jesus College, Cambridge.

London:

All Hallows', Barking, 1675–7. Cost, £220. Later displaced by Gerard Smith's organ, 1720. Destroyed 1940.

All Hallows', Lombard Street, 1703. The first organist was Renatus Harris, jun. Case and old pipes now at All Hallows', Twickenham.

Chelsea Hospital Chapel, *c.* 1691. Case remains. The organ went to Crediton, where it was displaced by a Harrison organ.

Christ Church, Newgate Street, 1690. Destroyed 1940.

Christ's Hospital, Newgate Street. The Hall, 1690.

"Popish Chapel", Whitehall, 1686–8. Cost, upwards of £1,100. Organ presented to St. James', Piccadilly. Damaged 1940.

Queen's Chapel, St. James's Palace, before 1688. Now called Marlborough House Chapel. Organ given to St. Anne's, Soho, in 1699; removed thence to St. Michael's Paternoster Royal in 1780, and broken up in 1893.

St. Andrew, Holborn, 1699. Made out of a part of the rejected Temple organ. The few pipes which remained were destroyed in 1940.

St. Andrew Undershaft, 1696. The beautiful case remains.

St. Botolph, Aldgate, 1676. The case remains.

St. Bride, Fleet Street. Case destroyed 1940.

St. Dionis Backchurch, 1724. His last organ. The organ was removed to St. Mark's, East Walworth, and the case was left here, but the pipes were removed to Darenth Training Colony, Dartford, Kent. It seems probable that this organ was largely by Renatus Junior.

St. Dunstan, Stepney. Case destroyed in 1879.

St. John's Chapel, Bedford Row. Case now at Thaxted Church, Essex.

St. Lawrence Jewry, 1684–5. Cost, £400 exclusive of the case. The instrument was removed to the Wesleyan Chapel, Horseferry Road (now the Training College Chapel), Westminster, 1875. The case (enlarged) was one of the finest in London until it was destroyed in 1940.

St. Martin-in-the-Fields. Repairs only costing £10.

St. Mary, Lambeth, 1701. Some pipework and carving remain.

St. Mary, Whitechapel, 1715. Of doubtful origin.

St. Michael, Cornhill. Cost, £325 and the old organ. Case destroyed in 1860.

St. Saviour, Southwark, 1703. Now the Cathedral (doubtful).

St. Sepulchre's, Holborn Viaduct, Snow Hill, 1670. A part of the case still survives, but the chaire case disappeared when the organ was removed from the west gallery.

Temple Church, 1684. Not accepted.

See page 157 *et seq.*, and St. Andrew, Holborn.

Newcastle: St. Nicholas, now the Cathedral, *c.* 1676. The two cases remain, one of them enlarged.

Norwich:

Cathedral, 1689. The case was spoilt in 1833 and altered in 1899 and 1914; it was burnt in 1939.

St. Peter Mancroft, 1707. Case removed to Parish Church, Great Yarmouth, in 1875, where it was destroyed by enemy action in 1940. Much of the pipework was incorporated in Messrs. Hele's organ at St. Simon's, Plymouth.

Oxford: Magdalen College Chapel. 1672, repairs costing £10; 1690, enlargement costing £150. This was the organ that was given to Oliver Cromwell and set up at Hampton Court; returned to Oxford in 1660 and sold to Tewkesbury Abbey in 1737.

Salisbury: Cathedral. (*a*) The pre-Restoration organ repaired by T. and R. Harris, *c.* 1660. (*b*) A small new organ with four and a half stops in 1669. (*c*) A new organ of four manuals and forty-six stops. No part of the case or pipework remains.

Wells: Cathedral, 1679–80. Harris was paid £20, which included £10 for 102 pipes, and 1*s.* "his men to drink".

Winchester:

Cathedral, 1693–4. A rebuild of Thomas's organ of 1655 in the old cases at a cost of £425; part of the organ, after being in use at Christ Church, Lancaster Gate, W., from 1852 till 1884, went to St. Peter's, Southsea.

The College. An instrument costing £55, afterwards called "Bishop Ken's organ".

St. Mary's College Chapel. Repaired in 1664 and rebuilt in 1864–5.

Windsor: Wolsey Tomb House, 1686–8.

Worcester: Cathedral. (*a*) T. Dallam's old organ repaired in 1666. (*b*) A new organ built the same year by Thomas and Renatus Harris, costing £428; a few pipes remain in the present organ; the chaire case is now at Mistley Church, Essex.[1]

A note on the Temple Organ

About the end of the reign of King Charles II the Societies of the Temple, being determined to have erected in the church an organ as complete as possible, had been in treaty with Smith for that purpose, when Harris (who, from this and subsequent proceedings, seems to have had some warm supporters among the Benchers of the Inner Temple) was introduced to their notice, and both of these eminent artists were backed by the recommendations of such an equal number of powerful friends and celebrated organists, that the Benchers were unable to determine among themselves which to employ. They therefore (as appears by an order in the books of the Temple, dated February 1682[2]) proposed that "If each of these excellent artists would set up an organ in one of the Halls belonging to either of the Societies, they would have erected in their Church that, which, in the greatest number of excellencies, deserved the preference". Smith, thinking that he had been selected as the builder of the organ before the introduction of Harris, and not a little chagrined by this proposal, used every exertion to have the above order rescinded, and thus avoid the competition to which it would expose him.

Harris built his organ on the south side of "The Communion Table" and Smith erected his on the screen between the round church and the nave.

"Dr. Blow and Mr. Purcell" were employed to show off Smith's organ, and a similar service for Harris was performed by Baptist Draghi, organist to Queen Catherine. The contest continued for nearly a year, and, as neither of the builders had been paid for their work, they "were almost ruined".[3]

There was some acrimony between the rival builders and their partisans and it is said that Harris's supporters even went so far as to cut Smith's bellows. The Benchers of the Middle Temple were inclined to terminate the contest by giving a decision in favour of Smith, but those of the Inner Temple were not willing to concur without further consideration "by impartial judges".[4]

[1] This list is prepared from notes kindly supplied by the late Rev. Andrew Freeman to which the author has added further material.

[2] Note that the legal year which was used in all public instruments and state papers commenced on 25th March (from 1300 until 1st January 1753). Consequently this date would be February 1683 according to our present mode of computation. Edmund Macrory, *A Few Notes on the Temple Organ* (London, 1861).

[3] The facts concerning the "Battle of the Organs" are from the letters of Dr. Tudway, who was alive at the time, to his son. Burney in his *History of Music* says in error that *Lully* demonstrated Harris's organ, because he misunderstood Tudway's reference to *Baptist*. The error has been repeated frequently. See also Sir John Hawkins' *History of Music*, vol. ii, p. 795. Tudway's letters are in the Bodleian Library.

[4] The records are still preserved by the respective societies. Reprints of significant extracts are given in Macrory's booklet.

"At length," says Burney, "the decision was left to Lord Chief Justice Jeffreys, afterwards King James the Second's pliant Chancellor, who was of that Society (The Inner Temple) and he terminated the controversy in favour of Father Smith; so that Harris's organ was taken away without loss of reputation, having so long pleased and puzzled better judges than Jeffreys."[1]

Macrory says: "There is nothing in the books of either Society to corroborate this statement, derived by Burney from a letter written by Dr. Tudway."

Jeffreys was not Lord Chief Justice at the time of the decision, as he became Lord Chancellor in 1685, and continued until 1690 in that office.

Rimbault, in *The Organ,* suggests that Jeffreys gave the casting vote, as it is probable that, in view of the detailed accounts of the controversy in the records of the societies, some mention of Jeffreys would have appeared had he been solely concerned in making the decision.

Harris removed his organ and re-erected it in his workshop in order to show it to his clients. Eventually a portion of it was used to make the organ at Christ Church Cathedral, Dublin, and the remainder was erected in St. Andrew's, Holborn.[2] The termination of the "battle" was the end of 1687 or the beginning of 1688. The deed of sale is still preserved and bears the date 20th June 1688. Smith received £1,000, of which half was paid by each society.

Here follows the schedule of stops taken from the agreement which is headed:

"*Mr. Bernard Smythes Bargaine and Sale of ye Organ in ye Temple Church to both ye Societys of ye Temples.*

Great Organ

1.	Prestand of mettle	61	pipes	12 foote	Tone
2.	Holflute of wood and mettle	61	,,	12 foote	,,
3.	Principall of mettle	61	,,	06 foote	,,
4.	Quinta of mettle	61	,,	04 foote	,,
5.	Super octavo	61	,,	03 foote	,,
6.	Cornett of mettle	112	,,	02 foote	,,
7.	Sesquialtera of mettle	183	,,	03 foote	,,
8.	Gedackt of wainescott	61	,,	06 foote	,,
9.	Mixture of mettle	226	,,	03 foote	,,
10.	Trumpett of mettle	61	,,	12 foote	,,
		948			

Chair Organ

11.	Gedackt wainescott	61	,,	12 foote	,,
12.	Holflute of mettle	61	,,	06 foote	,,

[1] Burney, *History of Music,* vol. iii, p. 437. Reported to Burney by Roseingrave, organist of St. George's, Hanover Square.

[2] Handel was frequently seen listening to this part of the instrument in its new home. The portions of Harris's organ which remained were destroyed by fire in the air-raids of 1940.

13.	A Sadt of mettle	61 ,,	06 foote ,,
14.	Spitts flute of mettle	61 ,,	03 foote ,,
15.	A Violl and Violin of mettle	61 ,,	12 foote ,,
16.	Voice humane of mettle	61 ,,	12 foote ,,
		366	

Ecchos

17.	Gedackt of wood	61 pipes	06 foote Tone
18.	Sup. octavo of mettle	61 ,,	03 foote ,,
19.	Gedackt of wood	29 ,,	
20.	Flute of mettle	29 ,,	
21.	Cornett of mettle	87 ,,	
22.	Sesquialtera	105 ,,	
23.	Trumpett	29 ,,	
		401	

With 3 full sets of keyes and quarter notes.
Ber. Smith.

Sealed and delivered in the presence of
Geo. Mincett. Tho. Griffin. Richard Cooke."

At this time all organs were tuned to mean-tone temperament or something approaching it. Although the thirds and sixths were in tune, the powers of modulation were limited. The quarter notes (which meant separate action and pipes in respect of each) gave a G♯ and D♯ distinct from A♭ and E♭ respectively. The appropriate short keys were divided into two portions of about equal lengths and the back part was raised and controlled the extra notes. The "quarter tones" accounted for the apparently modern compass of sixty-one notes, which in fact only represented little more than four octaves.[1]

A manuscript notebook in the Inner Temple Library[2] which does not contain a clue to its author's identity contains the following passage:

"The Organ in the Temple hath quarter notes, which no organ in England hath, and can play any tune; as for instance, ye tune of ye 119 Psalm,[3] and severall other services set by excellent musicians, which no other organ will do. It hath several excellent stops, as the Cremona stop, ye Trumpet stop, the Voice Humane, which last stop is set to Mr. Gascell's voice, who can reach one of the deepest basses in England. These three stops, tho' pleasant to the ear, are of no duration, and must be tuned two or three times a month, which is chargable, and cannot be performed but by an organ maker; but commonly the organists beyond sea are better skill'd

[1] The evolution of the systems of tuning the organ and temperament is discussed on p. 283 *et seq.*

[2] Entitled "Notes on Gunnery, Sir C. Wren's Dial, The Temple Organ etc.".

[3] In F minor.

in the art of tuning their instruments, which few or none in England do understand. Mr. Smith's metall for his pipes is composed of tin, lead and copper. The pipes that are made of wainscoat are better and more durable than those that are made of deal. Mr. Smith says that he can make metall pipes speak like those made of wood, and those of wood to speak like those of metall. The Humane stop is made with tongues of Brass."

Some details of this instrument as it evolved from the time of Smith, which at one period of its history was the finest in London and was finally completely destroyed by enemy action in 1940, may not be out of place here.

Originally, the Temple organ consisted of great and choir organs, ranging from FFF (twelve feet) to C^3 in alt omitting FFF♯, GG♯, AA♯ and DD♯ in the bass, and an echo to middle C continued by a small choir-bass, the whole being supplied with wind from three diagonal bellows.

The echo organ was enclosed in a wooden box to make its tone soft and "distant", and it only needed the further step of providing a shutter or door to the box to make a rudimentary swell organ. This latter was done at the Temple in 1729–30 by Christopher Schrider, Smith's son-in-law. In 1741 John Byfield, who then had the charge "of keeping the organ in tune and repair" added a new swell containing six stops to fiddle G the horn going to tenor F. The following is the list of these stops.

Open diapason	Horn
Stopped diapason	Trumpet
Cornet, 4 ranks	Hautbois

Many changes were effected in 1843 by Bishop, and the organ was taken from the screen and placed in a spacious chamber on the north side of the oblong church, where it remained until it was destroyed in 1940. Amongst other improvements a new building frame was provided, the swell was continued to tenor C and the quarter tones added, an octave and a half of FFF pedals were laid down, and an octave of CCC return pedal pipes applied to them.[1] Various composition pedals for controlling the stops and couplers were also provided. T. J. F. Robson made a CCC to tenor F pedal-board with three independent pedal stops. At the same time the old manuals with black naturals and white short keys were removed and new claviers supplied, and in 1856 the same builder reconstructed the instrument "from the ground". Three years later the societies decided that the organ should be complete in every respect, and Edmund Schultze [*sic*], whose organ at the 1851 Exhibition was much admired, was asked to send a number of his flue stops, including his "Lieblich" stopped pipes and his string-toned stops. At the same time the bellows were worked by Joy's Patent Hydraulic engines. The organ then contained forty-seven speaking stops and twenty couplers and other accessories. From 1843 E. J. Hopkins (who collaborated

[1] See p. 189

PLATE 15a.

The Fugger Chapel of St. Anne, Augsburg. Earliest German Renaissance case, 1509–12. Destroyed during the last war

PLATE 15b.

The Steinmeyer organ in Passau Cathedral. Claimed to be the largest church organ in Europe. Main organ, 1929

PLATE 16.

Console at City Hall, Hull, by John Compton, 1951. The stops have translucent fronts illuminated from behind. When pressed a stop comes on, when pressed again it goes off

PLATE 17.

The large console of the Atlantic City Organ, U.S.A., (the largest in the world) designed by Senator Emerson Richards. (1929–31)

PLATE 18.

Blowing the Halberstadt Cathedral Organ in the Sixteenth Century (from Praetorius: Plate 26)

with E. F. Rimbault in the writing of the well-known organ-book) had been organist. Later the instrument was reconstructed by Rothwell of Harrow and was known for its smooth, musical tone. In 1953–54 the fine Harrison organ built for Lord Glentanar in his residence near Aberdeen was given by him and installed in a spacious chamber in the repaired church.

A Note on the Choir Organ in English Organs

The modern use of the term choir organ is a corruption of "chair organ", and, in the words of the New Oxford Dictionary, "in printing seventeenth-century documents even writers of repute have erroneously alleged that (the word choir) was the original".[1] Here follow some early references to the chair organ. There are no records of the use of choir organ until more recent times. Indeed, even were the organ used for the express purpose of accompanying the choir, it would originally have been spelt "quire", a form still retained by the Prayer Book. There is no historic use of the equivalent of the word "choir" in European usage. The manual division which approximated to the English chair organ would be called positif (positiv). The "grand choeur" an innovation made in France in the second half of the nineteenth century referred to the organ *chorus* which was used with the grand orgue and gave it great power and brilliance because it contained loud reeds and mixture stops. The small organs, separate from the main instrument, which are found in the chancels of European churches, are called by such names as petit-orgue, epistelorgel, chancel-organ, or sanctuary organ. Here follow some examples of the use of the word *chair*.

1606–7. Account book in King's College Chapel[2] (mentions pypes, armes and scutchens of the chayre organ).

The cathedral records through the country abound in documents which make reference to the chair organ. Two of these, which are typical, appear in the accounts of Worcester Cathedral:

> 1613. "In the Chaire organ, 1 principal of mettal, 1 diapason of wood."
>
> 1666. "He shall set up in the choyre a double organ consisting of great organ and chair organ."

The articles of agreement signed by Father Smith in respect of the organs which he built in many churches and cathedrals refer to a chair organ. Extracts from the Durham manuscripts give "A good, perfect tuneable and harmonious Great Organ and Chair Organ", and in 1690 a reference to "Chear Organ by articles". In 1610 John Yorke made "a new chaire orgaine"

[1] Hopkins and Rimbault (op. cit.), Grove (corrected in the present edition by the author) and innumerable others make the same mistake, e.g. Hawkins, *History of Music* (1776), vol. iv, p. 150: "We in England call it the Choir and by corruption the Chair Organ." Hiles, *Catechism of the Organ* (1878): "The first, or lowest manual, which is called the Choir Organ, contains pipes of a narrow measure, and a soft, delicate and somewhat penetrating tone."

[2] Edited by Carter (Cambridge, 1867).

at Trinity College, Cambridge. Although[1] the word "choir" began to appear in the eighteenth century the older word was often retained:

> 1760–88. W. Boyce, *Cathedral Music*, vol. xii: "It is recommended . . . to play the Full Chair Organ."
> 1796. Green, *History of Worcester*, vol. i, p. 114: "On this side the lesser or chair organ is seen."

It is a great pity that musical historians have almost always transcribed the word "chair" wrongly and thereby altered its meaning. In original documents relating to English organs it is of frequent occurrence.

The meaning of the words "chair organ" becomes apparent when we consider the organ's origin. It was placed at the side of and later behind the organist's seat for the main organ. No doubt some of the positive organs of the continental churches were placed in the organ galleries with the larger organs so that an organist could go from one to another quite easily. He would turn with relief from the heavy action of the large organ to a less exhausting period of playing on the positive. The positive could stand in front of the main organ from the observer's point of view. It was at the back of the organist and thus earned the name "rückpositiv" in the old German organs. For a century or more no attempt was made to play it from a row of keys above or below that of the large organ. The organist had to turn round or turn aside to play it, and during the service he would "take a turn" on the smaller instrument. Eventually organ-builders were able to bring the action of the small organ under the organist's seat so that he could play it from a row of keys near that of the main organ. For centuries in many churches abroad no attempt was made to effect a similar convenient arrangement in the stops of the small organ. Even today in many churches in France, Belgium, Germany and Austria the stops of the rückpositiv can only be changed by the organist getting off his seat and walking to the front of the gallery. Organ-builders found that a beautiful effect both to the eye and ear could be obtained by placing the small organ in a case in front of and below that of the main organ.

In the specifications of sixteenth- and seventeenth-century German organs the rückpositiv (i.e. positive organ at the back of the organist) is sometimes given as *Positiv in stühl*—positive in the case which forms the organist's "throne".[2]

It is clear that the origin of the words "chair" organ is either that this small organ was placed near or behind the organist's chair or that it was the organ that took a *turn* or that was *turned to* as a contrast to the large organ. The organist would often have to turn physically before he could play it. It is impossible to say which was the original meaning; certainly it was not choir organ and all evidence seems to point to the meaning, believed by the writer, that the origin of the word implied that the positiv organ was the one that

[1] Chapel accounts of Trinity College, Cambridge, given by G. F. Cobb, *History of the Organ in the Chapel of Trinity College* (*Cambridge*).
[2] See Appendix, Specification No. 1.

"took a turn". There are many spellings of the old word chair=a helper, one who takes a turn: char (as in charwoman), chare, chore, chewre. The German is kehren and the Dutch keeren. The New Oxford Dictionary gives "to turn away to", "to turn aside", "to turn back again". It was the organ that "took a turn" or was "turned to".[1]

John Snetzler

The most honoured place in later eighteenth-century organ-building in England is occupied by John Snetzler, born in Schaffhausen (Switzerland) on April 6th, 1710.

Our knowledge of Snetzler's early life is largely due to Burney, who was well acquainted with the organ-builder. He says that as a young man Snetzler worked with Egedacher of Passau, who in 1731–3 made a new organ of three manuals and thirty-nine speaking stops of which ten were on the pedal. Burney says that Snetzler made some of the front pipes and also the vox humana and octave dulciana in the little organ, which are the two best solo stops that the instrument contains. Snetzler knew about the Viennese organs, and it is likely that he must have visited them. He urged Burney to go to St. Michael's Church in that city to see the organ "on account of the singular disposition of its keys".[2] It is unlikely that Snetzler was a master organ-builder before he came to England, for we next hear of him at Haarlem, where he was helping Müller to build the famous organ in the Church of St. Bavon (1735–8).[3] There is no record of his arrival in England nor of what he did on the completion of the Haarlem organ. No mention of him occurs in any European document which we have found. It was believed that he built the organ in Chesterfield Parish Church in 1741, a date which has often appeared in English accounts of his work, but the church records give the date 1756 for the building of this Derbyshire organ. He made certain repairs to the organ in St. Nicholas's Church (now the Cathedral) in Newcastle in 1749, and may have helped other English builders before this. In letters written to the Moravian brethren at Fulneck, near Leeds, in 1747–8, he says, "I am new to the trade." No doubt he had heard that England was favourably disposed to German musicians and technicians at this time. Burney left London for health reasons in 1753, gave up his post at St. Dionis Backchurch and went to St. Margaret's Church, King's Lynn, where he immediately took steps to secure a new organ and recommended Snetzler as the builder.[4]

Thus, before this date Snetzler must have given Burney confidence in his sterling qualities as an organ-builder in London. The Lynn organ, followed by Burney's increasing support, established the builder's fame and, in

[1] The word "chair" as a helper or one who takes a turn (i.e. char) is of frequent occurrence in seventeenth-century English; e.g. 1626: Fletcher, *Fair Maid of Inn*, vol. iv, ii; "The witches of Lapland are the devils chairwomen." 1662: Fuller, *Worthies*, L, 2: "It is no good huswifery to hire chairwomen."

[2] Burney, *The Present State of Music in Germany*, etc. (1773), vol. i, p. 78.

[3] See specification No. 17.

[4] *Grove's Dictionary of Music* (1908 ed.) gives 1755 as the date of Snetzler's establishment in London, but the actual date was 1747.

Burney's words, "he gave such a specimen of his abilities that he was soon called to almost every quarter of the kingdom".[1] Snetzler introduced a version of the old German stop known as dulciane or dulciana, a flue stop of narrow scale and cylindrical shape.[2]

Sir John Sutton[3] says:

> "His instruments are remarkable for the purity of their tone and the extreme brilliancy of their chorus stops, which in this respect surpassed anything that has been heard before in this country, and which have never since been equalled. His reed stops were also much better than those built before his time. His organs, though they are more brilliant than their predecessors, fall short of that fullness of tone which characterised those of Schmidt, Harris, Schreider, etc., but they are nevertheless most charming instruments."

Sutton would have been able to hear many of the Snetzler organs in almost their original state. Few had been rebuilt or modified before he wrote his little work. He says that Snetzler introduced longer keys than had been usual before the middle of the eighteenth century, with very narrow sharps and flats "like the new Piano Forte keys" and that they had a piece of ivory or bone let in along the length of the raised keys, leaving the sides of them black like the naturals.

Burney says that German builders seemed to do better work out of Germany than in their own country, and he finds qualities in the works of Smith and Snetzler which are not apparent in the larger organs of Germany. Snetzler made many organs for English churches between 1747 and 1781. Towards the end of his working life he took as a partner an organ-builder called Jones. Sir John Sutton (who did not know Snetzler) says that by 1782 the organ-builder had saved sufficient money to enable him to return to his native country to retire, but "having been so long accustomed to London porter and English fare, he found in his old age that he could not do without it, so he came back to London, where he died",[4] on Sept. 28th, 1785.

Here is a list of the organs made or repaired by Snetzler in England:

Moravian Church, Fetter Lane, London, 1747.

Moravian Church, Fulneck, Leeds, 1748 (rebuilt Binns, 1929).

[1] Burney, *History of Music*, vol. iii, p. 348.

[2] Wedgwood, *Dictionary of Organ Stops* (London, 1907), says that Snetzler introduced "bearded" dulcianas (i.e. those with cylindrical bars fixed between the "ears" at the pipe mouth). Snetzler's "dulcianas" were plain dolce or dolcan stops such as had been made in Germany for nearly two centuries, or were small-scaled cylindrical stops.

[3] Sir John Sutton, op. cit.

[4] Burney's letter to Dr. Callcott, dated January 1803, printed in full in *The Musical Times* for September 1904. Snetzler's workshop was behind Rose St. (later Manette St.) and the north-east side of Greek St., Soho, London. It was later taken over by Henry Bevington and is mentioned by Dickens in *A Tale of Two Cities*. See Sumner, W. L., "Snetzler's First English Organs", *The Organ*, Jan. 1954.

Newcastle Cathedral, 1749 (swell organ).
St. Mary's Church, Finchley, 1749.
R. C. Church (no former organ), Lewisham, 1750.
St. John the Evangelist, Smith Square, Westminster, 1750 (probably made by Snetzler and provided by Thomas Griffin).
Picton Castle Chapel, Pembrokeshire, 1750.
Eton College Chapel, 1751.
Mersham le Hatch, Kent, Caldecott Community, 1754.
St. Margaret's Church, King's Lynn, 1754 (Dr. Burney's organ, specification No. 24).
St. Paul's, Sheffield, 1755.
St. Mary's, Lowgate, Hull, 1755.
Sculthorpe Parish Church, Norfolk, 1756 (German toe pedals).
Parish Church, Chesterfield, 1756 (pipework still in use).
Parish Church, Doncaster, 1756 (repaired and tuned).
Lodge Canongate, Kilwinning, Edinburgh, 1756.
Shaw House, Newbury, 1756 (former organ).
St. Nicholas's Church, Whitehaven, 1756 (now at Arlecdon).
Barnsley Parish Church (doubtful).
Duke of Bedford, Woburn, 1756 (now at Long Melford).
German Lutheran Chapel in the Savoy, London, 1757 (afterwards at Cleveland Street, W.). (The first English organ with pedals "up to C", i.e. FFF to C, nineteen notes. Rebuilt by Walker; destroyed 1940.)
Gloucester Cathedral, 1757 (repairs).
St. John at Hackney, London, 1757 (former organ).
Leatherhead, Surrey, 1760.
Buckingham Palace, London, 1760 (now at Eton College).
Christ Church, Broadway, Westminster (Old Church), London, 1760.
Little Plumstead Church, Norfolk, 1760 (later at Horsefair Chapel, Bristol).
Southwell Cathedral, 1762. Removed 1890.
Bureau organ now in possession of the Dolmetsch family, Haslemere, 1764.
Ludlow Parish Church, 1764.
Christ Church, Cambridge (Mass., U.S.A.) 1764 (pipes used for bullets during the "Revolution").
Trinity Church, New York, 1765 (destroyed by fire, 1776).
St. Peter's College (sic.), Cambridge, 1765.
Swithland Church, Leicester, 1765.
Halifax Parish Church, 1765–6.
Octagon Chapel, Bath, 1767.
Beverley Minster, 1767 (case now in south aisle).
St. Michael's Episcopal Church, Charlestown, South Carolina, U.S.A., 1767.
Rushworth and Dreaper Collection, Liverpool, 1767 (chamber organ).
Brookthorpe Church, Glos., 1768.
Louth Parish Church, 1769.

Stafford, Teddesley Hall, 1769.
Elland (Halifax) All Saints', 1770.
St. Mary Magdalen, Richmond, Surrey, 1770.
Burton-on-Trent Parish Church, 1771 (case remains).
Andover Parish Church, 1772 (traditionally by Snetzler).
Edmonton Church, 1772 (possibly by the elder England).
St. Martin's Church (now the Cathedral), Leicester, 1774 (some pipework still in use).
St. George's, Hanover Square, London, 1774 (case remains).
St. Margaret's Chapel, Bath, 1775 (destroyed by fire in the factory of Clarke and Son, Bath, in 1889).
Scremby Church, Lincs., 1775.
Earl of Scarborough, Sandbeck, 1775 (now at Handsworth, Yorkshire).
Nottingham, St. Mary's Parish Church, 1777 (the remains of the pipework is at St. Andrew's Church).
Birmingham Cathedral, 1777 (enlarged and restored).
Rotherham Parish Church, 1777 (case and pipes still remain).
Nottingham, St. Peter's Church (present case only).
West Bromwich: St. Andrew's Church, 1777.
Cobham Hall, Kent, 1778.
Wymistay Hall, Wrexham (2 organs).
Woodhill, Herts., 1780.
Scarborough Parish Church, 1780.
St. Mark's Woodhill, Hatfield, 1780.
Belfast: St. Anne's Cathedral, 1781 (now in Clarence Place Hall).
Windsor: St. George's Chapel Royal, 1781.
Armagh Cathedral, Ireland.
Banbury Parish Church (case destroyed).
Bath: Moravian Chapel.
Bath: New King St. Chapel (formerly belonging to Mr. M. Hemmings).
Blickling Church, Norfolk (formerly in Hall).
Buntingford Church (now at Beeleigh Abbey).
Cambridge: Old All Saints' Church (renewed 1864).
Chester Cathedral (former choir organ).
Hillington Church, King's Lynn.
Huntingdon: St. Mary's Church and probably also All Saints' Church.
London: Buckingham Palace (now in Marlborough House Chapel and rebuilt).
London: German Calvinist Church in the Savoy.
London: St. Etheldreda, Ely Place, Holborn (later in St. Anthony's, Lordship Lane, E. Dulwich).
Norton (Sheffield) (now in Hastings Unitarian Chapel).
Painswick Church, Glos. (from 1814).
Pontefract Church, Yorks.
Theddingworth Church, Leics.
Tiverton Parish Church.
Whaddon Church, Cambs.

York: All Saint's Pavement.
Windsor: St. George's Chapel (small vestry organ).[1]
Norwich Cathedral (small organ).
Barber Institute, University of Birmingham.
Private organ: John Holmes, Monasterevan, Eire.
St. Etheldreda, Norwich.

Other English Organ-builders of the Eighteenth Century

Christopher Schreider was a German in the employ of "Father" Smith and later his son-in-law and foreman. After the death of Smith he succeeded to the business, and in 1710 became organ-builder to the Chapels Royal. His name is often spelt Schrider. He was born in Leopoldsberg, the son of Christopher and his wife Anne. He died *c.* 1754.[2]

Schreider spent most of his time maintaining his father-in-law's organs, but he also made the instruments at the following places:

Chapel Royal, St. James's, London, 1710.
St. Mary Abbot's, Kensington, 1716.
Finedon Parish Church, Northants, 1717.
St. Martin-in-the-Fields, London, 1726. (The organ case and some pipework are now in Wotton-under-Edge Parish Church.)
Westminster Abbey, 1730 (part probably in Kilkhampton Church, Bude).
St. Mary Magdalen, Bermondsey, London.
Whitchurch, Shropshire.
Hampton Court Chapel.

Christian Smith and Gerard Smith

Two of Father Smith's nephews did much repair and maintenance work and built some new organs, which include the following:

Christian Smith: Tiverton, Devon, 1696. Boston, Lincs, 1717.
Gerard Smith: Bedford Parish Church, 1715. All Hallows', Bread St., 1717. St. George's, Hanover Square, 1725. Little Stanmore Church, Edgware. Repairs at Lincoln Cathedral, 1702.

[1] This list is not exhaustive. There are several chamber organs in private hands and probably more exported organs.

[2] Chamberlayne, *Magnae Britanniae Notitia* (1754). "Organ Maker, Mr. Christopher Shrider, son of the late Mr. Shrider."

Webb, *Collection of Epitaphs* (1775), vol. ii, p. 76: "On the celebrated Mr. Christopher Shrider:

"Here rests the musical kit Shrider
Who organs built when he did bide here:
With nicest ear he tun'd 'em up;
But Death has put the cruel Stop:
Tho' Breath to others he convey'd
Breathless, alas! himself is lay'd.
May he, who us such keys has giv'n
Meet with St. Peter's keys of Heav'n!
His Cornet, Twelfth, and Diapason
Could not with Air supply his weasand:
Bass, Tenor, Treble, Unison,
The loss of tuneful kit bemoan."

Paul Micheau

A West-countryman whose real name was Mitchell. He built the organs at St. Mary Arches, Exeter, St. Mary Major, Exeter, and elsewhere in Devon, at the end of the 18th century.

Thomas Schwarbrook[1]

This eminent German organ-builder was employed by Renatus Harris. Early in the eighteenth century he left London and settled in Warwick. The last notice of him occurs in 1752 when he was given an order for £300 to repair the organ in Worcester Cathedral. He invented "a harpsichord with flute pipes as a principal to it". His chief instruments were:

St. Alfege, Greenwich, 1706 (repairs).
St. Philip, Birmingham (now cathedral), 1715.
St. Chad's, Shrewsbury, 1716 (removed in 1794).
St. Mary's, Warwick, 1717 (the case remains).
Holy Trinity, Coventry, 1732.
St. Michael's, Coventry, 1733. (This was Schwarbrook's masterpiece and cost £1,400. It contained stops named *harp, lute* and *dulcimer*, but in consequence of the "difficulty of keeping the strings in tune" they were removed in 1763.)
Magdalen College, Oxford, 1740.
Lichfield Cathedral (removed in 1789).
Stratford-upon-Avon Church, 1745 (now removed).
All Saints', Northampton (now removed).
Wells Cathedral (repairs only), 1724–8.
St. Mary's, Nottingham (removed to Uppingham Parish Church in 1777, where the case remains).

Schwarbrook also repaired the organ in St. Cuthbert's Church, Wells, adding trumpet and cornet stops, and he extended the organ in the Vicars' Hall, "sinking the pitch a lesser third to bring it nearer to concert pitch."

The Abraham Jordans, Father and Son

Dr. W. B. Gilbert in his *Antiquities of Maidstone* shows that the Jordans were an ancient family known in this town early in the fifteenth century.

> "Thomas Jordan resided [in 1477] at the ancient family seat in Stone Street, called for some centuries 'Jordan's Hall'. Many members of the family have at various times been concerned in the affairs of Maidstone, and one of the Jordans in the eighteenth century was a distiller in the town. Having a genius for organ-building, he removed to London, where he made many fine instruments."

[1] His name is also spelt Schwarbrick and Swarbrick. *Henry* Schwarbrook was organist of Hereford Cathedral in 1730, but it is not known whether he was related to Thomas.

Sir John Hawkins in his *History of Music* says:

"About the year 1700 one Jordan, a distiller, who had never been instructed in the business, but had a mechanical turn, and was an ingenious man, betook himself to the making of organs and succeeded beyond expectation. He had a son, named Abraham, whom he instructed in the same business; he made the organ for the chapel of the Duke of Chandos, at Cannons, near Edgware and many organs for parish churches."

The important invention of the swell and its introduction in the organ of St. Magnus Church, London Bridge, as announced in *The Spectator*, 8th February 1712, has been dealt with elsewhere in this work (p. 191 *et seq*). In the *London Journal* of Feb. 7th, 1729–30, the Jordans advertise an organ with a reversed console only 3 ft. high.

The Jordans built the following organs:

St. Michael's, Paternoster Royal, London, 1700 (removed in 1798).
Fulham Church, Middlesex, 1701.
St. Antholin's, Watling Street, London, 1703.
St. Saviour's (now the Cathedral), Southwark, 1703.
The Chapel of the Duke of Chandos at Cannons, 1720. (Handel often played this organ: it was removed in 1748 to Holy Trinity Church, Gosport, where, after enlargements, including one by Hill in the present century, it still remains.)
St. Magnus the Martyr, London Bridge, 1712.
Chelsea "College", 1715.
Holyrood Parish Church, Southampton, 1731.
St. Luke's, Old Street, 1733.
Parish Church, Maidstone, Kent, 1746.
St. Benet Fink, Threadneedle Street, London (later in Malmesbury Abbey).
St. Dunstan's, Fleet Street, London.
St. Paul's, Shadwell, near London.
The Portuguese Chapel, London.
The Abbey, Bath.
Covent Garden Theatre, London.
St. George's, Botolph Lane, London.

Richard Bridge

Rimbault[1] says that Richard Bridge was probably trained in the factory of the younger Harris. According to an advertisement in the *General Advertiser* for 20th February 1748, "Bridges, organ builder" resided in Hand Court, Holborn. Burney says that he died before 1776. He is known to have built organs at:

[1] Hopkins and Rimbault, op. cit.

St. Paul's, Deptford, 1730.
Christ Church, Spitalfields. This is esteemed the maker's best instrument.
St. Bartholomew the Great. (Case and organ replaced in nineteenth century.)
St. George's in the East. (Destroyed in 1940 raids.)
Cuper's Gardens, Lambeth, 1740.
St. Anne's, Limehouse. (Burnt in 1851.)
Canterbury Cathedral, 1752, (repairs).
Enfield Church, Middlesex, 1753. (Case is dated 1752.)
Faversham Church, Kent, 1754.
St. Leonard's Church, Shoreditch, 1757.
Eltham Church, Kent.
Spa Fields Chapel, Clerkenwell.
St. James's Church, Clerkenwell. (Removed to Beccles in Suffolk, 1796.)
Parish Church, Paddington.
Trinity Church, Newport, Rhode Island, U.S.A.
Worcester Cathedral (enlargement), 1752.

The composer, G. F. Handel, seems to have favoured the organ-builder Bridge. Handel wrote to Jennens, the compiler of the words of *The Messiah*, on September 30th, 1749:

"Sir,

"Yesterday, I received your letter, in answer to which I hereunder specify my opinion of an organ which I think will answer the ends you propose, being everything that is necessary for a good and grand organ without reed stops, which I have omitted because they are continually wanting to be tuned, which in the country is very inconvenient, and should it remain useless on that account, it would still be very expensive althou' that may not be your consideration. I very well approve of Mr. Bridge, who without any objection is a very good organ-builder, and I shall willingly (when he has finished it) give you my opinion of it. I have referr'd you to the flute stop in Mr. Freeman's organ being excellent in its kind, but as I do not refer you in that organ, The system of the organ I advise is, (Vizt The Compass to be up to D and down to Gamut, full Octave, Church Work).

"One row of keys, whole stops and none in halves.

Stops

An Open Diapason—of Metal throughout to be in Front.
A Stopt Diapason—the Treble Metal and the Bass Wood.
A Principal—of Metal throughout.
A Twelfth—of Metal throughout.
A Fifteenth—of Metal throughout.
A Great Tierce—of Metal throughout.
A Flute Stop—such a one as in Mr. Freeman's Organ.

"I am glad of the opportunity to show you my attention, wishing you all health and happiness, I remain with great sincerity and respect,

Sir,

Your most obedient and humble
Servant,
"George Frederic Handel."

The organ was transferred to Great Packington Church, and a second manual was added by Snetzler. The organ is still in good condition.

John Byfield, Junior

"In consequence of the many new churches that were erected at the commencement of the eighteenth century an equal number of organs was required, which induced many persons who were totally unskilled in the art and mystery of voicing organ pipes to become builders. To prevent, therefore, the sad consequences which must have naturally followed, a coalition was formed between the three eminent artists of the day. Byfield, Jordan and Bridge, who undertook to build organs at a very moderate charge, and to apply their united talents to each; the result of which was a fair, though moderate, compensation to themselves, and superior instruments to our churches. The organ in Yarmouth Parish Church, Norfolk, 1733, and in St. George's Chapel in the same town, were made in this way." A curious figure, Thomas Griffin, also comes on the scene. This man, a barber by trade, and entirely without musical qualifications, was elected Gresham Professor of Music in 1762, and held the office until 1771. He was also recorded as an organ-builder, but was actually an organ *provider*.[1] It seems likely that he obtained his instruments from Snetzler, Byfield, Jordan and Bridge. He lived in Fenchurch Street, London, and provided organs in a singular way. In consideration of an annuity granted to him for life, he provided an organ for the contracting parish, and engaged to pay an organist as long as his own annuity was regularly paid to him. In this way he contracted for organs with the authorities of the following London churches: St. Helen, Bishopsgate, 1744; St. John the Evangelist, Westminster; St. Margaret Pattens 1750; St. Michael Bassishaw; St. Mildred, Bread Street, 1744; and St. Paul, Deptford. Byfield built organs in the following places:

St. Botolph's, Bishopsgate, London, 1750.
Christ Church Cathedral, Dublin, 1751.
St. Mary's Church, Rotherhithe, 1764.
St. John's College, Oxford, 1768.
Charlotte Chapel, Pimlico, London, 1770.
Drury Lane Theatre, 1769.
Magdalen College Hall, Oxford.
Woolwich Church, London (?).
St. John's Church, Cardiff.

[1] Hawkins, *History of Music*. Hopkins and Rimbault (op. cit.) found a note in the handwriting of Dr. Benjamin Cooke, organist of Westminster Abbey, stating that Byfield died in 1774.

Highgate Chapel, London.
St. Bartholomew-the-Less, London.
The Chapel of Greenwich Hospital.
Berwick Street Chapel, Soho, 1768.
The Sheldonian Theatre, Oxford, 1768.
Barking Church, Essex, 1770.
Newbury Church, Berkshire, 1770.
St. Mary's Church, Islington, 1771.
St. Lawrence's Church, Reading, Berkshire, 1771.
The last six organs were partly the work of Green.

Glyn and Parker of Salford, Manchester, built many organs in Lancashire. They had more than a local fame, for they also erected instruments in churches at Prestbury, Cheshire; Leek, Staffordshire; Manchester Collegiate, 1730, and in London.

Parker, Thomas of Gray's Inn "Lane", built some London organs, including that which displaced "Handel's" organ at the Foundling Hospital (1768).

Samuel Green

Green was born in 1740 and became a partner of John Byfield the younger, the son of John Byfield, senior (of Harris and Byfield), and a great grandson on his mother's side of Renatus Harris. Sir J. Sutton (and others who have copied him) says that Green was in all probability brought up in the establishment of Byfield, Bridge and Jordan, to which we have referred on the previous page but as regards the only organs that have been ascribed to their "firm" (those at the Parish Church and St. George's Chapel, Yarmouth), the contract in both cases was given to Jordan. Byfield senior, and Jordan junior, both died when Green was a mere stripling, so that he cannot have owed much to either of these; but Richard Bridge seems to have been living a few years later, and either he or the younger Byfield may have had Samuel as apprentice. Byfield seems to have been the more likely master since he took Green into partnership in or about 1770, when the younger man was about thirty years of age. Together they made or remade about a dozen instruments, and then, in 1772, Samuel set up on his own account. Byfield may have retired at this time, for we hear no more of his activities, and he died in 1774.

It is worth noting that there were other good builders in the field. John Snetzler, though over sixty, was still active and continued to build organs for another decade. Both Richard Bridge and Thomas Schwarbrick had probably been dead for some years, but George England senior had been established for more than ten years and Richard Parker of Salford for an even longer period. Crang and the two Hancocks found work both in London and the provinces, but Green soon stepped into the front rank and retained his position until his death in 1796. Beginning with some church and chamber instruments of moderate size, he achieved considerable success and notoriety with his fine organ at St. Katherine's-by-the-Tower, London. Here he gave the swell organ the hitherto unprecedented compass of forty-six notes, from gamut G upwards to D. Next year came the first of his seven Cathedral organs, that at Bangor. He does not seem to have attracted the notice of George III until Snetzler had retired, but thereafter Green stepped into the old man's shoes and into the king's heart. No two contemporary builders could have differed more in their tonal ideals, but the royal preference was markedly shown when Green was directed to remove the pipework from a fairly recent Snetzler organ in the king's possession in order to substitute pipework of his own.

Green built or rebuilt more than sixty organs, but he died a poor man.[1]

An echo of the penurious state of the Green household is found in an editorial note in *The Christian Remembrancer* for January 1834, which runs:

> "Mr. Samuel Green, organ-builder to the King, died at Isleworth, Sept. 14, 1796 at the age of 56. He left a wife and two daughters, one of whom is still living, and receives a pension of 20 *l.* per ann. by the kindness of his Majesty George III. This is her sole dependence."

After Green's death, his widow carried on the business in partnership with Benjamin Blyth, who had been Green's foreman. The style of the firm was Green and Blyth, and subsequently Blyth and Sons. Benjamin died in 1840 and his son, James Blyth, in 1847. The family seems to have abandoned its connection with organ-building, but continued to live in the same premises in Church Street, quite close to the church, until 1908.

Tonally, Green's organs were soft and sweet, and for this they were widely acclaimed during his lifetime. Sir John Sutton's verdict,[2] though perhaps expressed too forcibly, could not have been very wide of the mark:

> "The writer is obliged to confess that he cannot join in the general admiration of Green's Organ-building. He certainly carried his system of voicing the pipes to the highest degree of delicacy; but what he gained in that way he lost in the general effect of the instrument. In his diapasons, though the quality of tone is sweet, at the same time it is very thin, and his chorus is entirely destitute of either fulness or brilliancy of tone. His choir organs are pretty toned, and would make nice chamber organs, but they want firmness. One would suppose that Green was anxious in his instruments to emulate the tone of a musical snuff-box rather than that of an organ. . . . His chamber organs are very nice instruments (in short all his organs are chamber organs on a large scale). . . . He unfortunately brought in a style of organ-building which had many imitators, and from which the trade is only just recovering."

Green was particularly fond of the dulciana, a small-scaled cylindrical stop developed by Snetzler after his introduction of the slightly outward-tapered pipes of dolcan or dolce quality under the name of dulciana. The invention of the cylindrical dulciana is often ascribed to Green, but Freeman[3] has

[1] A letter in *The Gentleman's Magazine* for June 1814 gives a list of forty of his organs and refers to his penury. The letter is signed H.O. and addressed from Salop, April 30 [1814].

[2] *A Short Account of Organs* (London, 1847).

[3] Andrew Freeman, Samuel Green, *The Organ*, vol. xxi.

found evidence that it was Snetzler who devised it and Green who popularised it. Like John Harris before him, and Lincoln after him, Green made frequent use of spotted metal in thin sheets for his pipework. Dr. Hopkins[1] truthfully says: "Father Smith could no more have obtained Green's playful, light and musical tones from his thick pipes, than could Green have produced powerful and ringing tone from his thin pipes. . . . Green was aware of this, particularly in regard to bass pipes: hence his great enlargement of the scale; though, from the thinness of their material, they would not bear so much blowing." Green's peculiarly musical tone was obtained by large-scale pipes with low mouths, closely nicked and lightly blown. He and England followed Father Smith's practice in the treatment of the pipes of his mixture stops, making the feet of the duplicate ranks of different lengths to avoid interference.

Although Snetzler sometimes used keyboards with "white" naturals for his chamber organs, Green is said to have been the first to make this practice general in organs of all sizes.[2] Green adopted the Venetian swell, which had been in use in harpsichords for some years, and enclosed the whole organ at St. George's Chapel, Windsor, in a general swell-box. Green's delicately voiced pipework was not the kind that could be effective under total enclosure, and the experiment was not a success. In 1836, forty years after the death of its maker, the first "general swell" was swept away. Green was the innovator of a number of ingenious organ mechanisms. He used the stop Keraulophon in the Heaton Hall organ.

St. George's Chapel, Windsor, by Samuel Green, 1790

This organ was enclosed in a large swell-box with the swell organ in a smaller box inside the larger one. The compass of the great and choir organs was carried down to FFF 12 ft. as in Green's organ at Greenwich and in those which he restored at Magdalen College, Oxford, and York Minster. Compass: Great and choir FFF no (FFF♯) to E in alt., fifty-nine notes Swell tenor F to E in alt., thirty-six notes.

Great Organ (11 *stops*)	*Choir Organ* (6 *stops*)	*Swell Organ* (7 *stops*)
Open diapason	Stopped diapason	Open diapason
Open diapason	Dulciana (from FF)	Stopped diapason
Stopped diapason	Principal	Dulciana
Principal	Flute	Principal dulciana
Twelfth	Fifteenth	Cornet, 3 ranks
Fifteenth	Bassoon	Trumpet
Sesquialtera		Hautboy
Mixture, 2 ranks	Pedals "up to C"	
Cornet to mid C, 4 ranks		
Trumpet		
Small trumpet (clarion)		

[1] Hopkins and Rimbault, op. cit.

[2] Sutton, *A Short Account of Organs*, p. 83; but instances can be quoted where Green used "black" keyboards.

It would seem that Alexander Cumming, F.R.S., a clockmaker, should have the credit of inventing horizontal bellows, since he wrote about it in 1762 and introduced it into an organ constructed under his direction in 1787, the year when Green first used it in one of his instruments, that at St. Thomas's, Ardwick, Manchester. Moreover, Green preferred diagonal bellows for his larger work; it was in his chamber instruments that he found the horizontal type advantageous.

Green was a good reed-voicer, who sought perfection rather than novelty. Hautboy and trumpet on the swell, a trumpet on the great, a bassoon or, more rarely, a vox humana on the choir were the limits of his achievements in this direction. The four- and five-rank cornet on the great organ was found in most of his instruments. The lowest rank of the five-rank cornet was of 8-ft. pitch, that of the four-rank cornet was of 4-ft. pitch. The three-rank cornet was merely the treble continuation of the sesquialtera. The days of the cornet as a solo stop were already numbered, but the cornet voluntaries, trumpet voluntaries and flute voluntaries, were to continue for some years.

Organs by Byfield and Green

Berwick St. Chapel, Soho, London, 1768.
St. John's College Chapel, Oxford, 1768.
Sheldonian Theatre, Oxford, 1768.
St. Peter's-in-the-East, Oxford, 1768.
Drury Lane Theatre, London, 1769 (burned in 1809).
Barking Church, Essex, 1770 (the case remains).
Ely Cathedral, 1770 (repairs).
Charlotte Chapel, Pimlico, London, 1770.
All Saints' Parish Church, Wigan, 1770.
St. Mary's, Islington, London, 1771.
St. Nicholas's Parish Church, Newbury, 1771.

Organs by Samuel Green

Sleaford Parish Church, Lincs., 1772.
Fairfield Church, Manchester, 1772.
Parish Church of St. Matthew, Walsall, 1773 (rebuilt Walker, 1952).
Bruton Parish Church, Williamsburg, Virginia, U.S.A., 1775.
Parish Church of All Saints, Isleworth, 1776 and 1792.
New College Chapel, Oxford, 1776 and 1794.
Appleford Church, Berkshire, 1777.
Parish Church of St. Mary, Leigh, Lancs., 1777.
The Music School, Oxford, 1777.
St. Botolph, Aldersgate Street, London, 1778.
St. Katherine's Collegiate Church, London, 1778.
Bangor Cathedral, 1779.
Walton (probably Walton in Suffolk), 1779 ?
Abbey Church, Wrexham, 1779.

College Chapel, Winchester, 1780.
St. Olave's, Hart Street, London, 1781.
Parish Church, High Wycombe, 1783.
Canterbury Cathedral, 1784.
Cashel Cathedral, 1786 (case now in Wicklow Parish Church).
East Bradenham Church, near Dereham, 1786.
St. Mary Magdalen, Old Fish Street, London, 1786.
Wells Cathedral, 1786.
Dinmore Manor Chapel (formerly at Moccas, Hereford, 1786).
Edith Weston Church, Rutland, 1787.
St. Thomas's, Ardwick, Manchester, 1787.
Nayland Church, Essex, 1787.
Wisbech Parish Church, Cambs., 1787.
St. Mary-at-Hill, London, 1788.
St. Peter's Church, Stockport, 1788.
Parish Church, Tonbridge, Kent, 1788.
Greenwich Hospital Chapel, London, 1789.
Cirencester Parish Church, 1790.
Brattle Street Church, Boston, U.S.A., 1790.
Lichfield Cathedral, 1790.
St. Michael, Cornhill, London, 1790.
St. George's Chapel, Windsor, 1790.
Heaton Hall, Manchester, 1790 (restored 1952).
Rochester Cathedral, 1791.
Lacey Green Church, Bucks., 1792.
Tamworth Parish Church, Staffs., 1792.
St. Peter-le-Poer, London, 1792.
Salisbury Cathedral, 1792 (now in St. Thomas's, Salisbury).
Opera House, Covent Garden, London, 1794.
The old Parish Church, Bolton, Lancs., 1795.
St. Mary's Parish Church, Chatham, 1795.
Old Heathfield, Sussex, 1795 (rebuilt Walker, 1866).
Broad Court Chapel, Drury Lane, London, 1796.
Convent of Notre-Dame, Plymouth, 1796.
Episcopal Chapel, Aberdeen.
Barnsley Church, Glos.
St. Michael's Church, Bath.
Camborne, Cornwall.
Coombe Abbey, near Coventry.
Trinity College Chapel, Dublin (choir retained, remainder to Durrow Church).
St. Ethelbert, Falkenham, Suffolk.
Hereford Cathedral (repairs only).
Kingstown Church, Jamaica.
Broad St. Chapel, Islington, London.
Foundling Hospital, London (repairs).
Freemason's Hall, London.

St. Mark's, Coburg Road, Camberwell.
Loughborough Parish Church.
Attingham Park (Birmingham University Adult Education Centre).
Malvern Priory Church.
Pomfret (Pontefract) Parish Church.
St. Petersburg (now Leningrad).
Tiverton Parish Church (additions).
Windsor Castle (the favourite instrument of George III), thence to Emmanuel Church, Weston-super-Mare.[1]

Greenwich Hospital, by Samuel Green, 1789, Swell to FF.

Great Organ (11 stops)		*Choir Organ* (5 stops)		*Swell Organ* (8 stops)	
	pipes		*pipes*		*pipes*
Open diapason	59	Stopped diapason	59	Open diapason	48
Open diapason	59	Principal	59	Stopped diapason	48
Stopped diapason	59	Flute	59	Dulciana	48
Principal	59	Fifteenth	59	Principal	48
Flute	59	Bassoon	59	Dulciana principal	48
Twelfth	59		——	Cornet, 3 ranks	144
Fifteenth	59		295	Trumpet	48
Sesquialtera, 3 ranks	117			Hautboy	48
Mixture, 2 ranks	118				——
Cornet to mid C, 4 ranks	116				480
Trumpet	59				
	——				
	883				

Total 1658

The England Family

George England started building organs about 1750. He learnt his trade under Richard Bridge, whose daughter he subsequently married. He had a brother, John England, who worked as an organ-builder with Hugh Russell, *c.* 1784, and did work at the church of St. Mary Woolnoth, London. George Pike England, the son of John, did excellent work between 1788 and 1814. Hopkins describes the scaling of the diapason chorus of the organs of the elder England in the following words.[2] "George England made the principal one pipe smaller than his open diapason, his fifteenth two pipes narrower, and every rank of his mixtures to a varied scale."

In a four-rank compound stop, comprising seventeenth, nineteenth, twenty-second and twenty-sixth, he would make the seventeenth a small scale, the nineteenth rather larger, the twenty-second a larger scale and powerfully voiced, and the twenty-sixth small again, and voiced almost as a dulciana. This last rank, nevertheless, made itself heard, and gave to the mixture a sound as of bells. England's mixtures were of a very silvery and sparkling

[1] A fuller account of these organs and some notes concerning their subsequent histories is given by A. Freeman in *The Organ*, vol. xxiii, pp. 110, 153, and vol. xxiv.
[2] Hopkins and Rimbault, op. cit., 3rd Ed., p. 154.

quality, though not so bold as Smith's, nor so full as Harris's, on account of their different composition and smaller scale. His larger organs commonly had the advantage of four 8-ft. stops and three 4-ft. stops, which, in conjunction with the lighter mixtures, presented a two-fold modification greatly in favour of a well-balanced tone; though, from the greater comparative firmness thus imparted to the medium work, they are generally quite capable of "carrying" a 16-ft. stop of light intonation. A five-rank cornet was an invariable constituent of all but his smallest great organs, and this in addition to other chorus work consisting of anything from three to seven ranks. Cornet voluntaries in which this compound stop was used as a solo were in great favour at the time. England's usual reeds were a trumpet on the great organ, trumpet and hautboy on the swell and a vox humana on the choir. His larger organs included a clarion on both great and swell, and occasionally, as at St. Stephen's Walbrook, a French horn on the choir. The vox humana was usually placed on the choir, but once, at Ashton-under-Lyne, on the swell and once, at St. Mildred's Poultry, London, on the great organ.

Organs by George England

Dulwich College Chapel, London, 1760 (the case and some ranks of pipes remain in the present organ, rebuilt in 1888 by Lewis and in 1908 by Norman and Beard, and by Walker in 1954).
St. Matthew's, Friday Street, London.
Long Acre Chapel, London, 1763.
Gravesend Parish Church, Kent, 1764.
St. Stephen's Walbrook, London, 1765 (the original case was saved when the church was damaged in 1940 by enemy action; rehabilitated 1954).
Ashton-under-Lyne Parish Church, 1770.
Stockport Parish Church, 1775.
St. Mildred's Poultry, London, 1778.
St. Michael's Queenhithe, 1779.

George England also repaired the organ at the church of St. Mary Woolnoth, London, in 1765, and he did similar work in other London churches.

By J. England and Russell

All Hallows, London Wall.
St. Mary Aldermary, Queen Victoria Street, London, 1781.
Llewenni (near Denbigh), Lord de Blacquiere, 1782.
Cambridge Congregational Chapel, Glos., 1784.
German Lutheran Church, Goodmansfields, London, 1795.
Christ Church, Chelsea (case from St. Michael, Queenhithe).
Bromsgrove Parish Church, etc.

George Pike England had a workshop from 1794 (and probably earlier) at 9 Stephen Street, Rathbone Place, London. He died in 1816.[1] He was

[1] His name appears in the account books of All Hallows the Great, Upper Thames St., in this year.

followed by his foreman and son-in-law, Nicholls, though there is evidence from the account books of All Hallows the Great, Upper Thames Street, that his widow, Ann England, continued under her own name for a few years longer.

G. P. England's Organs

St. George's Chapel, Portsmouth, 1788.
St. John's Church, Portsmouth, 1789.
Moravian Chapel, Fetter Lane, London, 1790 (casework now at Yoxford Church, Suffolk).
The Adelphi Chapel, London, 1791.
St. James's Church, Clerkenwell, London, 1792 (an early use of pedal "pull-downs"; the date of the organ is usually wrongly given as 1790[1]).
Warminster Parish Church, 1792 (the fine case is still in existence).
Gainsborough Parish Church, 1793.
Blandford Forum Parish Church, 1794 (the case still survives).
Newington Church, London, 1794.
St. John's Parish Church, Margate, 1795.
St. Peter's Church, Carmarthen, 1796.
St. John's Church, Hackney, 1796.
St. Margaret's Church, Lothbury, London, 1801.
St. Paul's Chapel (Trinity Parish), New York, 1802 (the case still remains).
St. George's, Colegate, Norwich, 1802.
Sardinian Chapel, Lincoln's Inn Fields, London, 1802 (broken up when Kingsway was made).
Newark Parish Church, Nottinghamshire, 1803.
St. Martin Outwich, London, 1805.
Sheffield Parish Church (now Cathedral), 1805.
Stoke Newington Parish Church, London, 1806.
South Lambeth Chapel, London, 1808.
Hinckley Parish Church, 1808.
St. Mary-the-Virgin, Bishop's Cannings, Wilts, 1809.
Richmond Parish Church, Yorkshire, 1809.
St. Thomas, Stourbridge, *c.* 1809.
Lancaster Parish Church, 1811.
Ulverston Parish Church, Lancashire, 1811.
Shifnal Parish Church, Shropshire, 1811.
St. John's Church, Chichester, 1812.
St. Stephen's Church, Norwich, 1813. Now in Cawston, Norfolk.
Islington Chapel of Ease, London, 1814 (now St. Mary Magdalene, Holloway Road). (The organ was rebuilt in 1867 by Henry Willis, who was organist at the church for some years. The case of Spanish mahogany remains. Restored by N. P. Mander, 1947.)
A chamber organ belonging to the Marquess of Anglesey sold by Christie's in 1905.
Unitarian Church, Canterbury.

[1] See p. 187.

Lincoln Cathedral Choristers' School.
Church of the Holy Innocents, Lamarsh, near Sudbury.
Beccles Parish Church, Suffolk, 1796.
St. James's, Poole, 1797.
St. Philips', Birmingham (now the Cathedral), 1805 (rebuild of Schwarbrook's organ of 1715).
Chichester Cathedral, 1806 (rebuild).
Portuguese Chapel, South Street, London, 1808 (extensions).
St. Mary Woolnoth, London, 1808 (new swell and other repairs).
Grantham Parish Church, 1809 (rebuild).
St. Nicholas, Great Yarmouth, 1812 (extensions).
All Hallows, Barking-by-the-Tower, London, 1813 (extensions).
Durham Cathedral, 1815 (additions completed by Nicholls).
St. Mary's, Haverfordwest (rebuild ?).

Minor repairs were effected by England in the organs at Greenwich Parish Church; Southwell Cathedral; St. Katherine Coleman, London; St. Andrew Undershaft and St. Clement Danes, London; St. Peter Mancroft, Norwich. England for an annual fee of £6 each had the tuning and oversight of a number of organs. His business was continued by his son-in-law, Nicholls; and James Butler and Joseph Walker (q.v.) both claimed "descent" from England.

John Avery

It does not seem possible to find much concerning the work of this builder. He is said to have been a "dissipated character",[1] but he was an excellent workman. Organs known to have been built by him were at:

St. Stephen's, Coleman Street, London, 1775.
St. Michael's Mount, Cornwall, 1786.
Croydon Parish Church, 1794 (destroyed with the church by fire in 1866).
Sevenoaks Parish Church, 1798.
Winchester Cathedral, 1799.
St. Margaret's Church, Westminster, 1804.
King's College Chapel, Cambridge, 1804. (Some of Dallam's work was incorporated in this instrument; the case was (and is) the original one erected by Chapman and Hartop in 1606.)
Carlisle Cathedral, 1808.
Great St. Mary's Church, Cambridge; repairs and extensions.

Avery also did work on the organs at Westminster Abbey and Leominster Priory.[2] He died while working on the Carlisle organ.

Crang and Hancock

Crang came from Devonshire and became a partner with Hancock, a reed-voicer, who added new reeds to many of Father Smith's organs. "Crang

[1] Hopkins and Rimbault, op. cit., p. 153.
[2] See p. 184.

appears to have been chiefly employed in altering the old echo organs into swell organs."[1] He made this improvement in the organs of St. Paul's Cathedral; St. Peter's, Cornhill; St. Clement Danes and other London churches. He built the organ in Stoneleigh Abbey, 1761. There were two Hancocks: John Hancock, organ-builder of Wych Street, London, who died near Maidstone in January, 1792;[2] and James Hancock, who was alive in 1820 and probably for some years thereafter. The firm built organs at:

St. John's, Horsleydown, 1770.
Barnstaple Parish Church, Devon 1772.
Chelmsford Parish Church (now the Cathedral), 1772.
St. George the Martyr, Queen's Square, London, 1773.
St. Vedast, Foster Lane, London.
Brompton Chapel, London.
St. Margaret's, Leicester (improvements to Smith's organ).
St. Mary's, Scarborough.
St. Mary's Cray, Kent.

Parsons, James worked in and around Plymouth. He rebuilt the organ in St. Andrew's Church, Plymouth, in 1726.

Parsons, Anthony, of Sheffield, worked in Yorkshire, Derbyshire and Lincolnshire. He repaired the Lincoln Cathedral organ, 1729–34.

Parsons, George, of 25 Duke St., Bloomsbury, London, did work in Walsall, Wolverhampton, Bilston, Coventry, Cardiff, and St. Magnus, London Bridge, 1809–29.

Parsons, Samuel, of 2 Little Russell St., London, made barrel organs and built the organ in St. Anselm's Church, Kennington Road, London, *c.* 1840.

The Development of the Pedal Organ in England

It is not a little surprising that more than four hundred years after music for an organ with an independent pedal had been written and played in Germany there were still important places in England where the pedal clavier had not been adopted or its use was despised.

Although the long-manual compasses often supplied tones of graver pitch than the lower notes of the 8-ft. stops of modern organs, they could only be played by neglecting the demands of well-spread chords in the middle of the compass. Nevertheless, several players, such as Dr. Philip Armes of Durham of the mid-nineteenth-century period, gave the organ a sonority by this means which it did not possess when the "long octaves" were swept away and the standard CC-manual compass was introduced with a quite inadequate pedal of perhaps only one stop to support it. The pedals were originally short-toe pedals, and the heel could not be used to play them. Thus the English organs stood in unhappy contrast to those fine structures in Northern Germany described by Praetorius in 1619.

[1] Hopkins and Rimbault, op. cit., p. 149.
[2] W. B. Gilbert, *Memorials of the Collegiate Church of Maidstone.*

Nicholas Forkel (1749–1818) had written in his life of Bach:[1] "The Pedal is an essential part of the Organ; by this alone it is exalted above all other instruments; for its magnificence, grandeur and majesty depend upon it. Without the Pedal this great instrument is no longer great; it approaches those little organs called in Germany Positifs, which are of no value in the eyes of competent judges."

Occasionally the shortcomings of the English organ were apparent as is shown in the following extract,[2] which deals with a little-known episode in the life of the great astronomer Herschel.

> "About this time (1765) a new organ for the parish church of Halifax was built by Snetzler, which was opened with an oratorio by the well-known Joah Bates. Mr. Herschel and six others were candidated for the organist's place. They drew lots how they were to perform in rotation. My friend Herschel drew the third lot. The second performer was Mr. Wainwright, afterwards Dr. Wainwright, of Manchester, whose finger was so rapid that old Snetzler, the organ builder, ran about the church exclaiming, 'Te tevil, te tevil, he run over te key like one cat, he vil not give my piphes room for to shpeak.' During Mr. Wainwright's performance I was standing in the middle aisle with Herschel. 'What chance have you,' said I, 'to follow this man?' He replied, 'I don't know. I am sure fingers will not do.' On which he ascended the organ loft and produced from the organ so uncommon a fulness, such a volume of slow, solemn harmony, that I could by no means account for the effect. After this short extempore effusion, he finished with the Old Hundredth psalm tune, which he played better than his opponent. 'Aye, aye,' cried old Snetzler, 'tish is very goot, very goot indeed. I vil luf tish man, for he gives my piphes room for to shpeak.' Having afterwards asked Mr. Herschel by what means, in the beginning of his performance, he produced so uncommon an effect, he replied, 'I told you fingers would not do' and produced two pieces of lead from his waistcoat pocket. 'One of these,' said he, 'I placed on the lowest key of the organ, and the other upon the octave above; thus by accommodating the harmony I produced the effect of four hands instead of two. However, as my leading the concert on the violin is their principal object, they will give me the place in preference to a better performer on the organ; but I shall not stay long here, for I have the offer of a superior situation at Bath, which offer I shall accept'."

No earlier account of the use of pedals in an English organ than the following appears to be extant. It is from the Wages Book, No. 45, preserved in the library of St. Paul's Cathedral:

[1] Ch. iv of Forkel's *Life of Bach*, in an English translation, appears in *The Bach Reader* (David and Mendel, London, 1946).

[2] Extract from the *History and Antiquities of Doncaster and its Vicinity*, by Edward Miller, Mus. D. (Doncaster, *c.* 1804). Miller composed the tune "Rockingham".

"1720–21 Xtopher Shrider Musical Instrumt. Maker for Cleaning and Repairing the Organ, all the pipes and Movements and for adding sevll. new Springs	45. 0. 0.
For Adding six large Trumpet Pipes down to 16 foot tone to be used with a pedal or without	36. 0. 0.
For the Pedal and its movements	20. 0. 0.
For adding the Loudning and Softning (that is) the Swelling Note & its movements & other things thereto belonging	12. 0. 0.
	113. 0. 0.
Deduct on this bill	13. 0. 0.
	£100. 0. 0."

It is a matter of some curiosity that many historians of the organ have given the date of the introduction of pedals into English organ-building sixty or seventy years after this. In *Account of the Handel Commemoration of* 1784 Burney says: "On Handel's first arrival in England, from Green's[1] great admiration of this master's style of playing, he had literally condescended to become his bellows blower, when he went to St. Paul's to play on that organ, for the exercise it afforded him in the use of the pedals."

It will be recalled that in 1712 Renatus Harris tried to persuade the Cathedral authorities to commission him to erect an enormous organ in the west end of St. Paul's Cathedral with six manuals and a large independent pedal organ of continental proportions.

The introduction of pedals caused no great stir, and for another century or more few organs were equipped with as much as a row of twelve pedal pipes. Indeed, as late as 1860, when Holdich built a pedal organ of ten stops for his instrument at Lichfield Cathedral, Spofforth, the organist, protested: "You may put them there but I shall never use them."[2] At the Temple Church, which was regarded as one of the half-dozen most important places in the country for its organs and organ-playing, pedals were not introduced until 1843, when the organ was rebuilt by Bishop. Only an octave and a half of FFF pedals were laid down and an octave of CCC "return"[3] pedal pipes were actuated by them. Various stories were told about the introduction of pedal pipes at Westminster Abbey and no records are available which clear

[1] Maurice Green was organist at St. Paul's from 1718 to 1755.

[2] Lichfield Cathedral pedal organ, CCC to E, by Holdich, 1860.

Double double open diapason	32
Double double open diapason	16
Montre	16
Grand bourdon	16
Octave	8
Superoctave	4
Sesquialtera	1½
Mixture	2 ranks
Grand trombone	16
Grand trumpet	8

[3] See p. 189.

up the difficulties. Certain it is that sometime during the latter half of the eighteenth century thirteen large-scale unison pedal pipes from GG were added. It is believed that Dr. Benjamin Cooke composed his service in G for the opening of the instrument with the new improvement, and the organ part contains passages appropriate to the pedals. The date of the service is 1778, and if the pedal pipes were added at this date they would have been the work of Thomas Knight, for Avery, who is usually credited with this innovation at Westminster Abbey, did not start work there until 1790.

In 1757 John Snetzler built a three-manual organ (with a swell organ from fiddle G to F) and pedals from FFF to C (nineteen notes) as a part of the original organ at the German Lutheran Chapel in the Savoy, which was the church he attended. (In 1878 the old chapel was demolished, and the organ taken to a new building in Cleveland Street, W.1, where the instrument has been rebuilt at different times by Gray and Davison, August Gern, and the present firm of Walker, and was destroyed during the last war.)

The late introduction of the pedals in England was due to the type of instrument specified by our "Masters of Music", who were insular and rather jealous where continental ideas were concerned. Both Smith and Harris would have been capable of building satisfactory pedal organs, and, as a young man, Snetzler had worked on some of the largest German and Dutch instruments. Even in the second decade of the nineteenth century only nine of thirty-three cathedral and abbey organs in Britain had pedals, and in all but two of these cases they were pull-downs acting on the great organ keys.

In view of Snetzler's claim concerning the German pedals fitted to the Savoy organ, it would seem that the St. Paul's pedals were only those of the short-toe type and probably not more than an octave of pull-downs. The earliest date which can be found for the introduction of pedals into England is therefore 1720, and thus Hopkin's statement that pedals "were not introduced into England until nearly the close of the eighteenth century" requires qualification.

Some references to organ pedals in English eighteenth-century musical publications probably show the continental influence, and do not mean that even octaves of the pedals were of frequent incidence in English organs. In Tans'ur's *Elements of Music Displayed* (London, 1767) is found: "To play on an organ is to press down the several keys with the Fingers (or if Pedals, with the Feet)."

Grassineau's *Musical Dictionary*[1] (London, 1740) is partly an English version of an earlier French work (*Brossard's Dictionary*, Paris, 1703) and we need not be surprised when we read that "Usually the longest pipe (of the organ) is sixteen feet, though in extraordinary organs 'tis thirty-two: the pedal tubes are always open though made of wood and lead". The use of the word *tubes* as a translation of *tuyaux* and the word *lead* for *pipe-metal* seems to be indicative that the translator knew little about organs. The passage cannot be interpreted to mean that independent pedal stops

[1] Another part of the dictionary comes from the *Cyclopedia* of Ephraim Chambers, 1728, and the article may have been the work of Pepusch.

were known in England in 1740; nor did any 32-ft. pipes exist in England at the time.

There is an interesting reference to organ pedals in Rees's *Cyclopedia* (London 1805), in which we read: "Scarce two organs in the kingdom have their pedals alike, either in respect of their number or position." A diagram of the two-octave pedals at St. Paul's Cathedral is given, which "might serve as a model for other English organs".

In 1800 the English did not know the music of Bach, his predecessors and that of the French school of organ composers. Little need was felt for an independent pedal part, and the idea of playing a solo chorale melody with the feet was entirely unknown. The Bach "pedal fugues" were a source of wonder to those who heard them played by Samuel Wesley. In the latter half of the nineteenth century, leeway was made up by the magnificent pedal organs of Willis, Schulze and Cavaillé-Coll and the fine playing on the pedals, probably unmatched throughout the world, of W. T. Best.

Sir George Smart played the organ at St. George's Chapel, Windsor, for the funeral of King William in 1837. In order to accommodate a few more people in the organ loft, "R. Gray was sent down to Windsor to remove some of the pipes and board over the others".[1] The pedal pipes had been added since 1830. At the 1851 Exhibition Sir George Smart, then a vigorous old man of seventy-five years, who had played at the coronations of William IV and Victoria (for which latter he received a fee of £300), was asked to try one of the organs with pedals. "My dear Sir," he replied, "I never in my life played upon a *gridiron*."[2] At Lincoln Cathedral J. M. W. Young, appointed organist in 1850, was the first to make use of the pedals.[3]

More interesting is the notebook of Henry Leffler, organist of the Church of St. Katherine-by-the-Tower, who visited practically every British organ of note between the years 1800 and 1810.[4] Of thirty-three British cathedrals and abbeys at the time only two, those at Westminster and Hereford had a few separate pedal pipes.

In 1844[5] it is recorded that Mendelssohn cancelled an engagement to play pedals and a swell organ to tenor C.[6] Until Bishop built a new organ at his organ compositions at the Hanover Square Rooms because the organ was not fitted with "German pedals".

In 1884 the organ at Canterbury Cathedral had only one octave of short Southwell Minster in 1890 there were no separate pipes on the three-manual organ. Spofforth, who had been a pupil-assistant there, later became organist at Lichfield Cathedral, where he refused to use the large pedal organ provided

[1] *Journals of Sir George Smart*, 1837 (London, Longmans, 1907).

[2] Sir John Goss (1800–80), organist of St. Paul's Cathedral, chided the late skilled amateur, E. G. Meers, because he was practising the pedals, saying: "You charm with your fingers not your feet" (told to the author).

[3] Reported by his successor, Dr. G. J. Bennett.

[4] The chief contents of his notebook were edited by C. W. Pearce as *Notes on English Organs* (London, 1911).

[5] Notices in the London papers during June 1844.

[6] S. W. Harvey, *The Organs of Canterbury Cathedral* (Canterbury, 1910).

by Holdich. It is surprising that Smith, Harris and Snetzler, who had all worked on large pedal organs abroad, should not have been able to leave a single example in England, though Harris tried valiantly.[1]

The following account is interesting because it reveals an attempt to advance the English organ in several ways.

St. Mary Redcliffe, Bristol

"To all Organists, Masters in Musick, and Gentlemen who are Judges or Lovers of the Organ.

"Gentlemen—Mr. Strahan, who drew the design for the organ-case, which was lately erected in St. Mary Redclift Church in Bristol, having thought fit to be at the expence of its being engraved (for Sale) and having given a very imperfect Account of the internal Contents, for want of desiring Information from us, the Makers of it, we think it reasonable to give the following Account of it; and are, Gentlemen, Your humble Servants, J. Harris and J. Byfield, Red-Lion Street, near Holborn, London, Feb. 1728–9.

"This instrument is Consort Pitch; the Compass or Extent of the great Organ, is from Double C-fa-ut, D-la-sol in Alt, compleat long Octaves, containing 63 keys and has the following stops, viz. two open Diapasons of Metal, one stop'd Diapason, one Principal, a grand sexquialtera of five ranks, a Trumpet, a Clarion, a Cornet of five ranks, and Twelfth, a Fifteenth and Tierce. The last three stops are only from double Gamut to D-la-sol in Alt.

"The Chair or Choir Organ, is from double Gamut to D-la-sol in Alt, being long Octaves, containing fifty-six keys, and has the following stops, viz, a stop'd Diapason, a Principal, a Flute Almain, a Flute, a Bassoon, and a grand Sexquialtera of three ranks.

"The Ecchoes (which are made to swell or express Passion) are from Gamut to D-la-sol in Alt, being fourty-four keys and has the following stops, viz. the open Diapason, the stop'd Diapason, the Principal, the Flute, a Cornet throughout the keys, a Trumpet, a Hautboy, a Vox Humane and a Cromhorn.

"This organ contains 26 stops and 1928 valuable speaking pipes, which are considerably more than either the organ in St. Paul's Cathedral or that in St. Martin's Church in London contain, and are as well perform'd in every respect, notwithstanding this Organ cost no more than £1,000 which is vastly less than the price of either of the others, altho' the Compass of St. Martin's is only from double Gamut to D-la-sol in Alt, and St. Paul's has (we think) only the two Diapasons and Trumpet, so low as Redclift Organ; and neither of those stops contain either the Double double C-fa-ut sharp or Double double D-sol-re sharp which are expensive pipes.

"Besides the C sharp and D in Alt, are not in any of the Stops of St. Paul's organ although it cost three times the price of this.

[1] See p. 151.

"N.B.—There are Pedals to the lower Octave of this great Organ, notwithstanding the touch as good as need be desired; and there is an Invention, which by drawing only a Stop, makes it almost as loud again as it was before (or play in a double Manner) tho' there are no new Pipes added to the Organ, or any keys put down by it. This great piece of work was compleated with the time agreed upon, and was finished in little more than a year and a Quarter, and was approved of as an excellent ton'd Instrument, by those Gentlemen whom the Parishioners made choice of to be the Judges of it, as it has ever been by all Persons that have play'd upon it."[1]

Gerber in his *Lexicon der Tonkünstler* erroneously states that G. ("the Abbé") Vogler introduced pedals into England. In an article on Vogler in *Grove's Dictionary of Music* (1922) J. H. Mee repeats this statement and adds, also in error, that "their introduction by the organ-builder England certainly belongs to the year of Vogler's visit (1790)". England's organ, planned in 1790 for St. James's Church, Clerkenwell, was not built until 1792, as is evident from an inscription on the instrument. Moreover, we have already quoted a document which shows that the organ originally did not have pedals.[2]

Pearce[3] quotes a lecture, the manuscript of which he read, given by Samuel Wesley (1766–1837), in which, speaking of improvements in organ-

[1] Thus, the organ at the church of St. Mary Redcliffe, Bristol, built in 1726 by Harris and Byfield, was notable in a number of ways: it had pedals; it had the first known coupler in England; the great organ had a compass of sixty-two notes, complete from 16-ft. C.; the swell consisted of nine stops; and eight of the twenty-six stops were reeds, more than a quarter of the total. A copy of this advertisement is preserved in the church. The younger Harris and Byfield built other organs between 1726 and 1743 and thereafter Byfield worked alone until 1757: St. Thomas, Bristol; St. Mary, Shrewsbury; Haverfordwest Parish Church; Grantham Parish Church; St. Lawrence, Reading; St. Bartholomew-by-the-Exchange, London; St. Mary-le-Tower, Ipswich; St. Thomas, Lewes; Ranelagh Gardens, London; Archbishop Tenison's Church, Regent St., London; an organ now in Truro Cathedral; Christ Church Cathedral, Dublin; Doncaster Parish Church, and many improvements. They also built the organ in the New Music Hall, Fishamble St., Dublin (1742). The instrument was later removed to St. George's Church, Douglas, Isle of Man.

[2] An account of Vogler's performances at the Pantheon is given in *The Gazetteer* and *New Daily Advertiser* for 8th, 22nd and 29th May 1790.

[3] *The Evolution of the Pedal Organ* (1927). In the article "Organ" in *Grove's Dictionary of Music*, which has persisted in its original form until recently, E. J. Hopkins says that the organ at St. James's Church, Clerkenwell, was the first English instrument to have had pedals. He further says that it was built by G. P. England in 1790. Apart from the fact that this instrument was not the first in England to have pedals, two other facts are important: (*a*) the church of St. James's, Clerkenwell, was not built until 1792; and (*b*) a memorandum by J. Butler, apprentice to G. P. England, which was shown to Dr. C. W. Pearce by H. Harford Battley of Canterbury and gives the specification of the organ and its correct date, 1792, makes no mention of pedals. (This memorandum was printed in the issue of the *Musical Standard* for 25th August 1866, vol. v, p. 117.)

It may be that Vogler added pedals which he had brought with him, or which he had had made on the spot, to the Pantheon organ in order to exercise himself to the full at his concerts at which he used this organ. Burney, in Rees's *Cyclopedia* under the heading "Vogler", says that the latter also enclosed the whole organ. The Pantheon and its contents were destroyed by fire during January 1792 (*Gentleman's Magazine*, 25th January 1792).

building in his day, he said he "could well remember the time when the only organ in London to which pedals were affixed was that in the German church in the Savoy, built by Snetzler". It is evident that if indeed the organ at St. Paul's Cathedral no longer had pedals, they had been allowed to fall into disuse or had been removed because of the indifference or antagonism of the organist. In fact, so insular and conservative were many English organists that the pedals were not used even when they were provided.

An early British enthusiast for pedal-playing was Dr. Edward Hodges, organist of St. James's Church, Bristol, and later of old Trinity Church, New York[1] (from 1839). Many of the early pedals, which acted only on the lower-manual keys and did not control any pipes of their own, consisted only of an octave of short wooden projections from the case of the organ. They were called toe pedals to distinguish them from the German pedal claviers, such as Snetzler provided for the organ at the German Lutheran Church of the Savoy in London. The former were "clumsy pieces of wood measuring from an inch to an inch and a half in width, and varying in length from a few inches to about two feet, only with the latter could both toe and heel be employed". Dr. Hodges had his pedals made of iron or brass, "with a sort of rail about the size of a lead-pencil running along the top of each pedal, so that he could reach over and easily play a third with his toe".[2]

Hodges also devised polyphonic pedal pipes, an example of which was shown by Ducci in his organ at the Great Exhibition of 1851 and later were perfected and used by John Compton in recent years.

Hodges describes these pipes[3] as "on the flute principle . . . in one of the sides of the pipe, apertures are cut, near which pallets or stoppers are affixed so as to cover or close them tightly. These pallets are respectively made to open upon the depression of their corresponding pedals, and to shut by means of springs or balance weights when the pedals are released. In this there is, of course, a double action—the wind pallet or air-valve being opened at the same time that the tuning pallet is adjusted. This action, which would be too heavy for the fingers, is scarcely sensible to the feet". One such pipe was made by John Smith, a Bristol organ-builder, and was placed in the organ at St. Mary Redcliffe, Bristol. (Smith also built a new organ at St. James's Church, Bristol, in 1824 under the direction of Hodges, then the organist of the church. This instrument contained the first pedal stop in England of 32-ft. tone and this was a double-stopped diapason, whose lowest pipe of C was 16 ft. in length. This organ also contained the first swell-octave to great coupler made in this country. It had four manuals, two of which belonged to choir organs, one at the back of the player, and the other inside the great case.)

In 1829 J. C. Bishop built what was then a large organ with three pedal stops with a range of two octaves each (twenty-five notes), the only "16-ft. stop" extended to GGG 21 ft. and the "unison" pedal pipes to GG 10ft., with a trombone of the same pitch. A manual keyboard on the left-hand side of

[1] F. Hodges, *Life of E. Hodges* (New York, 1896).
[2] A. H. Messiter, *A History of the Choir and Music of Trinity Church, New York* (New York, 1906).
[3] *Quarterly Musical Magazine and Review* (1827), vol. ix.

the three main keyboards acted on the pedal organ. E. J. Hopkins reported that he had seen a copy of Handel's chorus, "'But the waters overwhelmed their enemies', arranged for three performers", a duet for the manuals and the bass part played by a third performer at the side keyboard.[1] This was at St. James's Church, Bermondsey.

In 1823 the York Minster organ built by Ward had thirteen stops to FFF and two to FFFF, but its design was awkward and uneconomical.

Pearce[2] gives the following measurements for some of the earlier English pedals:

Date		*Width of Pedal key. Inches*	*Width from Centre to Centre. Inches*
1827	Dr. Hodges's pedal-board	1	$2\frac{1}{2}$ or $2\frac{1}{4}$
1801	St. Margaret's Lothbury (G. P. England)	$1\frac{1}{2}$	$2\frac{3}{4}$
1829	St. James's, Bermondsey (J. C. Bishop)	$\frac{7}{10}$	$2\frac{7}{8}$
1830	St. James's, Clapham (J. C. Bishop)	$\frac{7}{8}$	$2\frac{3}{4}$
1850-4	St. Mary Woolnoth (Groves and Hill)	$\frac{3}{4}$	$2\frac{3}{8}$
1881	W. E. Dickson in *Practical Organ-Building*	1	$2\frac{1}{2}$
1882	Royal College of Organists	—	$2\frac{3}{8}$
after 1851	Wesley-Willis pedal-board	$\frac{3}{4}$	$2\frac{3}{4}$

The *bourdon*, ubiquitous in later years, under the name of *double-stopped diapason*, was first used in England as a pedal stop early in the nineteenth century by Gray in the organ of St. Patrick's Roman Catholic Church, Soho Square, London, when he added eleven pipes, and soon after this two octaves of such pipes from CCC upwards were fitted to England's organ in St. Matthew's, Friday Street, Cheapside, London.[3]

For many years of the nineteenth century in England any independent pedal organ consisted of a single stop, a wooden open diapason of large scale, which was labelled "pedal pipes".[4] At first this pedal stop was a downward extension as far as G of the great manual. For example, in the Avery organ (1798) at the Parish Church, Sevenoaks, Kent, one of the great open diapasons went down to G♯ on the manual and was continued to GGG ($10\frac{2}{3}$ ft.) by large wooden pipes actuated by the pedals only. At various times during the century when old organs were repaired and extended, the old G pedal compasses were continued downwards to the present bottom note C. In order to save the expense of the five large pipes necessary to do this, pipes sounding the octave of the true pedal pitch were often used. This inartistic makeshift, known as *return pedal pipes*, meant that the lowest note in a short-

[1] *Grove's Dictionary of Music*, editions until 1922.
[2] C. W. Pearce, *The Evolution of the Pedal Organ* (London, 1927).
[3] This church was destroyed in 1881.
[4] At the time of writing this book there remain a considerable number of pedal stops still labelled in this way.

pedal compass of an octave or so was in the middle of pedal keyboard. The simplest of bass melodic lines played on such a pedal would be grotesquely distorted.

In the eighteenth century there were at least two organs with a great-manual compass from CCC upwards. Both the organs at St. Paul's Cathedral and St. Mary Redcliffe, Bristol, had "pull-down" pedal keys, but the latter had in addition a "spring of communication" or sub-octave coupler, which gave octaves downwards on the pedals, which, according to Leffler, had "a bad effect".

A first step towards the evolution of an independent pedal organ was the introduction of a drum-pedal. In this a single pedal key admitted wind to certain pipes which were tuned so that beats were produced which were thought to have the effect of a drum roll.[1] At Christ Church, Spitalfields, there were four pipes, two of which were tuned to CC and two tuned to the semitone below. Amongst others, G. P. England's organ in St. John's Chapel, Portsmouth Common, built in 1788, also had a drum pedal. At Westminster Abbey at the beginning of the nineteenth century there were thirteen open wood pipes from GGG to GG independent of the manuals. Although they had the same pitch as the manual diapasons, "by reason of their scale and the absence of upper partials they produced a tone quality which produced an effect of deeper pitch".

The Compasses of old English Organs

Some instruments had "short-octave" GG manuals for great and chair (choir) manuals; others had GG manuals with long octaves. Some great and choir keyboards descended a note lower to FF; occasionally others went as low as CCC; whilst the present lowest manual note of CC was also to be found. Not infrequently the echo organ and the later swell, which replaced it (or enclosed it), only went as low as middle C or fiddle G.

For at least one hundred and fifty years, up to the Restoration of the Monarchy in 1660, the manual range was usually four octaves from CC, the present bottom key. Often the lowest CC♯ was omitted, as such a bass note could not be used in the days of unequal temperament in tuning. After the Restoration there was a tendency to extend the manual compasses downwards, and in view of the fact that most English organists held out against the introduction of pedals, a sorely needed 16-ft. bass could sometimes be supplied by the left hand, though as regards the proper spacing of notes in the other parts, the right hand was set an impossible task, and the proper flow of independent parts in counterpoint was inhibited. In spite of the apparent downward extension of the manual compass, a number of pipes were sometimes omitted, as they would rarely be required in the restricted range of keys which would be tolerable on an instrument tuned to mean-tone temperament.

[1] The thunder pedal was popular in continental organs in the eighteenth century and, using the same principle of the heterodyning of the notes of large pipes, was found on some of the French instruments of Cavaillé-Coll and in German and Swiss organs. In Schulze's Doncaster organ of 1862 the thunder pedal caused the six lowest notes of the organ to sound simultaneously.

With *short octaves* only one extra pipe below CC was required. This additional key was placed immediately to the left of the CC key and had pipes sounding GG assigned to it. GG#, AA#, BB, and CC#, four notes not often required, were omitted, and the pipes sounding AA were assigned to the CC# key. The low thirteen keys of the keyboard would play as follows:

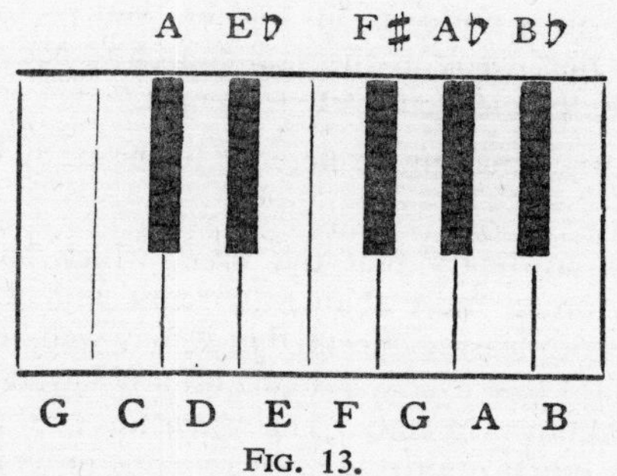

FIG. 13.

With *long octaves* at least one of the notes omitted in the short octave system was included. The short-octave keyboard beginning on GG and ending with F had fifty-five pipes per rank, and if only the GG# were omitted with the long octave keyboard there would be fifty-eight pipes in each rank. Short octaves were made in small European organs also.

THE INTRODUCTION OF THE SWELL ORGAN

It will be recalled that in Harris's proposal in 1712 for a west-end organ for St. Paul's Cathedral one of the six manuals of this instrument was "to be adapted for the emitting of sounds to express Passion by swelling any Note, as if inspir'd by Human Breath; which is the greatest Improvement an Organ is capable of, except it had articulation". In the same pamphlet he claims to have introduced this feature into the organ he set up at Salisbury Cathedral in 1710, and to have shown it "five years since" to Mr. Philip Hart, a well-known London organist. There is no record that Harris actually fulfilled his claims before Abraham Jordan, father and son, made a small swell organ for their instrument at St. Magnus's Church, London Bridge. At this period the pipes belonging to the third or echo manual were often placed in a box to give an effect of distance. Jordan made a sliding shutter to the front of the box and this could be opened and closed by means of a pedal. The device found immediate favour in England and, before the more modern Venetian swell fronts were invented, the lid of the box was hinged and worked by ropes, as an alternative to Jordan's method. In these early swells the indiscreet use of the pedal would lead to loud banging from the inside of the organ.[1]

The following advertisement appeared in *The Spectator* for 8th February 1712:

[1] It seems probable that Jordan knew of earlier swell-organs in Spain and Portugal.

"Whereas Messrs. Abraham Jordan have, with their own hands, joynery excepted, made and erected a very large organ in St. Magnus' Church, at the foot of London Bridge, consisting of four sets of keys, one of which is adapted to the art of emitting sounds by swelling the notes, which never was in any organ before; this instrument will be publicly opened on Sunday next, the performance by Mr. John Robinson. The above said Abraham Jordan gives notice to all masters and performers that he will attend every day next week at the said church to accommodate all those gentlemen who shall have a curiosity to hear it."

Again we find Burney making a reference to the tardy introduction of the swell in Germany:

"It is very extraordinary that the *swell*, which has been introduced into the English organ more than fifty years, and which is so capable of expression and of pleasing effects, that it may well be called the greatest and most important that ever was made on any keyed instrument, should be still utterly unknown in Italy. The *touch* too of the organ, which our builders have so much improved, still remains in its heavy, noisy state; and now I am on this subject I must observe that most of the organs which I have met with on the Continent, seem to be inferior to ours built by Father Smith, Byfield, or Snetzler, in every thing but size. As the churches there are often immense, so are the organs; the tone is indeed somewhat softened and refined by space and distance; but when heard near, it is intolerably coarse and noisy; and though the number of stops in these large instruments is very great, they afford but little variety, being, for the most part, duplicates in unisons and octaves to each other, such as the great and small 12ths, flutes and 15ths: hence in our organs not only the touch and tone, but the imitative stops are greatly superior to those of any organs that I have met with."[1]

"Before I left England, Mr. Snetzler had told me, that I should doubtless find *swells* in Berlin organs, though he was not certain that this improvement, which was English, had been adopted in other places on the continent: for Mr. Handel, several years ago, had desired him to describe, in writing, the manner in which the swell was produced, that he might send it to a particular friend in Berlin, who very much wished to introduce it there.

"But I enquired in vain of musical people in that city, whether they knew of any such machine, as a swell, worked by pedals, in any of their organs; no such contrivance had ever been heard of, and it was difficult to explain it."[2]

The Venetian Swell Shutters, now commonly used, were first adapted for organs by Green (q.v.), but they had been used a few years before this by English harpsichord makers.

[1] C. Burney, *The Present State of Music in France and Italy* (2nd ed. corrected, London, 1773). The passage quoted is from notes written on 18th November 1770 in Rome.

[2] C. Burney, *The Present State of Music in Germany and the Netherlands.*

PLATE 19a.

Totentanzkapelle, Lübeck, Marienkirche. J. Stephani 1475. J. Scherer 1557 (rückpositif). Destroyed Palm Sunday 1942

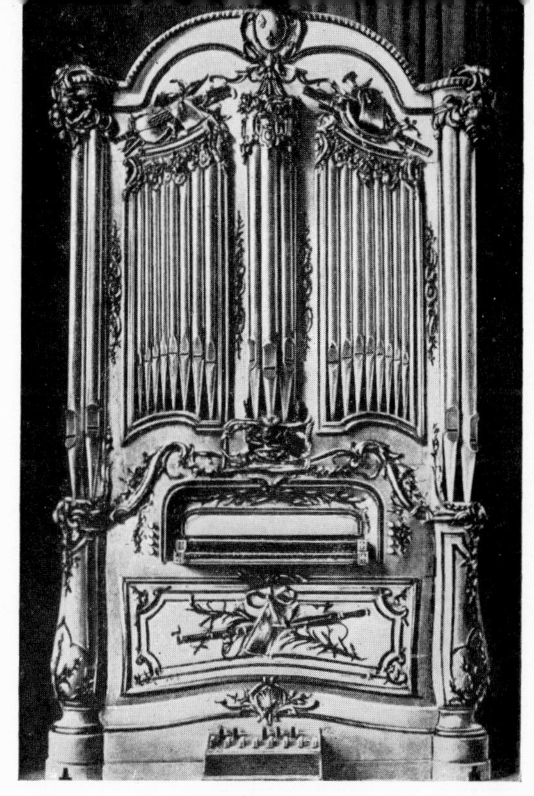

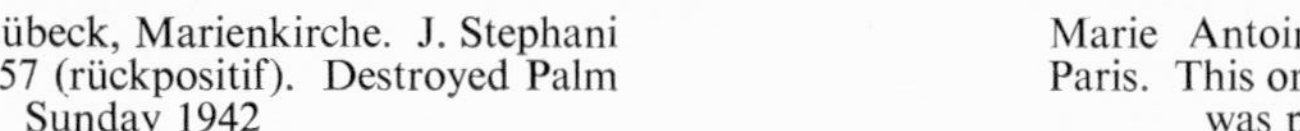

PLATE 19b.

Marie Antoinette's organ now in St. Sulpice, Paris. This organ, built by Nicolas Somer in 1756, was played by Mozart and Gluck

PLATE 20a.

La Ferté Bernard, France. Case by Evrard Baudot

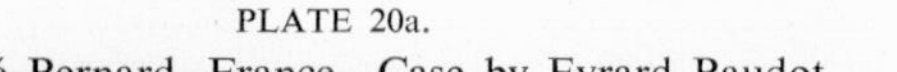

PLATE 20b.

Snetzler Case, c.1760. St. Peter's Church

PLATE 21a.

St. Sulpice, Paris. (Clicquot—Cavaillé Coll.) The largest organ in France

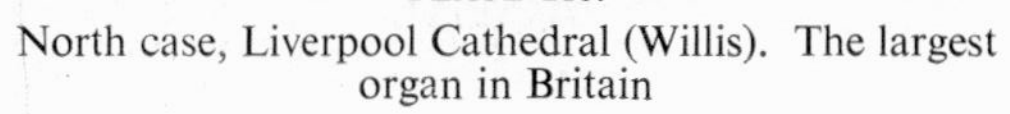

PLATE 21b.

North case, Liverpool Cathedral (Willis). The largest organ in Britain

PLATE 22a.

Chartres Cathedral, case by Foubert and Bely 1542–51

PLATE 22b.

The organ in the church of St. Stephen's Walbrook, London. (1765, case by the elder England. Organ

The swell principle seems to have been discovered independently by the Spanish builders, as we have already noted, not long before the Jordan swell at St. Magnus's Church. The fine effect of an enclosed reed chorus was first known to the Spanish, whence it passed many years later to Cavaillé-Coll and so to Henry Willis in England. Thus, the typical English "full-swell" effect can be traced to early eighteenth-century Spanish organs where 16-ft., 8-ft., 4-ft. and even quint reeds of brassy tone were known.

The Jordans were almost anticipated by Thomas Mace, as the following passage will show:

Thomas Mace's Table Organ[1]

"Now as to the description of this Table Organ, I cannot more conveniently do it than first in giving you a view of it by this figure here drawn, and then by telling you all the dimensions and the whole order of it. I mean my second which is the largest and best, and take as here followeth; Two of such organs only (I believe) are but as yet in being in the world, They being of my own contrivance, and which I caus'd to be made in my own house and for my own use as to the maintaining of Public Consorts etc.

"It is in its bulk and height of a very convenient, handsome and compleat table size (which may become and adorn a Nobleman's dining room, and all of the best sort of wainscot).

"The length of the leaf is 7 foot and 5 inches.

"The breadth 4 foot and 3 inches.

"The height 3 foot, inch, and better.

"Beneath the leaf, quite round, is handsome carved and cut work about 10 inches deep to let out the sound and beneath the cut work, broad panels so contrived that they may be taken down at any time for the amending such faults as may happen, with two shelved cupboards at the end behind to lock up your Musick Books etc.

"The Leaf is to be taken in Two pieces at any Time for conveniency of tuning or the like neatly joyn'd in the midst.

"The keys at the upper end being of Ebony and Ivory, all covered with a Slipping Clampe (answerable to the other end of the table) which is to take off at any Time when the organ is to be us'd and again put on, and lock'd up, so that none can know it as an organ by sight but a compleat new fashioned Table.

"The Leaf has in it 8 desks cut quite through very neatly [answerable to that upstanding one in the figure] with springs under the edge of the Leaf, so contriv'd that they may open, and shut at Pleasure; which (when shut down) joyn closely with the Table Leaf: But (upon occasion) may be opened, and set up, (with a spring) in the manner of a desk, as your books may be set up against them.

[1] From *Musick's Monument or a Remembrancer of the Best Practical Musick Both Divine and Civil that has ever been known to have been in the World*, "Tho. Mace, one of the Clerks of Trinity College in the University of Cambridge. Printed by T. Ratcliffe & N. Thompson for the Author 1676." Facsimile, Paris 1958.

"Now the intent of those desks, is of far more excellent use, than for meer [*sic*] desks; For without those openings, your organ would be but of very slender use, as to Consorts, by reason of the closeness of the leaf. But by the help of them, each desk opened, is as the putting in of another Quickning, or Enlivning stop; so that when all the 8 Desks stand open, the Table is like a little Church Organ, so sprightfully lusty and strong, that it is too loud for any ordinary private use. But you may moderate that by opening only so many of those desks as you see fit for your present use.

"There are in this Table Six Stops.

"The first is an Open Diapason, The second a Principal, The third a Fifteenth, The fourth a Twelfth, The fifth a Two & Twentieth and The Sixth a Regal.

"There is likewise (for a Pleasure and Light Content) a Hooboy Stop, which comes in at any time, with the foot; which stop (together with the Regal) makes the Voice Humane.

"The Bellow is laid next the ground; and is made very large, and driven either by the Foot of the Player, or by a cord at the far end.

"Thus I have given you a short description of this most incomparable and super excelling instrument, not doubting, but when it is well pondered and considered upon, it will be approved of and brought into use.

"And if any Person (upon the reading of this description) shall be desirous to purchase such an instrument, I believe I can procure for him the very same, which I have thus described &c. For my unhappiness has been such (by reason of my deafness) that I have (of late years) parted with it; and it is (at this time I think) to be sold, so that if any person send to me about it I shall do him the best service I can in it. And indeed it is a Very Very Jewel."

It will be noted that the Hautboy stop was controlled by the foot, and that it was possible for the performer to blow the instrument while playing it, in the same way. Had Mace thought of controlling the opening of one or more of his "8 desks" by means of a foot pedal he would have anticipated, in a more subtle way, Abraham Jordan's first swell in the organ of St. Magnus-the-Martyr, London Bridge (1712), by thirty-six years.

CHAPTER VI

THE ORGAN IN THE NEW WORLD

PEDRO DE GANTE, who was born in Flanders in 1480, theologian and musician, probably a half-brother of the Emperor Charles V, founded a school in Mexico City in 1524.[1] He introduced the liturgical music of the Roman Church and trained the natives in the construction and playing of musical instruments. He built an organ in 1527, probably of the positive type which was then found in the south European countries. This was almost certainly the first real organ to be heard in the new world. Many of the Mexican churches had organs which were played by the "Indians", who had studied in the school. This art was localised in some of the old Aztec towns; it was not progressive and did not extend to other parts of the North American continent.[2]

About two decades after the landing of the Pilgrim Fathers in New England came the English Commonwealth and the wholesale destruction of organs throughout the Kingdom in accordance with the ordinances of the Houses of Parliament of January 1644. The idea of the unsuitability of organs in worship became a deep-rooted conviction in the minds of the settlers, and in many quarters it lasted for at least two and a half centuries. Towards the end of the seventeenth century some of the chief churches in America, such as King's Chapel in Boston; Trinity Church, Newport Rhode Island and Trinity Church, New York, were established. The first organ in New England is connected with the history of King's Chapel, Boston. It was sent to America at the order of Thomas Brattle (born on 5th September 1656, graduated at Harvard "College" in 1676, in a class of three, and treasurer of the college from 1693 until his death on 18th May 1713), who while he was not an Episcopalian was rather too progressive in spirit to be regarded as an Independent. The organ was for use in his home and for the entertainment of his friends. The Rev. Samuel C. Green of Salem, says in his Diary, in 1711: "I was at Thomas Brattle's in Cambridge, heard his organ and saw strange things in a microscope." Brattle left this organ in his will (probated 23rd May 1713) to Brattle Street Church, being "given and devoted to the praise and glory of God in the said church, if they shall accept thereof, and within a year produce a sober and discreet person that shall play skilfully thereon and make a loud noise; otherwise to the Church of England in this town, on the same terms and conditions; and on their non-acceptance or discontinuation to use it as above, unto the College; and on their non-

[1] C. S. Braden, *Religious Aspects of the Conquest of Mexico*, Durham (N.C.) (1930); and E. Hague, *Latin American Music*, Santa Ana (Cal.) (1934).

[2] Mexican art, including that of the organ-case, is considered in the important work by P. Keleman, *Rococo and Baroque Art in Mexico*.

acceptance or discontinuation as before, I give the same to my nephew, Thomas Brattle". Not even a pitch pipe was allowed in Brattle Street Church. The organ, as being especially identified with Popery, was most abhorred, and a law had been enacted in 1675 prescribing that no one should play "on any kind of instrument except the drum, the trumpet and the jew's harp". Thus the organ was offered to Queen's Chapel (later King's Chapel), and the records of the church note: "At a meeting of the Gentlemen of the Church, this 3rd day of August, 1713, Referring the Orgain's Giveing them by Thomas Brattle, Esq., Decsd, voted that this organ be accepted by the church." In February 1714 before the organ was erected in the church it was voted "That the churchwardens write Col. Redknap (of London) and desire him to go to see Mr. Edward Enstone, who lives next door to Mr. Masters, on Tower Hill, and discourse him on his inclination and ability to come over and be the organist at thirty pounds per annum. This money, which, with other advantages as to Dancing and Musick etc, will, we doubt not, be sufficient encouragement, voted that the organ be forthwith put up."[1]

The organ must have been the work of one of the finest English builders, for Thomas Brattle would only be content with the best. The organ was in constant use at King's Chapel until 1756, when a new organ from England took its place. The Brattle organ was sold to St. Paul's Church, Newburyport, where it was used for eighty years. In 1836 it was bought for $450 by St. John's Church, Portsmouth, N.H., for use in their new mission chapel in State Street. It was reconstructed (*c.* 1831) and a new case was provided for it and in this form it is now preserved.

By a curious coincidence the second oldest American organ found a permanent home in another Portsmouth—that in Rhode Island. Richard Bridge, who in 1730 had the largest organ in England to his credit, exported a smaller instrument. In 1729, after a passage of five months, Dean Berkeley, later Bishop of Cloyne, landed at Newport on Rhode Island, with the purpose of founding a college at Bermuda. He took a great interest in Trinity Church in that town and often preached from its pulpit. The promised funds from England to fulfil his purpose did not arrive, Berkeley sailed back from Boston in 1731, and soon after his arrival he sent out the organ to the church as a token of his regard for it.

The organ is first mentioned in the church records of 25th February 1733:

"Voted: that the Church Wardens write to Mr. Charles Theodore Perchival, in Boston, to acquaint him that the organ is arrived for the Church, and that he is desired to come up here and assist us with his advice, in putting the same up, and that he shall be satisfied for his assistance in the affair. . . .[2]

[1] From the records of the church.

[2] The Annals of Trinity Church give a number of letters written with the hope of obtaining more stops from England. One (October 1753) addressed to Richard Bridge gives the specification as stop diapason, principal, flute, fifteenth and human voice, half-stops, cornet (treble), trumpet (treble), open diapason (treble), echo trumpet, stop diapason, open diapason—all half stops. The same letter also says: "We waited so long in hopes an organ builder might accidentally come here, but

"Voted: that Capt. Jonathan Thurston and Capt. Richard Mumford are appointed to go about to get subscriptions for £250 to defray the charges of setting up the organ and satisfying Mr. Perchival and Mr. Munday for their assistance in said affair, painting ye church and securing the tower from injury from the weather."

Only one of the keyboards survives and it is in the possession of the Newport Historical Society. There are twelve stops with six on each side. Paper labels, of which some are missing, beside the knobs indicate which stops they control. The following are still discernible: open diapason, principal, flute, stop diapason, fifteenth, trumpet, tierce treble, tierce bass. The compass is fifty notes (CC, no CC♯, to D^3) and below the keyboard on the front of the key frame is the builder's inscription and the date: "Ricardus Bridge, Londini, Fecit, *MDCCXXXIII*". The case of the organ, now flanked by larger pipes, still remains in the church. At intervals efforts were made to obtain further pipes for the organ from England, but without success; and there is no record of tuning or repairs done to the instrument to 1835. After this it was only "put in complete repair" and in 1844 it was replaced by a new one made by Henry Erben of New York.

The old organ, apart from the diapason, stopped diapason and flute and the case was set up in Grace Church, Brooklyn, N.Y., by Erben in 1845; in 1850 it was purchased by Miss Sarah Gibbs for St. Mary's Church, Portsmouth, R.I.; and in 1894 it was displaced by a larger instrument. Erben's organ (with the three Bridge stops) was in use in Trinity Church until 1880 when a two-manual instrument by Hook and Hastings was erected. Its specification was not unlike that of many English instruments of the same period.

Great Organ		*Swell Organ*		*Pedal*	
Bourdon bass	16	Open diapason	8	Open diapason	16
Bourdon treble	16	Viola	8	Bourdon	16
Open diapason	8	Stopped diapason	8		
Dulciana	8	Violina	4	*Couplers*	
Melodia[1]	8	Flûte harmonique	4	Swell to pedal	
Octave	4	Bassoon	8	Great to pedal	
Twelfth	$2\frac{2}{3}$	Oboe	8	Swell to great	
Fifteenth	2	Reversible pedal		Two composition pedals to great	
Trumpet	8	Great to pedal			

The old Erben organ was enlarged and Hook and Hastings rebuilt it in Kay Chapel, an adjunct of Trinity Church. This in turn was displaced by a large two-manual organ by the same builders (great, twelve stops; swell, fifteen stops; pedal, five stops).

---

as there is no one expected now, we hope for credit of your organ, you'll repair this to your satisfaction." C. T. Perchival was the son of Johann Pachelbel.

An illustrated monograph of this organ and its history written by W. King Covell of Harvard University was published in London in 1935 (Musical Opinion Office).

[1] A typical American stop of the late nineteenth and early twentieth centuries.

"It is characteristic of America that an old organ is disposed of entirely, and a wholly new instrument installed in its place. This tendency, naturally, is not discouraged by the builders. At times it may be advantageous that it does not encumber a new instrument with old material, some of which may not be equal in quality to the new work; again it leads to needless waste. If, for example, the Berkeley organ had been rebuilt rather than displaced, a most interesting instrument would have been preserved."[1]

The present organ is the work of the Skinner organ company; it was built in 1929 at the cost of $15,375. Its specification is here given as an example of the "late romantic" American organ. It is beautifully made, and the individual stops are well-voiced and regulated, but it lacks the proper development of fine choruses, and there is insufficient mutation and mixture work for so large a number of unison ranks.

Specification [*Trinity Church, Newport, R.I.*]

Great Organ		*Choir Organ*		*Swell Organ*	
Bourdon (pedal)	16	Dulciana	8	Diapason	8
Diapason	8	Unda Maris	8	Salicional	8
Erzähler	8	Concert Flute	8	Voix Céleste	8
Flûte harmonique	8	Flute	4	Aeoline	8
Octave	4	Clarinet	8	Rohrflöte	8
Grave mixture 2 ranks		Tremolo		Flûte triangulaire	4
				Mixture 3 ranks	
				Trumpet	8
				Flugel horn	8
				Tremolo	

Pedal Organ	
Diapason	16
Bourdon	16
Octave	8
Gedeckt	8
Flute	4

18 unison and octave couplers.
Balanced swell pedals to swell and choir.
Crescendo pedals.
Many other accessories.
Compass: pedal 32 notes. Manuals: great 61 notes, swell and choir 73 notes.

Apart from the instruments already mentioned in the Catholic missions, the honour of building the first organ in America belongs to New York City, where in 1737 John Clemm erected an instrument of three manuals and twenty-six stops at a cost of £520 in Trinity Church.[2] It can hardly have been a success, for in a quarter of a century it was offered for sale and a new organ was imported from England to take its place. The church and organ were destroyed in the great fire of 1777 and another English organ (a three-manual organ by Holland of London built in 1791) was used in the rebuilt church until the latter was taken down in 1839. On the completion

[1] King Covell, op. cit.

[2] America is very rich in organ history and it is pleasing to think that present progress has not obscured interest in old organs. Happily, there is a vigorous Organ Historical Society which publishes *The Tracker*.

of the present church in 1846 Henry Erben built an organ under the supervision of Dr. Edward Hodges (1796–1867), a distinguished organist who had lately come from Bristol, England.[1]

Here is the specification of the organ in Old Trinity Church, New York, 1846.

Trinity Church, New York

Great Organ
Strong open diapason
Clear open diapason
Stopped diapason
Strong principal
Bright principal
Flute
Double octave
Twelfth
Sesquialtera
Mixture
Trumpet
Clarion

Choir Organ
Stopped diapason
Dulciana
Principal
Flute
Fifteenth
Clarinet
Bassoon

Swell Organ
Double diapason
Open diapason
Dulciana
Stopped diapason
Principal
Cornet
Hautboy
Trumpet
Vox humana

Swell Bass
Dulciana
Serpent

Solo Organ
Double diapason
Horn diapason
Gamba
Melodia
Harmonic flute
Tuba mirabilis
Cornopean

Pedal Organ
Grand double open diapason
Grand open diapason

Compass
Great Organ CCC to f^3 in alt., 66 keys.
Choir CC to f^3 in alt., 54 keys.
Swell ten C to f^4 in alt., 54 keys.
Swell bass: two octaves.
Pedals: 2 octaves.
Couplers: 11, including swell bass to pedal. Great to pedal 16 ft., great to pedal 8 ft., pedal pipes in 32-ft. pitch, pedal pipes in 16-ft. pitch.

Henry Erben, born in New York in 1800, was one of the best American organ-builders of his day. His organ at Trinity Church lasted until 1924, when it was displaced by a new organ built by the Skinner Organ Company (the bottom octave of the 32-ft. stop was the only part of the old organ which was retained).

Claims for the honour of building the first organ in America have been made for Gustavus Hesselius, a Swedish painter (1682–1755), who settled in America in 1711. No organ certainly made by him is known. Dr. Christopher Witt, who joined the Hermits of Wissahickon in 1704, seems to have built an organ while he was with them and this he took to Germantown in

[1] Faustina Hodges, *The Life of Dr. Edward Hodges* (New York, 1896). For an account of his life in England before he settled in America, see "The Organs and Organists of St. James Church, Bristol", *The Organ*, vol. xxviii, p. 75. Hodges was later known as "the Father of American Cathedral Music".

1708. Robert Harttafel of Lancaster and David Tanneberger built some of the first organs in America. Tanneberger, said to be the best of the early organ-builders, made an organ for the Lutheran Church in Zion, which gave satisfaction until it was destroyed by fire in 1794.

When the Brattle organ was removed from the King's Chapel, Boston, in 1756 it gave place to one which became almost equally famous because of its durability. It was made by Adrian Smith of London. (It has been said that it was approved by Handel.) It cost £500 and continued in use in the church until 1860, when it was reconstructed and enlarged by Messrs. Simmons and Wilcox of Boston. The old case and eleven stops of the original organ continued in use until 1884, when a Hook organ took its place. Sumner Salter[1] mentions an instrument brought up from Newport R.I. in 1736, probably the third organ in the country, at Christ Church, Boston, a church famous for having been Paul Revere's signal station.

In 1752 Thomas Johnston[2] of Boston built an organ for Christ Church, which was thought to have been the first example of an instrument built in America until the Clemm organ became known. The Johnston organ was rebuilt in 1834 and again in 1883 it was rebuilt and enlarged by Hutchings of Boston.

In 1743, an organ built by J. Clarke of London, and purchased by subscription, was imported and set up in St. Peter's Episcopal Church, Salem. In 1754 it gave way to one by Thomas Johnston, "the American Father Schmidt," of one manual and six stops. Messrs. Hook and Hastings had in their possession a portion of this early specimen of American manufacture, including the name board, on which is inscribed in German text, executed in ivory "Thomas Johnston, fecit, Boston, Nov. Anglorum, 1754". The old London organ was presented to St. Michael's Episcopal Church in Marblehead.[3] He was succeeded by William M. Goodrich, a prominent New England organ-builder.

John Snetzler exported a number of organs, including one which was erected in Christ Church, Cambridge, in 1764, but the metal pipes were used by the patriot troops of the revolution and made into bullets.[4]

"In 1790, the old Brattle Street Church in Boston capitulated to the organ party being the first Independent Church in America to admit an organ. So great was the opposition, however, that when the vessel containing the organ arrived below in the harbour, a wealthy gentleman of the parish, who had refused to subscribe towards it, offered to pay into the treasury of the church,

[1] Sumner Salter, "Early Organs in America", *Musical Opinion* (May, 1892).

Note on the Royal Port Organ. An organ exhibited at the U.S. National Museum, Washington, D.C., formerly at Port Royal, was claimed to date from 1700. (See *The Organ*, vol. xxvii, p. 133, for an illustration.) Documents found by Wm. King Covell clearly prove that the organ could not have been built at Port Royal before *c.* 1750.

[2] Often spelt Johnson in church records.

[3] Johnston may have been an Englishman. He died in 1767, aged 59. An account of his life and work will be found in *Organs and Organ Builders of Christ Church, Boston, 1736–1945* by Mary Kent Davey (Babcock, Mass., Diocesan Library, No.7. Boston, 1946), and of Henry Erben in *The Diapason*, Dec. 1952.

[4] See page 165.

for the benefit of the poor, the whole cost of the organ and freight, if it might be thrown overboard below the lighthouse. As the minister himself, Rev. Dr. Thatcher, was luckily an advanced thinker on the subject of music, and in favour of the organ, he refused to be bought off by his wealthy parishioner."[1] The organ was built by Samuel Green[2] at a cost of £400 and was used until the church was taken down in 1872. An organ by G. P. England was erected in St. Paul's Chapel, Trinity Parish, New York, in 1802. An organ by Avery (who had fitted separate pedal pipes to the organ in Westminster Abbey in 1793) was erected at Salem in 1800. As early as 1740 there were two organs in the Moravian Church, Broad Street, Philadelphia. More than a century after this the South Reformed Church, New York (1846), had a three-manual organ with pneumatic lever action, independent pedal and a vox humana.

Even before the arrival of the energetic Dr. Hodges an interest in organ-playing had arisen in America. In 1809 Andrew Law wrote an *Art of Playing the Organ* which ten years later went into a second edition. In 1792 Raynor Taylor, who had as a choir boy sung at Handel's funeral in London, came to Baltimore where he gained fame by his improvisations. Many English organists settled in America in the early part of the nineteenth century and later Germans and other Europeans added to their number. Native Americans born later in the first half of the century showed skill as organists. The first concert organist in America was George W. Morgan (1822–92) from Gloucester, England, who became famous by his masterly playing from the year 1859 on the organ in Tremont Temple, Boston. This was a four-manual instrument of seventy speaking stops, by Hook and Hastings, and on it the representative works of Bach were played, probably for the first time in America.

The most important event in organ matters near the time of the Civil War was the erection of the large Walcker organ in the Music Hall at Boston. The Boston Music Hall was opened in 1852 and at the start had a small and inadequate organ, but the "Music Hall Association" raised a sum of $60,000 to provide a monumental organ. A committee of four, including E. J. Hopkins of the Temple Church, London, under the chairmanship of Dr. Upham, visited various organ-builders including Willis, Hill, Gray and Davison and Robson in England, and Schulze, Ladegast, Weigle and Walcker in Germany. A contract was signed with Walcker of Ludwigsburg, and the organ was under construction for a period of five years in the German factory. It was carefully examined and played upon by the committee in the factory and was taken down and sent to Rotterdam, where it was shipped in the brig *Presto* for Boston. It had a very stormy journey of three months, and both ship and organ were in peril of being lost. Seven months were taken in erecting the organ, and finally it was opened on 31st October 1863[3] with recitals

[1] Sumner Salter, op. cit.

[2] See page 176.

[3] I have extracted this information from the records of the Walcker firm, still preserved at Ludwigsburg. The session at which the organ was transferred to the Music Hall Association was private, and George W. Morgan, organist of Grace Church, New York, played Rossini's "Overture to William Tell".

during the following months by J. Knowles Paine, Eugene Thayer, B. J. Lang and other celebrated organists.

The organ created much interest in America. It was a large and well-designed instrument with proper choruses on each of its manuals and a fine pedal organ. Although little first-rate *organ* music was played on it, apart from some of the larger works of Bach, arrangements of orchestral and other instrumental pieces brought good music to the notice of the public. After twenty years of service the organ was eclipsed by public interest in the Boston Symphony Orchestra founded in 1881, and three years later the instrument was sold for the small sum of $5,000. It changed hands again in 1897, when it was bought by E. F. Searles of Methuen for the trifling sum of $1,500. In more recent years the organ has come into the sympathetic hands of the Aeolian Skinner Organ Company. A new console has been supplied, but the old one has been preserved. With a few improvements the organ remains as it was, and concerts are given in the Methuen Hall of the organ factory.[1] The great organ is remarkably fine even by the standards of the best organ-builders in history. More recently the instrument has been restored by G. Donald Harrison. The instrument directly influenced the tonal schemes if not the mechanical work of a number of American organ-builders including the large firms of Hook and Hastings, Hutchings and Roosevelt. It is interesting to speculate what trends would have been discernible in American organ-building had Willis of England, or Cavaillé-Coll of Paris been chosen to build the instrument. It is noteworthy that originally six of the twenty pedal stops were enclosed. The instrument, though not the largest, was one of a considerable number of fine large-scale instruments built by the firm of Walcker over a period of a century.

Many large organs were built in U.S.A. in the later part of the nineteenth century and in the beginning of the twentieth, both by native builders such as Skinner and by Europeans settled in America, such as Austin of Northamptonshire in England and Möller of Denmark. Much ingenuity was shown in the matter of reliable pneumatic and electric actions and in new forms of stops and stop control. Perhaps too much attention was paid to the console and too little to the improvement of tonal schemes taken as a whole.

A number of other organ-builders who worked in America during the nineteenth century are worthy of mention. John Geib, who had built the organ in St. Mary's Church, Stafford, England, in 1790, emigrated to America about ten years later. He first worked in Philadelphia and went to New York, where he set up in Barclay Street as a maker of organs and small square pianos. It is curious that the organ, believed to have been the work of G. P. England, exported to New York and set up in St. Paul's Chapel, Trinity Parish, in 1802, has a case strikingly like that of the Geib organ at Stafford. (It seems possible that Geib erected the organ in St. Paul's Chapel and made the case.) Geib built an organ for St. George's Church in Beckman Street,

[1] A detailed analysis of the contents of the instrument was given by W. King Covell of Harvard University in *The Organ*, vol. xi (1931). Oliver Wendell Holmes wrote about this organ. See also E. Flint, *The Great Organ in the Methuen Memorial Music Hall*, Methuen, Mass., 1954.

New York, in 1802, and in 1810 he built one for Grace Church, Lower Broadway, New York, which had the most handsome case in America and was destroyed by fire three years later.

Thomas Hall, originally of Philadelphia, settled in New York in 1820 and joined forces with his brother-in-law, Henry Erben. In 1824 partnership was dissolved and Erben carried on business on his own account and for sixty years had the best business in the district. His mechanical and tonal work was of a very high standard. He built one hundred and forty-six organs in New York City and several hundreds for many other parts of the United States. His finest instrument was that built in 1846 under the supervision of Dr. Edward Hodges. The manual compass was carried down to 16-ft. C. A seven-stop solo organ was added by Erben in 1869, and with little attention the organ remained as Erben left it until 1907. Meanwhile Thomas Hall had entered into partnership with La Bagh, and about 1865 James Kemp joined the firm, which, amongst others, built the organs in Baltimore Cathedral and in St. Thomas's P. E. Church, Church of the Strangers and Trinity Chapel in New York.

R. T. Ferris was a builder who made good plain substantial instruments at Calvary Baptist Church, New York Broadway Tabernacle, and elsewhere.

Thomas Robjohn, with his brother William, learned with Gray and Davison in London. He was a first-class mechanic and voicer, but suffered from lack of funds. He constructed the organ in the South Reformed Church, New York, making an independent pedal of seven stops. Robjohn and his brother went into employment with Odell. Thomas died in 1875 and William in 1879. In 1834 G. Jardine, related to Jardine the organ-builder of Manchester, began work in New York. He had four sons and two grandsons and for sixty years they built organs in many parts of the States. The instruments had good but cheap cases. In 1900 the firm went out of business on the death of three brothers.

About 1840 the firm of Stuart and Brother built some small but fairly good instruments such as that at the Broadway Tabernacle in New York.

After the year 1859 J. H. and S. Odell built no less than two hundred organs in New York and five hundred elsewhere. Their work was distinguished by its tonal and mechanical worthiness. Examples of their four-manual instruments were found at Temple Emmanuel, St. Nicholas Dutch Reformed Church, Second Christian Science Temple of New York, and the First Baptist Church of Newark, New Jersey.

One of the greatest of American organ-builders in the later nineteenth century was Hilborne L. Roosevelt, who flourished from 1872 until his death in 1886.[1] He had a factory in West 11th Street, New York. He built many large organs, and the firm did useful work with electric action, adjustable stop control and other mechanical devices. Notable achievements were the organs at the Garden City Cathedral (four manuals, one hundred and fifteen stops) and Grace P.E. Church and Calvary P.E. Church, New York. His brother Frank continued the business on a larger scale until 1893. Amongst other

[1]A cousin of Theodore Roosevelt, the President.

large organs he built the Auditorium organ at Chicago (four manuals, one hundred and seven stops). On his retirement the firm's patents were purchased by Farrand and Votey of Detroit.

From 1850 Alex Miles made some small but good organs. The firm of Davis and Sons originated from Morgan Davis, who first made pianos in the employ of Broadwood in London. He built an organ in Calvary P.E. Church, New York. The action was Barker lever and the stops were arranged in the form of a cross.

Francis Engelfroid, from the year 1853, built organs of German type of an old-fashioned kind. His best work was in the St. Vincent de Paul R.C. Church, New York.

Reuben Midmer came from England at sixteen and served his apprenticeship with Hall of Newark, N.J. He set up as an organ-builder in 1860 in Brooklyn. His son took control in 1895. Later the firm was jointly controlled as the Midmer Losh Organ Company. In the nineteenth century the firm, directed by father and son, built thousands of organs, including one hundred and thirteen in Brooklyn alone. Examples of their work were to be heard at St. Francis Xavier's R.C. Church, St. Anthony's R.C. Church, Brooklyn, First Congregational Church, Poughkeepsie, New York. The firm left New York and had establishments in Merrick, Long Island, Boston and Chicago. Within the last fifty years Midmer Losh have been responsible for some of the most important organs in America. The largest organ in the world, the seven-manual colossus at the Convention Hall, Atlantic City, designed by Emerson L. Richards, is the work of this firm.

Here are some of the more important inventions of organ-builders working in America in the late nineteenth and early twentieth centuries.

John T. Austin

A universal chest providing a constant wind pressure. Inspection of the action was possible by walking inside the chest which was really a large room full of pressure wind, through an air lock. The system was not widely used except by its inventor.

A "concertina" pneumatic motor for working the swell shutters.

An adjustable combination action and simplified electric-key action contained in a compact console, which "opened" so that easy adjustment of every part was possible. Each key had a "toggle" or top resistance touch produced by a spring.

Robert Hope-Jones

A unit chest so that each rank of pipes could be played at several pitches and from any manual.

Sforzando mechanism, causing the swell shutters to close slightly as soon as a chord or note has commenced to sound.

Swell shutters constructed of laminae with air-spaces between. Swell shutters with grooved edges to give a sound-trap joint. Swell shutters of aluminium with a vacuum cavity. A pizzicato action, automatically releasing the notes as soon as they are sounded.

E. M. Skinner

The "whiffle-tree" action box for moving the swell shutters. This device has been imitated by other builders in America and Europe. A rapid organ action using the "pitman" chest. Multiple-wound electro-magnets for coupling devices. A range of new and beautiful tone colours including the French horn, which has been widely used elsewhere, erzähler (a kind of gemshorn).

W. E. Haskell (a senior member of the Estey firm)

A means of producing a satisfactory open flue tone from pipes of half length by the use of a smaller diameter tube, closed at one end, in the pipe.

Saxophone, tuba and "labial clarinet" produced from flue stops, and for use in districts where visits by the tuner are rare.

Pneumatic couplers.

George Jardine's relief-pallet for lightening key touch was invented in 1850 and was used in the Church of the Annunciation in New York in 1853. *Hilborne Roosevelt* and *Charles Haskell* collaborated to produce new forms of ventil wind-chests and adjustable combination action. Hilborne Roosevelt patented his electro-pneumatic action in 1869. Originally he used mercury cup contacts, covering the surface of the mercury with glycerine to prevent oxidation. His electric action needed comparatively heavy current and he needed a separate battery for each octave of the organ. In 1872 and 1898 *J. H. Odell* patented "pneumatic tube actions", the latter being an exhaust pneumatic system.

P. Wirsching, W. B. Fleming, G. Hutchings and *F. W. Hedgland* developed various new tubular pneumatic and electro-pneumatic actions towards the end of the nineteenth century. Many others from Germany, Scandinavia, Switzerland and Holland brought with them European ideas and started organ-building in America.

Casavant Frères

The Casavant firm has been the leading organ-building establishment in Canada for more than half a century. Joseph Casavant, a French Canadian, was an organ-builder in a small way who made his first organ in St. Hyacinthe, Quebec Province, in 1837, but his business was discontinued at his death. Two of his sons visited France and worked in the factory of Abbey in 1878–9.[1] On their return to Canada they re-established the factory in St. Hyacinthe and built organs which were superior to most American organs. The Casavant brothers combined the mechanical ingenuity of the Abbey family with the magnificence, blend and unity of Cavaillé-Coll's organs. By 1924 over 1,050 instruments had been built by the firm, including many large organs of four manuals. Their instruments are found in every part of Canada and in some American cities. A fine example of their larger work is found in the Church of the Sacred Name of Jesus, Maisonneuve, Montreal. A feature of the Casavant organs is the full harmonic development of the chorus reeds

[1] W. L. Sumner, "John Abbey, Organ-builder", *The Organ* (January 1950). The Casavant brothers worked with the sons and grandson of the English founder of this French firm.

with their powerful basses, and the properly planned mixture work. The organ consoles are more sumptuously appointed than those of most American organs.

During the first three decades of the twentieth century the American organ advanced in mechanical and electrical devices and in the equipment of its detached console. In spite of the addition of some new solo voices by such artists as Skinner and Haskell, the standards concerning chorus work set by Roosevelt a generation before were forgotten. The influence of Hope-Jones, who had turned the organ into an unsatisfactory "one-man orchestra", was even more intense and widespread than it was in England. Unit organs in which a few ranks of highly individual tone-quality were extended to give 16-ft., 4-ft., 2-ft. and even other higher pitch effects, and were each made playable from more than one manual keyboard and the pedals, led to the Wurlitzer type of cinema-organ with its attempt at orchestral effects. Even when there was no unification or extension, except on the pedals, it was not often possible to find a clear, well-conceived diapason chorus with proper mixtures and mutations, or a full swell organ of the type to be found at St. Paul's Cathedral, London, throughout the length and breadth of the States.

It was thought necessary, even in small organs, to have a vox humana, gongs, chimes and other "percussion stops". Consequently it was difficult or impossible to play much of the historical organ music on the majority of American instruments. Even E. M. Skinner made diapasons of the "leather-lip" phonon type which ruined any attempt to produce a satisfactory great-organ flue chorus.

Nevertheless, with these limitations, thousands of organs, many of considerable size, with over a hundred speaking stops, were made by Skinner of Boston; Austin of Hartford, Conn.; Möller of Hagerstown, Maryland; Estey of Brattleborough, Vermont; Kilgen of St. Louis; Hillgreen Lane of Alliance, Ohio; Midmer Losh, Merrick, Long Island; Wanamaker, Kimball, Chicago; Hall, West Haven, Conn.; Pilcher of Louisville, Kentucky.

Leading European organists, though pleased with the ease of the console arrangements and the mechanical perfection, found the tonal ensembles of most American organs sadly defective. A number of other forces came together to initiate a renaissance of organ-building in America. Musicological research in many of the U.S. universities brought to the attention of American musicians the glories of the European organ music of the last four centuries. Many American organists and designers, notably Emerson Richards, had made a thorough study in Europe of the tonal structures of the finest organs. Holtkamp, an organ-builder of Cleveland, for many years had produced organs which were modern versions of the small seventeenth-century German baroque instruments. It was left to G. Donald Harrison, an Englishman and formerly a director of the English firm of Willis, to produce a new type of instrument, sometimes large in size, but always showing the tonal characteristics of the true organ of tradition. It would not be accurate to describe these instruments of the Aeolian-Skinner Company, of which Mr. Harrison became the artistic director, as neo-Baroque organs. At times the tone suggests the French ideal rather than the German. The instruments are characterised by "clarified" ensembles in all the manual choruses and on the pedals. The mixture, cornet and mutation schemes are ingeniously contrived, there are adequate pedal organs of independent pipes, capable of solo work, in addition to the production of clear, definite bass lines. The positive organ is a real foil to the great. High pressures are eschewed, and there is a proper balance and blend of flue and reed stops. There are mixture and mutation stops for colouring the foundation work, for building tonal pyramids as well as for adding brilliance and for locking flue and reed tone together. Mr. Harrison's work is to be heard at a number of U.S. universities, in the Tabernacle at Salt Lake City, Utah, and elsewhere. (See also specification 43.) The instruments have the advantages of modern wind supply, action and stop control, but the pervading "open wood", the opaque diapason, and the tonal "hotch potch" of the choir organ of the earlier twentieth-century English cathedral organ are quite foreign to these modern American organs. Though quite unmistakably the conception of the man who designed them, Harrison's instruments show more affinity to some of the organs of Steinmeyer of Öttingen, Germany, built about 1930, than to those of any other organ-builder.

There is immense scope for organ-building in U.S.A. Until recently thousands of churches in central U.S. had only suction reed organs (miscalled in England "American organs") and these are still not uncommon in isolated places. Between the wars nearly 2,500 organs were made each year in U.S.A.

The largest organ in the world is the instrument at the Convention Hall, Atlantic City, New Jersey, U.S.A., and it is not likely that it will be exceeded in size for many decades, if at all. Only the most brief account of it can be given here and indeed an exhaustive description would fill a book of considerable size. The hall in which the instrument stands is 500 ft. long, 300 ft. wide and 138 ft. high and it has seating accommodation for 41,000 people. The organ was designed by Senator Emerson Richards, built by Midmer-Losh Inc. of Merrick, Long Island, and much of the voicing was carried out by Henry Vincent Willis, a grandson of Father Willis. In order to cope with the special acoustic conditions of the hall extraordinary pipe-scales and designs had to be used and wind pressures up to 100 in. The organ occupies eight large chambers in six sections of the hall and it speaks through ornamental grilles. Within these chambers are fourteen large swell-boxes. Any set of swell-shutters can be switched to any of the six balanced pedals (the seventh pedal is a stop-crescendo). The shutters can also be switched in reverse, so that one pedal may be closing some of the shutters while at the same time it is opening others.

There are two consoles, one containing seven manuals and 1,250 stop-keys, and the other five manuals and 678 stop-keys. The former rests upon a revolving dais placed at the right of the stage extension and the other console is movable and can be brought near to the first when desired. Both consoles are entirely electric in action.

The total power of the blowers is 400 h.p. and the wind pressures vary between $3\frac{1}{2}$ and 100 in. w.g. The action current is generated by a 4-h.p. set delivering 143 amperes at 14 volts d.c.

The keyboards of the seven-manual console are in the following order from the lowest:

Choir organ	CCC to C 85 notes
Great organ	CCC to C 85 notes
Swell organ	GGG to G 73 notes
Solo organ	CC to C 61 notes
Fanfare organ	CC to C 61 notes
Echo organ	CC to C 61 notes
Bombarde	CC to C 61 notes

The console has been most ingeniously designed so that all the keys and stop-keys are within convenient reach of any performer of normal size. Each keyboard has been set at the most appropriate angle for ease of playing and the stop-keys have been arranged in concave quadrants on each side of the player. The designer of the instrument describes its major tonal schemes as follows:

Great organ: An immense flue chorus of surpassing brilliance.

Grand great: An upwards extension of certain ranks of the pedal organ to give additional weight and body to the tone on the great organ side of the auditorium, and also to provide materials for the complete compass of the seven-octave great-organ keyboard.

Great solo (duplexed): (1) Organ tone for accompanimental use against solo stops of other departments.

Great solo (duplexed): (2) Imitative orchestral section.

Swell: A blaze of fiery reeds and upper work.

Swell choir (duplexed): A division comprising quiet flue stops and quiet reeds.

Choir (unenclosed): A miniature great organ.

Choir (enclosed): A large accompanimental section of varied tone colours.

Grand choir: Extended ranks from the pedal organ, selected to provide material for the complete compass of the seven-octave choir manual and to give firmness and body to the general effect on the choir-organ side of the auditorium.

Solo: Largely a super swell organ with reeds striking through the ensemble.

Fanfare: A reed and flute section.

Echo: A large and varied antiphonal section (a full-length 32-ft. contra violone is included on the echo pedal).

Brass chorus: For reinforcement of the several reed sections.

String organ, 1: A powerful string division, many of the stops having two ranks.

String organ, 2: Broad orchestral tone; a number of stops possess two ranks.

String organ, 3: Ethereal, keen, but quiet tone.

Gallery organ, 1: The battery of 100 in. reeds.

Gallery organ, 2: Big flute chorus.

Gallery organ, 3: Bold Schulze diapason chorus.

Gallery organ, 4: A powerful wood-wind section.

Pedal organ: This immense department is mainly situated in the large chambers left and right of the stage, but ample pedal basses are placed in the other chambers to provide for the manual stops in these localities. The chorus, mixture and mutation stop schemes are far greater than have ever been conceived before. An example is the tromba family of reeds complete from 32 ft. to a tromba seventeenth $3\frac{1}{5}$ ft., which, like many other things in this remarkable work, is unique.[1] [See Plate 17.]

In the last two decades some hundreds of organs of enlightened design have appeared in America and many of these have been completely new instruments of considerable size. Amongst the firms, which undertake work on the largest scale throughout the American continent, are the Aeolian-Skinner Company of Boston, Mass.; Austin Organs Inc. of Hartford, Conn.; Holtkamp Organs, Cleveland, Ohio; M. P. Möller Inc. of Hagerstown, Md.; Schantz Organ Co. of Orrville, Ohio; Schlicker Organ Co. of Buffalo, N.Y.; Reuter Organ Co. of Lawrence, Kans.; Hillgreen, Lane and Co. of Alliance, Ohio; Estey of Brattleboro', Vermont; Wicks Organ Co. of Highland, Illinois. The last firm specialises in direct-electric action and in modern console design. In Canada, Casavant Frères, of St. Hyacinthe, continue to build organs of fine quality and on a large scale. In the U.S.A. there are some hundreds of other worthy builders such as Odell, Mudler Hunter, Tellers, Lowell, Dennison, Thompson-Allen, La Marche, Kilgen, McManis, Gress-Miles, Doerr, Blanton and Delaware. Moreover, in the person of Robert Noehren there is combined the organ-virtuoso player, the scholar, musicologist and organ-builder. In all fields of the art of the organ, America is no longer dependent on an eclecticism of the best which Europe can offer, but is developing an indigenous movement which is the largest and the most vigorous in the world.

[1] An account of this instrument has been given by R. Whitworth in four issues of *The Organ*, vol. xxvii (1947–48), but even this does not include a complete specification, nor does it attempt to describe the tonal effects of this vast organ. The Moller organ at West Point Military Academy Chapel with its remarkable "harmonic division" must also be mentioned.

CHAPTER VII

THE ORGAN FROM THE TIME OF BACH TO THE PRESENT

The Eighteenth Century

Both the French and German organs reached their apogee in the early years of the eighteenth century. Thereafter, during that century, many large organs were built in Europe, but they had little effect on the art of music, and musicians looked elsewhere for their media of expression. The close of the eighteenth century and the beginning of the nineteenth was a period of decadence as far as the organ art was concerned. The romantic revival in the fourth and fifth decades of the nineteenth century represented a break with tradition. The organ needed higher wind pressures and powerful reeds which necessitated the development of mechanical aids to the fingers of the organist in the work of opening the pallets which admitted wind into the pipes. Thus the development of pneumatic and later electrical actions went hand in hand with new ways of "raising the wind". The new intermediaries between performer and pipes permitted the detachment of the console, with the keyboard and stops, from the main instrument the division of the instrument into parts placed in different positions in the building. (It must be stated that remarkable feats of detachment of consoles and dividing organs into parts had been performed in Italy by Serassi in the eighteenth century.)[1]

The romantic-symphonic movement led to a second period of decadence at the end of the nineteenth century and the beginning of the twentieth. The instrument lost its identity; its traditional music was forgotten or misunderstood, it became an inefficient imitation of the orchestra, and the glories of the restrained flue choruses of the seventeenth century, with their possibilities of kaleidoscopic tonal changes, made by using the variety of harmonic ingredients then provided, were despised. Let us not imagine that there has been continuous progress in the organ as a musical instrument. The superb equipment of the organ as a machine and the elegance and convenience of a console of modern design, do not stand in the place of artistic tonal appointments bearing the mark of all art works, that of unity in diversity.

Only in recent years have we in Britain, America, France and Germany shown signs of recovery in this matter of organ aesthetics.

Amongst the most famous large organs of the eighteenth century was that at the Church of St. Bavo, Haarlem, Holland, built by Christian Müller of Amsterdam and completed in 1738 (see specification, No. 17).[2] The sons of

[1] Nor must Green's Handel Commemoration Festival Organ of 1784 with its "long action" in Westminster Abbey be forgotten.

[2] W. L. Sumner, "The Organ in the Church of St. Bavo, Haarlem", *The Organ*, vol. xv, p. 19. The instrument is mentioned by Burney in his *State of Music in Germany*, etc., vol. ii, pp. 303 et seq.

Schnitger also built large organs in Holland, as at Zwolle, about this time and F. C. Schnitger had constructed some notable instruments, as at Alkmaar, in the north of that country. Gabler, who lived in the town of Ravensburg, in Swabia, built a number of large organs in Germany in the latter part of the eighteenth century. His most famous work was the instrument in Weingarten Abbey (see specification, No. 18).[1] This organ, with 6,666 pipes, seventy-six speaking stops, and a number of open 32-ft. ranks and four manuals and pedals, was justly celebrated throughout Europe. (Gabler also built the organs in Ochsenhausen Abbey and in Wittenburg.)

The Spanish organ developed as a number of fine reed choruses, mixtures, and quiet flue-work. The organ of the Chapel Royal, Madrid (1778), was as good as anything in Europe at that time. It was from the eighteenth-century Spanish instrument that A. Cavaillé-Coll learnt the grandeur of organ-reed choruses.

In Italy the organ had remained faithful to its generous diapason choruses with very complete mutation ranks and with little attention to the development of the pedal organ. The singing of the Mass and the playing of the works of the old Italian masters demanded little else. Nevertheless, the Serassi family produced much larger and more versatile instruments in the Bergamo, Como and Milan districts.

There were three generations of the Serassi family who produced notable organs, but the greatest of these organ-builders was Joseph, who was born at Bergamo in 1750. His first great work was the double organ in the Church of Sant' Alessandro de Colonna at Bergamo. Each side of the organ contained the pipes of two manuals and a part of the pedals, making a total of eighty-four speaking stops of which thirty were "foundation" stops (i.e. stops of 4-ft. pitch or greater), and fifty-four were reeds, mutations and mixtures. The length of the tracker action under the very wide chancel was 163 ft., but it is said that the action was responsive and not heavy to play upon.[2] In 1792 Serassi made an organ of eighty-two speaking stops for the Ducal Church at Colorno, and in 1800 he built an instrument of three manuals and eighty-six speaking stops for the Church of the Annunciation at Como. In the early years of the nineteenth century he built large organs at Sant' Eustorgio (1808) and Saint Thomas (1813) at Milan.[3]

In Scandinavia, later to import many organs of German manufacture, Cahmann was constructing fine instruments in the eighteenth century. Three famous names mark the latter part of the eighteenth century in France so soon to be disturbed by the Revolution. François Henri Clicquot (Paris),

[1] Franz Bärnwick, *Die grosse Orgel im Münster zu Weingarten* (Weingarten 1922); Robert Weber, *Die Orgeln von Jos. Gabler und Joh. Nep. Holzhey* (Kassel, 1936); Paul Smets, *Die grosse Gabler-Orgel der Abtei Weingarten* (Mainz, 1940).

[2] M. Hamel, *Nouveau Manuel Complet du Facteur d'Orgues*, vol. iii, p. 482 (Paris, 1849).

[3] Serassi left a number of accounts of his work including: *Descrizione ed osservazioni pel nuovo organo posta nella chiesa dell' Annunziata di Como* (Como, 1808); *Sugli organi* (Bergamo, 1816).

Jean-Baptiste Lefebvre (Rouen) and Dom François Bédos de Celles (Toulouse, Bordeaux, Paris). The last wrote the remarkable work *L'Art du facteur d'Orgues* between 1766 and 1778, which was a detailed, authoritative and well-illustrated work on the construction of the organ and its use.[1]

Other notable builders who worked in France at this time were Dallery, Legros, Dupont (Lorraine), Riepp (q.v.), Lépine, the Cavaillé family (Guyenne and Languedoc), and Isnard.

In the early part of the nineteenth century, before Cavaillé-Coll had burst upon the world of organ-building in France, John Abbey,[2] an Englishman born in Whilton, Northamptonshire, in 1785 and formerly employed by Érard, was the most important figure. He introduced Cumming's system for making wind reservoirs, perfected methods of voicing and improved devices for mechanical stop changing.

The Cliquot (Clicquot) family originally came from Meaux. Clicquot, who built the organ in the Chateau Chapel at Versailles in 1711, was given a royal warrant by Louis XIV. He also built or rebuilt the organs in the cathedrals of Rouen (1686–9), Saint Quentin (1701–3), and Blois (1704). In 1713 the direction of the factory passed to his son, Jean Baptiste, and father and son were responsible for repairing the organ in Laon Cathedral (1714–16). Another son, Louis Alexandre, who died in Paris on 25th January 1760, rebuilt the organs at Houdan (1734) and Chevreuse.

The most famous member of the family was François Henri, the son of Louis Alexandre, who was born in Paris in 1728 and died there in 1790. He was known throughout Europe for the quality of his low-pressure reeds and mixtures. He succeeded his father in 1760 and became associated with Pierre Dallery in 1765. His most capable workmen were Lair, Isnard, Laurent, Brachet, and Gillier, who collaborated with him at St. Medard, Paris (1767), and St. Gervais, Paris (1764–8). The most beautiful organs in the churches of this city before the Revolution were the work of Clicquot:

The church of the Jacobins, Rue St. Dominique, 1771.
Sainte Chapelle, 1771.
St. Nicolas des Champs, 1776.
St. Merry, 1781.
St. Sulpice, 1781.
Notre Dame, 1784.
St. Leu, 1786–8.

He restored the organs in the cathedrals of Versailles (1761), Nantes (1784), and began the construction of the organs at St. Nicolas du Chardonnet, Paris, and the cathedral at Poitiers, which might have been his *chef d'œuvre*.

The work of Clicquot may still be heard in the restored organs of St.

[1] A facsimile of this work was printed in 1936 by Bärenreiter of Kassel. It is also contained in Hamel's *Facteur d'Orgues* (Manuels Roret, Paris, 1849) and in the German works of Töpfer and his later "editors".

[2] W. L. Sumner, "John Abbey", *The Organ* (January 1950).

Nicolas des Champs, St. Gervais, and St. Merry, in Paris. Much of Clicquot's work was superseded by that of Cavaillé-Coll; some was destroyed in the Revolution or neglected and ill-treated so that it was unrecognisable by the middle of the nineteenth century.

We give the specification of one of Clicquot's largest organs:

The Organ in the Church of St. Sulpice, Paris, 1781

Positif
First Clavier: A to E

Bourdon	16
Montre	8
Bourdon	8
Flûte	8
Prestant	4
Nasard	3 [*sic*]
Doublette	2
Quarte de nasard	2
Tierce	$1\frac{3}{5}$
Larigot	$1\frac{1}{3}$
Fourniture	4 ranks
Cymbale	5 ranks
Cornet	5 ranks
Trompette	8
Cromorne	8
Basson	8
Clarinette	8
Clairon	4

Bombarde
Third Clavier

Cornet	5 ranks
Bombarde	16
Bombarde	8
Clairon	4

Grand Orgue
Second Clavier

Montre	32
Montre	16
Bourdon	16
Montre	8
Bourdon	8
Flûte	8
Prestant	4
Tierce	$3\frac{1}{5}$
Nasard	3 [*sic*]
Quarte de nasard	2
Doublette	2
Petite tierce	$1\frac{3}{5}$
Nasard	$1\frac{1}{3}$
Fourniture	4 ranks
Second fourniture	6 ranks
Cymbale	4 ranks
Cornet	5 ranks
Voix humaine	8
First trompette	8
Second trompette	8
Clairon	4
Second clairon	4

Pédale
FFF to E: 36 notes

Flûte	16
Bourdon	16
Flûte	8
Second flûte	8
Nasard	6
Flûte	4
Bombarde	24
Bombarde	16
Trompette	8
Second trompette	8
Clairon	4

Récit
Fourth Clavier

Flûte	8
Cornet	5 ranks
Hautbois	8
Trompette	8

Echo
Fifth Clavier: C to E

Bourdon	8
Flûte	4
Cornet	5 ranks
Trompette	8
Clairon	4

Total: 64 stops,
4328 pipes.

The case which now contains the Cavaillé-Coll instrument (1858–63) cost 36,000 livres, including the carved figures. It was designed in 1776 in Corinthian style by Jean François Chalgrin. The organ built under the direction of Dom Bédos was probably the finest completed work of François Henri Clicquot and cost 40,000 livres.[1] The large grand orgue with its 32-ft. stop will be noted. The remarkable compass of the pedal (thirty-six notes) and the

[1] W. L. Sumner, "The Organs of the Church of St. Sulpice, Paris", *The Organ*, vol. xiv, pp. 141 et seq. See also Norbert Dufourcq, *Les Clicquot*, Paris, 1942.

wealth of chorus work and quiet mutation stops are also important features. The methods of using such an instrument are given by Dom Bédos in his great work on organ construction.[1] The flue-work had a light homogeneous quality, later to give way to the gambes (of geigen diapason quality), the harmonic flutes and montres of Cavaillé-Coll which blended quite well. The French reeds of the eighteenth century were a marvel of rapid speech, and though they had no great power, except in the bass, they blended admirably together and with the flue-work; but they did not stay long in tune.

Jean-Baptiste Nicolas Lefebvre of Rouen built an organ of five manuals and pedals, fifty-three speaking stops, in 1761 in the Church of St. Martin at Tours. He also built large organs at Honfleur and Havre. Lefebvre and his nephews built large organs at Caen in Normandy. The organ at the Church of St. Étienne in that town had sixty-three speaking stops, five manuals, a pedal clavier of thirty notes and eleven bellows, each 1 metre by 2 metres.[2]

After the death of Gottfried Silbermann, the most important organ-builder in Germany was Charles Joseph Riepp (1710–75), who was born on 24th January 1710 in Eldern. His best-known instruments are at the Ottobeuren Abbey, at Salem and Dôle. He was "naturalised" a Frenchman in January 1747 and built organs at Dijon, Besançon, Beaune, Toul and elsewhere in France.[3]

His two organs in Ottobeuren Abbey are extremely beautiful instruments and have been carefully conserved by Steinmeyer of Oettingen. The Benedictine Abbey is known as the "Swabian Escorial"; it is richly decorated and the two instruments, the "Trinity" organ in the gallery and the "Holy Ghost" organ at the side of the chancel with their late-Baroque cases and rich carvings blend perfectly with their surroundings. The tonal effects are surpassingly beautiful. The four-manual console of the "Trinity" organ is in a kind of arcade which goes through the middle of the organ, and it would be difficult to conceive a worse place for the organist to hear his instrument. (see specifications, No. 20).

Riepp earned more money as a vintner than as an organ-builder: he was interested in catering and left a long list of organ stop-combinations in which he compared them with the courses at a meal. "The organ-builder is, after all, only a wind-cook."

A few of his "melanges" are quoted[4] (Specifications Nos. 20 and 21). For the first set he does not give the uses of the combinations:

(1) Great principal 8 ft., copel 8 ft.
(2) Great bourdon 16 ft., principal 8 ft., copel 8 ft., pedal principal 16 ft.
(3) For chorale preludes: great bourdon 16 ft., principal 8 ft., copel 8 ft., octave 4 ft., nazard $2\frac{2}{3}$ ft., octave 2 ft.; or:

[1] See pp. 380 et seq.
[2] Hamel, op. cit., vol. iii, p. 453.
[3] A complete list is given by Joseph Worsching in his monograph *Die beruhmten Orgelwerke der Abtei Ottobeuren* (Mainz, 1941).
[4] Quoted extensively in Paul G. Anderson, *Orgelbogen*. See also H. Stubington: four articles in *The Organ*, vol. xxxviii, 1958–9.

(4) Great bourdon 16 ft., principal 8 ft., copel 8 ft., octave 4 ft., octave 2 ft., mixtur, cymbel.
(5) Jeu de tierce: great bourdon 16 ft., principal 8 ft., copel 8 ft., octave 4 ft., nazard $2\frac{2}{3}$ ft., octave 2 ft., tierce $1\frac{3}{5}$ ft.
(6) For a fugue: great octave 4 ft., cornet V, trompete 8 ft., clairon 4 ft., pedal bombarde 16 ft., trompete 8 ft., clairon 4 ft.
(7) Solo: flet 4 ft., copel 8 ft., serpent 8 ft. Solo: flut travers bourdon 3rd claviere mit vox humana.
(8) Solo: great vox humana 8 ft., copel 8 ft., octav 4 ft. Accomp: positiv copel 8 ft., octav 4 ft., nazard $2\frac{2}{3}$ ft.
(9) Solo: great gamba 8 ft., octave 8 ft., octave 4 ft. Accomp: echo flet 8 ft., copel 8 ft.
(10) Tierce en taille: positiv copel 8 ft., principal 4 ft., nasat $2\frac{2}{3}$ ft., superoctave 2 ft., terz $1\frac{3}{5}$ ft., larigot $1\frac{1}{3}$ ft.
(11) Positiv copel 8 ft., principal 4 ft., gamba 4 ft.
(12) Echo: serpent 8 ft., flet 4 ft.

In the last section both wine-marketing and organ-building appear. The form is humorous, but the stop-combinations can be taken quite seriously:

First, various stops are presented in this manner: Principal 16 ft.—a steak. Bourdon 16 ft.—bread in soup. Principal 8 ft.—rice in soup. Gedackt 8 ft.—beef-steak. Octave 4 ft.—wine. Flute 4 ft.—an hors d'oeuvre. Quint $2\frac{2}{3}$ ft.—pickled cabbage. Octave 2 ft.—salt. Mixtur and cymbel—various spices. Cornet—caper sauce. Vox humana—ox tongue. Bombarde—boar's ham. Cornet de recit—pheasant. Larigot—thin custard. Salicional—sugar bread, a sweet loaf. Echo cornet—coffee. Gamba 4 ft.—liqueur, and so on. The pedal organ is burgundy, whereas the positive organ provides confections for ladies' parties. Quint and tierce are nothing in themselves, but with the appropriate foundation they provide confections for men.

And then he tells one how various occasions are to be catered for: first, a usual meal, which must be devoured with gravity, since large lumps must be eaten slowly, or they get stuck in one's throat. This is naturally a chorale registration like No. 4. If something more solid is desired, reeds must be added. If the organist can manage the pedal bombarde in a solo with this combination, this will make a meal for a general or a prince of the Church or a conventual meeting. He suggests a fugue combination No. 6 for an organists' luncheon, and the organ-builder gets the 'jeu de tierce'. For ladies' tea-parties he serves a cornet-solo on the echo division, accompanied by principal 8 ft. and copel 8 ft. on the great. Officers, on the contrary, get a trumpet solo on the positiv. A German with good taste can be pampered with great gamba 8 ft., copel 8 ft., and prestant 4 ft.; positiv salicet 8 ft., copel 8 ft. and gamba 4 ft.; pedal sub-bass 16 ft., flute 8 ft. and flute 4 ft. Great flute 8 ft. and copel 8 ft. and positiv salicet 8 ft. and copel 8 ft. and pedal flute 8 ft. could be a suitable food for old men, but infants and students must have either a vox humana solo or else great vox humana 8 ft., copel 8 ft., prestant 4 ft., nazard $2\frac{2}{3}$ ft.; positiv salicet 8 ft., copel 8 ft., flet 4 ft., nazard $2\frac{2}{3}$ ft.; or simple positiv copel 8 ft., prestant 4 ft., gamba 4 ft., pedal flet 8 ft.

Delikatessen for organ lovers: "basse de cromorne" positiv cromorne 8 ft., prestant 4 ft.; great bourdon 16 ft., montre 8 ft., prestant 4 ft.; pedal flet 8 ft. (bass solo on positiv). A quartet will be most appropriate for highly skilled organists and musicians. Menu: great bourdon 16 ft., principal 8 ft., copel 8 ft., prestant 4 ft.; positiv copel 8 ft., prestant 4 ft., cromorne 8 ft.; récit cornet V; pedal sub-bass 16 ft., flet 8 ft., gamba 8 ft. And for those who are not in the least interested in organ playing one can serve something on the echo; it will please their taste best.

Of hardly less importance were the organ-builders Holzey, Courtain and the Egedacher family.

Johann Nepomuk Holzey was born on February 26th, 1741, lived in Ottobeuren, where he was the custodian of the Riepp organs, and died there on September 17th, 1809. His organs were beautiful, both to the ear and the eye. His best works are to be found at Rot an der Rot (two organs *c.* 1790), Neresheim, Kloster Weissenau, Kloster Ursberg and (probably) Kloster Holzen in Bavaria.

Jacob Courtain, between the years 1780 and 1800, built a number of fine organs in a more restrained style, with splendid tone and good cases, in Westphalia, the Lower Rhine, the Duchy of Bentheim, Osnabrüch, Oldenburg and Emmerich.

The Egedacher family built many fine organs in the Passau and Salzburg districts, from the beginning of the seventeenth century to the end of the eighteenth.

Amongst some hundreds of organ-builders in eighteenth-century Europe, who did notable work, were the Bossard family, which produced many organs in Switzerland (St. Urban, Muri, Einsiedeln, Solothurn, Frauenthal, Estavayer, Neuheim, Zug, St. Augustin at Zurich, etc.). The work of Römer, Kober, Panzner, Sippus, Mallek and Christoph, amongst others in Austria, of the Stumm family in the mid-Rhine district, and R. A. Mooser at Fribourg should not be forgotten.[1]

George Joseph Vogler

An interesting figure in European organ-building appeared in the person of George Joseph Vogler ("the Abbé") (1749–1814). This versatile musician divided his considerable energies between a number of interests, but he failed to leave a permanent mark on any of them. Virtuoso on the organ, composer of music in many forms, acoustician,[2] writer, traveller, inventor, theoretician, priest and teacher, he accomplished a colossal amount of work in his sixty-five years. Little is known of him in the English-speaking world save that he or his works inspired Browning's well-known poem, though the poet could not have known him. Vogler was born in Würzburg, but travelled constantly; he settled in Stockholm for a time and spent his later years in Mannheim and Darmstadt, where he founded music schools. He "simplified" organs and gave organ recitals wherever he went. He visited London in

[1] Lists of these, with some accounts of their works, are given in the books of Quoika and Eberstaller.

[2] G. J. Vogler, *Data zur Akustik* (Offenbach, 1800).

1790; he was entrusted with the organ in the Pantheon, and his performances drew crowds.[1]

In 1740 G. A. Sorge,[2] a German organist, had discovered differential tones, and in 1754 Giuseppe Tartini, the violinist, published an essay entitled *Del terzo suono nella natura* ("The third sound in Nature"). Tartini's tones are heard when two notes are sounded together; a third sound is generated, which, as Helmholtz showed a century after their discovery, has a frequency of vibration which is the difference of those of the two tones producing it. Hence such tones are often called "difference tones". By employing ranks of pipes of 16-ft. and $10\frac{2}{3}$-ft. pitches it was possible to obtain a 32-ft. sound without the aid of a 32-ft. pipe. The sound thus generated is a poor substitute for the subtle tone of the real, large pipe because the higher generating pitches are too much in evidence. The pedal organ *Quint* as a part of the flue chorus of the pedal organ was known to organ-builders centuries before its advocacy by Vogler.

Free reeds were used in 1780 by a Copenhagen organ-builder named Kirsnick, whose assistant, Rackwitz, showed Vogler how to make them, in Stockholm. Vogler demonstrated his free reeds wherever he went, and the later development of the harmonium and American organ must be ascribed to his influence.

Vogler arranged the pipes of his organs in the order of the notes of the keyboard, with the largest pipes on the left of the wind-chest. Not only did he destroy the pleasant symmetrical appearance of the pipes, but from the mechanical point of view such a loading of the sound-board caused a bad distribution of the weight, and defects in key and stop action often became apparent.

He attracted the general public by his organ music and opera performances, appealed to the savants by his *Data zur Akustik* and to the religious world by his proposals to reduce the cost of organ-building.

In 1784 he built a portable organ, known as the orchestrion, and toured Europe with it. It contained 900 pipes, and was enclosed in a swell-box. He used free reeds instead of reed pipes, and it is difficult to know how these stood in tune with the flue pipes. In Holland it was acclaimed, but in Prague it was said to be a failure.

[1] The "Grove" account of the life and work of Vogler by J. H. Mee, and Professor Schafhautl's *Abt George Joseph Vogler* (Augsburg, 1888), give a remarkably full treatment of his life and works. The story of the introduction by Vogler of pedals into England given by Mee is not accurate. His typical programme was a *Pastoral Festival Interrupted by a Storm* by J. H. Knecht (1792) which was known to Beethoven and was the precursor of Beethoven's Pastoral Symphony (*Orgel sonate: die unterbrochene Hirtenwonne*), Variations and Fugues on Themes of Handel, descriptive and programme music of his own composition. It is significant that the same Knecht wrote a book on organ-playing. In this (*Orgelschule*, 1795) he says: "The organ can be regarded somewhat as an imitation of a large orchestra. The advantage a large organ has over an orchestra is that of having a 32-ft. and not only 1-ft. and $\frac{1}{2}$-ft. stops, but compound stops, adding a piercing quality to its sonority. For unusual combinations as they occur in 'gallant playing' you can skip from one to three octaves between two stops, and combine a 16-ft. stop with a 2-ft. stop. This will produce a striking effect." Thus Knecht and Vogler anticipate the romantic decadent organ style of the nineteenth century.

[2] George Andreas Sorge, *Die Natur des Orgelklangs* (1771).

His chief proposals for the simplification of organs were:

(1) To limit the number of large, expensive pipes.
(2) To use free (harmonium-type) reeds instead of reed pipes.
(3) To arrange pipes in semitonal order on the chests and not in the usual symmetrical manner.
(4) To cut down the number of multi-rank mixtures.

We will deal with these briefly.

Doubtless the late-eighteenth-century organ-builders had misunderstood the fine tradition of compound stops in the German organs of previous days. Mixture and cornet stops were often voiced too loudly, they more easily went out of tune, and their presence in organs was frequently not an unmixed blessing. Vogler waged war against them and thereby started a movement which was to end nearly a century after in the works of Hope-Jones, which scarcely had a stop above 4-ft. pitch. Vogler did not understand the genius of the great Baroque period of organ music and he sowed the seeds of the "symphonic" organ, the orchestral arrangements and the third-rate descriptive organ fantasia. On the whole, his legacy as far as organ-building was concerned was not good.

Gerber[1] says that he introduced pedals into England on the evidence that in the year of his visit (1790) the organ at St. James, Clerkenwell, was built. Hopkins[2] says that this instrument was the first English organ known for certain to have had pedal pull-downs and he gives this date. In this he was in error, for there were earlier examples of the pedal in England. Also, according to a memorandum of J. Butler (apprentice to G. P. England), the organ was actually built in 1792, and certainly the church was not consecrated until 10th July of that year.[3]

An example of Vogler's system could be seen in his modifications of the tonal scheme in the organ of St. Peter's Church, Salzburg, which dated from 1618, by Daniel Haill.

Original Scheme			*Vogler's Scheme*		
Hauptmanual		*Pipes*	*Hauptmanual*		*Pipes*
Principal	8	45	Principal	8	45
Coppel	8	45	Nassat	5⅓	45
Gamba	8	45	(to give 16-ft. effect with principal)		
Oktav	4	45	Gamba	8	45
Flöte	4	45	Principal	4	45
Quinte	3	45	Gedackt	4	45
Superoktav	2	45	Quint	2⅔	45
Kornett	(4) 5 ranks	127	Terz	3⅕	37
Cimbel	(1) 4 ranks	135	Terz	1⅗	28
Mixtur	(2) 8 ranks	270	Oktav	1	45

[1] *Lexicon der Tonkünstler* (Leipzig, 1790).
[2] Hopkins and Rimbault, op. cit.
[3] C. W. Pearce, *Notes on English Organs*, quoting the memorandum of Butler which he had seen in the possession of H. Harford Battley of Canterbury.

Vorderes Manual
(*Positiv*)

Coppel	8	45
Principal	4	45
Flöte	4	45
Superoktav	2	45
Quinte	$1\frac{1}{3}$	45
Cimbel	($1\frac{1}{2}$) 4 ranks	135

Pedal

Subbass	16	18
Gamba	16	18
Grossbass	16	18
Principal	8	18
Oktav	4	18
Mixtur	(4) 4 ranks	72
Posaune	8	18

Vorderes Manual

Coppel	8	45
Principal	4	45
Flöte	4	45
Superoktav	2	45
Quint	$1\frac{1}{3}$	26

Pedal

Gambabass	16	18
Nassat	$10\frac{2}{3}$	18
Principal	16	18
Principal	8	18
Principal	4	18
Principal	2	18
Principal	1	18
Fagott	8	18

Thus Vogler saved 525 pipes and left 780. His method of synthesising tone by the use of harmonics (mutation stops) again anticipated the work of Helmholtz in the second half of the nineteenth century.[1]

The Nineteenth Century

The beginning of the nineteenth century did not show any signs of a bright future for the organ in Europe and America, in the later years of the century.

The large organs which had appeared sporadically in several places in Germany and Holland were regarded as monuments to the past. The fine work of Bach and his immediate pupils was latent, and for the time had been forgotten owing to an increasing interest in orchestral and other forms of music. The delights of opera and the orchestra confined the organ to the accompaniment and embellishment of the various forms of the church service. The organ of the nineteenth century owes much to Mendelssohn, because of his interest in the half-forgotten works of Bach, his own compositions which show a spontaneity which is unfortunately lacking in most original works for the organ and for his own organ-playing at public concerts in Germany and England. In England, the organ was used as an accompaniment to the services in cathedrals and some of the larger churches. Organ-building showed little or no improvement on the work of Snetzler. Little money was devoted to the building and repair of organs. Many churches relied on other wind and stringed instruments to provide the modest accompaniment to their psalmody.

The organ was nearly always placed on a gallery at the west-end of the church or on the chancel screen in a cathedral. We have a very clear picture

[1] Hermann Spies, *Abt Vogler und die von ihm simplifizierte Orgel von St. Peter in Salzburg* (Mainz, 1940).

of the organ in the British Isles as it was in the first two decades of the nineteenth century, in the notebook of J. H. Leffler, organist of St. Katherine-by-the-Tower, London, whose hobby was to travel the country, examining the organs and making notes of their contents and conditions. His work is very remarkable when the difficulties of travelling in those days are recalled.[1]

Germany did not fall so low in its organ tradition as did France, though the same infection of triviality and dullness was in evidence even in the lands of Bach, Mozart and Beethoven. Many of the fine French organs of Clicquot escaped serious damage in the Revolution; indeed, some were repaired and tuned so that they could provide music for the secular festivities which took place in the Temples of Reason into which the churches were converted. At the Church of St. Sulpice and Notre Dame Cathedral in Paris the instruments were used for the accompaniment of pagan orgies.

In the "post-Waterloo" period many of the churches were restored to Christian worship, but the organs were allowed to fall into disrepair. Few organ-builders were at work and these were content to continue with little art or science. No attempt was made to continue the fine work which had been described in the monumental *L'Art du Facteur d'Orgues* by Dom Bédos in 1770, which gave an exhaustive account of the pre-Revolution organ, with minute details of the construction of every part of the instrument and advice on the use of the various stops.

In the earlier years of the nineteenth century, the music which was played on the instrument during Mass reflected the light triviality of the secular life of the time. Mercier in *Tableau de Paris* reports "on joue durant l'élévation de l'hostie et du calice des ariettes, sarabandes . . . des chasses, menuets, romances, rigaudons". The Revolution and the later military achievements of Napoleon were remembered in the churches with the organic imitations of thunder and canon "pour célébrer le Dieu des armées !" There was a voice crying in the wilderness at the Church of St. Germain l'Auxerrois in Paris where Boely (1785–1858) had introduced a few of the works of Bach, but for his pains he soon lost his post, as the result of an "economy cut".

The second half of the nineteenth century was a good one for the leading organ-builders, although in England and Germany organ composition and the use of the instrument, with regard to its true genius, were not in such a happy position. Most of the leading French organ composers were content to take the Cavaillé-Coll organ as they found it and develop "symphonic" compositions, which were often out of keeping with the historic development of the instrument on which they were played. The organ works of César Franck, Widor, Vierne and Guilmant show this tendency, though it must be admitted that the first was sometimes able to rise above the limitations imposed by the instrument, and the scholarly research of the last was a starting point towards a better understanding of the French organ which had culminated with the work of the builder Clicquot and had been forgotten after the Revolution.

[1] C. W. Pearce published the notebook of Leffler in *Notes on English Organs*, London, (1912).

Aristide Cavaillé-Coll

Aristide Cavaillé-Coll[1] was born at Montpellier in France on 4th February 1811, and his ancestry in the organ-building profession could be traced as far back as 1700. Aristide's father, Dominique Cavaillé-Coll, had some fame as an organ-builder in Languedoc, and his grandfather, Jean-Pierre Cavaillé, had built some large organs in Barcelona. Aristide took the name Coll from his grandmother. Like his younger English contemporary, Henry Willis, Aristide learnt the voicing of harmonium-type free-reeds while still in his 'teens, and the Frenchman had the added advantage of experience with the Spanish organs with their batteries of rank upon rank of reeds.

Between them Dominique and Aristide evolved an expressive reed organ, a precursor of the harmonium, known as the Poikilorgue. Another son, Vincent, two years older than Aristide, also assisted his father for a time, but had little subsequent interest in organ-building. Aristide showed early gifts for mathematics, physics and engineering, adapted Watt's linkages, which he thought he had invented anew ("a system of parallelograms"), for steadying the motion of horizontal bellows and feeders, and at the age of twenty-two was awarded a prize for the invention of a circular saw which became popular in France.

Father and son both turned to the task of making the organ more expressive. At Lerida a swell-box was fitted to the echo organ. The organ-builder Abbey had applied composition pedals to his organs, but the fixed combinations of stops which they controlled were not thought to be ideal by the Cavaillés, who insisted that an organist should show his individuality, like a chef, by his "mélanges". The coupling of one manual to another had hitherto usually been performed by taking hold of two knobs, one at each end of the keyboard, and pulling the whole clavier forward. Aristide's father had almost found a practical and easy way of coupling manuals without moving the keyboards, but it was left to the son to devise the "pédale d'accouplement". By this means, stops prepared on one manual could be added to another without holding up the march of the music. In France, the grand orgue manual is supreme, but the other divisions of the instrument stand in such relation to it that it is not only worth while to add them successively for crescendos and tonal changes or to subtract them for diminuendos, but in Cavaillé-Coll's symphonic organs this is the normal procedure.

On 28th September 1832, the composer Rossini visited Toulouse, where at this date the Cavaillé-Coll factory was at work in the Rue des Recollets, and suggested that father and son might do well in Paris. The idea appealed to young Aristide, and, persuaded by the professors of Rhetoric and Physics at the Academy of Toulouse, he made the journey in the autumn of 1833. A leading French engineer, M. Borel, examined the young man in mathematics and science and was so pleased with his remarkable knowledge that letters of introduction to leading scientists and musicians in the capital were forthcoming. Thus Aristide was able to make the acquaintance of the physicists

[1] Cavaillé-Coll C et E, *Aristide Cavaillé-Coll, ses origines, sa vie, ses oeuvres* (Paris, 1929). W. L. Sumner, "Cavaillé-Coll and the organ at St. Denis Abbey", *The Organ*, vol. xxvi (1946), p. 22.

Savart and Cagniard Latour, and the musicians Cherubini, Berton and Baron de Prony. Berton was the chairman of a commission which was to select the builder and decide all details for a new and large organ desired for the basilica of St. Denis, near Paris. Pierre Erard, John Abbey, Callinet and Dallery, the four leading organ builders in France, had already submitted plans, but Aristide's seriousness, his obvious competence and engineering ability had so impressed those who had met him that he was pressed to submit his plans. In the three days remaining he produced a complete scheme for a new instrument, together with all measurements and calculations, without communicating with his father and only ten days after his arrival as a visitor to Paris. The contract was awarded to Cavaillé-Coll, who thereupon assumed the direction of the firm at the age of twenty-two, with the active support of his father and the less active help of his brother, Vincent.

The St. Denis organ was not finished until 1841 and several smaller instruments had been completed while the larger one was still in the process of construction. Barker's pneumatic lever (q.v.) was applied to the action of the instrument in 1837 in the course of its construction, and this type of action remained a standard for almost all the larger French organs for nearly a century.[1] The St. Denis organ showed the fine engineering qualities which distinguished all Cavaillé-Coll's work. This instrument was the starting point of a great school of French organ composition and playing. The symphonic style was inaugurated and, in a remarkably uniform way, persisted for some decades.

Soon after the successful opening of the St. Denis organ, Napoleon III, in the time of the Empire, ordered that the cathedral organs throughout France should be rebuilt, in order to curry favour with the Church, and suggested that Cavaillé-Coll should be given the work. In spite of the mechanical and tonal advances and the beautiful cohesion of the various divisions of the organ, the steady wind pressures, the aids to registration and a large measure of standardisation, something was lost and was not to be found again for nearly a century. Cavaillé-Coll tended to regard the mutations of the pre-Revolution builders as a poor makeshift dictated by the feeble wind supplies and non-imitative reeds of those days. Cavaillé-Coll thought that his higher pressure reeds were in every way better than those of Clicquot. It was not until Cavaillé-Coll's later life that Guilmant and other scholars were able to insist that he should supply a sufficient quantity of mutation ranks to serve the compositions of the old French and German masters. Even so, the French organs were more adequately supplied with these essential ranks than were the contemporary English instruments. The St. Denis organ was inaugurated on 21st September 1841, and a commission appointed by the Minister of Public Works examined and tested it in every detail. This body was formed from the leading organists, Lefébvre and Simon, engineers and scientists including Poncelet and

[1] J. Adrien de la Fage, *Orgue de l'église royale de Saint-Denis* (2nd édition, Paris, 1846). The Paris factories of Cavaillé-Coll were successively at 14 Rue Neuve Sainte Georges, in the Rue de Vaugirard, and 15 Avenue de Maine, Paris.

Séguier and musicians including Cherubini, Spontini, Berton, Auber and Halévy.[1]

Cavaillé-Coll used different wind pressures for flue and reed stops, and used increased pressures of wind to maintain the power and quality of the trebles of some of the ranks of pipes. His voicing of orchestral reeds and imitative string-toned stops reached a high degree of perfection. He devised and improved new types of flute stops. The metal flûte harmonique, with holes pierced half-way along the cylindrical pipe body, can be traced back to Praetorius (1619) at least; but Cavaillé-Coll said that he was led to develop this tone by experimenting with pipes bored with holes at different distances along the bodies in order to make a musical scale with pipes of the same diameter and length. Occasionally, in his large organs, ranks of mutation harmonics for building complex and effective tone colours were provided by him. The septième $4\frac{4}{7}$-ft., the seventh harmonic of the 32-ft. fundamental which he placed on the pedal division at Notre Dame Cathedral, gave a remarkable quality to the flue-work which Louis Vierne, the organist from 1900 to 1937, described as "like a muster of double-basses". The use of mutation ranks by organ-builders until the time of the Revolution was for the production of non-imitative and characteristic organ tone, but Cavaillé-Coll used such ranks of pipes for the synthesis of orchestral colours. The full organ in a Cavaillé-Coll instrument was a rich blaze of reed tone of a free type, rendered brilliant by the éclat of mixture stops. There was a complete break here with the traditional organ in which the manual reeds would lend colour and brightness to the flue tone but would not engulf it. Only the pedal reed would be all-powerful and then only in a number of cases. Cavaillé-Coll adopted the compensated double-fold reservoirs first used by Cumming and introduced into France by John Abbey. By careful calculations, he was able to plan sufficient blowing equipment to produce wind of several pressures in ample quantity for the largest demands which could be made on his organs, even when they were used harmonically with all the couplers drawn. One of the few real improvements to the organ since the year 1700 has been the perfection of means to secure sufficient wind at constant pre-determined pressures. Before the time of Cumming's invention, fluctuations in wind pressure took place as the reservoirs emptied, and often showed a slight rise as the reservoir collapsed. When diagonal bellows fed directly into a wind trunk considerable skill on the part of the blowers must have been necessary, not only to keep up a continuous wind supply but also to maintain the speech of the pipes.

Cavaillé-Coll extended the manual compasses to A and provided inter-

[1] "C'est à l'église abbatiale de Saint-Denys en France qu'était né, vers 1140, le grand portail gothique tel que les maîtres d'oeuvres en reproduiront le modèle dans nombre de nos cathédrales aux xiie, xiiie et xiv^e^s. C'est à la même église que naquit sept siècles plus tard l'orgue romantique (1841), tel que les facteurs en répandront la formule dans toute l'Europe jusqu'en 1914. Le portail du xiie était une oeuvre anonyme. L'orgue du xixe est sorti des mains d'Aristide Cavaillé-Coll. Il marque une révolution dans l'Art du Facteur d'Orgues." Norbert Dufourcq, Professeur d'histoire de la Musique au Conservatoire national, in *L'Orgue* (Paris, 1948). This is true only as far as concerns France.

manual and often sub- and super-octave couplers in addition to pedal to manual couplers in respect of all the manuals. Often, he separated the chorus reeds and mixtures on a "grand-choeur" manual, which could be added to the 16-ft., 8-ft., and 4-ft. flue-work confined to a grand-organ manual. The *plein jeu* of the old great organs vanished. Batteries of 16-ft., 8-ft., and 4-ft. reeds were added to the grand organ, and the small récit was enlarged and made expressive by being placed in a swell-box. Cavaillé-Coll soon perceived the thrilling effect of the use of 16-ft., 8-ft. and 4-ft. reeds of brilliant tone under expression in a swell-box. Henry Willis, his younger English contemporary, was soon to develop the characteristic English "full-swell", so beautifully exemplified in his organ at St. Paul's Cathedral, London, in 1872.[1] No doubt Cavaillé-Coll had appreciated the arresting effect of the batteries of reeds in the Spanish organs which he knew in his early years. He extended the compass of the hautbois by adding a basson, and changed the tone of the old organ hautbois to one of a more orchestral flavour. The cromorne, so useful for the playing of the music of the seventeenth- and eighteenth-century masters, gave place to the clarinet; the voix humaine, an example of the old "schnarrwerk" and a useful timbre-creator, was transferred as a solo stop to the récit expressif. Undulating stops, formed by adding slightly mistuned ranks to those of quiet "string" or salcional tone, became popular on the récit expressif or positif divisions of the organ. All these things offered fearful temptations to those who approached the organ in a "symphonic-romantic" mood without reference to its musical tradition.

Cavaillé-Coll produced an open metal foundation stop which was unlike the English diapason in tone. It was called "montre", because the traditional stops of that name appeared as the pipes in the organ case; and usually the 16-ft. montre in Cavaillé-Coll's organs provided the large, speaking show pipes, though the pipes of the stops of that name were not always visible in the organ case-work. He cut slots in the back of these pipes because, as he said, careless tuners would otherwise have pinched the pipes as a means of tuning them. The slots produced a hard quality of tone, which nevertheless blended well with the rest of the flue-work and with the reeds. Henry Willis adopted the same practice with many of his diapasons, but only to secure, as he hoped, a better blend and not to facilitate tuning. (Modern cylindrical tuning slides would have rendered such treatment unnecessary.) The romantic-symphonic organ was more tractable and easy to manage than its predecessors. In the hands of Cavaillé-Coll and Henry Willis, who were first-class structural engineers as well as tonal artists, it became a worthy, durable and noble instrument of music in spite of some shortcomings.

Cavaillé-Coll secured a large measure of standardisation and uniformity in his organ-console arrangements. Composers could write their works with a knowledge of the nature of the instrument for which they were writing. They would have a good idea of the actual sounds which would be produced when they suggested certain schemes of registration with Cavaillé-Coll's

[1] Remaining (1962) as it was, apart from an improvement in the swell-pedal mechanism, and still superb in its effect.

PLATE 23.

St. Stephan's, Karlsruhe. Two views. Organ by Klais, 1957

PLATE 24a.
Liverpool Cathedral, new Willis Nave Console 1940. The couplers are below the music desk

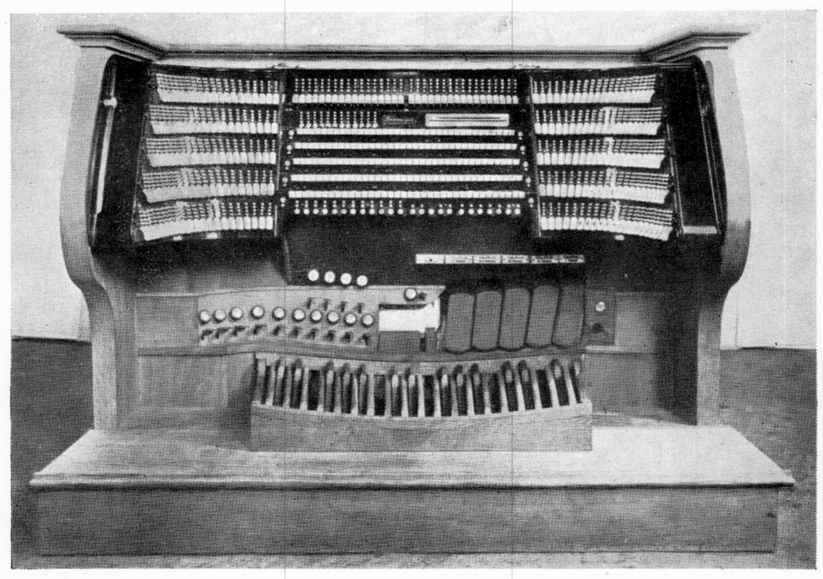

PLATE 24b.
Passau Cathedral, Bavaria. Organ by Steinmeyer. Note the rollschweller above the centre of the pedal-board and free-combination buttons above each stop key

organs in mind.[1] In a four-manual Cavaillé-Coll organ the order of the manuals from the lowest was: grand, positif, récit expressif, bombarde. The bombarde controlled loud reeds (and in some cases loud mixture stops). Later, following the Spanish custom, these reeds were placed horizontally with their open ends facing into the church. In 1875, Cavaillé-Coll fitted a swell-box for the pipes of a second manual to the organ in the Palace of Industry at Amsterdam.

In most of his larger church organs (and in many small instruments) the console was detached a little way from the instrument so that the organist sat with his back to the organ and could look over the console into the church or auditorium. The ventil system of stop control was applied to many of his larger organs. When a stop was drawn at the console nothing further happened until wind was admitted to the drawstop machines by pressing a ventil pedal or by drawing a ventil knob. This enabled the organist to prepare stop selections on various manual divisions or subdivisions of the organ and to bring them into operation as occasion required. The ventil system was superior to the English fixed composition, combination piston or pedal systems, for it enabled the French organist to show his individuality in the compounding of his tone-colour *mélanges*.

Over six hundred organs built by Cavaillé-Coll have been listed.[2] In Paris those at Notre Dame, Saint-Sulpice, La Madeleine, Sainte-Clotilde, Saint-Vincent de Paul, La Trinité and Saint-François-Xavier retain the tonal qualities which he gave them, the changes made to them have been of the nature of restorations and small additions have not altered their chief characteristics. Cavaillé-Coll fervently wished that he might be allowed to build a giant organ for St. Peter's, Rome, but, in spite of all his efforts, this did not materialise. Many other cathedrals and churches in France have Cavaillé-Coll organs, but some have been allowed to deteriorate. No comparable figure has arisen in France since the death of this great organ-builder on 13th October 1899 in his eighty-ninth year.

In England some of his work still remains.[3] His finest organ, in the Albert Hall, Sheffield, was destroyed by fire in 1937, but it had not been used as a concert instrument for some years. The organ at Manchester Town Hall, which was made famous by the playing of the late Kendrick Pyne, was rebuilt as a five-manual organ by Wadsworth of Manchester. The Paisley Abbey organ was much enlarged by Norman and Beard. The organs at Blackburn Cathedral and Bellahouston Church are largely by this builder. The "Grand orgue de 32 pieds" which formerly stood in Ketton Hall, Rutland, is now in Parr Hall, Warrington. There is a small instrument in Farnborough Abbey; and the organ at the Church of Notre Dame, Leicester Place, London, after war damage, has been restored. A number of organs contain vox humana

[1] W. Goodrich, *The Organ in France* (Boston, U.S.A., 1917). The theme of this work is the need for a non-literal translation of registration directions on French organ music when this is played on American or English organs.

[2] A complete list of his organs is given as an appendix to Cavaillé-Coll C et E, *Cavaillé-Coll—Ses origines, sa vie, ses oeuvres* (Paris, 1929).

[3] The account of this in the biography of Cavaillé-Coll is not accurate.

and orchestral reed stops ordered from him, for insertion, when English organs were built or enlarged.

Various devices were employed in different countries to aid the organist in controlling his stops. Cavaillé-Coll had a system of ventil pedals whereby stops could be prepared on a "laye" or sound-board and brought into operation when required. Sometimes one keyboard would control more than one sound-board. Even the pipes of the great organ (grand orgue) could be isolated from their own keys, leaving to sound only those of other coupled manuals. Further, a system was devised so that prepared stops would actuate the corresponding sliders (and cause the pipes to sound when the keys were pressed) *only* when wind was admitted to the drawstop machines by means of a pedal.

The manual claviers were extended to fifty-four notes, then to fifty-six, and finally to sixty.

Cavaillé-Coll never lost sight of the need for a second manual which should be comparable in its number of stops, though not in power, with the grand (great) organ. He never starved the tonal resources of his grand organ to provide a large swell division, although in his later instruments the heavy reeds were playable from a separate clavier known as the Bombarde.

The great merit of the romantic organ was the facility which it gave to an easy performance. The introduction of the pneumatic lever, which was followed by various tubular-pneumatic actions, lightened the touch of the keys to that of a grand pianoforte. The energy of the organ wind was also used to move the sliders of the stops, and there were new devices for moving the stops in groups and for quickly altering the registration scheme. These improvements were not always unmixed blessings. Very often, long tubular actions produced a sluggish emission of sound and destroyed all proper attack. In this the pneumatic lever was superior, and a well-made action gave instant response. Facilities for stop-changing were not infrequently abused by organists, and good rhythm, phrasing and architectural form in their music were sacrificed to restless tonal changes.

The organs of Cavaillé-Coll inaugurated a school of symphonic organ playing and composition marked at the outset by the works of César Franck (1822–90), Camille Saint-Saens (1835–1921) and followed by Charles Marie Widor (1845–1937), Alexandre Guilmant (1837–1911), Louis Vierne (1870–1937), Eugene Gigout (1844–1925), Theodore Dubois (1837–1924) and others. In spite of Widor's assertion that "after Cavaillé-Coll came the proper playing of the works of Bach",[1] the symphonic French organ was not ideal for playing the works of the Thuringian master. Widor did not know of the great Baroque tradition which found its apogee in the organs of Arp Schnitger in North Germany.

The Cavaillé-Coll organ exercised considerable influence in England. Indirectly, Henry Willis absorbed many of the French builder's ideas to the extent of making the great organ at the Royal Albert Hall (1871–2) practically a copy of the grand orgue and its chorus at the Church of St. Sulpice, Paris.[2]

[1] Preface to Pirro, *L'Orgue de Bach* (Paris, 1896).

[2] W. L. Sumner, "A great similarity", *Musical Opinion* (July 1936).

After this date the French influence was not so apparent, but the romantic orchestral style of organ playing still held sway. In particular, W. T. Best, who praised the work of Cavaillé-Coll, became famous for his orchestral arrangements and his superlatively clever playing of them at St. George's Hall, Liverpool. He was, of course, equally brilliant in the playing of genuine organ compositions, of which few were known other than those of Bach, Handel and Mendelssohn, but always the style of playing tended to be orchestral.[1]

The break with tradition was complete until the researches of Pirro (1869–1948) and Guilmant (1837–1911), at the turn of the century, showed what treasures of organ music were latent, and further revealed the inadequacy of the romantic organ for giving proper expression to these works of the greatest periods of organ composition.

It is necessary to pay tribute to the positive qualities of the organs of the symphonic period. New and beautiful voices both of flue and reed stops were heard in the instrument; the voicing and regulation of each rank of pipes reached a perfection which had not hitherto been obtained. The organ progressed as a piece of engineering and it became more easy to control. The development of the principles of Cumming and the increasing use of "mechanical" blowing with water, steam and gas engines and, later, electrical power had ensured that it had a regular and ample supply of wind.

The Willis combination pistons and the Cavaillé-Coll "registres de combinaison", which enabled prepared selections of stops to be brought into combination when required, by the use of pedals, were very valuable to the thoughtful organist.

Cavaillé-Coll remained faithful to the pneumatic lever and did not favour tubular systems. The firms of Daublaine and Callinet, Abbey, Merklin, Gutschenritter built many organs of the romantic type with tubular-pneumatic action. In Canada, in the latter part of the nineteenth century the Casavant firm of St. Hyacinth, Quebec, took the contemporary French organ as their model, but improved it by developing a reliable electric action. In Germany more and more 8-ft. stops of string and principal tone were added to organs; in English organs more unison diapasons and solo stops.

The Organ in Britain

The English organs were very small compared with those of France, Germany, Holland and Italy. For the first decade of the century, the two largest British organs were those in St. Paul's Cathedral and York Minster with twenty-seven stops each. Holland, Germany and Italy possessed instruments of sixty stops and upwards. Hamburg, for instance, had five 32-ft. organs, and there were some hundreds of instruments with independent pedal organs of considerable size in Germany. Canterbury Cathedral had twenty-four stops; Durham, Lichfield, Rochester and Salisbury had twenty-three each; and Bristol, St. Patrick's, Dublin, Hereford, Wells, Winchester, and

[1] H. Heathcote Statham, *The Organ and Its Position in Musical Art* (London, 1909).

Westminster had twenty-two. Cork, Chichester, Exeter, Gloucester and Norwich twenty each, and the rest less than twenty. There were no pedals on the cathedral organs at Bristol, Canterbury, Carlisle, Chester, Durham, Ely, Exeter, Gloucester, Lincoln, Norwich, Oxford, Peterborough, Wells, Chichester and Worcester, and only two cathedrals had separate sets of pedal pipes.

In the later part of the century in England a new and opulent civic pride resulted in the building of town halls in many towns and cities. There had been, in the 'forties, a revival in the Church of England, and new organs were required not only for the hundreds of new churches which were springing up in the industrial districts but also as replacements or renewals in the cathedral and collegiate churches. The organ-playing of W. T. Best in St. George's Hall, Liverpool, the work of Henry Smart (1813–79), John Stainer (1840–1901) and George Cooper (1830–92) in London and the formation of the College of Organists (now the Royal College of Organists) gave great impetus to the study of the instrument. The organ tutors of Rinck (1770–1846), Cooper, Best and, finally, the "best selling" Primer of Stainer, published by Novello, found ready buyers. An organ often became a mark of ecclesiastical and civic pride. Strange it was that so little attention was paid to the case with which it was clothed. Hideous designs, usually in unpleasant colours on flat rows of front pipes, replaced the artistic cases of the seventeenth and eighteenth centuries and stood in unhappy contrast to those which still beautified the cathedrals and churches of Europe. In spite of the numbers of organs which were erected between 1850 and 1900, few showed any attempt at economical and effective tonal design, and there was no definitive English school of organ-playing and organ composition. Individually, English organists were technically the best in the world, but so long as Handel's choruses, orchestral compositions and a few of the major works of Bach, played in a manner which showed little insight, were the stock-in-trade of these great players, little real progress could result. Nevertheless, English players, using the Wesley-Willis radiating and concave pedal-board, set a standard which was unrivalled throughout the world. Henry Willis, senior, in England, and Aristide Cavaillé-Coll in France, rivalled one another in producing organs which were not only integrated and beautiful instruments of music but also showed qualities of durability, engineering skill and attention to detail which were hardly to be matched elsewhere.

The state of the English organ in the middle of the nineteenth century is reflected in the fourteen instruments erected in the Crystal Palace for the 1851 Exhibition in Hyde Park, London. At this time not many English organs had pedals: with few exceptions they were small one- and two-manual organs. No standards concerning manual compasses had been worked out; barrel organs were still popular in small town churches, and no organ had been conceived in terms of the great European tradition of organ music. The accompaniment of the church service in an unsubtle manner on the manuals and the playing of extracts from Handel's oratorios were the measures of the capacity of many organists. An account of the organs in the 1851 Exhibition is found in *Musical Instruments in the Great Industrial Exhibition of 1851*, by

William Pole,[1] F.R.A.S., organist of St. Mark's, Grosvenor Square, and published in the same year. Eleven of the organs were English and there was one each from France, Germany and Italy.

The organs which had the greatest subsequent effect on British organ-building were those of the young Englishman, Henry Willis, and the German, Edmund Schulze, who had brought an instrument made by the firm founded by his father at Paulinzella in Central Germany.

The Willis organ, which was the starting point of many improvements in the British organ, had three manuals and seventy stops. It was the first large organ of the type which was to dominate British organ-building for the rest of the century, at least. The swell department, which had twenty-two stops, had a family of dulcianas (16-ft., 8-ft., 4-ft. and 2-ft.) and a three-rank "dulcimer". Barker's pneumatic action, as improved by Willis, was applied to the great and swell organs; an ingenious device was used for lightening the touch of the choir manual; and a roller-valve was applied to the action of the large pedal stops. Pneumatic "pistons", in the form of brass discs placed between the manuals, were the forerunners of the modern ivory studs which are used for controlling the stops in groups. The swell-bellows were placed inside the swell-box in order to prevent air from forcing open the shutters when the organ was in use. Part of this organ formed the nucleus of an instrument which Willis later erected in Winchester Cathedral, and the pipes can be heard there, at present, in an organ which has been rebuilt by Hele and Harrison, successively.

The Schulze instrument was a revelation in the flue choruses on each manual and the tonal output of its few pedal stops. The lieblich gedeckt stops, of smaller scale than the English stopped diapasons, immediately became popular and since that time have been used in practically every organ, however small, built in this country. The Schulze organ went to Northampton, was erected in the Town Hall and subsequently enlarged by a French firm. The cost of the instrument was £210. Strange to relate, this little masterpiece of organ-building was taken down and lost.

Gray and Davison, of Pentonville Rd., London, who were leading organ-builders, supplied a three-manual instrument which was sold to the Church of St. Anne, Limehouse. The swell organ extended to tenor C, and below that note the keys acted upon the choir organ. The swell to pedal thus acted in 4-ft. pitch, and it is remarkable that Dr. Pole refers to its value in Bach chorale-preludes where a 4-ft. solo is required on the pedals. Unfortunately few professional organists of the time would follow him in this matter. There was a great-to-swell sforzando pedal,[2] the swell pedal acted on a double set of Venetian louvres, and the pedal organ was supplied with a higher pressure of wind than the rest of the organ.

The Hill organ contained a nine-stop great organ from double diapason to

[1] William Pole was later Professor of Engineering in the University of London and was largely responsible for drawing up the syllabuses for the Musical Degrees of that university. The church at which he was organist is now known as St. Mark's, North Audley Street, London.

[2] This coupled the manuals so long as the pedal was depressed. Thus an accent could be given momentarily to a chord.

three-rank sesquialtera and two reeds, a swell organ with five 8-ft. stops intended to show the builders' voicing specialities, one of which was a tuba on 11-in. wind. The pedal organ was twenty-nine "open wood" 16-ft. pipes and the whole instrument was enclosed. The stops were controlled by a double row of stop-keys at the sides of the manuals which were "something like those of the manual claviers", and they acted on the sliders by means of pneumatic levers. The keys of one row brought the stops on and those of the other row took them off.[1]

The firm of Ducroquet of Paris, which was later absorbed in the house of Merklin-Schütze et Cie, exhibited a small organ with a reversed console, and excellent reeds on a higher pressure than the flue-work (see specification, No. 33). The English firm of Bishop showed a small organ of five stops with concussion-bellows and composition pedals; and the firm of Walker also provided a one-manual organ with nine registers of beautiful flue stops, for which the firm has always been notable.

G. M. Holdich, then a leading builder and one who had produced many instruments of considerable size, exhibited a three-stop organ with a diaocton (diocton) stop (an octave coupler that acted through the entire compass), thus necessitating the provision of an extra octave of pipes at the top of the compass.

A. and M. Ducci of Florence showed a small one-manual organ with six manual stops and one pedal pipe. This pipe, which served as the organist's seat, was about four feet long, seven inches broad and twenty inches deep, and, by means of valves which opened and closed orifices, it was made to yield twelve different notes. (A Baristate,[2] made on the same principle, was a portable instrument composed of three or four of these multiple-note pipes blown by the performer and played by means of a keyboard, was intended to supplement the deeper notes of the orchestra, and is said to have won high praise from Rossini.) The polyphone pipe used at the early date of 1851 is interesting, because in recent years, methods of polyphoning large pipes and "cubes" have been a feature of the Compton organs in England.

Gray and Davison, and Bryceson supplied barrel organs which could be

[1] It has often been stated that this instrument went to Turvey, Bedfordshire, where there is a small old Hill four-manual organ. Actually, the exhibition organ went to the Wesleyan Church, Pitt Street, Barnsley, Yorks, where it has been enlarged.

[2] "In Messrs. Ducci's organ in the Exhibition the pedal notes, twelve in number, beginning with 16-ft. C, are said to have been all produced from one pipe about 4 ft. long, contained in the stool on which the organist sat. It is stated that the makers have found a means of so varying the proportions and make as to cause a stopped-pipe 4 ft. long to sound a 16-ft. note of 8 ft., a 32-ft. note of 2 ft., an 8-ft. note, and so on; and, secondly, they have made the same pipe speak different notes by opening holes situated at certain distances in one of its sides, on the principle of the flute and other orchestral wind instruments. By applying, therefore, the pedal-keys to move valves covering these holes, the whole range of an octave of pedal notes is produced by a simple and inexpensive means" (Tomlinson, *Cyclopædia of Useful Arts* (1855), vol. ii—volumes dealing with the exhibits at the Great Exhibition, 1851). A writer in *The English Mechanic* (25th December 1868) says of this device: "A whole octave of excellent pedal tones can be obtained from two pipes", as "was ocularly and auricularly demonstrated by an organ-builder in the Italian department of the Great Exhibition of 1851".

used in houses for entertainment purposes or in small churches for accompanying the singing of hymns. The mechanical organ of Dawson worked by perforated pasteboard (like that of the Jacquard loom) instead of barrels. "It has the disadvantage of admitting the wind gradually into the pipes, and cutting it off gradually from them, the effect of which is a disagreeable wavering at the commencement and termination of the note."[1]

An "enharmonic organ" designed by Perronet Thompson, not intended for church or concert use, had forty-two different sounds to the octave distributed on three claviers. It was an attempt to show how purer intervals, unobtainable on the twelve-note octave of the tempered scale, could be obtained in many keys. The instrument was given to the South Kensington Science Museum.

Forster and Andrews of Hull exhibited an instrument with one manual, and pedals with a single stop. This was a model to demonstrate a transposing device. Ten different keys, five up and five down, were made available by the turning of a handle which moved the action a semitone at a time.

Until the end of the first half of the nineteenth century organists were not easily found for the smaller and country churches in England. Barrel organs, on which a number of hymn and psalm tunes could be played by means of pins on the surface of a slowly rotating cylinder, became popular, and many hundreds were made. The firm of Theodore Bates in Ludgate Hill, London, specialised in this type of work, and the founder of the Walker firm made small one-manual organs which were both finger and barrel organs. Some barrel organs still survive and occasionally are used in divine service. A large specimen of an instrument of this type is to be seen in Brightling Church in Sussex. Dom Bédos, in his *L'Art du Facteur d'orgues*, gives diagrams and a description of a barrel organ and he gives the method of pinning the barrels to make a particular tune and such organs must have been used for solo purposes in French churches and private houses before the Revolution.[2]

As is shown by the pages of the *Musical Times* (London), there seems to have been a superfluity of organists towards the seventies of last[3] century, and the smallest stipend or honorarium would attract a considerable number of applicants in most parts of the country. Many amateurs were content to give their services free. Thus, few barrel organs were required, and many were destroyed or were rebuilt as "finger organs". Some dozens stand silent and forgotten in churches in England.[4]

[1] Pole, op. cit.

[2] These exact descriptions enabled Arnold Dolmetsch to deduce the note values of certain ornaments in his research on the playing of old music. See his book on the performance of seventeenth- and eighteenth-century clavier music, *The Interpretation of the Music of the seventeenth and eighteenth Centuries* (London, 1915, 1944).

[3] P. A. Scholes, *The Mirror of Music*, vol. ii, p. 602 (London, 1947).

[4] The increasing demand for small but easily played organs from the middle of the nineteenth century led to the design by the Rev. J. Baron of Upton Scudamore (J. Baron, *Scudamore Organs*, 2nd ed., London, 1847) of a number of instruments which consisted of a single rank of open-diapason pipes, or of such a rank

Other Organ Builders of the 19th Century

After 1850 the organ became very popular, not only for leading congregational singing, but as a solo instrument, in secular buildings. Towards the end of that century there was also much work for organ-builders in Scotland and the Carnegie funds later provided many instruments. Composers turned out enormous quantities of "original organ music" and voluntaries, for the most part of third-rate quality. Arrangers turned popular operatic, vocal and instrumental pieces into organ and harmonium music. Such "organ-fodder" did much to bring the instrument into the low esteem of sensitive musicians. The traditional tonal structure of the instrument and its great heritage of real organ music were often forgotten.

Allen, William, built the organs in Peterborough and Lincoln Cathedrals and the "oratorio organ" in Covent Garden Theatre in 1810. A fine pedal stop by him taken from the Lincoln organ can still be heard in the organ at St. Bees' Priory Church.

Allen, Charles, of Soho, built some good chamber organs until *c.* 1860.

Bewscher and Fleetwood, a Liverpool firm who did some good work in various parts of the country at the beginning of the nineteenth century.

Bishop, J. C., the founder of a firm which is still in existence. He established a factory in London and introduced composition pedals for changing the stops (an improvement on the old shifting movements which shut off groups of pipe ranks by means of sliders). Bishop invented the Clarabella stop, a type of wide-scaled hohlflöte, and he used concussion bellows, which were fitted to the wind-trunks, near the organ sound-boards, to overcome the inertia of masses of air when sudden demands were made on the wind supply of a particular section of an organ.

The organ cornet, so misunderstood by English eighteenth-century builders and players (even Dr. Burney !) was suppressed by Bishop. Although this was a retrograde step, he cannot be blamed for this, as most specimens had become intolerable, shrieking mixtures. The firm was known successively as Bishop, Son and Starr; Bishop, Starr and Richardson; Bishop and Starr; and Bishop and Son. The quality of the woodwork of this firm was first-class. They were in charge of the organ at St. Paul's Cathedral for a time, and later built large organs at St. Mary's Church, Nottingham (1872), and Southwell Minster (1890). These instruments were subsequently reconstructed by others.

---

with the addition of a 4-ft. principal. Henry Willis made many such small organs.

In the second half of the century, the free-reed instruments, such as were made at an earlier date by Erard and Cavaillé-Coll in France and W. E. Evans (with whom Willis worked) in England, had been developed into harmoniums and reed ("American") organs. In the former the wind is blown through the reeds, but in the latter it is sucked into them from the outside air. Many dozens of thousands of such instruments, cheap, light in weight, readily transportable and standing in tune year in and year out, were made and sold in the U.S. and in Canada. The Mustel harmonium made in France, when played by a master, sounded remarkably like a small Cavaillé-Coll instrument in some of its moods, when it was heard in the resounding spaces of a large French Gothic church.

Booth, Joseph, of Wakefield, who is remembered as the inventor in 1827 of "puff bellows" for lightening the touch (q.v.), a precursor of pneumatic action.

Cumming, Alexander, F.R.S. (1733–1824), a clockmaker and mechanical constructor. (His name is often wrongly spelt Cummins in literature on the organ.) He improved organ bellows and wind reservoirs by using "inverted folds" so that pressure was maintained at any position of rise or fall. He built a machine organ for the Earl of Bute,[1] and the organ in Christ Church Priory, Hampshire, England, in 1788.

Eagles, John, a London organ-builder who had a factory at Hackney and did considerable work about the middle of the nineteenth century in churches in the East End of London and Essex. An example of his work (1858) exists in Preston near Wingham, Kent.

Flight, Benjamin, the son of an organ-builder of the same name, was born about 1767, and was for some time in partnership with his father. About 1800 he went into partnership with Joseph Robson. The factory was in Lisle Street, Leicester Square, London. After dissolving partnership they removed to 36 St. Martin's Lane, reverting to the original title of Flight and Son. The famous Apollonicon organ, which could be played simultaneously by a number of performers, was built by them, but when public interest in large instruments waned, it was broken up. Flight died in 1847. A Flight organ can still be heard in Harwich Parish Church, Essex.[2] Robson continued alone and then with his son until 1876.

Gray, Robert, established an organ factory in London in 1774. He was succeeded by William Gray (d. 1820) and afterwards by John Gray. After 1838 John Gray took Frederick Davison into partnership under the title of Gray and Davison. The firm still exists. Tonally, their nineteenth-century work, particularly the flue-work, is very beautiful. Examples may be heard in Sherborne Abbey, St. Pancras Parish Church, London, the High Pavement Chapel, Nottingham, Clumber Chapel and elsewhere. Much pipework of these builders has been incorporated in later organs by others.

Hamilton, David, the real inventor of the pneumatic lever (q.v.). An Edinburgh organ-builder and organist of St. John's Episcopal Church, Edinburgh. In 1851 he published *Remarks on Organ Building and the Causes of Defective Instruments*.

Holland, Henry, of London and Bath, did some minor work in various parts of the country. He built the organ in St. George's, Bloomsbury, London, in 1788. He learnt his trade with the elder England, and was in partnership with Jones.

Knight, Thomas, added the swell to Chichester Cathedral organ in 1778.

Lincoln, Henry Cephas, was born in 1789 and died in 1864. He was the son of John Lincoln, an organ-builder with whom he worked from an early

[1]A. Freeman, "The Earl of Bute's Machine Organ", *The Organ*, vol. xxiv, pp. 109 et seq.

[2] W. L. Sumner, "Two Essex Organs", *The Organ*, vol. xxviii. An account of the work of this firm is given by B. B. Edmonds in *The Organ Club Handbook*, No. 6 (1960).

age. His factory was at 196 High Holborn, London. He used Dom Bedos's great work on organ-building as a guide. His best-known work was at Brighton Parish Church and Pavilion. He built organs in Wells, Exeter, Worksop, Nottingham, Bakewell, Swinton, Painswick, Rye, Stafford, Luton, Bristol, Jersey, Guernsey and many in London and district, etc.

Renn and Boston. This Manchester firm, in the early part of the nineteenth century, supplied organs to many churches in Yorkshire, Lancashire and the North of England. F. W. Jardine (d. 1907) joined the firm in 1843 and it was later known as Kirtland and Jardine, and Thorold and Smith. It is still actively engaged in the trade as Jardine & Co. It absorbed the Holdich interests.

Russell, Hugh, was the father of William Russell, born in 1777, who subsequently became organist of the Foundling Hospital. A son, Timothy Russell, also an organ-builder, constructed a number of instruments in London, his last organ being that at St. Philip's, Arlington Square, in 1858.

Seede, Brice, a Bristol organ-builder of much repute in the middle of the eighteenth century. His successors were Richard Seede (*c.* 1787); John Smith (*c.* 1820), one of the first to make 32-ft. pedal stops in English organs; Joseph Munday (*c.* 1836); and W. G. Vowles, the head of a distinguished firm of organ-builders. (An example of their work may be heard in the Chapel of Mansfield College, Oxford.)

It is not necessary to give an exhaustive list of organ-builders who were at work in the later part of the nineteenth century. The chief figures were Willis, Walker, Hill, and, as far as foreign organs were erected here, Schulze of Paulinzella, Cavaillé-Coll of Paris, and Walcker of Ludwigsburg.

In addition to those firms of longer standing which were at work at the beginning of the century we ought to mention some later figures in the same century.

Holdich, George Maidwell, named after the Northamptonshire village in which he was born, whose work was good, with first-class flue choruses in the true organ style. Like many of his contemporaries, he was eclipsed by Henry Willis. He built many organs, an example of which was a fine instrument with a proper pedal organ in Lichfield Cathedral.[1]

Bryceson Brothers of London were early in the field with improvements to organ action. They rebuilt many organs in London and its environs. They built organs with electro-magnetic action in London. The large organ in Mr. Holmes's residence in Regent's Park, now in a monastery at Fort Augustus, Scotland, was their work. Their organ in Rugby School Chapel (1872) was notable.

Bevington, Henry, and Sons. They built two thousand one- and two-manual organs with clear diapason choruses including mixtures. Many of their organs are still in use in country churches. Their pipework was usually worth

[1] An account of his work is given in *The Organ Club Handbook*, No. 6 (1960) by B. B. Edmonds.

incorporating in rebuilt organs. They occupied premises in Greek Street and Rose Street, Soho, London, from 1794.

Jones, Henry. A London organ-builder, of Fulham Road, who did solid, durable work. His instrument at the Westminster Aquarium (on the site of the Westminster Central Hall) was his chief work. Many of his generously planned organs still exist in country churches.

Young, Maley and *Oldknow*, who did work in the West of England, Channel Islands etc.

Lewis, Thomas Christopher, of Ferndale Road, Brixton (also a bell founder). He built a large number of fine organs, many of which are still extant in almost their original condition. The firm was absorbed by that of Willis after the first European War. His fluework was particularly notable, and his diapason choruses and gedackts owed much to Schulze. The quality of his pipework was admirable and he used large quantities of tin in making his alloys. Structurally his instruments were durable and worthy. Magnificent as were his diapason choruses, they were limited in variety and not ideal for the playing of real organ music. Examples of his work may be heard at Southwark Cathedral, London; Westminster Cathedral Chancel Organ; St. Peter's, Eaton Square, London; St. Mary's, Beverley. Much of Lewis's pipework has been incorporated in rebuilt organs. The best work of Lewis and his firm was from 1860 to 1900.

Other English disciples of Schulze were *Thomas Pendlebury* of Leigh, who built some first-rate organs in Lancashire and made wooden pedal stops of beautiful string tone, and *James Jepson Binns*, of Meanwood, Leeds, who cared for the Schulze organ in St. Bartholomew's Church, Armley, Leeds, for many years. Binns's work was well made and, in particular, his wood pipes were of excellent quality. He was at work before the effect of the modern tonal renaissance had made itself felt. His individual flue stops were usually of good quality. He built many moderate-sized organs to two or three standard specifications. His largest organ was that at Yarmouth Parish Church, England, which was destroyed during the last war. Instruments by Binns may be heard at the Albert Hall and Castlegate Church, Nottingham; in Stoke Parish Church; Reading University; St. Aidan's Church, Leeds; and elsewhere. He died in 1929.

We have already mentioned the work of Edmund Schulze (1823–1878). His 1851 Exhibition organ which went to Northampton was followed by the building of a large chamber organ for the wife of T. S. Kennedy, the Leeds alpinist. This instrument, with some additions, is now in the Church of St. Bartholomew, Armley. A large organ at Doncaster Parish Church, with a great organ and pedal scheme which were unique in England, though common in Germany, was extended in the early part of the century by Norman and Beard and rebuilt by Walker between the wars. Schulze also built a fine instrument at Tyne Dock and others at Hindley Parish Church (near Wigan) and at Charterhouse School.[1] The Hindley organ

[1] A part of this organ was incorporated in that at Holy Trinity, Marylebone, London.

has been partly revoiced by Pendlebury. Schulze supplied small instruments and ranks of pipes elsewhere in England; and the organ, now destroyed, at the Temple Church, London, was enriched by his flue pipes. Schulze's influence was considerable, particularly in the North of England, in fact, it determined completely the type of organ made by the Yorkshire and Lancashire builders.

Telford, William, of Dublin. A large firm which flourished particularly in the mid-nineteenth century. Telford built the original organ in Radley College and adjudicated at the 1851 Exhibition.

Henry Willis

It can hardly be disputed that Henry Willis was the greatest of the nineteenth-century British organ-builders, but there were others who achieved notable work and some mention of these will follow. Henry Willis, the son of a North London builder, was born on 27th April 1821. Willis at an early age became friendly with George Cooper, later the sub-organist of St. Paul's Cathedral, and the two boys learnt to play the organ and to read the old open scores of those days without lessons but with a few hints from Attwood, the cathedral organist. In 1835, when he was fourteen years of age, Willis was articled for seven years to John Gray (afterwards of Gray and Davison). During his apprenticeship he invented the special manual and pedal couplers which he used in all his instruments for over sixty years. Willis tuned the organ at St. George's Chapel, Windsor, and was encouraged by the organist, Sir George Elvey. While still an apprentice, Willis was appointed organist of Christ Church, Hoxton; later he became organist of Hampstead Parish Church, where he had built an organ; and for nearly thirty years he was organist of the Chapel-of-Ease, Islington, from which he resigned only after he was well over the age of seventy. In spite of the claims of his work in many parts of the British Isles, he would often travel one hundred and fifty miles on a Saturday in order to be present at the Sunday services. In his younger days he also played the double-bass and performed at the provincial musical festivals of 1871 and 1874. After his apprenticeship expired he lived in Cheltenham for three years, where he assisted a musical instrument-maker, W. E. Evans, formerly of Norfolk Street, Sheffield. They produced a two-manual free-reed organ with two and a half octaves of pedals. This was a precursor of the "American" organ. Evans was a genius in reed-voicing and undoubtedly, as in the case of Cavaillé-Coll, Willis owed his superlative skill in voicing organ reeds to his early experience in obtaining the most musical results from the brass tongues of harmonium-type reeds. Willis met Samuel Sebastian Wesley at Cheltenham and this led to the rebuilding of the Gloucester Cathedral organ in 1847, which marked the establishment of Willis as an independent organ-builder. "It was my stepping stone to fame; the swell, down to double C, had twelve stops and a double Venetian front. The pianissimo was simply astounding. I received £400 for the job, and I was presumptuous enough to marry."[1]

[1] From an interview with Willis published in the *Musical Times* (May 1898).

For the Great Exhibition of 1851 in the Crystal Palace, then in Hyde Park, Willis erected the largest of the organs shown in the building. Patrons had lent him money to finance such a magnificent instrument, which brought him much fame and set the seal on his ability and revealed his qualities not only as a maker and voicer of organ pipes but as an engineer and inventor as well. The instrument had three manuals and pedals, seventy speaking stops and seven couplers. There were twenty-two stops on the swell organ, the manual compass extended to G "in altissimo" and the pedals from CCC to G (thirty-two notes). There were other important features which went a long way towards revolutionising the control of the instrument. Brass discs, since known as *pistons* inserted in the key-slips between the manuals, replaced the composition pedals which drew the stops "in blocks". Barker-lever pneumatic action was applied to the manuals, and, to use Willis's words, "that Exhibition organ was the great pioneer of the improved pneumatic movement. A child could play the keys with all the stops drawn. It never went wrong". (A large part of this instrument was erected in Winchester Cathedral as a four-manual organ and most of the pipework functions to this day in spite of rebuilds at various times by Hele and Harrison.)

The Exhibition organ was the means of procuring Willis the order for the organ at St. George's Hall, Liverpool, which became a Mecca for music lovers, before the days of frequent orchestral tours, owing to the superb skill of William Thomas Best as a player, particularly in the symphonic and orchestral style.

Willis had serious differences with S. S. Wesley, the "expert" retained by the Liverpool Corporation, who wanted both the pedals and manuals to begin at GG. Willis accepted a compromise and built the organ with manual compass a fourth longer than at present, but with a CC pedal. Willis got the idea of the radiating and concave pedal-board from Schulze's organ at the Great Exhibition. When inspecting the German instrument, in company with Wesley, the latter suggested that Schulze should not only have made his pedal-board concave but should have made his pedals radiate from an imaginary centre behind the player's back. Willis gave Wesley full credit for the idea, and the radius of curvature for the concavity was made equal to that of the "imaginary" radius of the radial pedals measured to the fronts of the sharps: 8 ft. 6 in.

Willis was instrumental in obtaining for W. T. Best the organist's post at Liverpool, and it is surprising that Best forgot, in his later years, what he owed to the organ-builder. Willis was largely responsible for showing English organists of the latter half of the nineteenth century how to play the pedal organ, and in fact played a separate pedal clavier at an important service at St. Paul's Cathedral in 1872 on the occasion of the Thanksgiving Service for the recovery of the Prince of Wales.

Willis also built two large organs of similar design for the Alexandra Palace, North London (the first was destroyed by fire); the large organ in the Albert Hall, London, in 1871–2; the organ in St. Paul's Cathedral, divided into two sections (1872) and later extended, and a section added in the north-east quarter-gallery of the Dome in 1899. Of a thousand organs which he built or rebuilt were included the organs at Truro, Salisbury, Exeter, Oxford, Winchester, Canterbury, Lincoln, Durham, Carlisle, St. David's, Glasgow, Wells, Gloucester, Hereford Cathedrals and many large concert and church organs in the British Isles and abroad. Willis brought the characteristically English swell organ with its chorus reeds and mixture to a high pitch of perfection. His voicing produced beautiful imitative reed tones and in this he was helped by his brother, George. The choruses of flue stops were clear and well-balanced, but the chorus reeds, beautiful though they were, tended to engulf the fluework of the organ. Towards the end of his life he felt, to some extent, the prevailing influence which tended to strip the organ of its chorus work, but his instruments never lacked vitality, cohesion and brilliance. The English organ at the time lacked properly developed pedal and choir organs, but in his largest instruments Willis produced adequate divisions for these important parts of the organ. His organs had a fine engineering quality; he developed pneumatic action, firstly by improving the Barker lever and later by improving a tubular action which he had seen in France. This enabled him to divide the organ at St. Paul's Cathedral, London, in 1872, but he continued to improve his pressure system of pneumatic action. In 1888 he applied electric action to his organ at Canterbury Cathedral. This was exceedingly reliable and only ceased working when the instrument was taken down for rebuilding shortly before the Second European War. It is well to point this out, for the Hope-Jones "electric-organ" at Worcester Cathedral (built after the Canterbury instrument) was showing signs of complete collapse after twenty-four years' service.

Willis's organs may be called "romantic", "symphonic" or "orchestral", but there was always a foundation of genuine organ-tone which can be obtained in no other way. Most organists played little genuine organ music of first-rate character in the nineteenth century, but relied on Handel's choruses, orchestral arrangements, original compositions in the style of Mendelssohn (and not often as good as the works of that composer). Willis and Cavaillé-Coll had much in common in their aesthetic outlook and both worked at a time when the historical significance of the genuine organ and its characteristic had been forgotten. Nevertheless, it is surprising how little modification to the tonal scheme of a Willis organ is necessary to bring it up to date, and most old Willis organs contain examples of voicing which have not been surpassed.

Willis's methods can be studied in the organ at St. Paul's Cathedral, London (and incidentally, in the same instrument the ideal way of conserving, extending and refurbishing an organ in the work of the grandson of the original builder, the present Mr. Henry Willis). The magnificence of the swell organ, with only twelve stops, which stands against the stone pier in the South Case, the peerless orchestral reeds on the solo organ, the virility of the chorus reeds, the refined clarity of the soft stops, the brilliance of the diapason chorus, the definition of the pedal stops and the amazing blend of the whole, make the instrument outstanding in the world. The choir mutation stops, the altar organ and the diapason organ in the south-east quarter-gallery, all by the present Henry Willis, complete this exquisite tonal picture.

Willis died in London in February 1901 and was buried in Highgate Cemetery. He was assisted in business by his two sons, Henry and Vincent. The former took over the business, but, owing to the ill-health of his father, the present Mr. Henry Willis took charge of the firm before the First European War. Vincent Willis, an ingenious inventor of many tonal and mechanical improvements, left the firm in 1894 and continued on his own account. He specialised in the construction of player and residence organs, but also patented devices for tuning pipes, illuminated stop-heads, various types of organ actions, some of which, with little modification, are in use today, and organs working on attenuated air.

In his lifetime Willis had built or rebuilt the organs at many cathedrals, churches, concert and public halls in Britain. Much of his work remains practically untouched as far as the tonal side is concerned. It is not easy, even today, to think how the magnificence of his organ in Truro Cathedral could be excelled.

Hill & Son and Norman & Beard Ltd.

John Snetzler commenced organ-building in England before the middle of the eighteenth century. He was succeeded by his foreman, a Swede named Ohrmann, in 1780. In 1790 Ohrmann took a partner, W. Nutt, who was afterwards joined by Thomas Elliot about the year 1803. Elliot built many durable and fine-toned instruments, including those at Montreal Cathedral, Waterford Cathedral, Christ's Hospital, London, York Minster, All Saints' (now the Cathedral), Derby. In 1825 Elliot took William Hill, his son-in-law, as partner. Hill was born in Spilsby, Lincs., in 1789, where there is a memorial window to him in the church.

Upon the death of Elliot in 1832 Hill remained alone until 1837, when he was joined by Frederick Davison, who left the next year to become a partner of John Gray. The firm was then known as W. Hill & Son and from its workshops went the organ at Birmingham Town Hall, in which the tuba was the first high-pressure reed to be made in this country. Amongst other notable instruments were the reconstructed organ in Westminster Abbey, the large instruments in Melbourne Town Hall, Edinburgh Reid Hall, and the small four-manual organ in Turvey, Bedfordshire, England.

On the death of William Hill, in 1871, his eldest son, Thomas, sustained and increased the reputation of the firm. The fine instruments, some of which have been rebuilt, at Beverley Minster, Trinity, King's and St. John's Colleges, Cambridge, Ely and Lichfield Cathedrals, Sydney Town Hall and the Queen's Hall, London (the last destroyed in 1940), belong to this period. (The organ at Beverley Minster is still one of the most musical and charming of English organs. It is most beautiful to both ear and eye and should be better known.) Thomas Hill died in 1893 and Dr. Arthur George Hill, M.A., Litt.D., F.S.A. (1857–1923), became head of the firm. His two folio volumes *Organs and Organ Cases of the Middle Ages and Renaissance*, and his own designs for the cases of instruments built by his firm, did something to restore to England a sense that an organ case was a desirable and beautiful piece of church furniture. Many of the nineteenth-century organs by other builders had disfigured churches and even cathedrals, with their rows of metal tubes, often made more objectionable to the eye by being hideously diapered with unpleasant colours.

During the régime of Dr. Hill the firm built or rebuilt the organs at Manchester Cathedral, the celestial organ at Westminster Abbey (out of commission at the time of writing this book); the organs at Chester Cathedral, the pro-Cathedral, Dublin, the University of Edinburgh, Selby Abbey, and many others of smaller size. In 1916 the firm was amalgamated with that of Norman and Beard of Norwich and London. Large organs by this firm will be found at Peterborough Cathedral, Southwell Minster, Melbourne Town Hall, Norwich Cathedral, Holbrook School near Ipswich, the Dome, Brighton, and in many other places, in Britain, Canada and elsewhere abroad.

J. W. Walker & Sons

Joseph William Walker was a "parlour apprentice" to George Pike England from about 1818. He completed for W. A. Nicholls (England's son-in-law) some of the contracts the firm had on hand at England's death. He was successively in business at 5 Bentinck Street, Soho (1827), 166 High Holborn (1831), 27 Francis Street, W.C. (1838). He died in 1870, aged sixty-eight. He had four sons and a daughter, Sarah, who used to mark the barrels prior to pinning, in the early days of the firm, when many barrel organs were produced. All the sons were apprenticed to their father, but the three elder brothers died comparatively young, leaving Mr. James John Walker single-handed until such time as his own sons were old enough to learn the business.[1]

J. J. Walker died soon after the incorporation of the firm (14th June 1920), leaving E.F., J.H.P., F.P. and R.H. as directors. The firm has excellent premises at Ruislip, Middlesex, and continues to do major work.

J. W. Walker erected this little "barrel and finger" organ in London in 1836.

Open diapason to tenor C.
Dulciana to fiddle G.
Stop diapason, treble and bass.
Principal throughout.
Fifteenth throughout.
Compass from GG to F with GG♯.
An octave of sliding German pedals.
Shifting movement (an early type of "composition" pedal).
Two barrels.

Walker also made a "dumb organist", a mechanical player placed above the organ keys.

Major instruments by the firm can be found at Bristol Cathedral (1907), Lancing College Chapel (1914), The Church of the Sacred Heart, Wimbledon

[1] This information has been taken from the records of the firm.

(1912) (see specification, No. 36), St. Margaret's Church, Westminster (1897), Royal College of Music (1901), Harrow School Chapel (1921). The damaged instrument at Holy Trinity, Sloane Square, London, and the completely destroyed organs at the Crystal Palace, Sydenham, London, and at the Public Hall, Ipswich (formerly at the Exeter Hall, London), were first-rate examples of the work of the same firm.[1] The diapasons of the firm had a magnificent "rolling" tone, and, although overscaled at times for modern tastes, were beautiful in quality. The mild string-toned stops, flutes and imitative reeds were also noteworthy. Old Walker organs such as those at Romsey Abbey, Hants, England, and at St. Mary's, Portsea, should be regarded as national treasures and treated accordingly when rebuilding is contemplated. Recent major work of the firm includes the organs at the City Temple and St. Columba's Churches, London, and Ampleforth College, York.

Robert Hope-Jones

The work of Robert Hope-Jones, a telephone engineer who took up organ-building on his own account and later in connection with a number of English and American firms, has been the cause of uncritical encomiums on the one hand[2] and wholesale condemnation on the other. The Hope-Jones organ was a "one-man orchestra," and obviously a poor substitute for a muster of orchestral players. New and extreme tone-qualities were added to the instrument, diaphones were used to supply basses of smooth quality and immense power, diapasons were provided with leathered lips and blown with high wind pressures so that there was no blend between one rank of pipes and another and the organ was stripped of the remains of its crowning glory: its mutations and mixtures. The organ was often distributed in thick concrete swell-boxes in various parts of the church or auditorium, and the whole was controlled by electric action from a small movable console which was usually comfortable to play, apart from the "springy" touch of the keys which, of course, was not peculiar to Hope-Jones' organs or even to those with electric action.

The organs built or designed by Hope-Jones represent the logical conclusion of a pernicious tendency which had been creeping into organ design since the early days of Cavaillé-Coll. If an instrument is conceived on romantic-symphonic lines the tendency is to forget the claims of the great historic organ music which so perfectly suited the genuine instrument, with its proper choruses, its synthetic possibilities with its mutation ranks and its unforced musical tone. The repertoires of English and American organists, towards the end of the nineteenth and at the beginning of the twentieth centuries, had been based on orchestral transcriptions or on romantic original pieces. Even Willis felt the symphonic tendency towards the end of his life, although he stood out against its worst aspects. The scholarship of Guilmant and other musicologists was necessary before even a modest equipment of mutation stops could be obtained from Cavaillé-Coll in some of his moderate-sized

[1] These two instruments were destroyed by fire, not by enemy action.
[2] See G. L. Miller, *The Recent Revolution in Organ-building* (New York, 1913).

organs, and, even so, the French symphonic organ persisted until the twentieth century and is not unknown today.

It is not unfair to say that apart from the development of a few extreme tone qualities, which, in any case, were known to Thynne, Vincent Willis, Pendlebury and Franklin Lloyd, Hope-Jones's influence on organ design both in England and in America was entirely unfortunate. The cinema organ of *c.* 1925–1930, as made by Wurlitzer, with its few extended ranks of pipes, its "traps" and effects, its high-pressure enclosed pipework and its convenient reliable electric action, was the direct result of the work of Hope-Jones.

Robert Hope-Jones was the third son of William Hope-Jones of Hooton Grange, Cheshire, England. His mother, Agnes Handforth, was the daughter of the rector of Ashton-under-Lyne. Robert was born on 9th February 1859 and was physically weak as a child, but from an early age he showed considerable inventive genius. As a young singer, organist and electrical experimenter his enthusiasm knew no bounds. He was honorary organist and choirmaster of St. Luke's, Tranmere, and St. John's, Birkenhead, at which latter church he provided the organ with electric console and action so that, if necessary, it could be played from outside the church door.[1] At this time Hope-Jones was employed by Laird Bros., engineers and shipbuilders of Birkenhead, but later he became chief electrician of the Lancashire and Cheshire (afterwards the National) Telephone Company. There can be no doubt that the science of electro-acoustics benefited greatly from the ideas of his fertile mind. He invented the diaphone which was used by the Canadian Government for its fog signal stations and has come into general use since that time.[2] Later he was to modify the diaphone for use as a sound producer in his organs. In 1889 Hope-Jones resigned from the telephone company in order that he could devote more of his time to the "improvement" of the church organ. Thereafter, either working on his own or in association with other organ-builders, he built a number of organs with extreme non-blending qualities of tone, convenient stop-key consoles with a useful stop-switch to assist registration and electric action which was not always reliable. His Worcester Cathedral organ worked for a quarter of a century and examples of his work, with some modification may still be heard in the McEwan Hall of Edinburgh University, St. George's, Hanover Square, and elsewhere. Hope-Jones left for America in 1903, but licensed a number of English organ-builders to use his inventions. In the U.S.A. he worked with Skinner at Boston, and in 1907 the "Hope-Jones Organ Company" was founded, but soon met financial disaster, in spite of the fact that it was supported by Mark Twain. The patents and plant of this company were acquired by the Rudolph Wurlitzer Co. in 1910 and the Wurlitzer unit organ, so well known in England in the between-war period, owes its origin to Hope-Jones. This ingenious but wayward inventor took his life in 1914. He made

[1] A photo of Hope-Jones, clad in cap and gown, actually doing this appeared in *The Organ*, vol. xiv, p. 221. With good organs such a feat seems entirely unnecessary!

[2] The invention of the diaphone has also been claimed for the firm of Blackett and Howden.

genuine advances in the electrical side of organ mechanism, though there were other more reliable workers in this field. He did much damage to the tonal structure of the organ both in England and America.

The short-lived firm of Michell and Thynne in the later years of the nineteenth century produced a few instruments remarkable for the beauty of their flue stops, in particular, the flutes and string-toned stops. The "Grove" organ at Tewkesbury Abbey was their largest work, and it is hoped that it will be restored in the near future. Whiteley and Fletcher copied and extended Thynne's work on the voicing of such stops as viol sourdine and zauberflöte. A beautiful small example of their combined efforts, in an attractive organ case, may be heard in the Church of the Cowley Fathers at Oxford, England.

Worthy of mention are the organs of Cavaillé-Coll's foreman, August Gern, who stayed in England after having erected one of his master's instruments in the Carmelite Church, Kensington. Most of his organs have been rebuilt, but his work may still be heard, amongst other places, in Alfreton Parish Church and St. Catherine's Church, Nottingham.

The Twentieth Century and the Neo-Classical Organ

Some voices were raised against the evil wrought to the tonal structure of the organ by Robert Hope-Jones on both sides of the Atlantic. Notably Thomas Casson[1] (1842–1910), originally a banker of Denbigh in Wales, insisted on the necessity of proper chorus work in the organ, adequate pedal organs and stop-control. He did not build any large and notable instruments, but he founded the Positive Organ Company, a London firm which produced a considerable number of small one-manual organs, with a few beautifully voiced stops, and bass and melody devices to obviate to some measure the need for pedals and a second manual. Lt.-Col. George Dixon of St. Bees, England, a student of the works of Willis and Schulze, did much in the first half of the twentieth century both through his influence in the designs of some of the Harrison organs and through his writings, to advance sound modern tonal design.

Before the First European War and for some years after it the American organ had felt too strongly the influence of Hope-Jones. With him the organ was a "one-man orchestra" and was developed as such by Rudolph Wurlitzer. The effect on the playing of real organ music was bad, and a hundred organs of the first quarter of the century might not yield one on which a good account of the finest organ music could be given. This has changed, and America is in the forefront of organ design and playing and in the scholarship which is necessary to trace the historical nature of the aesthetic of the organ.

Holland and Scandinavia were less touched by the Romantic movement than other countries. In Germany and France there still remained examples of the great eighteenth-century organs, although many of them were in an

[1] The father of Sir Lewis Casson, the distinguished actor. Casson's published works were well-known though his advice was not always followed: *The Modern Organ* (1883); *Reform in Organ-building* (1888); *The Pedal Organ* (1905); *Modern Pneumatic Mechanism* (1908).

unrestored and unusable condition. In particular, there were many old Schnitger organs in the north of Germany, and in Saxony examples of the work of G. Silbermann and his school.[1] Musicologists and organists in several parts of the world became interested in these old instruments through a new knowledge of the music which was composed for them which appeared. The Dutch preserved the integrity of their organ choruses and mutation ranks. The Swiss organ of this period showed a combination of both French and German influences.

Occasionally, one saw in the shortcomings of the symphonic organ the need of a sane return to the ideals of an earlier period. In 1880 Debierre in France added some mutation stops to the organ of the Church of Notre-Dame-de-Bon-Port at Nantes. Sometimes in the organs of Puget of Toulouse, Merklin at Lyons and Mutin, the successor of Cavaillé-Coll, in Paris we find a timid addition of these important stops. There was no understanding of the real functions of these registers. Until the whole aesthetic of the organ had been rediscovered in its historical setting, and scholarly musicians had considered the great heritage of the organ music of the past, the time of the revival was not yet. Although Widor, his pupil Albert Schweitzer and the musicologist, André Pirro, began a study of the inner meaning of Bach's music, in particular his choral-preludes, Widor did not realise the shortcomings of the Cavaillé-Coll organ. Schweitzer had written a booklet showing the inadequacies of the larger nineteenth-century organs for the playing of the works of the great Thuringian master.[2]

At the beginning of the century a few organs, such as that at St. Patrick's, Dublin, were built by Willis's son. The firm of Harrison in Durham was beginning to be known over the country for the excellence of their constructional work, their elegant and durable consoles, for the refinement of their voicing and the meticulous regulation of their pipe ranks. By rebuilding a number of large Willis and Hill organs in British cathedrals they produced an instrument which came to be regarded as the British cathedral organ of the twentieth century. The writer must admit that the rolling open wood stops of the pedal organs, the contrasted reed tones of swell and great organ and the beautiful voicing of the soft stops were useful for accompanying large congregations or smaller choirs, but the instrument was not, by its nature, ideal for rendering the traditional music of the organ. The highlight of Harrison's own work at the time this book was written was their instrument at St. Mary Redcliffe, Bristol, England. There is an aristocratic elegance about their instruments and they are always comfortable and easy to play.

John Compton was at work at this time and was developing his electric action and his methods of scaling and voicing pipe ranks which were suitable for extension organs.

The Norwich firm of *Norman and Beard* built many organs, particularly in East Anglia, and elsewhere, both in England and in the dominions,

[1] Paul Rubardt, *Alte Orgeln erklingen wieder* (Leipzig, 1937).

[2] A Schweitzer. *Deutsche und französische Orgelbaukunst und Orgelkunst* (Leipzig, 1906).

including the organs of Norwich and Chelmsford Cathedrals, Grantham Parish Church and Colchester Town Hall.

We must also note the firm of Wilkinson of Kendal who built a number of organs in the north-west of England, including a large instrument for Preston Town Hall; the firm of Brindley of Sheffield, who did considerable major work earlier in the century in England and abroad (and owed much to German methods of voicing and console equipment); Forster and Andrews of Hull, whose instruments were well and spaciously built; Abbott and Smith of Leeds, who reconstructed the large instrument in the Town Hall of that city. Wadsworth of Manchester, Percy Daniel of Clevedon, Arnold of Thaxted, Slater of Buckhurst, Browne of Canterbury, Cousans of Lincoln, Taylor of Leicester, Conacher of Huddersfield, Martin of Oxford are examples of those who have worthily sustained the tradition of individuality and craftsmanship which distinguishes the best organ-making. In the West Country, Hele of Plymouth built and continue to build many organs of considerable size. The large instruments of St. Peter Mancroft, Norwich, and St. James's, Paddington, London, were their work.

We should also note Nicholson & Co. of Worcester. This firm was founded about 1840, and in the year 1844 installed an organ in the Shire Hall, Worcester, consisting of three manuals with fifty-three speaking stops. Both the great and swell organs contained a double open diapason *metal throughout*; there was a five-rank mixture on great, swell and choir organs. The swell also contained a 16-ft. trombone and the pedal could boast a 32-ft. open wood and a three-rank mixture. There was a pneumatic lever attachment and ten composition pedals. This was a remarkable achievement for the time. More recent work can be found in Birmingham Cathedral; Manchester College, Oxford; Leominster Priory; St. Clement's Church, Oxford; St. Margaret's Church, Leicester, etc.

Nicholson and Lord of Walsall had an extensive connection, particularly in Staffordshire; their most famous instrument was the fine organ in Walsall Town Hall.

Bird, Walter J., built many organs in the Birmingham district.

R. Spurden Rutt & Co., Leyton, London, E. For half a century this firm has built and rebuilt many fine instruments, such as those at the churches of St. Martin-in-the-Fields, London; St. Magnus, London Bridge; Wesley's Chapel, City Road; and the large four-manual organ, destroyed during the last war, in the City Temple, Holborn, London.

W. C. Jones is a reed voicer whose beautiful chorus reeds may be heard in the organs of a number of builders.

Many supply houses in Europe and America make parts for organs. Notably amongst these are Aug. Laukhuff of Weikersheim in Wurttemburg, who makes pipes, consoles, mechanism and blowers. Eisenschmid of München (Munich) makes consoles; Stinkens of Zeist near Utrecht, pipe-work of all types; Reisner of Hagerstown, U.S.A., consoles and electrical work; Holt of Birmingham, small electrical parts, etc. Other firms specialise in organ-blowing: British Organ Blowing (B.O.B.) of Derby and Watkins and Watson (Discus) of London; Orgoblo, U.S.A.; Laukhuff (Ventus, etc.) in Germany, etc. The superb organ keys of ivory made by Herrburger Brooks of Long Eaton, England, are world famous.

Practically every city and cathedral town boasts one or more organ-builders, and it must be remembered that a number of artists working in a smaller way and not yet, so to speak, attaining cathedral status have constructed some beautiful instruments.

Noel Mander, of St. Peter's Organ Works, London, E.C.2. Representative works are at St. Lawrence Jewry (new), St. Pancras Parish Church (rebuild), St. Michael, Croydon (rebuild and enlargement), St. Leonard's, Shoreditch, St. Mary's, Rotherhithe, St. John the Evangelist, Upper Norwood (restoration). He is notable for his sympathetic and scholarly treatment of old organs by Smith, Snetzler, Bridge, Green, England, etc., and for his small organs of standard design.

Roger Yates, of Bodmin, Cornwall. Amongst his beautiful organs, new and rebuilt, are those in the parish churches of Ilkeston (Derbys.), Ruddington (Notts.), Oakham (Rutland), Kilkhampton (Devon), Kegworth (Leics.), and a number of interesting small instruments.

After the First World War, Willis III absorbed the business of Lewis, Hill amalgamated with Norman and Beard, and Compton was at work in London. Cinema organs were in demand, and several firms, especially those of Compton, Hill, and Norman and Beard, made a large number. *Rushworth and Dreaper* of Liverpool did a considerable amount of major work in various parts of Britain. Representative organs by this firm may be heard at Christ's Hospital School at Horsham, Stowe School, Buckinghamshire, Malvern Priory, St. Mark's, North Audley Street, London, the Town Hall, Blackburn, and Guildford Cathedral. The firm of *Alfred Hunter* of London, which had produced many good organs such as those at Wimbledon and Bangor (N. Ireland) Parish Churches, Hertford College Chapel, Oxford, Magdalene College, Cambridge, the Lower School, Eton, was later absorbed by that of Willis. Their finest organ is in St. James's Church, Spanish Place, London.

The renaissance in tonal design did not come until Henry Willis, the grandson of the founder of the firm, and John Compton, who used the principle of extension, studied more closely the traditional tone structure of the instrument and made a careful inspection of the finest instruments abroad. The typical English "full swell" was retained, but proper development of the choir organ and pedal organ, together with a more versatile great organ, were sought. With the production of convenient and reliable electric action, the control of the instrument became easier and more satisfactory in response. Willis adopted a "toggle" or "top-resistance" touch for his manual keys, which assisted "clean" playing and banished the indefinite, spring touches of some of the old pneumatic actions.

Typical instruments of Henry Willis III are the largest organ in the British Isles, that at Liverpool Cathedral, and those at Westminster Cathedral,

Kirkwall Cathedral, St. Jude's, Thornton Heath, Sheffield City Hall and many rebuilt instruments, such as those at St. Paul's, Salisbury, Hereford, Canterbury and Glasgow Cathedrals, the organs at King's College, Strand, Southwark Cathedral, Stonyhurst College, St. Mary's Church, Reading, All Soul's Langham Place, London, and many others.

John Compton built the organs at Downside Abbey and the B.B.C. studios, and rebuilt those at Derby Cathedral, Holy Trinity, Hull, and many others. By extending many of the ranks he was able to produce super and sub-unison effects. Although extended ranks can never replace separate registers, it must be admitted that nowhere in the world have better extension organs been produced than those of his firm, and the practical renaissance of tonal design in Britain is due partly to his influence.

In the late nineteenth century and until the beginning of the Second World War, Germany produced more organs than any other European country, and, moreover, had a vigorous export trade to surrounding countries, to Africa and South America, and even to Britain.

One of the greatest of the German firms is that of Walcker.

In the year 1781, a young organ-builder, Eberhard Walcker, commenced work in Cannstadt, in the Dukedom of Wurttemberg, and built an organ for the Evangelical Lutheran Garrison Church of Ludwigsburg. This instrument was followed by several others in the same area. The founder's son, Eberhard Friedrich Walcker (1794–1872), established the business in Ludwigsburg in 1820, and came under the influence of Joseph Vogler (the Abbé Vogler). His first organ was a one-manual and pedal instrument of romantic design in Kochersteinsfeld, Wurttemberg. After thirteen years Walcker produced one of the most remarkable instruments of the early nineteenth century in Frankfurt, where the firm was to erect at least forty organs. Here in St. Paul's Church was a large instrument,[1] known to Mendelssohn, of advanced romantic type, built almost a decade before the first large organ of Cavaillé-Coll, and two decades before that of Henry Willis. (See Specification No. 76.)

Walcker experimented with draughts in large chimneys in order to gain experience in the voicing of very large open pipes. The fame of the firm soon reached every country of the world (at least 200 organs were exported to Britain) and many of the largest organs in the world were made by them, including the 124 speaking stop organ (1883), which still attracts many hearers in the Cathedral of Riga in Latvia, and the organs at Ulm and Vienna Cathedral. After the death of E. F. Walcker the firm was managed by Oscar Walcker, who felt the influence of the Alsatian Organ Reform Movement and in 1909 built the organ of 105 speaking stops in St. Reinoldi's Church in Dortmund to the design of Albert Schweitzer. (This organ was entirely destroyed in the 1939–1945 war and a new, large instrument of interesting design (opus 3700) has been erected by the same firm.) Oscar Walcker was responsible for the Praetorius organ in Freiburg University, constructed

[1] The firm publishes a house magazine which gives accounts of new organs and contains other articles of interest.

according to the principles laid down by Michael Praetorius in his *Syntagma Musicum*, vol. ii, 1619, and for the historical, eclectic organ in Hans Sachs Hall, Gelsenkirchen.

Wilhelm Sauer founded an organ-building firm, which produced many large organs in Germany and Central Europe. After studying in Germany, England, France and Switzerland, Sauer worked with Walcker and Cavaillé-Coll. Until the year 1932 the firm had produced 1,600 organs, including those which had displaced Bach's instruments in Leipzig: later Sauer joined Oscar Walcker. The larger organs built by Sauer include those at Breslau Centenary Hall (200 speaking stops, 1913); Magdeburg Town Hall (131 speaking stops, 1928); Berlin Cathedral (113 speaking stops, 1904); Berlin, Kaiser-Wilhelm-Gedachtnis-Kirche (102 speaking stops, 1920); Sofia, Concert Hall (70 speaking stops, 1937).

Also of the "Walcker School" were the organ-builders Weigle, Link and Steinmeyer, of which the last developed the most notable business in Bavaria, and has constructed, in the twentieth century particularly, some of the largest and finest organs in Europe, such as those at Passau and Trondheim Cathedrals.

Friedrich Ladegast (1818–1905), who was befriended by both Walcker and Cavaillé-Coll, built organs of notable size and quality and was early in the field with various types of pneumatic action, free-combination and general crescendo action. His organ in Merseburg Cathedral (Specification No. 75) made possible the performance of the major organ works of Franz Liszt, who championed the organ-builder against all others.

Fürtwangler and Hammer of Hanover built many organs. Kemper, of Lübeck, produced some beautiful neo-Baroque instruments and conserved some of the old Schnitger organs. Laukhuff of Weikersheim specialised in pipe and action-making on a large scale. Other nineteenth-century firms of importance were those of Schulze, Jehmlich and Reubke. The firms Rover and Gobel have done major work in the north of Germany and in the Danzig district. In Austria, Rieger and Mauracher were the leading builders. In Italy the leading builders are now Tamburini, who built the large five-manual organ in Messina Cathedral, and Mascioni, who built an organ of one hundred and eighty speaking stops in Milan Cathedral, working under government orders, in collaboration with Tamburini. Mascioni made an admirable rebuild of the historic organ at St. Mary Major's, Trent. No firm as great as the nineteenth-century firm of Batz and Witte has yet appeared in Holland. Klais of Bonn built considerable numbers of first-rate organs in the Cologne district and in Belgium until the time of the Second World War. Markussen, of Apenrade, has done much work in Denmark and Sweden, and in 1940 Angster built a five-manual organ of one hundred and seventy-two speaking stops at Szeged, Hungary.

Switzerland is noted for the number of its fine west-end organs in good cases. The greatest part of the work is done by the two firms of Kuhn and Goll, but the firm of Metzler must also be mentioned. Amongst many notable organs, in churches and concert-halls, those in Berne Minster, the Musical Hall, Zurich (Kuhn), Engelberg (135 speaking stops—Goll), Einsiedeln,

Fribourg, Zurich (Predigerkirche), and Lucerne (Hofkirche) are justly famed.

Since the death of Cavaillé-Coll no comparable figure has arisen in France. Nevertheless, much enlightened work, particularly in the matter of tonal design, has been done. Cavaillé-Coll was followed by Charles Mutin, but the firm ceased to exist before 1940. The chief French organ-builder (though he did not work on the scale of a Willis, or a Steinmeyer) was Victor Gonzalez, who reconstructed many organs, including those at Rheims Cathedral and St. Eustache, Paris. He died in 1956. Others worthy of note are Gloton and Debierre of Nantes, Merklin of Lyon and Puget of Toulouse. Rochesson of Pontoise specialises in restorations of old organs, and Roethinger of Strasbourg has reconstructed over five hundred instruments. The firm of Abbey, established by an Englishman early in the nineteenth century, is now defunct.

Alexandre Guilmant edited old French organ music[1] and produced on the modern organ an ancient atmosphere. It was necessary to revive the art of Silbermann, of Arp Schnitger, of Clicquot, of Lefebvre, without forgetting the debts owed to Cavaillé-Coll.

The restored organs at St. Gervais, played by many generations of Couperins, and St. Nicolas des Champs, Paris, both five-manual instruments, and the organ in the chapel at Versailles, renewed with all the characteristics of the Louis XIV epoch, were most important links with the pre-Revolution art in France. In France all the leading organ-builders felt the Baroque influence in the work which they did between the wars. In particular Roethinger of Strasbourg, Gloton and Debierre of Nantes, Ruche of Lyon, Puget of Toulouse and most of the Swiss builders produced work in accordance with these principles once latent and then brought to light. In England, apart from an improvement in the design of choir organs and better equipped pedal organs in the works of Henry Willis (the grandson of the founder of the firm), and the provision of a more liberal mutation and mixture scheme in the organs built on the extension system of John Compton, little was done on the tonal side. In America Donald Harrison, an Englishman and formerly a senior member of the Willis firm, and W. Holtkamp, who had inherited the old German tradition, developed a type of instrument which showed an historical eclecticism. All improvements in wind supply, action and manufacturing techniques were permitted.

The leading British, American and German organ-builders use electro-pneumatic action for all but the smallest of new organs. The Germans still make tracker organs, and the Barker lever is still used in France. Pressure-pneumatic action has never been popular in France, but is still occasionally used in England, and some thousands of instruments with both pressure and exhaust pneumatics are still working in England. A return to lighter wind pressures and well-made tracker action would have some advantages in smaller organs. Direct electric action (q.v.) is sometimes used in America, but less frequently in England and Europe.

The Société des Amis de l'Orgue, formed in Paris in 1926, studied carefully the problems of restoring the old organs which had survived in a

[1] Alex Guilmant, *Archives* (Schott, Mainz, 1901).

neglected condition from the eighteenth century. Once again the works of Clicquot and Lefebvre spoke and revealed the beauties hidden in the works of the seventeenth- and eighteenth-century organ composers. The scholarship of Guilmant in his editions of old French music (*Archives*) had shown the inadequacy of the symphonic organ for such works. Pirro, the musicologist, Schweitzer,[1] the organist and philosopher, and Mathias, the canon of Strassbourg, had studied the essential spirit and character of the old works.

In Germany, Hans Henny Jahnn discovered the potentialities of the old Schnitger organ in St. Jakobi Church, Hamburg, and in the even older "Totentanz" chapel organ in St. Mary's Church, Lübeck. In 1926 Willibald Gurlitt designed a small organ, which was built in Freiburg University, on the details given by Praetorius in his *Syntagma* (1619). From 1927 onwards facsimile editions of the works of Praetorius, Dom Bédos, Mattheson, Adlung and Werckweister were produced in Kassel, and at a slightly later date editions[2] of the works of Schlick appeared in Mainz. Karl Straube, in editing the works of the old German organ composers in 1926, took the opportunity of correcting the wrong ideas which he had shown in his editions of 1904 for the "romantic" organ.[3] Organ-builders were not slow in producing instruments which, they hoped, would deal with all types of music. Organ conferences, which were attended by organ-builders, composers, players and clergy, musicologists and architects, were held in several parts of Germany.[4] Karl Kemper, of Lübeck, built many fine neo-classical organs at Hamburg, Danzig and Frauenburg, and he restored many of Schnitger's works. Walcker and Steinmeyer and other large firms favoured the eclectic organ, but ensured that a proper proportion of registers of the eighteenth-century type should be found on each instrument. The Walcker instrument at Recklinghausen, of eighty-eight speaking stops, and built in 1927, is an interesting example of an attempt to combine the characteristics of the Praetorius and Silbermann organs with modern developments. Steinmeyer produced a most interesting neo-Baroque instrument at St. Luke's, Munich, and found that it was a suitable medium for the performance of all serious organ music.

Since the end of the Second World War all new and restored German organs have tried to recapture the spirit of the organ of 1700. Wind pressures have been lowered to 3 in. or less, and the instruments are richly supplied with soft mixture and mutation stops in great variety. Often this has been the making of a virtue out of the necessity of economising in metal and timber, but the tendency was already at work before the war, and most German organists are convinced that the instrument of the period 1870–1916 was too large and too loud.

The significant feature of organ design in Europe and America in the last twenty years has been a return to the ideals of the organ as it grew "naturally", until the end of the time of Bach. The North German "Orgelbewegung"

[1] And later the missionary and doctor.

[2] See the bibliography.

[3] Preface to *Alte Meister des Orgelspiels* (Leipzig, 1926).

[4] A notable example was that held in Freiberg in Saxony from 2nd to 7th October 1927, the proceedings of which were published in a book of considerable size, *Bericht über die dritte Tagung für Deutsche Orgelkunst*. (Kassel 1927.)

(organ movement) in the third decade of the present century influenced the organ-builders of neighbouring countries, particularly Holland and Scandinavia. The aesthetic of this type of organ was worked out by the directors of such organ-building firms as Marcussen of Aabenraa and Frobenius of Lyngby, in Denmark, Flentrop of Zaandam, Pels of Zaandam, Holland, Rieger of Schwarzach Vorarlberg, Austria, and Klais, Kemper, von Beckerath, Walcker, Steinmeyer, of Germany. American and British organists travelling in Europe were considerably influenced by these organs of the classical revival. The impact of this influence was great in America where hundreds of new organs were erected every year; and even in England, known for its conservatism in organ design, some new organs such as those at the Royal Festival Hall, the Italian Church, Hatton Garden, St. Clement Danes and All Hallows-by-the-Tower Churches, London, St. Helen's Church, York, and others, showed the same influences, though not often to the extent of adopting mechanical action and the precise disposition of each section of the instrument with respect to the architecture of the organ itself and in relation to the building in which it stands. It must be confessed that this would not always be possible or desirable when the principal function of the organ is the accompaniment of church services in England.

The ideals of the so-called "neo-classical" system of organ-building have been set forth by the late Sybrand Zachariassen (1900–60).[1] The organ is to be erected, if possible on a west gallery, so that the whole construction enters into a geometric system which puts every part into its own place and makes the organ and the church appear as a whole. Tonally, the best disposition of the organ will always be that in which the pipework of each single division stands directly behind the case front. In every case, small as well as large, we should eschew organs disposed in the customary deep, open-topped cases. For tonal reasons, the divisions of an organ must be built into the shallowest possible cases (for manual divisions from 2 ft. 6 in. to 4 ft. deep, and perhaps more for the pedal pipes). The layout of the organ must be subordinate to such a plan of erection, and must not render this impossible at the outset. The swell organ in a two-manual organ should be placed above the great. If the swell organ is placed at the back of a deep case the sound will be indirect, lack freedom, liveliness and the necessary balance to the great. If there is insufficient height, great and swell can be erected on a common slider-chest with double the number of grooves and pallets. Absolute tonal balance is obtained by thus building the two divisions together; and the further advantage accrues, that this disposition claims very little space and the divisions do not get out of tune with one another by reason of temperature changes.

When it is absolutely impossible for the pedal organ to be erected at the sides of the manual divisions, it must be given its place behind them, but

[1] In a paper read before the International Congress on Church Music in Berne (see the *Organ Club Handbook*, No. 6, London, 1960). Similar ideas are put forward in J. E. Blanton's important American book, and in various publications of the German Gesellschaft der Orgelfreunde. It will be noted that Mr. Zachariassen does not recommend total exposure of the pipework.

separated from them by its own free-standing case. The intervening space between affords a good tuning passage and increases the accessibility of the organ.

(The swell is not actually regarded as the second most important division of the organ, and some authorities would leave it out altogether.)

Where height is sufficient the divisions of the organ will be erected one above the other so that naturally one arrives at the arrangement of divisions as Rückpositiv (chair organ), Brustwerk (front organ), Hauptwerk (great organ) and Oberwerk (upper organ).

The smaller Brustwerk, the longest pipes of which are only 2 ft., will be built into its own case below the great organ sound-boards and immediately above the music desk. This division of the organ will be provided with doors in front, so that it can be used as an open division or a miniature swell organ according to taste. The longest pipes of this organ are only 2 ft. long if the bottom octave of the stopped 8 ft. rank is outside the case. The 4 ft. rank is also stopped, but the 2 ft. rank is open. About 3 ft. 3 in. to 4 ft. is sufficient for the length of this front organ and the 2-ft. pipe length is sufficient for the height.

The Rückpositiv (chair organ), placed behind the seat of the organist, occupies the most favourable position among the various divisions of an organ, for no division can sound more freely into space, for which reason its voices make the best solos of the organ. The Rückpositiv with its bright, concentrated tones and smaller radiation area should make a good tonal balance with the broad "back-cloth" of the great organ, when this latter is used as a contrast or an accompaniment to the chair organ. In place of, or, better, in addition to, the chair organ, a manual division can be placed above the great organ.

The pedal organ ought also to have its place directly behind the case front. It will then be erected at the sides of the manual divisions, either in free-standing pedal towers, or left and right of the main case, at the same level as the great organ. Free-standing pedal towers require a considerable amount of space, and are therefore only seldom feasible. In order to restrict the surface area occupied by the organ as much as possible, it is appropriate to keep the lower part of the main organ case narrow. Where the height suffices, the pedal organ can be installed in the projecting sides of the case, cut over the lower part, for instance. In larger pedal organs it is best to divide the smaller pedal stops, mainly used for Cantus Firmus (solo) purposes, from the larger and to erect them separately on a Cantus Firmus chest. This Cantus Firmus division of the pedal organ can then be placed in the lower part of the organ, or even between the Brustwerk and Hauptwerk, where it can sound forth freely unhindered by the larger pedal stops. If there are no other possibilities a small pedal organ can be erected with the great organ on a common soundboard. This has the advantage that the "borrowed" pedal stops can be arranged easily.

The cases surrounding the pipework have the essential task of focusing the tone and giving it resonance, so that it sounds forth gathered together from the case front. It is extremely important that these cases be kept as shallow as possible in proportion to their breadth and height. The wall of the building should never be used as the rear wall of the organ. This is also to be avoided for reasons of temperature, since the rear wall of the building absorbs heat and throws the pipes out of tune. Also, for a similar reason, there should remain sufficient space between the top of the organ and the roof of the church, for warm air will often collect here.

Many of the most advanced thinkers in matters of organ design believe that the frequent practice of erecting entirely exposed organs and pipes, though supposed to conform with the tenets of functionalism and modern architecture, is bad from a tonal standpoint, since the tone is therefore lacking in the concentration so necessary to it.[1] The disposition of the parts of the organ which has been noted here is in accordance with the natural growth of the instrument and is not exclusively baroque. (Chair organs existed in the Gothic and Renaissance.) Not only are the divisions of the organ separated in space, but their principal choruses are founded on parent pitches which may be 16 ft., 8 ft., 4 ft., 2 ft. for pedal, great, chair and upper organ respectively. On these principals are built choruses which terminate with mixture, scharff, zimbel and small-scaled trumpet, each chorus as complete as possible in itself. There will also be as good a selection as possible of stops of wide scale, such as röhrflote, quintaton, completed upwards by a cornet, sesquialtera or separate imitation stops such as nazard and tierce and reeds such as schalmei and regals. The pipework should be planted on slider chests and played by mechanical action. With the slider chest it is possible to bring the ratio of space required by the pipework and that required by the wind-chest into the best agreement. With the slider chest, the onset of speech is much quieter and finer than on the pneumatic chest, and the pipes which are to blend with one another do this best when they stand on the same channel, and, in a sense, draw their breath from the same source.

The great significance, which a purely mechanical connection between key and pallet has from the standpoint of playing technique, is well-known. In spite of the air-cushion which the grooves create between pallet and pipe, the voicing is influenced for better or worse by the manner in which the wind enters the groove. With a mechanical action the languids can be given a position more favourable for the onset of speech and so for the tonal quality, and on such a chest voicing can be done far better without nicking, which in any case should be employed as sparingly as possible, because over-nicking renders the tone smooth, dull, characterless and confused. It should also be pointed out that full wind-voicing with open feet has an exceedingly favourable influence on blending, tone quality and clarity. The good effect of the grooves on blend is partially lost if the windway from the pallet to the locus of sound-formation is very reduced at the pipe foot. (Some organ-builders are unwilling to build slider chests with mechanical action because

[1] Zachariassen voiced all his stops rather fiercely, since he believed that in time the tone would lose its edge and the whole instrument would coalesce as a unity. For a time slats of absorbing material, to be removed later, were placed inside the wooden cases.

they have standardised their actions to electro-pneumatic operation and have found slider chests susceptible to climatic changes.) In the slider chest it is of the greatest importance that the slides have constant air tightness between the table and top board, otherwise the wind pressure will vary and the pipe-work will constantly alter in pitch. In the old form of slider chest constructional air-tightness was secured because the humidity of the air in the church did not vary greatly, but with modern space heating this no longer obtains and so materials and methods of construction, on which humidity and temperature changes have little effect, must be used. (Many ingenious methods have been used by Marcussen, Flentrop, Rieger and others for improving and maintaining the function of the slider chest in adverse atmospheric conditions.) While employing weather-fast material for each of the slides and dividing strips, two narrow slides, separated by a strip, can be used for each stop, according to the method of Cavaillé-Coll. With such narrow slides, movement or warping of the top-board is much less noticeable than with broad slides, because the span of the top board is shorter. Also, with doubled slides, there is twice the usual gap between the holes in each of the two slides, which practically excludes the dangers of ciphers.

The decisive factors for the weight of touch in mechanical action are, first and foremost, the size of the pallet opening and the wind pressure on the pallet at rest. If the pallet opening is larger than necessary it can be decreased by narrowing the opening rather than shortening it, and perhaps even by increasing its length. Obviously, coupling will increase the weight of touch, but it is quite natural that the louder tone should require a stronger key pressure. The European and American purists in organ design are prepared to do without stop combination action in order to preserve mechanical action for the slider mechanism. Some designers, while retaining slider-chests and tracker action for the manuals, use electro-pneumatic drawstop and combination mechanism and electro-pneumatic action for the pedals. However, it is desirable to work the whole key mechanism of an organ by the same system. With quick-speaking stops which possess characteristic initiation transients, differences in the speed of organ mechanism, over which the organist has no control, are painfully obvious.

Even the architectural arrangement of an organ depends on the disposition of the divisions, for front and organ case are to be an organic part of the organ and not a screen erected in front of it. The arrangements of a front can be solved if its outer profile is identical with the case which surrounds the inner division, and inserts the pipes of the largest principal in that division in the framework of the front, divided into large and small pipe fields. If these pipes are purposely arranged in groups, then almost automatically we arrive at a beautiful organ front, which, if need be, can further be decorated with profiles and ornaments. But the pipes should never be made over-long, for the front thereby acquires an unnatural and unseemly aspect. The use of over-long pipes is never necessary, and if the major principal pipes cannot find room in flat pipe fields, they can be set up in round or pointed towers. The towers not only serve to enliven the pipe front, but they also have a natural purpose. By this logical arrangement of the case front the set-out of the organ in its divisions becomes clearly recognisable, which creates a valuable and lively contact between the listener or onlooker and the organ.

It is not expected that the ideals of the "organ-movement", as given above in quotations from the late distinguished head of the Marcussen firm, will be accepted in their entirety by all those who are responsible for building new or rebuilding old organs.

Nevertheless, there is a general desire for smaller instruments, more intimate and more responsive to the full range of subtle touches of the sensitive player, for characteristic and characterful ranks of organ pipes both on manuals and pedals, for the production of the myriads of beautiful tones, obtainable by no other methods, by the use of mixtures, cornets and mutation stops with those of lower pitches. The high cost of organ-building, if nothing else, would demand that any given expenditure of money should result in the maximum potentiality for the production of beautiful tones.

An organ built on these principles is the very antithesis of an instrument crammed into an inadequate organ chamber, with ranks of pipes, placed wherever there is space for them, their tones masked by all manner of obstructions, and the slow, characterless tones of so many of the pipes controlled by slow tubular pneumatic action. Truly, when the smaller English organ was taken down from its gallery in the nineteenth century and was buried away in its sepulchral chamber we could say Ichabod!

There seems no reason why it should not be possible to design an organ which will serve many purposes well, if not ideally. The severely-designed, uncompromising neo-classical instrument may be admirable for the performance of organ music composed up to the year 1750, but it is of limited use for church service work and unsuitable for the performance of the works of the romantic and modern composers. The organ compositions of Liszt, Franck, Brahms, Reger, Rheinberger, Widor, Tournemire, Karg-Elert, and many others are not negligible and an organ on which they cannot be played is not a universal instrument, but it must be admitted that some organ designers, who are suspicious of eclecticism, would be prepared to accept severe limitations in particular instruments in order to obtain purity of style.[1]

What of the future of the organ?

There are no indications as yet that electrical devices have been able to imitate the major effects of the genuine pipe organ, in particular its major choruses. No doubt the prevalence of the loudspeaker in our daily lives has blunted the ears of many to the subtle beauties of really first-rate organ tone, and in view of the complexities and expense of the real organ there will be a temptation to the uncritical to purchase electrical substitutes. It is better to regard these latter as separate instruments than as imitations of the organ.

[1] It is extraordinary how cathedral, university and other organists, organ critics and professors of music, in the first four decades of this century were not only blind to the terrible shortcomings of the decadent-Romantic organ in Britain, but were loud in its praises. At present there are hopeful signs of an enlightenment in some cathedrals, churches and the universities (Oxford, Cambridge, Nottingham, Manchester, Newcastle, etc.), but it is remarkable that a completely new and expensive organ, at least half a century out of date in design before a note was played on it, could appear recently in another English university!

It cannot be doubted that the future will bring great improvements in the electronic organ and that it may displace the more expensive pipe organ where the retention of the latter necessitates large expenditure to keep it in repair or to effect its rebuilding.

Interest in the organ of tradition has never been so strong as in America at present. In Germany, the cost and shortage of material, the better disposition of pipework and the use of mutation and subtle mixture stops have resulted in some smaller but more musical organs in recent productions. Few new large organs can be built in England for reasons of the present high costs of materials, but rebuilds of existing instruments with more enlightened adaptations of the pipework and some additions of small ranks of pipes have produced many worthy instruments. The conservation of the finest instruments of the past, as regards their tonal appointments, is a useful task. The craft of organ-building at its best should be jealously preserved. It has a long and honourable history. A first-class organ is a combination of inspired design, worthy materials and skilled craftsmanship. Each organ worthy of a name should possess its own personality.

PLATE 25a.

The old Flemish organ (1602) at Carisbrooke Castle, Isle of Wight

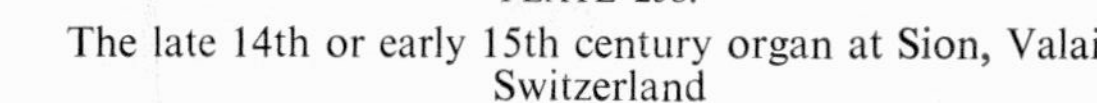

PLATE 25b.

The late 14th or early 15th century organ at Sion, Valais, Switzerland

PLATE 26.

Two small organs

The Premier. Cousans, Lincoln   The Denham. Mander, London

SECTION 2

CHAPTER VIII

THE PRINCIPLES OF THE CONSTRUCTION OF THE ORGAN

"*See, our huge house of the sounds*
Hushing its hundreds at once."

BROWNING.

THE ORGAN must be thought of in relation to the size and purposes of the building in which it is erected. It must have the "unity in diversity" of all works of art, it must be reliable and durable as a machine, and it must put the minimum of difficulties between the player and the proper interpretation of his music. Few organs attain all these desirable qualities. Many instruments are spoilt because they have not been well conceived in terms of their environment; others are marvels as machines, but fail as real instruments of music; while still more are beautifully voiced but lack unity and balance. The organ is the largest of all instruments and should present a pleasing, harmonious aspect to the eye. A good instrument is worthy of adornment with a fine case. In this section we propose to consider how it may be possible to realise all these ideals in practice.

THE POSITION OF THE ORGAN AND SOME ACOUSTICAL CONSIDERATIONS

It is a well-known fact that an organ of indifferent quality will sound tolerable or even well in a resonant building, and that even a fine instrument will sound unimpressive and dull in unsuitable surroundings. Instances of the former are found in many of the large continental Gothic churches; examples of the latter, such as the fine instrument in Sheffield City Hall, are well known in England.

Organ tone may be trapped and absorbed by the walls of an unsuitable organ chamber. Again, in a building with walls of absorbent material or in one which contains heavy carpets and drapings, the sound is too quickly turned into heat instead of being reflected from the walls, ceiling and other surfaces of the building and dying away slowly in a manner which could be represented by a logarithmic curve.

The general sustaining of the sound of a note, until it finally dies away beyond the threshold of audibility, is known as reverberation. An echo may result from reflection from a single distant plane surface. Concave surfaces which are sometimes found in ceilings may also cause uneven distribution of the sound and its concentration at focal points.

Long waves from low pedal notes tend to bend round corners more than the short waves from high notes. Also, short waves are broken up and scattered more than long waves when they strike rough plane-reflecting surfaces, such as stone or brick walls. Many churches and other large buildings have satisfactory acoustical properties when they are empty, but when they are filled with people all music seems to be flat, soft and lifeless. An organist must be prepared for this possibility when rehearsing his music in an empty church or hall. Some of his most beautiful quiet effects may count for nothing when the building is full, even if the audience keeps as silent as possible. High notes and harmonics are more readily absorbed by walls than low notes and ground tone. An organ sounds less brilliant in the distance than it does near its pipes.

The following table gives the coefficients of absorption of various materials for various frequencies, compared with an open window as standard, i.e. complete absorption of sound.

Material	*Absorption Coefficients*						
Frequency / pitch	64 8 ft.	128 4 ft.	256 2 ft.	512 1 ft.	1024 6 in.	2048 3 in.	4096 1½ in.
Open window	1·00	1·00	1·00	1·00	1·00	1·00	1·00
Audience (seated)	·35	·72	·89	·95	·99	1·00	1·00
Thick brick or stone wall	·021	·024	·025	·031	·042	·049	·07
Brick wall (painted)	·011	·012	·013	·017	·020	·023	·025
Pine wood	·064	·098	·110	·100	·081	·082	·110
Cushions	·230 to ·370	·280 to ·610	·390 to ·620	·540 to ·760	·470 to ·910	·270 to ·730	·160 to ·470
Hair felt	·090	·100	·200	·520	·710	·660	·440
Plaster or hollow tile	·012	·013	·015	·020	·028	·040	·050
Tiles	·012	·013	·018	·029	·040	·048	·053

It must be remembered that the sound from various types of organ pipes is emitted as follows:

Reeds and diaphones: from the top with slight but characteristic radiation from the body.

Open flue pipes: from the mouth, from the top and body vibrations.

Stopped flue pipes: Mouth and, to a lesser extent, body.

There is no universal agreement concerning the optimum conditions of reverberation in auditoria. A period of less than ·5 sec. may be suitable for speaking, but for musical purposes it would be too little and produce a dead, lifeless effect. A reverberation period of a second, or very slightly more, is a suitable compromise period, which will still leave a fairly rapid melodic line clear and will carry the tones sufficiently to enable them to develop their qualities.[1] For massive effects a period of two seconds is not too much, but even this would produce difficulties if fairly rapid contrapuntal music were played. These times are given for auditoria which are filled. In empty buildings they may be doubled, at least. Under the dome of St. Paul's Cathedral the reverberation period for fairly loud organ music is upwards of 10 sec. Under these conditions the effect of the organ is majestic, but part-writing cannot be heard in fast organ music. A dead building is an acid test for an organist. Any defects in his touch and registration become painfully apparent.[2]

In view of the screening effect of many ranks of pipes planted parallel to one another, a considerable proportion of the output of the pipes at the back does not reach the front of the organ. It is desirable that much sound should be permitted to escape above the organ. An organ chamber should be lofty and the roof above the organ should be so shaped that the sound is projected into the building. A spacious design for the instrument itself will prevent cramping of the pipes and the screening of the pipes by other parts of the organ.

The great organ-builders of the past realised that the whole structure of the instrument was capable of forced vibration and sound transmission. The worthy, liberally planned and well-joined woodwork of the instruments, apart from the pipes, contributed not a little to the success of the organ. This was particularly in evidence in the structures erected by G. Silbermann, E. Schulze and A. Cavaillé-Coll. It must be admitted that remarkable feats have been performed by modern organ-builders in overcoming, to some extent, the natural disadvantages arising from the use of small "unit" chests and concrete chambers.

In the latter part of the nineteenth century many English organs were taken from their west-end galleries and crammed into inadequate chambers at the side of the chancel. Sometimes good side-chapels were spoilt by the new home given to the organ. To make matters worse, the removal of the organ was often made the opportunity to secure its enlargement. New ranks of pipes, new mechanisms, new small sound-boards, were multiplied. The appearance of the church was marred, the pipes spoke in a cramped position, and there was not sufficient area for the egress of the sound.

Organs should not be so placed that their sounds can only reach the body of the church by travelling under low chancel arches. Buried organs are rarely successful, and even though special curved surfaces of hard reflecting material are used much of the sound is lost. Organs are better if they are placed at a

[1] The Sabine-Eyring formula is $t = \frac{.05\ V}{-S \log_e (1-a)}$ where t = time in seconds; S = total surface area in square feet; V = volume in cubic feet; a = average coefficient of absorption. See also "Acoustics for Musicians" by the present author in Hinrichsen's *Musical Year Book* (1945–6), pp. 342 et seq.

[2] As candidates at examinations of the Royal College of Organists know only too well!

reasonable height. A gallery or floor raised some 10 ft. from the main level of the ground of the building may produce a great improvement in the effect of an organ placed on it. For an organ of medium size at least 20-ft. in height above its base should be allowed. 16-ft. open stops can then stand with sufficient room above them. It is usually better to forgo one or two ranks of pipes in an organ so as to give others adequate speaking room if organ chambers are too small. Ideally, an organ should not be in a chamber: it should be placed fairly high near a solid reflecting wall, or it should stand on a screen so that its pipes are surrounded on all sides and at the top with free air.

An organ should be built on the north side of a church or in a chamber on the north side of the chancel rather than at the south side. Temperatures are more constant on the north side. If a church is heated by certain modern

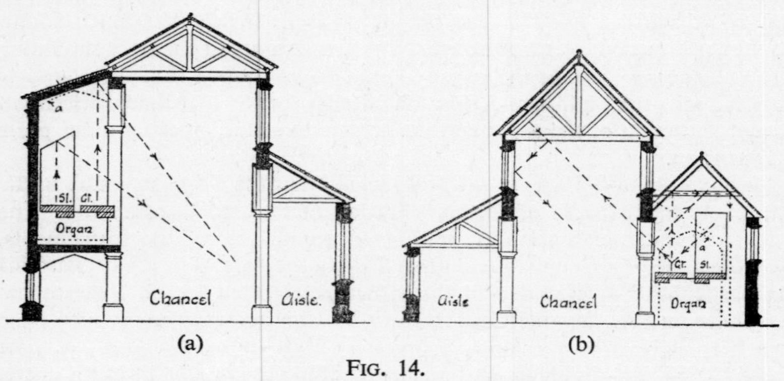

(a) (b)

FIG. 14.

A. A section of a good organ-chamber (after F. Webb.) (Dotted line at "a" represents aisle or transept opening).
B. A section of a bad organ-chamber (after F. Webb.) (Dotted line at "a" represents aisle or transept opening).

methods (hot air, gas, electricity, central heating) and there is no adequate attention to the relative humidity of the atmosphere, an organ, particularly one in which there are large slider sound-boards, may suffer considerable damage. A 55–65 per cent humidity is reasonable from every point of view. Damp organ chambers are equally undesirable. Organs should be planned so that every pipe and all the mechanism are readily accessible for tuning and adjustment. The interior of an organ should give the same impression of functional efficiency as an automatic telephone exchange or a modern electrical generating station, and this can only result from sound planning and engineering skill. It was always a pleasure to explore the interiors of the organs of Father Willis and Cavaillé-Coll, for instance.

Organ chambers cannot be considered without reference to organ cases, with which we shall deal briefly later in this section. Rows of plain or painted metal pipes unrelieved by any framing woodwork cannot be considered to be an ideal cover for an organ, though many of the pipes of different types of the great and positiv organs may be arranged to give a pleasing visual ensemble instead of a formal case. The organs may sound and look well under these conditions. Many recent American and German organs are arranged in this manner.

The Organ Case

It is satisfactory to note that in England attention is being paid to the appearance of the organ, and something is being done to redeem it from the unsightly rows of zinc "chimney-cans", or the hideously diapered fronts of painted tubes which were such a feature of later nineteenth-century instruments. The problem is not to be solved by placing the instrument in concrete chambers and hiding the swell shutters by means of ornate screens. A good organ should be seen as well as heard. Magnificent examples of organ cases abound on the Continent and some have been preserved from the fifteenth century. A good organ case solidly made of well-seasoned wood of high quality may even enhance the tone of the instrument by acting as a radiating surface. A badly designed case may prevent the egress of sound but hardly to the extent that is found in organs which have been packed away in "organ chambers" at the sides of a chancel. *Acoustically* there can be no doubt that the west-end position in the gallery of a large church is the best, but if the organ must needs go in the chancel it should be on the north side by preference, and should have ample room above it with generous openings facing both into the church and chancel. The screen, separating chancel and nave, where this exists, is an excellent place to put an organ, for it can be both seen and heard. Usually, it is only possible to put a part of the overgrown modern organ in such a screen case, and the rest of it is disposed in the choir-aisles, above the choir stalls or in the triforia. Such arrangements can be seen at Exeter, Norwich, Southwell, Beverley Minster, Manchester (until its damage by enemy action), Lincoln, Ripon, Gloucester, Wells and elsewhere.

The reaction against organ casework which took place in Germany between the wars led to the use of organ pipes of all types, without enclosing woodwork, to make pleasing designs. The natural logarithmic curves of a set of organ pipes were exploited. There is nothing to impede the sound, and the combination of tin, copper, plain metal, woods of various types, are used to give a pleasing appearance.[1]

An artistic appearance can be given to an organ by remembering that the small or medium-scaled organ flue-pipe is not only pleasing in itself but should be treated as the unit, or building-stone, of the case. In other words, it is not sufficient just to design an elaborately carved wooden structure and then to frame a few pipes within it. As in other art works, there must be unity in conception. Elaborate carving and sumptuous decoration are secondary considerations and, without a feeling of wholeness and balance, may prove to be irritating and ridiculous.

Organ cases can be studied in the fine works of Arthur Hill, Andrew Freeman, and Walter Kaufmann, but there are a few cardinal principles in case design which must be recorded.

[1] Nevertheless, modern opinion does not always regard this as ideal.

(1) The artistic principle of unity in diversity must be preserved and the case should be designed as a cohesive whole.

(2) No pipe-ends should be allowed to appear above the top of the woodwork. "No really good case has ever yet been designed in any style or period in which this has been allowed to happen."[1]

(3) The lower part of the case which is separated from the beams on which the pipes stand (known as the *impost*) is less important than the upper, but it should match the woodwork in colour and it should be dignified, well joined, and may be decorated with restrained carving, and panelling.

(4) If possible, the upper-part should overhang. In the old organs the bellows were at the back of the case and outside it, and so the lower part contained the simple mechanism only. The overhang, which may be supported by brackets, can be used to add to the artistic appearance of the instrument. The top of the woodwork which hides or canopies the ends of the pipes is known as the cornice and may contain ornamental carving or cresting work. The cornice, like the impost, may be broken so that its parts are at different levels.

(5) Pipes are arranged in (*a*) towers; (*b*) in flats, i.e. so that their feet are planted in a straight line; and (*c*) curves. Carved panels may be placed between compartments of organ pipes, but if the former are too wide the effect will usually be heavy and unsatisfactory. Any group of pipes which is used as a unit in a case, i.e. a flat or a tower, should show a natural sequence, i.e. their tops, mouths and feet should respectively form a continuous straight line or curves. There should be no sudden transition from a pipe to one which is much smaller or larger. Thus the designer has three lines which he can control in using pipes for his case: the line of the ends of the feet, the mouths and the tops; and he can use them in all sorts of combinations. With modern methods of conveyancing or of setting off individual pipes on unit chest-blocks most, if not all, of the visible pipes can be used to give music.

(6) Circular bands round groups of pipes in towers or round single pipes usually look bad. Pipes of tin as are found on the Continent look excellent without further decoration. Spotted-metal, and even zinc pipes, have a satisfactory appearance, but those which have too much lead and antimony in their composition soon tarnish to an unpleasant dark-brown colour or to black. Gilding pipes is an expensive process, but such pipes are effective against oak or mahogany. "Silver" or aluminium paint invariably produces a cheap and unpleasant appearance, but a mixture of aluminium and bronze or copper paint produces tolerable effects. Tin pipes with gilt mouths look attractive. The painting of organ pipes with blues, greens and browns is now entirely out of fashion. There are certain exceptions to this: the organ at Beverley Minster, for instance, with its rich brown case and pipes decorated with gilt and scarlet, has an entirely pleasing and sumptuous appearance.

Some of the neo-Gothic cases had very pleasing decorations on the woodwork, and occasionally the painted doors or wings which were characteristic of the early cases of Germany, Italy and Spain (and probably of England)

[1] B. B. Edmonds, *The Organ Club Handbook* (London, 1947).

FIG. 15. The Smith-Wren organ case at St. Paul's Cathedral. Carvings by Grinling Gibbons. Divided and rebuilt by Willis, 1872. (North Side.)

have been revived. Embossed pipes such as those at Tewkesbury Abbey (Milton Organ) and Nettlecombe Court can be very beautiful.

An organ is usually the most expensive piece of church furniture and it should be beautiful to the eye as well as to the ear.[1]

"Although eminently desirable, an organ is not a necessity in any church; there is, therefore, no excuse for admitting one to be a disfigurement. It follows that no new instrument should be permitted to be installed if it be ugly or mean-looking. An organ should not look like a large rectangular box with pipes standing along one or more of its sides. Where there is sufficient height the proportions of an organ can be vastly improved by making it more lofty and less deep than is customary in England. An organ of moderate size, properly cased in at the sides and at the back, can be one of the most beautiful features in any church. Front pipes should appear 'natural' by displaying as much as possible of their true speaking lengths. Light from the rear should not be allowed to show through the pipes or carving. The effect of many fine cases is spoilt by neglecting this point. Some of the best cases of all periods were enriched with gold and colour. Many seventeenth- and eighteenth-century cases have been vastly improved by having their carved 'pipe-shades' lavishly gilt; for instance as at St. Peter's, Cornhill, and St. George's, Hanover Square, London.

"The chancels of our older churches were not constructed to hold organs of more than a few stops, or more than a mere handful of singers. Many of them have insufficient room for a harmonium without overcrowding, yet somehow or other an organ and a choir have been packed in because it is felt that this is the correct place for them. Side-chapels were not meant to be organ chambers, and their use as such is bad architecturally, devotionally and musically. An organ standing in the open (such as the west-end of the nave) is far more effective than it would be if it were packed into an organ chamber. For this reason, if for no other, the west-end position for an organ, if at all possible, is nearly always the best, and in a loft, if there is sufficient height.

"Other positions that might be considered are:

(*a*) Under the easternmost arch of the nave arcade—this for a somewhat small instrument.

(*b*) Under the westernmost arch of the nave arcade, where the organ might project farther back into the aisle and so be of larger dimensions.

(*c*) At either end of an aisle. Here the keyboards should be placed so that the player can see the altar.

(*d*) In a shallow, open transept, at floor level or in a loft.

[1] A. G. Hill, *Organ Cases and Organs of the Middle Ages and Renaissance* (London, 1883 and 1891); A. J. Freeman, *English Organ Cases* (London, 1921), *Church Organs and Organ Cases* (London, 1945); W. Kaufmann, *Der Orgelprospekt*, 2nd ed. (Mainz, 1948, Eng. trans. 1961); G. Servières, *La Décoration Artistique des Buffets d'Orgues* (Paris, 1928); F. H. Sutton, *Church Organs*, 3rd ed. (London, 1883); J. Norbury, *The Box of Whistles* (London, 1877); John E. Blanton, *The Organ in Church Design* (Texas, 1956). See also the articles of Andrew Freeman and E. E. Adcock in *The Organ*.

(*e*) Divided into two or more portions. This is readily done by means of modern actions, but it is more expensive.

(*f*) On the chancel screen. This is not recommended in a church unless the arch be very large, so that the organ looks small by comparison; or very low, so that the organ stands against what is virtually the blank east wall of the nave.

"An organ hidden from sight may induce a feeling of mystery, even of mystification, but so, too, would a hidden pulpit or a hidden altar. A hidden or buried organ is a lost opportunity of enriching a church with a noble article of furniture."[1]

Loudness.

The subjective phenomenon of loudness varies in a logarithmic, and *not* in a direct manner with the intensity or energy of the generating source of the sound. If x and y are the energies of a source of sound before and after its increase in energy.

$$n = 10 \left(\log.\frac{y}{x}\right) \text{ decibels}$$

If the energy is doubled, $n = 10 \log. 2 = 3$. Thus, two ranks of organ pipes of similar output will only produce a sound with a 3-decibel level above that produced by one rank. The decibel scale is measured from the average threshold of hearing, but this varies with the pitch of the note, and therefore a loudness measure (phon) is used by matching the loudness with that of a 1,000-cycle note. Except in the case of low notes, the phon and decibel scales are practically the same.

(The acoustic output of the Boston Symphony Orchestra has been adjusted to phon-meter readings: $ppp = 20, p = 53, f = 75, fff = 95$.)

A doubling of intensity at any level only leads to an increase of 3 phons; e.g.

5 phons + 5 phons = 8 phons; 100 phons + 100 phons = 103 phons.
Gedackt, 40 phons.
Claribel flute, 50 phons.
Small diapason, 60 phons.
Great trumpet, 65 phons.
Tuba, 70–5 phons.

A good swell-box will enable the loudness level to be raised by 13–15 phons above the value when closed.

An increase of apparent loudness and majesty in organ tone is not to be thought of by adding unison to unison, but rather by gradually increasing the intensity of the harmonics of the tone in correct order. The use of the swell pedal to alter the power of a loud 8-ft stop, or a mixture of 8-ft. stops, is almost certain to lead to subjective flattening of the tone. As Dr. H. Lowery[2] has pointed out, and as a number of artistic players have found by experiment, slight additions of tone made after a period of quiet playing are more effective

[1] Andrew Freeman, *Church Organs and Organ Cases* (S.P.C.K., 1945).
[2] H. Lowery, "Weber's Law and the Organ", *The Organ*, vol. xxi, pp. 29 et seq.

than considerable additions of tone after a period of *mf* or *f* playing. Loudness is purely subjective to the listener and cannot be measured in terms of stop-knobs or swell-shutter angles, in an absolute manner.

An estimate of the number of speaking stops in an organ designed with proper chorus work is given as follows:

$$\frac{\text{The cubic content of the church in cubic yards}}{200} = \text{A}^{1}$$

$$\frac{\text{The number of seats in the building}}{25} = \text{B}$$

$$\text{Approximate number of speaking stops} = \frac{\text{A} + \text{B}}{2}$$

[1] If the volume of the building is given in cubic metres it should be divided by 150.

CHAPTER IX

THE PRODUCTION OF SOUND IN THE ORGAN

"—every soun(d) n'is but of aire reverberation."
The Summoner's Tale—CHAUCER.

SOUND travels at a rate of about 1,100 ft. a second at 60° F. Changes of atmospheric pressure do not greatly affect this speed, but it increases with a rise of temperature and decreases with a fall in temperature. The pitch of any note (neglecting certain subjective considerations) is determined by the frequency of the vibrations producing that note. The product of the wave length of the compressional waves in the air (or other sound transmitting medium) and the frequency of vibration is equal to the speed of the sound.

Any elastic body, such as a column of air, has a natural period of vibration. A cylindrical column of air in a tube, closed at one end, can be made to vibrate by means of a tuning-fork having the same, or nearly the same, natural frequency as that of the air column. A wave of compression going down the tube is reflected back at the closed end and up through the tube, and is followed by a wave of rarefaction. Thus the length of the tube has to be traversed four times in each complete cycle. A stopped pipe is approximately a quarter of the length of the wave of the note to which it will resound or which it will produce (e.g. as in the case of blowing across the open end of a hollow key). In the case of a pipe, which is open at both ends, a wave of compression will travel the whole length of the tube, swing out some distance into the open air and, owing to the elasticity of the air, will change its phase and travel back along the tube as a wave of rarefaction, provided that the tuning-fork or other supplier of energy is in time with it. Thus, an open pipe is about half as long as the wave length of a sound which it produces. In the middle of the column of air which is vibrating there will be a point or region of no motion, and this is called a node. The places of greatest movement of the air particles at the open ends of the tube are called antinodes. In a stopped pipe there will be a node at the closed end and an antinode at the mouth. Actually, the antinodes are somewhat outside the limits of the tube. An end correction has to be added to the tube length. In other words, the "speaking length" of an organ pipe is less than would be expected by dividing the note wave-length by four in the case of pipes closed at one end, and by two in the case of an open pipe. Corrections become large as tube diameters increase.

A stretched string, vibrating under tension between two fixed pegs, not only vibrates with an antinode at the middle and nodes at each end, but tends, particularly if touched at certain positions along its length, to vibrate in other ways so that it splits up into fractions ($\frac{1}{2}$, $\frac{1}{3}$, $\frac{1}{4}$, $\frac{1}{5}$, etc.) of its length. Its tone quality will not only contain its fundamental note, given by the vibration of its complete length, but will contain harmonics or partial tones given by wave-lengths of $\frac{1}{2}$, $\frac{1}{3}$, $\frac{1}{4}$, $\frac{1}{5}$, etc., of its fundamental, and therefore frequencies 2, 3, 4, 5, etc., times that of the fundamental.

Helmholtz, in 1865, in his *Tonempfindungen*,[1] believed that the harmonic contents, both as regards their number and strength, determined the quality or tone-colour of a note.[2] The harmonics are known to be important factors, but there are others, such as groups of inharmonic frequencies, usually of no great power, together with initiation and collapse transient tones, of which account must be taken in all musical instruments.

A vibrating column of air will also produce partial vibrations. A column which is narrow in proportion to its length will tend to produce a larger proportion of harmonics than a wider column, because, in the former case, there will be less end-correction and the column of air inside the tube then tends to break up into simple fractional lengths necessary for the production of harmonics. In a pipe open at both ends, with a node in the middle, there is a full series of harmonics which fall off in relative intensity according to the scale (width : length ratio). In the case of the pipe stopped at one end, only the odd harmonics are produced, because the end of the pipe must be a node and changes from compression to rarefaction are only possible at the open end.

		Open pipe length in ft.	*Harmonics*	*Vibrations per sec.*
CC	fundamental	8	1	$64 \times 1 = 64$
C	octave	4	$\frac{1}{2}$	$64 \times 2 = 128$
g	twelfth	$2\frac{2}{3}$	$\frac{1}{3}$	$64 \times 3 = 192$
c^1	fifteenth	2	$\frac{1}{4}$	$64 \times 4 = 256$
e^1	tierce	$1\frac{3}{5}$	$\frac{1}{5}$	$64 \times 5 = 320$
g^1	nineteenth	$1\frac{1}{3}$	$\frac{1}{6}$	$64 \times 6 = 384$
$b\flat^1$	flat twenty-first	$1\frac{1}{7}$	$\frac{1}{7}$	$64 \times 7 = 448$
c^2	twenty-second	1	$\frac{1}{8}$	$64 \times 8 = 512$

and so on.

Here we have considered the bottom note of an open 8-ft. manual stop and its harmonics. It must be pointed out that the vibration rates which have been given, although not far removed from those actually employed, are hypothetical and have been chosen merely to show the principle of the simple multiples which are found in the frequencies of harmonics. (The International Standard Pitch, 1939, gives $a^1 = 440$.) Apart from the octaves, all harmonics are out of tune with the notes of the tempered scale; the twelfths and nineteenths are not seriously out, but the tierces and flat twenty-firsts are badly out of tune. We shall discuss this later when we deal with tuning and mixture work.

[1] Translated by Ellis as "The Sensations of Tone". As has been pointed out in the historical portion of this work, organ-builders had anticipated Helmholtz by at least three centuries.

[2] Helmholtz used the words "clang-tint" instead of "tone-colour".

After this short introduction, we can now deal with the forms of organ flue pipes. In this type of pipe, air is admitted through a foot, issues in a flat sheet from the flue and, passing the mouth of the pipe, impinges on an upper lip. Formerly it was believed that the air in travelling upwards vibrated in and out of the mouth to form an "air reed" which produced vibration in the column of air in the pipe and in its turn was controlled by it; or that the column of air selected, from the many sounds of the wind-rush, a frequency to which it would resound. A sound can be produced even when the pipe body of a properly voiced pipe is removed, if the mouth parts, including the upper lip, are left. Actually, edge tones are produced by two streets of vortices at the front and rear of the sheet of wind as it passes upward to be divided by the upper lip. The note of the edge tones and that of the natural frequency of the pipe are coupled together. The rate per second at which each of the alternate eddies in the street of vortices strikes the edge is the frequency of the note produced. The vortices, rotating alternately inwards and outwards, give the sheet of wind, if rendered visible by smoke and photographed with a high-speed cinema camera, a curious wriggling motion. The pitch of the edge tone is somewhat modified by that of the tube, but is chiefly determined by the distance of the upper lip from the flue, i.e. the height of the mouth. The coupling of the vibrating column of air and that of the edge tones of the mouth is usually rather loose since there is damping in both systems. If an attempt is made to force the control of the mouth tone by an ill-matched air column there will be a tendency for the column of air to break up into segments and the note will fly up to a higher harmonic. This can be done by gradually increasing the wind pressure at the flue until the frequency of the vortices suddenly changes.[1]

When a set of organ pipes is made it must first be planned:

(*a*) in scale to suit the building in which the organ is to be placed;
(*b*) in relation to the other stops on the same division;
(*c*) in relation to the other divisions of the organ; and
(*d*) so that the pipes of a rank or set stand in proper relation to one another.

The old organ-builders to the end of the seventeenth century often made and voiced the pipes in the actual church in which the organ was to speak.

An organ pipe is sensitive to its acoustical surroundings, and its tonal output can vary within very wide limits according to the powers of absorption of its surroundings. It has been said that the best stop in an organ is a good building with sufficient but not excessive reverberation. The tone of an organ pipe is somewhat modified by the worthiness of the structure on which it stands. We have already noted that the excellent joinery of well-seasoned wood of first-rate quality used by Schulze for his building frame and soundboards contributed something to the general musical effect of his instruments.

[1] E. H. Barton, *Sound* (London, 1922). Alex Wood, *The Physics of Music* (Cambridge, 1945). E. G. Richardson, *The Acoustics of Orchestral Instruments and the Organ* (London, 1937). D. M. A. Mercer, "The Physics of the Organ Flue Pipe", *Am. Journal of Physics*, vol. xxi, no. 5, pp. 376–86.

This should be remembered when ranks of organ pipes on small unit chests are enclosed in concrete chambers.

When an organ pipe is voiced, it is not only necessary to secure a particular tone regulated in quality and power between one pipe and the next in the rank, but it is also necessary to secure prompt speech without undesirable initiation transients. The "coughing" pedal bourdon which begins with an unpleasant quint tone must be known to all who have heard a small commercial pipe organ. (Occasionally, of course, a "chiff" or "bubble" may be encouraged by the voicer at the onset of the speech of a pipe, but this is in order to produce orchestral imitations and is often ill-advised. Further, it must be pointed out that not all the characteristic tones of the Baroque organs commenced with such transient tones.) A stop must be voiced on a sound-board of the type (or nearly of the type) on which it is to speak. The cutting or pressing of nicks parallel with the pipe-body, in the languid and the lower lip, will cause secondary eddies to form, and these can be made to prevent the pipe from speaking until the wind pressure has built up itself in the foot. Only the minimum of nicking should be done, otherwise the tone of the pipe will be windy. The harmonic development of a tone can be assisted somewhat by varying the type of nicking. Fine nicking, close together, will assist the formation of string tone. The type of nicking must also depend upon the distance of the lower lip from the languid. To a certain point the energy of the note is determined by the width of the wind sheet, provided that the foot hole is wide enough, but many other factors then come into play. If the flue is widened the upper lip must be pulled out so that it is still in a position to separate the rows of eddies. Widening the flue also lowers the pitch of the mouth tone. If the languid is raised or the upper lip is pushed in, the lip is then ineffective in separating the rows of eddies, and the speech is slow in maturing and tends to be rich in overtones. The note is then said to be slow and bright. On the other hand, if the languid is depressed or the upper lip pulled out the speech is quicker, duller and tends to overflow to a harmonic when the pressure is increased. An open flue pipe of normal diapason tone should not easily overblow to a harmonic.

Sometimes an inverted languid is used and the bevel is then on the underside. Nicking is then not usually necessary, because a convergent orifice has been produced. Modern methods of voicing for neo-classical organs require less and less nicking.

With small-scaled pipes it was possible to produce tones rich in harmonics, of non-imitative string tone, by fine nicking and pressing in the upper lip or raising the languid, but the pipes were always very slow of speech. The discovery of the "harmonic" bridge, misnamed "beard", revolutionised the voicing of flue organ pipes of string or geigen tone and ensured firmness of speech in other flue stops.

The cylinder of wood or metal (or half cylinder with the curved part facing inwards) is fixed between the ears of the pipe, which may be cut away above or below the bridge. This acts as a front baffle and stabilises the tone by inhibiting vortex formation. Thus the tone of the pipe can be kept so that the fundamental is preserved in proper relation to the harmonics. The bridge must not be too big in diameter, otherwise the tone is throttled; and its exact position in relation to the mouth must be found by the voicer. Other devices such as the "frein harmonique", invented by Gavioli, in which a flat plate of metal is fixed in front of the mouth and held by the attachment to the pipe-foot, have a similar effect.

The height of the mouth or "cut-up" must be considered as a fraction of its width. Thus we talk of a cut-up of 1 in 5, meaning that the rectangle of the mouth is five times as broad as it is high. In the case of some flute stops the upper lip is curved or even semicircular and a compromise height must be arrived at. A wide mouth, assuming a copious wind supply, will give a louder tone but produce difficulties of adjustment of a wind stream which is no longer almost flat but convex to the voicer. Narrow mouths are much more easy to treat and permit of much greater latitude in cut-up. The higher the mouth the duller is the note produced by a given wind pressure, but if the latter is increased beyond a certain limit the note will "fly off" to a harmonic. The quality of the tone and the nature of its speech can be modified to some extent by the shape and treatment of the upper lip. A bevelled and sharp upper lip will encourage the formation of overtones, whereas a thick lip made of heavily-leaded alloy or a lip which has been covered with soft leather will discourage overtone formation. The use of leather makes voicing easy, permits the use of higher pressures, but produces an unpleasant, heavy, non-blending quality of tone, heard only too often in some English cathedrals. Happily, there is an overdue reaction against this type of tone.

The shape and scale and material of the pipe will not have been determined by the voicer, but it will be remembered that these are fundamental to its final tone and power.

There is not only a loss of power at the antinode outside the mouth of a pipe, but there is also a loss at the top where the wave swings outwards into the open air. Vincent Willis, the son of Father Willis, produced double languid pipes, the spaces between the languids being open to the air at the back of the pipes, in order to increase the power of diapasons without spoiling the tone by leathering the lips. A fine example of a stop so treated, made by Henry Willis III, may be heard in the organ at Westminster Cathedral, London. Again, various devices have been suggested to stabilise the antinode formation at the top of the tube and thus increase the power of the pipe without it over-blowing to a harmonic. Henry Willis uses a small metal cylinder of diameter different from that of the pipe placed at the top of the tube. This he calls his "compensator amplifier" and it permits the use of higher wind pressures in flue stops while it preserves the character of the quality of the tone of the stop.[1]

Reed pipes

The construction of a typical reed stop will be understood from the diagram. Organ reed stops are of two kinds: those which have a metal tongue which vibrates inside a rectangular opening without touching its sides, and those

[1] A related device known as the "tubeon" had been used occasionally in the earlier years of the century by Grindrod.

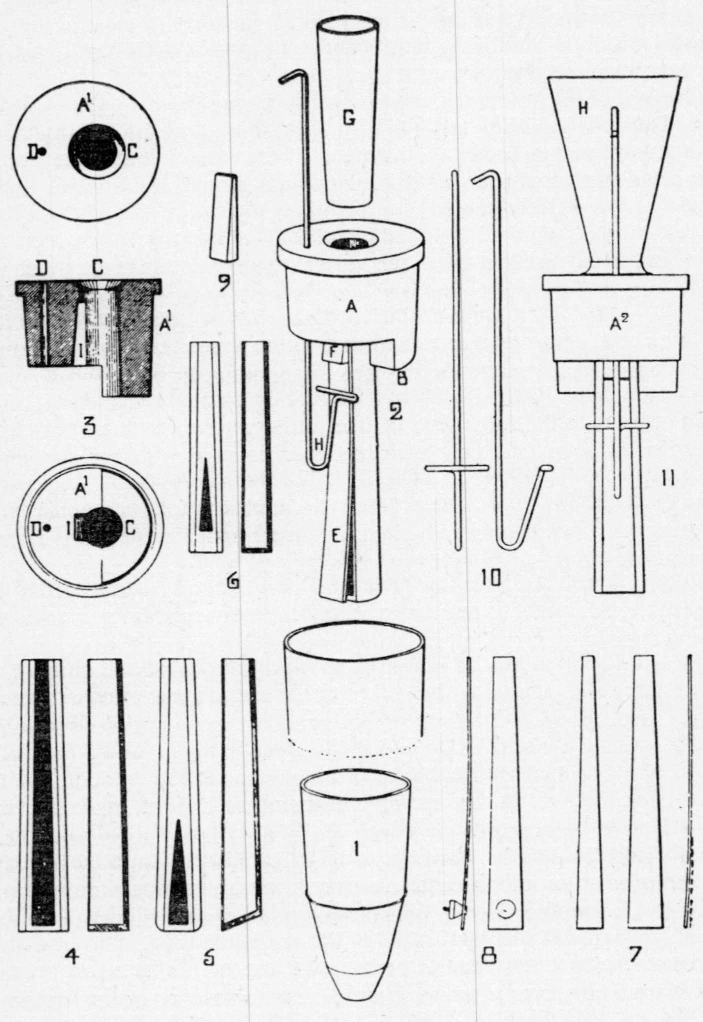

FIG. 16. A Reed Pipe and its Parts (after Audsley).

1. Part of boot. 2. Block, shallot, reed, tongue and tuning wire. 3. Block. 4, 5, 6, Shallots. 7. Brass reed tongues. 8. Reed tongue with weight (Willis). 9. Wedge for fixing tongue. 10. Tuning wires. 11. The parts put together. (The conical tube is not shown.)

which beat against a metal plate alternately opening and covering a hole cut therein. The former are known as free reeds and are hardly known in Britain; the latter are known as "beating" or "striking" reeds.

Like the flue pipe, the organ reed pipe is a coupled system between the vibrations of the reed and those of the air column in the tube. Either of them can be made to control the other within certain limits; for instance, the pipe may be sharpened in pitch by shortening the effective length of the tube or by shortening the vibrating length of the tongue.

Bonavia Hunt[1] gives the following list of the factors which may control the power and quality of a reed pipe.

Thickness of tongue.
Length of tongue.
Shape of tongue
Curve of tongue.
Weighting the end of the tongue.
Shape of the shallot (i.e. the tube against which the tongue beats).
Shape of orifice of shallot.
Length of orifice.
Position of orifice (arranged by filling in part of its base).
Area of boothole.
Size of boot and block.
Length of boot.
"Bleeding" the boot (i.e. boring a small hole therein).
Shape of tube or resonator.
Length of tube.
Thickness of tube.
Material of tube.
Scale of tube at tip and at top.
Capping and slotting top of tube.
Adding bell or flare to tube.
Adding other appendages.

The principal vibrating systems of the reed stop are the movement of the reed and that of the air in the tube. For normal reeds of the Willis type these should be coupled at resonance, that is, so that their natural frequencies do not differ greatly. If such a reed is taken and the tuning spring is pushed down, the pitch of the note will be raised, but it will also change in quality, becoming stifled, more horn-like, and more close in tone until finally "choking" takes place. If, on the other hand, the tuning spring is raised, the pitch of the note is lowered and the tone becomes freer and more "splashy". There is a considerable degree of mutual control of the reed and tube, but this cannot be pushed beyond certain limits or the pitch will change suddenly. If the tube is made two or three times as long as would be required for normal resonance and the pressure is raised, the tongue still determines the note, which becomes rich and harmonic. (From the foregoing it will be appreciated that if there is *much* movement of the tuning spring a change of tone quality as well as

[1] *Modern Studies in Organ Tone*, p. 91, London, 1933.

pitch will result. Many organs after frequent tuning have reeds in which it is difficult to find two notes of the same quality. When reeds are made their tubes have to be carefully cut to length in order to secure correct pitch with a particular tone quality. Reeds are mitred in order to prevent dust from falling into the shallot and thence to the tongue, or in order to reduce the height of the pipe.)

The method of making the tongue from rolled brass (or, rarely, aluminium or some elastic alloy) is not easily acquired. The tongue is so curved that it covers and uncovers the hole in the shallot gradually by a rolling and unrolling process. The curve varies from parabolic to logarithmic according to the type of tone. Each tongue is made empirically by the voicer by rubbing the tongue screwed on a wooden block with a steel rod or burnisher. It is then tried in the reed stop. In large bass reeds the tongues have to be long and attempts to control them by lengthening the tubes cause the note to fly up. Father Willis and his brother George solved the difficulty by screwing brass weights to the tongues. This is a difficult technique and it is not surprising that less able voicers have used weights "chattertoned" to the tongues or have glued on pieces of felt. Thin tongues (other things being equal) tend to produce richer notes than thicker tongues.

It is not possible to produce a tone which is both powerful and beautiful with wind pressures suitable for the fluework. A wind pressure of from 7 in. (upwards to 25, 50 or even more under extreme circumstances) is necessary to give the tongue the necessary amplification of movement for the purpose. Father Willis and his brother George produced reeds, both for chorus and solo purposes, on pressures of 8 in. and upwards, which have not yet been exceeded in beauty.

Nevertheless, it must be stated that the remarkable feats of Cavaillé-Coll in France and the Willis brothers in England tended to obscure the beauties of a low-pressure reed which, although it did not possess the arresting and thrilling orchestral tones of the symphonic organ, was eminently musical and made a perfect blend with a flue chorus without engulfing it. Such reeds were made by Clicquot in France before the revolution, by Gray and Davison, England, Green and a number of others, both in England and in France. It is pleasing that such reed voicing is being cultivated again for these low-pressure stops were truly organic in character.

The tone of the reed stop is also dependent on the shape of the orifice cut in the flat face of the shallot. Three main types of shallots are in use in the organs:

(*a*) The open shallot. This extends the entire length of the tongue and is useful for producing a loud tone rich in harmonics, such as that of a trompette.

(*b*) The closed shallot. Such a shallot is not really closed; its shape is like that of a narrow frustum of a cone, and the opening is triangular. This is a popular type, and by using small-scaled tubes and high wind pressures it is possible to obtain a brilliant tone from it.

(*c*) The "filled-in" shallot. The opening is made higher up the body of the shallot and the tongue, placed in the usual position with respect to the face of the shallot, closes the orifice before it has completed its downward stroke. The harmonics of its extreme end are thus not in evidence and such a shallot is used for producing tromba, horn or other smooth reed tone. [See Fig. 16.]

The type of tone is also influenced by the nature of the metal used in making the various parts of the reed. The boot and block should be heavy and solidly made, and the reed tubes should be made of an alloy rich in tin. A certain reinforcement is desirable at the point where the tube fits into the block, and in order that there shall be a proper transformation of the energy of the wind which passes the reed, the tubes should have a critical bore at the tip. Many of the coarse-toned commercial reeds were too wide at this point. It is easy to show, by acoustic theory, that a conical tube will reinforce the harmonics in their natural series. Thus conical tubes, whether straight or mitred, are used for pipes of trumpet tone, but the power obtained from a pipe varies to a certain extent with the width of the tube. Wooden tubes can be used, and zinc is often used for larger pipes. The diameter of a loud trumpet or trombone 16-ft. CCC pipe at the top would not be greater than 8 in.

The swell oboe may be made with a "close" tone, although the writer feels that when it is the only reed in a small organ it should be voiced to have considerable vitality so that it can be used as a miniature chorus-reed. The tube consists of a narrow cone surmounted by a conical bell which is partially covered at the top by soldering on a regulating cap or shade. If the cap is opened the reed can be tuned to give a louder and brighter note, but if the cap is closed to a certain extent, the tone becomes smoother and weaker.

The orchestral oboe has a thin cylindrical tube with a bell, and the opening in the shallot is very narrow. If a "double-bell" is fitted to an orchestral oboe type of reed its tone is then changed to that of the cor anglais.

A logarithmically flared tube will tend to encourage all overtones, whether harmonic or otherwise. Such tubes made of brass are used by Henry Willis III in his trompette militaire stops.

Stops of clarinet type have cylindrical tubes which reinforce the odd-numbered harmonics only. The clarinet tube is half length and is capped. Some pipe-makers solder the cap so that it covers the top of the tube completely and make a slot below it. A thin tube encourages overtones, but produces less volume. With extremely thin tubes we obtain musette tone.

The vox humana is a type of clarinet with a short tube, usually of eighth length, although Willis made his of quarter length. (It must be pointed out that the basses of chorus reeds can be made with half length reeds. The magnificent double swell reed in St. Paul's Cathedral is so made.)

The modern Skinner-Willis French horn has large "filled in" shallots, with weighted tongues. The tone is extremely close and a wind pressure of 6 in. minimum is required. A more usual pressure is 25–30 in. The tone of this reed should be both soft and smooth, imitating the orchestral instrument in its quieter moods.

The Valvular Reed and Other Devices

At its best this is a producer of powerful pervading tone. It was invented by Hope Jones and improved by Compton. It is useful particularly in enclosed spaces for producing *mf* or *f* basses, and it has been adapted to give smooth horn tones of 16- and 8-ft. pitch. The diaphone does not blend well and its fundamental note is too fat to form the basis of a tonal superstructure. Its use is strictly limited and it forms no part of a neo-classical or even eclectic tonal design.

Amongst other devices for the production of sound in the organ, the following may be mentioned.

(1) Haskell bass-pipes. If a cylinder of metal, closed at one end, and of the correct length and diameter, is placed inside an 8-ft. pipe so that the open end of the cylinder is near the mouth of the pipe, the latter can be voiced to give a 16-ft. note of violone tone. This saves the cost of real 16-ft. open basses (and this is a large item) in small or moderate-sized organs.

(2) The tone of bourdons is often improved by adding 8-ft. dulciana "helpers".

(3) Polyphonic pipes. If a hole is cut in a flue pipe, opposite to the mouth if it is a stopped pipe and either here or at the other end in an open pipe, the effective vibrating air-column is shortened (or what amounts to the same thing as regards pitch, the mouth area is increased). Thus the pitch of the note is raised. If the hole is closed by a pallet the original note is restored. Thus, two (or more) pedal notes may be obtained from one pipe, and the mechanism by which the hole is opened and closed is cheaper than a separate pipe.

(4) Under-energised pipes. It has been possible to voice large-scale stopped pipes so that their volume of tone adjusts itself, to some degree, to the amount of tone which is given by other pipes which are sounding at the same time. This was particularly useful when only a few pedal pipes were provided. The adjustments, made empirically, to the mouth-parts of the pipes were so arranged that the wind sheet was only partially interrupted by the upper lip when the pipe was sounding alone. The matter is also interesting when the speech and function of the large-scale flutes of the classical organ are considered.

At first sight it might appear that the tone of an organ pipe will be dependent only on the size and the shape of the vibrating air column and the nature of the method of setting it in motion (that is, the vibration of the tongue in a reed pipe and the edge-tone of the flue pipe). There are other factors which are important: (1) the materials of which the pipe is made; (2) its immediate environment in the organ; and (3) its acoustical environment in the building in which it speaks and even its precise position and orientation with respect to its environment.

The Materials from which Organ Pipes are Made

In the past many materials have been used for making organ pipes. Woods of every kind, lead, tin, iron, copper, glass, brass, silver, paper and even sized fabrics. The list given by Schlick in 1511[1] is impressive. Seidel[2] says that "gold, silver, brass, copper, alabaster, glass, clay and paper" were used for the

[1] Schlick, Spiegel, op cit. [2] Seidel, Orgelbaukunst.

purpose; and Dom Bédos[1] says that flue stops have even been made of ivory. Today and for a number of centuries tin-lead alloys and wood are and have been the chief materials for pipes less than 4 ft. long (and in the past much longer). Sheet or beaten copper has been used for making some of the light-pressure stops of the Baroque type, and brass was sometimes employed for the tubes of the old regal reeds. Hard-rolled zinc has become a favourite material for the manufacture of large open flue pipes and string-toned basses, larger than 4 ft. It looks well, is easily worked and is more durable than the organ metal of tin and lead. In the hands of any but a skilful voicer it tends to produce a hard, "desiccated" and "hungry" tone. Normally, it should not be used for pipes of less than 4 ft. in length.

The lead-tin alloy, known as "metal", varies in its constitution. Formerly, almost pure tin was used for medium and small-sized pipes, and in continental organs for the front pipes, whatever the size. It retained its superb silver-like appearance and it helped to produce a bright, clear tone. Heavily leaded alloys were used for dull flute tones and the pipes of the cornet ranks. Tin is far more expensive than lead, and in England economies were perforce effected in recent times by the increasing use of the latter metal. Antimony is not helpful in the production of good tone—it gives rigidity to a heavily leaded alloy and the pipes quickly tarnish in a characteristic manner. A little copper in the pipe metal is not harmful. Cornish tin was much sought after in France, even when lead was used, to a greater extent, in England for organ pipes. Cavaillé-Coll and Silvermann used tin alloys of upwards of 95 per cent of the metal for their narrow-scaled flue pipes, and for front pipes almost pure tin. For certain diapasons and flutes in England alloys containing 70 per cent of lead and more are often used, and for string tone only 45 per cent to 50 per cent tin. Alloys with as little as 35 per cent and as much as 65 per cent of tin can be run into sheets which have a spotted appearance. This is known as spotted metal and is often considered to be a "hall-mark" of satisfactory pipe metal. The large spots contain lead and tin in combination in definite chemical proportions. Plain metal contains 20 per cent tin.

A physical analysis of the effect of pipe materials on tone quality has confirmed what artist organ-builders have found in centuries of empiricism.[2] Of the various alloys used in the experiments, a "fifty-fifty" mixture of tin and lead gave the best reinforcement of the first seven harmonics, with wood second, and galvanised-iron and other materials far behind. Steel only served to reinforce the eighth to the eleventh partials. Silver and gold organ pipes do not produce qualities of tone as pleasing as those of pipe metal. It is, of course, by no means certain that in these days of "tailor-made" alloys it will be impossible in the future to compound new mixtures of metals suitable for organ pipes.

Wood Pipes

With regard to wood, lengths of well-seasoned straight-grained oak, mahogany, pear, pine for small pipes and pine for the larger, gave good re-

[1] Dom Bédos, op. cit.

[2] Boner and Newman, *Journ. Acoustic. Soc. America*, vol. xii, p. 83 (1940).

sults. Such timber of the correct quality is not now easy to obtain in England, but it is still available in U.S.A. and in Germany. Wooden pipes are more trouble to make and to adjust properly, but if they are kept reasonably free from extreme damp they are more durable than those of metal. The great Haarlem organ (Muller, 1738) originally contained metal pipes only.

In view of the difficulty of obtaining good timber of first-rate quality and thoroughly seasoned, together with the skill necessary for fitting the parts and voicing a set of pipes, wooden pipes are not employed as often as they ought to be. Both Schnitger and Henry Willis used comparatively few wooden pipes, and the latter claimed that he could obtain the tone which he wanted for his flute stops from metal pipes. Compenius made his celebrated organ at Frederiksborg Castle, near Copenhagen, with many wooden pipes, and the adjustment of the small mouths of the upper notes of some of the higher-pitched stops must have called for infinite patience. Various kinds of wood have been employed for making pipes, and all organs should have some ranks of such pipes, if possible. Apart from a wooden great-organ claribel or stopped diapason, many moderate-sized British organs only have wooden stops on the pedals, where usually they need the addition of some metal ranks in order to give clarity and definition to the pedal line. Wooden pipes are made (1) four-sided; (2) three-sided (triangular); (3) cylindrical; (4) pyramidal and inverted pyramidal. The four-sided open and stopped pipes are the most common, but triangular construction is used for some flute-toned ranks and occasionally, as in some Schulze organs, cylindrical wooden pipes were used for the construction of orchestral flutes.

The construction of a wooden pipe will be apparent from the diagrams. The cap which fits on the front of the pipe needs careful adjusting, with some trial and error before it can be screwed or glued on. The mouths of wooden pipes cannot be manipulated in the same easy way as the soft lead-tin alloys of the metal pipes. The timber used in the construction of large 32-ft. pipes should be of adequate thickness. For smaller pipes oak, mahogany, pine and pear woods are used. The pieces must be glued together carefully and held in cramps until the glue has set. Screws should be avoided as far as possible, but they may be used for fixing the caps in large

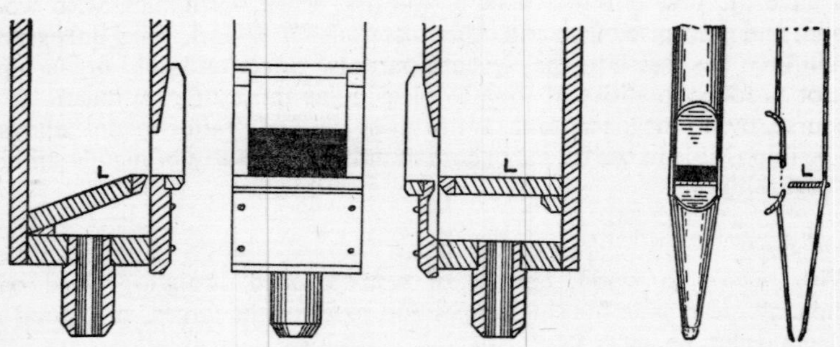

FIG. 17. Wood and metal flue-pipes (the languids are marked L).

pipes. Everything must be of extremely well-fitted and worthy construction, and where there are stoppers these should be made airtight with a covering of soft leather.

Hopkins[1] describes the construction of wooden pipes as follows: "The body consists of a right-angled tube, formed of four planed boards, the cross-section of which is not usually a square but an oblong. At the lower end the body is closed by the block (which is the first part of the pipe to be made) and is nearly divided in two by a deep cutting called the *throat*. The block and throat are closed in front by the cap, a piece of hard wood hollowed out, leaving the two sides and the bottom edges to be glued or screwed to the sides and block of the pipe. The upper edge of the cap recedes a little to form the wind-way. The pipe-foot is a cylindrical, conical or four-sided tube introduced at the bottom of the tube to serve as a conductor of wind into the pipe and to act as a support thereto.[2]

"The proportion of the breadth as compared with the depth of wood stopped pipes is varied very much, according to the quality of tone that is desired to be produced. Father Smith and Richard Bridge frequently made their stopped pipes nearly square, the former sometimes making the proportions of the block of his CC stopped diapason 5 in. by 4¾ in. The German builders make some of their wood pipes narrow and deep as in the Lieblich Gedact, the CCC pipe of which measures 5 in. by 3⅜ in., while those for other stops are made wider than they are deep, as in the Hohl flöte, the tenor pipe of which is made 1 13/16 in. deep and 2 7/16 in. wide. A pipe that is nearly square gives a full and weighty tone, one that is narrow and deep, a soft and sweet (lieblich) tone, and one that is shallow and wide a powerful and hollow tone.

"In working together the separate parts of an open wood pipe the sides are first glued and nailed or pinned to the block, and when the glue has thoroughly set the back and front are attached to the edges of the sides by similar means. The pipe-foot is then glued in, and when the pipe is voiced (by carefully adjusting the top of the block and cap, 'nicking' these, and adjusting the size of the foothole) the cap is fastened on."

Formerly, colossal scales for 16-ft. wooden stops were proposed in an endeavour to obtain great power from one or two ranks of pedal pipes.[3] Such curious constructions produced only windy, unmusical tone. Following the German usage, the scales of the CCC open 16-ft. pipes can be 8 in. by 10 in., 9 in. by 11 in. or 10 in. by 12 in. at the largest. Poorly voiced, large stopped basses tend to speak the twelfth partial before settling down to their proper notes. This may be overcome by adjusting the hole in the pipe-foot or by fitting a baffle, adding a roller-bridge and adjusting the wind pressure. A "cut-up" (of the upper lip) which is too high, cannot be adjusted without remaking the pipe.

[1] Hopkins and Rimbault, op. cit., p. 108.

[2] Practical details of actual pipe construction may be found as follows: W. E. Dickson, *Organ Building*, pp. 10 et seq.; G. A. Audsley, *The Organ of the Twentieth Century*, pp. 416 et seq.

[3] L. G. Hayne, *Hints on the Purchase of an Organ* (London, 1865). Therein internal measurements of 16 ft. pipes were given as 18 ins. x 20 ins., and 22 ins. x 24 ins.

Metal Pipes

Hopkins[1] describes the time-honoured practice of casting the sheets of lead-tin alloy as follows: "The ingredients are melted together in a copper and then cast into sheets, a process effected by pouring it in a molten state into a wooden trough, and running the trough rapidly along a bench faced with tick. The metal escapes from the trough through a narrow horizontal opening at the back, leaving a layer of metal behind it as it proceeds; and the wider the cutting is, of course the thicker will be the sheet of metal produced. After being cast to an approximate thickness, the metal is planed down to the precise thickness required. It is then cut into portions of the shape necessary to give to the pipes the required size and form and is thus finally worked up." Although organ-builders still cast their own "metal" sheets, they buy zinc and copper in sheet form from the manufacturers. A few pipe-makers are still at work in Britain, and some organ-builders obtain their pipes from the professional pipe-makers. All practical organ-builders, worthy of the name, should be able to voice, regulate and adjust finally in the organ the pipes which they use.

Here follows an analysis of a number of typical pipe metals of various builders who have done work in England.[2]

Builders	*Date*	*Pipes*	*Place*	*Tin* %	*Lead* %
J. Loosemore	1665	Double diapason	Exeter Cathedral	100	0
T. Harris	1637	Diapason	Tewkesbury Abbey	98	2
B. Smith	1687	Diapason	Temple Church, London	91	9
B. Smith	1687	Great Diapason	St. Mary's, Cambridge	30	70
G. England	1789	Diapason	St. John's, Portsea	30	70
B. Smith	1666	Principal	Westminster Abbey	23	77
B. Smith	1697	Principal	St. Paul's Cathedral	22	78
J. Snetzler	1777	Diapason	St. Mary's, Nottingham	14	86
R. Harris	1678	Diapason	Chichester Cathedral	10	90
A. Cavaillé-Coll	*c.* 1870	Front pipes	Blackburn Parish Church	91	9
A. Cavaillé-Coll	*c.* 1870	Inside pipes	Blackburn Parish Church	76	24
E. Schulze	*c.* 1865	Trombone	St. Bartholomew's, Armley, Leeds	56	44
E. Schulze	*c.* 1865	Piccolo	St. Bartholomew's, Armley, Leeds	50	50
H. Willis	1877	Clarion	Durham Cathedral	50	50
H. Willis	1872	Diapason	Royal Albert Hall	90	10
T. C. Lewis	*c.* 1890	Diapason	St. Nicholas, Newcastle	47	53

[1] Hopkins and Rimbault, op. cit., p. 99.

[2] This analysis was made by Lt.-Col. George Dixon, M.A., and was published in *The Organist and Choirmaster* for 15th January 1909.

In view of the phenomenon of *eutexia* by which lead-tin and other alloys may have a melting-point lower than that of either or any of the constituents, soldering is not always an easy operation. Father Smith's solders sometimes contained bismuth.

The Scales of Organ Pipes

The word *scale* is commonly used to give the diameter of the tube of an organ-pipe at the top, but it is obvious that this, as an absolute measure, will be useless unless it is related to the length or pitch of the pipe. Scales are given as diameters at 8-ft. C, 4-ft. C and so on. It will readily be understood that the proportions of each organ pipe in a set cannot be maintained throughout the compass. A pipe which speaks an octave above another has half its speaking length, and if other proportions were preserved it would have half its diameter, and the volume of air in the tube would be only an eighth of that of the tube an octave below. Clearly, as we went up the scale (even though tone quality were preserved), there would be a great falling off in power. The energy required to give a perception of equivalent loudness is less as we go up the scale, but it is much greater than we should obtain by using pipes which were in all dimensions proportional to one another.[1]

The medieval organ-builders made two or more octaves of organ pipes of similar diameter by rolling the metal on the same mandril. Hence the tone of the set of pipes was sharp and stringy in the bass, and dull and fluty in the treble. When the notes of a melody rise they usually are subjected to a slight crescendo. Thus, any apparent falling off in power of a rank of pipes, as we go up the scale, is a serious fault. Moreover, when heard at a distance, the lower notes of a single rank of pipes or a whole instrument seem louder in comparison with the trebles than they do when heard near to the organ. Thus it is necessary to preserve both the quality and power of the trebles of a rank of pipes and yet allow enough substance of tone in the bass and sufficient musical quality and breadth in the middle register. The manner in which the diameters of a set of pipes decrease progressively is a most important factor. It is a matter that can only be considered in relation to other factors of voicing and design. Hundreds of years of empiricism have been necessary to give modern scales, and it must be confessed that even today many badly scaled ranks of pipes are made. The builders of eighteenth-century organs often duplicated the treble pipes: this was not often satisfactory. (It is possible to have two similar pipes working at the same time and mutually destroying their tones and at best the increase in loudness is only 3 decibels.) Cavaillé-Coll divided the sound-boards of his reeds and used higher pressures for the trebles. Father Willis was able to devise scales so that this was not necessary, but he did not favour the heavy reed basses of the French organs or the ponderous basses of some of the German organs. In many Willis organs there is a distinct crescendo as the scale is ascended. This

[1] The scaling of organ-pipes until the end of the eighteenth century has been fully dealt with by Dom Bédos (op. cit.); J. G. Töpfer, *Lehrbuch der Orgelbaukunst* (Weimar, 1855); and C. Mahrenholz, *Die Orgelregister* (Kassel, 1932) and *Die Berechnung der Orgelpfeifen Mensuren* (Kassel, 1938).

was sometimes overdone, but it was remarkably effective when there was no swell-box.[1]

The scaling of organ-pipes depends on the size and acoustical qualities of a building, the sensitivity of the average human ear at different pitches and the nature of the tone quality of the pipe.

We have seen that instead of the pipe diameter halving on the twelfth note (i.e. octave) it must halve on a higher note.

A scaling ratio favoured by the nineteenth-century German organ-builders, including Schulze, for open flue pipes was known as $\sqrt{8} : 1$. This meant that the *areas* of the *cross*-sections of any pipe and its octave were in the proportion $\sqrt{8} : 1$. Here the pipe diameters halve on the sixteenth note *above* any particular pipe. Each note is wider than the next by a certain factor, and the scale, like that of the pipe lengths, is logarithmic. Thus, at the octave the pipe *widths* will be $2^{\frac{12}{16}}$ or $2^{\frac{3}{4}}$ to 1 (as the octave is the twelfth note above). The areas of the cross-sections at the octaves: $(2^{\frac{3}{4}})^2 = 2^{\frac{3}{2}} = \sqrt{8} =$ 2·83 to 1.

For string-toned stops, halving the diameter on the twentieth note is favoured; for many reeds the thirty-eighth pipe; for other fluework the seventeenth pipe.

Here are some simple examples:

	Diameter halves on	*Octave areas* Ratios
Flue	sixteenth pipe *above*[2] given note	2·83 to 1
	seventeenth pipe ,, ,, ,,	2·66 to 1
	twentieth pipe ,, ,, ,,	2·3 to 1
Reed	thirty-eighth pipe ,, ,, ,,	1·55 to 1

An easy way of calculating pipe diameters is demonstrated in the following example. Suppose that if the diameter of a CC pipe is 6 in. and the rank halves on its sixteenth pipe, it is required to find the diameter at AA the ninth note above CC.

$$\text{Required diameter} = \text{diameter at CC} \div 2^{\frac{9}{16}}$$
$$= 6 \div 2^{\frac{9}{16}} = 4{\cdot}1 \text{ in.}$$

If the logarithms of the diameters of a set of pipes, with uniform scaling, are plotted on graph paper as equi-distant vertical lines and the tops of these lines are joined, the slope of the straight line which results gives a measure of the manner in which the pipe scales "halve". Before the "factory-organ" of the nineteenth century became common, organ pipes were often made in the actual building in which they were later to speak. Thus the tone of the organ evolved by patient trial and error as well as by tradition and artistic experience in ecological adjustment with its surroundings. Immense time and care were given by organ-builders to all stages of this work, within the church itself. The scalings, which they used for their pipework, were ob-

[1] At Truro Cathedral the solo and choir organs are unenclosed, but in that resonant building it is difficult to realise this, because the solo tones seem to become louder as the melodies rise, and vice versa.

[2] i.e. the seventeenth note inclusive, giving sixteen semitone intervals (e.g. c to e).

tained empirically; and the blend which they secured was in keeping with the acoustics of the building and the response of the sensitive human ear. These were known as "mixed scalings".

TEMPERAMENT AND TUNING

The need for temperament in the tuning of a keyboard instrument, with the arrangement of black and white notes, which is found in the organ or piano, is readily seen when we think that twelve intervals of a tempered fifth make seven octaves. A pure fifth which does not produce beats between its two notes has a vibration ratio of 2 : 3 or $\frac{3}{2}$; the corresponding octave ratio is 1 : 2 or 2. But there is a difference between $(\frac{3}{2})^{12}$ and $(2)^7$, and this difference between twelve fifths and seven octaves is known as a Pythagorean *comma.* The fifths are slightly too sharp and thus, when the frequencies of the notes are not determined by the player and he has to accept the limitations of the twelve notes of the organ or pianoforte keyboard octave, each upward fifth must be narrowed or flattened slightly if the errors are to be distributed *proportionally* through the compass, and in every key. Such a scale is known as the equally tempered scale and in it only the octaves are in tune; every other interval, to a greater or lesser extent, is out of tune. It is universally adopted for the tuning of organs and pianofortes, though in practice some tuners tend to allow a slightly greater consonance to some of the major keys with few sharps or flats. This probably accounts for key-colour, a quality formerly said to be associated with different major or minor keys, e.g. the key of B major was said to be bright and hard, that of D♭ tender, noble and full of emotion. No doubt, a great deal of this was purely subjective associationism on the part of the listener. In an organ which has been tuned to real equal temperament, as well as is humanly possible, no key colour can be heard.

Again we could start at C and arrive at B♯ above it by going up three major thirds:

$$\left(\frac{5}{4}\right)^3, \text{ but } \left(\frac{5}{4}\right)^3 \left(= \frac{125}{64}, \text{ the interval of three major thirds}\right)$$

falls short of the octave ratio of 2, $\left(\frac{128}{64}\right)$

(The difference is known as a *diesis.*)

We can make a simple diatonic scale by taking C, E, G, with pure third and pure fifth and adding the dominant triad G, B, D, and the sub-dominant F, A, C; but other intervals, obtained by modulation, would be sadly out of tune. Moreover, the intervals of a second, C to D and F to G and A to B, are larger than the seconds D to E and G to A. With instruments where the performer has some control over the pitch of the notes which he is playing, but not in keyboard instruments, he modifies his intervals slightly to suit the nature of the melody which he is playing, and for purposes of modulation. At first sight it might appear that if, instead of the twelve notes of the present keyboard octave, it were possible to provide sufficient keys to give pure intervals in all keys, all difficulties of temperament would be solved (provided, of course, that the keyboard could be played). This is not the case, for successive modulation changes without the use of enharmonic changes (i.e. change of note without change of pitch) might commit the music to a continuous change of pitch as it progressed, and it is necessary, in most music, that a general pitch norm should persist throughout its performance.

Because of this, and in order to provide a keyboard which is convenient to play, and an octave which does not comprise too many pitches (and therefore pipes to each rank in an organ) the scale has to be tempered.[1]

The Mean-Tone Temperament

This temperament, or something approaching it, was employed in organs from medieval times and was used in England in many organs until nearly the end of the nineteenth century. Owing to the influence of Werckmeister in 1688 and John Sebastian Bach in the early eighteenth century, it was gradually abandoned for a system which was nearer to equal temperament. Pianos in England were tuned to mean-tone temperament until 1842, and the large organ at Liverpool City Hall was tuned to this temperament for a number of years after its opening in 1855 because of the insistence of S. S. Wesley. Many compositions such as Mendelssohn's first Sonata in F minor, Op. 65, could not be played on it. In the keys of B♭, F, C, G, D, and A major and G, D and A minor the effect of unenclosed great and choir organs was quite charming but would probably have seemed insipid to many people today.

In mean-tone temperament the major thirds are in tune, and the fifths are slightly narrow, and the differences between the major and minor seconds are smoothed out, which is the reason for the expression "mean-tone". The relative consonance of intervals in these keys has been secured at the cost of dreadful dissonances elsewhere. For instance, the differences between C, B♯ or D♭♭ have become great, the difference between A♭ (which is not provided by the scheme) and G♯ is considerable. The G♯ is nearly three-fifths of a semitone away from the just major third with C, and nearly one-third of a semitone from the just fifth with E♭. This interval, which hurts the ears even of the uninitiated, was known as the "wolf".

Equal Temperament

This is now almost universally employed in the pianoforte and organ, but owing to "rule of thumb" techniques of tuning, mathematical accuracy is not attained and many instruments still produce the perception of key-colour, which theoretically should not arise.[2] With this temperament only the octaves are in tune and every other interval has a constant pitch ratio according to its kind throughout the compass, i.e. the semitones are a twelfth part of the octave, the tones are twice the semitones, the major third four semitones, the fifth seven semitones.

[1] "Enharmonic organs", with more than twelve notes to the octave, are in the University of Edinburgh (McClure organ), the Teyler's Museum, Haarlem, Holland, and the Science Museum, South Kensington, London.

[2] The writer has shown that the phenomenon of key-colour does not appear when pure tones in a scale tuned perfectly to equal temperament are used. *Musical Times* (March 1934).

The pitches of each note can be determined logarithmically from a fixed C or other note as follows:

$$
\begin{aligned}
C &= N \times 2^{\frac{0}{12}} = 261{\cdot}62\\
C\sharp &= N \times 2^{\frac{1}{12}} = 277{\cdot}18\\
D &= N \times 2^{\frac{2}{12}} = 293{\cdot}66\\
D\sharp &= N \times 2^{\frac{3}{12}} = 311{\cdot}12\\
E &= N \times 2^{\frac{4}{12}} = 329{\cdot}63\\
F &= N \times 2^{\frac{5}{12}} = 349{\cdot}22\\
F\sharp &= N \times 2^{\frac{6}{12}} = 369{\cdot}99\\
G &= N \times 2^{\frac{7}{12}} = 391{\cdot}99\\
G\sharp &= N \times 2^{\frac{8}{12}} = 415{\cdot}30\\
A &= N \times 2^{\frac{9}{12}} = 440{\cdot}00\\
A\sharp &= N \times 2^{\frac{10}{12}} = 466{\cdot}16\\
B &= N \times 2^{\frac{11}{12}} = 493{\cdot}88\\
C^{1} &= N \times 2^{\frac{12}{12}} = 523{\cdot}25
\end{aligned}
$$

(where N is frequency of vibration of C).

With equal temperament the fifths are slightly narrow and the upward thirds are considerably "sharp", but unlimited modulation is possible, and (theoretically) intervals in all keys are equally mistuned. Equal temperament evolved slowly by the progressive widening of the thirds.

Tuning the Organ

Flue pipes are tuned by decreasing or increasing the effective length of the air column to secure sharpening or flattening respectively. Reed pipes can often be tuned in the same way, but the method of tuning depends on their particular type.

Stopped and half-stopped flue pipes are tuned by pushing down the stopper to sharpen them. Formerly open flue pipes were tuned by dilating the tops with a cone to sharpen them and closing the tops with a hollow cone to flatten. This practice still persists, and the pipes are damaged by a fraying of the tops and by breaking them at their feet. Cylindrical, open pipes should be fitted with short, hollow cylinders of metal, known as tuning slides, which can be knocked up or down to flatten or sharpen the pitch. Large pipes in the organ case have slots cut in their backs and they can be sharpened by pushing the metal at the bottom of the slot away from the pipe. Large open wood pipes have a piece of wood screwed at the back and top, so that it can be moved to cover or uncover a rectangular slit at the back. Sometimes small pipes have to be tuned at the mouth, but this should be avoided if it is at all possible. The ears at the sides of the mouth are opened out to sharpen the pipe and closed to flatten its pitch.

Frequently, the tuning of reeds is done by knocking down the tuning spring or wire to sharpen the note and knocking it up to flatten it, by means of a tool known as a "reed-knife". They can also be tuned by adjusting the effective speaking length of the tube or by opening or closing the cap or slot at the tops of pipes which are so fitted. It must be remembered that the tone and not only the pitch of a reed pipe, depends on the coupling of the tongue vibration with that of the pipe. Not infrequently, after a few years of unenlightened tuning, we find the reed-work of an organ badly out of regulation. The Willis chorus reed pipes were carefully cut to length when they were made. Some reed tongues are voiced so that they are susceptible to tuning at the spring. Tuners, particularly in badly-planned instruments, often do what is expedient instead of what is right. If reed tongues have been given a distributive curve they must be tuned at the slot.

An experienced tuner knows the difficulty of tuning and adjusting a large organ. If the instrument has been badly designed there is sometimes a tendency for one pipe to draw another in tune, or for changes of pitch to take place when many pipes are played together. Thus, a poor organ may sound terribly out of tune when chords are played with many stops drawn, but when it is tried, note by note, nothing appears to be wrong. An organ pipe is very sensitive to its surroundings; and, in addition, in old or poorly designed organs, there may not be enough wind at the pipe feet, when many stops are drawn.

Mixture stops are sometimes provided with separate sliders so that each rank may be tuned without interference from the others. Or small mops may be put in the pipes to silence them while the others are being tuned.

Mixture ranks should be tuned to give perfect intervals with their corresponding unison ranks.

Reed pipes are usually less sensitive to changes of temperature than flue pipes, but the latter, in spite of temperature fluctuations, stand in tune for longer periods. An organ tuned in a cold building will be found to be out of tune when the temperature rises. Some electric blowing-plants which are allowed to run for hours with very little use of wind, as happens when the organ is tuned, may progressively increase the temperature of the wind supplied to the instrument.

Usually the great-organ principal is first tuned as a rank, so that its notes have the correct absolute pitch and stand to one another in the relationship necessary to secure equal temperament. When an organ is made, a pitch pipe is provided so that, at any temperature, it will fix a pitch of a particular note of the instrument. Failing this, the organ should be tuned at a standard given temperature of about 60° F. with a standard tuning-fork having the 1939 pitch of A = 440 or its equivalent at some other note. The "bearings may be laid" by using fifths and octaves as follows: The octaves are tuned true, but the fifths slightly narrow. The "beating" of the fifths will be slightly less than one per second near middle C; and more, higher in the scale. When the principal is in tune as a rank, other flue ranks are tuned to it and finally the reeds are dealt with. In very large organs it is necessary to "lay the bearings" separately on several ranks, and a number of telephones are used to communicate with the man at the console. It must be added that fine regulation and tuning will make a great deal of difference to the apparent tone quality of the organ as a whole. Although very refined and experienced ears may be necessary to single out defects from a mass of tone, many others are able to realise that there are shortcomings in the general gestalt or mass-impression of an instrument of which the pipework needs regulating.

Schlick (Spiegel, 1511) says that fifths should be tuned slightly flat to accommodate the major thirds (in particular F-A, G-B♮, C-E), except G♯, which should be tuned to E♭. Thus the notes C♯ and A♭ must be avoided and transposition must be used. Schlick mentions transposition devices (clearly keyboards capable of a lateral movement).

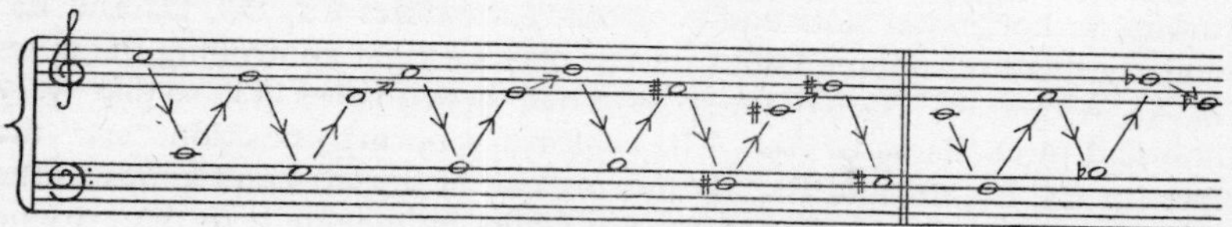

FIG. 18A. Tuning with fifths and octaves.

FIG. 18B. Tuning with fifths and fourths.

The change from mean-tone temperament in England came gradually. Although a system approaching equal temperament was introduced in 1846 by the pianoforte house of Broadwood, most tuners progressively widened the major thirds until, in 1869, the older temperament was finally abandoned. In the last decade of the nineteenth century there were still some parish church organs in England which had not been converted to equal-temperament tuning, although Snetzler's first English organs (*c.* 1747) were so tuned.

The mathematical problems of musical scales and temperament occupied the attention of the Trinity College "philosophers". It is not surprising that Robert Smith, the successor of Bentley in the Mastership of Trinity College, wrote a book entitled *Harmonics, or the Philosophy of Musical Sounds* (1749).

Bernard Smith, the organ-builder, had equipped two of his organs with "quarter notes", but only two such additional notes to each octave. "Doctor Smith's new principle" needed four additional notes to the octave in order to preserve reasonable consonance between the major intervals of the scale in all but the most remote keys.[1]

In 1768 a new organ was built for the Foundling Hospital, London, by Thomas Parker of Gray's Inn Lane at a cost of £670 "exclusive of the case" and "upon the new principle invented by the late Doctor Smith containing four additional notes to each octave".[2]

There were only two "demitones" on Father Smith's organ at the Temple Church and they provided additional notes of D♯ and A♭ which were played by separate black keys made by dividing the front of an ordinary black key from its rear portion. At the Foundling Hospital there were also additional

[1] Robert Smith described equal temperament "that inharmonious system of 12 hemitones which produces a harmony extremely coarse and disagreeable".

[2] It has often been stated by historians of music and frequently repeated elsewhere (e.g. Barton, *Textbook of Sound*) that this was the organ given by Handel, a governor of the hospital. Handel's organ was built by a "Doctor of Medicine", Justinian Morse, of Barnet in 1751, and was displaced by Parker's instrument.

sets of pipes for D♭ and A♯, so that there were sixteen notes and pipes to the octave. The supplementary tones at the Foundling Hospital were brought into service by an ingenious piece of mechanism which did not need alterations to the ordinary keyboards.

On the left hand of the player were three knobs, one for each manual, working in horizontal slots and controlling the notes C♯, D♭, D♯ and E♭. Similarly there were three knobs on the player's right controlling the notes G♯, A♭, A♯ and B♭. Each of the six slots had three notches in it, so that every knob had three places of rest. The central (or normal) position "set" the pipes for C♯, E♭, G♯ and B♭. By moving one of the left-hand knobs to the extreme left D♯ was substituted for E♭, whilst by moving it to the extreme right D♭ was substituted for C♯. In the same way, by moving one of the knobs on the right hand G♯ would become A♭, or B♭ could become A♯. The movement was outwards for sharps and inwards for flats, and each manual was under separate control. It is difficult for a modern listener, with ears blunted by equal temperament and thick unison stops, to imagine the beauty and clarity of organ pieces played on the transparent, rich mezzoforte of the old light wind diapason *choruses*, assisted in this case by intervals which were practically consonant. Gottfried Silbermann resisted the introduction of equal temperament because he believed that it would spoil the effect of his mixtures, cornets and mutation ranks which were tuned to just intervals. Hopkins traces the decline in mixture work in the nineteenth century to the progress of equal temperament as a method of tuning organs.

Beats in Tuning an Equally Tempered Scale

Fifths on 8-ft. rank:

A to E	7·6 in 10 sec.	Double for Principal 4-ft. e.g. A to E about 15 beats in 10 sec.
G♯ to D♯	7·15 ,, ,, ,,	
G to D	6·75 ,, ,, ,,	
F♯ to C♯	6·35 ,, ,, ,,	
F to middle C	6·00 ,, ,, ,,	

The pitch of a′ (the note in the second space of the treble clef) is taken as Standard International 1939, A = 440.

According to Ellis[1] the A frequencies of some organs of the past are as follows:

[1] A. Ellis, *History of Musical Pitch* (London, 1881). The deductions of Ellis have been challenged in some of his details, but there is no reason to doubt those which we have quoted here. See Arthur Mendel, "Pitch in the 16th and Early 17th Centuries", *The Musical Quarterly*, vol. xxxiv (1948), pp. 28, 199, 336, 575 et seq., and the section on Musical Pitch by the present author in *The Music Book* (Hinrichsen, 1952). The international standard A=440 is broadcast by the B.B.C. every evening before the start of the Third Programme.

The pitch of most of Gottfried Silbermann's organs was about half a tone higher than the present pitch of A=440: that of Arp Schnitger's ¾ of a tone. This was called Chorton (choir pitch). The Dresden and Zittau Silbermann organs were in kammerton (chamber pitch). In France the choir tone (ton de chapelle) was fixed in about the middle of the eighteenth century. The opera tone (opernton) varied and was sometimes a quarter or a half tone higher or lower than the choir tone. The

PLATE 27a.
An old spring chest at St. Cosmae, Stade

PLATE 27b.
The keyboards of the Compenius organ, 1610. At Fredericksborg near Copenhagen

PLATE 28a.

The Scherer-Schnitger organ at Cappel, North Germany.

PLATE 28b.

St. Magnus the Martyr, London Bridge. Original organ by Jordan, now by Spurden Rutt.

PLATE 29.

The old and new in Holland. *Left*, Oosthuizen, c.1530. *Right*, Doetinchem, Flentrop, 1952

PLATE 30

Two Austrian organs. The abbeys of Herzogenburg (*left*) and Heiligenkreuz (*right*)

M. Praetorius: suitable church pitch (1619). A = 424.
A. Schnitger: organs in Hamburg (*c.* 1688). A = 489.
Father B. Smith: low pitch at Hampton Court Palace (1690). A = 442.
Renatus Harris (1690) and S. Green (*c.* 1790): organs. A = 428.
G. Silbermann (1720) and Spanish organs (eighteenth century). A = 415 to 420 (chamber-tone).
Cavaillé-Coll (1859): Ste. Clotilde, Paris. A=444.

Strasbourg organs by Andreas Silbermann were tuned to this opera tone which was half a tone lower than the choir tone. The chamber tone of Gottfried at the Catholic Court Church in Dresden is $\frac{1}{4}$ tone lower than the usual chamber tone. The additional lower note in the "chamber-toned" organs cost more in tin than most of the rest of the organ pipe-work. This is said to have caused Zacharius Hildebrand to die of worry when he was building the organ in the Church of the Three Kings in Dresden Neustadt. Silbermann was the first to build large organs in kammerton. Contius's (Cunzius's) Halle organ (1716) had a transposing device.

The higher pitches of the cheaper organs were not considered ideal, but resulted from the necessity of saving the expense of tin for the large pipes.

CHAPTER X

THE TONAL STRUCTURE OF THE ORGAN

"*And even things without life, giving sound, whether pipe or harp, except they give a distinction in the sounds, how shall it be known what is piped or harped*" (1 Corinthians xiv. 7).

AN ORGAN is not merely a collection of beautifully voiced stops: it must show unity in its separate divisions and unity in the whole of its tonal structure.

Enough has been said in the historical portion of this work, in particular the chapter on the baroque organ and the accompanying specifications which will be found in the appendix, to show that the organ of the sixteenth to the eighteenth centuries was properly supplied with choruses of flue tone on two, three or four manuals and on the pedals. Loudness was not sought by adding 8-ft. ranks together and finally by swamping everything with unison reeds. The sensation of loudness, when necessary, was produced by spreading the acoustic energy amongst ranks of different pitches. The 8-ft. diapason rank was not the norm of tone, but the open flue chorus was the chief tonal attribute of the instrument. Reeds were used for adding colour and brilliance and, in the Silbermann organs, a greater definition to the pedal organs. The tonal structure of many British and American organs has suffered because of the romantic-orchestral movement of the later nineteenth and early twentieth centuries, which overlooked the true nature of the instrument with its choruses, its tonal "pyramids" and its wealth of quiet mixtures, mutations and low-pressure reeds. In the hands of a Willis or a Cavaillé-Coll the organ still remained a musical instrument, in spite of the break with tradition, but with Hope-Jones, on both sides of the Atlantic, it became a feeble imitation of the orchestra.

Much lost ground has still to be made up and some prejudice overcome before we can hear again, as a commonplace, in our cathedrals and churches the classical music of the organ as it should sound. This does not mean that we should strip the instrument of all the examples of progress in reed and flue voicing which have appeared in the last century, but it does require that even in a small instrument there should be choruses on two manuals and a more versatile and independent pedal organ.

The twentieth-century British organ is deficient in brilliances. The brilliances of its swell- and great-organ choruses soon become tiring and are often destructive of classical organ music. The study of the seventeenth- and eighteenth-century organs has reminded us of the musical qualities that are inherent in reed and flue stops on low wind pressures.

Nevertheless, in spite of the decadence of the early twentieth century, both in England and elsewhere, it would be unwise to throw away the remarkable achievements of the nineteenth century in England, France and Germany. The beautiful flue choruses on the great organs made by Walker, Willis, Hill, Gray and Davison, and others of lesser fame, still represent some of the most attractive aural experiences of the discerning musician. The fine chorus reeds of the Willis firm; the solo reeds of Willis and Cavaillé-Coll; the soft string tones of Thynne, Walker, Pendlebury, Schulze, Willis and others; the fine wood basses of Schulze, Pendlebury and Binns; and the soft flue work of Schulze, Harrison and almost every other organ-builder of note, are not to be cast aside foolishly. Moreover, the magnificence of the conception of the organ on a grand plan, evinced in the work of Cavaillé-Coll, Lewis, Willis, Hill and Schulze, is something which must largely remain our envy because of present-day expense, but it is certainly an ideal at which to aim. It must be remembered that many organs, which are claimed as the work of rebuilders, have retained the majestic conception and layout of the original structures.

We still have a number of old organs remaining to us, and when the reconstruction of these has to be considered it is fervently to be hoped that any pipework which is still usable will be retained in the rebuilt instrument. Tin, which should be a chief ingredient of pipe metal, is now exceedingly expensive, and the modern organ-builder has often to do the best he can with inferior metal. Some of the eighteenth- and nineteenth-century pipework was of almost pure tin, and today this represents a considerable sum of money in material. When an organ is rebuilt as an extension instrument the owner should assure himself that valuable pipework is not removed and replaced by coupling mechanism. It should be remembered that only the pipes of the organ are heard and all the elaborate console fittings will not add more voices to the instrument. Unfortunately, some old pipework cannot be used in rebuilt organs because it has been ruined by years of tuning or excessive nicking. All pipes of open metal above 4-ft. C should be fitted with tuning slides.

The Great Organ

The nucleus of a great organ in the English style is its diapason chorus. In order of importance, in a scheme of minimum type, the stops would be open diapason, octave or principal, fifteenth, double diapason (or, less preferably, bourdon), mixture of three ranks, twelfth. On all small two-manual organs it would be necessary to add (but not as a part of the diapason chorus) a quiet unison stop or two, such as a dulciana, a claribel flute and a 4-ft. gemshorn or harmonic flute. If a reed is added to a small great organ it should be a trumpet, which will complete the brilliance of the division, and not a tromba of close-tone which pulls down the mean of brilliance when it is added. Some judgment is required here, for many organists would like to have a great reed which shows tonal contrast to that on the swell organ, and one which could be used for tuba effects. A close-toned reed will not blend with a bright diapason chorus, and we do not recommend one. The lack of resources in the average large English great organ is soon apparent when the problems concerning *mf* choral accompaniment and the playing of classical organ music arise. There should be a secondary great organ with a proper harmonic structure of its own, capable of giving a quiet brilliance. This lack of a varied and quiet brilliance is a failing of the average English organ, and it is not to be remedied by the mere provision of a handful of soft flute-toned mutation stops on the choir organ, useful as these are. Both John Compton and the present Henry Willis have been alive to this shortcoming and have gone far to remedy it in their more recent instruments. A secondary diapason chorus, on a separate sound-board so that it could be played with the great organ, if necessary, and from the choir manual, as a contrast to the larger chorus, would be very valuable. This would permit a much better interpretation of the works of Bach than is possible on most organs at present in England. Where the positive organ is asked for, as in the Fugue in E flat by Bach, the swell fluework (or what is worse, the full swell organ with the box closed) and the usual choir-organ flue stops are not suitable for this purpose. There are some divided great organs in England, for example at Norwich Cathedral, and their value is readily apparent. There will be no need for divided great organs when adequate positive organs are provided.

Swell Organ

The full swell organ, as introduced by the first Henry Willis, is a unique organ effect and should not be dispensed with. It has something in common with the tone of the récit of the larger Cavaillé-Coll instrument, but here the reeds are of a different quality. Willis perceived, in the early fifties of last century, that the incomparable effect of the full swell organ was due principally to a double chorus reed and a mixture of bright tone. An early example of this appeared in the organ at Wallasey Church, Cheshire, England. At St. Paul's Cathedral the peerless effect of the full swell organ is due to the chorus reeds used with the mixture; and the rest of the fluework can be put in without the loss of effect. (It ought to be added that the swell organ is very shallow from back to front and is backed by the solid stone piers of the cathedral. The swell shutters are actuated by the "infinite speed and gradation" swell mechanism invented by the Willis firm and this adds to the effectiveness of the crescendo.)

It is doubtful whether the tonal structure of the quieter part of the swell organ, as made by Henry Willis, has yet been improved. He used restful and mild string tones and sometimes a vox angelica of the same type of tone. The lieblich gedeckts were firm and bright, and the diapasons were free from the sharp and cutting tone which is often found under the name of geigen or violin diapason. It is a pity that so many organ-builders have added very keen string tone to swell organs, as this does not blend with the rest of the fluework. The value of a swell bourdon is as near to zero as can be found in an organ stop. Often its function is entirely negative, because it only serves to thicken and to clog the tones of the other stops that are drawn. On the other hand, on an open sound-board it might make a stop of some utility for use on the pedal organ, although even here a very quiet dulciana might be more effective.

Ideally, a swell-box, its shutters and its pipe ranks contained within should be so designed that, when the box is slowly opened, the tone should seem to become brighter with comparative little increase in the ground tone, but with a gradual addition of harmonics. This is Nature's way of making a crescendo, and it is rarely simulated in a swell organ. When 8-ft. tone, which is not sufficiently bright, is subjected to a crescendo by means of swell shutters there is always the sense of the subjective flattening as there is when "close" tromba tone is added to bright fluework. The uncertainty of pitch of a choir or congregation, which is being accompanied on a swell organ, with much swell-pedalling, is well known, and is cured as soon as the organist transfers to the bright tone of an unenclosed choir or great organ.

Choir Organ

The English choir organ, with its small but sound design in the seventeenth and early eighteenth centuries, was forgotten when the swell organ became the second manual in the two-manual schemes of the nineteenth century. When a third manual was provided it tended to control a hotch-potch collection of quiet flue stops and a solo reed or two. All attempts at a tonal structure on the choir organ were abandoned, except in the largest instruments. Certainly it was no longer a worthy successor to the fine rückpositiv sections of the Renaissance and Baroque periods; and when its pipes were placed in a swell-box its shortcomings were often even more apparent.

The choir organ would be more useful if it could contain, as in the old positives, a small, quiet, open-flue chorus, some flutes with flute and gemshorn mutations and some quasi-imitative reeds. If there is no solo organ it could control quiet solo reeds and the tuba. Sometimes the great-organ tromba is borrowed for use as a solo reed and made playable on the choir. When this is done its tone should not be stifled in a belief that it will then serve a dual capacity. Its primary function is to complete the great-organ chorus, and its tone should not be spoilt in an endeavour to adapt it for other purposes. The artistic value of the close-toned powerful tuba is very slight at its best, and negative at its worst.

The Solo and Bombarde Organs

The bombarde manual was known in France before the Revolution and controlled one or more loud reeds. Usually, this manual could be coupled to the pedals so that a penetrating reed tone was available to mark out a slow cantus firmus. The bombarde organ was developed by Cavaillé-Coll as a reed section. In the largest British organs, after the First World War, the bombarde organ, as at Liverpool Cathedral, was a tuba organ with a powerful mixture. It could be added to the great organ for special effects or used in contrast to the full great-organ chorus.

Sometimes the bombarde organ is combined with the solo organ. The latter is a nineteenth-century development and originally consisted of a few unrelated solo voices. The typical early Willis solo organ would consist of clarinet, orchestral oboe, harmonic flute and tuba. In the larger twentieth-century organs, the solo organ was often made to contain choruses of keen string-toned stops and sets of mutation stops, which could be used for synthesising new tones. In addition, developments in voicing have produced beautiful new tones such as the French horn. Large solo organs, well equipped with orchestral tones, were a feature of the Harrison organs of the early twentieth century.

Echo Organ

An echo organ must be considered a luxury. It should be a separate small organ playable from two manuals and pedals, placed at some distance from the main instrument and voiced with the utmost refinement. It is a mistake to make an echo organ of 8-ft. stops only; it should have a proper chorus of low-pressure stops as at Doncaster Parish or at St. Bartholomew's Church, Armley (although these examples are not detached from the main instruments). The addition of a percussion stop to the resources of an echo organ enhances its effect. The celestial organ at Westminster Abbey, in the triforium above Handel's tomb, was a charming section, in effect a two-manual and pedal organ playable from the main console.[1] When the tonal resources of an organ are planned, an echo organ will take a very low priority.

The Pedal Organ

It was a far cry from the magnificent pedal organs of the seventeenth century in the north German organs to the single octaves of pedal pipes which were so often the only representatives of separate pedal tonal resources in nineteenth-century English organs. Henry Willis provided adequate independent pedal organs in his large instruments, such as those at the City Hall, Liverpool, and the Albert Hall, London. In the second half of the century, Holdich, Jones, Walker and Hill in England, Roosevelt and others in America, were making reasonably adequate pedal divisions. Even the symphonic German and French organs had fairly good equipment, although there was a tendency to think of the pedal organ solely as a bass provider for the manual-stop combinations; and the melodic aspect of the pedal, which was so evident in Baroque organs, was overlooked.

A suitable pedal organ, for a moderate-sized instrument, should have an adequate number of 16-ft. and 8-ft. ranks of flue tone, a loud or moderately loud reed and a softer reed in 16-ft. and 8-ft. pitch which can be obtained by borrowing from the manuals. Large pedal pipes, whether flue or reed, are now exceedingly expensive, and it will be found, on most modern large organs, that their numbers are not great in comparison with those of the rest of the instrument. 16-ft. ranks are often extended upwards to 8-ft. pitch, 4-ft. pitch and even 2-ft. pitch and downwards to 32-ft. pitch (or by the coupling of quint pipes are used to give 32-ft. acoustic tone). In addition, every available manual 16-ft. stop on a separate sound-board is available for borrowing on the pedals. Thus a pedal scheme which looks very impressive on paper is obtained by extension from a few ranks and by borrowing from the manuals. As the extension of pedal stops does not usually produce the missing notes which are apparent in extension or octave coupling on the manuals, it is not ideal, but is often the best which can be done because of exigencies of finance and the availability of materials and space. All derivations

[1] At the time of writing this book this part of the organ is not connected up.

A CLASSIFICATION OF ORGAN STOPS ACCORDING TO THE PIPE-WIDTHS

	Very narrow	*Narrow*	*Normal*	*Wide*	*Very wide*
			Flue Stops		
Open	Aeoline	Cello	Bauerflöte	Doppelflöte	Blockflöte
	Cymbel	Dulciana	Bassflute	Flageolet	Nachthorn
	Dolce	Flachflöte	Choralbass	Gemshorn	Cor de nuit
	Harmonika	Fugara	Contrabass	Glöckleinton	
	Viola	Gamba	Open flute	Hohlflöte	
	Violin	Geigen		Jubalflöte	
	Viol	Harfenprincipal	Octave	Gross-Mixture	
	Vox Célestes	Holzflöte	Open Diapason	Cornet	
		Mixture	Principal	Kupferflöte	
		Piccolo	Schw(i)egel	(Copper flute)	
		Salicional	Sifflöte	Nasard	
				Italian principal	
		Schweizerflöte	Spitzflöte	Traverse (Quer) flute	
		Spitzgamba		Rauschpfeife	
		Violflöte		Sesquialtera	
				Starkflöte	
		Violon		Tertian	
		Scharff		Waldflöte	

A CLASSIFICATION OF ORGAN STOPS, ACCORDING TO THE PIPE-WIDTHS—*contd.*

	Very narrow	*Narrow*	*Normal*	*Wide*	*Very wide*
Stopped	Fernflöte Zartflöte Zauberflöte	Liebl. gedackt Quintade Singend gedackt	Stopped diapason Gedacktpommer Spitzgedackt	Bourdon Untersatz Subbass	
Half-stopped		Rohrquintade Spillflöte	Rohrflöte Rohr gedackt	Koppelflöte	
			Reed Stops		
Cylindrical bodies	Geigendregal Krummhorn Kopregal (Knop) Rankett Sordun	Dulcian	Clarinet	Zink	
Tapered bodies		Bombarde English horn Fagotto Oboe Schalmei	Trumpet (Tuba)	Field Trumpet Horn Posaune (Tuba)	
Cone-shaped body with tubes		Cornet Musette Bärpfeife			

should be clearly marked on the stop knobs. Pedal organs should have proper flue choruses at two or more powers, reed tone and solo flutes and reeds of 4-ft. pitch for the playing of chorale preludes. The chief weakness of most British pedal organs of the twentieth century is the indefinite effect of too much bourdon and open-wood tone. A quiet violone 16-ft. and a louder metal contra-bass 16-ft. will go far to remedy this. The old German pedal organs were as clear and precise in tone as that of the great organ. Ideally, the pedal organ should be able to establish a definite melodic line, without the use of the great-to-pedal coupler, against the full fluework of the great organ.

Real 32-ft. tone, while it should add great fullness and depth to the other pedal flue stops, should not be too loud for use with the quiet swell-organ stops. An acoustic-bass, made by adding a bourdon at an interval of a fifth to an open wood stop, can never yield this subtle effect; but where acoustic conditions are helpful it might be tolerable in combination with other stops. Mr. Compton's acoustic cubes with polyphone devices (i.e. a number of orifices capable of control by pallets to give separate notes) yield real 32-ft. tone of no great power. Valve oscillators and loudspeakers have been used to augment pedal tone, but usually these only serve to reveal the superiority of the real pipework.

The principles which we have discussed are illustrated in the organ specifications printed in the appendix and it is not necessary to give any further examples here.

A Glossary of Organ Stops

Acoustic bass (harmonic bass). A device whereby a resultant 32-ft. effect is obtained by playing a 16-ft. open pedal stop with a corresponding fifth rank usually obtained from bourdon pipes. The tones, first discovered by Sorge, a German organist, later became well known as "Tartini's tones" and were used by the Abt Vogler (q.v.) in his "economical" methods of organ-building. The two generators of each differential tone are usually too loud, and the resulting 32-ft effect lacks the subtlety of the genuine stop. Sometimes the effect is obtained from a single rank of bourdon pipes by taking the note of the interval of a fifth above or a fourth below the given note which is to be "quinted". The effect is usually not good and tends to destroy the clarity of the pedal line.

Acuta. Latin: acutus = sharp; German: akuta, scharf. A sharp mixture (q.v.).

Aelodicon (Greek). A free reed stop of 16-ft. pitch. (Example: the Walcker organ at Riga Cathedral.)

Aeoline. Latin: aeolina; German: äoline; French: éoline. Usually a small-scaled flue stop of the gamba class with delicate intonation. Occasionally in German organs it is a soft free-reed stop.

Aequale. A unison or principal stop. 8 ft.

Apfelregal. An old stop of the regal or "schnarrwerk" class with a globular or apple-shaped resonator.

Baarpijp. In Dutch organs this appears as a flue-stop of gemshorn type.

This may be a false derivation from bauerpfeife (peasant flute), or it may come from the Dutch baar (= bright).

Bärpfeife. A "bear-pipe". A regal of gruff sound.

Bachflöte. A gemshorn (q.v.).

Baryton. A tenor vox humana, or an old type of tenor viola (viola di bordone).

Bass. In general, the prefix bass refers to the 16-ft. version of a stop which is normally found in unison pitch, e.g. bass tuba or bass clarinet. Bass flute, on the contrary, is usually of 8-ft. pitch.

Basset-horn. See Corno di bassetto.

Bassflute. In British organs it is usually an 8-ft. upward extension of the pedal bourdon. Occasionally, it is an open wood flute of 8-ft. pitch. The German name for this stop is Flötenbass.

Bassoon. Italian: fagotto; French: basson; German: fagott; Spanish: bajon. A small-scaled reed stop intended to imitate the tone of the orchestral instrument. In French organs it is often regarded as the bass of the hautbois and a single 8-ft. rank then appears as basson-hautbois. The favourite pitch of this stop in English organs is 16 ft. and it is usually called fagotto or contra-fagotto. It is used as a solo stop, a quiet pedal reed or the double reed of a small swell organ. As a solo stop it has a dry but not unpleasant effect. Berlioz says that the orchestral instrument "tends towards the grotesque—the character of its high notes is somewhat painful". Handel uses it to produce an eerie, cadaverous effect in the Witch of Endor episode in *Saul*.

Bauerflöte, *bauernflöte* (German: peasant flute). A stopped flute of 8-ft., 4-ft., 2-ft., or 1-ft. pitch. It is found in German organs of the last two and a half centuries. It is sometimes used as a part of a chorus of "gedeckt" stops.

Bell-diapason. French: flûte à pavillon. A stop invented in France and introduced into England at the 1851 Exhibition. A flaring cone is soldered to the end of the cylindrical tubes of the diapason pipes. The tone is really that of a loud flute. Willis used such a stop in the Albert Hall (London) organ in 1871.

Bell-gamba. A small-scaled string toned stop. A bell or open cone is soldered to the top of the cylindrical tubes. The stop is obsolete, as it gives considerable trouble in making and voicing it; but good examples have an attractive, soft intonation said to resemble that of the old viola da gamba. The stop was a favourite of the Bevington firm.

Bifara (*piffaro*). An open stop with two mouths, so arranged that a "célestes" or tremulant effect is produced by the beating of the slightly different notes of each mouth. Walcker made the stop of two ranks of single-mouthed pipes: an 8-ft. gedeckt and a soft 4-ft. string tone. Now, such a stop would hardly be considered a justifiable way of "tying up" two pipe ranks.

Blockflöte (German). See Recorder.

Bombarde. (1) A section or manual division of an organ containing powerful chorus reeds and usually mixtures. (2) A loud reed stop of 16 ft. usually found in pedal organs. The stop is popular in France, and Cavaillé-Coll used four bombardes in both the organs at Notre Dame and St. Sulpice in Paris. The bombarde derives its name from the mediaeval reed instrument which was probably the forerunner of the fagotto. The organ bombarde is usually much louder than might be expected in the case of any stop related to the more quiet fagotto.

Bombardon. A pedal stop of 16-ft. or 32-ft. pitch with a tone quality between those of the bombarde and bassoon.

Bourdon (French); Italian: bordone; German: bordun or brummbass (bourdonner = French: to buzz). Usually stopped 16-ft. pipes of wood playable from the pedals. In many small British organs it is the only 16-ft. rank of pipes available and often is extended upwards to give bass flute 8 ft. In spite of its ubiquity, its droning tone quickly becomes monotonous. When it is not skilfully voiced it commences its speech with a transient harmonic (twelfth), which is irritating and unmusical. The stop is sometimes made in 32-ft. pitch, for use both on the pedal and in large great organs. Manual bourdons of small scale under the name of lieblich bourdons are frequently found in British organs of the last century. As swell-organ stops, their use is very limited, and for such a purpose they are omitted by enlightened organ-builders. Metal bourdons of 8-ft. pitch, of slightly fuller tone and larger scale than the usual gedeckt, were used by Cavaillé-Coll in his "swell" divisions and are good stops for combining with others of soft intonation. For wooden bourdons, a scale has to be chosen so that the pipes do not, on the one hand, produce a windy, muddy tone and, on the other, one in which the odd numbered harmonics are too prominent. The large-scale bourdons known as Hayne's-tubs (after Dr. L. G. Hayne, a precentor of Eton College, *c.* 1870) are not now made. The largest pipe of a 16-ft. bourdon made by Lewis for the Public Hall, Glasgow, was 5⅛ in. in width and 6⅜ in. in depth, with a mouth 3⅞ in. in height and a square-cut upper lip $\frac{11}{16}$ in. in thickness. The largest pipe of Schulze's lieblich bourdon 16 ft., at Hindley, near Wigan, England, has a rectangular section 3⅜ in. by 5 in., with a mouth 3¾ in. high. The bourdon is also popular as a quiet, great-organ double stop, whence it is often derived to the pedals.

Bazuin. A stop found in Dutch organs of 32-ft. or 16-ft. pitch of posaune quality.

Bratsche (German = Viola).

Buccina. An obsolete name for the posaune (q.v.)

Calcant (German: tread). A signal or bell for the organ-blower ("bellows-treader").

Campana (Italian). German: glöcklein. A stop of 1-ft. or 6-in. pitch, repeating at every octave, intending to suggest the sound of bells when it is combined with other stops. The stop is also called campanelli (Walcker), campanette and campanilla (Spain).

Bryceson used such a stop (1-ft. pitch) in the Church of St. Paul at Rusthall, Kent, in 1876. High-pitched mutation stops would now be used for obtaining soft bell-like effects, if these were needed.

Carillon. (1) A mixture, usually of three ranks (octave, fifth and third sounding, the last being kept fairly prominent), to suggest the clang of bells. A good example is found on the Cavaillé-Coll organ at Manchester Town Hall. Such effects are now synthesised by the use of appropriate mutation stops. (2) A set of tubular bells struck by hammers which are worked by the pneumatic or electric action of the organ. (Example, the organ at the Albert Hall, Nottingham.)

Cart. Anglicised form of quarte (de nasard) used by Renatus Harris.

Celesta. A series of metal plates or tuning-forks usually of 4-ft. pitch. They are struck by hammers worked by pneumatic or electric action.

Céleste (French). See Voix céleste.

Celestina. A soft open wood flute of 4-ft. pitch invented by William Hill of London. Willis used metal pipes of somewhat louder tone in his organ at the Albert Hall, 1872.

Chalumeau (French). German: schalmei; English: shawm. A soft-toned reed stop supposed to imitate the old shawm, a forerunner of the clarinet. The stop would blend with and colour up fluework, and this is not usually possible with the modern clarinet. The stop is not often found in modern British organs, but its use is becoming general elsewhere.

Chamade (French). A name applied to reed stops to show that their tubes are laid horizontally. In Spain the loud reed pipes project fanwise horizontally from the case of the organ. In France the trompette en chamade is usually contained within the organ case.

Chimney-flute. French: flûte à cheminée; German: rohrflöte (q.v.).

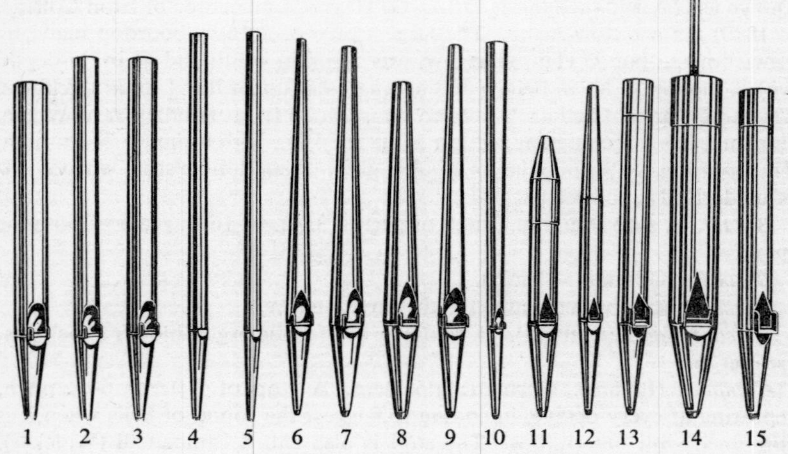

FIG. 19. Baroque Organ Pipes.

From left to right: 1. Nachthorn. 2. Schwiegel. 3. Sifflöte. 4. Querflöte. 5. Schweizerpfeife. 6. Spitzflöte. 7. Blockflöte. 8. Gemshorn. 9. Flachflöte. 10. Dulcianflöte. 11. Koppelflöte. 12. Spillflöte. 13. Quintade. 14. Rohrflöte. 15 Gedackt Pommer.

Choral bass. A flue pedal stop of open pipes of fairly powerful intonation and usually of 4-ft. or 2-ft. pitch. In German organs it is used for solo purposes, e.g. to sustain the melodic line in a choral prelude.

Cinq (Dutch). See Zinck.

Clairon (French). A reed stop of large scale and 4-ft. pitch. The octave of the trompette. Called Clarion in British organs.

Clarabella. An open wood stop of 8-ft. pitch commonly found on the great divisions of small organs. The stop was invented by J. C. Bishop of London about 1840 and was often used in his organs. The tone of the clarabella is full and sweeter than the German hohlflöte. It should not be mixed with diapason tone. It makes a good unenclosed solo voice in the tenor and upper parts of the compass.

Claribel flute. A stop of 4-ft. (or 8-ft.) pitch used by Henry Willis in his great organs. Willis made the stop of metal from middle C and harmonic above G. He left some beautiful specimens.

Clarinet. A favourite solo reed stop in British organs. The resonators are cylindrical. The stop is usually found in the choir or solo divisions. Sometimes the stop, as bass clarinet, is made in 16-ft. pitch and is also playable from the pedals. The stop is often quite imitative of some aspects of its orchestral prototype, but the tone of the best Willis corno di bassetto is usually fuller and richer and gives a better imitation of the orchestral instrument in its chalumeau register. The stop is very useful for solo work, and occasionally it has been used as a double reed in small swell organs. See also Labial clarinet.

Clarinet flute. A flue stop of interesting tone but not of wide application. It was sometimes made by Gray and Davison in London and Estey in America. An overblown gedeckt of small scale, with a "beard", produces a tone, rich in the odd harmonics, which has a reedy quality.

Clarion mixture. A powerful mixture stop designed by Walker to stand in place of a great-organ clarion reed. There were two examples in the Church of Holy Trinity, Sloane Square, London.

Clear flute. German: hellflöte. An open wood stop of 4-ft. pitch. This indefinite name was first introduced by Jardine of Manchester.

Compensationsmixtur. A German stop invented by Wilke, an organist of Neu-Ruppin. It was a compound stop intended to overcome any tendency to dullness in the flue stops of a pedal organ by adding suitable harmonics. The stop has not had a wide application.

Concert flute. See Orchestral flute.

Contra. A prefix applied to organ-stop names to indicate that the pitch is 16-ft. in the manual or 32 ft. in the pedal.

Contrabass. French: contrebass. A fairly powerful, open flue-pedal stop of metal or wood in 16-ft., imitating as closely as possible the tone of the double-bass. The stop is found in many French organs such as those at the Madeleine and St. Sulpice, Paris. When it is well-made the stop is remarkably definite in tone and has something of the magnificent "bite" of the stringed instrument. It has been used by the present Henry Willis, as in the organ at St. Paul's Cathedral, and it gives remarkable definition to the pedal fluework.

If it could displace the rolling "open wood" of the English cathedral organ of a generation ago, an increase in the musical potentialities of the instrument would result.

Coppel, koppel, copel. A clear-toned open, metal flute, often made with inward-tapered tops to cylindrical bodies. The stop was frequently found in baroque and post-baroque German and Austrian organs. It was intended to be a binder of the tones of other stops or an 8-ft. fundamental on which to erect "tonal pyramids" with mutation ranks.

Copula (Latin). A coupler.

Cor Anglais. Italian: corno inglese; English: English horn. The stop is usually called cor anglais in British organs. It is a reed stop of 8-ft. pitch. In England and America it is made with beating reeds, but in Germany and France free reeds have been used. The stop is of metal, of narrow scale, and at the end there is a "bell", made from two truncated cones of metal, in imitation of the orchestral instrument. When it is well made it is a beautiful solo voice with a suggestion of the tender melancholy of the orchestral instrument, used by Franck and Dvorak in the soft movements of their symphonies. It is possible to synthesise, to a certain extent, a cor anglais tone by using the choir-organ 4-ft. flute, nazard and tierce. Other constituents of such tones may be found by experiment on sufficiently large organs.

Cordedain. A quiet flute stop of 4-ft. pitch used in some of A. Silbermann's organs.

Cor de nuit (French). German: nachthorn. (Usually called cor de nuit in English organs.) An open or closed flue stop of wide scale, usually of 8-ft., but sometimes of 4-ft. and 2-ft. pitch. When it is well made, its tone has an attractive, quiet reediness, although it is a flue stop. A poor cor de nuit has a tone not different from that of a dull 8-ft. bourdon. An example of a good cor de nuit is to be heard in the altar organ at St. Paul's Cathedral, London. (Henry Willis III.)

Cormorne (French). A reed stop of 8-ft. pitch which was very useful for solo and combination purposes in the positiv divisions of French Baroque organs. The name has been spelt cromorne, crumhorn, cromhorne, crommehorne, etc.; but later builders, such as Cavaillé-Coll, labelled the stop "cromorne" as though the name were a corruption of krummhorn. The cromorne was a true organ voice and as such it is a pity that it has tended to become obsolete. It is probable that the word krummhorn is derived from crooked horn. The krummhorn is amongst the oldest of organ tones: a small-scale clarinet of penetrating tone.

Cornet (see also Mixture stops). The cornet is a compound stop which has been known abroad for five centuries and in England since the Restoration of the Monarchy. The stop was originally made with wide scale-pipes of a metal which contained a large percentage of lead. The dull tones of the individual ranks coalesced to give a composite reedy tone, the brilliance of which, usually not great, varied with the number and type of voicing of the ranks. The cornet was not used with the clear tones of the "principal chorus" of narrow scale, but was classed with the "wide" or "female" stops and was used for solo purposes either alone or in combination.

In Smith's organ (1684) at the Temple Church, London, there were two cornets, and Harris frequently used it in his own organs. The German and French traditions of organ music and organ playing were unknown in England, and in the eighteenth century the cornet was much abused. Rambling "original compositions for the organ", known as cornet voluntaries, which used the stop as a solo, became popular. The cornet was placed on a separate wind-chest above the main great organ. Then it was known as the mounted cornet.

Usually, the composition of the cornet was maintained throughout the compass, though sometimes it was a short compass stop or had a sesquialtera bass. It consisted of 8-ft., 4-ft., $2\frac{2}{3}$-ft., 2-ft., $1\frac{3}{5}$-ft. ranks, but sometimes the 8-ft. rank was omitted and at other times the harmonic series was carried to more acute pitches. The old cornet was useful in playing the melodies of the chorales. In the nineteenth century its nature and purpose were not understood. Sometimes it was used to cover up the breaks in the diapason mixtures, which was not its proper function. Again, it was made of diapason or small-

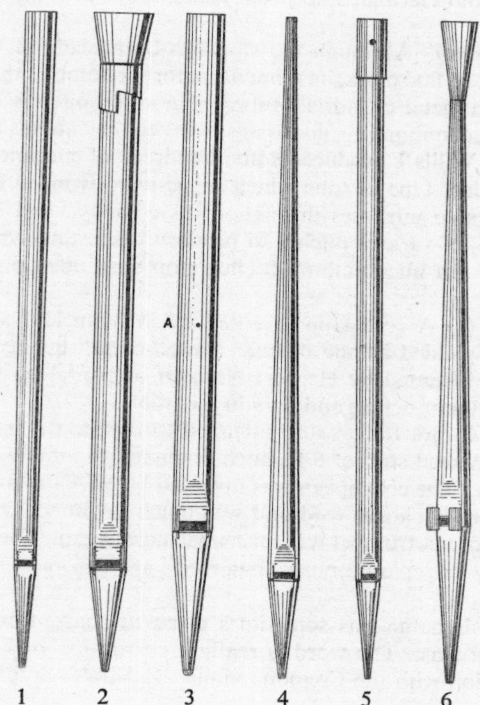

FIG. 20. Flue Pipes.

1 Dolcan. 2. Horn diapason. 3. Flûte Harmonique (Hole at A). 4. Gemshorn. 5. Keraulophon. 6. Bell Gamba.

scaled pipes as "harmonics" or as a second mixture. The choir-organ mixture, made from dulciana pipes, and including third-sounding ranks, is sometimes called echo-cornet. It is better to have a proper small-scaled choir mixture of octave and fifth-sounding, and to split the cornet into its separate mutation ranks.

A dulciana cornet (five ranks):

CC to BB	19	22	24	26	29
C to B	12	15	17	19	22
c^1 to b^1	8	12	17	19	22
c^2 to c^4	1	8	10	12	15

Compound stops of the viol class are usually called cornets de viols.

The real organ cornet is returning to the neo-classical organs now being built in America, France and Germany. Cornets on both the great organ and the positive are necessary for the correct performances of the organ music of the sixteenth, seventeenth and eighteenth centuries.

Cornett. An old German solo pedal reed stop of penetrating tone in 4-ft. or 2-ft. pitches.

Corno di bassetto. Although the stop has been made in Germany from small-scaled closed flue pipes, its more usual form resembles that of a clarinet, a reed stop with metal cylindrical tubes. The usual pitch is 8 ft., but 16-ft. stops are not uncommon in solo organs, whence they are also derived to the pedals. Henry Willis I produced some hundreds of specimens of this stop with a rich clarinet type of tone which suggested a wooden tube. The stop is excellent for solo purposes throughout its compass, and it will combine with other stops of various pitches to produce interesting synthetic tones.

Corno dolce. An uncommon 8-ft. flue stop with open pipes of outward taper.

Corno flute. (1) A reed stop invented by William Hill. It had wooden resonators and yielded a tone of quiet "swell-oboe" quality. (2) An open metal flue stop invented by Herbert Norman of Norwich. Its quality was horn-like in the tenor octave and fluty in the treble.

Cornamusa. A rare Italian stop intended to imitate the bagpipes.

Cornopean. A reed stop of 8-ft. pitch, intended to imitate the tone of the cornet à pistons. The cornopean was invented by William Hill. It became a popular swell-organ chorus reed and was much favoured by Willis. Sometimes the swell-organ trumpet was misnamed cornopean. The tone should be thin and brassy in separate notes, but reedy and resonant when played in chords.

Cremona. This name was sometimes given to coarse-toned clarinets on English great organs. The word is really a corruption of krummhorn and has no connection with the Cremona violin. Example: Smith's organ at the Temple Church.

Cromorne (French). German: krummhorn. See Cormorne.

Cymbale. A high-pitched mixture of octave- and fifth-sounding ranks and breaking at every octave. It adds considerable further brilliance to the full fluework of a great organ. Excellent examples by Willis are found on the organ at St. Paul's Cathedral, London. A cymbale should blend with and add brilliance to the chorus reeds of the organ. (See Zymbel.)

A cymbale (seven ranks):

CC to BB	15	19	22	26	29	33	36
C to B	12	15	19	22	26	29	33
c^1 to b^1	8	12	15	19	22	26	29
c^2 to b^2	1	5	8	12	15	19	22
c^3 to c^4	Double	1	5	8	12	15	19

Cymbelstern (German: Cymbal-star). An old German organ stop of the sixteenth, seventeenth and eighteenth centuries. A gilded wooden star, to which small bells or jingles were attached at its points, was caused to revolve when the stop was drawn. The famous Weingarten organ (q.v.) contained such a device. Sometimes the bells were tuned to give C″, g″, c‴ etc.

Decima (Italian). A tierce or tenth, $3\frac{1}{5}$ ft.

Diapason (Greek. διαπασῶν = from first to the last note).

"Through all the compass of the notes it ran,
The Diapason closing full in man."

(Dryden: "Song for St. Cecilia's Day.")

The nearest equivalents are the German prinzipal, the Italian principale and the French montre (show pipes), but the tones of the English nineteenth-century diapasons by Walker, Hill, Gray and Davison are quite distinct from these European unison ranks of open pipes. In old English organ-music the word "diapasons" meant the 8-ft. open and stopped diapasons.

The characteristic tone of the English organ is that of a chorus of diapasons. Diapason tone is neither that of the flute on the one hand nor that of the string-toned stop on the other. A blend of these two last types yields a composite type of tone, but it is not that of the true diapason. The French montres, the pipes of which often form part of the casework of the instrument, are not true diapasons, and the German prinzipal is usually harder in tone quality than the English stop. Nevertheless there are many varieties of diapasons to be found in British organs, whether of the present or the past two or three centuries. If an organ is to have one stop, that stop will be a diapason of 8-ft. pitch, but this does not imply that the 8-ft diapasons are the most important stops on larger organs. The 8-ft. diapasons should be regarded as parts of larger choruses, in which there is blend and no outstanding voice, and a properly balanced relationship with the rest of the instrument. There has been an unfortunate tendency to regard the tone of diapasons and diapason choruses almost as ends in themselves and not means of making music. A loud, brilliant diapason chorus, released in chords, has a thrilling and highly emotional effect on many people, but always it must be considered in relation to the playing of organ-music and the accompaniment of church services.

There are eight rough divisions of diapason tone which may be given as follows:[1]

[1] This is adapted from the classifications made by the Rev. Noel Bonavia-Hunt, M.A., who has devoted a long life to the study of organ tone; in particular, the diapasons.

Early German and English.
Baroque German and French.
Nineteenth-century German.
Nineteenth-century English.
Nineteenth-century French.
Geigen diapasons.
English and American "foundation" type.
Specially treated twentieth-century types.

Diapason pipe diameters in inches; ratio 1: $\sqrt{8}$, halving on seventeenth pipe:

	CC	C	c^1	c^2	c^3	c^4
Large scale	6·60	3·93	2·33	1·39	·82	·49
	6·32	3·76	2·23	1·33	·79	·47
Medium scale	6·06	3·6	2·14	1·27	·76	·45
	5·56	3·3	1·96	1·16	·69	·41
Small scale	5·10	3·03	1·80	1·07	·64	·38

Bonavia-Hunt[1] gives the following details concerning diapasons by E. Schulze with $\frac{2}{7}$ mouth (i.e. mouth width: circumference of pipe) and "cut-up" 1 in 5 (i.e. ratio of height to width of mouth), except at Leeds:

	Diam. at CC	*Tenor C*	*Mid. C*
Parish Churches at Tyne Dock and Leeds	No.1. $6\frac{1}{4}$ in.	$3\frac{3}{4}$ in.	$2\frac{1}{4}$ in.
St. Bartholomew's, Armley, Leeds	No. 1 (wood-bass)	$3\frac{3}{8}$ in.	$2\frac{1}{8}$ in.
St. Peter's, Hindley, Lancs.	No. 1. (wood-bass)	$3\frac{1}{4}$ in.	2 in.
St. George's, Doncaster	No. 2.	$3\frac{1}{4}$ in.	$2\frac{1}{4}$ in.

Hill's nineteenth-century diapasons had thicker languids than the old English diapasons, a low cut-up and small footholes. Bonavia-Hunt suggests that the top lip should be burnished and the footholes enlarged, but there were quieter diapasons which were eminently musical, and when they were considered as a part of a diapason chorus they were very satisfactory. Of course, more power than they gave is required in large buildings, especially if there is lusty congregational singing. It should be kept in mind that where this is so the massed voices in themselves produce large volumes of 8-ft. tone.

Of the "early" German and English pipework (i.e. sixteenth and seventeenth centuries), Bonavia-Hunt gives the following notes:

The wind pressure was not often more than $2\frac{1}{2}$ in. There were thin, obtuse-angled languids and a cut-up not greater than 1 in 5, with a mouth not less than a quarter of the pipe diameter. The nicking was shallow and the lips were vertical. The tone was singing and refined. The diapasons of Green were beautiful, but far too light for subsequent tastes.

Bonavia-Hunt gives the following method of calculating the diameters

[1] N. Bonavia-Hunt, *The Modern British Organ* (London, 1948).

of the lowest octave of a diapason. Take the diameter at tenor C and increase it by $\frac{1}{8}$ in. to G♯ and thence by $\frac{1}{4}$ in. to CC; e.g.:

T.C.	B	A♯	A	G♯	G	F♯	F	E	D♯	D	C♯	CC
$3\frac{1}{2}''$	$3\frac{5}{8}''$	$3\frac{3}{4}''$	$3\frac{7}{8}''$	$4''$	$4\frac{1}{4}''$	$4\frac{1}{2}''$	$4\frac{3}{4}''$	$5''$	$5\frac{1}{4}''$	$5\frac{1}{2}''$	$5\frac{3}{4}''$	$6''$

A simple graphical method with a logarithmic curve can be used to graduate the increases in diameter. The same authority suggests that a suitable scale for a 16-ft. zinc pipe (i.e. the bottom note of a pedal metal open diapason) is 10 in., with a $\frac{2}{9}$ mouth. Nevertheless, it must be remembered that the principal choruses of the old masters, such as Schnitger, were made by using mixed scaling. The uniform scaling generally is associated with the romantic organ and the influence of Töpfer.

Diapason phonon. A very powerful diapason made by leathering the upper lip of a thick metal, large-scale open stop and increasing the wind pressure. The stop is associated with the name of Hope-Jones. It is difficult to think that it has any artistic value.

Diaphone. A valvular reed, invented by Blackett and Howden and developed by Hope-Jones, and of more use as a fog horn, for which it is valuable, than as a voice in the organ. Nevertheless, when it was improved and refined by John Compton, it had some value as a powerful and pervading pedal stop, and as a smooth horn-like tone on the manuals. It was used to a considerable extent in cinema organs, where a few ranks of pipes on fairly heavy wind-pressure were extended to many pitches.

Dolcan, Dolkan. An open metal stop with a slight outward taper. It has a quiet charm, and is useful both as a soft accompanimental register and for *pp* solo effects. The stop was known in the sixteenth century and was the precursor of the modern cylindrical dulciana.

Dolce. A soft and sweet-toned stop favoured by nineteenth-century German organ-builders, and made both with small-scaled pipes and with those that were slightly tapered outwards. Sometimes the stop has a string tone, but it is better to make it so that it has a gentle, horn quality. Although Snetzler occasionally used the stop in his English organs, it is rarely found now in its true form; and those stops that are labelled dolce in modern instruments usually have a soft tone of no particular character.

Donner. A thunder effect in German organs, made by playing some of the large bass pipes together.

Doppelflöte. A large-scale, open flute with two mouths opposite to one another. The stop has a full musical tone, is not easy to make and is not often found in England. It was frequently made by Roosevelt in America, and a fine specimen by Henry Willis III is found in the organ at Liverpool Cathedral.

Doppelkegel-Regal. 8 ft. and 4 ft. on manual and 2 ft. on pedal. A regal with a double-cone (i.e. barrel-shaped) resonator.

Double. When it is used as an adjective, the word usually means the 16-ft. version of an 8-ft. manual stop or the 32-ft. version of a stop which is normally thought of as a 16-ft. pedal stop. Thus a double-clarinet is a 16-ft. manual stop and a double open diapason is a 32-ft. pedal stop.

Doublette. A French, open-flue stop of 2-ft. pitch on the manuals, and in European organs sometimes found as a 4-ft. stop on the pedals. Willis used it in the organ at St. George's Hall, Liverpool, in both 2-ft. and 1-ft. pitches.

Dudelsack (German = bagpipes). A regal of musette tone.

Dulcet. An octave dulciana of quiet tone and of 4-ft. pitch. The stop was a favourite with the English organ-builder, Green, who liked tones of soft and refined intonation.

Dulcian (*dolcian, dulzian*). A soft reed stop found on both manual and pedals in German organs of the last four centuries. The tone is not unlike that of the bassoon; and the small-scaled resonators are usually made of wood.

Dulciana. A very popular stop in British organs. It was first used in England in Snetzler's organ at King's Lynn. The stop, as made by Willis, was a soft and refined open diapason of small scale, but many organ-builders give it a slightly nasal or string quality. It is of frequent occurrence on the great organs of two-manual instruments and on the choir organs of larger instruments. The best English dulcianas have a sweet, silvery and cantabile quality.

Dulciana pipe scales, diameters in inches:

CC	C	c^1	c^2	c^3	c^4	
3·25	2·05	1·29	·81	·51	·32	ratio 1:2·519
3·38	2·13	1·34	·84	·53	·33	
3·34	2·05	1·25	·77	·47	·29	ratio 1:2·66
3·48	2·13	1·31	·80	·49	·30	

Dulciana flute. A small-scaled metal open stop with a pronounced flute quality in its soft voice.

Dulciana mixture. A soft compound stop formed of dulciana pipes and often found on choir organs or on the swell organs of smaller instruments.

Dulciana Principal. A soft principal made by S. Green.

Dulcimer. A percussion stop used by Thomas Schwarbrook in the organ at the Church of St. Michael, Coventry, in 1733. The device was removed in 1763 because of the "difficulty of keeping the strings in tune".

Dulzflöte; dulcianflöte 8 ft. A dulciana with outward taper and quiet string tone.

Dulzgedackt 8 ft. and 4 ft. A metal stop which tapers outwards towards the top and is closed with a metal canister, which is sometimes fitted with a chimney. This useful construction has been used in Germanic countries and more recently in America.

Duodecima (Latin). A quint or twelfth $2\frac{2}{3}$-ft.

Echo. This word, when it is used before that of a stop name, usually implies a softer version of a more common register; e.g. echo bourdon, echo dulciana, echo gamba, etc. The word is also applied to a whole manual division. Formerly, the distant effect was produced by enclosing the stops of this section in a box which was permanently closed, but now it usually refers to a distant swell organ of quiet stops placed at some distance from the main instrument.

English horn. See Cor anglais.

Erzähler. A stop invented by E. M. Skinner of America in 1904. It is of gemshorn type, and was so-called because "it had a pleasant garrulousness".

Euphone, Euphonium. A reed stop of 8-ft. or of 16-ft. pitch intended to imitate the tone of the brass instrument of the same name. The German organ-builders made the stop with free reeds: its tone should be open, smooth and full.

Fagotto. See Bassoon. It is not infrequently found on English organs as a double swell reed under the name of contra fagotto.

Feldflöte, Feldpfeife. An assertive, open-flue stop with a penetrating tone. It is not often made now, and there are no regrets at its departure from organ specifications.

Fernflöte (German: distant or echo flute). A small-scaled quiet flute. The Schulze example at St. Mary's, Tyne Dock, is of spitzflöte type. A modern example is found on the altar organ at St. Paul's Cathedral, London.

Fifteenth, superoctave. A 2-ft. pitch stop of open-diapason pipes on the great organ and 4-ft. on the pedals. The fifteenth is a part of the diapason chorus of the organ.

Flachflöte. A German stop of 8 ft., 4 ft., and 2 ft., of wood or metal, and made of small-scaled, cylindrical or conical pipes. The stop was frequently found in the northern German organs of the seventeenth century, when it was sometimes made with shallow wooden pipes. Hence the name "flat-flute".

Flageolet. A medium-scaled metal flue stop of 2-ft. or 1-ft. pitch. The tone should be liquid, clear and penetrating. Sometimes the name is given to the piccolo, but the flageolet should have a softer tone. Often both the fifteenth and the piccolo are too loud, except for use with fairly full combinations.

Flautino (Italian). An even quieter stop than the flageolet, found in 4-ft. and, more rarely, 2-ft. pitch.

Flauto (Italian). This word for a flute usually has attached to it a fanciful word, e.g. amabile, amoroso, dolce, traverso, etc.

Flügelhorn. A large-scaled 8-ft. reed stop, which has a full, round tone. (Flügel = winged).

Flûte bouchée harmonique. A stop of zauberflöte type made by Rushworth and Dreaper.

Flûte à cheminée (French). English: chimney flute; German: rohrflöte (q.v.).

Flûte conique. See Spitzflöte.

Flûte harmonique. A stop invented by Cavaillé-Coll in his early days and first used in his organ at St. Denis Abbey, near Paris. The principle of the stop seems to have been known to Praetorius (1619). In a moderate-scale open metal pipe, a hole is bored half-way along the cylindrical tube. The chief tone yielded by such pipes is the octave or first harmonic, and the quality of the note is full and satisfying. The stop at once became popular and was used by Willis, sometimes to the extent of three such registers in quite small organs of as many manuals. The harmonic principle can also be applied to closed pipes, but the hole is then made at a distance of two-thirds or three-fifths of the way along the pipe tube. Although the stop has for many years been a favourite on the great organs of the English instrument, care must be taken to see that it is not allowed to disturb the purity of the diapason chorus. It is useful as a solo stop.

Flûte à pavillon. A large-scale metal flue stop of 8-ft. pitch with cylindrical bodies surmounted by inverted conical bells or pavillons. The stop was first introduced into England at the 1851 Exhibition by the French builder Ducroquet, and it quickly became popular. It is not often made now, but is occasionally found in French and English organs of a generation ago. In England it is sometimes called bell diapason. The tone of the stop is that of a combination of diapason and flute with a suspicion of reediness in its voice.

Fourniture (French). English: furniture. We have already dealt with the origin of this stop (p. 50). The furniture is a mixture stop of octave- and fifth-sounding ranks, which may be added to the diapason or reed chorus when extreme brightness is desired. The stop was found in the larger organs by both Cavaillé-Coll and by Willis in the nineteenth century, but then there were third-sounding ranks.

French horn. Only in the present century has the French horn shown any real resemblance to its orchestral prototype. In the eighteenth and nineteenth centuries the stop might produce almost any reed tone, from that of a regal to that of a small trumpet. E. M. Skinner of America devised a high-pressure reed stop with filled-in shallots and thick tongues, which gave a remarkable imitation of the orchestral instrument in its quieter moods. Even the "bubble" at initiation has been copied, and it is difficult to believe, on hearing the stop, that its sounds are really produced by reeds. Some excellent examples have been made by Henry Willis III and Harrison in Britain. (See Horn.)

Fugara.[1] An open wood or metal stop of 8-ft. or 4-ft. pitch of rather indefinite tone, half string and half reed, which is often found in German organs. It was frequently made by the firm of Walcker.

Full mixture. A powerful, compound stop belonging to the diapason chorus and made from octave- and fifth-sounding ranks.

Gamba (Italian). French: gambe; German: gambe. Although this is one of the most common stop names, and is very often found in the smallest of organs, it is a curious corruption of viola da gamba—a viol held between the legs. The stop should be made of small-scaled metal pipes of good metal, which contains a very large proportion of tin. The older German stops were slow of speech, but the modern stop can be voiced with a harmonic-bridge at the mouth and an amplifier at the top, so that it does not need the help of another flue stop to ensure prompt speech.

Gambette (French). An octave gambe.

Gedampftregal (German). A muted regal.

Gedeckt (German). A covered (stopped) pipe. After the appearance of the Schulze examples at the 1851 Exhibition, the lieblich gedeckt (sometimes spelt gedact or gedackt) tended to displace the old English stopped diapason. This was not an unmixed blessing, for the sweet tones of the smaller-scaled German stops, though very beautiful in themselves, did not have the general utility of the earlier English stops. Gedeckts are found in all pitches from 32 ft. to 2 ft. and are made both from wood and from metal. There are

[1] Fujara (Bohemian)=hirtenflöte: a shepherd's pipe of reedy tone.

various patterns, e.g. rohrgedeckt, with perforated stoppers and a subtle tone with prominent twelfth and seventeenth harmonics; kleingedeckt (a 4-ft. stop of quiet tone), grob or grossgedeckt, stillgedeckt, etc.

Gedecktbommer or *gedecktpommer*. A gedeckt which is so overblown that the twelfth is very prominent in its voice. An example of the stop is found in the Görlitz organ made by Casparini in the year 1703. Sometimes the stop has been called quintaton, and the beautiful pipes made by Thynne and called Zauberflöte are of this class, though the Baroque stop is of different quality.

Geigen (German: a violin). Geigenprincipal, geigenprinzipal: violin diapason. An open metal stop of scale and treatment half-way between that of a diapason and a gamba. The stop, which is singularly effective as a swell-organ diapason, has a rich, stringy diapason tone which blends well with both the flue- and reed-work of the swell organ. The scale of the stop at CC would be between 4 in. and 5½ in. It has sometimes been used as a second great-organ diapason on English organs, and in Europe it is not infrequently one of the unison stops of the chief manual of a large organ. An enclosed family of geigen stops is of considerable utility in the swell division of a large organ.

Gemshorn (German: a goat-horn). French: cor de chamois. An open stop usually of metal, with pipes which have a taper inwards towards their tops. They are conical in form when made of metal and pyramidal when of wood. The gemshorn is usually of 8-ft. or of 4-ft. pitch in America and England, but in German instruments it is sometimes found as a 16-ft. pedal stop, and recently Skinner of America has made some 32-ft. examples: in Holland it appears as a 2-ft. flute. The stop is sometimes used as a 4-ft. swell-organ stop, and Henry Willis III used it as a great-organ stop of this pitch in preference to a second principal in his "model" organ. The stop has a beautiful tone when it has been properly made: the composition of its harmonics varies with the degree of taper and other factors in its voicing. Audsley[1] gives the following scale for a gemshorn:

CC pipe 4·96 in. at the mouth and 1·62 in. at the top
C pipe 3·13 ,, ,, ,, ,, ,, 1·02 ,, ,, ,, ,,
c[1] pipe 1·90 ,, ,, ,, ,, ,, 0·64 ,, ,, ,, ,,

In a large organ, a family of gemshorns is a most desirable addition to the tonal resources of the instrument.

Gemsrohrflöte, 8 ft., 4 ft. and 2⅔ ft. or 2 ft. A chimney flute with a tapering chimney. The tone is piquant and interesting.

Glockenspiel (German). French: carillon; Italian: campanella. A mechanical stop formed of dish-shaped bells, spiral rods, steel bars or bell-metal tubes sounded by a hammer action.

Glockleinton (German = little bells). A two-rank compound stop, 2 ft. and 1 ft.

Grand. Prefix applied to (1) organ, meaning great-organ section or chief organ (French); and (2) to single stops, meaning (*a*) of large scale, e.g. grand open diapason, or (*b*) of 16-ft. compass on the manuals or 32-ft. on the pedals,

[1] G. A. Audsley, *Organ Stops* (New York, 1921).

e.g. grand cornet, a set of harmonics belonging to the 16-ft. series or grand bourdon, a pedal 32-ft. bourdon.

Gravissima (Latin). A 64-ft. stop made by using the differential tones generated by playing a quint rank 21⅓-ft. pitch with a stop of 32 ft. pitch. The resultant tones so made have no separate musical existence, but add a little to the depth of the full diapason chorus of a very large organ. The former organ at Bremen Cathedral by J. F. Schulze had such a stop, and the device was used by Hope-Jones in his organ at Worcester Cathedral and by Willis at Liverpool Cathedral.

Grob or *gross*. As a prefix before a stop name, it refers to (*a*) a stop of large scale or (*b*) a 16-ft. version of a stop more usually found in 8-ft. pitch.

Halbprinzipal (German). A half principal, that is, a 4-ft. open stop. The German principal was of 8-ft. pitch, and the equivalent English stop was the diapason. English organ-builders omitted the prefix halb and called the 4-ft. stop, illogically, principal. The more correct term, octave, is now replacing the word principal for the major 4-ft. rank on larger British organs.

Harfenprinzipal (German). A small-scaled open stop usually made of tin, giving a "dry", string tone which is intended to imitate the tone of the plucked harp strings. An echo geigen.

Harfpfeife, 8 ft. A stop with a delicate salicional-type of tone. The small-scaled pipes have a slight inward taper towards the top. Cf. Sylvestrina.

Harmonia aetheria (Greek). A small or echo mixture of small-scaled pipes sometimes found in German organs. The ranks, which do not break, are twelfth, fifteenth and seventeenth, or twelfth and seventeenth. There is a two-rank example by Schulze in the organ at Doncaster Parish Church, and the firm of Walcker made a number of examples in Germany earlier in the century.

Harmonic. See also Flûte harmonique. Used as an adjective to qualify the name of an organ stop, the word usually refers to a pipe body which is twice (or a larger multiple of) the length of the pipe as it speaks normally. When the harmonic principle is applied to flue stops the formation of nodes is assisted by boring small holes at appropriate distances along the pipe body. In reed stops the hole is not necessary as the considerable energy of the reed blown by high-pressure air will cause the air column to break up into vibrating segments. The tone of harmonic stops is richer and fuller than those of ordinary construction but the blending capacities are sometimes impaired.

Harmonic bass. See Acoustic bass.

Harmonica, harmonika. An open flue stop of small scale, usually of wood, and so voiced that its tone is a delicate combination of flute and string. Schulze left specimens in the organs at St. Bartholomew's Church, Armley, Leeds, and at Doncaster Parish Church. The stop occurs fairly frequently in organs of German make, and is sometimes the softest stop in the instrument. A suitable scale for square pipes (internal widths) is:

CC	C	c^1	c^2	c^3	c^4
2·84	1·74	1·06	·65	·40	·25

(halving on the eighteenth pipe) and with a wind pressure of only 1½ in. to 2½ in.

Harmonics. A mixture stop intended to reinforce the natural harmonics of the diapasons. The composition of the stop varies with different builders, but contains third and flat-seventh sounding ranks as well as octaves and fifths. The ranks are open and of small scale and the thirds and flat sevenths need careful adjusting. The stop is a modern, and usually not very successful, attempt to limit the number of compound stops on a great organ.

Harp. This is not a true organ stop, but is sometimes made as a percussion stop for large organs. Bars of wood or metal placed over hollow resonators are struck by hammers worked by pneumatic or electro-pneumatic action. An early attempt to put percussion stops of this type on organs was that of Thomas Schwarbrook, who fitted the organ at St. Michael's Church, Coventry, with string stops, harp, lute and dulcimer (probably with harpsichord action), in 1733.

Hautboy. French: hautbois; Italian and German: oboe. The stop has been popular in British organs during the last half-century or more as the swell reed of small organs. Its tone varies from organ to organ, and no attempt was made to imitate the orchestral oboe, unless the stop was labelled orchestral oboe, in which case it was usually found in the solo or choir organ. The hautboy, as made by Henry Willis III is a small-scaled metal conical reed stop with a smooth yet telling tone and is admirable as a quiet solo. With octave couplers and a 4-ft. principal or small mixture it may give "miniature full swell" effects. The stop does not usually blend well with other 8-ft. flue stops, and it is much abused by organists. If only one reed is available for a swell organ it is better for it to be made so that it inclines to trumpet tone. In England, the stop is made as a striking reed, but in France and Germany it is sometimes a free reed. Its tone is then reminiscent of that of a well-made reed organ or harmonium. No sweeping statement can be made concerning the tone of the so-called organ oboe, but we have heard very unmusical effects produced by attempts to combine some specimens of this stop with 8 ft. flue stops.

Hellflöte. A bright or clear flute.

Hohlflöte, hohlpfeife (German). French: flûte creuse; Dutch: holfluit, holpijp. A hollow-toned flute, made in 16-ft., 8-ft., 4-ft., and 2-ft. pitch, properly of open, wooden pipes of moderate scale. A family of such stops exists on the organ at Liverpool Cathedral. The stop blends quite well, but a good diapason should not need its help. It is popular in English great organs, instead of the clarabella or claribel flute. The tone should be full, and slightly dull, but it should have no suspicion of coarseness in its voice.[1]

Hohlschelle (German: hollow bell). A now obsolete German stop of the quintaton type (q.v.).

Horn. The old orchestral horn stop made by Harris in 1724 for St. Dionis Backchurch and in 1730 by Bridge for Christ Church, Spitalfields (both in London), were stops of trumpet quality but with a certain stifling of the tone caused by the use of thick metal tongues and partially closed tubes. The orchestral horn is best copied, as far as is possible, in its quieter moods. On English and American organs it is then usually labelled French horn (q.v.).

[1] Not to be confused with holzprinzipal—a wood diapason.

E. M. Skinner of America, who was remarkably successful with his French horn, gives the following data [Tenor C pipe]:

Length of resonator=3 ft. $3\frac{1}{2}$ in.
Internal diameter at top=$1\frac{9}{16}$ in.
Length of reed from underside of block=$2\frac{3}{16}$ in.
Width of tongue at free end=$\frac{7}{16}$ in.
Width of tongue at block=$\frac{7}{32}$ in.

The reed shallot is of closed form, its perforation being about $1\frac{3}{16}$ in. long, commencing about $\frac{3}{8}$ in. from the lower end. The wind pressure is 12 in.; in other specimens this varies from 8 in. to 50 in. It is an effective solo organ stop when it is carefully voiced.

Horn diapason. An open diapason stop of moderate scale, in the tubes of which at the top and back are cut slots. (Not all diapasons so treated are called horn diapason.) A hard quality of diapason tone results and this is said to have good blending properties. It is impossible to know what type of tone to expect when one is confronted with such a stop name, commonly found in Messrs. Walker's swell and great organs of the late nineteenth century. Some of the diapasons of Henry Willis I were slotted, as were the montres of Cavaillé-Coll, but doubtless the intention of this was to secure good blend with their reed stops.

Hornlein or *Hornle.* A two-rank compound stop: 2 ft. and $1\frac{3}{5}$ ft. or $1\frac{3}{5}$ ft. and 1 ft.

Italian principal. A large-scale open stop of 8-ft. pitch and of diapason-flute tone.

Jubalflöte. An open flue stop of 8-ft. or 4-ft. pitch, occasionally found in German organs. It is found in 8-ft. or 4-ft. pitches on the celebrated early eighteenth-century organ at the Church of SS. Peter and Paul, Goerlitz, made by Casparini.

Jungfernregal (German). An old regal of soft tone in 8-ft. and 4-ft. pitch. A member of the schnarrwerk class.

Kälberregal. An old regal stop with a tone like that of a lowing calf (hence the name).

Keraulophone (from the Greek κέρας = a horn, and αὐλός = a pipe or flute). A flue stop of quiet tone improved by Gray and Davison and first used by them in 1843 in their organ at St. Paul's, Knightsbridge, London. The name was applied occasionally to reed and flue stops in German organs in the late eighteenth century. Samuel Green made a flue stop of this name for the Heaton Hall organ. The stop is made of cylindrical pipes of medium scale and is fitted with a perforated tuning-slide. If it is true to its name, the stop is a quiet flute with a slight reedy intonation. It is not likely that new examples of the stop would now be made.

Kinura (Greek: κινύρα = a harp). A very small-scaled reed stop rather like a thin orchestral oboe in tone, made by Hope-Jones. The stop cannot be recommended for general use.

Klein (German: small). Applied as an adjective to imply small-scaled or 4-ft. pitch versions of other organ stops, e.g. kleingedeckt, kleinflöte.

Knopfregal (German: knob-regal). An old regal with small spherical resonators.

Kopf Trompete (German). Cor anglais (q.v.).

Koppel. See Coppel.

Krummhorn. See Cormorne.

Kutzialflöte. An open flute of 4-ft., 2-ft., or 1-ft. (and rarely 1⅓-ft.) pitches, sometimes found in German organs at the beginning of the nineteenth century.

Labial klarinette, 8 ft. A flue stop whose pipes have double-barrel shape with a constriction or waist in the middle of the tube.

Larigot (French. From l'arigot: a flageolet). A mutation stop, usually of flute tone, useful for synthetic tone-building. Its pitch is 1⅓ ft. on the manuals and 2⅔ ft. on the pedals. It is of some antiquity in France and was first used in England in 1670 by Renatus Harris in the organ of St. Sepulchre's, Holborn (Snow Hill), London. It is a most useful ingredient of synthetic solo tones and gives a "piquant" flavour to other soft tones. A stop of this pitch is known as nineteenth or in Italian organs decima nona, but then the pipes are open. The stop was called Largo in the Brustwerk of the organ at St. Paul's University Church in Leipzig in Bach's time.

Lieblich (German: lovely). An adjective, applied usually to stopped flute stops, used to indicate that their tone is particularly sweet. The lieblichflöte, lieblich gedeckt, lieblich bourdon are of smaller scale and softer tone than the respective flute, stopped diapason and bourdon.

Lieblich gedeckt (*gedackt*, *gedact*) (German). A soft, sweet-toned stopped diapason which became popular in England after Schulze exhibited his organ at the Exhibition in 1851. The stop has never lost its popularity in British swell organs; families of such stops were made by Lewis for his larger choir organs. The stop is made of wood or metal, or of metal with wooden stoppers.

Schulze's 8-ft. stop in the choir organ at the Church of St. Peter, Hindley, near Wigan, England, has the following measurements (ratio 1:2·66):

	CC	C	c^1	c^2	c^3	c^4
Width	2·13	1·31	·80	·49	·30	·20
Depth	3·08	1·89	1·15	·71	·43	·27

Audsley[1] says: "The height of the mouth is an important factor in the production of the lieblich gedeckt tone. In no case should it be less than half its width in height, while it may with advantage exceed its width in height, as in the stop in the swell of the Hindley organ, the CC pipe of which has a mouth 2⅛ in. wide and 2¼ in. high. The thickness of the upper lip is another factor in the production of satisfactory tone. This may vary in the CC pipe, from ¼ in. to ½ in. (the thicker lip producing the smoother tone) and be cut square or have carefully rounded edges: and the lip may be straight or arched. Pipes having mouths of so great a height in proportion to width require a copious supply of wind, desirably of moderate pressure, for their proper speed. The manual stop should speak on wind of 3½ in. and the pedal stop on wind of from 4 to 5 in." (See also Gedeckt.)

[1] G. A. Audsley, *Organ Stops* (New York, 1921), p. 181.

Lleno (Spanish). A mixture.

Locatio (*Lokatio*) (Latin = distributed). Name for mixture in the fifteenth and sixteenth centuries.

Lochgedackt (German = perforated gedackt 4 ft. or 2 ft.). A very wide-scale metal gedackt, with a hole punched in the top of the canister at the top. The stop is used on both manual and pedal. The tone is not unlike that of a nachthorn.

Lute. See Dulcimer.

Major bass. A bourdon of 32-ft. sometimes known as untersatz or grand bourdon. In England it is sometimes a 16-ft. open wood stop.

Meerflöte (German). See Unda maris.

Melodia. A large-scale open stop of 8-ft. pitch. The stop has poor blending properties, but is a favourite in earlier twentieth-century American and Canadian organs as a full-toned flue solo stop. Now such stops are not often made. The term is applied to a moderate-scaled open flue stop of normal design.

Messingregal (German). An old German regal stop which was supposed to suggest the tone of brass instruments, and hence it derives its name.

Mixture. German: mixtur; Italian: ripieno; Spanish: lleno. The mixture was originally that part of the great-organ flue chorus which was left when ranks of lower pitch were separated from it. The medieval organ could be regarded as one large mixture. Today the word mixture is sometimes misused. A mixture should consist of octave and fifth-sounding ranks with suitably contrived breaks in the ranks when it is no longer feasible to carry such small pipes upwards to the end of the compass. (This, of course, is not the only reason for the breaks, as the mixture has different functions in different parts of the compass.) A well-equipped organ will have mixtures on three manuals and the pedals at least. Mixtures supply to an organ a tonal quality in the chorus which can be obtained in no other way and is peculiar to the instrument. Mixtures have been misunderstood and abused in England for nearly one and a half centuries and it is only in recent years in Britain and the U.S.A. that their nature and function as an essential part of even a small organ have been grasped. The loud screaming voices of so many of the nineteenth-century mixtures in cheap commercial organs culminated in the final heresy of Hope-Jones who swept them away from his organs and thereby took away from the organ its main distinguishing feature, that of a proper chorus of open flue pipes.

True mixtures should not contain third-sounding or ranks other than those sounding octaves and fifths.

Mixture with five ranks:

Break	I	II	III	IV	V
1. CC to BB	19	22	26	29	33
2. C to B	15	19	22	26	29
3. c^1 to b^1	12	15	19	22	26
4. c^2 to b^2	8	12	15	19	22
5. c^3 to c^4	1	8	12	15	19

Mixtures may be made of many degrees of power, and a good selection of compound stops should be found in large organs.

Mixtures: (*a*) Are a part of the harmonic content of the flue choruses of the organ.
(*b*) Can be used to give *depth* to the trebles, brilliance in the middle of the compass, and definition to the bass.
(*c*) Spread the acoustic energy and, when properly made, give an impression of power without loudness.
(*d*) Act as a complement to other upper ranks and compound stops.
(*e*) Act as a bridge between the fluework and chorus reedwork of the organ, binding the whole tone mass together.
(*f*) Help to produce the scintillating blaze of tone characteristic of the organ, by the clash of their perfect intervals and resultant tones with the tempered notes of the scale.

The characteristic tone of the English full swell is due to its unison and double chorus reeds and its mixtures.

It is often more subtle to arrange the breaks of a mixture on notes other than B to C.

Here is another example:[1]

CC to BB	15	19	22	26	29
Tenor C to mid-F	8	12	15	19	22
Mid-F♯ to treble D	1	5	8	12	15
Treble D♯ to top C	Sub. octave	1	5	8	12

Mollterz. A tierce of pitch a minor third above an octave or double octave. It is made in ${}^{1}_{7}{}^{2}_{7}{}^{8}$-ft. pitch by Walcker as a pedal stop.

Montre (French). The show pipes of the French organ, and thus the stop derives its name. It is the nearest (though not very near) equivalent of the English diapason. The pipes are usually made of almost pure tin and preserve a silvery brightness which gives a superb appearance against the beautiful French organ cases. Montres are of the 32-ft., 16-ft. and 8-ft. pitches. The octave 4-ft. is often called prestant.

Mounted cornet. See Cornet.

Musette (French). German: sackpfeife. A thin-toned reed stop often of 4-ft. pitch of tone not unlike that of an orchestral oboe. The stop has little general utility: its tone should resemble that of a small bagpipe and in a very large instrument it might conceivably be of use as a distinctive quiet solo voice of a pastoral character.

Mutation stops. Strictly speaking, mutation stops *change* the name of the note which is played, e.g. nazards (twelfths) and tierces are mutations, but 4-ft., 2-ft. and 1-ft. stops are not. There is a modern tendency to call all ranks of pipes of less than 4-ft. pitch mutation stops, particularly those which are used for synthesising other tone qualities.

[1] See also page 512.

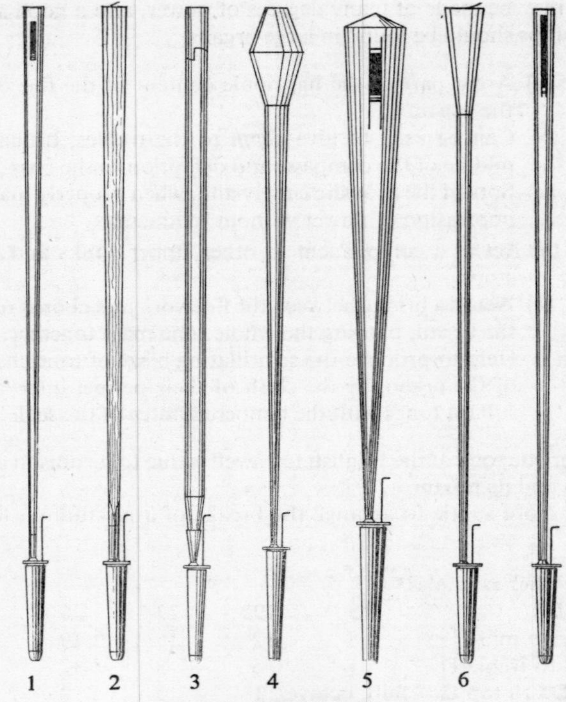

FIG. 21. Some Solo Reeds.

1. and 2. Bassoon. 3. Clarinet. 4. Cor Anglais. 5. Horn. 6. Oboe. 7. Orchestral Oboe.

Nachthorn (German). See Cor de nuit.

Nasard (*nazard*) (French). German: nasat; Italian and Spanish: nasardo. An important mutation stop of $2\frac{2}{3}$-ft. pitch on the manuals and $5\frac{1}{3}$-ft. pitch on the pedals. The stop is of wider scale and softer tone than the great-organ twelfth, and is sometimes made of stopped or gemshorn pipes. It is a necessary ingredient of the piquant tones used in the French and German organ music of the Baroque period. It is found in positive, choir and echo organs. A synthetic clarinet may be made by adding nasard and tierce to a quiet 8-ft. flute and a synthetic cor anglais by substituting a quiet 4-ft. flute for the 8-ft. rank. The Spanish nasardos is usually a quint mixture. The word nasard is derived from nasal, the quality of tone which the stop was supposed to suggest.

Nason. A 4-ft. stop of closed pipes made by German organ-builders in the seventeenth and eighteenth centuries. The tone has a pronounced twelfth in its harmonic content, which gives it a reedy or slightly nasal quality. One of the two old stops in the organ at Westminster Abbey is a nason. It is the 4-ft. counterpart of the English stopped diapason.

Nineteenth. A part of the harmonic series of the diapason chorus of 1⅓-ft. pitch on the manuals and 2⅔-ft. pitch in pedal organ. The rank of pipes may form a part of a mixture, but it should be of diapason scale and therefore not suitable to form part of a cornet.

Oboe. See Hautboy.

Oboe-flute. A name given by the late William Hill of London to an open wood flute of 4-ft. pitch with a slightly reedy intonation.

Oboe horn (*cor-oboe*). A stop used by Hope-Jones in the organ at Llandaff Cathedral. It is a hybrid of a close-toned trumpet and a "swell" oboe. The stop was occasionally made by Norman and Beard under the name of cor-oboe.

Ocarina. An open metal flue stop of 4-ft. pitch with a hollow tone. The stop must be regarded as a freak. Examples were made by Anneessens of Belgium for the organ at St. Mary's, Bradford, England, and by Amezua for Seville Cathedral.

Octave (1). The correct name for the chief 4-ft. diapason stop on the manuals and 8-ft. on the pedals. It is customary now in large British organs to call the second open diapason stop of 4-ft. pitch by the name of principal. (2) Used as an adjective, the word octave implies a 4-ft. version of an 8-ft. manual stop or the 8-ft. version of a 16-ft. pedal stop.

Octavin. An open metal flue stop of 2-ft. pitch found in French organs, e.g. those at the Church of St. Sulpice, Paris, and the Cathedral of Notre-Dame.

Offenbass (German: open-bass). An open pedal stop of 16-ft. pitch of wood or metal.

Open diapason. See Diapason.

Ophicleide (German. ὄφις = a serpent; κλεῖς = a key, i.e. a keyed serpent). A powerful reed stop, supposed to imitate the tone of the brass orchestral instrument. Willis left some fine specimens on the manuals of 8 ft., and of 16 ft. on the pedals of his larger organs, such as that at St. George's Hall, Liverpool. Pressures of 10 in. to 25 or more inches of wind are employed for these stops.

Orchestral. This adjective implies hopefully that the tone of a particular stop is intended to imitate, as far as possible, its orchestral prototype. The orchestral bassoon and orchestral oboe as organ stops are made with smaller-scaled tubes than those of the swell oboe. The orchestral clarinet is voiced in imitation of the chalumeau register of the orchestral instrument.

Orchestral flute. French: flûte traversière; Italian: flauto traverso; German: concertflöte. Schulze, Cavaillé-Coll and Willis have made some excellent orchestral flutes with open, small-scaled, cylindrical wooden tubes and small mouths. Square, rectangular and triangular constructions have also been used.

Orlo, cro orlo (Spanish). A reed stop of 8-ft. pitch of musette character.

Panflöte (Pan flute). A rare pedal flue stop of 1-ft. pitch; e.g. the organ in Lund Cathedral, Sweden.

Pastorita. The Italian name for a cor de nuit.

Pauke. The drum pedal found in old German organs whereby two coarse wooden pipes of loud tone were caused to sound together.

Perduna (German). A bourdon.

Philomela (nightingale). A sweet-toned flue stop of small scale and high pitch. The name was also applied to a loud double-mouthed open flute.

Phoneuma. A small viol pipe fitted with a roller bridge and voiced to speak as an echo quintaten. It was made by J. W. Whiteley and used by Hope-Jones.

Physharmonika. A German stop of 16-ft. and 8-ft. pitch made from harmonium reeds without resonators. The stop is not popular, as its pitch is not affected by changes of temperature and therefore it will not stand in tune with the rest of the pipework of the organ.

Piccolo. A flute stop of 2-ft. or 1-ft. pitch. Sometimes it is made harmonic. The stop is useful as a fifteenth or twenty-second in a series of harmonic ranks on a choir or positive organ. Willis made a number of examples of 2 ft. for his swell organs, where they were of limited value.

Piffero (Italian: fife).

Pileata (Latin). A gedeckt.

Plein-jeu (see also the section on registration). A mixture with octave- and fifth-sounding ranks and six or seven ranks. The plein-jeu is a large true mixture with sub-unison and unison ranks in the treble. The example here analysed is that made by Cavaillé Coll for the organ of Manchester Town Hall.

CC to E	15	19	22	26	29	33	36
F to e^1	8	12	15	19	22	26	29
f^1 to e^2	1	8	12	15	19	22	26
f^2 to b^2	1	5	8	12	15	19	22
c^3 to f^3	Double	1	5	8	12	15	19
f♯ to c^4	Double	Double Quint	1	5	8	12	15

Pommer. See Gedeckt-pommer.

Portunal. An open wood stop of medium scale of 8-ft. and 4-ft. pitch. The finer examples have bodies with a slight outward taper and a slight reediness in their voices. The stop is occasionally found in German organs.

Posaune. A loud reed stop of trumpet type with free and brassy tone. It is found at 8-ft. pitch on the manuals and 16-ft. pitch on the pedals. It is of frequent occurrence: Henry Willis left some excellent examples.

Prestant. A French 4-ft. stop equivalent of the English principal. It is so-called because it "stands in front", i.e. it forms part of the exposed pipework of the organ case. The Dutch stop of this name is usually of 8-ft. or 16-ft. pitch.

Principal. A name still used for the octave diapason or 4-ft. stop on manuals and 8-ft. stop on the pedals. See also Octave.

Prinzipal (German). Italian: principale. The nearest equivalent to the English open diapason on German and Italian organs.

PLATE 31a.
Wilma Jensen at West Point, U.S.A., Möller organ

PLATE 31b.
Dr. Marilyn Mason at her house organ, Ann Arbor, U.S.A. Note the functional nature of both organ and console

PLATE 32a.

Salzburg Cathedral, Austria. Console by L. Eisenschmid of Munich

PLATE 32b.

Lady Susi Jeans at her neo-baroque house organ

PLATE 33.
St. Lawrence Jewry, London. The City Guild church organ by Mander, 1957.
Main case

PLATE 34a.

The chapel, Massachusetts Institute of Technology. Organ by

PLATE 34b.

Kath. Pfarrkirche. St. Peter Bevel–Vilich bei Bonn. Organ

Prinzipal diskant, diskant prinzipal. A diapason type of stop of 8-ft. pitch reinforcing the treble octaves of the main open flue stop. The stop is not now made, since proper scalings are used which prevent the characteristic falling off in power of the upper octaves of the old 8-ft. diapason stops.

Progressio harmonica. A mixture stop in which the number of ranks increases from bottom to top of the compass. The nineteenth-century German organ-builder, Ladegast, made a number of such stops, the idea of which was to enrich the treble of the organ.

Pyramidon. A stop invented by the late Rev. Sir F. Gore-Ouseley and made by Flight. A wooden flue stop with pyramidal resonators was made to yield a 16-ft. bourdon tone, the CCC pipe measuring 2 ft. 3 in. square at the top and 8 in. square at the mouth line, with a speaking length of 2 ft. 6 in. The stop took up too much sound-board room and, having no tonal advantages, was soon discarded.

Quartane. See Rauschquinte.

Quarte de nasard (French). The fourth above the nasard, i.e. the double octave or fifteenth. A stop, in the harmonic series on positive or grand orgue, of 2-ft. pitch.

Querflöte. A traverse flute, 8-ft. pitch, imitating as far as possible the tone of the orchestral instrument.

Quint. French and German: quinte; Italian and Latin: quinta. A stop of $5\frac{1}{3}$-ft. pitch on the manuals and $10\frac{2}{3}$-ft. pitch on the pedals. A part of the harmonic series of the 16-ft. and 32-ft. pitches. A quint $5\frac{1}{3}$ ft. adds body and depth to a great organ which is already supplied with 16-ft. ranks and good upper work. A quint $10\frac{2}{3}$-ft. on the pedals when used with 16-ft. ranks gives a resultant 32 ft., which may be quite effective if sufficient other stops are drawn.

Quintadena. A small quintaten (q.v.). The stop is often found in old Dutch organs.

Quintaten. A "covered" (stopped) flue stop which speaks its twelfth almost as prominently as the ground tone. The word is derived from quintam tenentes (holding the fifth). The stop was well known in Germany in the sixteenth century and is described by Praetorius. It has become popular in recent years as a light choir-organ 16-ft. rank. It is often made playable from the pedal organ, where it has the grip and definition of a double bass played quietly.

Ranket, racket. An obsolete reed stop of 16-ft. and 8-ft. pitches found in early baroque organs. A type of regal stop which was imagined to imitate the old instrument of the same name.

Rauschflöte, rauschpfeife (German: rustling flute). A two-rank mixture of the eighteenth century made from open pipes of 2-ft. and $1\frac{1}{3}$-ft. pitch ranks.

Rauschquinte (German: rustling quint). A two-rank mixture of $2\frac{2}{3}$-ft. and 2-ft. pitches respectively. The distinguishing feature is the interval of a fourth between the ranks, which accounts for the name quarte or quarta given to it by the old German builders.

Recorder (English). German: blockflöte. An old English stop of flute tone intended to represent that of the recorder or flûte à bec. It was popular in the seventeenth-century organs of Dallam and Loosemore. A modern example, voiced to imitate the tone of one of Canon Galpin's instruments, is found in the organ at Chelmsford Cathedral.

Regal (German). French: régale; Italian: regale. An old reed stop made with various patterns of resonator which qualify the tone but do not sensibly control the pitch. The stop belongs to the schnarrwerk class which is explained in this book in the section on the baroque organ.

Regula (Latin). An open metal stop of diapason class.

Reim. A rarely found reed stop of soft tone and 16-ft. pitch used by Schulze in the pedal organ at Bremen Cathedral in the middle of the nineteenth century.

Ripieno (Italian. Literally, filling up). A mixture.

Rohrflöte, rohrschelle. Chimney flute. French: flûte à cheminée. The German words, though often half anglicised to rohr flute, are usually used in English organs. The stop has been known for four hundred years. It belongs to the half-stopped class of flue pipes. The metal canister which covers the fairly wide-scaled stop is pierced and a length of open metal tubing is soldered to it. There are various modifications of this, including one where the tube or chimney is soldered so that it goes downwards into the body of the pipes. Sometimes a long wooden stopper is used in which a hole is bored, or a horizontal hole may be made through the stopper connecting with a vertical hole so as to produce a T-shaped hole in the stopper. The finest characteristic tone is produced by the external metal chimney, which adds a subtle "formant" to the tone of the stopped pipe.

Rohrgedackt, 16 ft., 8 ft., 4 ft. or 2 ft. Similar to Rohrflöte in construction but darker in tone.

Rohrpommer, 16 ft., 8 ft., 4 ft. or 2 ft. Similar in construction to above stop, but bright, quinty with "acid edge".

Rohrquintadena, 16 ft., 8 ft., 4 ft. or 2 ft. More lively in tone than Rohrgedackt.

Rohr Schalmei, 8 ft. A low-pressure reed with intense, pungent and hollow sound. See the diagram at the end of this section.

Sackbut. A 32-ft. trombone used by Hill in the pedal organ at York Minster in 1833.

Sadt (German: zackt=pointed). Used by Smith for a stop, believed to be of gemshorn character, in the organ at the Temple Church, London, in 1688.

Salamine. An echo salicional used half a century and more ago by Meyer of Hanover and Forster and Andrews of Hull.[1]

Salicet. An octave salicional.

Salicional, salcional (Latin: salix=a willow). Names given to 8-ft. and 16-ft. open cylindrical metal stops of small scale with delicate, stringy intonation. The stop is popular in Europe, England and America and is frequently found to be the softest stop on the swell organ. It should be made of a metal very rich in tin. A suitable scale for an organ of moderate size would be:

CC	C	c^1
3·21	1·97	1·20

[1] An effect inspired by the sound of the sea-waves off the coast of Salamis.

The stops should be of the utmost refinement and should blend well with other quiet stops.

Sanftgedeckt (German). A soft lieblich gedeckt.

Saxophone. A stop rarely found outside America which may be either reed or flue. The reed stop is usually a large-scaled clarinet, and the flue stop invented by Haskell of the Estey Organ Co. is a medium-scaled open wood stop fitted with "harmonic bridges". The stop can have little claim to be placed in a modern organ of economical design.

Schalmei (Chalumeau). A reed stop, supposed to imitate the tone of the old shawm.

Scharf (German). Dutch: scherp. A bright high-pitched mixture commencing with fifteenth, nineteenth and twenty-second ranks. When added to the full flue chorus with normal mixture it imparts great brilliance; it also gives great brightness to the reeds.

Scharfgeige. Viole d'orchestre (q.v.).

Scharfpfeife. Dolcan (q.v.).

Schweizerflöte, schweizerpfeife (German: Swiss flute). An open flue stop of 8-ft., 4-ft. and 2-ft. or sometimes 1-ft. pitch, of small scale and yielding a quiet tone of string-flute hybrid.

Schweizergedackt (Swissgedackt), 8 ft., 4 ft., 2 ft. or 1 ft. A small-scaled metal gedackt of bright tone.

Schweizer-Spitzgedackt, 8 ft., 4 ft or 2 ft. A small-scaled spitzgedackt.

Schweizer trompete (Swiss trumpet). A powerful trumpet: tuba mirabilis.

Schwiegel, schwägel (German). A flute stop with cylindrical bodies surmounted by truncated cones and having a quiet interesting tone. In Germany it is found in 8-ft., 4-ft., 2-ft. and 1-ft. pitches.

Septerz. See Terzsepta.

Septième. A mutation stop of $2\frac{2}{7}$-ft., $1\frac{1}{7}$-ft. pitch on the manuals and $4\frac{4}{7}$-ft. on the pedals. The stop was used in England in 1850 by Jackson at Liverpool Collegiate Institution as sharp twentieth, though it might have been happier to have called it flat twenty-first. The stop was used by Cavaillé-Coll in his larger instruments. The $4\frac{4}{7}$-ft.-pitch rank on the pedal organ at Notre Dame Cathedral was said by the late organist, L. Vierne, to give it "the richness of a muster of double basses". The stop is increasingly found in the choir or positive divisions of British and American organs.

Septuadecima (Latin). A seventeenth $1\frac{3}{5}$-ft. pitch.

Seraphon. The name of a class of powerful flue stops with wide mouths and working on fairly high pressures of wind invented by the late W. F. Weigle of Stuttgart. The stops are of dubious artistic value.

Serpent. A reed stop of 16-ft. or 8-ft. pitch with a tone between those of the bassoon and trombone. The stop is supposed to imitate the old sixteenth-century instrument of the same name and is related to the zinken. The stop is sometimes found in Germany, but the only British example known to the writer is at the Castlegate Congregational Church, Nottingham, in the pedal organ.

Sesquialtera, sexquialtera. Originally a stop with two ranks of $2\frac{2}{3}$ ft. and $1\frac{3}{5}$ft. respectively (twelfth and tierce), giving an interval of a sixth. The sesquialtera is not primarily a producer of brilliance but adds a reedy rich colour to the fluework; it is useful in building a tonal bridge between flue and reed stops. Sesqui means a ratio of 3 to 2, which would be suggested by the heights of the two ranks on the sound-board. In German and Dutch organs the ranks are of principal scale; in old English organs the sesquialtera was often 17, 19, 22, and was used as a bass for the cornet and as a chorus mixture. Sesquialteras have been made with four and five ranks; e.g. by John Snetzler in 1777 for the organ at St. Mary's Church, Nottingham.

Four ranks:

CC to G	15	17	19	22
G♯ to g^1	12	15	17	19
$g♯^1$ to top	8	12	15	17

Seventeenth. French: tierce; German: terz; Italian: decima settima. A mutation stop of $1\frac{3}{5}$ ft. on the manual and $3\frac{1}{5}$ ft. or more rarely $6\frac{2}{5}$ ft. on the pedals; thus being the fifth harmonic or seventeenth interval in the 8-ft., 16-ft. and 32-ft. pitches respectively. The stop is called seventeenth when it is found in British great organs (but more often it has no separate existence but is a part of a sesquialtera or other compound stops). As a quiet mutation of open diapason or gemshorn tone on the choir or positive organ, it is usually called tierce. The stop is useful in synthetic tone-building, but as it tends to produce a reedy growl it needs carefully adjusting to the other mutation and octave stops in power and tone. The French tierce is usually a flute.

Sext. A stop having the twelfth and tierce of the sesquialtera but made with ranks of flute type.

Sifflöte (German). French: sifflet. A small-scaled open metal stop of 2-ft., 1-ft., or, more rarely, of $1\frac{1}{3}$-ft. pitch found in German organs of the last three centuries.

Soave. An Italian stop of 8-ft. pitch giving a soft and beautiful tone.

Sordon. French: sourdine; Italian: sordini. A soft gedeckt of 16-ft. or 8-ft. pitch.

Spillflöte, spindelflöte. A half-stopped open flue pipe of 8-ft., 4-ft., or 2-ft. pitch. The body of the metal pipe is cylindrical, but it is surmounted by a conical portion rather like a pipe-foot inverted, and hence the whole pipe is spindle-shaped. The stop has been in use in Germany since the beginning of the sixteenth century. It has a beautiful, quiet tone and it is a pity that it is not often made in England.

Spitzflöte. French: flûte à fuseau; English: spire flute. In British organs the stop is usually called spitzflöte or spitz flute. An open metal flue stop of 8-ft., 4-ft., or 2-ft. pitch tapering towards the top and not unlike the gemshorn in shape, but is more pointed. The spitzflöte must be regarded as a half-closed stop and the fifth harmonic can be heard in its voice. Töpfer gives the dimensions of the 8-ft. CC pipe as $4\frac{3}{5}$ in. diameter at the mouth and $1\frac{1}{2}$ in. at the open top. The spitzflöte has an interesting, telling and attractive tone with more harmonic development than the usual English gemshorn.

Spitzgamba, 8 ft. and 4 ft. A gamba of tapered construction: an interesting string-tone.

Spitzgedackt, 8 ft. and 4 ft. A spitzflöte which tapers to a very narrow top, closed with a small stopper. The tone is quiet, dark and interesting.

Stentorphone (from the Greek: loud voice). A large-scaled, loud open flue stop of 8-ft. pitch and not of much artistic value in any organ of reasonable size. It was found on large American organs, but was invented by Weigle (of Stuttgart).

Stilles Regal, 8 ft. and 4 ft. A quiet vox humana.

Stillgedeckt. A quiet gedeckt.

Stopped diapason (English). German: gedeckt; French: bourdon; Spanish: tapada, tapadillo. The stop is not really a diapason but a stopped flute. It was found as the second 8-ft. stop in English great, choir and swell organs until the smaller-scaled lieblich gedeckts became popular after 1851. The stop was usually made of wood and had a tone which did not cloy as quickly as the more modern lieblichs.

Suabe flute (Swabian flute). A wooden quadrangular open stop of 4-ft. pitch with inverted mouths, invented by William Hill of London. It is occasionally found in British great and choir organs.

Suave flute (Latin *suavis:* sweet, pleasant). An open wooden flute stop with a cylindrical dowel attached to the upper lip.

Suavial. 8 ft. and 4 ft. open flute. See above.

Sub-bass. German: subbass; French: soubasse, sous-basse. A 32-ft. bourdon found on the pedal division and more rarely on great organs. It was used by the German firm of Walcker.

Sub-bourdon. See Sub-bass.

Sub-prinzipal (German). French: principal bass. The equivalent English stop is double open diapason 32 ft. The stop is the chief open flue pedal rank of 32-ft. pitch. It may be made of metal, in which case it may appear in an imposing organ case, or it may be made of wood. In the organ at the Church of the Sacré-Coeur, Montmartre, Paris, it is called flûte 32-ft.

Super octave. A fifteenth or doublette of 2-ft. pitch.

Sylvestrina. A stop first made in Germany at the beginning of the nineteenth century. Mr. Henry Willis III frequently uses a quiet, gemshorn-like stop of flute-string tone of this name in his choir or swell organs.

Tapadillo, tapado (Spanish). The equivalent of a stopped diapason or gedeckt.

Teneroon. A name used in England in the nineteenth century to denote an incomplete stop. The name of the organ stop was derived from the tenor bassoon or alto fagotto, but was later applied to flue stops as well as reeds of incomplete compass. Sometimes the name was given to a 16-ft. diapason.

Terpodion (from the Greek *to delight* and *a song*). The stop, occasionally made by Schulze (there is an example on the organ at Doncaster Parish Church), is made from small-scaled open metal flue pipes, but it has a slightly reedy intonation. Its tone was supposed to imitate that of an instrument invented in 1816 by Buschmann of Berlin, in which pieces of wood were struck by hammers by means of a type of pianoforte action.

Tertian, terzian. A compound stop of two quiet ranks of open pipes sounding the interval of a minor third. The ranks are of $1\frac{3}{5}$-ft. and $1\frac{1}{3}$-ft pitch respectively if they belong to the 8-ft. series. In eighteenth-century German organs the stop sometimes had three ranks: 4-ft., $3\frac{1}{5}$-ft. and $2\frac{2}{3}$-ft. pitches.

Terz septa. A two-rank compound stop: $1\frac{3}{5}$ ft. and $1\frac{1}{7}$ ft.

Tibia (Latin: a pipe). The word tibia is usually qualified by some other word when it is used to represent a rank of organ pipes. Hope-Jones called his louder bourdons tibia clausa, for instance. The tibia has fallen into disrepute, as it was associated with the tonal ideas of this builder, and it was a favourite of the cinema organist for producing loud penetrating flue solos (usually with tremulant). The word itself is innocuous, but it has come to mean a quality of tone which stands out of balance with the rest of the fluework of a properly designed organ. Nevertheless, some beautiful specimens of normal flue voicing are to be found under this name, particularly when the builder or organist has a penchant for translating the stop names into the Latin tongue, e.g. the organ at St. John's Church, Torquay, until 1951.

Tierce. See Seventeenth.

Traversflöte (German). Italian: flauto traverso. A stop often made by Edmund Schulze in 4-ft. and 8-ft. pitches and intended to imitate the orchestral flute in tone quality. The narrow-scale produces a pleasant reediness in the tone.

Tremulant. Although it has fallen into low esteem because of its wearisome and inartistic use by cinema organists of the past generation, it was a respected and important device in the organs of the Renaissance and Baroque periods. Samuel Scheidt (1587–1654) describes it as "a dignified stop and one of importance on the organ", and also at the beginning of the seventeenth century Compenius made an adjustable tremulant for the organ at Frederiksborg, Denmark, and the organist was (and is) able to adjust it at the console. He gives the following hints on its use ("for motet, pedaliter or manualiter"), 1597:

(*a*) Gedackt 8 ft., flachflöte 2 ft., tremulant.
In the pedal subbass only.
(*b*) Gedackt 8 ft., sifflöte 1 ft., tremulant.
In the pedal subbass.

In the early years of the seventeenth century the tremulant was used with the plein-jeu at times, and it was commonly combined with "Le larigot" (i.e. a combination with a pronounced fifth): Gedackt 16 ft., principal 8 ft., larigot $1\frac{1}{3}$ ft.

Two types of tremulant were in use in both France and Germany: the "tremblant fort" and "tremblant doux". Scheidt's regard for the tremulant went so far that he actually tried to imitate its effect in one of his pieces in the *Tabulatura Nova.*[1] The popularity of the tremulant in the sixteenth century

[1] p. 62. "Bicinium imitatione Tremula Organi duobus digitus in una tantum clave manu, tum dextra, tum sinistra."

waned a little in the next century. Mertel,[1] in 1666, said the use of the device should be confined to sad and penitential songs and during the Sanctus. At the Halberstadt Convocation in 1693 it was decreed that the tremulant must not be used with the full organ "as its beating will shake up the instrument and send it out of tune". In 1670 the Church Superintendent of Leisnig forbade its use altogether.

Lebègue (1630–1702) recommended the use of the tremulant with the vox humana as an imitation of the human voice. Gigault (1624–1707) gave instructions for the playing of preludes of festive character on full organ, with or without reeds, with the use of the stop.[2] Dom Bédos (1709–79) mentions its use in several ways: it could even help to cover up irregularities in the reed tone. Bach's insistence on the proper adjustment of the tremulant on the Mühlhausen organ is well known.[3]

Trichterpfeife (German = funnel pipe). A Dolcan (q.v.).

Trichterregal. An old German regal with a funnel-shaped resonator, from which it derives its name.

Tromba. This was the name used by Italian organ-builders to denote stops of the trumpet class. In Britain it has come to mean a loud reed of 8-ft. or of 16-ft. pitch with a "close" tone, in contrast to the free tone of the trumpet or the French type of trompette. Although it may be desirable to seek contrast amongst loud reeds, it must be remembered that if tromba tone is made too "close" it will fail to blend with the flue chorus of the organ. Some English great organs with trombas and leathered diapasons produce a dull, wearisome and an inartistic sound. (See the section on reed-voicing.)

Trombone. A stop of 8-ft. and 16-ft. pitch on the manuals and 16-ft. and 32-ft. pitch on the pedals. (In the last case it is usually called contra-trombone.) The stop, perhaps of slightly closer tone than that of the normal organ trumpet (though it may very well be a trumpet), is intended to imitate the loud brass orchestral instrument, and is often the loudest reed stop on the organ, unless there is a tuba.

Trompette. This usually implies a loud reed stop of very free tone, as is found in the French organs made by Cavaillé-Coll.

Trompette en chamade. A reed stop whose tubes lie horizontally and sometimes project from the organ case as in the Spanish organs.

Trompette militaire. A stop, made by Henry Willis III, with flaring brass tubes, and of very free, loud tone, intended to imitate the tone of the French cavalry trumpets. An example may be heard in the Dome organ at St. Paul's Cathedral.

Trumpet. A normal, organ chorus reed of moderate or loud tone. The characteristic tone of the English full swell-organ is due to a family of trumpets, including one of 16-ft. pitch, and a flue mixture. The old Spanish organs, those of Cavaillé-Coll and of the Willis and other English and American firms, contain many magnificent specimens of such stops. The trumpet can

[1] *Orgelschlüssel.*
[2] Lady S. Jeans, "The Tremulant", *Musical Times* (London, March 1950).
[3] W. L. Sumner, "The Organ of Bach", *The Organ* (July 1950).

be used both for chorus and for solo work. (See also the section on reed stops.)

Tuba, tuba mirabilis (mirabilis=Latin: wonderful). A very loud high-pressure stop of the trumpet class intended to act as a powerful solo stop. In the classical organ music there is very little work for it to do and always it must be used with restraint. It is useful in some modern organ music and in accompanying large congregations, for very occasional use. The tuba is effective when coupled to the pedals in order to produce a very telling *fff* bass line.

Tuba clarion. A tuba of 4-ft. pitch.

Tubasson. A name used by French and Belgian organ-builders for a 16-ft. pedal stop of trombone type.

Twelfth. A stop of $2\frac{2}{3}$-ft. pitch, which is part of the diapason harmonic series, and is sometimes united to the tierce to form the sesquialtera. When a softer, wider-scaled stop of this pitch is found on the choir or positive organ it is called *nasard* or *nazard.*

Twenty-second. A stop of 1-ft. pitch, thus giving the third octave above the note played. It is commonly incorporated with the mixture, but it sometimes appears independently as in the organ at Notre Dame Cathedral, Paris. The stop was called two and twentieth by old English builders, e.g. at St. John's College, Cambridge, by Dallam.

Unda maris (Latin: wave of the sea). A stop of the celeste type in which two 8-ft. ranks of quiet tone and properly of flute quality, though gambas, viols, and dulcianas are used, slightly mistuned so that there is a gentle beating or heterodyning of the ranks. Sometimes the stop consists of one rank only, tuned slightly flat to the organ. This is drawn with some other soft rank of pipes in order to produce the céleste effect. Although such stops are popular with romantics, they soon become wearisome, irritate the sensitive and cultured ear and are to be regarded as one of the fancy effects of the organ. Nevertheless, this is a genuine organ stop.

Untersatz (German). A sub-bourdon. See Sub-bass.

Viol. French and German: viole. A name somewhat loosely applied in organ nomenclature and often qualified with other terms. The tone of the stop does not usually resemble that of any member of the old family of stringed viols. Small-scaled, open pipes of pure tin, or of a metal very rich in tin and fitted with beards, roller bridges, etc., produce a quality of tone which is of the gamba class, and is often designated viol.

Viola. A gamba type of stop of 4-ft., or 8-ft. pitch and intended to imitate, as far as is possible, the stringed instrument of the same name.

Viola da gamba (Italian). The correct name for the organ stop usually called gamba. Usually it means almost any stop of string tone, but originally it was intended to represent the old stringed instrument, held between the legs when it was played. From this it derives its name.

Viola d'amour. A 4-ft. or 8-ft. stop of string-tone which, if it is true to its name, is of refined tone, resembling to some degree that of the seven-stringed instrument of the same name. Willis made some good specimens, e.g. in the organ in King's College Chapel, London (in 8-ft. pitch!).

Viole céleste or *Violes célestes* (French). A stop made from two ranks of viol pipes, one of which is tuned slightly sharp to the other.

Viole d'orchestre (French). A small-scaled string-tone stop, invented by William Thynne of London, and at the time of its manufacture giving the closest imitation of such tone then achieved. It must be regarded as an exaggerated effect as far as the organ is concerned and therefore should not find a place on a small organ where a salicional or gamba would be of much greater general utility. Nevertheless with a family of such stops on a solo or choir organ and octave couplers some beautiful effects, for occasional use, may be obtained.

Viole sourdine. An attenuated viol tone of beautiful quality invented by Thynne. An example may be heard in the large organ at Tewkesbury Abbey, England.

Violetta (Italian). A 4-ft. viol.

Violin. An open metal stop of 8-ft. pitch which is intended to represent the tone of the violin. This, of course, is quite impossible, but violin stops can be made so that they have a satisfying string quality and a certain amount of "body". Willis III and others have made effective violin stops by using a small-scaled rank of thin string tone and giving it more tonal substance by adding to it a stop of gedeckt character.

Violin diapason. See Geigen diapason.

Violoncello, cello (Italian). French: violoncelle. An open flue stop of wood or metal and in 8-ft. pitch, which is intended to imitate the tone of the stringed instrument. It is found both on manuals and pedals, but is popular as an octave stop on the latter. Some excellent specimens were made by Schulze and his admirer Pendlebury, of wood, and these have a quality hardly to be found in those of metal.

Violone (Italian). French: violon basse. An open flue stop of non-imitative string tone sometimes found as a quiet 16-ft. pedal stop, where it is a welcome change from the ubiquitous bourbon; or on the great and swell organs as a flue double.

Vogelgesang (German). Latin: avicinium. A stop found in old German organs intended to imitate the warbling of birds. Two or three small open pipes were bent over so that their tops were immersed in water in a small bowl.

Voix céleste (French). Latin: vox coelestis. A beating stop with two ranks of pipes of mild string tone, one of which is tuned slightly sharp to the other so that there is a pleasant tremolo effect because of their heterodyning.[1]

Vox angelica (Latin). German: engelstimme. A stop of céleste type with very refined intonation and a slow beat. Father Willis's specimens, such as that on the organ at St. Paul's Cathedral, have a pleasant, restful quality of which the ear does not soon tire.

Vox humana (Latin). French: voix humaine; Italian: voce umana; German: menschenstimme. A stop of great antiquity, originally belonging to the regal or schnarrwerk class. The stop, as made at present, is a type of clarinet with very short tubes—a usual length is about an eighth of that which would

[1] The out-of-tune rank usually extends to Tenor C only in such stops.

be required for normal resonance. A small hole is usually pierced at the top of the small pipe-bodies. Some organ-builders use tubes of conical or other shapes. The old stops of this name were only made tolerable, even to the undiscerning ear, by their elevated positions in large churches and their enclosure in boxes. The stop was a favourite, when used with the tremolo as a solo register. When properly made it has a use in genuine organ-playing. When combined with other ranks, it is a timbre-creator and is of value when coupled to the pedals as a quiet, colourful reed capable of qualifying other louder tones. Vox humanas tend to go out of tune easily and their small resonators have little influence on the pitch of their vibrating reeds. The voce umana can be an open diapason céléste in Italian organs.

Waldflöte (German). Latin: tibia sylvestris; Dutch: woudfluit (forest flute). An open flute of 8-ft., 4-ft., 2-ft., or, rarely, of 1-ft. pitch, usually made of wood and less often of metal. Some excellent examples were made by Walcker of Germany and Walker of London.

Waldhorn (German). As usually made, this is a stop of moderate power, of 8-ft., and 16-ft. pitches, and of "closer" tone than that of the trumpet. Henry Willis III has made some good specimens for the swell organs of some of his larger instruments.

Weidenpfeife (German = willow pipe). Salicional (q.v.).

Wienerflöte (German: Vienna flute). A soft, open wood flue stop of delicate tone and usually found in 8-ft. or 4-ft. pitch. Such pipes, speaking on a pressure of wind of 2 in. or less, have a beautiful effect whether they are used alone or in combination with other soft stops.

Xylophone. A percussion stop, not strictly "organic" in character, but which was frequently found in organs of the romantic age in America, and in cinema instruments. Four octaves of rosewood bars, over metal cylindrical resonators, are struck with hammers, usually operated by electric action.

Zartflöte (German. Literally, delicate flute). Originally a soft flue string-flute hybrid, but as made by Whiteley at the end of the nineteenth century it was a type of quintaton fitted with harmonic bridges.

Zartgeige (German = delicate string tone). See Aeoline 8-ft.

Zarthorn, 8-ft. and 4-ft. A regal of delicate tone.

Zauberflöte (German. Literally, magic-flute). A stopped harmonic stop, invented by William Thynne of London, and subsequently imitated by a number of other builders. A stopped pipe is overblown, and a small hole is bored about two-fifths of the way along its body; its chief tone is then the harmonic twelfth of a gedeckt pipe of the same size.

Zink, zinck, zinken. A reed stop, usually of 2-ft. or of 1-ft. pitch, deriving its name from the old trumpet-like instrument. The stop is usually found on the pedal organ, and is of fairly frequent appearance on old Dutch organs, such as the famous instrument in the Church of St. Bavon at Haarlem. A zynck, such as was used by Casparini, had been made in Germany since 1620 and was actually a form of sesquialtera. Other old reeds, which easily got out of tune, were also replaced by compound flue stops.

Zymbel. A German mixture stop, which derived its name from the Greek

Kymbalon. Originally it contained only octave or octave and fifth-sounding ranks, but, later, the Terzzymbel which contained a third-sounding rank appeared. Generally, the sound of the Zymbel was sharper than that of the mixture. Sometimes a four- or five-rank stop, known as Zymbel-scharf, was made.

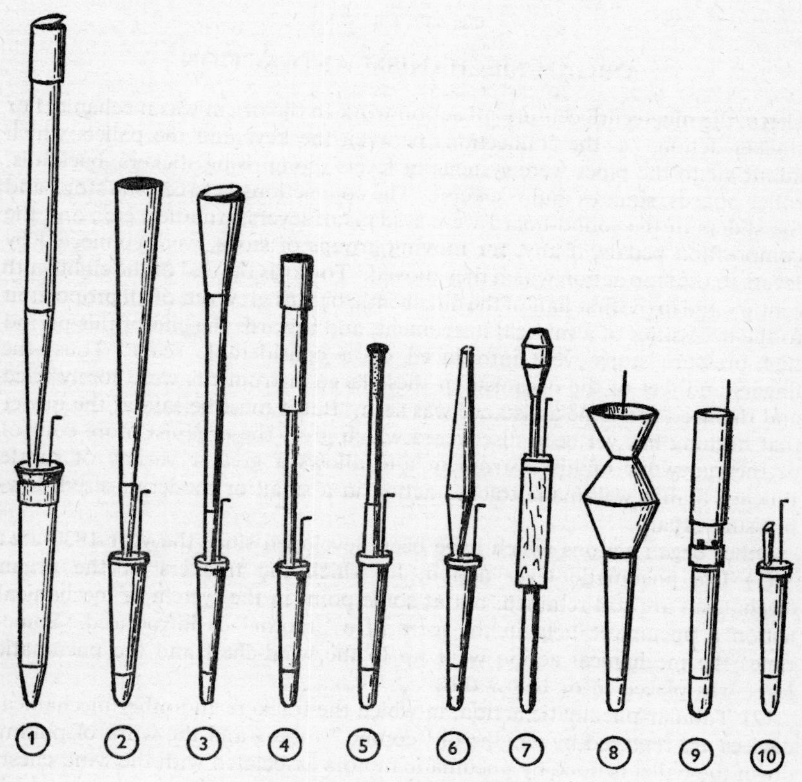

FIG. 21a. Old Reed Pipes.

1. Dulzian. 2. Trompette. 3. Oboe. 4. Rohr Schalmei. 5. Krummhorn. 6. Musette. 7. Finnish regal. 8. Bärpfeife. 9. Rankett. 10. Regal.

CHAPTER XI

ORGAN MECHANISM AND ACTION

UNTIL the nineteenth century all action work in the organ was mechanical or tracker action, i.e. the connections between the keys and the pallets which admit air to the pipes were systems of levers (comprising stickers, backfalls, roller-boards, squares and trackers). The connections between the stops and the sliders in the sound-board were systems of levers, trundles, etc., and the composition pedals, if any, for moving groups of stops, were connected by levers to the stop action which they moved. Towards the end of the eighteenth century and in the first half of the nineteenth, organs grew out of all proportion to the necessities of a musical instrument, and towards the end of this period high-pressure stops were introduced on a considerable scale. Thus, the fingers and feet of the organists of these large instruments were sorely tried and the need for some assistance was seen. But it must be said at the outset that nothing has yet been discovered which gives the organist more control of the pipework of his instrument and allows a greater variety of subtle touches than a well-made tracker action in a small or moderate-sized, low-pressure organ.

Other organ actions which have been developed since the year 1830 are:

(1) The pneumatic lever action, in which the trackers of the organ mechanism are still retained, but at some point in the system of mechanical action a pneumatic help in the form of a "motor" is introduced. Sometimes the mechanical action went up to the wind-chest and the pneumatic lever was placed in or below this.

(2) Tubular-pneumatic action, in which the trackers and other mechanical devices are replaced by lengths of "compo" tubing and the work of pulling down the pallet is done by pneumatic motors associated with the wind-chest. Tubular-pneumatic actions may be divided into two types: (*a*) that in which pressure wind available at the key-ends is sent into the tubes when the respective keys are pressed, and (*b*) that in which the pressing of a key allows a motor in or near the wind-chest to discharge its air into the atmosphere via a tube leading to the console. The former type is called *pressure-pneumatic* and, although it requires a supply of pressure wind in the console, it is usually the superior type of action. The latter was quite popular because there was no need to supply wind to the console in a separate wind trunk. In order that there shall be satisfactory repetition in such an action a "bleed-hole" of fairly critical size has to be made in the first small ("primary") motor in order that it shall fill quickly when the key is again raised.

(3) Electro-pneumatic action. In this the connections between the keys and the wind-chest are electric wires (usually in a cable), but the electro-

magnets open small valves which control the movement of pressure wind into or out of pneumatic motors which do the heavy work of pulling down the pallets. In a similar way the sliders of the draw-stop action are worked by powerful pneumatic motors which are themselves controlled by small primary motors and electro-magnets. There may be electric relay and coupling mechanism in the console or in a separate chamber.

(4) Direct electric action. Here the valves which admit air to the pipes are worked directly by electro-magnets or solenoids. Such action is usually confined to small organs or to pipes of 4 ft. or less. Nevertheless, the American firm of Wicks has been successful with direct electric action for organs of all sizes. Large amperages of low-voltage current would be required for larger organs and larger pipes, and this is not often a feasible proposition. It is usual to give the heavier work of organ action of whatever type to pneumatic motors.

There are other ways of classifying organ action: (*a*) there are slider-chests, in which a single pallet serves for all the pipes played by a particular key on each sound-board; and (*b*) sliderless-chests, in which each pipe has its own valve and each rank of pipes stands on what is, in effect, a separate air-supply or chest, to which the wind is admitted when the stop controlling that rank of pipes is drawn or put on.

Slider-chests have certain disadvantages in spite of their simplicity of construction. (*a*) They are susceptible to changes of climate: sliders tend to stick in humid atmospheres and slip or warp in dry conditions. Moreover, the large lengths of wood from which such chests are made tend to warp, crack or leak after years of climatic change. In order to retain slider-chests, modern European builders are showing much ingenuity both in design and the use of materials. (*b*) The inertia of a large and long slider is such that it cannot be moved in or out at the same speed as the opening of a small pallet. When any sliders are to be moved by using composition pistons or pedals much power has to be used and there is sometimes a loss of speed. Modern players demand that stop and piston action shall work at practically the same speed as key action. (*c*) The sliderless-chest is necessary where individual ranks are to be extended, and it is also necessary or more convenient if they are to be transferred or duplexed so as to be playable from another manual or from the pedals.

It ought to be mentioned that stops which have been voiced on slider voicing-machines do not commence their speech properly when they are transferred to sliderless or "unit" chests where the valves are immediately under the pipe-feet. This is because an unsteady wave of compression and rarefaction in the pressure-air enters the pipe-foot and may reach the flue just as the pipe is trying to settle down to stable speech. In the slider-chest the channel of air above the pallet acts as a damper to the inrushing wind. There is no reason why pipes should not be voiced just as satisfactorily for use on unit-chests, but there can be no doubt that the slow-speaking diapason of the Schulze type prefers a slider-chest constructed on liberal lines.

All organ-builders have their own modifications and mixtures of these basic systems. It should be asked of an organ-action:

(*a*) That it is fairly easy to construct without elaborate parts.
(*b*) That it is reliable, even after considerable periods when it is not used or of neglect.
(*c*) That it is not unduly affected by damp and temperature changes.
(*d*) That it can be inspected and adjusted without disturbing other parts of the organ.

(It might surprise the uninitiated to know that organ actions have been produced in Germany, America and in England which needed the removal of all the pipework from a sound-board in order to adjust the valve of a single pipe. When all the pipework had been returned, after the adjustment had been made, it was not unusual to find half a dozen more defects in an instrument which had been erected for twenty or thirty years.)

Mechanical Action

We have already seen in the historical portion of this work how the discovery of the slider-chest gave the organist control over single ranks of pipes and enabled him to choose the ingredients of his tonal "mélanges". There are still many thousands of slider-chests in use throughout the world and, in fact, they are now made to an increasing extent. They have the advantage

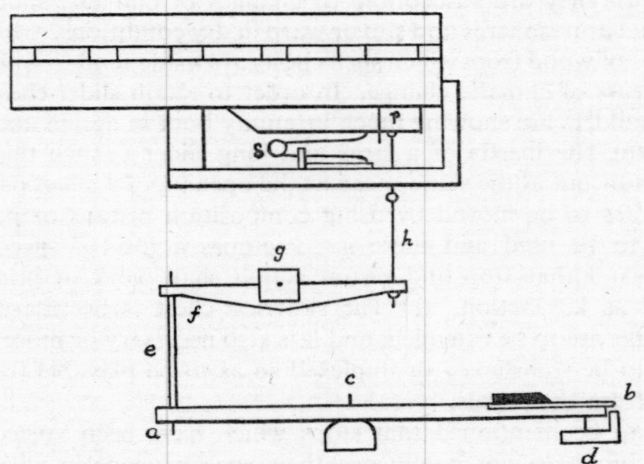

Fig. 22. Diagram of Simple Tracker Action.
a b key; *c* and *d* key pins; *e* sticker; *f* backfall; *g* backfall bridge; *h* tracker; *p* pallet; *s* spring. The pipes are supported in wooden rack-boards. (See p. 337.)

of simplicity in design, durability and the possibility of planting the pipes on good wooden structures which are not without effect on the general tonal quality of the organ. On the other hand, they require considerable quantities of the finest wood, are often susceptible to atmospheric changes, particularly of humidity, and may be ruined completely in time by a fault due to the shrinkage of wood with age. Moreover, a slider, and its mechanism represent a mass which has considerable inertia, and it is difficult or impossible to obtain a mechanical stop action which will work a slider with the same rapidity as a key action.

Historically, the slider-chest combined with direct mechanical action is of great importance. The diagram is practically self-explanatory. When the key is depressed a system of wooden levers causes the pallet or valve to be opened, and air from the wind-chest is admitted to the channel of the particular note, over which the pipes are planted. But no pipe can speak until the slider belonging to its row or rank is also drawn. The action of the slider may be imagined by thinking of a perforated Meccano strip drawn between two similar strips. A movement of the sandwiched strip can be arranged to make the sets of holes coincide, or, alternatively, the holes may be closed. Obviously, in the sliders of the organ, the holes vary in size along the sliders according to the size of the pipes which are planted above them.

As a rank of sixty-one pipes is longer than a five-octave keyboard it is necessary to use some mechanical device for transmitting the motion of a key to a point which is not in the same plane vertically above it but is displaced laterally. Moreover, it is not usual with mechanical actions and slider sound-boards to plant the pipes in the order of their corresponding keys on the manuals. Historically, a favourite way of planting the pipes was to start with the CC pipe on the extreme left and the CC♯ pipe on the right and work

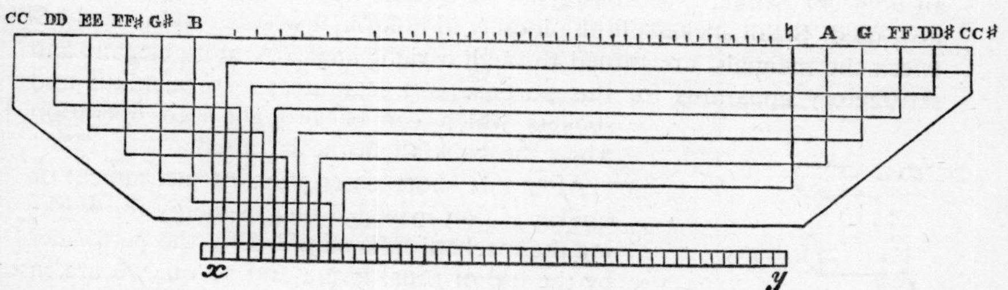

FIG. 22A. By means of a roller-board the movements of the keys of the keyboard *xy* are transmitted to the pallets.

inwards from both ends so that the pipe tops gave a convex curve with the smallest in the middle. The weight of the pipes was then distributed symmetrically by this arrangement.

CC DD EE FF♯ GG♯ → ← GG FF DD♯ CC♯, etc.

The left side of the organ, looking at it from the front, was called the CC side, and the right side the CC♯ or the sharp side. The large-scale pipes of an open diapason might tend to be "crowded off" the sound-board or they might be required as montres for exposure in the casework of the organ. Their feet are then connected by metal tubing to the corresponding holes in the sound-board. The tubing should be of generous diameter otherwise the speech of these pipes will be slow. (With pneumatic and electric actions some builders would give these pipes their own mechanism.)

The mechanical action of the key can be transmitted laterally by

(*a*) a roller-board, an invention, which, as we have seen in the historical portion of this work, greatly assisted the development of the large organ as an instrument which could be played conveniently from a keyboard of reasonable size.

(*b*) a frame, whereby the sequence of the notes was preserved and there was a spacing out, so that pipe diameters were not limited by key widths. Here the backfalls are splayed in a fanlike manner, only those in the middle of the compass being parallel to one another.

The sliders which shut off or open the wind to the pipe ranks are moved by levers and trundles. The coupling of manuals and pedals is achieved by a set of stickers, backfalls and trackers which are brought into action when the backfall frame is raised by drawing the coupler. Octave couplers are made by using small roller-boards and stickers. Inter-manual coupling was effected in organs until the end of the eighteenth century by drawing one manual forward by means of knobs on each key frame, so that small projections on the ends of the keys of one manual engaged with the key ends of an adjacent manual. Various types of tracker inter-manual couplings are now used. Small stickers, fitting loosely in holes in a wooden rod placed between the manuals, are turned through a right angle. A more elegant and satisfactory apparatus for this purpose is a separate set of backfalls and stickers which can be brought into operation when the backfall frame is raised.

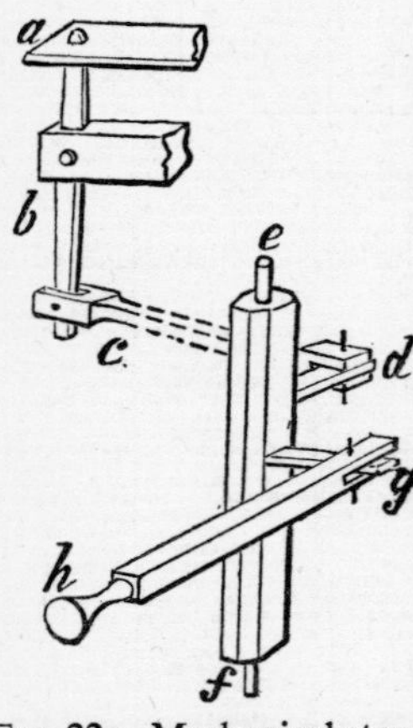

FIG. 22B. Mechanical stop action. The movement of the stop-knob *b* is transmitted by means of the trundle *ef* to the end of the slider *a*.

After this short description of mechanical or tracker action in which all the energy for working the mechanism is supplied by the performer by the use of rods, levers and so on, we are in a position to understand the devices which have been developed for relieving the performer of some of the labour by supplying pneumatic, electro-pneumatic or electrical intermediaries between the keys and the pipes. It must be remembered that such intermediaries may only be supplied to a part of the organ mechanism; e.g. a small organ may have mechanical action for the manuals and stops but pneumatic action for the pedals. A large organ may have pneumatic action for stops, pedals and three manuals but there may be electric action to a fourth manual whose pipes are some distance away. On the whole, it is better to be consistent in the use of an action where a new organ is concerned, but whereas it is often possible to make a direct connection between the manual keys and sound-boards, pneumatic tubing has often been the means of simplifying the connections between the pedal-board and pedal pipes placed at the side of the instrument.

Pneumatic Actions

The first pneumatic action in any instrument came almost unawares without any realisation of its importance. In 1827, Joseph Booth, a Wakefield organ-builder, used a pneumatic auxiliary action in the organ at Attercliffe Parish Church, Sheffield, to play some bass pipes of a GGG compass open

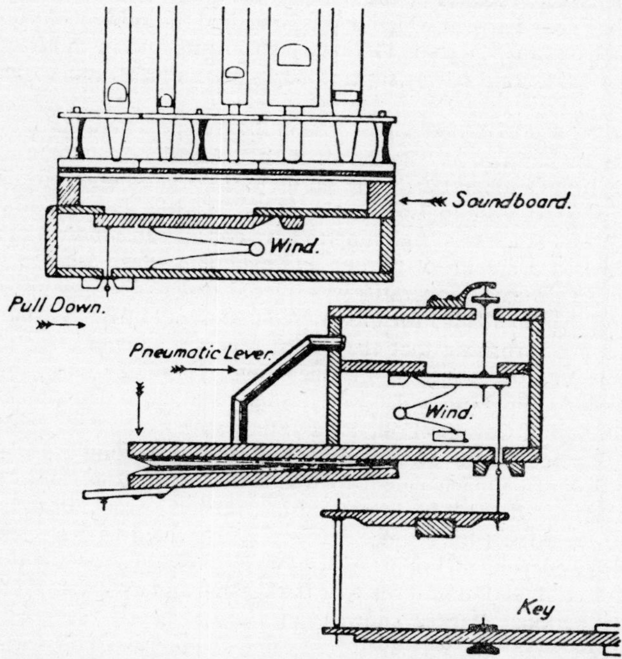

Fig. 23. Hamilton's original type of pneumatic lever action: later improved by Barker and Willis.

diapason which were separated from the main great organ.[1] From the pipe-hole on the main sound-board which normally would have fed the pipe, he led the wind through a conveyance into a small circular bellows, and these "puffs", as he called them, opened the pallets. The leakage of air in the system sufficed to cause the bellows to collapse when the wind supply ceased.[1]

In 1835, David Hamilton, organ-builder to the Queen, of Edinburgh, applied a complete pneumatic action of the lever type to the organ at St.

[1] Hopkins and Rimbault, op. cit.

John's Episcopal Church in that city. The apparatus was designed and made in the year 1833 and is now preserved in the Royal Scottish Museum, Edinburgh. It was shown and described at the Birmingham meeting of the British Association for the Advancement of Science in 1839.[1]

A principle which has been essential to many types of pneumatic action, still in use at the present day, is the internal motor which collapses when the extra pressure within the wind-chest forces the air from it through an orifice opened to the atmosphere. This device was worked out by Hamilton in 1861, independently of other workers in a similar field, and was used in his organ in the Augustine Congregational Church in Edinburgh.[2]

The invention of the pneumatic-lever has long been credited to Charles Spackman Barker, because of the fame of Cavaillé-Coll's instrument at St. Denis Abbey near Paris in which it was first used, its subsequent use in the large French organs, in some German instruments and in those of Henry Willis from 1851, until it was superseded by the latter's tubular pneumatic actions.

C. S. Barker was the eldest son of Joseph Barker and a nephew of the artist, Thomas Barker, known as "Barker of Bath". Charles Spackman was born in Bath on 10th October 1804.[3] He set up as an organ-builder in his native city, after a short visit to London in 1832. Having seen the Bramah or hydraulic press, which was beginning to have considerable industrial application, he devised a system of pistons and cylinders which worked by compressed air. This crude apparatus was offered first to the organist of York Minster and then in 1834–5 for use in the large organ at Birmingham Town Hall. It is not surprising that the device was not accepted, for it needed considerable improvement. In the meantime, Hamilton had produced a more convenient apparatus which was strangely similar to that which Barker, at the invitation of Cavaillé-Coll, fitted to the organ at the Abbey Church of St. Denis, Paris, after the organ-builder had started erecting the instrument. Barker took out a French patent for the action in 1839, and Cavaillé-Coll thereafter applied it to all his important instruments. Later, Barker directed the firm of Ducroquet for a time. Barker experimented with electric-action, but was largely dependent on Dr. Albert Peschard of Caen for his information on this subject. It is doubtful whether Barker was an innovator of pneumatic or electric action. Barker showed an instrument of his at the Paris Exhibition of 1855 and was awarded a first-class medal and was made a Chevalier in the Imperial Order of the Légion d'Honneur. He left Paris at the time of the Franco-Prussian war and built several organs in Dublin

[1] In a monograph published in 1851 entitled *Remarks on Organ Building and the Causes of Defective Instruments*, by David Hamilton, Organ-builder to the Queen (Edinburgh, Hamilton and Müller), the author says: "Many years ago he discovered a new principle in mechanism, which he applied for relieving the weight of touch in large instruments. . . . He afterwards found the identical invention (in all its details the same as his model) applied in the grand organ of the church of St. Denis and that of the Madeleine . . . under the name of 'pneumatic-lever'."

[2] The records are preserved in the books of the Hamilton firm.

[3] The records of the Barker family are preserved in the Victoria Gallery and Municipal Libraries, Bath.

(where he was on occasion aided by Hilborne Roosevelt, the American organ-builder). He died at Maidstone on 26th November 1879.

Camidge, the organist of York Minster, wrote to Barker in 1833:

"To such an instrument as ours it (the pneumatic lever) would certainly be very important, where four organs have to be played occasionally by one set of keys, and I should be most happy to recommend its adoption. Mr. Hill, of the late firm of Elliot and Hill, has erected our organ, and, I assure, the playing it is no sinecure; it is most laborious work to go through a grand or last voluntary with the whole power of the instrument. Such a difficult touch as that of York Cathedral organ is doubtless sufficient to paralyse the efforts of most men, I assure you. I, with all the energy I rally about me, am sometimes inclined to make a full stop from actual fatigue in a very short time after the commencement of a full piece."

"In the year 1845, Prosper-Antoine Moitessier, an organ-builder of Montpellier, France, patented what he called 'abrégé pneumatique', an organ action in which all back-falls and rollers were replaced by tubes

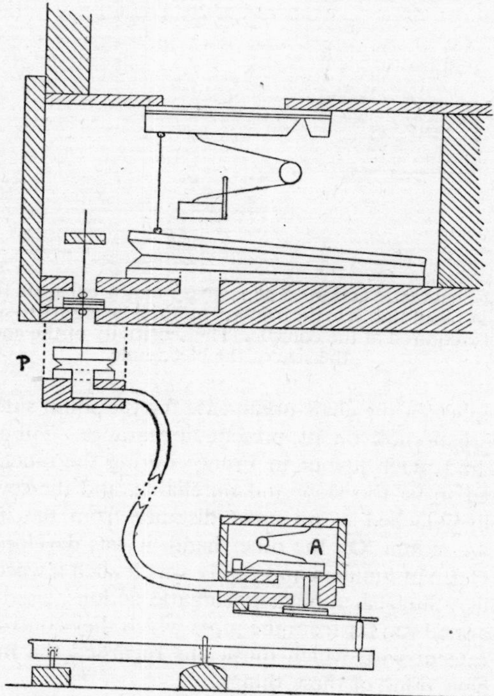

FIG. 24. Pressure-pneumatic action. When a key is depressed, wind from the key touch box (A) in the console goes to the primary pneumatic (P) in the organ via the pneumatic tubing between console and organ.

operated by exhaust air. In 1850 he built with this action an organ of 42 speaking stops for the church of Notre Dame de la Dalbade, at Toulouse. In 1866, Fermis, schoolmaster and village organist of Hanterire near Toulouse improved on Moitessier's action by combining tubes conveying compressed air with the Barker lever. An organ was built on this system for the Paris Exhibition of 1867, which came under the notice of Henry Willis, by which he was so struck that he was stimulated to experiment and develop his action which culminated in the St. Paul's organ in 1872."[1]

Thus, the division of the organ at St. Paul's Cathedral into two sections (made by cutting in half the case, which stood on the former chancel screen,

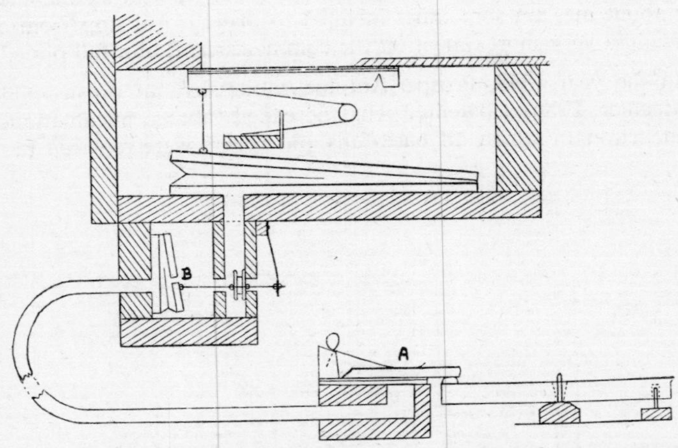

Fig. 25. Exhaust-pneumatic action. The primary motor exhausts through the key touch box at A. A bleed-hole B in the primary motor is necessary to secure repetition. No wind supply is required at the console. The sensitivity of the action depends on the size of the bleed-hole.

and adding a replica of the chair-organ case for the south side) became possible and the organ took on its present appearance. Tubular pneumatic action did not find much favour in France during the nineteenth century; it was considered to be too slow and unreliable, and the reversed consoles of Cavaillé-Coll, detached at no great distance from the instrument, did not need such an action. On the other hand, it was developed by English, American and German builders and rarely was it such a worthy mechanism as that of Willis. Sluggish tubular-pneumatic actions, used with consoles which were separated too far from the pipes which they controlled, did much to reduce the esteem with which musicians regarded the instrument. The French would have none of these things.

[1] Dr. Gabriel Bédart, Professor of Physiology, University of Lille, in an article in *Musical Opinion* (London, July 1908). In 1867, E. Horsell Pulbrook, of Tooting, London, patented an ingenious but complicated pneumatic action which required both pressure and exhaust wind for its operation.

Electric Actions

Electric action was first regarded as a novelty, but it was soon obvious that electric wires and cables were less bulky than masses of "compo" tubing and that, as far as the electrical portion of the instrument was concerned, its response was instantaneous. Many of the early actions were unreliable, but the chief difficulty was a lack of a proper supply of low-voltage electric current. Electric batteries had a way of running down during a Sunday service, and the compound-wound dynamo generator had not then been used. Many electric actions were seen not to have been as bad as they were thought to be, when electric power of sufficient amperage and at about 14–15 volts was available from a reliable rotary generator.

The idea of using electric action in the organ is as old as the electro-magnet itself, for its inventor, William Sturgeon, tried to open the pallets of an organ built by his friend, William Wilkinson, in 1826. The experiment showed that electric power from batteries was not sufficient to do this. Some other means had to be found to do the heavy work.[1]

Electric action was suggested by Du Moncel, Froment, and afterwards by MM. Stein et fils, and in 1885 a not very successful action was shown at the Paris Exhibition. Dr. Gauntlett, who was a London organist and whose hymn-tunes are still popular, suggested that replicas of all the organs of the Crystal Palace Exhibition should be made and played by electricity from one console. In 1852 he took out a patent for an electrical connection between the keys and the pallets of an organ.[2]

The first successful use of electricity was in an *electro-pneumatic* action, and the majority of actions which are called *electric* today are really *electro-pneumatic*, i.e. an electro-magnet or solenoid is used to open a small valve, which in turn lets wind into a pneumatic motor (which may act as a relay for a larger motor) and thus the pallet or pipe-valve is opened. This type of action was first devised by Dr. Albert Peschard (1836–1903), a Caen lawyer, and was made by Barker in 1861. A joint patent was taken out in 1862 and the action was successfully applied in the organ of the Collegiate Church, Salon, near Marseilles, in 1866.[3]

In 1867 Henry Bryceson, of London, exhibited an organ in the Exposition Universelle in Paris and saw the electro-pneumatic action which Barker had applied to the organ at St. Augustin's Church, Paris. On returning to England Bryceson began experimenting and produced the first successful electric action in England at the Theatre Royal, Drury Lane, London. The chief difficulty was to find adequate batteries to supply electric current for the purpose. Later, this organ was removed to the Polytechnic Institute, Regent Street, London, where it was the object of much curiosity. The same firm

[1] This information is from the records of the firm which is still active in the same district (Kendal, England).

[2] J. W. Hinton, *Story of the Electric Organ* (London, 1909).

[3] Peschard produced documentary evidence to Dr. Hinton to show that he had communicated his ideas to Barker in 1861 and that Barker had stolen these from him. Certainly Barker never gave Peschard his due, and the latter did not make a sou from his plans and experiments (J. W. Hinton, op. cit.).

built a large and beautiful organ in the Chapel of Rugby School in 1872. The electric action was reliable and the instrument was not rebuilt until 1910.

German organ-builders were also experimenting. Weigle applied a direct electric action in the organ at Echterdingen, near Stuttgart, in 1870, but it was a failure, owing to the need for heavy currents and the oxidising of the key contacts. J. W. Goundry produced a fairly successful action in 1863, and

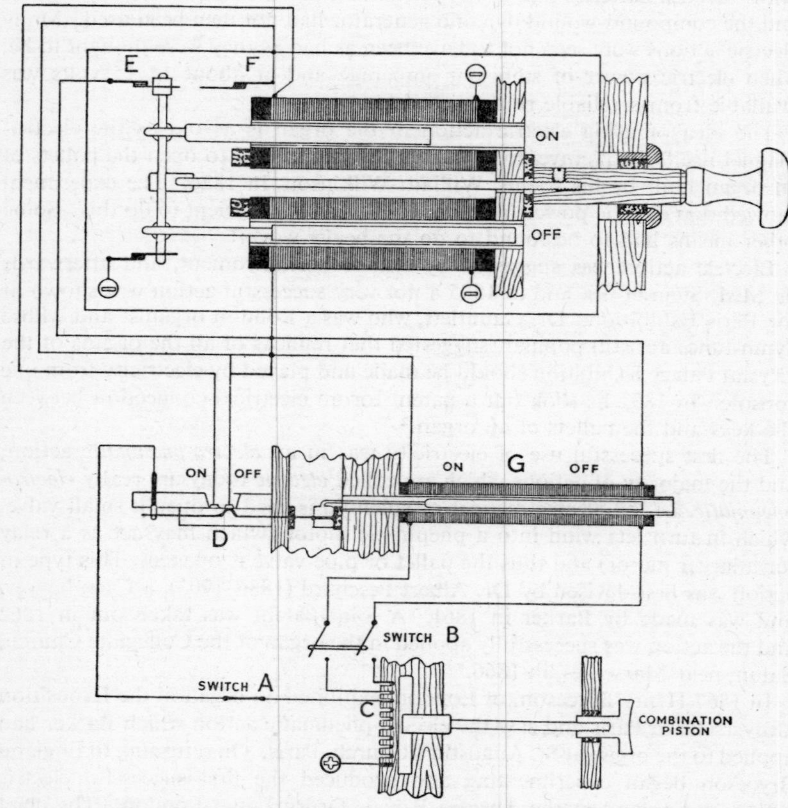

FIG. 26. Willis adjustable piston mechanism, using switches and solenoids. This is one of many methods of drawing stops to a preconceived system in use. No wind is required in the console with such an electrical system. Designed by A. Thompson-Allen.

in the following year he experimented with a method for opening the pallets with water-power governed by electro-magnets. W. G. Trice, an Englishman working in Italy, produced some fine organs in Genoa and district about 1890. All these had electric action.

Towards the end of the century a number of French builders took up electric action, and Merklin built successful electro-pneumatic instruments as in the choir organ at St. Clotilde, Paris, in 1888; St. Jacques de Haut-Pas, Paris, in 1889; choir organ of Notre Dame Cathedral, Paris, in 1890. Schmoele and Mols produced some successful electric actions in Antwerp in 1881; Voit and Sons, Durlach, in 1885. Walcker in Germany and Hilborne Roosevelt in America were producing remarkably effective electric actions by the end of the century. We have already mentioned Hope-Jones in the historical portion of this work. His work sometimes appeared to be unreliable, but often his actions would have been generally satisfactory had electric current of sufficient amperage been available. Cavaillé-Coll stood aloof from electric action and indeed preferred Barker-lever pneumatics to the improved British tubular type. Henry Willis only used electric action when no other means was possible. He did not like detached consoles. His electric action, made in 1886 in the organ of Canterbury Cathedral, which was placed in the triforium, was entirely reliable. It continued working until the instrument was taken down for rebuilding before the last war and would have continued working for an indefinite time. The key-contacts were made to work in mercury cups and the wires therefrom were arranged side by side in a frame, like trackers. The magnets were large

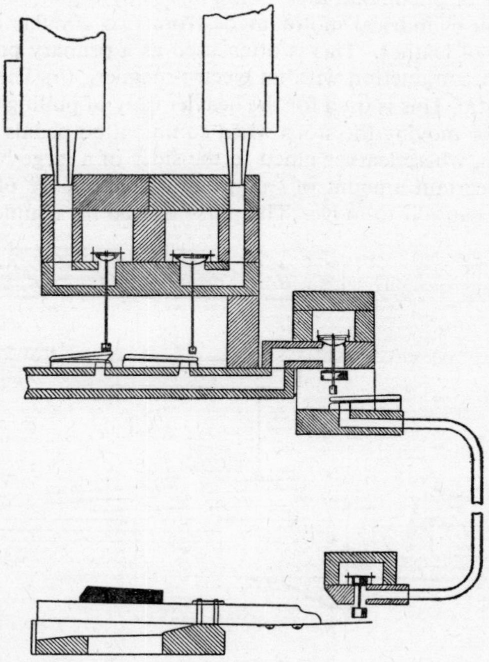

FIG. 27. Walcker Kegellade chest without springs. The valves are cone-shaped (hence the name Kegellade). The mechanical Kegellade was patented in 1842, the pneumatic type here depicted in 1890. The valve on left is raised.

and wound with wire of substantial gauge. Here again Willis's fine engineering skill revealed itself. Although Hope-Jones's Worcester Cathedral organ was built after that of Willis at Canterbury, its action collapsed completely after less than twenty-five years of service.

The pallet-chest with its sliders is still made in spite of the introduction of other types, but with its possibilities of warpings, leakages and "runnings", it has been displaced to a large extent by some form of sliderless- or ventil-chest in which each rank of pipes or stop is fed separately by the wind supply (which is controlled by the stop when the latter is put on and off). In ventil-chests a simple, round valve of wood, faced with cork and leather and about double the diameter of the hole which it covers, may be used; or the valve may be a cone of wood which fits into a hole of conical shape and is raised against the wind pressure. Such "kegellade" or "cone" chests were widely used by Walcker after 1842, but they were introduced about the year 1780 by the German builder, J. S. Hausdörfer. It must be pointed out that organ pipes should be voiced on a machine which has the type of chest on which they will speak when they are placed in the organ. The aerodynamics of the entrance of wind from the pipe-foot to the flue are often critical in regard to the initiation of speech of the pipe.

Various types of pneumatic motors are in use by organ-builders: (*a*) The pill-box or small cylindrical motor made from two circular discs of wood and a rectangle of leather. This is often used as a primary pneumatic for a first stage, or in conjunction with an electro-magnet. (*b*) The triangular or bellows pneumatic. This is used for the heavier duty of pulling down a pallet, moving sliders or moving the stops when combination pedals or pistons are used. (*c*) Purses, where leather glued to the sides of a large hole in a block of wood has a certain amount of "play" and a difference of air pressures on its faces will cause it to move. The purse is used for coupler mechanism,

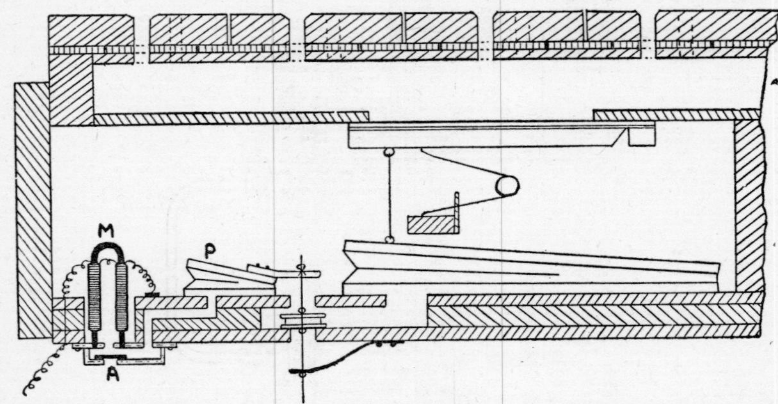

Fig. 28. Diagram to show action of electro-pneumatic key action and slider chest. The armature A of the magnet M controls the flow of pressure wind from the chest to and from the primary pneumatic P which in its turn controls the wind to the large pneumatic motor which pulls down the pallet.

ventils, and instead of the larger triangular pneumatics for opening the valves of large pipes. To an engineer trained in the use of metals, the fine white leather of the organ-builder may not seem, at first sight, very durable material; but pneumatic actions, preserved from extremes of climate, dust and dirt, and from destruction by living organisms, will often last for half a century and perform their cycles of functions many hundreds of thousands of times. (It must be mentioned that "rubberised cloth" is quite unsuitable for reliable and durable pneumatic work.) In fact, some organ-builders prefer to have pneumatic movements for working the combination action, where many

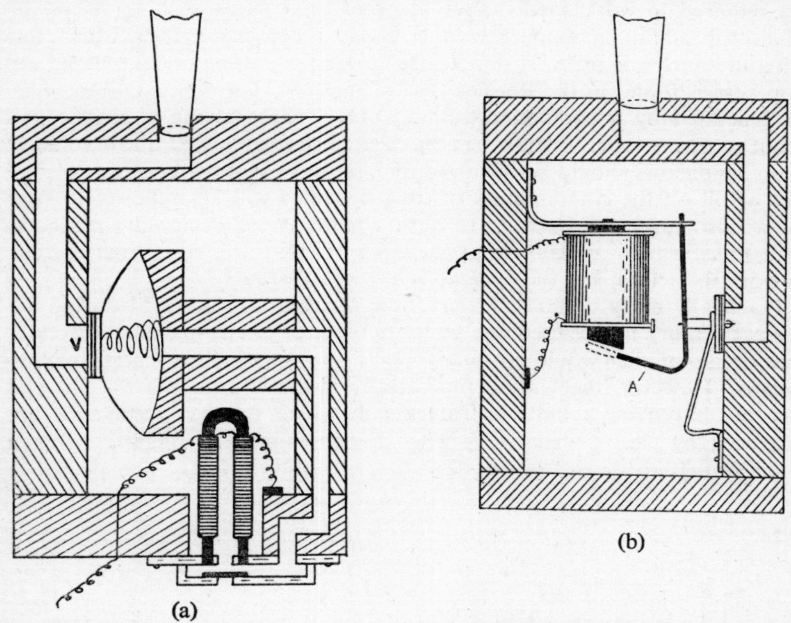

FIG. 29A. Electro-pneumatic action for separate unit pipes of moderate size. The purse pneumatic is faced with a flat valve V.

FIG. 29B. Direct electric action for unit pipes. Note the design of the rocking armature and the shape of the magnet pole face.

stops have to be moved, rather than to have all-electric console movements. It must be stated that stop-keys controlled by Reisner-type magnets or the luminous stop-heads of the Compton type make small demands on the low-voltage electrical supply when the pistons are used, and in the latter case no current is used for drawing a stop-knob. The translucent stop-head (first used by Vincent Willis) is put on by a touch and taken off when it is touched again. Many all-electric consoles, with draw-knobs, use a solenoid and plunger armature for controlling the movement of each stop when the combination pistons are used.

A number of types of electro-magnet and solenoid are used in modern organ-building. They are now made by supply houses as standard equipment, but a number of British, American and German organ-builders maintain separate small plants for making their electrical equipment, relays, etc. The most commonly used piece of electrical equipment is the action-magnet which works at about fourteen volts. The disc armature acts as a valve which controls a primary pneumatic.

Solenoids with plunger armatures are used where a longer travel and more power are required. Double solenoids are used for working stops and in certain types of adjustable "composition piston" mechanism. Where magnets are required to work small valves or other movements such as relays, in all-electric action, a magnet with a bevelled pole-piece, over which the armature moves, is used. A double use of this for putting on and taking off stop-keys is found in the Reisner type of magnet. The action current may be generated by a compound-wound D.C. dynamo giving a pressure of about fourteen volts. It must be remembered that with such a low voltage, main conductors should be of substantial gauge to avoid voltage drops, and dirt or oil on the commutators of such dynamos will be sufficient to stop the action current altogether. In most organs, Westinghouse dry rectifiers, with transformers working from the A.C. mains, will give enough current to work the action, and the dynamo is now obsolescent.

Practically every organ-builder of note throughout the world during the present century has devised one or more types of electro-pneumatic action, Few organ-builders would now make electro-pneumatic slider-chests for new organs. However, there are comparatively few new organs in Britain and Europe, but many rebuilt instruments in which tubular pneumatics are displaced by electro-pneumatics when the instrument is rebuilt. Often a good plan is to fit electro-magnets to the existing primary pneumatics at

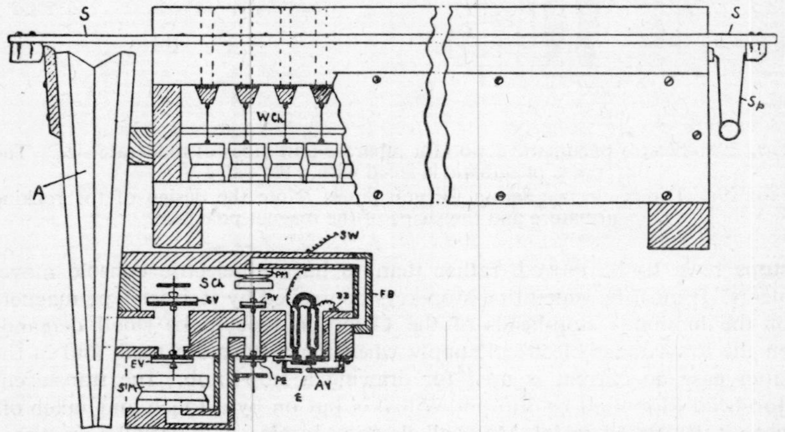

FIG. 30. Electro-pneumatic stop action for drawing slider (after R. Whitworth). The magnet armature (AV) controls the supply of wind to the primary pneumatic (PM) which in turn controls the secondary pneumatic motor (SM). The slider is drawn against a spring by the large triangular pneumatic (A).

the wind-chest, and to use electro-pneumatic machines for working the sliders (either single large pneumatic motors which open the slider against a spring, or double pneumatics which will both open and close it). A new console which may be detached from the instrument and, if required, a considerable number of couplers and other accessories, all conveniently contrived electrically, may be provided. The change inside the organ and the saving of space are quite remarkable when hundreds of feet or even miles of pneumatic tubing and elaborate coupler mechanism are replaced by thin electrical cables. Again, when the large wind reservoirs and their feeders give way to the smaller wind regulators (although this is not always advisable) the saving of space is even more pronounced.

In old organs, the stops were rarely changed during the performance of a movement, but today organists in Britain and America expect stop and piston action to take effect as quickly as key action. It was therefore necessary to devise a type of chest which would permit registration changes to be made so that they could be "played" on the beat without disturbing the phrasing and rhythmic flow of the music. Such a chest is known as the pitman chest because it contains a type of completely mobile valve known as a pitman[1]

A good electro-pneumatic action should have the following positive properties:

(1) It should be prompt and reliable in key and stop action, even if it is not used for a number of weeks.

(2) It should be durable and should not be affected by environmental changes of temperature and humidity.

(3) It should be capable of adjustment without disturbing other mechanism or the pipes mounted on the main wind-chests.

(4) It should be of such design that it can be constructed by any good worker with wood and pneumatic motors.

A pitman-chest, though not unique in this way, when properly made, certainly fulfils these desiderata.

Amongst other subsidiary mechanisms in the modern organ is reversible action. It is used for both pedal and piston actions. Alternate similar movements of the pedal and piston bring the mechanism into operation and remove it. Pistons and pedals controlling "great to pedal", other couplers, "full organ reversible", are of frequent occurrence. Usually the "full-organ" piston will not move the stops and a small red light should become visible to show that the piston is in operation. Pneumatic reversible action depends on the working of a "poppet", but with electric action a simple reciprocating switch or Reisner-type magnets, where more elaborate control is required, may be used.[2]

[1] In 1897 C. F. Brindley of Sheffield patented a pneumatic-pouch action (Pat. Eng. 13,764) which anticipated the actual pitman action, which was first used by Hutchings and Votey at the Flatbush Dutch Reformed Church, Brooklyn, New York, in 1899. The action was improved and used by Skinner in the U.S.A. and later by Willis in England.

[2] The reader interested in modern electric actions will find an exceedingly clear exposition well illustrated in R. Whitworth's *The Electric Organ*, 3rd ed. (1948).

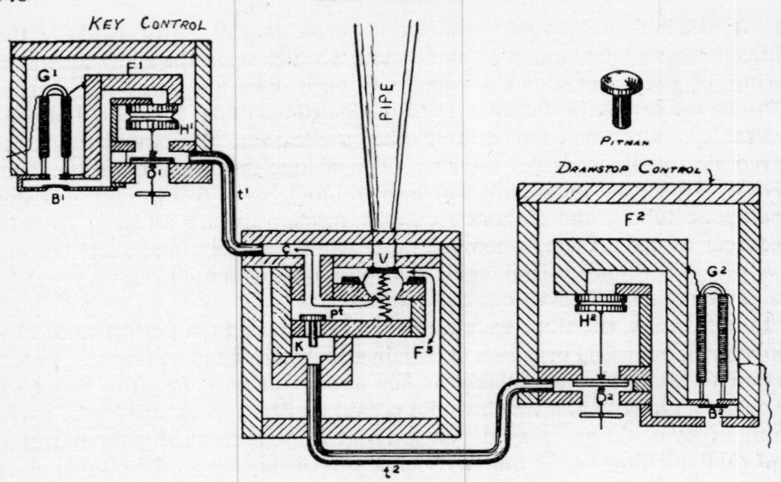

FIG. 31. Theoretical Diagram of a Pitman Chest.

F1, F2, F3 are charged with pressure wind and the pipe will not sound until the channel C is exhausted and the pressure of wind in F3 will collapse the membrane and valve V against the spring. The Pitman valve fits loosely in its seating. If the stop is on and a note off, the long groove common to a number of pipes is exhausted but the Pitman prevents the pressure falling within the membrane (purse). If the stop is off and a note on, the Pitman rises and prevents an escape of wind through channel C. Only when both K and C are exhausted will the pipe sound. The pipe boring is at the side of the channel and a *plan* would show that it does not go through it. The method of actually making up the chest in working drawings is given by R. Whitworth *The Electric Organ*, 3rd edition, or W. H. Barnes *The Contemporary American Organ*, all editions.

CONSOLE EQUIPMENT[1]

One of the most interesting and yet at times disturbing aspects of organ-playing is that there are hardly two organs alike. Occasionally, designs for small instruments have been evolved by their makers and a few such instruments have been made to the same pattern, but in the ordinary way each instrument presents its own problems and possibilities. No standard console has been agreed upon by organ-builders, but individual firms have produced consoles which, in spite of different stop-lists, have shown a certain amount of standardisation. The consoles of Cavaillé-Coll and his tonal schemes showed such family likeness that organists who were familiar with one such instrument would find no difficulties when they were confronted by others

---

Perhaps it should be pointed out that much thought has to be given to the arrangement of circuits in electric actions. Unless each movement is fed and energised separately, particularly in coupler mechanism, electric current may flow in circuits which are not anticipated and various unwanted notes will sound.

[1] A scientific account of the factors of console design has been given by G. R. Bamber in *The Organ Club Handbook*, No. 6, 1960; reprinted in *The Organ*, 1961.

of the same builder. The consoles of Harrison and the present Henry Willis show a certain amount of standardisation.[1]

Until the middle of the nineteenth century the key and stop arrangements for playing organs were usually simple and crude. In many cases it was difficult for an organist to change the stops while he was playing, unless he had the help of one or more assistants. Even now a number of large European organs are no better equipped. Organists who are responsible for certain details of the console equipment of the organs at which they preside do not agree concerning the nature of the control mechanism of the organ. Some players prefer to have stop-keys, and others like to have stop-knobs on vertical jambs at angles of 45 degrees to the key length. The standard modern Willis console uses stop-knobs for the speaking stops and tilting tablets over the top manual for the couplers, which are arranged according to a consistent plan. It has been customary, for nearly a century, in English organs to place the swell-organ stops on the left jamb and the great-organ stops on the right. Beyond that, stops have been grouped to suit the organ-builder's design, but usually more stop-knobs are placed on the left jamb than on the right, presumably from a belief that the left hand is more often free to deal with them than the right. Sometimes couplers are grouped with the departments which they augment and at other times they are arranged in a separate group. Composition pistons with ivory heads, arranged in rows in the key-slips under the respective manuals whose stops they control, are usual in British and American organs. Adjustable pistons are favoured by British and American organists. To adjust the stop combinations the requisite stops are drawn, the piston on which the combination is required is pressed at the same time that a locking piston is also pressed. The adjustable piston then "carries" the stops which are fixed to it until the combination is changed by a similar process. Some builders, such as Willis, provide a cancel piston, which puts in all the stops, and a reversible piston, which gives full organ without moving the stops. Light indicators are provided to show the organist that stops are sounding, even if the knobs are not drawn or the stop-keys put down. A similar arrangement is used when there is a *stop-crescendo* pedal or *rollschweller*, which brings on the ranks of pipes in chorus order without affecting the stops. Blind combinations which do not move the stops have been popular in German organs, but the modern trend is against this.[2]

[1] Some keyboard measurements (Willis, 1939) follow: Length of naturals (white keys) $5\frac{1}{2}''$; width $\frac{7}{8}''$, covered with solid ivory plates $\frac{1}{8}''$ thick. Length of sharps (black keys) $3\frac{1}{2}''$; width $\frac{3}{8}''$. Sharps $\frac{1}{2}''$ above the level of naturals. Distance between sharps $\frac{11}{16}''$. Total length of a manual keyboard of 61 notes $= 2'\ 9\frac{1}{2}''$. Overlap of manuals about $1\frac{1}{2}''$. Distance between manuals $= 2\frac{1}{4}''$ to $2\frac{1}{2}''$. Depth of manual touch $\frac{5}{16}''$ to $\frac{3}{8}''$. Top resistance touch 4–$4\frac{1}{2}$ oz., touch at bottom $2\frac{1}{2}$ oz.

[2] Ingenious devices for controlling the stops have appeared in great quantity since 1850. As an example we print an extract from a patent of 1857 for an *adjustable* stop-crescendo pedal.

Henry Willis, Patent No. 376, 1857, Improvements in organs:

"A crescendo pedal for adding stops successively. The principle comprised a cylinder similar to that of a musical box and with pins tapped into it. There were placed at the console two lever pedals, one for control of a crescendo of the stops,

The console arrangements of the Cavaillé-Coll organs were simple. The foundation stops, on a particular manual, were grouped on one sound-board; and the reeds, mixtures and mutations (jeux de combinaison) were placed on a separate "laye" or sound-board. Ventil pedals were provided so that wind was admitted to the second chest at a desired time and only then would the stops sound. An extension of this principle was made in the larger organs by the same French builder. When stops were drawn, the sliders which controlled the pipes were not affected until wind, controlled by ventil pedals, was admitted to the draw-stop machines which were arranged in groups. Thus the organist could disconnect the sliders from the stops, and while playing on one combination could prepare for another, which would become operable when the wind was let into the draw-stop machines. Hope-Jones had an electrical version of this device, whereby the current was permitted to flow in the stop circuits by pressing a switch-key or pedal. The stops were then able to operate the sliders, and, again, when the current was cut off, a new combination could be prepared without upsetting the stops which were in use. The nineteenth- and twentieth-century German organs often used a system of "free-combinations". Under each stop or stop-key small studs or diminutive stops were provided for each of the free combinations. When these small knobs or studs were drawn, nothing happened until the appropriate pedal or stop-key was put into operation, when the tones fixed on the free-combination come into operation without disturbing the actual stops or stop-keys drawn. The Anglo-American system of pistons, adjustable at the console, is the most expensive; but it can be cheapened by using a simple switchboard in which there is a switch for each stop on the organ, or division of the organ, for each adjustable piston; that is, the total number of switches is equal to the number of adjustable pistons multiplied by the number of stops. Each switch may be placed in three positions—on, neutral, off. The functions of the switch at the first and third positions are obvious: in the neutral position the stop, if on, will not be taken off, and if off will not be put on by a particular piston.[1]

Opinions vary concerning swell pedals, their nature, position and action. In the nineteenth century, most swell-boxes were fitted with horizontal swell shutters and these were controlled by a simple pedal which was placed on the

---

and the other for the de-crescendo or reverse movement of the same stops. As the crescendo pedal was depressed, a brass cylinder would be rotated through the medium of a toothed gear. The pins on the cylinder, as they came beneath a beam of levers, would lift an opposing lever, which would impart an impulse of wind into a pneumatic drawstop machine, and this would cause the soundboard sliders to be pushed into the 'on' position. On depression of the decrescendo lever, the same cylinder would be reversed. The pins which engaged the 'on' levers would pass by these levers without lifting them when the cylinder was moved in the reverse direction. This was effected by what are described as 'tumbling pieces', fitted on the ends of the levers so engaged. A different set of pins on the cylinder, which similarly passed the 'off' levers during the advance on the crescendo, would then operate the 'off' levers on the return journey of the cylinder. By changing the positions of the pins the device could be made selective both as to the stops effected, and the orders by which they came on or were taken off."

[1] To an increasing extent organ-builders are avoiding the neutral position.

right above the extreme sharp pedal keys. The pedal returned and the box closed when the foot was removed, but the pedal could be fastened down at one or more positions by means of notches in a piece of wood with which it could be made to engage. Such a pedal discouraged the abuse of the swell on the organ, and, in spite of its disadvantages, it could be used for the production of excellent sforzando and phrasing effects which do not always come so readily with a more recent type of pedal. Present-day organists usually prefer centrally-placed swell-pedals of rectangular or "shoe" shape, on which the whole foot can be placed. The pedal stays at any position and so the swell shutters, which are balanced, or placed vertically, can be opened to any extent desired by the performer, and left in any position after the foot has been removed. This type of swell pedal has undeniable advantages, but it is also true that it is rarely so susceptible to its use for producing subtle nuances of dynamic change and sforzando as is the older type. Even in quite large organs, direct mechanical connection between the swell pedal and the shutters which it controls is often possible. Movements working with ball-bearings, and other devices to reduce friction, have all been used to secure good mechanical connections. Often, electro-pneumatic intermediaries have been applied between the pedal and the shutters. Hope-Jones and others used a system in which swell shutters, starting with some of small width, were opened successively as the swell pedal was put into operation. It has been found more satisfactory, however, to evolve systems of control whereby all the shutters move simultaneously. Methods of swell-shutter control are legion, but few are satisfactory. A favourite device is to arrange that, as the swell pedal is opened, pressure air passes successively into a number of tubes, each of which leads to a pneumatic motor or small bellows. The movements of these bellows are compounded together to open the swell shutters. Such an arrangement is bound to be jerky, and at least eight stages are required even for the crudest working. (It must be remembered that the first small distance travelled by the shutters counts for more in the corresponding increase of tone than much larger distances travelled later on.) An improvement on these simple "jerks" is the "whiffle-tree" action which has been improved by Skinner and Willis. In this, at least sixteen and sometimes thirty-two pneumatic motors, coupled together mechanically, are used for opening the swell shutters. At the console the swell pedal operates a similar number of contacts and each motor in the swell engine has a magnet and a primary pneumatic. The connection between the swell pedal and the organ is a number of wires in the main cable. Hydraulic connections between swell pedal and shutters have been used with success. The pedal works a piston which drives a liquid from a cylinder through a tube to the organ, where the liquid forces the movement of a piston which is connected to the swell shutters. Very little use has been made of the floating pneumatic lever invented by Vincent Willis for working swell shutters. In this simple "servo-mechanism" the movement of the heavy shutters can be made to follow faithfully that of a light rod attached to the pedal.

The Willis "infinite speed and gradation"[1] swell pedal is a complete depar-

[1] Patent Brit. 428,448 (8.9.1933) Henry Willis and Aubrey Thompson-Allen.

ture from ordinary swell-pedal mechanism and requires a new technique of swell-pedalling. When the foot is removed from the swell pedal it returns to its neutral position by the action of two springs and in doing so does not affect the position of the swell shutters. The amount by which the pedal is pushed forward is a measure of the *speed* at which the shutters open, and the amount it is pushed backwards from its neutral position is a measure of the speed at which they close. In other words, the position of the swell shutters at any instant is not necessarily related to the position of the pedal, and therefore visual indicators have to be provided to show the positions of each set of swell shutters. The device is so arranged that the shutters are held tightly closed when this is desired. Organists differ in their appreciation of this ingenious system.

There is no consensus of opinion throughout the world concerning organ pedal-boards. The use of the Wesley-Willis radiating and concave board, with radii of both radiation and concavity equal to 8 ft. 6 in., is general in

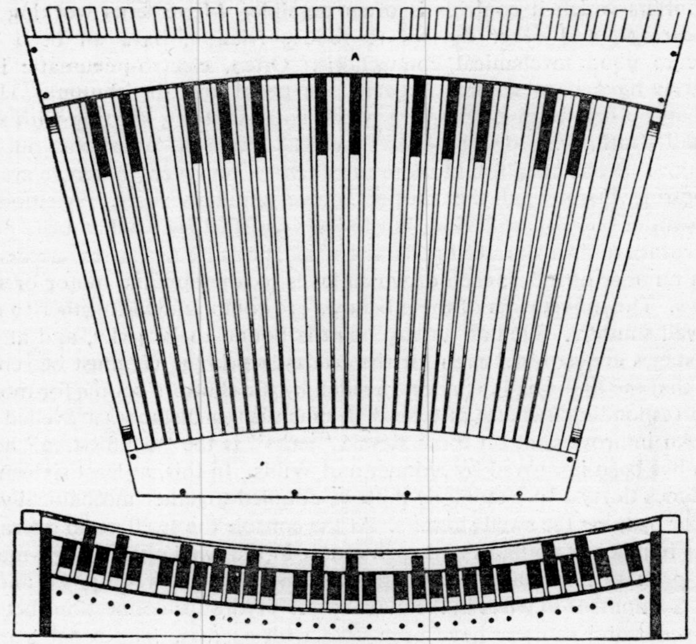

FIG. 32. The Willis Pedal Clavier.

A concave and radiating pedal-board is now in general use in English-speaking countries (often with a compass of 32 notes CCC to G which is larger than the original Willis clavier here illustrated). In Europe such a clavier finds little acceptance. The placing of the board should give the pedal DD key exactly under middle D of the manuals. The distance from the top of the middle natural key to the lowest manual should be 2′ 6½″. The height of each sharp above the level of the naturals is 1¼″, the distance between centres of adjacent naturals at the sharps is 2⅜″, the radii of both arcs of radiation is 8′ 6″. Width of keys ⅞″. Depth of touch ⅝″. Weight of touch at front of sharps 3 lbs.

PLATE 35.

A house organ in Munich, made by Dip.Ing. Karl Bormann in 3,200 hours (1956–9). *See* Spec. 100

England and America (with small modifications such as those of the Audsley-Willis and Ellingford-Willis). This form of pedal-board has met with no general acceptance in France and Germany, where straight and flat or straight and slightly concave pedal-boards are favoured. French and German organists claim that these types of pedal-board enable the feet to be passed behind one another with more playing room and more precision than is possible with the British type. Organs should be equipped with adjustable benches so that the organist can adjust both height and distance from the keys to suit himself.

Organ keys differ from one maker to another, and it is surprising that even the octave length is not quite standard. Usually the natural keys are somewhat shorter than pianoforte keys and the sets of keys are arranged with a certain amount of overhang to facilitate thumbing a melody on one set of keys while the rest of the hand is playing on another. Again, in four- or five-manual organs the distance between the top and bottom manual is thus shortened. In British and American organs the top manual is made to tilt towards the player and the lower manual to tilt upwards. The angle of tilt is graduated between intermediate manuals. It has been customary, by the best English organ-builders during the last century, to make the sharp keys of ebony and to cover the natural keys with thick single-piece plates of unbleached ivory. The consoles of Hill, Willis and Harrison, amongst others, during the present century, have been particularly sumptuous, and even the stop-knobs have been turned from solid ivory. In durability and appearance these have not been rivalled in the world. The arrangement of manuals in British organs is consistently: choir, great, swell, solo, echo or bombarde, from bottom to top, but in large organs there is the possibility of transferring sections of the organ to particular manuals; and certain ancillary or "floating" divisions can be made playable from any one of several manuals. In a similar way, sets of swell shutters can be worked from a particular swell pedal or swell pedals by adjusting a pedal switch-plate. If necessary, all the swell-boxes may be controlled by the same pedal. In France the Cavaillé-Coll organs usually have the grand orgue as the lowest manual, followed by the positif and the récit, but, as in Germany, there is no consistent arrangement. In twentieth-century German organs the manuals are often marked I, II and III. Reading upwards these correspond roughly with hauptwerk (great), positiv (choir), schwellwerk (swell).

A key action which works directly against a spring is not ideal: it is reminiscent of the harmonium and does not assist clean playing. Accordingly, some builders fit a "toggle" spring and action to each key. This can be arranged to give a touch similar to that of a well-made tracker action. The resistance to the finger is about 4 oz. at the top, but a pressure of only 2½ oz. is necessary to keep the key depressed.

Tremulant

There are two types of tremulant: (*a*) the fan, and (*b*) the tremulant which imparts a pressure wave to the air in a wind trunk which supplies a chest of pipes. In the former type, which is little used, a rotating fan, revolving slowly along a horizontal axis and driven by a pneumatic turbine, disturbs the air near the pipes whose tone it is intended to affect.

The usual pattern of tremulant is a vibrating pneumatic motor which opens and closes an air port. The device is connected by a wind trunk to the sound-board. The tremulant was highly esteemed in organs built until the end of the eighteenth century. Dom Bédos distinguishes between the "strong" and the "gentle" tremulant. Father Willis and others made tremulants in which the speed of the beating was controllable by the organist. The tremulant has come into low esteem in the twentieth century by its incessant use by inartistic cinema organists. Nevertheless, if it is used very occasionally it may serve to increase the emotional effect of a short passage played on one or more 8-ft. stops. In the sixteenth and seventeenth centuries the tremulant was regarded as a very important aid to tone production in the organ.

The Extension Organ

Extension or transmission organs are those in which some or all of the pipe ranks are used in more than one pitch and are also made available for use on more than one manual and on the pedals. The transference of a stop, so that it becomes playable on more than one manual and pedal at its normal pitch, is spoken of as borrowing or duplexing. Nearly all organs in Britain use extension as far as the pedal organ is concerned. Even apparently quite large pedal organs often control comparatively few independent pipes, and stop-knobs are multiplied by extension and manual-borrowing. In Germany and France this is less evident. An extension organ is said to be one where there is much manual extension. The extension system has been developed in its most satisfactory manner by John Compton in England. It is now hardly used in the United States. Mr. Compton has always insisted that extension can only be properly applied when there is a proper complement of pipe ranks to start with. When only four or five ranks are available it is not artistic to try to extend them to make an organ whose console may look impressive. It is far better to use the money which would be spent on elaborate electrical mechanism for the small extension organ on two or three more ranks of real organ pipes. In Mr. Compton's organs a considerable part of the mechanism of the extension instrument is made from standardised electrical equipment. A typical scheme is given in specification No. 41, and the derivation of the ranks can be seen. By the skilful combination of the parent pipe ranks at different pitches the missing notes, which occur when most chords are played with octave couplers, are usually avoided. Extension organs are not infrequently built so that the pipework is entirely enclosed in two or more swell-boxes. Each pipe can be considered a unit, and it has its own action. Between the console and the instrument there is an elaborate "switching" system, often with thousands of contacts, so that each rank of pipes can be used in several pitches. It is, of course, possible to place such relay mechanism in the console, but often it is placed separately and may even be in the organ itself. Many extension organs have been built in small con-crete chambers and, as they do not contain sound-boards and massive building frames, the tone is not enhanced by the forced vibrations of solid, large pieces of wood as in the organs of Schulze and Cavaillé-Coll, or indeed in those of almost any master organ-builder of the nineteenth century. It is therefore quite remarkable that the Compton organs are so effective in spite of the difficulties which arise from poor sites and, in many cases, poor acoustical environment. The writer believes that the extension organ as such has no future, but that the principles of extension will continue to be used to enhance the possibilities of existing pipework when organs are rebuilt in England. It must be stated that the majority of British builders used extension sparingly and some eschew manual extension altogether. Many of the finest European and American organs do not contain extended ranks, even on the pedal organ.

The Wind Supply

We have seen how the ancients not only used water for stabilising the air pressure of their organs but, in the late Alexandrian and Byzantium periods, as a source of power both for blowing the organ and playing it automatically. Water wheels and windmills have been used for blowing organs since the sixteenth century of our era and probably even before this. Such methods were obviously inconvenient for blowing the majority of church organs.

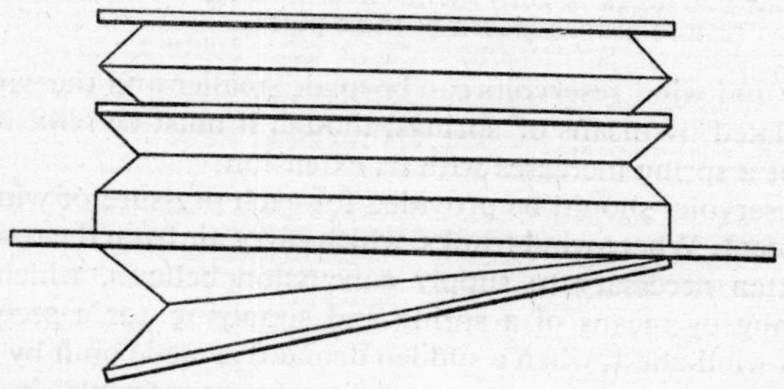

FIG. 33. Wind reservoir with Cumming's improvement (inverted folds) and feeder.

Hand and foot blowing by teams of men was the method employed until the middle of the nineteenth century, and in France and elsewhere until the present century, even for large organs.[1] Even today some small organs in England and abroad are still blown by hand, but the number decreases every year.

An early method of blowing large organs is shown in Plate 18, which is taken from Praetorius's *Syntagma* (q.v.). It can readily be imagined that there would be considerable fluctuations of wind pressure but, because of the general scale on which everything was planned, and the cushioning effect of large masses of air in the wind trunks and chests, a regular supply of wind could be produced by skilful blowers. There were no reservoirs to hold the wind and to adjust its pressure, and these were not in evidence in the organs

[1] The organ at the Cathedral of Notre Dame, Paris, was not supplied with an electric blower until after the first European War.

pictured by Dom Bédos, *c.* 1770 (q.v.). The blowing of small organs, from the fourteenth century, was sometimes effected by pulling on a rope which was connected with the bellows: this was known as "pulling or drawing the organs". It is difficult at times to distinguish between references to the blower and to the player in old manuscripts.

The invention of Cumming (q.v.), of the inverted bellow folds, was a great step forward in the production of a steady wind supply. We must distinguish between the *reservoir* which was improved by Cumming's invention and the feeders or bellows which pump in the air. Usually both feeders and reservoir are loosely described as "bellows". With modern mechanical blowing no bellows feeders

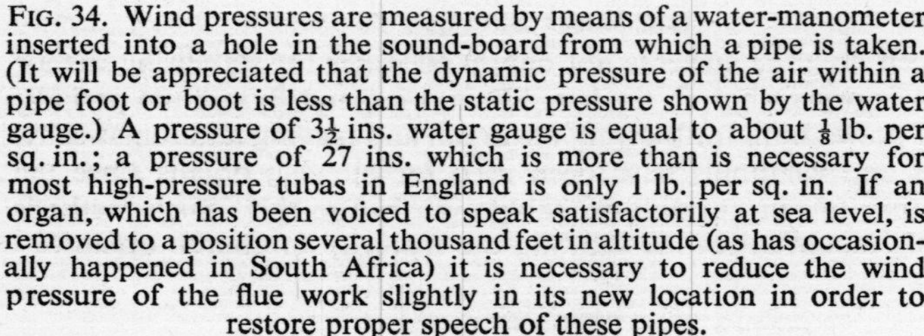

FIG. 34. Wind pressures are measured by means of a water-manometer inserted into a hole in the sound-board from which a pipe is taken. (It will be appreciated that the dynamic pressure of the air within a pipe foot or boot is less than the static pressure shown by the water gauge.) A pressure of 3½ ins. water gauge is equal to about ⅛ lb. per sq. in.; a pressure of 27 ins. which is more than is necessary for most high-pressure tubas in England is only 1 lb. per sq. in. If an organ, which has been voiced to speak satisfactorily at sea level, is removed to a position several thousand feet in altitude (as has occasionally happened in South Africa) it is necessary to reduce the wind pressure of the flue work slightly in its new location in order to restore proper speech of these pipes.

are necessary and wind reservoirs can be made smaller and the wind pressure may be regulated by means of springs, though it must be remembered that the tension of a spring increases with its extension.

Separate reservoirs should be provided for each pressure of wind required in the instrument. Where wind trunks, which carry air from the reservoirs, are long it is often necessary to supply concussion bellows, which are small bellows closing by means of a spring and supplying, for a second or two, extra air to a wind-chest, when a sudden demand is made on it by the playing of a full chord. In modern organs, wind pressures vary from 2½ in. to 25 in. or more. Many small or old instruments work on a single wind pressure of 3 in. to 4 in. Moderately large instruments may have 3½ in. for the fluework and 5 in. or more for the pneumatic action and the reedwork. Each inch of wind pressure represents 5·3 lb. weight of loading of the horizontal surface of the reservoir for each square foot; and cast iron, lead or other weights or spiral springs must be provided accordingly.

Early in the nineteenth century, water mains, which were becoming common in England and in favourable circumstances were capable of supplying water at a pressure of 30 lb. per square in., were used to actuate blowing cylinders which moved the bellows feeders.

Large instruments of the mid- and later nineteenth-century, such as those at the Alexandra Palace, London, and St. George's Hall, Liverpool, were blown by steam power, and Henry Willis invented large-diameter blowing cylinders to replace the bellows feeders. Such a method of blowing was obviously inconvenient to an organist requiring the use of the instrument at short notice.

The early hydraulic engines which did not differ greatly in design from steam cylinders were crude and jerky in action, but between 1860 and 1870 David Joy, a Middlesbrough engineer, devised a "fluid-driven slide valve", which was a great improvement. The device could be attached to existing feeders, if necessary, and the rising reservoir could readily be made to regulate the supply of water. Even today when the hydraulic blower has practically vanished from English organs, it is still found in some places in America where the churches are exempt from water rates! In London and a few other places, hydraulic power became available at 750–1,000 lb. per square inch, and this was used occasionally for organ-blowing. For a time two tiny blowing cylinders, with mechanism devised by Mr. Vincent Willis, were used in the organ of St. Paul's Cathedral, London. Gas engines became popular in many parts of the world in the late nineteenth and early twentieth centuries. When a gas engine was used for organ-blowing, the plant had to be set up at some distance from the organ and in a special chamber, usually outside the building in which the organ stood. Many organs were ruined, over a period of years, by the action of oil and gas fumes sucked in with the air of the blower and delivered to the organ. This, of course, could be avoided by a proper arrangement of the blowing apparatus, but it occurred quite often and much damage was done, in particular, to the leather of the pneumatic action.

Mains electricity is now almost universally employed for organ-blowing. At first, electric motors drove the feeders of the "bellows" by worm and pinion gear, but later the old leather feeders were rendered obsolete by supplying air from centrifugal compressors directly to the reservoirs. Fans rotating in an

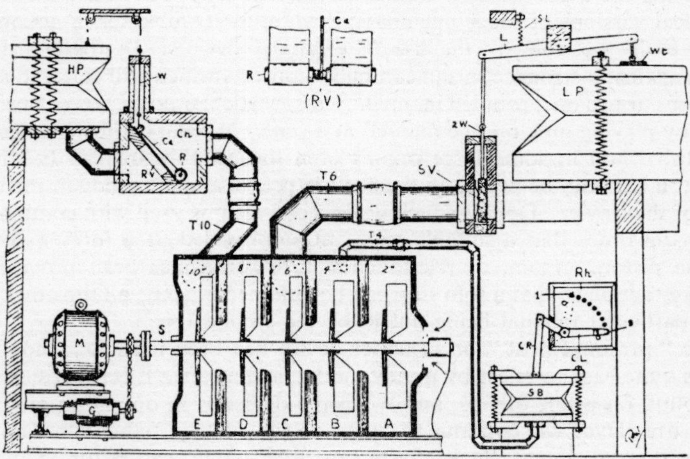

FIG. 35. A modern blowing plant with action-current generator (G). The wind can be drawn from the multiple fan in stages so that reservoirs for high and low pressures may be supplied. The supply of wind is regulated by the valves in the trunks (R.V). The controlling rheostat (Rh) is actuated by the rise and fall of the bellows (SB). Lengths of flexible leather coupling in the wind trunks prevent any vibration from the fan being transmitted to the organ. (Drawn by R. Whitworth.)

airtight casing and driven by electric motors had been used for blowing blast and other furnaces from 1880 or before, and Robert Hope-Jones used a similar device for blowing the organ in St. John's Church, Birkenhead, in 1887. The single stage fan was improved in 1902 by L. B. Cousans, of Lincoln, who introduced his Kinetic blower. This worked at the relatively slow speed of 1,000–1,400 revolutions per minute and was coupled directly to the electric motor. The principle of the multi-stage fan was that air which was thrown from the periphery of a fan and thus compressed was taken by ducts to the centre of the next fan on the same spindle: thus each fan increased the pressure by 1½ in. or 2 in. of wind. The pressure wind could be tapped off at any stage and piped to appropriate reservoirs. Blowers are made so that they adjust their power automatically to the wind which is being taken from them. Moreover, even large plants can be started and stopped by simple push-button control at the organ console and the starting rheostat is actuated automatically. It was customary to drive the low-voltage dynamo (14–15 volts), which supplied current for the organ action, by a belt from the blowing motor. Organ-blowing plants for the smallest organs can be obtained in insulated boxes, so that they may be placed within the organ itself, outside the instrument and in the church, or even above the pipes of the great organ, and yet no noise is apparent in the building. There is now no longer any need to endure noisy organ-blowing plants.

The modern organ is replete with electrical devices which may prove convenient to an organist who is thoroughly familiar with a particular instrument, but may add to the difficulties of a visitor. Some of these aids to playing are made possible by the use of electricity, but others are merely electrical versions of older pneumatic apparatus. Double-touch actions are made easily possible by the use of electrical devices. In these a deeper touch against a stronger spring can make contacts which will cause to sound the stops drawn on a coupled manual. Thus, particular notes can be "brought out" by playing only on one manual at a time. A pedal can be coupled to a solo tuba, and in some large organs even the pedal-board can be divided so that a bass can be played in the bottom octave and a melody in the upper part of the clavier. Double-touch devices can also be used with combination pistons in order that a suitable bass can be provided by a further pressure on the piston. Again, double-touches have sometimes been provided on stop-key action so that a solo stop can be obtained quickly, all the other stops on a particular manual being put in by the second touch.

The "prolongement" or sustainer device has been used for many years and is quite easy to effect by purely mechanical means. Electrical sustainers are found on a few organs, and when the device is in operation any notes which are played will continue to sound on a particular manual until another key is pressed down. Such effects are occasionally called for in modern compositions and improvisations.

A Note on the Development of Combination Action

There is evidence that devices which shut off a part of the organ were in use in England before the Commonwealth. In the eighteenth century, the favourite method of shutting off a part of the full organ was the use of a separate set of sliders known as a "shifting movement", which was often employed by Snetzler. Bishop, in 1809, had a crude form of "composition" pedal for drawing fixed groups of stops—and it is unfortunate that the term "composition" has tended to persist in the English-speaking countries.

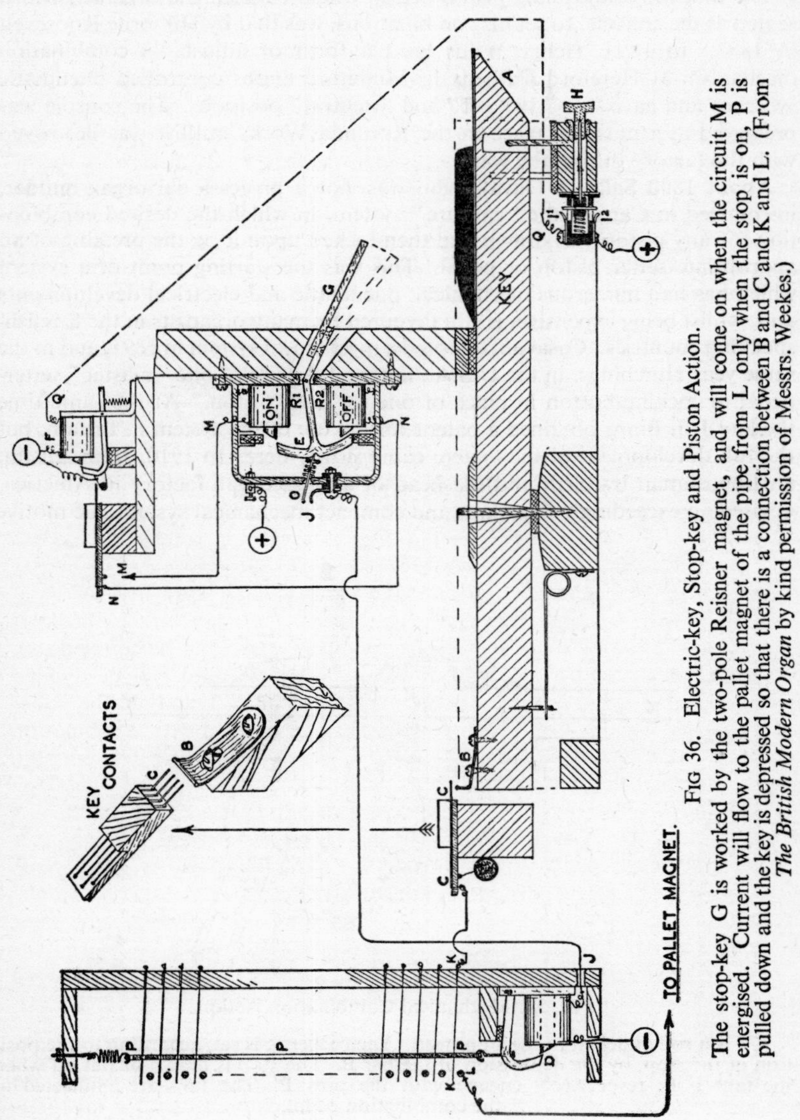

FIG 36. Electric-key, Stop-key and Piston Action.

The stop-key G is worked by the two-pole Reisner magnet, and will come on when the circuit M is energised. Current will flow to the pallet magnet of the pipe from L only when the stop is on, P is pulled down and the key is depressed so that there is a connection between B and C and K and L. (From *The British Modern Organ* by kind permission of Messrs. Weekes.)

In 1847, Henry Willis first used thumb-pistons (Manor Chapel, Bermondsey) and improved them for his organ in the Great Exhibition of 1851 (see page 229). An adjustable system was employed at St. George's Hall, Liverpool in 1854, and was used until the organ was rebuilt in the present century. The adjustments could readily be made by a tuner.

The first fully adjustable piston action which enabled the organist, whilst seated at the console, to set his combinations, was that by Hilborne Roosevelt in 1882. In 1893, Henry Willis used a form of adjustable combination mechanism at Hereford Cathedral. Miniature knobs controlled pneumatic switches and gave "on" or "off" and "neutral" positions. The console was preserved as a museum piece in the Rotunda Works until it was destroyed with the factory during the war.

About 1890 Salluste Duval, who was not a professional organ-builder, introduced in Canada the "capture" system, in which the desired combination for any piston was drawn and then locked upon it by the pressing of an appropriate setter piston or pedal. This was the starting point of a system which has had numerous mechanical, pneumatic and electrical developments and, whilst being expensive, is still favoured by many organists in the English-speaking countries. Casavant adopted a mechanical system in 1891, and in the same year Hutchings, in the U.S.A., initiated the use of one "master" setter-pedal or locking-button in place of one for each piston. At the same time the late J. J. Binns obtained a patent for the use of the system in Britain, but the full development of the system came slowly here. In 1910, John Austin, an Englishman by birth and the head of a large organ factory in America, devised an exceedingly ingenious and compact mechanical system, the motive

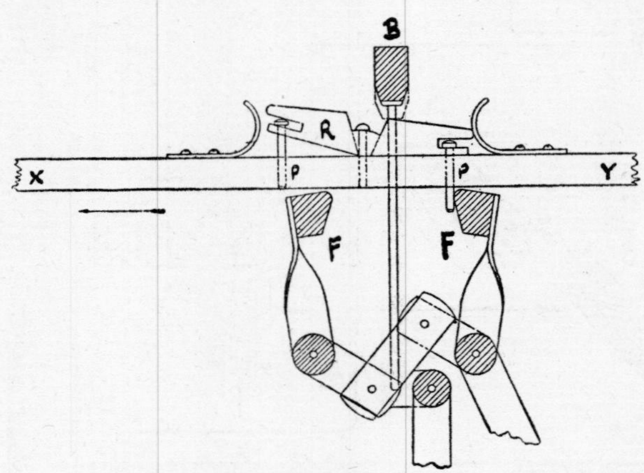

FIG. 37. Mechanical Combination Action.

XY is a rod attached to the stop-head. The rocker R is set, according to the position of the stop, by the depression of the bar B. The stop is drawn or put off when the fans F_2F_1 respectively engage with the pins P. The fans are connected to the combination pedal.

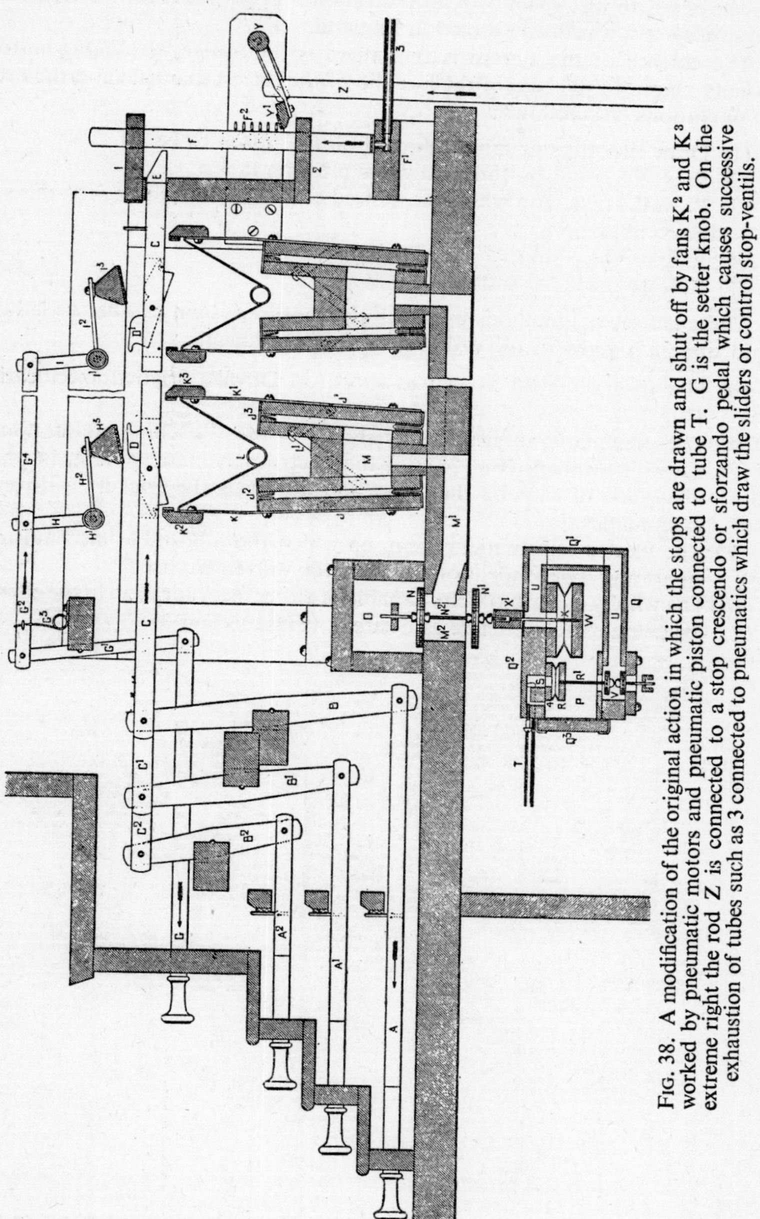

FIG. 38. A modification of the original action in which the stops are drawn and shut off by fans K^2 and K^3 worked by pneumatic motors and pneumatic piston connected to tube T. G is the setter knob. On the extreme right the rod Z is connected to a stop crescendo or sforzando pedal which causes successive exhaustion of tubes such as 3 connected to pneumatics which draw the sliders or control stop-ventils.

power of which was given by a large solenoid. From 1922, the all-adjustable capture system was firmly rooted in England.

The essence of the system is that there is one setter or locking-button, usually placed to the bass of the key slip of the lowest manual; and the cycle of operations is as follows:

(1) Draw the stops or tablets desired on the piston to be set.
(2) Press the setter-button, and while pressing it—
(3) Press the piston on which the desired combination is to be set—this sets the combination.
(4) Release the piston.
(5) Release the setter-button.

There are several methods by which the capture system can be carried out and these are given in the order of their development:

(*a*) The all-mechanical system as shown in Duval's original specification (Fig. 37).
(*b*) The pneumatic application, as shown in the Wirsching adaptation of Duval's principle (Fig. 38); or the electro-pneumatic system, in which the work of moving the stops and adjusting the rockers is done by pneumatics.
(*c*) The electro-pneumatic system, on which the adjustable mechanism is apart and independent of the drawstop movement itself.
(*d*) The wholly electric system, capable of either incorporation in the console or using remote control as desired. (Figs. 36 and 39).

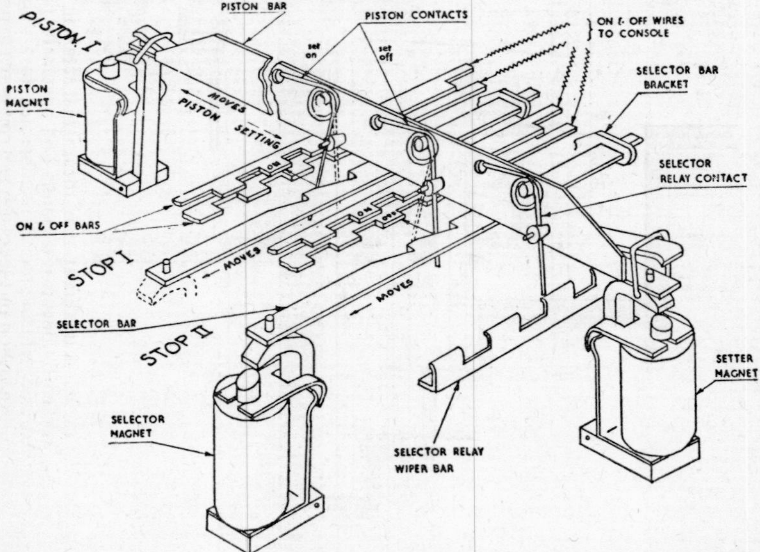

FIG. 39. Diagram of selector mechanism for all-electric combination action (Hill, Norman and Beard), showing one piston movement on two selector movements.

SECTION 3

CHAPTER XII

THE STUDY AND USE OF THE ORGAN

"*In my eyes and ears the organ will ever be the King of Instruments.*"
—W. A. MOZART (*letter written on* 18.10.1777).

"*I maintain that an organist, who is a master of his instrument, is a virtuoso of the highest order.*"—L. VAN BEETHOVEN (1770–1827).

"*To play the organ properly one should have a vision of Eternity.*"
—CHARLES-MARIE WIDOR (1845–1937).

NO INSTRUMENT is capable of such noble and dignified effects as the organ, and also, on the other hand, offers such temptations to triflers. The modern organ, with its multiplicity of devices for controlling the stops, its attempts at orchestral imitations and its possibilities of powerful dynamics, offers attractions to the inartistic player with feeble musical feeling.

The thoughtful student of the organ will acquire a reasonably good pianoforte technique before approaching the larger instrument, will start with the study of simple pieces in trio form rather than with harmonised chorales, and use perhaps only single stops on two manuals, and an 8-ft. stop on the pedals. Much organ-playing fails because organists are either unable to hear or have not acquired the habit of listening critically to their own playing. If they begin by engulfing themselves in masses of sound the matter becomes even more difficult. It is a useful, though sometimes humiliating experience, to practise a piece of music and record it, so that it can be replayed to the performer. Organists would do well to hear others play the instruments at which they preside, noting carefully the stop combinations which are used and judging the effect from various parts of the buildings in which the instruments stand.

Rhythm and clarity, the phrasing of each passage so that its musical potentialities are realised, and an overall conception of the form and architecture of the music are basic necessities of all musical performances. The organist should listen carefully to music performed with other media, such as the string quartet and the orchestra, and consider whether in his own instrument he is realising the fundamental necessities of art. Suitable organ registration should be used to enhance the artistic appeal of the music, but good rhythm and phrasing should never be sacrificed to obtain registration changes. On modern organs these can often be effected with as much precision as that of the key action. The swell pedal and combination pistons should never be used to sully and detract from the natural climaxes which are inherent in the musical structure of organ compositions, such as the organ fugues of Bach.

From the earliest times good organ-playing has been associated with the ability to extemporise. Unfortunately, owing to the nature of the English church services it has tended to be lightly esteemed in Britain, but it is still part of the requirements for the Diplomas of the Royal College of Organists and is practised in the services of the Roman Catholic churches abroad, particularly in France. It is also a feature of the interludes played in some of the German and Dutch protestant churches. Improvisation often tends to degenerate into a rhythmless meandering, amorphous and unmusical. Much careful study must be undertaken before success can be achieved in this important part of the organist's art. Here again previous practice at the piano is desirable, for then there are no temptations to try to replace poverty of ideas and musical invention by changes of tone colour; moreover, the transient tones of the piano do not allow the sequence of slow, suspended chords which is a feature of so much poor organ extemporisation. The student will acquire a thorough knowledge of musical form, of counterpoint, harmony and their applications, and he will find that these studies and that of improvisation will have mutual benefit one to another. The simplest forms, played with a few stops of traditional organ tone, should be attempted at the start. Attention should be paid to the proper shape and speed of the composition. Simple canons between manual and manual, and manual and pedals, should lead to simple trios and, later, fugues. It is easy to allow a flamboyant imagination and the resources of a large modern organ to produce wearisome fantasias of no musical value. Discipline and hard work are necessary, as well as the ability to evolve effective musical themes, before good improvisations can be produced. Before commencing to play, the organist should have a clear idea in his mind of (*a*) his musical form; (*b*) the speeds, rhythms and times; (*c*) the principal themes; (*d*) the registration which will be employed. No doubt other ideas are suggested to him as he plays, but these should only be used if they enrich his plan, and usually they will have to be drastically pruned.[1]

Phrasing and Manual Touch

The insistence, in the nineteenth century, on continuous legato-playing with elaborate systems of finger changing, as given in John Stainer's *Organ Tutor*, together with slow pneumatic actions, led to a dull, unimaginative and inert style of performance which is so often associated with church-service playing. It is neither possible nor would it be necessary to join the notes of a melody played on a loud reed; and it is only too easy, on the other hand, to produce an indefinite overlap on stops of the lieblich gedact type. Dr. Eaglefield Hull,[2] in a systematic work, divided organ touches into:

A. *connected*

Legato
Legatissimo or portamento
Glissando

[1] Marcel Dupré, *Cours complet d'improvisation à l'orgue* (Paris, Leduc, 1947).
[2] A. E. Hull, *Organ Playing: Its Technique and Expression* (London, 1911).

B. *disconnected*

Staccatissimo
Brillante or mezzo staccato
Marcato ($\frac{3}{4}$ note lengths)
Non-legato
The action of the hand and arm used for rapid changes of manuals, or of the body in releasing long final chords on heavy organs.

Good phrasing should be complementary to good touch, both in attack and release, and one cannot be considered apart from the other. In view of the nature of the steady sound-emission of the organ pipe, the matter cannot be learnt at the piano; although it must be admitted that listening to good phrasing on the piano is very helpful since it enables the performer to take cognizance of the problem. Much practice on a small tracker organ, using only one or two quick-speaking flute or diapason stops placed on an open sound-board quite near to the performer, in a building without resonance, is ideal. Such conditions are an acid test of a good player. In the seventeenth and eighteenth centuries in Europe all organists would regard such skill as a part of their technical equipment. Careful listening is necessary on the part of the player, and if the keyboards of the instrument are unsuitably placed with respect to the pipes, there is an added difficulty. Slow pneumatic actions have tended to destroy, and often to render impossible, good touch and phrasing in organ-playing. When slow pneumatic actions, or even actions which are partly pneumatic, are made to control slow-speaking manual pipes and ponderous basses, any possibility of using the organ as an eloquent and poetical instrument has disappeared. A moderate-sized low-pressure organ with transparent flue choruses, adequate mutation stops and bright reeds of no great power, all controlled by well made and nicely adjusted tracker action, is the medium *par excellence* for playing the real music of the organ. Barker-lever action (especially the improved floating lever such as was made by Vincent Willis) approaches tracker action in its power of permitting the player to feel that he is in contact with the pipes. Slow exhaust-pneumatics, controlled by keys with spring or "harmonium" touch, are the greatest stumbling blocks to artistic organ playing. Well-made pressure pneumatics, with no great length of tubing between the keyboard and the sound-board, are better, and electro-pneumatic actions with promptly working pneumatic motors are better still. The tracker or top-resistance touch can be simulated by using toggle springs in the key action, and this can be so made that a force of 4 oz. or even 4½ oz. is necessary to overcome key top resistance, while 2½ oz. will suffice to keep the key depressed. The fact remains that for sensitive playing, with every variety of touch, the small tracker organ cannot be rivalled by any other mechanism. Here the player has full control of the pallet and its speed of opening (if he has sufficient skill), and this involves careful listening and fine muscular adjustments.[1] He will adopt the type of attack

[1] In the *Organ Tutor* of the late Sir Percy Buck exercises are given for producing subjective effects of accent by carefully adjusting note values.

which suits different qualities of tone, different styles of music and the acoustical environment of the instrument. A flute on an open sound-board will stand quick playing, whereas a keen string, particularly if enclosed, may have to be "caressed" into speech. Even diapasons vary considerably in possibilities of attack, from the leisurely onset of speech in a Schulze diapason to the smart, precise attack of a Father Willis diapason. The organist will also pay attention to niceties of key release, a matter which is just as important as attack.

Although the steady tone emission of the organ must be relieved and varied by every means at the organist's disposal, it is necessary to be able to secure a good legato, as far as the flue-work and quiet reeds, such as the oboe and clarinet of the organ, are concerned. Nineteenth-century exercises with copious finger changing can be ignored, as there is much simple contrapuntal organ music which will serve to lay down a much better style. Hull[1] says: "The legato touch should be first practised with slow passages and the simplest fingering. It is best acquired with the fingers only very slightly curved. The old school of legato players used very flat fingers—a sort of clinging touch. The fingers always feeling the keys. . . . Muscularly, the action is this:—the fingers supply the connection, whilst the hand overcomes the key resistance. . . . The resistance of the organ key and the speed of the passage will always influence the touch. In quick legato passages the fingers will assume a more rounded position, and in very fast scale-work, in order to prevent a blurred result, the 'brillante' muscular action must be used to secure the legato effect." In resonant places, such as St. Paul's Cathedral, London, the reverberation of the building tends to blur and overlap joined tones, and to join those that are played with detached touches.

Occasionally, the use of the thumb for playing on the manual immediately below that used by the rest of the hand is called for, particularly in late-romantic organ music, such as Widor's Fifth Symphony. Surprisingly, it has never been exploited to give a sustained "inverted-pedal" by using a 4 ft. or 2 ft. stop.

Every legitimate device of organ touch is sooner or later necessary to secure the proper phrasing of a passage of organ music. Yet this is not all. Musicianship, study and insight are necessary and each phrase must be studied in relation to the composition as a whole. In some editions of organ music, curved lines have been often used by the composer merely to group notes in an arbitrary manner or to give the music a finished appearance. These are *not* phrasing marks. In certain types of music the swell pedal can be used as an aid to phrasing, but its value is not to be compared with that of good touch and careful attention to note lengths. Very little use of the swell pedal for phrasing purposes was called for in the original Willis organs, for there was a sense of crescendo on going up the scale of many of the stops. Like many other devices on the organ, the use of the swell pedal is effective in the inverse ratio of the number of occasions on which the box is opened and closed. Care must be taken in contrapuntal music not to destroy the phrasing of one melody by swell-pedalling on another with which it is combined.

[1] A. E. Hull, ibid.

The swell pedal has other uses and we may summarize these as follows:

(*a*) It can be used to adjust the relative dynamics of various sections of the organ.

(*b*) It can be used to produce "dissolving" tonal effects by using two swell pedals, so as to give simultaneous crescendi and diminuendi respectively on two coupled manuals with contrasted tone-colours.

(*c*) Occasionally, its use to produce a sforzando by a momentary pressure on the pedal, preferably of the old trigger type, is effective.

(*d*) A crescendo of the tones of an accompanimental section will give a subjective sense of diminuendo in an unenclosed solo register and vice versa.

(*e*) The swell pedal may be used to "cover up" the addition of stops to its own manual or to one to which an enclosed division is coupled.

It is fatally easy to begin organ-playing with hymns and simple four-part harmony. After a good grounding on the pianoforte, with such works as Bach's forty-eight preludes and fugues and his suites, trio playing should be started on the organ, using single 8-ft. stops on two manuals and pedals, and enlivening such registration with the judicious addition of 4-ft. tone.

A small or moderate-sized organ, in which mechanical action controls the speech of a well-designed tonal structure, composed of highly characteristic tones of quick-speaking pipes, is ideal for the sensitive playing of the finest organ music. Clarity and individuality of tone will have replaced the characterless, ponderous, slow-speaking sounds of unmusical organs. An instrument of enlightened design, with the pipe-work quite near to the player, will respond perfectly to the skill and sensitivity of the artist-organist. The meticulous control of note lengths, of the speed of attack and release of each note, in relation to the type of organ-tone employed, is a fundamental requirement. The articulation of the organ should be eloquent and poetic.

Such organ playing, which will ensure the future of the art, demands careful attention to the problems of phrasing, note-grouping, the "playing" of rests, ornamentation and appropriate registration. The psychological impact of any sound of short duration is proportional to the product of its intensity and time value. Thus, a passage played staccato may seem to be an echo of one played legato on the same stop or stops. Each phrase presents considerable possibilities to players with insight. There must be a differentiation between the *arsic* (climbing or energetic) part of a phrase and the *thetic* (cadential, declining or restful). In harmonised chorales and hymn tunes these elements will be common to each of the parts, but in polyphonic music one part may rise while another falls. In each phrase, there is usually a peak and each note should tend towards it or fall away from it; but phrases will seem heavy if the stress is always near the end. The eloquence of a phrase may be increased by the neutral playing of an earlier phrase, and each phrase-end should be marked by a breathing space. Such sensitive playing has much in common with the beautiful speaking of poetry or prose and the art of the lieder singer. Poor registration and the stifling of the tone by swell boxes will inhibit such artistic performance by the organist. Natural organ tones, bright, clear and musical, built from the minimum of pipe-ranks (and with sparing use of more than one 8-ft. stop on each division of the organ at any time), will aid an artistic performance.[1]

The Use of the Pedals.[2]

The organist should sit in relation to the pedal keyboard so that he can readily command its extreme notes; and the seat should be high enough to give him the feeling that there is no sense of strain in reaching the natural keys and that they can be played comfortably by using the heels.

It was said of Bach[3] that his pedal technique was so good that he could play with his feet what others had difficulty in managing with their hands. The tone of the German pedal organs was just as bright and precise as that of the manuals and therefore any defects in pedal technique were cruelly exposed. Moreover, the pedal was used melodically and for supplying two-part harmony in some of the chorale preludes, in addition to its functions of supplying the bass. There is a tradition, which would be difficult to prove, that Bach never used his heels when playing, and German players tend to ignore the use of the heel even today. On the other hand, British and French players use the heel freely on the natural keys, and even use pedal glissandi on both sharp and natural keys.

It is not difficult to play on the pedals, and it seems to us that there is no need to work exercises which are designed to help the feet to hunt for the spaces between A♯ and C♯, D♯ and F♯, and so on. These spaces can be felt for, if necessary, without playing the notes. It is a good idea to begin with 8-ft. and 4-ft. stops or to obtain these by coupling to a manual.

A co-ordination of the spatial, muscular and aural senses should be the aim. The sense of sight should be occupied with the score. The difficulty is that of obtaining independence of hands and feet. The playing of psalm and hymn-tunes and the doubling of bass, already played by the left hand, on the pedals is a bad way of starting. Here again, simple trios and fugues are a firmer rock on which to build. Moreover, they will serve to show that the pedal is not always playing and that the phrasing of a pedal passage does not always coincide with that which is being played on the manual. Nothing is less artistic than the dragging of a heavy, indefinite pedal bourdon or "open-wood", played continuously throughout a whole composition or church

[1] See also Denis Vaughan, Preface to *Facsimile Edition of the Voluntaries of John Stanley* (Oxford University Press); Gordon Phillips, *The Technique of Trio-playing* and *Articulation in Organ Playing* (Hinrichsen).

The writer believes that much of the unpopularity of organ-recital between the wars was due to the wearying effect of masses of heavy 8-ft. tone on the manuals, and 16-ft. tone on the pedals and the excessive use of orchestral imitations, whose differences from their real prototypes were painfully apparent. The organ has its own splendour and dignity. It does not need to try to imitate the orchestra which is a composite instrument of its own genius, which sometimes lacks an adequate bass.

[2] Some excellent exercises to help in acquiring a good pedal technique are found in Ellingford and Meers, *The Science of Organ Pedalling* and in the organ tutors of W. G. Alcock (Novello) and H. Keller (Peters).

[3] W. L. Sumner, "The Organ of Bach" (London, 1954), quoted from Forkel.

service. It is to be hoped that the future will see better pedal stops which have good blending properties and precise, well-defined tone and pitch.

Pedal-playing should always be consistent with good harmony and counterpoint. In order to produce shapely melodies, written as the composer desired, it is better to eschew the use of the swell pedal and to play the pedal-board throughout with both feet. This does not mean that free pedalling in the lower part of the keyboard is not to be permitted occasionally in a verse of a hymn or a psalm, but it does imply that the correct march of a bass should not be destroyed by the use of queer inversions designed to keep the right foot on the swell pedal and the left foot on the lower octave of the pedal-board. Phrasing and touch, though sometimes rendered difficult by slow pneumatics and ponderous, over-scaled pipes, are just as important on the pedals as anywhere else. The organist will find by experiment just what types of pedal touch are possible on the instrument which he plays. A detached touch, played on a contre-bass or good metal open diapason with suitable mutations, will be a great relief from the monotonous legato of the bourdon and "open wood". Mendelssohn played the soft movement of his Fifth Sonata in B minor with an 8-ft. "string" stop on the pedals, played staccato. It is an excellent relief to play the pedals without 16-ft. tone when occasion permits it. Again, there is nothing more irritating to a cultured ear than a pedal bourdon droning in its lower regions at a distance of two octaves from 8-ft. manual tone to which it is supposed to supply a bass. There is no need to try to compare the organ with a string quartet, but the same principles of art and its media apply, and it is painful to hear all the qualities of artistic music thrown to the wind when it is played without insight on an organ.

Registration, or the Use of the Stops of the Organ

The art of combining the stops of the organ is no longer bound by the fixed rules of the sixteenth and seventeenth centuries. Almost every organ is different from all others, and even when small instruments have been produced to standard specifications, their acoustical environments, in the buildings in which they are used, will certainly be different. A writer for the organ cannot score the work with the same certainty as an orchestral composer. Nevertheless, the former is still able to indicate general effects and sometimes the type of tone colour which he has in mind. Some organ composers, such as Mendelssohn, Rheinberger and Reger, were interested in changes of dynamic or loudness, rather than of tone colour; whilst others, such as Cesar Franck, and arrangers of orchestral music for the organ, such as William Thomas Best, have called for specific tone colours. If the organist, trying to respect the wishes of the organ composer, slavishly follows the printed directions on the score with respect to the choice of stops, the effect may be unsuitable or even ludicrous. In his work entitled *Prière*, Cesar Franck asks for "trompette" tone, and the best way of fulfilling his demands on the majority of English organs would be to use the swell oboe. Usually the swell and great trumpets would be intolerably coarse for this keenly felt, introspective music. Franck had in mind the quiet, enclosed trumpet stop of beautiful quality in the récit (swell organ) at Ste. Clotilde, Paris.

The experienced organist tries to read the composer's intention from the music and then to translate it into sound, in terms of the resources of his own instrument, in the most fitting way possible. Widely different tone qualities and dynamics are to be found in different organs from stops with the same names; nor is there any proportional power factor between one manual and another in different instruments. The experienced organist will go through an instrument stop by stop and notice the balance between treble and bass, as well as the change in timbre which often occurs in different parts of the compass of the same stop. He will then try the stops in combination, and find any suitable stops which will give satisfactory effects when played an octave higher or lower than normal, either singly or in combination.

Organ pipes are very sensitive to their environment: output and tone quality will change according to the amount of sound-absorbing material in the vicinity. A scheme of organ registration which has been carefully prepared and practised in an empty church will often count for nothing when the building is full of people.[1] Some of the most beautiful effects of the softest stops of the organ may have to be sacrificed under these conditions. Different types of organ tone are elicited at different speeds from the pipes. Usually flute tone is precise and clear, gamba tone is slow, a German Baroque flue-chorus is almost as percussive as a harpsichord, reed tone may be slow or come on with "a crack", and diapason tone may vary between the leisurely initiation of a Schulze open diapason and the immediate response of a rank of pipes of the same name by Father Willis. The selection of stops, the type of manual and pedal touch which is employed to play them and the acoustical conditions at the time of playing must all be taken into account. The speed of playing, quite apart from the restrictions laid on it by the acoustical properties of the church or hall, is also modified by, and in its turn modifies, the choice of stops. Slow-speaking pedal stops, loud broad-toned tubas and other ranks of pipes with long initiation periods, are unsuitable for quick passages. Flute tone and certain types of diapasons, with or without 4-ft. and higher pitched stops, are usually suitable for rapidly moving passages.[2]

The perception of loudness which results from a vibrating system is not directly proportional to the output of energy, but rather to its logarithm. A rough "law", known as the Weber-Fechner Law of Sensation, states that an increase of energy in a source of sound (or of light, weight, etc.) which can just be perceived as an increase of sensation always bears the same ratio to the unaugmented output of energy.[3] A soft stop added to another soft stop of about the same output will give an increase of loudness which is comfortably perceptible. This is an increase of about three decibels. At a greater level of output the necessary addition of stops to give a sensation of just perceptible increase of loudness would be much greater. In planning ranks of organ

[1] It should be said that their clothes absorb many hundred times the acoustic energy which is taken in by their ears.

[2] In 1936 the writer investigated the speech of a 16-ft. open diapason stop during a recital in which the D major organ fugue of J. S. Bach was being played. An electrical recording was made and it was found that in some passages few of the pipes reached proper speech at the speed at which the music was being taken.

[3] Dr. H. Lowery, "Weber's Law and the Organ", *The Organ*, vol. xxi, pp. 29 *et seq*.

pipes, which can be added in progressive stages, a smooth build-up should result if the Weber ratio between each added stop and the whole output up to that point is maintained. The Weber Law further indicates that the first few millimetres travel of a swell-pedal, starting with the box closed, is more effective than a similar distance with the box partly open.

Much organ-playing is far too loud, and a long period of loud or moderately loud playing will lead the ear to adjust itself to this as a norm. The organist is then left with few further resources either to produce climactic effects or to obtain tonal variety. The use of single stops or combinations of a few stops, for an initial period, will give a feeling of enormous reserves of power and tone when louder combinations of stops are subsequently brought into play. It is usually bad policy to start an organ recital with a lengthy movement in which the organ is used at *f*, *ff*, and *fff* power. A gentle diapason and flute movement followed by a number of pieces which call for subtle, quiet tones will prepare the way for the display of the louder stops.

The sixteenth- and seventeenth century methods of dividing the stops into "narrow" (male) and "wide" (female) groups have disappeared, but certain facts known to the old builders and players are not without interest today. A diapason chorus is essentially of vertical, "male" and transparent tone. To add to it heavy unison diapasons which bear no relation to the rest of the tonal structure is to destroy blend and musical quality. Leathered diapasons, in particular, do not blend well, and the addition of flute tone to a diapason chorus spoils the freshness and clarity of the tone. Occasionally "massive" unison effects are required as a contrast to the more sprightly choruses, but thick foundation tone soon becomes wearying. It is only to be expected that a tone mass in which the energy is spread throughout a large frequency-range will be less exhausting and more interesting than one in which the energy is concentrated in a small frequency-range. The charm of the synthetic tones, built up from a quiet 8-ft. foundation by the addition of mutation ranks of the baroque organ, is thus explained. Heavy unison stops are of little use in an organ except for occasional solo purposes and they form no part of the choruses which are the peculiar characteristic of a real organ.

In much present-day organ-playing far too many 8-ft. stops are used simultaneously. When this is done the organist is being prodigal with his resources, and is often destroying the clear tone of individual registers and producing what has been aptly called a "mash of tone". Organ-builders ought to provide better selections of stops of the higher pitches, mutation and quiet mixture stops. Thick unison tone of indeterminate quality quickly tires the ear, and when this type of tone is released with a monotonous legato there is little wonder that the instrument is held in poor esteem by many musicians. When the organ is used for accompanimental purposes, the 8-ft. tone is supplied by the voices, and definite 16-ft. pedal melodic lines moving properly, together with manual upper-work, are more effective. It must be admitted that some interesting composite unison tones may be obtained by combining 8-ft. stops in pairs, such as gedeckt and salicional, but this is the exception rather than the rule. Good diapasons, flutes, reeds and string-toned stops are usually spoilt by the addition of other unison stops. Single

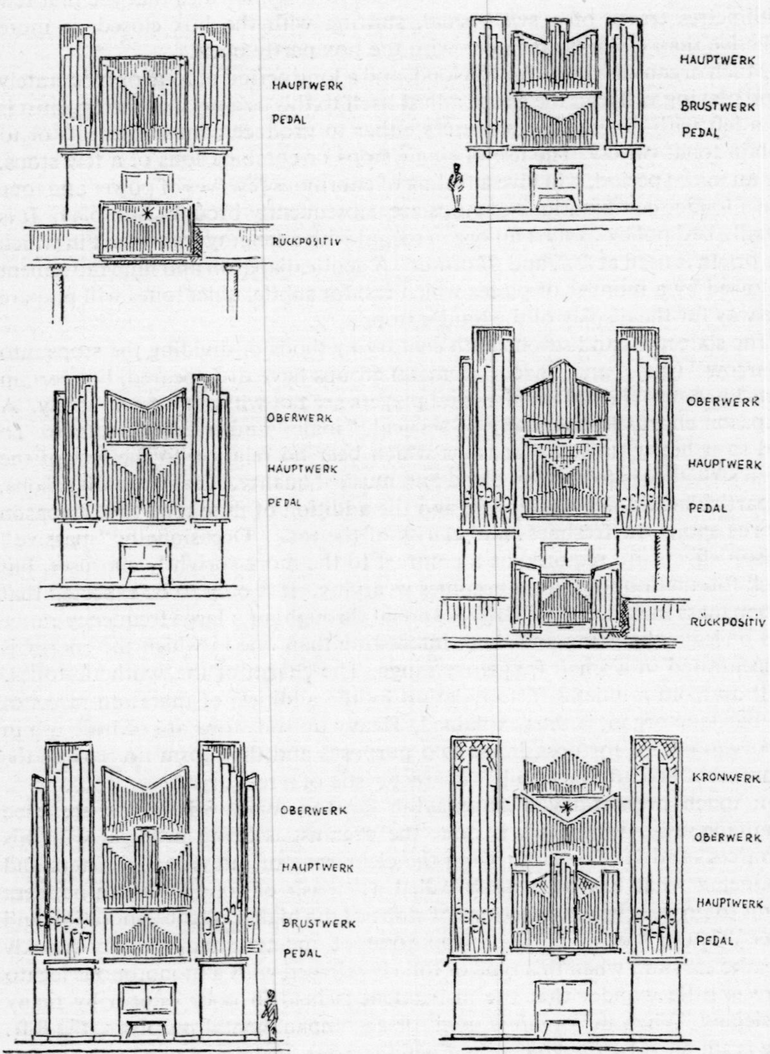

FIG. 40. The forms of the classical organ.

stops should be used where possible, and modern voicing is so good that this is an excellent practice. Good phrasing, and touch appropriate to the unalloyed tone will not only give the organist a lesson in listening to his own music but will provide relief to the hearer and increase the resources of even a small organ. Organists sometimes permit themselves to be submerged in a tone mass of a hundred or more pipes, all speaking at once. It is salutary to have to listen to single pipes breathing their sounds.

Similarly, the organist should draw the minimum number of stops to secure the effect which he wants. All those which are not essential should be put in.

On a good organ a "full organ" effect may be secured by the use of no more than half a dozen stops. The characteristic English "full swell" is obtained from two or three reeds and a mixture. Stops which are not a necessary part of a combination detract from its effect by spoiling its clarity and making it aurally opaque. In many organs, "full organ", secured by a few essential stops, is actually louder than when all the stops are drawn, because it is better to have a full wind supply to six stops than a partial wind to a dozen or more. Further, the chances of obtaining ranks of pipes in tune together are obviously greater when only a few are in operation, than when many are sounded together. This highly selective use of a few stops, usually of different pitches, increases the scope of even a small instrument.

In spite of their penetrating tone, stops such as the viol, the orchestral oboe and cor anglais do not travel well. To be effective at some distance from the instrument they need to be used at a greater power than is required to produce a good balance near the instrument. Modern chorus reeds and good diapasons make excellent solo stops, but they are little used as such. A tenor solo on a claribel or small open diapason is very effective in church accompanimental work. Good contrasts in tone should be used for the stops which accompany the organ solo voices. Strings and soft reeds will accompany the flute, and vice versa. The "fat" tone of the tromba is tolerable against a moderately loud, brilliant flue chorus. It is a great mistake to sully this transparent flue tone by coupling to it the swell reeds, which immediately remove the contrast. If the rank of pipes, which is used as the solo stop, is on an open sound-board, e.g. the great flute, it is possible to give the impression of a slight crescendo by reducing the power of the accompanimental tone obtained from an enclosed division. In using any solo-stop a proper phrasing of the melody is essential. It is necessary to let as many windows as possible into the long, dark wall of unrelieved organ tone. Although the swell pedal is a useful aid to phrasing, good players have always been able to make the tones of unenclosed ranks of pipes seem musical and satisfying. The skilful organist should be able to give the impression of diminuendo and crescendo on single unenclosed ranks of pipes by skilful use of note values, slight tempo-rubato and correct perception of melodic curves. In old organs many ranks of pipes give the impression of a crescendo when one plays from bass to treble. Such stops, if used for solo purposes, produce their own crescendo when the music rises and a diminuendo when it falls. The tone annihilation which results from the use of certain modern swell-boxes is inartistic. There is no virtue, apart from novelty, in starting a melody at zero and eventually making it just audible and then louder. This is quite inartistic and out of keeping with the need for preserving the integrity of each phrase of music.

Although the need to transcribe orchestral music for the organ is less justifiable than it was in the days of W. T. Best and E. H. Lemare (because of the development of good orchestral broadcasting and the greater availability of orchestras heard directly), the organ solo stops are worth careful thought. The seventeenth- and eighteenth-century organs were replete with non-imitative stops bearing the names of certain orchestral instruments, in particular trumpets and flutes. These always stood on open sound-boards and were often combined with other stops to produce the solo effects.

Modern voicing and organ-pipe design have produced solo stops which are beautiful in themselves and are capable of sustaining melodic lines without the help of other tones in combination. The organ can never be a substitute for an orchestra, and although it can give a remarkable palette of tone colours, its true genius lies elsewhere. Efforts, such as those of Robert Hope-Jones, to perfect a one-man orchestra, can only destroy the identity of the organ as an instrument and produce a machine which will provide short interludes in the cinema. In its own way the organ has a breadth and grandeur which the orchestra cannot rival, but the subtle effect of massed strings, the personal elements in orchestral solo playing, the attack of instruments played in groups, are not to be looked for in the organ which is at its best with simple "block or terrace dynamic." The critical ear trained to appreciate the nuances of orchestral playing will not hear much resemblance to the orchestral prototypes in the stops called orchestral oboe, horn, viol, trumpet; and, in spite of a somewhat closer imitation, the organ clarinet and flute leave much to be desired. The orchestral instruments form a sensitive living whole with their respective players. The organist can only open and close a valve which admits wind to a pipe, whose tone has been fixed once and for all by the organ-builder and by the acoustics of the building. Although it is necessary to enclose most, if not all, solo stops in a swell-box to give them the only dynamic control of which the organ is capable, something is lost by so doing. A natural crescendo, obtained from an orchestral instrument, is due to the increase in intensity and number of the harmonics rather than of the ground-tone. The constant use of the swell pedal applied to organ solo tone quickly becomes wearisome,[1] and with some tones produces subjective flattening.

In view of the fact that the addition of one unison stop to another of similar power produces little sensation of extra loudness, and sometimes a poor blend of tone, the organist should seek to vary not only the sensation of loudness but also the change of tone-colour by the addition of harmonics rather than of more ground tone. This was the secret of tone-building, both on manuals and pedals, in the organs before the nineteenth-century. These instruments, at first sight, seem to contain few 8-ft. stops on the manuals and 16-ft. stops on the pedals. In an orchestral instrument such as the horn, or

[1] An arrangement of the Larghetto from Mozart's Clarinet Quintet played on one of Willis's best clarinet stops became intolerable to the writer before the end of the movement.

the pianoforte, a crescendo is produced by a relatively small increase in the ground-tone and by a progressive addition of overtones.[1]

The effect of a mixture of lieblich gedeckt, salicional, geigen diapason and swell oboe is usually vile to the sensitive ear, yet it is often used, and even fixed as a stock combination on pistons! Voix célestes and other out-of-tune ranks do not make good accompanimental stops. They produce subjective changes of pitch in the solo voice, and this is intolerable to the cultured ear. Pneumatic and electric actions have enabled unison and other couplers to be provided in large numbers at no great cost. If a proper pedal organ has been provided, and this is unusual in English organs, even the great-to-pedal coupler loses some of its considerable importance. The swell-to-great coupler is a much abused stop. Many organists seem afraid to use the true organ diapason chorus of the great organ without the reedy background of the swell organ. Thus, they detract from the freshness of the full swell (reeds and mixtures) on the one hand, and the clear characteristic tones of the great organ on the other. As in other matters concerning registration, the printed advice given by composers and arrangers should be considered with a completely open mind by the musician-organist.

Octave and sub-octave couplers, which do so much to destroy the balance of the manual tones, should be reserved for special effects, especially in moderate-sized or large organs. Unless special additions have been made at one or both ends of the pipe ranks and sound-board, the playing compass is reduced by two octaves by the use of such devices. With carefully chosen chords the experienced organist will be able to produce arresting effects, for a short time, by playing on a good viol stop with sub- and super-octave couplers. On small organs, octave couplers are often used to simulate the effects obtained normally from larger organs, e.g. great to fifteenth (diapason and principal with octave coupler), a "full" swell (cornopean and principal with couplers), but such effects are often unmusical.

Even in a small organ, useful tone combinations can be obtained by combining stops experimentally and playing at octave or sub-octave pitches. In the "extension" instruments most of these possibilities have already been exploited in the instrument itself. As French and German organs, in many ways, are fundamentally different in tonal design from the majority of British organs, various artifices have to be used to produce optimum results when foreign organ-music is played. Moreover, it is unwise for the British organist to regard the European instruments as oddities and his own as normal. The British organ, with few exceptions, notwithstanding its mechanical excellence and the fine qualities of its individual ranks of pipes, was often an illogical hotch-potch. Often, loud French organ music seems top-heavy when it is played on an English instrument, and sub-octave couplers, even applied to heavy reeds, are necessary to restore the balance. Conversely, German organ music of the late romantic period may call for

[1] Writers, who have completely misunderstood the nature of these old organs, have asserted that the old organ-builders would not make more 8-ft. stops because they could not supply enough wind for them. This is quite incorrect. They designed the 8-ft. stops to stand in proper relation to the rest of the organ.

thick chords low in the keyboard, which sound unpleasant on the average English great organ. Here the use of the lighter 8-ft. stops, much upper work and octave couplers may be necessary.

In the opinion of many, the classical-baroque type of organ is still the best medium for the playing of Bach's works. This late seventeenth- and early eighteenth-century organ was a much less crude instrument than has been imagined by the unenlightened. The one undeniable improvement since the time of Bach is the supply of ample quantities of wind, at a steady pressure, by mechanical means. It would be unwise to close one's eyes to the resources of the modern organ, but some of these are fraught with danger for the Bach player. The full swell and the swell reeds find little use in the music of Bach. Again, the average English choir organ is not a suitable substitute for the German Positiv; and the small English pedal organs, even when they are helped out with couplers, are not adequate for Bach's music. Even when the English pedal organ is liberally equipped with 16-ft. and higher pitched stops the tone lacks the definition of the German pedal organ and is often ponderous and dragging. The 4-ft. reed, called for in some of the chorale-preludes, cannot even be supplied on the pedal organ of Westminster Abbey.

The stop-crescendo, rollschweller or walze is sometimes found on British and American organs. It was popular on German organs of the nineteenth century, but it never found favour in France, where the coupling of manual sections, of similar tone but different powers, was used to obtain crescendos and decrescendos. Some stop crescendos are adjustable so that the stops can be brought on in a desired order, and only certain selections of stops are then used. The stop-crescendo is capable of abuse; and the fine individual schemes of registration employed by the best French organists were not often apparent in those of the Germans. Nevertheless, it has its uses. It can provide quickly, without moving the stops, a level of organ tone on manuals and pedals, and while it is in use a new scheme of registration can be prepared by manipulating the stops, and this will become operable when the pedal or roller is returned to its zero point. On very large organs in resonant buildings the stop-crescendo can be used for producing fine effects by the addition of upper ranks, mixtures and reeds to ground tone. Such a crescendo, used very sparingly, is far more effective than that given by the swell-pedal, but the conditions for such an effect are only found very rarely, in the length and breadth of Europe.

The extension organ makes full use of every available rank of pipes throughout its range, but in the "straight" organ (i.e. the instrument without manual extension) many new tonal effects can be achieved by experimenting with stops or stop combinations by playing them an octave higher or an octave lower. The modern organ with its electric action usually provides couplers between all the manuals and often at 16-ft. and 4-ft. as well as at unison pitch (i.e. sub-octave, super-octave and unison couplers). On the whole, couplers are used far too much in modern organ-playing. Were the tonal resources of an instrument planned in a more satisfactory manner their use would not be so necessary. Not only is the swell-to-great coupler drawn too often, but in large instruments so is the solo-to-great, in order to bring on the tuba for the production of a final powerful climax. A tuba coupled to the pedal, for the final statement of a theme in a coda of a fugue, is far more effective than such a stop superimposed on the full tone of a great organ.

Bach's Registration

C. P. E. Bach remarked, in the obituary notice of his father, that John Sebastian never presided regularly at a first-rate organ. The instruments at St. Jakobi and St. Catherine, Hamburg, were the finest on which he played, and these must have been considered ideal by him. Buxtehude's large four-manual organ in the west end of St. Mary's Church, Lübeck, which Bach must have played, was inferior to the Hamburg instruments, and Buxtehude's hopes that he would have his organ rebuilt by Schnitger were not realised. We may therefore consider the "Jakobi-orgel" at Hamburg in more detail. (See Specification No. 7 in the Appendix.)

The fine pedal organ with flue and reed families based on stops of 32-ft. pitch first takes our attention. The principal pitch of the hauptwerk (great organ) is 16-ft., that of the oberwerk and rückpositiv (i.e. positiv organ at the back of the player) is 8 ft., and that of the brustwerk (breast work) is 4 ft. In smaller three-manual instruments we find the principal pitches are: pedals 16 ft., hauptwerk 8 ft., positiv 4 ft., and brustwerk 2 ft. It was still possible in this high baroque period to divide the stops into male and female groups, but the rigid rules for registration given by Praetorius were tending to go, and it is evident that Bach cared for none of these things and was more interested in what sounded well.

First, we will consider the actual documentary evidence concerning Bach's use of the stops, of which, unfortunately, there is very little.

The *Prelude and Fugue in E flat* (known in England as the "St. Anne") is marked *pro organo pleno*. This is undoubtedly the equivalent of the French *plein jeu*. It does not mean the full organ, in that all the stops are drawn. The small-scaled fluework on two manuals (hauptwerk and positiv) is drawn, and care is taken not to contaminate this with thick flutes or cornets, but the fourniture and cymbales are allowed. The tierce and third-sounding ranks are not permitted. To the full narrow-scaled pedal-flues the reeds of thin trumpet tone are added. Clarity on manuals and pedals is the keynote here. Opaque, leathered diapasons, "full swell with box closed", and an indefinite pedal held together by the "open wood" and coupled to the great organ, give the very antithesis of the scheme mentioned above and produce a curious and evil parody of this spacious music. An "organo pleno"[1] treatment also serves for the chorale-prelude *Wir glauben all' an einen Gott* (the so-called "Giant" Fugue) and similar works.

Bach's friend Walther brought away from the opening recital at Mühlhausen a copy of *Ein' feste Burg, ist unser Gott*, which had been marked in accordance with the registration of his master. Bach's scheme called for hauptwerk 16 ft. fagotto and rückpositiv sesquialtera. It is assumed, but it is not certain, that these stops were added to neutral flue-stops. This registration is clearly in the

[1] This term can be traced back to the "organo pieno" of the sixteenth- and seventeenth-century Italian organs.

style of some of the early French pieces in which there is a duo between a 16 ft. reed on one manual and a sesquialtera or small cornet on another.[1] At a later date (*c.* 1770) Dom Bédos gives this as a favourite recipe for a duo. In the chorale-preludes of Bach examples abound in which the pedal is used melodically, and quiet but bright flue and reed-toned stops (independent of the manuals) in 8-ft., 4-ft. and even higher pitches are essential.

In *Wo soll ich fliehen hin* (*O whither shall I fly*), *in E minor*, Bach gives Man I, 8 ft.; Man II, 16 ft.; pedal, 4 ft.; and in *Gottes Sohn ist kommen* (*The Son of God is come*), the registration is given as prinzipal 8 fuss, pedal trompete 8 fuss. The "prinzipal 8 fuss" would incline in tone to a quiet English small open diapason with bright, almost geigen tone, and the trumpet tone would be thin and bright like an early Willis cornopean. One would seek for such a tone on an English pedal organ for a long time. There can be no doubt that Bach used the stops of any organ which he played in a highly ingenious and imaginative manner. At Mühlhausen a set of 4-ft. bells of "quick", tinkling tone playable on the pedals was specified. In the chorale prelude *In dir ist Freude* (*In Thee is gladness*) there is a basso ostinato, seventeen times repeated, which is suggestive of bells. The author has heard this piece played on a German organ with bright *mf* flue stops and a definite pedal line to which was added a quiet cymbal and 4-ft. bells and it was performed with the necessary freedom and jollity. It took on a new meaning and seemed to reveal itself for the first time. Bach and his predecessors not infrequently call for pedale-doppio (e.g., the *Prelude in D*, the choral-preludes *Aus tiefer Noth* (*Out of the Deep*), *An Wasserflüssen Babylon* (*By the waters of Babylon*), and *Wir glauben all' an einen Gott, Vater* (*We all believe in one God, the Father*). The tone of the old German pedal organ was just as definite as that of the manuals, and usually this section commanded as many stops as that of the chief manual of the instrument.

References to organ registration in the works of Bach's contemporaries or successors are quite common. Adlung, a Bach pupil, says that registration varied with the seasons of the Church Year, and more stops were used at Christmas and Easter than during more solemn seasons. He goes on to say that the plein jeu should not be used too often. It must be remembered that the churches known to Bach, even including the brick-Gothic buildings of the north, had a homeliness which was not found in the large cathedrals of south and east Germany, of France and England. A quieter, unforced, but harmonically well-spread and crystal-clear organ-tone would be common in all Bach's churches in the early eighteenth century. The magnificence of the larger and more powerful Silbermann instruments was not common. Mattheson, of Hamburg, who was associated with the British Embassy, a friend of Handel and a prolific writer of textbooks on music and compositions for the organ and other instruments, wrote in *Das neu eröffnete Orchester* (1717): "Do not draw reeds with the manual fluework unless there is a reed on the pedal." He gives the following scheme for registering a chorale prelude on the organ at St. Catherine's Church, Hamburg.

[1] "Trompette en taille." It is known that Bach copied the whole of Nicolas de Grigny's *Livre d'Orgue*.

In werke (i.e. hauptwerk): trommete 16 ft., spitzflöte 8 ft., oktave 4 ft.; *or* in oberwerk: trommete 8 ft., zincke 8 ft., flöte 4 ft., nasat 3 ft. ($2\frac{2}{3}$).

In positiv: gedackt 8 ft. alone.

In pedal: dulcian 16 ft., subbass 16 ft., posaune 16 ft., prinzipal 16 ft., trommete 8 ft., cornett 2 ft.

J. S. Bach and the Technique of the Organ

"No one has ever tried out organs so severely and yet at the same time honestly as he. He understood the whole building of organs in the highest degree. When an organ-builder had worked conscientiously, and incurred losses by his work, he would persuade the employers to make amends. No one understood registration at the organ as well as he. Organists were terrified when he sat down to play on their organs and drew the stops in his own manner, for they thought that the effect would not be as good as he was planning it; but then they heard an effect that astounded them. [A marginal note goes on to add, 'These sciences perished with him.'] The first thing he would do in trying an organ was this. He would say, in jest, 'Above all, I must know whether the organ has good lungs,' and, to find out, he would draw out every speaking stop, and play in the fullest and richest possible texture. At this the organ-builder would often grow quite pale with fright."[1]

"All his fingers were equally skilful; all were equally capable of the most perfect accuracy in performance. He had devised for himself so convenient a system of fingering that it was not hard for him to conquer the greatest difficulties with the most flowing facility. Before him, the most famous clavier players in Germany had used the thumb but little. All the better did he know how to use it. With his two feet he could play things on the pedals which many not unskilful clavier players would find it bitter enough to have to play with five fingers. He not only understood the art of playing the organ, of combining the various stops of that instrument in the most skilful manner, and of displaying each stop according to its character in the greatest perfection, but he also knew the construction of organs from one end to the other."[2]

"In many old organs of Germany, e.g. in St. Catherine's Church in Hamburg, and in others, and even in many new, splendid organs of France, the reeds are present in fairly large numbers. The greatest organist and expert on organs in Germany, and perhaps in Europe, the late Kapellmeister Bach, was a great friend of the reeds, he for one must have known what could be played on them, and how. Is the convenience of some organists and organ builders really reason enough to scorn such stops, to call them names, and to eliminate them?

"In the organ of St. Catherine's Church in Hamburg there are sixteen reeds. The late Kapellmeister, Mr. J. S. Bach, in Leipzig, who once made himself heard for two full hours on this instrument, which he called excellent in all its parts, could not praise the beauty and variety of tone of

[1] From a letter written by C. P. E. Bach to Forkel (Hamburg, 1774).

[2] C. P. E. Bach and J. F. Agricola, *Obituary of Bach.*

these reeds highly enough. It is known, too, that the former organist of this church, Mr. Johann Adam Reinken, always kept them in the best tune.

"The late Kapellmeister Bach in Leipzig gave assurance that the 32-ft. principal and the pedal trombone (32 ft.) in the organ of St. Catherine's Church in Hamburg spoke evenly and quite audibly right down to the lowest C. But he also used to say that this principal was the only one as good as that, of such size, that he had heard."

"It is good to have the manuals (i.e. the length of the keys) as short as possible. For when there are three or four the player can go from one to the other with much more ease if the manuals are short. He can remain in a straight sitting position even if he wishes to play for any length of time even on the third manual (reckoning from the bottom up) of some organs, having long manuals. Anyone who is in the habit of placing his fingers properly will know that he need never stretch a finger out straight in playing. Why, then, does he need long manuals? As far as the width of the keys is concerned, it is known that particularly in Brandenburg the keys are made narrower than elsewhere, but no man has yet got his fingers stuck between the semitones. . . . "[1]

Organ registration in France in the late eighteenth century—given by Dom Bédos in *L'Art du Facteur d'orgues* and "read, examined, corrected and approved by the most celebrated and able organists of Paris, such as Messieurs Calvière, Fouquet, Couperin, Balbastre and others".

These registration suggestions should be read with reference to the organ of Clicquot in the Church of St. Sulpice, Paris (p. 213).

(1) If the reeds are unsatisfactory a bourdon may tend to correct matters, if they are too "sharp" in tone. If they are slow of speech an open 8-ft. and a nazard $2\frac{2}{3}$-ft. may help to remedy the trouble.

(2) If the reeds are out of tune or badly regulated a "strong" tremulant may (just possibly !) serve to distract the attention from the trouble. Such a tremulant, however, usually shows poor taste and needs the utmost discretion in its use.

(3) If the two 8-ft. registers are too soft for accompanimental purposes, add a 4-ft. flute, or, failing that, the prestant. Never add a 16-ft. stop.

(4) Never add tierce, nazard or quarte (de nazard 2-ft.) to the plein jeu. They stifle its brilliance, clarity and finesse.

(5) Do not add tierce, nazard or quarte to the grand jeu, for the reason given above. The beauty of the grand jeu depends on the reed stops.

(6) Often the prestant is too "sharp" in tone to add to the 8-ft. stops for accompanimental purposes: the 4-ft. flute is much better, if there is one available.

(7) Where "pédale de flûte" is specified it will be necessary to use flutes of 32 ft., two of 16 ft. and the 8-ft. and 4-ft. flutes all used together.

(8) A "jeu de tierce à la pédale" means the addition of nazards, quartes and

[1] J. F. Agricola, "Treatise on the Organ and Other Instruments", contained in Adlung's *Musica Mechanica Organoedi*.

tierces, to the foundation stops. This combination is useful for playing quartets or trios, and on other occasions according to the discretion of the organist.

(9) Some organists nearly always add a nazard to the cromorne, but this is hardly satisfactory, for if the cromorne is poor and out of tune there is no blending of stops, and if it is good the nazard is not necessary.

(10) Here Dom Bédos enjoins organists to study the peculiarities of their instruments, and to use taste and discretion. Even in the same rank of pipes some parts will be more useful than others. Again, the organist should choose his *mélange* according to the type of music which is being played. Here follow the hints on registration given by Dom Bédos.

(1) *Plein jeu.* All the montres, open 8-ft. stops, all bourdons, prestants, doublettes, fournitures, cymbales, both on the grand orgue and positif. The manuals may be coupled. On the pedals all the trompettes and clairons *or* the flue stops. The plein jeu should be treated with grave and majestic movement—"with great flights of harmony, interwoven with the art of syncopation, striking discords, suspensions, and new harmonic devices". The plein jeu of the positif needs "clear" playing.

(2) *Grand jeu.* The cornet, prestant, and all the trompettes and clairons of the grand orgue. Similar registration for the positif, which should be coupled to the grand (récit and echo should have the cornet also) pédale as given under (1). (Avoid the tremulant with this combination.)

(3) For a "duo". Dom Bédos gives eight different recipes for playing pieces with two parts:

(*a*) *Grand orgue* (left-hand): foundation stops from 32 ft. with nazards, tierces, quarte but *not* doublette. (This was known as "Grand jeu de tierce".) *Positif* (right hand; uncoupled): similar ingredients to the above.

(*b*) Right hand—cornet (*récit*); left hand—prestant and cromorne (*positif*), or instead of cornet (*récti*) a petit jeu de tierce on the grand orgue., i.e. two 8-ft. stops, prestant, nazard ($2\frac{2}{3}$ ft.) quarte and tierce.

(*c*) Right hand—cornet (*récit*); left hand—trompette (*positif*).

(*d*) Right hand-trompette (*récit*); left hand—jeu de tierce (*positif*).

(*e*) Right hand—cromorne and prestant (*positif*); left hand—jeu de tierce (*grand*). (Do not thicken the bass in this case.) This will also serve for a trio with two parts taken by the right hand.

(*f*) Both hands on grand orgue, using prestant and reeds. (Also useful for a "caprice".)

(*g*) Right hand—two 8-ft. stops, 4-ft. flute and nazard of positif, or, better still, the cromorne and prestant; left hand—two 16-ft. stops and clairon of the grand orgue.

(*h*) Right hand—cornet (*récit*); left hand—foundation stops of grand orgue with cromorne and prestant (keyboards coupled). Do not thicken the bass.

(4) For a slow and grave fugue. *Grand orgue*: prestant, all trompettes and clairons. *Positif* (coupled): trompette, clairon and cromorne. *Pédale*: as in 1 and 2. Do not add cornet or tremulant.

(5) For a quick fugue. Use grand jeu or the grand jeu de tierce (manuals

coupled). Do not in the latter case add clairon to grand orgue or cromorne to positif.

(6) For the tierce en taille (a tenor solo tierce):

(*a*) Accompany on two or three 8-ft. stops on the grand and the pedal fluework 16-ft., 8-ft., 4-ft.

(*b*) The solo is played on the positif with the following stops: two 8-ft., 4-ft. flute, nazard, tierce, quarte and larigot. The solo melody should be "singing" and "ornamented with taste".

(7) For the cromorne en taille (a solo cromorne). Accompany as under 6. Solo on positif with cromorne and prestant. (A jeu de tierce on the pedal gives a still better effect for the accompaniment.) Notice that the récit is capable of many solo effects and is more pleasing in the second octave than higher in the compass.

(8) *Solo trompette*. Accompaniment as above. Use the trumpet (positif alone, or if its tone is not good add the prestant. The second and third octaves are most effective.

(9) *A trio on two claviers*. Dom Bédos gives ten recipes:

(*a*) (i) Cornet de récit.
(ii) Cromorne and prestant positif.
(iii) Jeu de tierce pédale. (Do not keep more than an octave interval between bass and top parts.)

(*b*) (i) Jeu de tierce (positif) without larigot.
(ii) Trompette récit (or grand orgue).
(iii) Jeu de tierce or flues 16 ft., 8 ft., 4 ft., pédale.

(*c*) (i) Cornet de récit.
(ii) Jeu de tierce positif.
(iii) Pédale as above.

(*d*) (i) All 8-ft. stops of grand and positif coupled.
(ii) Trompette or cornet de récit.
(iii) Pédale as above.

(*e*) (i) 8-ft. grand orgue.
(ii) Positif cromorne and prestant.
(iii) Pédale as above.

(*f*) (i) Trompette de récit or grand.
(ii) Positif 8-ft. flute 4 ft. nazard.
(iii) Pédale as above.

(*g*) (i) Two 8-ft. and $2\frac{2}{3}$ grand orgue.
(ii) Cromorne and prestant.
(iii) Pédale as above.

(*h*) (i) Jeu de tierce positif.
(ii) Two 8-ft. grand orgue.
(iii) Pédale as above.

(*i*) (i) Cornet de récit or two 8-ft. flute and nazard.
(ii) Vox humaine, bourdon 8 ft. and flute 4 ft.
(iii) Pédale flûtes 16 ft. 8 ft., 4 ft.

(*j*) The tremulant may be used (i and ii) on all 8-ft. stops of grand and positif coupled and (iii) on flue stops of pédale.

(10) *A quartet on four keyboards.* This is hard (says Dom Bédos) owing to the necessity of playing on two keyboards with the same hand, and the difficulty of making the two upper parts "sing". He gives two suggestions:

(*a*) (i) Trompette de récit or two 8-ft. stops.
(ii) Petit jeu de tierce (grand orgue).
(iii) Cromorne and prestant of positif.
(iv) Pédale flûtes or jeu de tierce.

(*b*) (i) Cornet de récit.
(ii) Trompette and prestant of grand orgue.
(iii) Jeu de tierce positif.
(iv) Pédale flûtes.

(11) *A trio on three keyboards.* This is a modification of 10.

(12) *To play on the foundation stops of the organ.* All 8-ft. and 4-ft. stops, claviers coupled with pedal flue-work. Never use the tremulant.

(13) *A cromorne bass.* Use the positif cromorne and prestant to imitate the bassoon or the double-bass. Accompany with two 8 ft. stops on the grand orgue.

(14) *To play a musette.* If there is a musette stop, add to it the 8 ft. bourdon only; accompany with two 8 ft. stops, holding down the tonic and quint (dominant) bass with two lead weights, or play the tonic on the pedals. Two upper parts may be played on the same stops. If there is no musette use the cromorne without prestant.

(15) *To accompany the voice.* Adjust the power of the organ to that of the voices. With a large choir use the plein jeu and a pedal bass of trompettes and clarions. With several voices in harmony use all the 8 ft. stops; with weak voices the 8 ft. of the positif only. The voice should always dominate, and the accompaniment should only serve to sustain and embellish.

(16) *The use of the Bombardes.* The bombarde is never used alone; it may be added to the trompettes and clarions of the pedal, and, as in playing a plain-song melody, it may then be accompanied with the plein jeu, or if the character of the piece demands it, with the grand jeu. Again, the bombarde could be coupled to the other claviers (*i.e.* grand and positif) or slow and majestic effects, suspensions, points d'orgue and final cadences or chords. It may be added to the grand orgue reeds for a plain-song melody, but genius and discretion are necessary in order that the bombarde may be properly used.

APPENDIX I

A SELECTION OF ORGAN SPECIFICATIONS

Contents

A SELECTION OF ORGAN SPECIFICATIONS

1

Lübeck. Sixteenth century. From Praetorius (*Syntagma*). "*Onser lieben Frawen*" (*St. Mary's Church*). Built by M. Bartold. Three manual claviers: the two upper from D to $\bar{\bar{a}}$ and the lowest from C to $\bar{\bar{a}}$. The pedal from C to $\bar{d}$. "Item Coppei zum Pedal ound Manuali."

Oben in der Orgel Sind
(7 Stimmen)

1. Principal und ventile
2. Grossoctava
3. Kleinoctava
4. Ruschquint
5. Scharff zimbel
6. Superoctava
7. Mixtur

In der Brust
(5 Stimmen)

1. Regal
2. Zinck oder cornett
3. Krumbhorn
4. Baarpfeiffe
5. Gedact

Im Rückpositif
(20 Stimmen)

1. Gemshorner
2. Blockpfeiff 4
3. Principal
4. Zimbel
5. Mixtur
6. Superoctava
7. Principale
8. Feldpfeiffe
9. Octava
10. Borduna
11. Offenfloit 8
12. Gedact 8
13. Dulcian oder fagott 8
14. Querpfeiffe 4
15. Offenfloit 4
16. Octava 4
17. Superoctav
18. Mixtur
19. Dulcian oder fagott 16
20. Trommeten 16

In Pedal
(14 Stimmen)

1. Gross principal unter bass
2. Duppelt unter bass
   Ventile zu allen rohren bassen oben in der orgel; als dulcian bass, schallmeyen bass und cornet bass
3. Unter bass
   Ventile zu allen pfeiffen und bassen im stuel
4. Mixtur bass im stuel
5. Trommeten bass
6. Bassunen bass

7. Schallmeyen bass	10. Dulcian bass
8. Feldpfeiffen bass im stuel	11. Cornett bass
9. Klein octaven bass	12. Gross octaven bass im stuel
Ventile zum bassunen und trommeten bass im stuele	13. Dezehm bass im stuel
	14. Quintadehnen bass im stuel

The *case* of this organ survived until it was destroyed in an air raid on Palm Sunday night, 1942. The sizes of the rückpositif and pedal are remarkable. The smaller pedal stops "im stuel" (i.e. stuhl or chair) represent a chair organ playable from the pedals.

2

Lüneburg, St. John's Church. The organ built in 1549 by Jasper Johannsen of 'sHertogenbosch, Holland.

Hauptwerk
(Middle Clavier)

Prinzipal	16	Mixtur
Oktave	8	Scharf

Oberwerk
(Top Clavier)

Rohrflöte	8	wide scale	Prinzipal	4	narrow scale
Gedacktflöte	4	wide scale	Oktave	2	narrow scale
Nasat	$2\frac{2}{3}$	wide scale	Zimbel		narrow scale
Nachthorn	2	wide scale	Trompete	8	

Pedal

Prinzipal	16	Trompete	4
Oktave	8	Nachthorn	2
Sub-bass	(metal) 16	Bauernflöte	1

Rückpositiv
(Lower Clavier)

Prinzipal	8	narrow scale	Regal	8	reeds
Oktave	4	narrow scale	Bärpfeife	8	reeds
Mixtur		narrow scale	Schalmei	4	reeds
Scharf		narrow scale	Tremulant		
Quintadena	8	wide scale	Ventil to rückpositiv		
Rohrflöte	4	wide scale	Ventil to oberwerk		
Rauschpfeife	$2\frac{2}{3}$, 2	wide scale			
Sifflöte	$1\frac{1}{3}$	wide scale			

The flue chorus pitches of the hauptwerk, rückpositiv and oberwerk will be seen to be 16-ft., 8-ft. and 4-ft. pitches respectively. Sometimes at a later date the brustwerk had a principal pitch of 2 ft. The solo possibilities of the oberwerk, pedal and rückpositiv will be noted. The separation of the thin "prinzipal" scale stops and the wide-scale stop families is a feature of the organs of this period. The organ specified above shows affinities both to the "mixture" spring-chest organ as in the Hauptwerk, and the later slider-chest organ with its separation of the ranks of pipes as in the other sections of the instrument.

3

Toledo Cathedral, Spain. The organ built in 1549 by Juan Gaytan of Toledo.

Lower Manual
(57 notes)

Prinzipal	16	Clarin de campana	4
Oktave	8	Clarin claro	4
Oktave	4	Clarin brillante	2
Gedackt	16	Trompeta magna	16
Trompeta real	8		

Pedal
(13 notes)

Prinzipal	32	Oktave	2
Oktave	16	Oktave	1
Holzflöte	16	Bombarda	16
Oktave	8	Clarines reales	8
Oktave	4	Clarines	2

There were two pedal keyboards: one for the flue-work and one for the reeds.

Upper Manual
(57 notes)

Prinzipal	16	narrow scale
Oktave	8	narrow scale
Oktave	4	narrow scale
Mixture	8 ranks	narrow scale
Mixture	5 ranks	narrow scale
Scharf	8 rank	narrow scale
Gedackt	8	wide scale
Gedackt	4	wide scale
Rauschpfeife	$2\frac{2}{3}$, 2	wide scale
Sesquialtera	7–13 ranks	wide scale
Trompeta magna	16	
Trompeta real	8	
Bajoncilloy Clarin (clarion)	4, 8	
Violetas (Krummhorn)	8	
Querflöte (a 2-rank flute celeste)	8	

4

St. Wolfgang, Austria. Built by Michael Khall, Budweis, 1497.

Hauptwerk		*Rückpositiv*		*Pedal*	
Principal	8	Gedackt	8	Principal	16
Hölzern Octav	4	Flöte	4	Octav	8
Quint	3	Hölzern Principal	2	Zimbel	
Octav	2	Hintersatz			
Zimbel					
Scharfe Mixtur					

5

The University, Freiburg in Breisgau. The design and scales from M. Praetorius, "Organographia", *Syntagma musicum,* vol. ii, 1618. Built by Dr. Oskar Walcker in 1921.

Rückpositif

1. Quintadeena 8
2. Blockflöit 4
3. Gemshörnlein 2
4. Zimbel doppelt gar klein und scharff
5. Spitzflöit oder Spillflöit 4
6. Krumbhorn 8

Tremulant zum ganzen Werck, Coppel zu beyden Manualen Coppel des Pedals zum Rückpositiff.
Coppel des Pedals zum Oberwerck
Stern zum Zimbelglöcklin. Vogelgesang (Trummel).

Oberwerk

1. Principal 8
2. Octava 4
3. Mixtur 4 fach, dorinnen Octav 2′ Quint $1\frac{1}{2}$′
4. Grob Gedact Rohrflöt 8
5. Nachthorn 4
6. Schwiegelpfeiff 1
7. Rancket oder stille Posaun 16
8. Gemshorn 4

In der Brust

1. Klein lieblich Gedact flöit, Rohrflöit 2
2. Baerpfeiff 8
3. Geigend Regal 4

Zum Pedal

1. Untersatz starck 16
2. Posaunen Basz 16
3. Singend Cornet 2
4. Dolzianbasz 8

Names of flue stops in different languages.

English	*German*	*French*	*Spanish*
Open diapason	Prinzipal	Montre	Contras
Principal	Oktave	Préstant	Flautado
Fifteenth	Superoktave	Doublette	Octavo
Mixture	Mixtur	Fourniture	Nasardos
Sharp mixture (cymbale)	Scharf	Cymbale	Lleno

6

Grosshartmannsdorf. The organ built in 1741 by G. Silbermann, op. 45.

Hauptwerk

Prinzipal	8	Rohrflöte	8	Quinta	$2\frac{2}{3}$
Quintadena	8	Spitzflöte	4	Cornet	3 ranks
Oktave	4	Oktave	2	Mixtur	4 ranks

Oberwerk

Gedackt	8	Oktave	2	Tertia	$1\frac{3}{5}$
Rohrflöte	4	Gemshorn	2	Sifflöt	1
Nassat	$2\frac{2}{3}$	Quinta	$1\frac{1}{3}$	Cymbel	2 ranks

Pedal

Sub-bass	16
Posaun Bass	16
Oktav Bass	16

Silbermann left a MS. notebook with suggestions for registration on this organ:

Full organ: Hauptwerk without Quintadena, Spitzflöte and Cornet; Oberwerk without Gemshorn, Nassat, Tertia; all pedal stops.

Flute combinations: Rohrflöte, Spitzflöte, Gedackt, Rohrflöte.

Sifflöte combination: Gedackt, Rohrflöte, Sifflöte.

Quiet flute combinations: Quintaden and Spitzflöte; Rohrflöte and Spitzflöte; Principal and Spitzflöte; Gedackt, Rohrflöte and Gemshorn.

Cornet solo combination: Principal, Rohrflöte, Octave, Cornet accompanied by Gedackt, Rohrflöte or Gemshorn.

Nassat solo: Gedackt, Rohrflöte, Nassat accompanied by Rohrflöte and Spitzflöte.

7

St. Jakobi, Hamburg. The organ built in 1688–92 by Arp Schnitger.

Hauptwerk

Prinzipal	16	Gedackt	8	Flachflöte	2
Quintatön	16	Oktave	4	Rauschpfeife	3 ranks
Oktave	8	Rohrflöte	4	Mixtur	6–8 ranks
Spitzflöte	8	Superoktave	2	Trompete	16

Oberwerk

Prinzipal	8	Nasat	3 ($2\frac{2}{3}$)	Zimbel	3 ranks
Holzflöte	8	Oktave	2	Trompete	8
Rohrflöte	8	Gemshorn	2	Vox humana	8
Oktave	4	Scharff	4–6 ranks	Trompete	4
Spitzflöte	4				

Rückpositiv

Prinzipal	8	Nasat	3 ($2\frac{2}{3}$)	Scharff	4–6 ranks
Gedackt	8	Oktave	2	Dulzian	16
Quintatön	8	Sifflöte	$1\frac{1}{2}$ ($1\frac{1}{3}$)	Bärpfeife	8
Oktave	4	Sesquialter	2 ranks	Schalmei	4
Blockflöte	4				

Brustwerk

Holzprinzipal	8	Sesquialter	2 ranks
Oktave	4	Scharff	4–6 ranks
Hohlflöte	4	Dulzian	8
Waldflöte	2	Trechterregal	8

Pedal

Prinzipal	32	Rauschpfeife	3 ranks
Oktave	16	Posaune	32
Sub-bass	16	Posaune	16
Oktave	8	Dulzian	16
Oktave	4	Trompete	8
Nachthorn	2	Trompete	4
Mixtur	6–8 ranks	Kornett	2

Coupler: oberwerk to hauptwerk; Oberwerk tremulant.
Coupler: brustwerk to oberwerk.
The organ has been restored (1950) and is again in use.

8

Pellworm. The organ built in 1711 by Arp Schnitger.

Oberwerk

Principal	8	Spitzflöte	4	Rauschpfeife	
Gedackt	8	Oktave	2	Mixtur	5–6 ranks
Oktave	4	Nasat	$2\frac{2}{3}$	Trompete	8

Brustwerk

Gedackt	8	Gemshorn	2	Scharff	4 ranks
Waldflöte	4	Sesquialter		Dulcian	8
Oktave	2				

Pedal

Quintade	16	Nachthorn	2	Trompete	8
Principal	8	Mixtur	6 ranks	Cornett	2
Oktave	4	Posaune	16		

9

Neuenfelde. The organ built in 1683–8 by Arp Schnitger.

Hauptwerk

Quintade	16	Oktave	2	Mixtur	5–6 ranks
Principal	8	Spillflöte	2	Cymbel	2–3 ranks
Rohrflöte	8	Nasat	$2\frac{2}{3}$	Trompete	8
Oktave	4	Rauschpfeife		Vox humana	8
Spitzflöte	4				

Rückpositiv

Gedackt	8	Oktave	2	Tertian	
Quintade	8	Quinte	$2\frac{2}{3}$	Scharff	4–5 ranks
Principal	4	Sifflöte	$1\frac{1}{3}$	Krummhorn	8
Blockflöte	4	Sesquialter			

Pedal

Principal	16	Nachthorn	2	Posaune	16
Oktave	8	Rauschpfeife		Trompete	8
Superoktave	4	Mixtur	5 ranks	Cornett	2
Flöte	4				

10

The Church of Sts. Peter and Paul, Görlitz, Germany. The organ built in 1697–1702 by Eugen Casparini (Caspar or Gaspar).

Pedal Organ

1. Gross prinzipal bass	32 (24)	12. Mixtur	12–17 ranks
2. Octave bass	16	13. Mixtur	4–5 ranks
3. Contra bass	16	14. Bauernflöte (2 ranks)	$1\frac{1}{3}$, 1
4. Bordun sub-bass	16	15. Scharffs	2 ranks
5. Quintaden-bass	8	16. Helle cymbel (2 ranks)	$1\frac{1}{3}$, 1
6. Tubalflöte	8	17. Posaunen	16
7. Gemshorn-bass	8	18. Fagotti (Dulcian)	16
8. Gross-quinten-bass	6 ($5\frac{1}{3}$)	19. Krummhorn	8
9. Tubalflöte	4	20. Tromba	8
10. Jubal	4	21. Jungfernregal	4
11. Superoctav-bass	4		

Hauptwerk
(middle clavier)

22. Prinzipal	16	30. Offenflöte	4
23. Prinzipal	8	31. Decima nona	3 ($2\frac{2}{3}$)
24. Viola da gamba	8	32. Plockflöte	2
25. Vox humana (fiffaro)	8	33. Zynck (sesquialtera)	$2\frac{2}{3}$, $1\frac{3}{5}$
26. Rohrflötenquint	6 ($5\frac{1}{3}$)	34. Rauschpfeife	$2\frac{2}{3}$, 2
27. Superoctav	4	35. Mixtur (3 ranks)	$1\frac{1}{3}$, 1, 1
28. Salicet	4	36. Bombart	16
29. Gedackt pommer (Quintadena)	4		

Oberwerk
(lower clavier)

37. Quintaden	16	43. Sedecima	2
38. Prinzipal	8	44. Glöcklein-Thon	2
39. Onda maris	8	45. Super-decima	$1\frac{1}{2}$ ($1\frac{1}{3}$)
40. Octava	4	46. Cornett	(3 ranks) $5\frac{1}{3}$, 4, $3\frac{1}{5}$
41. Gedackte fluet doux	4	47. Scharffs	(2 ranks) 1
42. Spitzflöte	3 ($2\frac{2}{3}$)	48. Cymbel	(2 ranks) $1\frac{1}{3}$

Brustwerk
(upper clavier)

49. Gedackt	8	53. Quintnassat	$1\frac{1}{2}$ ($1\frac{1}{3}$)
50. Prinzipal	4	54. Sedecima	1
51. Octava	2	55. Scharff mixtur (2 ranks)	1, $\frac{2}{3}$
52. Plockflöte	2	56. Hautbois	8

We now give the specifications (11–15) of some of the better-known Bach organs:

11

St. Boniface, Arnstadt. The organ built in 1701 by J. F. Wender.

Oberwerk

1. Prinzipal	8	6. Quinte	6 ($5\frac{1}{3}$)	10. Trompete	8
2. Quintatön	16	7. Octava	4	Tremulant	
3. Viola da gamba	8	8. Cymbel	2 ranks	Cymbel stern (star with rotating bells)	
4. Gedackt	8	9. Mixture	4 ranks		
5. Gemshorn	8				

Brust Positiv

1. Prinzipal	4	4. Nachthorn	4	7. Mixtur	2 ranks
2. Gedackt	8	5. Quinte	3 ($2\frac{2}{3}$)	8. Octave	2
3. Spitzflöte	4	6. Sesquialtera	2 ranks	Manual und Pedal Koppel	

Pedal

1. Sub-bass	16	3. Flötenbass	4	5. Cornet bass	2
2. Prinzipalbass	8	4. Posaune	16		

The organ lasted until 1862, but a few stops and most of the case were incorporated in the present organ. The console is in the Museum of Bach relics in Arnstadt.

12

St. John's Church, Leipzig. The organ built in 1746 by J. Scheibe. The console of this organ still remains in the Museum.

Hauptwerk

1. Quintatön	16	5. Octava	4	8. Octava	2
2. Principal	8	6. Spitzflöte	4	9. Cornett	3 ranks
3. Grobgedackt	8	7. Quinte	3	10. Mixtur	4 ranks
4. Viola d'amour	8				

Oberwerk

1. Gedackt	8	4. Hohlflöte	4	6. Octava	2
2. Quintatön	8	5. Flauto traverso	4(?)	7. Sifflet	1
3. Principal	4				

Pedal

1. Sub-bass	16	3. Violonbass	8(?)	Tremulant
2. Octavbass	8	4. Posaune	16	Pedalkoppel

13 and 14

St. Thomas's Church, Leipzig. (*a*) The large organ, 1723. (*b*) The small organ at the same date.

(*a*) THE LARGE ORGAN

Oberwerk

1. Principal	16	7. Spiel-Pfeiffe	8
2. Principal	8	8. Sesquialtera	2 ranks
3. Quintadena	16	9. Mixtur	6, 7–10 ranks
4. Octava	4	Tremulant	
5. Quinta	3	Vogelgesang (bird song)	
6. Super octava	2	Cimbelstern	

Brustwerk

10. Grossgedackt	8	15. Cimbel	2 ranks
11. Principal	4	16. Sesquialtera	
12. Nachthorn	4	17. Regal	8
13. Nasat	3	18. Geigendregal	4
14. Gemshorn	2		

Rückpositiv

19. Principal	8	25. Rauschquinte	2 ranks
20. Quintadena	8	26. Mixtur	4 ranks
21. Lieblich gedackt	8	27. Spitzflöte	4
22. Klein gedackt	4	28. Schallflöte	1
23. Traversa	4	29. Krumbhorn	16
24. Violin	2	30. Trommet	8

Pedal

31. Sub-bass von metall	16	34. Schallmeyenbass	4
32. Posaunenbass	16	35. Cornett	3
33. Trommetenbass	8		

(*b*) THE SMALL ORGAN

Oberwerk

1. Principal	8	4. Octava	4	6. Mixtur	4–10 ranks
2. Gedackt	8	5. Rauschquinte	$2\frac{2}{3}$, 2	7. Cimbeln	2 ranks
3. Quintadena	8				

Brustwerk

8. Trichterregal	8	9. Suffloth	1	10. Spitzflöt	2

Rückpositiv

11. Principal	4	14. Nasat	3	17. Dulcian	8
12. Lieblich gedackt	8	15. Octava	2	18. Trommet	8
13. Hohlflöt	4	16. Sesquialtera 2 ranks			

Pedal

19. Sub-bass von Holz	16	Tremulant
20. Fagottbass	16	Cimbelstern
21. Trommetbass	8	(A rotating star in the case with small bells)

15

Weimar Castle. Built in 1719–20 by H. N. Trebs

Hauptwerk

Quintatön	16	Gedackt	8	Mixtur	6 ranks
Principal	8	Octave	4	Cymbel	3 ranks
Gemshorn	8	Quintatön	4	Glockenspiel	

Positiv

Principal	8	Kleingedackt	4	Sesquialtera	2 ranks
Viola di gamba	8	Octave	4	Trompette	8
Gedackt	8	Waldflöte	2		

Pedal

Gros untersatz	32	Principal bass	8	Trompeten bass	8
Sub-bass	16	Posaune bass	16	Cornetten bass	4
Violon bass	16				

16

Freiberg Cathedral, Saxony. Built in 1710–14 by Gottfried Silbermann

Hauptwerk

Bordun	16	Quinta	3 ($2\frac{2}{3}$)	Zimbel	3 ranks
Prinzipal	8	Superoktav	2	Trompete	8
Viola da gamba	8	Terz	$1\frac{3}{5}$	Klarine	4
Rohrflöte	8	Mixtur	4 ranks	Kornett	4 ranks
Oktav	4				

Oberwerk

Quintadena	16	Spitzflöte	4	Zimbel	2 ranks
Prinzipal	8	Superoktav	2	Vox humana	8
Bordun	8	Flageolett	1	Krummhorn	8
Quintadena	8	Mixtur	3 ranks	Echokornett	5 ranks
Oktav	4				

Brustwerk

Gedackt	8	Nasat	3 ($2\frac{2}{3}$)	Quinte	$1\frac{1}{3}$
Prinzipal	4	Oktav	2	Sifflöte	1
Rohrflöte	4	Terz	$1\frac{3}{5}$	Mixtur	3 ranks

Pedal

Untersatz	32	Oktav	8	Bombarde	16
Prinzipal	16	Superoktav	4	Trompete	8
Sub-bass	16	Mixtur	6 ranks	Klarine	4

This instrument is well preserved at the present day. Bach played a number of the Silbermann organs, in particular that at St. Sophia's Church, Dresden. Silbermann described the tone qualities of the sections of his typical three-manual instruments as follows:

(1) Hauptwerk von grossen und gravitatischen Mensuren.
(2) Oberwerk von scharfen und penetraten Mensuren.
(3) Brustwerk von delicaten und lieblichen Mensuren.
(4) Pedal von Starken und durchdringenden (penetrating) Mensuren.

17

The Church of St. Bavon, Haarlem, Holland. The organ built in 1735–8 by Christian Müller.

Great Organ

1. Prestant	16	9. Quint préstant	$2\frac{2}{3}$
2. Bourdon	16	10. Woud-fluit	2
3. Octaav	8	11. Tertian	(2 ranks) 1
4. Roerfluit	8	12. Mixtur	6–10 ranks
5. Viol di Gamba	8	13. Trompet	16
6. Roer-quint	$5\frac{1}{3}$	14. Trompet	8
7. Octaav	4	15. Hautbois	8
8. Gemshorn	4	16. Trompet	4

Positiv

17. Prestant	8	24. Sesquialtera	2–4 ranks
18. Quintadena	8	25. Mixtur	6–8 ranks
19. Hohlfluit	8	26. Cimbel	2 ranks
20. Octaav	4	27. Cornet	5 ranks
21. Fluit-doux	4	28. Fagot	16
22. Speel-fluit	$2\frac{2}{3}$	29. Trompet	8
23. Super-octaav	2	30. Regal	8

Boven (Echo) Organ

31. Quintadena	16	39. Flageolet	$1\frac{1}{3}$
32. Préstant	8	40. Sexquialtera	2 ranks
33. Baarpyp	8	41. Mixtur	4–6 ranks
34. Quintadena	8	42. Cimbel	4 ranks
35. Octaav	4	43. Schalmei	8
36. Flag (flach) fluit	4	44. Dulcian	8
37. Nassat	$2\frac{2}{3}$	45. Vox humana	8
38. Nacht-horn	2		

Pedal

46. Sub-principal	32	54. Holfluit	2
47. Prestant	16	55. Ruisquint	5 ranks
48. Sub-bass	16	56. Bazuin	32
49. Roer-quint	$10\frac{2}{3}$	57. Bazuin	16
50. Octaav	8	58. Trompet	8
51. Holfluit	8	59. Trompet	4
52. Quint	$5\frac{1}{3}$	60. Cinq	2
53. Octaav	4		

Compass: Manuals—CC to D in alt, 51 notes.
Pedals—CCC to tenor D, 27 notes.
Unison couplers.
Ventils to each manual and pedal.
Two tremulants.
Twelve bellows 9 ft. by 5 ft.

Added in 1961
Scherp 6–8 ranks to G. Organ
Mixtuur 6–10 ranks to Pedal

18

The second half of the eighteenth century was characterised by the building of many large organs in Europe, in particular in Germany and France.

The great instrument, built between 1736 and 1750, by Josef Gabler, of Ochsenhausen, in the Chapel of the Benedictine Monastery in Weingarten, was justifiably famous, though, in common with most of the organs of that and a slightly later period, it had little effect on the arts of organ-playing and composition. Organs became larger; the peculiar tone of the instrument with its subtle tone-building potentialities was tending to go. Organ cases became more restless and rococo in conception and florid in design.

The Abbey, Weingarten, Germany. The organ built by Joseph Gabler (completed in 1750). [See the frontispiece.]

Hauptwerk

(Manual I)

Praestant (49 pipes)	16	Hohlflöte (49 pipes)	2
Principal (49 pipes)	8	Sesquialter (9–8 ranks; 441 pipes)	2
Rohrflöte (49 pipes)	8	Mixtur (10–9 ranks; 465 pipes)	2
Piffaro (5–7 ranks; 319 pipes)	8	Cymbel (12 ranks; 588 pipes)	1
Oktave (1-2 ranks; 72 pipes)	4	Trompete (49 pipes)	8
Superoktave (2 ranks; 98 pipes)	2	Carillon	

Oberwerk

(Manual II)

Bordon (1–3 ranks; 86 pipes)	16	Salicional (49 pipes)	8
Violoncello (1–3 ranks; 86 pipes)	8	Hohlflöte (49 pipes)	8
Principal (49 pipes)	8	Unda Maris (49 pipes)	8
Koppel (49 pipes)	8	Mixtur (9–12 ranks; 552 pipes)	4

Kronpositiv
(Manual II)

Octave douce (49 pipes)	4	Vox humana (49 pipes)	8
Viola douce (2 ranks; 98 pipes)	4	Oboe (49 pipes)	4
Nasat (49 pipes)	2	Carillon 32 notes	
Cymbel (2 ranks; 98 pipes)	2	Tremulant	

Hauptpedal
(originally 20 notes from C extended to 28 in 1912 by Weigle)

Kontrabass (2 ranks; 40 (56) pipes)	32	Mixturbass (5–6 ranks; 108 pipes)	8
Sub-bass (20 (28) pipes)	32	Bombarde (20 (28) pipes)	32
Oktav (20 (28) pipes)	16	Posaune (20 (28) pipes)	16
Violonbass (40 (56) pipes)	16	La Force (one note C with 49 pipes)	
		Carillon (20 bells)	2

Pedal—Positiv

Quintatönbass (20 (28) pipes)	16	Kornettbass (11–10 ranks; 205 pipes)	4
Superoktavbass (20 (28) pipes)	8	Sesquialter (7–6 ranks; 125 pipes)	$2\frac{2}{3}$
Flute douce (20 (28) pipes)	8	Trompete (20 pipes)	8
Violoncello (20 (28) pipes)	8	Fagott (20 pipes)	8
Hohlflöte (20 pipes)	4		

Unterwerk—Echo
(Manual III)

Bordun (49 pipes)	16	Hohlflöte (2 ranks; 96 pipes)	4
Principal (49 pipes)	8	Piffaro dolce (2 ranks; 98 pipes)	4
Quintatön (49 pipes)	8	Superoktave (49 pipes)	2
Flöte (49 pipes)	8	Mixtur (5–6 ranks; 270 pipes)	2
Viola dolce (49 pipes)	8	Kornett (6–5 ranks; 269 pipes)	1
Oktave (49 pipes)	4	Oboe (49 pipes)	8

Epistel—Positiv
(Manual IV)

Principal doux (49 pipes)	8	Piffaro (5–6 ranks; 189 pipes)	4
Flute doux (49 pipes)	8	Flageolet (49 pipes)	2
Quintatön (49 pipes)	8	Kornett (11–8 ranks; 452 pipes)	2
Violoncello (49 pipes)	8		
Rohrflöte (49 pipes)	4	Cymbala (Cymbelstern) 3 bells	
Querflöte (49 pipes)	4	Cuculus (Cuckoo) 4 pipes	
Flauto traverso (2 ranks;		Nachtigall (Nightingale) 2 pipes	
98 pipes)	4	Tympanum (Drum) 4 pipes	

Stops added by Weigle in 1912 *on* 6 *in. wind pressure*[1]

Seraphon—Hornprincipal	8	Seraphon—Flöte	8
Seraphon—Fugara	8	Seraphon—Gamba	4
Seraphon—Violine	8	Tuba mirabilis	8
Seraphon—Gedackt	8		

Unison couplers. Original wind pressure, 2·75 in.

Total: 7,040 pipes and 55 bells.

[1] Removed at recent restoration.

The multi-rank mixtures were obtained by the duplication and multiplication of ranks of the same pitch. After years of neglect such mixtures produce fearful dissonances. The composition of the twelve-rank mixture on Manual I of the Weingarten organ is as follows:

C	1	1	1	1	$\frac{2}{3}$	$\frac{2}{3}$	$\frac{2}{3}$	$\frac{2}{3}$	$\frac{1}{2}$	$\frac{1}{2}$	$\frac{1}{2}$	$\frac{1}{2}$
c^1	2	2	2	2	$1\frac{1}{3}$	$1\frac{1}{3}$	$1\frac{1}{3}$	$1\frac{1}{3}$	1	1	1	1
c^2	4	4	4	4	$2\frac{2}{3}$	$2\frac{2}{3}$	$2\frac{2}{3}$	$2\frac{2}{3}$	2	2	2	2

19

Kirchheimbolanden. An early "romantic" organ built in 1746 by Stumm.

Hauptwerk (upper manual)

(CD—c^3, 48 keys)		Oktave	4	Terz	$1\frac{3}{5}$
Bordun	16	Flöte	4	Mixtur 4 ranks	
Prinzipal	8	Salizional	4	Kornett	$2\frac{2}{3}$, 2, $1\frac{3}{5}$
Quintadena	8	Quinte	$2\frac{2}{3}$	Trompete	8
Viola de gamba	8	Oktave	2	Glockenspiel (diskant)	

Pedal

(C–f, 18 keys with C♯)		Sub-bass	16	Posaune	16
Prinzipal	16	Oktave	8		

Unterwerk (middle manual)

Hohlflöte	8	Salizional	2	Vox humana	8
Principal	4	Quinte	$1\frac{1}{3}$	Flauto traverso (diskant)	8
Rohrflöte	4	Mixtur 3 ranks			
Oktave	2	Krummhorn	8		

Hinterwerk (lower manual)

Gedackt	8	Quinte	$1\frac{1}{3}$	Regal	8
Gedackt	4	Oktave	1	Violine (diskant)	8
Prinzipal	2				

Koppel hauptwerk to pedal.
Koppel unterwerk to hauptwerk.
Schwebung (tremulant).

20

The Trinity Organ at *Ottobeuren Abbey*. Built between 1754–66 by Karl Joseph Riepp.

Positif (C to d) (first manual)

Principal (a half-stop)	16	Flageolet	4	Fourniture	5 ranks
Flûte	8	Nazard	3 ($2\frac{2}{3}$)	Trompette	8
Copel	8	Quarte	2	Cromorne	8
Viole de gambe	4	Tierce	$1\frac{1}{2}$ ($1\frac{3}{5}$)	Voix humaine	8
Octave	4	Quinte	$1\frac{1}{2}$ ($1\frac{1}{3}$)	Clairon	4

All the stops except the octave 4, and the principal which was a half-stop draw in halves.

Grand Orgue (*Hauptwerk*) (C to d)
(second manual)

Copel	16	Tierce	3 ($3\frac{1}{5}$)
Flûte	8	Waldflet	2
Copel	8	Tierce	$1\frac{1}{2}$ ($1\frac{3}{5}$)
Principal	8	Cornet	5 ranks
Salicional	8	Fourniture	4 ranks
Gambe	8	Cimbale	4–6 ranks
Prestant	4	Trompette	8
Flageolet	4	Clairon	4
Quinte	3 ($2\frac{2}{3}$)		

Récit (C to d)
(third manual)

Cornet (5 ranks) 8

Echo (C to d)
(fourth manual)
[Draws in half stops]

Bass

Copel	8	Quinte	3 ($2\frac{2}{3}$)	Tierce	$1\frac{1}{2}$ ($1\frac{3}{5}$)
Flageolet	4	Quarte	2	Hautbois	8

Dessus

Copel	8	Larigot	($1\frac{1}{3}$)	Hautbois
Flageolet	4	Tierce	($1\frac{3}{5}$)	

Pedal (C-c)

Principal	16	Flet	4
Copel	16	Fourniture	5–6 ranks
Octave	8	Bombarde	16
Violoncello	8	Trompette	8
Quinte	6 ($5\frac{1}{3}$)	Trompette	4

Couplers, etc.: Clavier I, II
Trémolo doux I
Trémolo fort I
Trémolo doux II, III, IV
Trémolo fort II, III, IV

21

The Holy Ghost Organ, Ottobeuren Abbey. Built by Karl Joseph Riepp.

Positif
(first manual)

Copel	8	Flageolet	4	Fourniture	4 ranks
Flûte	8	Quinte	3	Cornet	3 ranks
Prestant	4	Doublette	2	Chalumeau	8

Hauptwerk
(second manual)

Copel	16	Gambe	8	Doublette	2
Principal	8	Salicional	8	Fourniture	4 ranks
Copel	8	Octave	4	Cimbale	3 ranks
Flûte	8	Flageolet	4	Cromorne	8

Pedal

Principal	16	Flet	4	Tremblant doux.	
Copel	16	Quinte	3 ($2\frac{2}{3}$)	Schiebekoppel.[1]	
Flûte	8	Basson	8		

22

St. Dionis Backchurch, London. The organ built in 1722–4 by Renatus Harris,

Great Organ
(13 stops)

	pipes
1. Open diapason	56
2. Stopped diapason	56
3. Principal	56
4. Twelfth	56
5. Fifteenth	56
6. Tierce	56
7. Larigot	56
8. Sesquialtera (4 ranks)	224
9. Cornet (to mid-C) (5 ranks)	135
10. Trumpet	56
11. French horn (to tenor D)	37
12. Clarion	56
13. Cremona (from choir organ, by communication)	
Total	900

Choir Organ
(7 stops)

	pipes
14. Open diapason (to mid-C) (by communication from 16)	27
15. Stopped diapason (to gamut G) (by communication from 17)	44
16. Principal	56
17. Flute	56
18. Fifteenth	56
19. Cremona	56
20. Bassoon	56
21. Vox humana	56
22. Clarion (from great organ)	
Total	407

Swell Organ
(7 stops)

	pipes
23. Open diapason	32
24. Stopped diapason	32
25. Cornet (4 ranks)	128
26. Trumpet	32
27. Clarion	32
28. Cremona	32
29. Vox humana	32
Total	320

[1] The manuals were coupled by drawing the upper one forward by pulling two knobs, one on each side of the keyframe. A new, large organ, known as the Marienorgel, was built in the west gallery by Steinmeyer in 1957. This organ can be played from a 3-manual tracker console or a 5-manual electric console.

Total number of pipes = 1,627.

Compass: great and choir—GG with GG♯ to D in alt., 56 notes.
Swell—fiddle G to D in alt., 32 notes.

Tenor D was a common lowest note for reed stops which were not of full compass. It was the tonic of the key in which most trumpet and other reed solos were written.

23

Christ Church, Spitalfields, London. The organ built in 1730 by Richard Bridge. This was the largest organ in England at that date.

Great Organ
(16 stops)

		pipes
1.	Open diapason	56
2.	Open diapason (to gamut G) then stopped and principal pipes	68
3.	Stopped diapason	56
4.	Principal	56
5.	Principal	56
6.	Twelfth	56
7.	Fifteenth	56
8.	Tierce	56
9.	Larigot	56
10.	Sesquialtera	280
11.	Fourniture	168
12.	Cornet (to mid-C♯) (5 ranks)	130
13.	Trumpet	56
14.	Trumpet	56
15.	Clarion	56
16.	Bassoon	56
	Total	1,318

(Compass)

Great and choir GG long octaves.
Without GG♯ to D in alt., 56 notes.
Swell, fiddle G to D in alt., 32 notes.
Drum pedal on C, 2 pipes.

Choir Organ
(9 stops)

		pipes
17.	Stopped diapason	56
18.	Principal	56
19.	Flute	56
20.	Fifteenth	56
21.	Mixture (3 ranks)	168
22.	Cremona	56
23.	Vox humana	56
24.	French horn (to tenor D)	37
25.	Hautboy (to tenor D)	37
	Total	578

Swell Organ
(8 stops)

		pipes
26.	Open diapason	32
27.	Stopped diapason	32
28.	Principal	32
29.	Flute	32
30.	Cornet (3 ranks)	96
31.	Trumpet	32
32.	Hautboy	32
33.	Clarion	32
	Total	320

Total pipes 2,216

24

St. Margaret's Church, King's Lynn. The organ built in 1754 by John Snetzler, to a specification approved by Charles Burney, the organist.

Great Organ

(Compass: GG to E in alt.)

1. Bourdon to CC	16	8. Sesquialtera	4 ranks
2. Open diapason	8	9. Fourniture	3 ranks
3. Stopped diapason	8	10. Cornet (to mid-C)	5 ranks
4. Principal	4	11. Trumpet	8
5. Twelfth	$2\frac{2}{3}$	12. Clarion	4
6. Fifteenth	2	Number of pipes in the great organ, 1,053.	
7. Tierce	$1\frac{3}{5}$		

Choir Organ

(Compass: GG to E in alt.)

13. Dulciana (metal)	8	18. Bassoon (up to [from] fiddle G)	8
14. Stopped diapason	8	19. Vox humana	8
15. Principal	4	Number of pipes in choir organ, 378.	
16. Flute	4		
17. Fifteenth	2		

Swell Organ

(8 stops plus 3 borrowed bass stops)
(Compass: Tenor F to E in alt.)

20. Open diapason	8	27. Hautboy	8
21. Stopped diapason	8	(*a*) Stopped bass	(from choir)
22. Dulciana	8	(*b*) Dulciana bass	(from choir)
23. German flute (mid-C)	4	(*c*) Flute bass	(from choir)
24. Cornet	4 ranks	Number of pipes in swell organ, 1,820.	
25. French horn	8		
26. Trumpet	8		

Pedals were added to the organ in 1852 by Holdich.

The compass of the great and choir extended half an octave below the present manual compass.

25

St. Martin-in-the-Fields, London. The organ built by Shrider (*c.* 1727).

Great Organ (10 stops)	*pipes*	*Echo Organ* (4 stops)	*pipes*	*Choir Organ* (6 stops)	*pipes*
Open diapason	55	Open diapason	32	Stopped diapason	55
Stopped diapason	55	Principal	32	Principal	55
Principal	55	Unison to Principal	32	Flute	55
Twelfth	55	Fifteenth	32	Fifteenth	55
Fifteenth	55			Vox humana	55
Sesquialtera	165			Clarion	55
Mixture	110				
Trumpet	55				
Bassoon	55				
Cornet (from C) (5 ranks)	135				

Pedals.

26

Parish Church of St. Mary, Nottingham. A favourite frontal design of Snetzler's. The organ built in 1777 by Snetzler.

Three sets of keys: Great and choir—GG (long octaves) to E.
Swell—tenor F to E.

Great Organ
(10 stops)

	pipes
Open diapason (No. 1)	57
Open diapason (No. 2)	57
Stopped diapason	57
Principal	57
Twelfth	57
Fifteenth	57
Sesquialtera (4 ranks)	228
Trumpet	57
Clarion	57
Cornet (from C) (5 ranks)	145

Swell Organ
(6 stops)

	pipes
Open diapason	36
Stopped diapason	36
Principal	36
Cornet (3 ranks)	108
Trumpet	36
Hautboy	36

Choir Organ
(6 stops)

	pipes
Open diapason	57
Stopped diapason	57
Principal	57
Flute	57
Twelfth	57
Bassoon	57

The Early Nineteenth-Century English Organ

27

St. Paul's Cathedral, London. The organ built in 1697 by "Father Schmidt" and placed on a screen at the west-end of the choir. A different compass for each of the three manuals.

Three sets of keys: Great—from CCC (no CCC♯) to C.
Swell—from tenor C to C.
Choir—from FFF (no FFF♯ nor GGG♯) to C.

Great Organ
(13 stops)

	pipes
Open diapason (No. 1)	60
Open diapason (No. 2)	60
Stopped diapason	60
Principal	60
Nason	60
Twelfth	60
Fifteenth	60
Tierce	60
Block flute	60
Sesquialtera (4 ranks)	240
Mixture (3 ranks)	180
Trumpet	60
Cornet (from C♯)	120

Swell Organ, added by Crang
(6 stops)

	pipes
Open diapason	37
Stopped diapason	37
Principal	37
Cornet (3 ranks)	111
Trumpet	37
Hautboy	37

Choir Organ
(8 stops)

	pipes
Stopped diapason	54
Principal	54
Flute	54
Twelfth	54
Fifteenth	54
Mixture (3 ranks)	162
Cremona	54
Vox humana	54

Pedals: Two octaves of "pull-downs".
No pedal pipes.

"A fine organ all through; sharp pitch."—H. Leffler, who noted this specification in 1800.

28

Westminster Abbey, London (as it was in 1810). An organ with pedal pipes, built in 1730 by Christopher Shrider.

Three sets of keys: Great and choir—from GG (long octaves with GG♯) to D.
Swell—with fiddle G to D.

Great Organ
(12 stops)

	pipes
Open diapason (No. 1)	56
Open diapason (No. 2)	56
Stopped diapason	56
Principal	56
Flute	56
Twelfth	56
Fifteenth	56
Sesquialtera (3 ranks)	108
Mixture (2 ranks)	112
Cornet (from C♯) (5 ranks)	130
Trumpet	56
Clarion	56

Swell Organ
(4 stops)

	pipes
Open diapason	32
Stopped diapason	32
Trumpet	32
Hautboy	32

Choir Organ
(5 stops)

	pipes
Stopped diapason	56
Principal	56
Flute	56
Fifteenth	56
Cremona	56

Pedal—13 pedal pipes from GGG to GG.

"The pedal pipes are open wood, unconnected with the keyboard; of very large dimensions, and though only unisons with the diapasons, from their increased size have the effect of a double diapason—from the quality of the tone. They were added at a later date."—H. Leffler.

29

Christ Church Cathedral, Oxford (as it was in 1810). A cathedral organ without a swell, built in 1680 by "Father Schmidt".

Two sets of keys: from GG (short octaves) to C.

Great Organ
(9 stops)

	pipes
Open diapason	50
Stopped diapason	50
Principal	50
Twelfth	50
Fifteenth	50
Tierce	50
Sesquialtera (3 ranks)	150
Trumpet	50
Cornet (from C) (4 ranks)	96

Choir Organ
(4 stops)

	pipes
Stopped diapason	50
Principal	50
Flute	50
Fifteenth	50

No Swell

30

York Minster organ, enlarged in 1823 by Ward of York, was designed by Dr. Camidge and was claimed to be the "largest and most complete instrument in Great Britain". The design was wasteful and ineffective.

Great Organ
(FFF to F, 60 notes. East sound-board)

Open diapason
Open diapason
Open diapason
Stopped diapason
Principal
Nason
Twelfth
Fifteenth
Sesquialtera (3 ranks)
Cymbal (3 ranks)
Cornet (mid.-C) (5 ranks)
Trumpet
Clarion

Choir Organ
(FFF to F, 60 notes)

Open diapason
Stopped diapason (wood)
Stopped diapason (metal)
Dulciana
Principal
Flute
Octave flute
Sesquialtera

Swell Organ
(FF to F, 49 notes)

Open diapason
Stopped diapason (metal)
Dulciana (metal)
Dulciana (wood)
Principal
Cornet
Trumpet
Hautboy

Pedal Organ
(FFFF (24 ft.) to CC, 19 notes)
(Placed in the interior of the stone screen, right and left of the organ)

Left Side

Double open diapason	24	German principal	12
Double stopped diapason	24	Sackbut	24
German stopped diapason	12	Trombone	12

Right Side

Double open diapason	24	Sackbut	24
Double stopped diapason	24	Trombone	12
German stopped diapason	12	Shawm	12
German principal	12		

Nave Great or West Sound-board in a case.

Open diapason
Stopped diapason
Principal
Harmonica
Twelfth
Fifteenth
Flageolet
Mixture (4 ranks)
Clarinet
Bassoon

Couplers
East great to keys.
Nave great to keys.
Swell to great.
Choir to great.
Great to pedals.
Choir to pedals.

Theatre Organs at the Beginning of the Nineteenth Century

31

Drury Lane Theatre, London. The organ built in 1769 by Byfield and Green for the lessees, Messrs. Stanley and Smith, at a cost of £180.

One set of keys: GG (long octaves) to E. Long movements.

Great Organ
(7 stops)

	pipes
Open diapason (from Gamut)	46
Stopped diapason	57
Principal	57
Flute	57
Fifteenth	57
Sesquialtera (3 ranks)	171
Trumpet	57

Swell Organ
(4 stops)
(On the same Manual)

	pipes
Open diapason	29
Principal	29
Cornet (3 ranks)	87
Hautboy	29

This was the organ used for the oratorio performances carried on after Handel's death by John Stanley, the blind organist of the Temple Church, and John Christopher Smith (Handel's amanuensis). The organ was burned with the theatre on 25th February 1809.

32

Hanover Square, Concert Room, London. The organ built in 1804 by Elliot at a cost of £700.

Two sets of keys: Great—GG (long octaves) to F.
Swell—tenor F to F.

Great Organ
(8 stops)

	pipes
Open diapason (No. 1)	58
Open diapason (No. 2)	58
Stopped diapason	58
Principal	58
Twelfth	58
Fifteenth	58
Sesquialtera (4 ranks)	58
Trumpet	58

Swell Organ
(3 stops)

	pipes
Open diapason	37
Stopped diapason	37
Hautboy	37

Pedals

Large pipes: CC to f♯, 19 pipes

33

The Great Industrial Exhibition (*Hyde Park*), *London.* The organ by Ducroquet, Paris, 1851.

Grand Orgue

Bourdon	16	Prestant	4
Montre	8	Plein jeu (12, 15, 19, 22, 26)	
Flûte à pavillon	8	Bombarde	16
Salicional	8	Trompette	8
Bourdon	8	Clairon	4

Pedal Organ

Flûte (open wood)	16	Bombarde	16

Récit (*Swell Organ*)

Flûte	8
Flûte harmonique	8
Viola di gamba	8
Bourdon	8
Prestant	4
Trompette	8
Hautbois et basson	8
Cor anglais	8

Six coupler pedals:
1. Great to pedal.
2. Great organ reeds on or off.
3. Entire great organ on or off.
4. Swell to great, unison.
5. Swell to great, octave.
6. Swell to great, sub-octave.

Compass: Manuals: CC to C in alt., 61 notes.
Pedal: CCC to C, 25 notes.

This organ shows the tendencies of "the symphonic and romantic" instrument, and it represents a complete break with the late eighteenth century French instruments. The individual registers were of great beauty and the full grand orgue was a cohesive mass of tone, and impressive. The instrument was not sold in England, nor apparently did it obtain any further orders for its maker.

A Nineteenth-century Romantic-symphonic Organ

34

The organ at *Ste. Clotilde, Paris.* Built by Cavaillé-Coll, as played by César Franck from 1859 to 1890.

Grand Orgue

Montre	16	Gambe	8	Plein jeu (5 ranks)	
Bourdon	16	Préstant	4	Bombarde	16
Montre	8	Octave	4	Trompette	8
Flûte harmonique	8	Quinte	$2\frac{2}{3}$	Clairon	4
Bourdon	8	Doublette	2		

Pédale

Sub-bass	32	Octave	4	Trompette	8
Contrebasse	16	Bombarde	16	Clairon	4
Flûte	8	Basson	16		

Récit-expressif

Swell Organ

Viole de gambe	8	Flûte octaviante	4	Basson-hautbois	8
Flûte harmonique	8	Octavin	2	Voix humaine	8
Bourdon	8	Trompette	8	Clairon	4
Voix céleste	8				

Positif

Bourdon	16	Salicional	8	Doublette	2
Montre	8	Préstant	4	Trompette	8
Flûte harmonique	8	Flûte octaviante	4	Clairon	4
Bourdon	8	Quinte	$2\frac{2}{3}$	Clarinette	8
Gambe	8				

35

Trinity Chapel, New York. The organ was built in 1870 by Messrs. J. H. & C. S. Odell from a specification prepared by Mr. W. B. Gilbert. It contained the 33 sounding stops, etc., mentioned below:

Great Organ

1. Contra gamba	16	6. Twelfth	3
2. Stopped diapason	8	7. Fifteenth	2
3. Open diapason	8	8. Sesquialtera (4 ranks, pure tin)	
4. Gamba	4	9. Trumpet (pure tin)	8
5. Principal	4	10. Clarion (pure tin)	4

Swell Organ

11. Bourdon	16	17. Principal	4
12. Stopped diapason	8	18. Mixture	4 ranks
13. Dulciana	8	19. Oboe	8
14. Salicional	8	20. Cornopean	8
15. Open diapason	8	21. Contra trumpet	16
16. Dulcet flute	4		

Choir Organ

22. Melodia	8	25. Concert flute	4
23. Dolce	8	26. Principal	4
24. Keraulophon	8	27. Clarionette	8

Pedal Organ

28. Sub-bourdon	32	31. Open diapason	16
29. Bourdon	16	32. Violoncello	8
30. Bell gamba	16	33. Trombone	16

Couplers, etc.: 1. Swell to great.
2. Swell to choir.
3. Choir to pedal.
4. Great to pedal.
5. Swell to pedal.
6. Signal to blowers.

36

The Church of the Sacred Heart, Wimbledon, London. The organ built in 1912 by J. W. Walker & Sons Ltd., Ruislip, Middlesex (enlarged in 1935).

Compass: Manuals—CC to C, 61 notes.
Pedals—CCC to F, 30 notes.

Great Organ

1. Double open diapason	16
2. Open diapason (No. 1)	8
3. Open diapason (No. 2)	8
4. Open diapason (No. 3)	8
5. Flauto dolce	8
6. Wald flute	8
7. Octave	4
8. Principal	4
9. Twelfth	$2\frac{2}{3}$
10. Fifteenth	2
11. Mixture	3 ranks
12. Trumpet	8

Swell Organ

1. Lieblich bourdon	16	9. Fifteenth	2
2. Open diapason	8	10. Mixture	3 ranks
3. Stopped diapason	8	11. Contra fagotto	16
4. Echo gamba	8	12. Trumpet	8
5. Voix céleste T.C.	8	13. Hautboy	8
6. Principal	4	14. Octave hautboy	4
7. Flute	4	15. Clarion	4
8. Dulciana twelfth	$2\frac{2}{3}$	Tremulant	

Choir Organ

(enclosed with the exception of Nos. 2, 7, 15.)

1. Contra gamba	16	9. Nazard	$2\frac{2}{3}$
2. Open diapason	8	10. Piccolo	2
3. Lieblich gedeckt	8	11. Tierce	$1\frac{3}{5}$
4. Gamba	8	12. Septième	$1\frac{1}{7}$
5. Dulciana	8	13. Clarinet	8
6. Vox Angelica T.C.	8	14. Orchestral oboe	8
7. Gemshorn	4	Tremulant	
8. Harmonic flute	4	15. Tuba	8

Pedal Organ

1. Double open diapason	(upper 18 notes from No. 4)	32
2. Sub-bass		32
3. Open metal		16
4. Open diapason		16
5. Bourdon		16
6. Lieblich bourdon	(from No. 1 swell)	16
7. Gamba	(from No. 1 choir)	16
8. Octave	(18 notes from No. 4)	8
9. Flute	(18 notes from No. 5)	8
10. Contra trombone	(upper 18 notes from No. 11)	32
11. Trombone		16
12. Fagotto	(from No. 10 swell)	16
13. Trumpet	(18 notes from No. 11)	8

Couplers

1. Choir to pedal	7. Swell octave
2. Great to pedal	8. Swell sub-octave
3. Swell to pedal	9. Swell unison off
4. Swell to great	10. Choir octave
5. Swell to choir	11. Choir sub-octave
6. Choir to great	12. Choir unison off

Accessories:

Five adjustable pistons to great and pedal.
Five adjustable pistons to swell and pedal.
Five adjustable pistons to choir.
Five combination pedals, duplicating great and pedal pistons.
Five combination pedals, duplicating swell and pedal pistons.
Double-acting pedal, controlling great to pedal coupler.
Balanced swell pedal.
Balanced choir pedal.
Tubular pneumatic action.
Electric blowing.

37

The organ in *St. Paul's Cathedral, London.* Henry Willis, 1872, 1900, 1930, 1949, 1960.

Compass: Manual—CC to C, 61 notes.
Pedal—CCC to G, 32 notes.

Great Organ

Double open diapason	16	Principal (No. 1)	4
Lieblich bourdon (1929)	16	Principal (No. 2)	4
Open diapason (No. 1) (1900)	8	Twelfth	$2\frac{2}{3}$
Open diapason (No. 2)	8	Fifteenth	2
Open diapason (No. 3) (17th century, Schmidt)	8	Fourniture	3 ranks
		Mixture	3 ranks
Open diapason (No. 4) (1900)	8	Trombone	16
Claribel flute (1946, new ten. C up)	8	Tromba	8
		Clarion	4
Quint (metal)	$5\frac{1}{3}$		

Solo Organ
(enclosed)

Open diapason	8	Trumpet	8
Viola da gamba	8	French horn (1930)	8
Viole Célestes		Corno di bassetto	8
Flute harmonique	8	Cor anglais	8
Concert flute	4	Doublette grave (8 and 15) (1960)	2 ranks
Piccolo	2		
Contra posaune	16	Mixture (12, 19, 22) (1960)	3 ranks
Contra fagotto	16	tremolo	

Tuba
(unenclosed dome N.E. Quarter Gallery)

Double tuba	16	Trompette militaire (1930)	8
Tuba	8	Tuba	8 } in chancel
Clarion	4	Clarion	4 } in chancel

Swell Organ

Contra gamba (wood and metal)	16	Fifteenth	2
Open diapason	8	Cornet	3 ranks
Lieblich gedact	8	Contra posaune	16
Salicional	8	Cornopean	8
Vox angelica (bass into salicional)	8	Clarion	4
Principal	4	Hautboy	8

Couplers

Great, swell, choir, solo, tuba to pedal
Swell to pedal 4 ft.
Solo to pedal 4 ft.
Altar on solo
Altar on choir
Tuba to solo
Solo to great
Solo to swell
Choir to great
Swell to great
Swell octave to great
Swell sub-octave to great
Swell to choir
Solo to choir
Tuba to choir
3 spares (under choir)
Tuba to great and pedal
Swell, sub. and super-octaves and spare
Solo, sub. and super-octaves and spare
Tremulant to altar
Couplers off
Pedal stops off
Great and pedal pistons coupled
Pedal pistons on great pistons
Doubles off
3 spares

Pedal Organ

Dome (N.E. Quarter Gallery)

Double open bass (wood) (ext. of open I)	32
Contra violone (metal) (1930)	32
Open bass (No. 1) (wood)	16
Open bass (No. 2) (wood)	16
Open diapason (metal)	16
Principal (wood) (ext. of open bass II)	8
Violoncello (metal)	8
Mixture	3 ranks
Contra bombarde	32
Contra posaune (wood)	32
Bombarde (metal)	16
Clarion (metal)	8

Chancel

Open bass (wood)	16
Contra bass (metal)	16
Violone (metal)	16
Bourdon	16
Open metal (from great)	16
Viola (from choir)	16
Octave (wood) (ext. of open bass)	8
Flute	8
Octave flute (extension)	4
Mixture (8, 12, 15, 19, 22)	5 ranks
Ophicleide (metal)	16

Choir Organ

(unenclosed)

Contra viola	16	Koppelflöte	4
Open diapason	8	Nazard (1930)	$2\frac{2}{3}$
Violoncello	8	Flageolet	2
Clarabella	8	Tierce (1930)	$1\frac{3}{5}$
Lieblich gedact	8	Larigot	$1\frac{1}{3}$
Dulciana	8	Cymbale (29, 33, 36)	3 ranks
Gemshorn	4	Trumpet	8

Altar Organ

(enclosed in its own swell-box)

Quintaten	16	Sylvestrina	8
Cor de nuit	8	Fern flute	4

(above four 1930)

Composition of Mixtures, etc.

Great

Fourniture:
CC to middle C (17, 19, 22)
Middle C♯ to treble F♯ (12, 15, 17)
Treble G to top C (8, 12, 15)

Mixture:
CC to tenor G (24, 26, 29)
Tenor G♯ to middle G (17, 19, 22)
Middle G♯ to treble G (10, 12, 15)
Treble G♯ to top C (3, 5, 8)

Swell

Cornet
CC to middle C (17, 19, 22)
Middle C♯ to treble F♯ (12, 15, 17)
Treble G to top C (8, 12, 15)

Pedal

Mixture:
17, 19, 22 throughout

Added in 1948:

Diapason Chorus
(*On Tuba Organ*)

Double open diapason	16
Open diapason, No. 1	8
Open diapason, No. 2	8
Octave diapason	4
Principal	4
Quartane (12, 15)	2 ranks
Cymbale (22, 26, 29)	3 ranks
Mixture (15, 19, 22, 26, 29)	5 ranks

(In South-East Quarter Gallery.)

Coupler

Diapason Chorus on choir

38

The Royal Festival Hall, South Bank, London. The organ built by Harrison & Harrison of Durham, England.

The organ is designed to be suitable for the performance of organ music of all periods and for combining with chorus and orchestra.

Emphasis has been placed on the need for a rich and varied ensemble, and to this end many characteristic classical registers have been introduced, some of them being treated deliberately according to the practice of other schools of organ-building.

Instead of grilles or the usual casework there is a functional front array, in which the pipes of the unenclosed positive organ will occupy a prominent place.

There will be five manual departments controlled from four keyboards, CC to C, 61 notes; and two and a half octaves of concave and radiating pedals, CCC to G, 32 notes; 102 speaking stops and 18 couplers, etc., making a total of 120 drawstops. This design is due to Ralph Downes, Esq.

Pedal Organ

(25 stops, 4 *couplers*)

1.	Principal	(20 from No. 53)	(5 wood, 7 zinc)	32
2.	Majorbass		(wood)	16
3.	Principal		(metal)	16
4.	Sub Bass		(wood)	16
5.	Quintadena	(from No. 73)	(wood and metal)	16
6.	Dulciana	(from No. 40)	(metal)	16
7.	Quintflöte		(wood and metal)	$10\frac{2}{3}$
8.	Octave		(metal)	8
9.	Rohrgedeckt		(metal)	8
10.	Quintadena	(from No. 73)	(wood and metal)	8
11.	Nazard		(metal)	$5\frac{1}{3}$
12.	Superoctave		(tin)	4
13.	Spitzflute		(metal)	4
14.	Open Flute		(metal)	2
15.	Septerz	(17, 21)	(metal)	
16.	Mixture	(12, 15, 19, 22)	(metal)	
17.	Sharp Mixture	(22, 26, 29)	(metal)	
18.	Bombarde	(20 from No. 19)	(zinc)	32
19.	Bombarde		(metal)	16
20.	Dulzian	(from No. 38)	(metal)	16
21.	Trumpet		(metal)	8
22.	Cromorne	(20 from No. 51)	(metal)	8
23.	Clairon		(metal)	4
24.	Schalmei	(from No. 52)	(metal)	4
25.	Kornett		(metal)	2

(i) Positive to pedal.
(ii) Great to pedal.
(iii) Swell to pedal.
(iv) Solo to pedal.

Positive Organ

(13 stops, 2 *couplers*)

(unenclosed)

26.	Principal	(metal)	8
27.	Gedeckt	(metal)	8
28.	Quintadena	(metal)	8
29.	Octave	(metal)	4
30.	Rohr flute	(metal)	4
31.	Quintflöte	(metal)	$2\frac{2}{3}$
32.	Spitzflute	(metal)	2
33.	Tierce	(metal)	$1\frac{3}{5}$
34.	Larigot	(metal)	$1\frac{1}{3}$
35.	Carillon (29, 38 : 1, 8, 10)	(metal)	
36.	Mixture (15, 19, 22, 26, 29)	(metal)	
37.	Scharf (22, 26, 29, 33, 36)	(metal)	
38.	Dulzian (in choir box)	(metal)	8
39.	Trumpet (in choir box)	(metal)	8

(v) Solo to positive.
(vi) Swell to positive.

Choir Organ

(14 stops, *tremulant*, 1 *coupler and* 1 *transfer*)

(enclosed in a swell-box)

40.	Dulciana	(metal)	16
41.	Open Wood	(metal)	8
42.	Stopped Wood	(wood and metal)	8
43.	Unda maris (AA) (2 ranks)	(metal)	8
44.	Spitz octave	(metal)	4
45.	Open Flute	(metal)	4
46.	Principal	(metal)	2
47.	Quintflöte	(metal)	$1\frac{1}{3}$
48.	Octave	(metal)	1
49.	Sesquialtera (26, 31)	(metal)	
50.	Mixture (29, 33, 36, 40)	(metal)	
51.	Cromorne	(metal)	8
52.	Schalmei	(metal)	4

(vii) Tremulant.
(viii) Octave (16-ft. and 8-ft. stops only).
(ix) Choir on solo.

Great Organ (20 stops, 3 *couplers and* 1 *transfer*)

53.	Principal	(metal)	16
54.	Gedackt pommer	(wood and metal)	16

55.	Diapason (2 ranks in treble)	(metal)	8
56.	Principal	(metal)	8
57.	Flûte harmonique	(wood and metal)	8
58.	Rohr Gedackt	(wood and metal)	8
59.	Quintflöte	(metal)	$5\frac{1}{3}$
60.	Octave	(metal)	4
61.	Gemshorn	(metal)	4
62.	Gedeckt	(metal)	4
63.	Quint	(metal)	$2\frac{2}{3}$
64.	Octave	(metal)	2
65.	Blockflöte	(metal)	2
66.	Tierce	(metal)	$1\frac{3}{5}$
67.	Mixture (15, 19, 22, 26, 29)	(metal)	
68.	Scharf (26, 29, 33, 36)	(metal)	
69.	Cornet (1, 8, 12, 15, 17–mid. C)	(metal)	
70.	Bombarde	(metal)	16
71.	Trumpet	(metal)	8
72.	Clarion	(metal)	4

(x) Positive to great. (xi) Swell to great.
(xii) Solo to great. (xiii) Reeds on solo (also affects No. 69).
(xiv) Transfer: Reeds and Cornet on solo manual (off great).

Swell Organ (20 stops, *tremulant and* 2 *couplers*)

73.	Quintadena	(wood and metal)	16
74.	Diapason	(metal)	8
75.	Gemshorn	(metal)	8
76.	Quintadena	(metal)	8
77.	Viola	(metal)	8
78.	Voix Célestes (AA)	(metal)	8
79.	Principal	(metal)	4
80.	Koppelflöte	(metal)	4
81.	Nazard	(metal)	$2\frac{2}{3}$
82.	Octave	(metal)	2
83.	Open Flute	(metal)	2
84.	Tierce (F)	(metal)	$1\frac{3}{5}$
85.	Flageolet	(metal)	1
86.	Mixture (22, 26, 29, 33)	(metal)	
87.	Zimbel (38, 40, 43)	(metal)	
88.	Hautbois	(metal)	8
89.	Voix Humaine	(metal)	8
90.	Bombarde	(metal)	16
91.	Trumpet	(metal)	8
92.	Clarion	(metal)	4

(xv) Octave (16-ft., 8-ft. and 4-ft. stops only). (xvi) Solo to swell.
(xvii) Tremulant.

Solo Organ

(10 stops, *tremulant and* 1 *coupler*)

93.	Diapason	(metal)	8
94.	Rohr flute	(metal)	8
95.	Octave	(metal)	4
96.	Wald flute (conical)	(metal)	2
97.	Rauschquint (12, 15)	(metal)	
98.	Tertian (17, 19)	(metal)	
99.	Mixture (19, 22, 26, 29, 33, 36)	(metal)	
100.	Basset Horn	(metal)	8
101.	Trompette harmonique	(metal)	8
102.	Clairon harmonique	(metal)	4

(xviii) Great to solo.
(xix) Great to solo.

Accessories

Eight combination foot pistons to the pedal organ.
Eight combination pistons to the positive organ.
Eight combination pistons to the great organ. (Pedal combinations by double touch.)
Eight combination pistons to the swell organ. (Duplicated by foot pistons.)
Eight combination pistons to the solo organ.
Eight general pistons to the entire organ. (Duplicated by foot pistons.)
(All above instantly adjustable by locking piston.)
One general cancel piston.
One cancel piston each to positive, great, swell, solo and pedal organs.
Reversible piston to *positive to great*.
Reversible piston to *swell to great*.
Reversible piston to *solo to great*.
Reversible piston to *great to solo*.
Reversible piston to *solo to swell*.
Reversible piston to *solo to positive*.
Reversible piston to *swell to positive*.
Reversible piston to *positive to pedal*.
Reversible piston to *great to pedal*.
Reversible piston to *swell to pedal*.
Reversible piston to *solo to pedal*.
} Duplicated by foot pistons.
One general crescendo pedal, with indicator, and adjuster switchboard.
Full organ pedal, with indicator.
Three balanced crescendo pedals to choir swell and solo organs.

Wind Pressures

Pipe wind from $3\frac{1}{4}$ to $3\frac{1}{2}$ inches.
Action: 12 in., to 15 in.

The drawstop jambs are concave, with a final angle of 25 degrees to the keyboards.

The stop handles have solid ivory fronts, the speaking stops being lettered in black and the couplers, etc. (indicated above in italics), in red.

The mechanism is on the builders' latest electro-pneumatic system.

The pitch will be A=440 vibrations.

The term "metal" throughout this specification, except where otherwise stated, denotes spotted metal of not less than 50 per cent tin.

The blowing plant is by Messrs. Watkins and Watson, of London.

39

St. Mary's Abbey, Tewkesbury, Gloucester, England. Organs rebuilt by J. W. Walker and Sons.

Brief Historical Notes on the Old Organs

The Milton Organ

Built for Magdalen College, Oxford, probably by Thomas Dallam about 1615 (two manuals, 13 stops). The case woodwork was probably made *c.* 1590. Presented to Oliver Cromwell about 1654 and moved to Hampton Court Palace. While the organ was there the poet Milton may have played upon it; there is no other reason for its name (Lord Macaulay's "Essay on Milton").

Moved back to Magdalen College, Oxford, about 1660. Renovated by Renatus Harris 1672 and 1690. Sold to Tewkesbury Abbey 1737. Additions by Holland 1796. Renovated by Willis 1848.

In the considered opinion of no less an authority than the late Rev. Andrew Freeman, the Milton organ probably contains more old pipework than any other 17th century instrument in the country.

Size of organ before the present scheme, 21 stops.

(Great 13; swell 6; pedal 2.)

The Grove Organ

Built by Michell & Thynne and placed in the concert room of the Inventions Exhibition, South Kensington, 1885. Moved to the Liverpool Exhibition 1886. Purchased by the Rev. C. W. Grove of Mythe House, Tewkesbury, and presented to Tewkesbury Abbey in commemoration of the Jubilee of Queen Victoria, 1887.

Size of organ previous to present scheme, 35 stops.

(Great 10; swell 9; choir 7; solo 4; pedal 5.)

Description of the Rebuilding Scheme

This comprehensive organ scheme, commenced in 1947, has been drawn up in consultation with H. Stubington, Esq., F.R.C.O., A.R.C.M., Organist and Master of the Choristers, and comprises the rebuilding and enlargement of the two historic organs in the Abbey (known respectively as "The Milton" and

"The Grove") together with an additional new organ of two departments (now called "The Apse Organ", since it is located in an overhead apse chamber on the east side of the south transept). The scheme also includes two detached consoles: one of two manuals, and one of five manuals, placed near together on a new console gallery.

An important point of the present scheme has been the retention of the inherent characteristics of the two old organs embodied (e.g. the old world quality of the Milton and the bold Schulze-like quality of the Grove) although at the same time their specifications have been considerably increased and embellished with more variety and tonal completeness.

The following main features of the scheme as a whole should be noted:

The Milton Organ. Provides a very complete and fine two-manual scheme.

The Apse Organ. Mainly associated with the Milton, thereby combining to provide a four-manual instrument on the south side, the Apse echo forming an enclosed choir and the Apse solo being of moderate power. The Apse organ also gives uses within itself as a two-manual as well as providing an echo department to the Grove.

The Grove Organ. A robust and complete four-manual instrument in the north transept.

The Small Console (two manuals) to play the Milton organ only for week-day services, teaching, etc.

The Main Console (five manuals) to play all three organs in various ways, i.e.

Milton and Apse organs together (Grove off).

Grove Organ alone (Milton and Apse off).

Milton, Apse and Grove organs together.

Note.—The two consoles are also usable simultaneously; one player for the Milton, and the other player for the Apse and Grove.

Complete Specification

Compass: Manuals—CC to C, 61 notes.
Pedals—CCC to G, 32 notes.

MILTON ORGAN

Milton Great Organ

1.	Double dulciana	16	10.	Tierce	$1\frac{3}{5}$
2.	Open diapason (No. 1)	8	11.	Fourniture (19, 22, 26)	3 ranks
3.	Open diapason (No. 2)	8	12.	Trumpet	8
4.	Stopped diapason	8	13.	Clarion	4
5.	Clarabella	8	14.	Cremona T.C.	8
6.	Principal	4	15.	Hautboy (from No. 23)	8
7.	Flûte harmonique	4	(i)	Swell to great.	
8.	Twelfth	$2\frac{2}{3}$	(ii)	Solo to great.	
9.	Fifteenth	2	(iii)	Echo to great.	

Milton Swell Organ

16. Open diapason 8
17. Flûte à cheminée 8
18. Salicional 8
19. Vox angelica T.C. 8
20. Principal 4
21. Flute 4
22. Mixture (15, 19, 22) 3 ranks
23. Double hautboy 16
24. Echo trumpet 8
25. Hautboy (from No. 23) 8
26. Octave hautboy (from No. 23) 4

(iv) Tremulant.
(v) Sub-octave.
(vi) Octave.
(vii) Solo to swell.
(viii) Echo to swell.
(ix) Great chorus reeds (transfer to swell).

Milton Pedal Organ

27. Open wood 16
28. Bourdon 16
29. Dulciana (from No. 1) 16
30. Bourdon quint (from No. 28) $10\frac{2}{3}$
31. Principal 8
32. Flute (from No. 28) 8
33. Dulciana (from No. 1) 8
34. Fifteenth (from No. 31) 4
35. Flute (from No. 28) 4
36. Trumpet 16
37. Double hautboy (from No. 23) 16
38. Hautboy (from No. 23) 8
39. Octave hautboy (from No. 23) 4

(x) Great to pedal.
(xi) Swell to pedal.
(xii) Great and pedal combinations off.

Note.—Couplers (ii), (iii), (vii) and (viii) refer to the Apse organ, and are not on the small console.

APSE ORGAN

Apse Echo Organ

40. Quintaton 16
41. Dolce 8
42. Unda maris T.C. 8
43. Cor de nuit 8
44. Dolcissimo 4
45. Flauto amabile 4
46. Harmonica aetheria (12, 15) 2 ranks
47. Voix humaine 8

(xiii) Tremulant.
(xiv) Sub-octave.
(xv) Octave.

Apse Solo Organ (all enclosed)

48. Lieblich gedeckt 16
49. Harmonic flute 8
50. Aeoline 8
51. Flute octaviante 4
52. Nazard $2\frac{2}{3}$
53. Piccolo 2
54. Tierce $1\frac{3}{5}$
55. Septième 1
56. Corno di bassetto 8
57. Orchestral oboe 8

(xvi) Tremulant.

58. Double horn 16
59. Horn (from No. 58) 8

(xvii) Sub-octave.
(xviii) Octave.

Apse Pedal Organ

60. Lieblich gedeckt (from No. 48) 16
61. Lieblich gedeckt (from No. 48) 8
62. Double horn (20 notes from No. 58) 32
63. Horn (from No. 58) 16

(xix) Echo to pedal.
(xx) Solo to pedal.

GROVE ORGAN[1]

Grove Great Organ

64. Sub-bourdon T.C. (from No. 66) 32
65. Violone 16
66. Bourdon 16
67. Open diapason (No. 1) 8
68. Open diapason (No. 2) 8
69. Claribel 8
70. Quint $5\frac{1}{3}$
71. Octave 4
72. Geigen principal 4
73. Tierce $3\frac{1}{5}$
74. Septième $2\frac{2}{7}$
75. Rauschquint (12, 15) 2 ranks
76. Mixture (19, 22, 26, 29) 4 ranks
77. Trombone 16
78. Tromba 8
79. Clarion 4

(xxi) Swell to great.
(xxii) Choir to great.
(xxiii) Solo to great.

Grove Swell Organ

80. Open diapason 8
81. Flauto traverso 8
82. Viol di gamba 8
83. Voix celestes T.C. 8
84. Geigen 4
85. Fifteenth 2
86. Mixture (12, 19, 22) 3 ranks
87. Sharp Mixture (26, 29) 2 ranks
88. Oboe 8

(xxiv) Tremulant.

89. Contra posaune 16
90. Trumpet 8
91. Clarion 4

(xxv) Sub-octave.
(xxvi) Octave.
(xxvii) Solo to swell.

Grove Choir Organ (unenclosed)

92. Bourdon (from No. 66) 16
93. Spitzflöte 8
94. Viole sourdine 8
95. Gedeckt 8
96. Gemshorn 4
97. Zauberflöte 4
98. Flautino 2
99. Larigot $1\frac{1}{3}$
100. Octavin 1
101. Scharf (26, 29, 33) 3 ranks
102. Clarinet 8

(xxviii) Swell to choir.
(xxix) Solo choir.
(xxx) Echo to choir.
(xxxi) Milton great on choir (with indicator).

[1] There seems to be no immediate prospect that this wonderful example of Victorian organ-building will be restored to use.

Grove Solo Organ (enclosed except No. 110)

103. Contra viola 16
104. Violoncello 8
105. Violoncello vibrato T.C. 8
106. Violetta 4
107. Concert flute 4
108. Cornetto di viole (10, 12, 15) 3 ranks
109. Orchestral trumpet 8
110. Tuba 8

(xxxii) Sub-octave.
(xxxiii) Octave.
(xxxiv) Great to solo.

Grove Pedal Organ

111. Contra violone (20 notes from No. 65) 32
112. Major Bass 16
113. Violone (from No. 65) 16
114. Dolce 16
115. Bourdon (from No. 66) 16
116. Octave 8
117. Major Flute 8
118. Super Octave (from No. 116) 4
119. Cornet (12, 15, 17, 19, 22) 5 ranks
120. Double Trombone (20 notes from No. 77) 32
121. Bombarde 16
122. Trombone (from No. 77) 16
123. Clarion 8
124. Octave Clarion (from No. 123) 4

Note.—No. 119 cornet. 15th and 22nd from No. 116. 12th and 19th one rank. 17th one rank.

(xxxv) Choir to pedal.
(xxxvi) Great to pedal.
(xxxvii) Swell to pedal.
(xxxviii) Solo to pedal.
(xxxix) Independent pedal (with indicator).

Note.—Coupler (xxxix) provides for the Milton pedal and Apse pedal to be used in conjunction with the Grove pedal.

(xl) Great and pedal combinations off.
(xli) Double touch canceller.

Note.—On the small console (xli) applies only to the Milton organ, and on the main console to all three organs.

Number of Pipes in Complete Specification

Milton organ	1,811
Apse organ	1,232
Grove organ	3,720
Total Number of pipes	6,763

THE SMALL CONSOLE
(two manuals)

Equipped with "Walker" stop-keys arranged over the manuals for stops Nos: 1 to 39 inclusive and Couplers, etc., (i) (iv) (v) (vi) (ix) (x) (xi) (xii) and (xli), thus operating Milton Organ only, 48 stop-keys in all.

Accessories

Four thumb pistons to great and pedal.
Four thumb pistons to swell.
Four toe pistons to great and pedal.
Four toe pistons to swell (*duplicating*).
Four general thumb pistons.
One reversible toe piston for pedal trumpet, 16 ft.
One reversible toe piston for great to pedal.
One reversible thumb piston for great to pedal.
One reversible thumb piston for swell to great.
Balanced swell pedal (*with indicator*).
Push button switch for Milton blower (*with indicator*).

THE MAIN CONSOLE
(five manuals)

Equipped with "Walker" stop-keys arranged on curved side jambs, for stops Nos. 1 to 124 and couplers, etc., (i) to (xli) inclusive, thus operating all three organs, 165 stop-keys in all.

Accessories

Six thumb pistons to choir (Grove).
Six thumb pistons to great and pedal (Grove).
Four thumb pistons to great and pedal (Milton).
Six thumb pistons to swell (Grove).
Four thumb pistons to swell (Milton).
Six thumb pistons to solo (Grove).
Four thumb pistons to solo (Apse).
Four double-touch thumb pistons to echo (Apse) (*giving Echo to pedal and Lieblich Gedackt* 16 *ft. only on second touch*).
Four general thumb pistons to Grove organ.
Four general thumb pistons to Milton and Apse organs.
Three general cancel thumb pistons to Grove, Milton and Apse organs, respectively.
Six toe pistons to great and pedal (Grove).
Four toe pistons to great and pedal (Milton).
Six toe pistons to swell (Grove) (*duplicating*).
Four toe pistons to swell (Milton) (*duplicating*).
Two reversible thumb pistons for great to pedal (Grove and Milton respectively).
Two reversible thumb pistons for swell to great (Grove and Milton respectively).
One reversible thumb piston for solo to great (Grove).
Two reversible toe pistons for great to pedal (Grove and Milton respectively).
One reversible toe piston for 32-ft. flue (Grove).

One reversible toe piston for 32-ft. reed (Grove).
One reversible toe piston for 16-ft. bombarde (Grove).
One reversible toe piston for 16-ft. trumpet (Milton).
Three controlling thumb pistons.
Three controlling toe pistons (*duplicating*).

Note.—These controlling pistons are labelled M., MG and G respectively. They bring the various sections of the organ into operation and cause the stop-department labels to be illuminated. For example, when piston G is pressed only the labels of the Grove departments are illuminated and any stops drawn on the Milton and Apse remain silent. In the operation of these pistons the Apse organ is included with the Milton.

Balanced swell pedal (Grove), *with indicator.*
Balanced swell pedal (Milton), *with indicator.*
Balanced echo pedal (Apse), *with indicator.*
Balanced solo pedal (Grove and Apse), *with indicator.*
Push-button switches for blowers of Grove, Milton and Apse organs respectively, *with indicators.*

Detached Consoles in Oak. Stop-key control with double-touch cancelling. All combinations on the main console adjustable by Walker Patented Selective Combination Mechanism arranged in a separate cabinet placed near the organist.

Electro-Pneumatic Action.
"*Discus*" *Electric Blowers* and transformer rectifiers.

WIND PRESSURES

			inches
Milton Organ	Great	Flues	$3\frac{3}{4}$
		Reeds	6
	Swell	All	$4\frac{1}{2}$
	Pedal	Flues	$4\frac{1}{2}$
		Reeds	6
Apse Organ	Echo and Solo		4
	Horn rank		6
Grove Organ	Great	Flues	$4\frac{1}{2}$
		Reeds	8
	Swell	Flues	5
		Reeds	8
	Choir	All	4
	Solo	Flues	6
		Reeds	16
	Pedal	Flues	5
		Reeds	16

40

The Organ in Norwich Cathedral. Specification of the organ as rebuilt and augmented 1899–1942. By Norman and Beard. Case by S. Dykes Bower.

(N = situated in north triforium. S = situated in south triforium. P = situated on the pulpitum.)

Pedal Organ

(CCC to G, 32 notes)

S	1. Double open wood (44 pipes)	32
S	2. Open wood (56 pipes)	16
	3. Open wood minor (from No. 1)	16
N	4. Open diapason (56 pipes)	16
N	5. Open diapason minor (from great)	16
N	6. Violone (44 pipes), wood	16
P	7. Contra viole (from solo)	16
N	8. Bourdon (56 pipes)	16
P	9. Lieblich bourdon (from great)	16
N	10. Dulciana (44 pipes)	16
S	11. Quint (44 pipes)	$10\frac{2}{3}$
	12. Octave wood (from No. 2)	8
	13. Principal (from No. 4)	8
	14. Bass flute (notes from No. 8)	8
	15. 'Cello (notes from No. 6)	8
	16. Dolce (from No. 10)	8
	17. Twelfth (from No. 11)	$5\frac{1}{3}$
	18. Superoctave (from No. 2)	4
	19. Fifteenth (from No. 4)	4
	20. Octave flute (from No. 8)	4
N	21. Harmonics (19, 22) (64 pipes) (2 ranks)	
	22. Bass trombone } 68 pipes (N and S)	32
	23. Ophicleide	16
	24. Clarion	8
	25. Octave Clarion	4
N	26. Trombone (from great)	16
P	27. Contra fagotto (from swell)	16
P	28. Schalmei (from choir)	16

Solo to pedal.
Swell to pedal.
Great to pedal.
Choir to pedal.
Echo to pedal.

Great Organ

(CC to C, 61 notes)

Primary:

(arranged out of sight in north triforium)

1. Lieblich bourdon, tenor C (from great No. 13)	32
2. Double open diapason (61 pipes)	16

3. Open diapason, large (61 pipes)		8
4. Open diapason, medium (61 pipes)		8
5. Quint (61 pipes)		$5\frac{1}{3}$
6. Octave (61 pipes)		4
7. Twelfth (61 pipes)		$2\frac{2}{3}$
8. Fifteenth (61 pipes)		2
9. Mixture (15, 19, 22, 26) (4 ranks) (244 pipes)		
10. Trombone	and on choir and through choir couplers (61 pipes)	16
11. Trumpet	(61 pipes)	8
12. Clarion	(61 pipes)	4

Secondary:

(arranged behind west case front on the pulpitum)

13. Lieblich bourdon (61 pipes)	16
14. Dulciana (43 pipes) (18 lowest notes from ped. dulciana)	16
15. Open diapason (61 pipes)	8
16. Geigen diapason (61 pipes)	8
17. Hohlflöte (61 pipes)	8
18. Geigen principal (61 pipes)	4
19. Stopped flute (61 pipes)	4
20. Fifteenth (61 pipes)	2
21. Harmonics (12, 15, 17, 19, 22) (5 ranks) (305 pipes)	

Solo to great.
Swell to great.
Choir to great.
Choir-swell to great
(by rocking tablet).

Swell Organ

(CC to C, 61 notes)

(arranged facing west on the pulpitum)

1. Contra geigen (61 pipes)	16
2. Bourdon (61 pipes)	16
3. Open diapason* (61 pipes)	8
4. Geigen diapason (61 pipes)	8
5. Rohr gedackt (61 pipes)	8
6. Salicional (61 pipes)	8
7. Voix celeste (2 ranks) (110 pipes)	8
8. Principal (61 pipes)	4
9. Lieblichflöte (61 pipes)	4
10. Twelfth (61 pipes)	$2\frac{2}{3}$
11. Fifteenth (61 pipes)	2
12. Mixture (15, 19, 22, 26, 29) (5 ranks) (305 pipes)	
13. Mixture* (17, 19, 21, 22) (4 ranks) (244 pipes)	
14. Oboe (61 pipes)	8
15. Contra fagotto* (61 pipes)	16

16. Horn* (61 pipes)	8
17. Trumpet* (61 pipes)	8
18. Clarion* (61 pipes)	4

Tremulant, Octave, Sub-octave, Unison-off } acting also through manual couplers.

Solo to swell.

Transfer great secondary to swell.

Transfer positif to swell.

*On heavier wind.

Choir Organ

(CC to C, 61 notes)

(arranged facing east on the pulpitum)

Positif:

(unenclosed)

1. Quintaten (61 pipes)	16
2. Double dulciana (from great)	16
3. Open diapason (partly very old) (61 pipes)	8
4. Chimney flute (61 pipes)	8
5. Bell gamba (61 pipes)	8
6. Principal (61 pipes)	4
7. Nason flute (61 pipes)	4
8. Octave quint (61 pipes)	$2\frac{2}{3}$
9. Superoctave (61 pipes)	2
10. Tierce (61 notes from harmonics) (4 ranks)	$1\frac{3}{5}$
11. Harmonics (17, 19, 21, 22) (4 ranks) (244 pipes)	

Choir Swell

(enclosed)

12. Violoncello (61 pipes)	8
13. Dolce (61 pipes)	8
14. Cor de nuit (61 pipes) } undulating	8
15. Unda maris (ten C) (49 pipes) } undulating	8
16. Gemshorn (61 pipes)	4
17. Nazard (61 pipes)	$2\frac{2}{3}$
18. Flageolet (61 pipes)	2
19. Schalmei (61 pipes)	16
20. Trumpet (61 pipes)	8

Octave, Sub-octave, Unison-off, Tremulant } Enclosed division only acting also through manual couplers.

Solo to choir.

Swell to choir.

Great Reeds

N 21.	Great trombone	16
N 22.	Great tromba	8
N 23.	Great clarion	4

Transfer great secondary to choir by rocking tablet.

Solo Organ
(CC to C, 61 notes)

(arranged in a swell box on the pulpitum and facing west)

1.	Contra viole (85 pipes)	16
2.	Viole d'orchestre (85 pipes)	8
3.	Octave viole (85 pipes)	4
4.	Viole celeste (2 ranks) (110 pipes)	8
5.	Harmonic claribel (61 pipes)	8
6.	Flauto traverso (61 pipes)	4
7.	Cor anglais (tenor C) (49 pipes)	16
8.	Orchestral oboe (61 pipes)	8
9.	Corno di bassetto (61 pipes)	8
10.	Vox humana (61 pipes)	8
	Tremulant	
11.	Orchestral horn (old tuba) (61 pipes)	8
12.	Orchestral trumpet (85 pipes)	16
13.	Orchestral trumpet (85 pipes)	8
14.	Orchestral trumpet (85 pipes)	4
	(unenclosed)	
15.	Tuba mirabilis (61 pipes)	8
	(on 20 in. wind pressure)	

Octave, Suboctave, Unison-off } Acting also through manual couplers, but not upon extended ranks.

Swell to solo.

Echo Organ[1]

(arranged out of sight on the triforium to south-east of altar)

1.	Sub-bass (12 pipes)	16
2.	Contra viola (49 pipes)	16
3.	Gamba (61 pipes)	8
4.	Zauberflöte (61 pipes)	8
5.	Unda maris (2 flute ranks) (110 pipes)	8
6.	Vox angelica (2 ranks, pure tin) (110 pipes)	8
7.	Viola (61 pipes)	4
8.	Harmonic piccolo (61 pipes)	2

[1] Not in use.

9. Harmonic trumpet (61 pipes) 8
10. Cornet (6 ranks) (366 pipes)
11. Vox humana (pure tin) (61 pipes) 8
12. Gongs (49 notes)

Tremulant.
Octave couplers.
Echo on choir.
Echo on swell.
Echo on solo.

The four-manual console, arranged on the north side of the pulpitum, has the following:

Accessory Controls

8 toe pistons to pedal organ.
8 thumb pistons to pedal organ (duplicating toe pistons and arranged to bass end of great key slip).
10 thumb pistons to great
10 thumb pistons to swell
10 thumb pistons to solo
10 thumb pistons to choir
} All with a selected pedal combination by optional second touch.
3 thumb pistons to echo.
1 knob disconnecting pedal second touch on manual pistons.
All combinations set at miniature switchboard by the console.
1 knob connecting great pistons to pedal pistons.
1 thumb piston to each manual cancelling all stops on that manual.
1 thumb piston cancelling octave couplers.
1 thumb piston general cancel.
"Doubles-off" by rocking tablet with luminous warning indicator.
On-and-off thumb pistons.

Great to pedal
Swell to pedal
Swell to great
Solo to pedal
Choir to pedal
Choir to great
Solo to great
Pedal solo
} Duplicated by toe pistons

Transfer couplers by rocking tablets.
Transfer positif to swell.
Transfer choir-swell to great (last 2 right of choir keys).
Transfer great secondary to choir.
Transfer great secondary to swell (last 2 right of great keys).
3 balanced swell pedals, choir, swell, and solo and echo.
3 push button switch controls and luminous indicators to main blowers.
Echo blower and tuba wind booster.

All the mechanisms are new, and rather more than half of the 6,655 pipes. The rest of the pipework is of various dates, beginning with a few of the Dallam pipes made at the Restoration in 1663, Renatus Harris in 1689, Byfield in 1760, Bishop in 1833, Norman & Beard in 1899, and the present day.

The great has been entirely remodelled and reconstructed as a primary and secondary section. The primary is arranged out of sight in the north triforium, and is intended for big foundational effects and for the accompaniment of the nave congregational singing.

Notes on the Organ Planning

The 1899 Norman & Beard organ was mainly disposed within the lofty Pulpitum or Screen Case. The swell was arranged behind the great, both facing south; to their west, the tuba; and below, the small solo swell box. To the east, some pedal stops, bourdon, dulciana, bass flute, etc., above the unenclosed and projecting choir organ. The metal pedal open formed a screen above the console, then on the south side. The bulky 32-ft. open wood, 16-ft. open wood and 16-ft. ophicleide were on the south triforium behind and above the player.

Such was the layout of the organ when in April 1938, it was extensively damaged by a fire in the pulpitum, only the triforium pedal stops escaping serious damage.

The new instrument, with enlarged and partially enclosed choir organ and greatly augmented pedal and solo organs, demanded serious consideration in the following requirements:

(1) Reduced pulpitum case-work, avoiding the former obstruction of the view of the distant east windows.
(2) Avoid cutting off the essential daylight from the triforium windows.
(3) A homogeneous layout, having the triforium sections desirably unencased and out of sight from the cathedral floor, and
(4) Meeting the diverse requirements of intimate fully choral daily choir services and festival nave services and occasional recitals in an unusually long and narrow building.

Due regard for the first and second requirements made it difficult to find a satisfactory solution to the third and fourth.

The south triforium layout was first improved by lowering the 32-ft. wood to the horizontal and out of sight, and building in quint, octave wood and clarion, the natural additions to the family of the original occupants of this site.

An open triforium site to the north of the pulpitum was chosen for the new pedal and primary great, avoiding undue temperature variation from sunlight. By careful planning, no windows are covered, and only a small screen of double dulciana pipes can be seen from below, and it is ideally situated to accompany nave services on festival occasions, and spaciously accommodated.

Thus was obtained the desired reduction in the bulk of the pulpitum section to conform to the ideal case proportions proposed by the architect. The disposal of the bulky pedal stops elsewhere but nearby allowed the adoption of a novel system of construction, the pulpitum organ consisting of four structural cells forming all-enclosing swell boxes for the pipes, windchests, reservoirs and actions of choir, swell and solo. The fourth box encloses the main relays and switch mechanisms for quietness of action, of wind and for cleanliness. The general layout of the whole instrument is both ingenious and economical.

The console is now placed on the north side balanced amidst the voices of the organ, yet away from the more aggressive ranks. The player has a direct view of the choir stalls, and by mirrors can see the nave, pulpit and lectern.

The location of the enclosed and open section of the choir organ facing east, together with careful organ planning and the unusual transfer intermanual couplers, enables these two sections to be used as a colourful accompanimental two-manual instrument for choir use. The provision of the large panelled screens to the north and south sides of the organ enabled the acoustic surroundings to be completed despite the lack of main casing.

41

Analysis of a small extension organ as made by the John Compton Organ Company, North Acton, London.

The whole may be enclosed in one swell chamber, or ranks 6, 7, 8, 9, or some of them, might be separately enclosed. Such separate enclosure would of course be used if additional ranks could be provided to form an effective independent swell organ.

	Rank	*Pitch*	*No. of pipes*	*Pedal*	*Great*	*Positif*
1.	Diapason	16	73	16	8	
2.	Principal	8	85		8 2	4
3.	Prestant	8	97	8	4 1⅓, 1	8
4.	Gemshorn	16	121	16	8, 2⅔, 2, ⅔, ½	16, 8, 4, 1⅓, 1
5.	Salicional	8	109	8	16, 4, 1⅓, 1	8, 2⅔, 2 ⅔, ½
6.	Bourdon	32	98	32, 16, 8	16, 4	8, 2⅔, 2
7.	Flute	8	73	4	8	4
8.	Trumpet	16	85	16	8, 4	
9.	Bassoon	16	85	16, 8	16	16, 8, 4

Specification of the organ analysed above

Pedal

1. Subbass	32	
2. Contrabass	16	
3. Gemshorn	16	
4. Bourdon	16	
5. Prestant	8	
6. Bourdon	8	
7. Bourdon	4	
8. Trombone	16	
9. Bassoon	16	
10. Hautboy	8	

Great

1. Contra Salicional	16	(12 from Gemshorn)
2. Bourdon	16	
3. Diapason	8	
4. Principal	8	
5. Gemshorn	8	
6. Flute	8	
7. Prestant	4	
8. Salicet	4	
9. Bourdon	4	
10. Twelfth	$2\frac{2}{3}$	
11. Superoctave	2	
12. Fifteenth	2	
13. Mixture (2 ranks)	$1\frac{1}{3}$, 1	
14. Cymbale (4 ranks)		
15. Bassoon	16	
16. Trumpet	8	
17. Clarion	4	

Positif

1. Double gemshorn	16	
2. Prestant	8	
3. Salicional	8	
4. Bourdon	8	
5. Principal	4	
6. Octave gemshorn	4	
7. Octave flute	4	
8. Nasard	$2\frac{2}{3}$	
9. Octavin	2	
10. Quinte	$2\frac{2}{3}$	
11. Doublette	2	
12. Scharf (4 ranks)		
13. Bassoon	16	
14. Hautboy	8	
15. Hautboy clarion	4	

The only case of manual unison borrowing (called duplication) is that of the 16-ft. bassoon, and the only cases of next-octave extension on either manual are in the great trumpet 8, 4, and the positif bassoon-hautboy 16, 8, 4.

Mr. Compton says: "I believe this will explain clearly the general principle of extension design that I prefer to recommend and use wherever possible. Unfortunately some organists prefer, even with such a limited amount of actual material, to spread the 'stops' over three manuals, but I deprecate this very heartily."

42(*a*)

The Church of All Hallows, Barking-by-the-Tower (*Guild Church of Toc H*), *London, E.C.* Organ by Harrison and Harrison.

The specification has been drawn up by Gordon Phillips, Esq., the organist of the church, in consultation with the builders.

The organ stands in the West Gallery, a similar position to that of the old organ, which was destroyed, together with the Church, by enemy action in 1941.

There are three manuals, CC to C, 61 notes, and two and a half octaves of pedals, CCC to G, 32 notes; 44 speaking stops and 16 couplers, etc., making a total of 60 drawstops.

Pedal Organ
(10 stops, 3 *couplers*)

1. Open metal	(metal)	16
2. Subbass	(wood)	16
3. Spitzflute (from No. 21)	(metal)	16
4. Octave (20 from No. 1)	(metal)	8
5. Bourdon (20 from No. 2)	(wood)	8
6. Superoctave (20 from Nos. 1 & 4)	(metal)	4
7. Mixture (22, 26, 29)	(metal)	—
8. Posaune	(metal)	16
9. Trumpet (20 from No. 8)	(metal)	8
10. Schalmei	(metal)	4

(i) Choir to pedal
(ii) Great to pedal
(iii) Swell to pedal

Choir Organ
(10 stops, *tremulant*, 3 *couplers and* 1 *transfer*)
(in a swell-box)

11. Stopped diapason	(metal)	8
12. Principal	(metal)	4
13. Rohrflute	(metal)	4

14. Octave	(metal) 2
15. Blockflute	(metal) 2
16. Sesquialtera (12, 17)	(metal) —
17. Mixture (26, 29, 33)	(metal) —
18. Cromorne	(metal) 8
(iv) Tremulant	
19. Harmonic trumpet (from Great)	(metal) 8
20. Harmonic clarion (from Great)	(metal) 4

(v) Swell to choir
(vi) Swell suboctave to choir
(vii) Suboctave
(viii) Choir to great

Great Organ
(11 stops, 2 *couplers*)

21. Spitzflute	(metal) 16
22. Open diapason	(metal) 8
23. Open flute	(metal) 8
24. Rohrflute	(metal) 8
25. Octave	(metal) 4
26. Stopped flute	(metal) 4
27. Quint	(metal) $2\frac{2}{3}$
28. Superoctave	(metal) 2
29. Mixture (19, 22, 26, 29)	(metal) —
30. Harmonic trumpet	(metal) 8
31. Harmonic clarion	(metal) 4

(Nos. 30 and 31 in a swell-box)
(ix) Choir to great
(x) Swell to great

Swell Organ
(13 stops, *tremulant and* 3 *couplers*)

32. Spitzflute	(metal) 8
33. Quintadena	(metal) 8
34. Viola	(metal) 8
35. Celeste (Ten. C)	(metal) 8
36. Principal	(metal) 4
37. Open flute	(metal) 4
38. Nazard	(metal) $2\frac{2}{3}$
39. Gemshorn	(metal) 2
40. Tierce	(metal) $1\frac{3}{5}$
41. Cymbel (29, 33, 36)	(metal) —
42. Fagotto	(metal) 16
43. Trumpet	(metal) 8
44. Clarion	(metal) 4

(xi) Tremulant
(xii) Octave
(xiii) Suboctave
(xiv) Unison off

Combination Couplers

(xv) Great and pedal combinations coupled
(xvi) General tutti

Accessories

Five foot pistons to the pedal organ.
Four pistons to the choir organ.
Five pistons to the great organ.
Five pistons to the swell organ.
One general piston enabling any stop or stops in the organ to be set thereon.
General cancel piston.
Reversible piston to *great to pedal.*
Reversible piston to *swell to pedal.*
Reversible piston to *swell to great.*
Reversible piston to *choir to great.*
Two reversible foot pistons to *great to pedal.*
Reversible foot piston to *swell to pedal.*
Reversible foot piston to *choir to pedal.*
Balanced crescendo pedals to choir, swell and great reeds.
All combination pistons are adjustable by switch.

Wind Pressures

Pedal flue work 3 inches; reeds 3½ inches.
Choir 3 inches.
Great flue work 3 inches; reeds 5 inches.
All swell 3 inches.
Action 12 inches.

42(*b*)

St. Clement Danes Church, London, W.C. Organ by Harrison and Harrison Ltd., 1958.

Manual compass 61 notes. Pedal compass 32 notes.

Pedal Organ
(8 stops, 3 *couplers*)

1. Diapason (20—CC to G—from No. 18)	16
2. Subbass	16
3. Octave	8

4. Recorder bass	4
5. Open flute	2
6. Trombone	16
7. Trumpet	8
8. Shawm	4

(i) Choir to pedal
(ii) Great to pedal
(iii) Swell to pedal

Choir Organ
(8 stops, *tremulant and* 1 *coupler*)

9. Stopped diapason	8
10. Principal	4
11. Spitzflute	4
12. Nazard	$2\frac{2}{3}$
13. Octave	2
14. Tertian (19, 24: 17, 19)	II
15. Cimbel (29, 33, 36: 12, 15, 19)	III
16. Cremona	8

(iv) Tremulant
(v) Swell to choir

Great Organ
(10 stops, 2 *couplers*)

17. Quintadena	16
18. Open diapason	8
19. Spitzflute	8
20. Octave	4
21. Rohrflute	4
22. Flageolet	2
23. Rauschquint (12, 15)	II
24. Sesquialtera (19, 24: 12, 17)	II
25. Mixture (19, 22, 26, 29: 8, 8, 12, 12, 15)	IV—V
26. Cornet (Mid. C)	V

(vi) Choir to great
(vii) Swell to great

Swell Organ
(11 stops *and tremulant*)

27. Rohrflute	8
28. Salicional	8
29. Celeste (AA♯)	8

30. Principal	4
31. Open flute	4
32. Spitzflute	2
33. Larigot	$1\frac{1}{3}$
34. Sesquialtera (26, 31 : 12, 17)	II
35. Mixture (22, 29, 33, 36 : 12, 15, 19, 22)	IV
36. Fagotto	16
37. Trumpet	8

(viii) Tremulant

Combination Coupler

(ix) Great and pedal combinations coupled

Accessories

Four combination foot pistons to the pedal organ.
Four combination pistons to the choir organ.
Four combination pistons to the great organ.
Four combination pistons to the swell organ.
Four general pistons, duplicated by foot pistons.
Reversible piston to choir to pedal.
Reversible piston to great to pedal
Reversible piston to swell to pedal.
Reversible piston to choir to great.
Reversible piston to swell to great.
Reversible piston to swell to choir.
Reversible foot piston to great to pedal.
Reversible foot piston to swell to great.
Reversible foot piston to pedal trombone.
General cancel piston.
All pistons to be adjustable by setter.
Pipe wind pressures: $2\frac{1}{4}$ to $3\frac{1}{4}$ inches.
Action wind: 10 inches.
Pitch: A = 440 (C—523.3) at 65 degrees Fahrenheit.
All contacts silver to silver.

42(*c*)

St. Thomas the Martyr (*University Church*), *Newcastle-on-Tyne.* Organ by Harrison and Harrison, 1961.

The specification was drawn up by D. E. Wright, Esq., B.Sc., Ph.D., the Master's Warden at St. Thomas' and the organist to the Chapel of King's College, in conjunction with the builders.

The manual compass is CC to A, 58 notes, and the pedal CCC to F, 30 notes; 62 speaking stops and 19 couplers, etc.

Pedal Organ
(15 stops, 4 *couplers*)

1. Double open wood	(acoustic)	32
2. Open wood		16
3. Violone		16
4. Subbass		16
5. Lieblich Bourdon	(from No. 51)	16
6. Principal		8
7. Flute		8
8. Octave quint		$5\frac{1}{3}$
9. Octave		4
10. Octave flute		4
11. Mixture		III
12. Trombone		16
13. Trumpet		8
14. Schalmei		4
15. Orchestral trumpet	(from No. 62)	8

(i) Positive to pedal
(ii) Great to pedal
(iii) Swell to pedal
(iv) Solo to pedal

Positive Organ
(11 stops, 2 *couplers and* 1 *transfer*)
(unenclosed)

16. Diapason		8
17. Quintadena		8
18. Gedackt		8
19. Principal		4
20. Rohr flöte		4
21. Nazard		$2\frac{2}{3}$
22. Gemshorn		2
23. Tierce		$1\frac{3}{5}$
24. Cimbel		III
25. Trompette		8
26. Orchestral trumpet	(from No. 62)	8

(v) Swell to positive
(vi) Solo to positive
(vii) Great reeds and cornet on positive

Great Organ
(12 stops, 3 *couplers*)

27. Double geigen	16
28. Open diapason I	8
29. Open diapason II	8

30. Stopped diapason	8
31. Octave	4
32. Wald flute	4
33. Octave quint	$2\frac{2}{3}$
34. Superoctave	2
35. Mixture	IV
36. Cornet (Mid C)	V
37. Trumpet	8
38. Clarion	4

(viii) Positive to great
(ix) Swell to great
(x) Solo to great

Swell Organ

(12 stops, *tremulant and* 4 *couplers*)

39. Diapason	8
40. Rohr gedackt	8
41. Salicional	8
42. Celeste (AA)	8
43. Principal	4
44. Spitzflute	4
45. Fifteenth	2
46. Mixture	IV
47. Oboe	8

(xi) Tremulant

48. Contra fagotto	16
49. Cornopean	8
50. Clarion	4

(xii) Octave
(xiii) Suboctave
(xiv) Unison off
(xv) Solo to swell

Solo Organ

(12 stops, *tremulant and* 1 *transfer*)
(enclosed)

51. Bourdon	16
52. Dulciana	8
53. Spitzflöte	8
54. Unda Maris (AA)	8
55. Nachthorn	4
56. Octave	2
57. Open flute	2
58. Quint	$1\frac{1}{3}$

59. Sifflöte 1
60. Sesquialtera
61. Clarinet 8
(xvi) Tremulant
62. Orchestral trumpet 8
(xvii) Great reeds and cornet on solo

Combination Couplers

(xviii) Great and pedal combinations coupled
(xix) Pedal to swell pistons

Accessories

Six foot pistons to the pedal organ.
Six pistons to the positive organ.
Six pistons to the great organ.
Six pistons to the swell organ (duplicated by foot pistons).
Six pistons to the solo organ.
One general cancel piston.
Four general pistons, affecting the whole organ.
Six switches coupling 1st, 2nd, 3rd, 4th, 5th and 6th pistons on all manuals.
Reversible piston to swell to positive.
Reversible piston to positive to great.
Reversible piston to swell to great.
Reversible piston to solo to great.
Reversible piston to positive to pedal.
Reversible piston to great to pedal.
Reversible piston to swell to pedal.
Reversible piston to solo to pedal.
Reversible piston to pedal trombone.
Reversible piston to solo orchestral trumpet.
Reversible foot piston to swell to great.
Reversible foot piston to great to pedal.
Balanced crescendo pedals to swell and solo organs.
All pistons are adjustable by setter button or switch.

Wind Pressures

Pedal flue work, 4 inches; reeds 5 inches.
Positive, 3 inches.
Great flue work, $3\frac{3}{4}$ inches; reeds 5 inches.
Swell flue work and oboe, $3\frac{1}{2}$ to 4 inches; chorus reeds, $3\frac{1}{2}$ to 4 inches.
Solo flue work and clarinet, 3 to 4 inches; orchestral trumpet, 12 inches.
Action, 9 to 12 inches.

43

The Mormon Tabernacle, Salt Lake City, Utah, U.S.A. The famous organ in the Tabernacle at Salt Lake City was built originally in 1867 by Joseph Ridges. It was rebuilt in 1900 and in 1916. In 1948 it was thoroughly renovated and enlarged by the Aeolian-Skinner Organ Company of Boston under the direction of G. Donald Harrison.

Great Organ
(unenclosed)

Sub principal (61 pipes)	16
Quintaten (61 pipes)	16
Principal (61 pipes)	8
Diapason (61 pipes)	8
Spitzflöte (61 pipes)	8
Bourdon (61 pipes)	8
Flûte harmonique (61 pipes)	8
Bell gamba (61 pipes)	8
Grosse quinte (61 pipes)	$5\frac{1}{3}$
Principal (61 pipes)	4
Octave (61 pipes)	4
Gemshorn (61 pipes)	4
Koppelflöte (61 pipes)	4
Grosse tierce (61 pipes)	$3\frac{1}{5}$
Quinte (61 pipes)	$2\frac{2}{3}$
Super octave (61 pipes)	2
Blockflöte (61 pipes)	2
Tierce (61 pipes)	$1\frac{3}{5}$
Septième (61 pipes)	$1\frac{1}{7}$
Full mixture (4 ranks) (244 pipes)	$2\frac{2}{3}$
Fourniture (4 ranks) (244 pipes)	2
Kleine mixtur (4 ranks) (244 pipes)	$1\frac{1}{3}$
Acuta (3 ranks) (183 pipes)	1
Chimes (p–f) (dampers on and off) (32 tubes)	

Choir Organ
(enclosed)

Gamba (68 pipes)	16
Principal (68 pipes)	8
Viola (68 pipes)	8
Viola celeste (68 pipes)	8
Dulcet (2 ranks) (136 pipes)	8
Kleine erzähler (2 ranks) (124 pipes)	8
Concert flute (68 pipes)	8
Prestant (68 pipes)	4
Gambette (68 pipes)	4
Zauberflöte (68 pipes)	4

Piccolo harmonique (61 pipes)	2
Carillon (3 ranks) (183 pipes)	$2\frac{2}{3}$
Rauschpfeife (3 ranks) (183 pipes)	2
Dulzian (61 pipes)	16
Orchestral oboe (61 pipes)	8
Cromorne (61 pipes)	8
Trompette (61 pipes)	8
Rohr schalmei (61 pipes)	4
Tremulant	
Harp } (dampers on and off)	8
Celesta } (dampers on and off)	4
Choir to choir 4 } on selected stops.	
Choir to choir 16 } on selected stops.	

Swell Organ
(enclosed)

Gemshorn (68 pipes)	16
Lieblich gedeckt (68 pipes)	16
Geigen prinzipal (68 pipes)	8
Claribel flute (68 pipes)	8
Gedeckt (68 pipes)	8
Viole de gambe (68 pipes)	8
Viole celeste (68 pipes)	8
Orchestral strings (2 ranks) (136 pipes)	8
Salicional (68 pipes)	8
Voix celeste (68 pipes)	8
Flauto dolce (68 pipes)	8
Flute celeste T.C. (56 pipes)	8
Prestant (68 pipes)	4
Fugara (68 pipes)	4
Flauto traverso (61 pipes)	4
Nazard (61 pipes)	$2\frac{2}{3}$
Octavin (61 pipes)	2
Cornet (3 ranks) (183 pipes)	$2\frac{2}{3}$
Plein jeu (6 ranks) (366 pipes)	$2\frac{2}{3}$
Cymbale (4 ranks) (244 pipes)	$2\frac{2}{3}$
Hautbois (68 pipes)	8
Voix humaine (68 pipes)	8
Harmonic trumpet (68 pipes)	8
Contra fagot (61 pipes)	32
Contre trompette (61 pipes)	16
Trompette (61 pipes)	8
Quinte trompette (61 pipes)	$5\frac{1}{3}$
Clairon (61 pipes)	4
Tremulant	
Swell to swell 4 } on selected stops.	
Swell to swell 16 } on selected stops.	

Positiv Organ
(unenclosed, first manual)

Cor de nuit (61 pipes)	8
Quintade (61 pipes)	8
Principal (61 pipes)	4
Nachthorn (61 pipes)	4
Nazard (61 pipes)	2⅔
Principal (61 pipes)	2
Spillflöte (61 pipes)	2
Tierce (61 pipes)	1⅗
Larigot (61 pipes)	1⅓
Sifflöte (61 pipes)	1
Septerz (2 ranks) (98 pipes)	1⅐
Scharf (3 ranks) (183 pipes)	1
Zimbel (3 ranks) (183 pipes)	½
Rankett (61 pipes)	16

Solo Organ
(enclosed)

Gamba (68 pipes)	8
Gamba Celeste (68 pipes)	8
Viole celeste (2 ranks) (136 pipes)	8
Flauto mirabilis (68 pipes)	8
Concert flute (68 pipes)	4
French horn (68 pipes)	8
English horn (68 pipes)	8
Corno di bassetto (68 pipes)	8
Tuba (68 pipes)	8
Tremulant	
Chimes	
Harp	8
Celesta	4
Solo to solo 4	
Solo to solo 16	

Bombarde Organ
(unenclosed, fourth manual)

Diapason (61 pipes)	8
Octave (61 pipes)	4
Grosse cornet (4–6 ranks) (306 pipes)	2⅔
Grande fourniture (6 ranks) (366 pipes)	2⅔
Bombarde (61 pipes)	16
Trompette (61 pipes)	8
Clairon (61 pipes)	4

Antiphonal Organ
(enclosed, fifth manual)

Diapason (68 pipes)	8
Gedeckt (68 pipes)	8
Salicional (68 pipes)	8
Voix celeste (68 pipes)	8
Principal (68 pipes)	4
Kleine mixtur (3 ranks) (183 pipes)	2
Trompette (68 pipes)	8
Vox humana (68 pipes)	8
Tremulant	
Antiphonal to antiphonal	4

Pedal Organ

Flûte ouverte (12 pipes)	32
Montre (12 pipes)	32
Bourdon (12 pipes)	32
Flûte ouverte (32 pipes)	16
Principal (32 pipes)	16
Contre basse (32 pipes)	16
Violone (32 pipes)	16
Bourdon (32 pipes)	16
Gemshorn (swell)	16
Gamba (choir)	16
Lieblich gedeckt (swell)	16
Grosse quinte (32 pipes)	$10\frac{2}{3}$
Principal (32 pipes)	8
Violoncello (32 pipes)	8
Spitzprinzipal (32 pipes)	8
Flûte ouverte (32 pipes)	8
Flauto dolce (32 pipes)	8
Gamba (choir)	8
Lieblich gedeckt (swell)	8
Quinte (32 pipes)	$5\frac{1}{3}$
Choral bass (32 pipes)	4
Nachthorn (32 pipes)	4
Gamba (choir)	4
Lieblich gedeckt (swell)	4
Blockflöte (32 pipes)	2
Grand harmonics (5 ranks) (160 pipes)	$10\frac{2}{3}$
Full mixture (4 ranks) (128 pipes)	$5\frac{1}{3}$
Cymbale (4 ranks) (128 pipes)	$1\frac{1}{3}$
Bombarde (32 pipes)	32
Contra fagot (swell)	32
Ophicleide (32 pipes)	16

Trombone (32 pipes)	16
Fagot (swell)	16
Dulzian (choir)	16
Posaune (32 pipes)	8
Trumpet (32 pipes)	8
Cromorne (choir)	8
Clairon (32 pipes)	4
Chalumeau (32 pipes)	4
Kornett (32 pipes)	2
Chimes	

Couplers

Coupler		Type
Choir to pedal		Pedal
Great to pedal		Pedal
Swell to pedal		Pedal
Solo-bombarde to pedal		Pedal
Antiphonal to pedal		Pedal
Solo to pedal 4		Pedal
Swell to pedal 4		Pedal
Choir-positiv to great',		Unison
Swell to great		Unison
Solo-bombarde to great		Unison
Antiphonal to great		Unison
Swell to choir		Unison
Solo-bombarde to choir		Unison
Great tutti to solo		Unison
Choir to great	4	Octave
Swell to great	4	Octave
Solo to great	16	Octave
Solo to great	4	Octave
Swell to choir	4	Octave

Combinations

Great	0, 1–8	Solo and bombarde	0, 1–8
Swell	0, 1–8	Antiphonal	0, 1–4
Choir and positiv	0, 1–8	Pedal	0, 1–8
General	0, 1–20. Eight duplicated by toe studs.		

Mechanicals

All manual to pedal unison couplers controlled by reversibles.
Great to pedal reversible toe stud.
Swell to pedal reversible toe stud.
Solo-bombarde to great reversible toe stud.

32 ft. bombarde reversible toe stud.
32 ft. bourdon reversible toe stud.
Coupler: choir expression pedal to swell expression pedal.
Swell expression pedal.
Choir expression pedal.
Solo expression pedal.
Antiphonal expression pedal.
Crescendo pedal.
Sforzando by toe stud reversible with light indicator.
Set button.
Tremolo cancel on crescendo pedal.
30 horse-power blower.
Wind pressures: $2\frac{3}{4}$, $3\frac{3}{4}$, 5, 7, 10, 15 in.

44

Organ for the *Boston Symphony Orchestra, Music Room at "Tanglewood", Stockbridge, Mass., U.S.A.* Built by Aeolian-Skinner Organ Company.

Great Organ
(61 notes)

Quintaten	16	Rohrflöte	4
Principal	8	Quint	$2\frac{2}{3}$
Spitzflöte	8	Super octave	2
Principal	4	Fourniture (3–5 ranks) (285 pipes)	

Positiv Organ
(61 notes)

Nason flute	8	(enclosed)	
Koppelflöte	4	English salicional	8
Nazard	$2\frac{2}{3}$	Gedackt	8
Nachthorn	2	Gemshorn	4
Tierce	$1\frac{3}{5}$	Trompette	8
Italian principal	1		
Cymbel (3 ranks) (183 pipes)			

Pedal Organ
(32 notes)

Geigen prinzipal	16	Nachthorn	4
Salicional (extension of 8 ft. salicional enclosed) (12 pipes)	16	Mixture (4 ranks) (128 pipes)	
		Bombarde (low CCCC) (1 pipe)	32
Quintaten (great)	16	Posaune	16
Spitzprinzipal	8		

45

Rheims Cathedral, 1938. A French "neo-classique" design by V. Gonzalez.

Pedale
(20 stops)

Principal	32	Grande fourniture	6 ranks
Flûte	16	Petite fourniture	4 ranks
Principal	16	Nasard	$2\frac{2}{3}$
Soubasse	16	Tierce	$1\frac{3}{5}$
Flûte	8	Bombarde	32
Principal	8	Bombarde	16
Bourdon	8	Trompette	8
Principal	4	Clairon	4
Flûte	4	Basson	8
Doublette	2	Buccine	2

Grand Orgue
(21 stops)

Montre	16	Cymbale	4 ranks
Bourdon	16	Cornet	5 ranks
Montre	8	Quinte	$2\frac{2}{3}$
Diapason	8	Quarte	2
Grosse flûte	8	Tierce	$1\frac{3}{5}$
Bourdon	8	Bombarde	16
Prestant	4	Trompette	8
Flûte à cheminée	4	Clairon	4
Doublette	2	Trompette	8
Grande fourniture	6 ranks	Clairon	4
Petite fourniture	5 ranks		

(The last two are "en chamade", i.e. horizontal, and are transferable to another manual.)

Positif
(16 stops)

Bourdon	16	Fourniture	4 ranks
Montre	8	Cymbale	3 ranks
Flûte	8	Nasard	$2\frac{2}{3}$
Bourdon	8	Tierce	$1\frac{3}{5}$
Salicional	8	Larigot	$1\frac{1}{3}$
Prestant	4	Trompette	8
Flûte bouchée	4	Clairon	4
Doublette	2	Cromorne	8

Recit Expressif
(20 stops)

Quintatön	16	Quinte	$2\frac{2}{3}$
Montre	8	Tierce	$1\frac{3}{5}$
Flûte harmonique	8	Flûte	1
Bourdon	8	Septième	$1\frac{1}{7}$
Dulciane	8	Bombarde	16
Voix céleste	8	Trompette	8
Prestant	4	Clairon	4
Flûte creuse	4	Hautbois	8
Doublette	2	Voix humaine	8
Fourniture	4 ranks	Tremblant	
Cymbale	3 ranks		

Echo
(10 stops)

Cor de nuit	8
Quintatön	8
Viole	4
Bourdon	4
Cymbale	5 ranks
Sesquialtera	2 ranks
Flûte	2
Ranquette	16
Chalumeau	8
Musette	4

Slider-chests and tracker action.
Unison couplers over the top row of keys.
Wind pressures: Echo and positif, 3 in.
Remainder of pipework, including reeds, $3\frac{1}{2}$ in.

46

Aalen Parish Church, Germany. A romantic organ rebuilt in neo-classical style.

(*a*) ORIGINAL SPECIFICATION

Manual I

1. Bourdon	16	8. Quinte	$5\frac{1}{3}$
2. Prinzipal	8	9. Oktave	4
3. Gamba	8	10. Fugara	4
4. Flöte	8	11. Flöte	4
5. Trompete	8	12. Oktave	4
6. Gemshorn	8	13. Mixture (4–6 ranks)	$2\frac{2}{3}$
7. Gedackt	8		

Manual II

14. Prinzipal	8	19. Kornett	8
15. Gedackt	8	20. Oktave	4
16. Salizional	8	21. Traversflöte	4
17. Äoline	8	22. Dolce	4
18. Klarinette	8	23. Flautino	2

Pedal

24. Prinzipal	16	28. Oktavbass	8
25. Violonbass	16	29. Violon	8
26. Sub-bass	16	30. Oktave	4
27. Posaune	16	Unison couplers	

(*b*) AS REBUILT

Hauptwerk

Gedacktpommer (from 1)	16	Trompete (new)	4
Prinzipal (from 2)	8	Quinte (from 13)	$2\frac{2}{3}$
Rohrflöte (from 19)	8	Koppelflöte (from 16)	2
Quinte (from 8)	$5\frac{1}{3}$	Mixtur (4–6 ranks) (new)	2
Oktave (from 9)	4		

Brustwerk

Trechterregal (new)	8	Terzian (from 13)	$1\frac{3}{5}$, $1\frac{1}{3}$
Rohrschelle (from 20)	4	Zimbel (3 ranks) (new)	$\frac{1}{6}$

Oberwerk

Lieblich gedackt (from 15)	8	Sesquialtera (from 19)	$2\frac{2}{3}$, $1\frac{3}{5}$
Gemshorn (from 6)	8	Oktave (from 12)	2
Krummhorn (new)	8	Nasat (from 17)	$1\frac{1}{3}$
Prinzipal (from 10)	4	Blockflöte (from 23)	1
Flötgedackt (from 7)	4	Scharf (4–6 ranks) (new)	1

Pedal

Posaune (from 27)	32	Choral bass (from 19)	4, 2
Prinzipal (from 24)	16	Mixture (4 ranks) (from 14, 29, 4, and 13 respectively)	$5\frac{1}{3}$, 4, $3\frac{1}{5}$, $2\frac{2}{3}$
Untersatz (from 26)	16		
Oktave (from 28)	8	Singend Kornett (from 6)	2

Some Small Organ Designs

47

St. Michael's Church, Essen. Choir organ built in 1940 by Klais of Bonn.

Hauptwerk

Lieblich gedackt	8	Principal	4	Nasat	$1\frac{1}{3}$

Positiv

Salicional	8	Rohrflöte	4	Oktave	2

Pedal

Sub-bass	16	Gedackt	8

48

Evangelical Church, Auerbach, in Saxony. The organ built in 1840 by Jehmlich.

Hauptwerk

Principal	8	Oktave	4
Gemshorn	8	Mixtur	2–3 ranks

Positiv

Rohrflöte	8	Waldflöte	2
Salicional	8	Terzcymbel	3 ranks
Praestant	4		

Pedal

Sub-bass	16	Principal	8	Choralbass	4

49

Theological Seminary, Neuhof. The organ built in 1936 by Kemper of Lübeck.

Unterwerk

Gedackt	8	Principal	4
Sifflöte	1	Quinte	$2\frac{2}{3}$

Oberwerk

Principal	8	Spitzflöte	4
Oktave	2	Mixtur	3 ranks

Pedal

Sub-bass	16	Quintade	8

50

The University, Königsberg. The organ built in 1928 by W. Sauer.

Oberwerk

Principal	8	Rohrflöte	8
Oktave	4	Gemshorn	4
Mixtur	4 ranks	Cymbel	3 ranks
Rankett	16	Krummhorn	8

Brustwerk

Violflöte	8	Quintade	8
Gedacktflöte	4	Principal	2
Nachthorn	2	Blockflöte	1
Sesquialtera	2 ranks		
Vox humana	8		

Pedal

Untersatz	16	Dulcian	16
Cornett	4	Principal	8
Rohrflöte	8	Gemshorn	4
Rankett	16		

51

A multum-in-parvo romantic design for a two-manual organ by Lt.-Col. George Dixon, M.A., T.D.

Great Organ
(3½ in. wind)

Bourdon (soft in bass)	16
Rohrflöte (soft in bass)	8
Geigen	8
Open diapason	8
Octave	4
Superoctave	2
Mixture (12, 19, 22)	3 ranks

Swell to great.

Swell Organ
(7½ in. wind)

Sound-board (carried up an extra octave)

Hohlflöte	8
Viole	8
Geigen principal	4
Cornet (12, 15, 17)	3 ranks
Corno di bassetto	16
Trumpet	8

(unenclosed)

Tromba	8

(a small tuba)

Octave couplers.
Octave alone.
Balanced swell pedal.

Pedal Organ

Sub-bass (from great)	16	
Flute (from great)	8	
Open diapason (4 in. wind)	16	one extended rank
Octave (4 in. wind)	8	one extended rank
Superoctave (4 in. wind)	4	one extended rank
Trombone (8 in. wind)	16	

Great to pedal.
Swell to pedal.

52

Another design by Lt.-Col. George Dixon, M.A., T.D. (tracker action to manuals).

Great Organ

Double salicional (12 from sub-bass)	16	Octave	$2\frac{2}{3}$
Rohrflöte (soft)	8	Superoctave	2
Open diapason	8		
Twelfth	4		

Swell to great.

Pedal Organ

Sub-bass	16	one rank
Flute	8	
Open diapason	16	one rank
Octave	8	
Superoctave	4	

Great to pedal.
Swell to pedal.

Swell Organ

Hohlflöte	8
Gamba	8
Geigen principal	4
Gemshorn	2
Sesquialtera	2 ranks
Corno di bassetto	16
Cornopean	8

Balanced swell pedal.

53

The Chapel, Clinique, 29 *Rue Georges Bizet, Paris.* The organ built by Gonzalez.

Manual I

Bourdon	8
Prestant	4
Plein jeu (15, 19, 22)	3 ranks

Manual II

Quintaten	8
Flûte ouverte	4
Cor de nuit	2
Sesquialtera (12, 17)	2 ranks

Pédale

Bourdon	8
Rankett	16

Some One-manual Organs

54

Leipzig Museum. The organ built *c.* 1720 by Gottfried Silbermann.

Gedackt	8
Principal	4
Octave	2
Quinta	$1\frac{1}{3}$
Cymbel	2 ranks

55

Willis Plainsong Organ, c. 1930.

Open diapason	8
Bourdon	8
Salicional	8
Gemshorn	4
Plein jeu (12, 15)	2 ranks
Pedal sub-bass	16

Octave coupler.
Manual to pedal coupler.

56

Glapthorne, Northants. The organ built *c.* 1934 by Roger Yates.

(unenclosed)

Bourdon	16
Open diapason	8

(enclosed)

Dulciana	8
Principal	4
Flûte couverte	4
Plein jeu (12, 15, 17)	3 ranks
Pedal bourdon	16

Octave coupler.
Manual to pedal coupler.

57

Carpentras Church, France. The organ built in 1583 by Marchand. (All the stops were divided.)

Montre	8	Nazard	$2\frac{2}{3}$
Flûte	8	Quinsième	2
Octave	4	Fourniture	4 ranks
Flûte	4	Cymbale	2 ranks

58

Histon, St. Andrew's Church. Organ rebuilt by Wm. Hill & Son and Norman & Beard Ltd., 1952 (an enlightened small design).

Pedal Organ

(Compass: CCC to F, 30 notes—an increase of 10 notes)

		pipes
1. Sub-bass	16	54
2. Echo Bourdon	16	30
3. Bass Flute	8 (from No. 1)	
4. Choral Bass	4 (from No. 1)	

Great Organ

(Compass: CC to C, 61 notes)

		pipes
1. Open Diapason	8	61
2. Gedeckt	8	61
3. Dulciana	8	56
4. Gemshorn	4	61
5. Nason Flute	4	61
6. Flageolet	2	61

Swell Organ

(Compass: CC to C, 61 notes)

		pipes
1. Viola da Gamba	8	56(FF)
2. Lieblich Gedeckt	8	61
3. Principal	4	61
4. Mixture (12 and 15)	2 ranks	122
5. Contra Oboe	16	61

(iv) Swell Octave
(v) Swell Sub-octave
(vi) Swell Unison Off
} Acting also through Swell to Great.

Accessories

Four Thumb Pistons to Great and Pedal Organs.
Four Thumb Pistons to Swell Organ.
One Thumb Piston to Swell to Great—Reversible.
One Thumb Piston to Great to Pedal—Reversible.
Four Toe Pistons to Great and Pedal Organs.
One Toe Piston to Great to Pedal—Reversible.
One General Cancel Piston.
Balanced Swell Pedal.
Blower Push-button Starter (silent momentary contact pattern).
Console Light Switch.
Action Current Voltmeter.

59

Wellington, New Zealand, 1913. Designed by F. J. Livesey, Esq.

Great Organ		*Swell Organ*	
Double salicional	16	Viol	8
(T.C. bass from pedal sub-bass)		Stopped flute	8
Claribel flute (soft)	8	Geigen principal	4
Open diapason	8	Mixture (12, 15, 19, 22)	IV
Principal	4	Contra fagotto	16
Twelfth	$2\frac{2}{3}$	Octave coupler	
Fifteenth	2		
Pedal Organ		3 couplers	
Sub-bass } extension	16	$3\frac{1}{2}''$ wind pressure	
Flute } extension	8	Tracker action	
Open wood	16		

60

A design by Cecil Clutton, 20 speaking stops, $3\frac{1}{4}$ in. wind pressure; 1940.

Great

Gedackt	(wood) 16				
Holzflöte	(wood) 8				
Diapason	8				
Octave	4				
Fifteenth	2				
Fourniture	V ranks				
CC	12	19	22	26	29
TC	12	15	19	22	26
C^1	5	12	15	19	22
C^2	5	8	12	15	19
C^3	1	5	8	12	15

Choir 16 ft. to great
Choir 8 ft. to great
Swell 8 ft. to great
Swell 4 ft. to great

Swell

73 note chest				
Viola				8
Geigen principal				4
Scharf				III ranks
CC	15	19	22	
$g^2\sharp$	1	15	19	
$g^3\sharp$	1	12	15	
$g^4\sharp$	1	5	8	
Krummhorn				16
Trumpet				8

Octave
Sub-octave
Unison off
Tremolo
Great to swell

Choir

Enclosed

Dulciana	8
Rohrflöte (metal)	8
Nachthorn (metal)	4
Gemshorn	2
Sesquialtera (12,17)	

Tremolo

Swell to choir

Pedal

Gedackt	32
Gedackt (from great)	16
Gedackt	8
Contra bass (extended)	16
Octave	8
Cornet (15, 19, 22, 24)	IV ranks
Krummhorn (from swell)	16
Posaune	(metal) 16
Great to pedal	
Choir to pedal	
Swell 8 ft. to pedal	
Swell 4 ft. to pedal	

61

The Church of St. Martin-in-the-Fields, London (a notable organ at the time of its erection). Built by Henry Bevington and Sons in 1854.

Great Organ
(CC to G)

			pipes
1.	Double diapason	16	44
2.	Double diapason	16	12
3.	Open diapason	8	56
4.	Open diapason	8	56
5.	Hohl diapason	8	44
6.	Stop diapason *bass*	8	12
7.	Claribel	8	44
8.	Quint	5⅓	56
9.	Principal	4	56
10.	Waldflute	4	44
11.	Decima	3⅕	56
12.	Twelfth	2⅔	56
13.	Fifteenth	2	56
14.	Sesquialtera	IV ranks	224
15.	Furniture	III ranks	168
16.	Mixture	III ranks	168
17.	Trumpet	8	56
18.	Clarion	4	56

Swell Organ

			pipes
19.	Bourdon *bass*	16	12
20.	Double diapason *treble*	16	44
21.	Open diapason	8	56
22.	Dulciana	8	44
23.	Stop diapason *bass*	8	12
24.	Stop diapason *treble*	8	44
25.	Principal	4	56
26.	Flute	4	56
27.	Twelfth	2⅔	56
28.	Fifteenth	2	56
29.	Sesquialtera	V ranks	280
30.	Trombone	16	56
31.	Cornopean	8	56
32.	Oboe	8	56
33.	Clarion	4	56

Choir Organ
(CC to G)

			pipes
34.	Bourdon *bass*	16	12
35.	Double diapason *treble*	16	44
36.	Open diapason	8	56

Pedal Organ
(CCC to F)

			pipes
46.	Great open diapason	16	30
47.	Bourdon	16	30
48.	Unison open diapason	8	30

37. Viol de gamba	8	44
38. Dulciana	8	44
39. Claribel	8	44
40. Stop diapason *bass*	8	12
41. Principal	4	56
42. Flute	4	56
43. Mixture	III ranks	168
44. Bassoon	16	44
45. Clarinet	8	44

49. Unison stop diapason	8	30
50. Principal	4	30
51. Quint and decima	$5\frac{1}{3}$	60
52. Twelfth and fifteenth	$2\frac{2}{3}$	60
53. Great trombone	16	30
54. Trumpet	8	30

9 composition pedals
3 to great
3 to swell
3 to choir

Couplers

55. Pedals to great
56. Pedals to choir
57. Pedals to swell
58. Swell to great
59. Swell to choir

The names of the great stops were engraved in white letters on a blue ground; of the swell in white letters on a red ground; of the choir in black letters on mother-of-pearl; of the pedal and couplers in red and black letters, respectively, on plain ivory.

62

Three Organs in Teaching Institutions

Salle Berlioz, Conservatoire National, Paris. Specification by M. Marcel Dupré, built by Jacquot-Lavergne.

Grand Orgue
(61 notes)

		pipes
1. Bourdon	16	61
2. Montre	8	61
3. Bourdon	8	61
4. Flûte harmonique	8	61
5. Prestant	4	61
6. Plein jeu (3 ranks)		183

Positif Expressif
(61 notes)

		pipes
7. Cor de nuit	8	61
8. Salicional	8	61
9. Flûte douce	4	61

Récit Expressif
(61 notes)

		pipes
14. Diapason	8	61
15. Flûte	8	61
16. Gambe	8	61
17. Voix céleste	8	61
18. Flûte Octaviante	4	61
19. Octavin	2	61
20. Plein jeu (3 ranks)		183
21. Basson	16	61
22. Trompette	8	61
23. Clairon	4	61
24. Basson hautbois	8	61

10. Nazard	$2\frac{2}{3}$	61
11. Quarte de nazard	2	61
12. Tierce	$1\frac{3}{5}$	61
13. Cromorne	8	61

Pédale
(32 notes)

Soubasse unit 16, 8 and 4 ft.
21, 22, 23 from Récit

Combinaisons par registres sur le fronton des claviers

Tirasse Grand Orgue	8	Récit/Grand Orgue	4
Tirasse Positif	8	Positif/Grand Orgue	4
Tirasse Récit	8	Récit/Positif	4
Tirasse Grand Orgue	4	Grand Orgue	16
Tirasse Positif	4	Positif	16
Tirasse Récit	4	Récit	16
Récit/Grand Orgue	16	Suppression Grand Orgue	8
Positif/Grand Orgue	16	Suppression Positif	8
Récit/Positif	16	Suppression Récit	8
Récit/Grand Orgue	8	Grand Orgue	4
Positif/Grand Orgue	8	Positif	4
Récit/Positif	8	Récit	4

63(*a*)

University of Nottingham (*Great Hall*, *Trent Building*). A romantic organ (1909), rebuilt with improved design by Willis (1957).

Great
(8 stops)

	feet	*pipes*
Douple open diapason	16	61
Open diapason I	8	61
Open diapason II	8	61
Claribel flute	8	61
Principal	4	61
Fifteenth	2	61
Mixture (17, 19, 22)	III	183
Tromba	8	61

Swell to great
Swell to great, octave
Swell to great, suboctave
Choir to great
Choir to great, octave

Swell
(10 stops)

	feet	*pipes*
Open diapason	8	61
Lieblich gedackt	8	61
Viola da gamba	8	61
Voix Célestes (GG)	8	54
Gemshorn	4	61
Sesquialtera (12, 17)	II	122
Mixture (15, 19, 22)	III	183
Contra fagotto	16	61
Trumpet	8	61
Clarion–oboe	4	61

Swell octave
Swell suboctave
Swell unison off
Swell tremolo

Choir
(7 stops)

Violoncello	8	61
Hohl flute	8	61

Pedal
(10 stops)

Resultant bass	32	—
Open bass	16	32

Dulciana	8	61
Lieblich flute	4	61
Flautino	2	61
Sext (12, 17)	II	122
Krummhorn	8	61
Choir octave		
Choir unison off		
Swell to choir		
Choir tremolo		

Gallery Pedal
(3 stops)

Gedackt	16	56
Gedackt	8	—
Gedackt	4	—

Bourdon	16	32
Octave	8	12
Bass flute	8	12
Super octave	4	12
Octave flute	4	12
Mixture (17, 19, 22)	III	96
Fagotto	16	SW
Trombone	16	32
Swell to pedal		
Swell to pedal, octave		
Great to pedal		
Choir to pedal		
Choir to pedal, octave		
Great and pedal combinations coupled		

Accessories

0–5 pistons to great.
0–5 pistons to swell.
0–5 pistons to choir.
0–5 toe pistons to pedal.
0–5 toe pistons to swell (dup.).
(All above except cancel pistons (O) are adjustable by setter buttons at the console.)

Reverser pistons for:
Swell to pedal, great to pedal, choir to pedal, swell to great, Swell to choir, choir to great.
Reverser toe piston for:
Great to pedal.
One piston for "octave couplers cancel".
One piston for "general cancel".

Balanced swell pedals, electro-pneumatic, to swell and choir.
Detached and mobile console, of standard "Willis" pattern, with its own casework.

Electric blowing with separate push-button starters at console for main organ and choir section.

Wind Pressures

Great fluework 4 inches, tromba 6 inches.
Swell, throughout, 5 inches; choir throughout 4½ inches.
Pedal 4½ inches; trombone 8 inches.

63(*b*)

University of Nottingham (*Portland Chapel*). By Henry Willis & Sons, Ltd., 1957.

The instrument consists of two manuals, CC to G, 56 notes, and a "Willis" concave and radiating pedal board, CCC to F, 30 notes.

There are 15 speaking stops, 3 couplers and tremulant, making a total of 19 registers.

Great
(5 stops)

1. Open diapason 8
2. Rohr flöte 8
3. Pianissimo 8
4. Principal 4
5. Quartane $2\frac{2}{3}$ and 2

Swell Positif
(6 stops)
(enclosed)

6. Gedackt 8
7. Viola da gamba 8
8. Gemshorn 4
9. Flageolet 2
10. Sext $2\frac{2}{3}$ and $1\frac{3}{5}$
11. Krummhorn 8
Tremulant

Pedal
(4 stops)

12. Major bass 16
13. Bordun 16
14. Octave 8
15. Choral bass 4

(all independent)

Couplers

Swell positif to great
Swell positif to pedal
Great to pedal

Wind pressure

$2\frac{3}{4}$ inches.
Mechanical action throughout except pedal mechanism—tubular-pneumatic

64

St. Mary's Baptist Church, Norwich, 1954. Built by Wm. Hill & Son and Norman & Beard Ltd. The organ case was designed by Mr. Stanley J. Wearing, F.R.I.B.A., F.S.A., and built by H. E. Taylor & Co. Ltd.

Great

Quintaton	16
Open Diapason	8
Geigen Principal	8
Quintade	8
Principal	4
Gedeckt	4
Twelfth	$2\frac{2}{3}$
Fifteenth	2
Harmonic Trumpet	8

(i) Swell to Great
(ii) Choir to Great

Choir

Enclosed Division

Dulciana	8
Dulcet	4
Dulcetina	2
Dulcet Twelfth	$2\frac{2}{3}$
Dulcet Tierce	$1\frac{3}{5}$
Viole d'Orchestre	8

Unenclosed Division

Stopped Diapason	8
Gemshorn	8
Koppel Flute	4
Harmonic Trumpet	8

(vi) Choir Octave
(vii) Choir Sub-octave
(viii) Choir Unison Off
(ix) Swell to Choir

Swell

Contra Viole	16
Geigen Diapason	8
Rohr Gedeckt	8
Octave Gamba	4
Super Octave	2
Harmonics	3 ranks
Double Trumpet	16
(iii) Swell Octave	
(iv) Swell Sub-octave	
(v) Swell Unison Off	

Pedal

Sub-bass	32
Open Wood	16
Bourdon	16
Quintaton	16
Echo Bass	16
Octave Wood	8
Bass Flute	8
Choral Bass	4
Trombone	16
Trumpet	8
(x) Swell to Pedal	
(xi) Great to Pedal	
(xii) Choir to Pedal	
(xiii) Swell Octave to Pedal	
(xiv) Great to Pedal Pistons Coupled	

Accessories

Four thumb pistons to great stops
Four thumb pistons to swell stops
Four thumb pistons to choir stops
Four toe pistons to pedal stops
Four toe pistons to swell stops
One general cancel thumb piston
One pedal trombone thumb piston
One great to pedal thumb piston and duplicated by toe piston
One swell to great thumb piston and duplicated by toe piston
One choir to great thumb piston
Two balanced swell pedals
Electric blower
Electric action
Manual compass CC to C—61 notes
Pedal compass CCC to G—32 notes

Three Modern Organs in Baroque Style

65

First Presbyterian Church, Baltimore, Md., U.S.A. Möller, 1940.

Positif (enclosed)

Nason Gedeckt	8
Spitzflöte	8
Nachthorn	4
Nasat	$2\frac{2}{3}$
Principal	2
Tierce	$1\frac{3}{5}$
Tremulant	

Oberwerk

Salicional	8
Rohrflöte	4
Mixture (29, 33, 36)	III
Cromorne	8
Tremulant	

Pedal

Nason Gedeckt	16
Spitzprincipal	8
Koppelflöte	4

66

Evangelische Kirche, Ludwigsburg, Germany. Walcker, 1953.

Hauptwerk		*Schwellwerk*		*Pedal*	
Flöte	8	Gedeckt	8	Sub-bass	16
Prinzipal	4	Blockflöte	4	Oktavbass	8
Rauschpfeife (12, 15)	II	Prinzipal	2	Choralbass	4
		Spitzquinte	$1\frac{1}{3}$	Flöte	2
Mixtur	IV–VI	Scharfzimbel	III	Fagott	8
		Oboe	8	Mechanical action	
		Tremulant		Slider chests	

67

Vamdrup Kirke, Jylland, Denmark. Frobenius, 1953.

Hovedwerk		*Brystwerk*		*Pedal*	
Principal	8	Traegedakt	8	Sub-bass	16
Rorfloijte	8	Rohrfloijte	4	Principal	8
Oktav	4	Principal	2	Nathorn	4
Quint	$2\frac{2}{3}$	Spidsquint	$1\frac{1}{3}$	Fagot	16
Oktav	2	Scharf		Mechanical action	
Mixtur				Slider chests	
Dulcian	8				

68

All Souls' Church, Langham Place, London. Rebuilt by Willis, 1951.

The instrument consists of Three Manuals, CC to C, 61 notes, and a "Willis" Concave and Radiating Pedal Board, CCC to G, 32 notes.

Pitch—C. 523 (A. 440), 60° F.

Great Organ
(13 stops, 2 *couplers*)

		feet		*pipes*
1. Double Open Diapason		16	(metal)	61
2. Open Diapason No. 1		8	(metal)	61
3. Open Diapason No. 2		8	(metal)	61
4. Open Diapason No. 3		8	(metal)	61
5. Wald Flute		8	(std. and open wood)	61
6. Principal No. 1		4	(metal)	61
7. Principal No. 2		4	(metal)	61
8. Stopped Flute		4	(std. metal)	61
9. Quartane (12, 15)		$2\frac{2}{3}$ & 2	(std. and open metal)	122
10. Mixture (17, 19, 22)		3 ranks	(metal)	183
11. Contra Tromba	H.P.	16	(metal)	61
12. Tromba	harmonic	8	(metal)	61
13. Clarion	trebles	4	(metal)	61

(i) Swell to Great
(ii) Choir to Great

Swell Organ
(14 stops, 3 *couplers and tremolo*)
(enclosed)

	feet		pipes
14. Open Diapason	8	(metal)	61
15. Rohr Flöte	8	(std. wood and metal)	61
16. Æoline	8	(metal)	61
17. Voix Célestes (bass No. 16)	8	(metal)	49
18. Fugara	4	(metal)	61
19. Flauto Traverso	4	(std. and open wood)	61
20. Flageolet	2	(metal)	61
21. Sesquialtera (12, 17)	2 ranks	(std. and open metal)	122
22. Dulzian	16	(metal)	61
23. Oboe	8	(metal)	61
24. Mixture (15, 19, 22) } H.P. harmonic trebles	3 ranks	(metal)	183
25. Waldhorn }	16	(metal)	61
26. Trumpet }	8	(metal)	61
27. Clarion }	4	(metal)	61

(iii) Swell Octave
(iv) Swell Sub-octave
(v) Swell Unison Off
(vi) Swell Tremolo to light pressure

Choir—Solo Organ
(13 stops, 5 *couplers and tremolo*)
(enclosed)

	feet		pipes
28. Quintaten	16	(std. wood and metal)	61
29. Open Diapason	8	(metal)	61
30. Violoncello	8	(metal)	61
31. Stopped Diapason	8	(std. wood)	61
32. Dulciana	8	(metal)	61
33. Unda Maris T.C. (bass No. 32)	8	(metal)	49
34. Flûte Couverte	4	(std. metal)	61
35. Nazard	$2\frac{2}{3}$	(metal)	61
36. Piccolo	2	(metal)	61
37. Tierce	$1\frac{3}{5}$	(metal)	61
38. Corno-di-Bassetto	8	(metal)	61
39. Flügel Horn	8	(metal)	61
40. Tuba (harmonic H.P.)	8	(metal)	61

(vii) Choir Octave
(viii) Choir Sub-octave
(ix) Choir Unison Off
(x) Swell to Choir
(xi) Great Reeds on Choir
(xii) Choir Tremolo to light pressure

Pedal Organ
(15 stops, 4 *couplers*)

		feet		*pipes*
41.	Sub-bass (ex. No. 45)	32	(std. wood)	12
42.	Open Wood Bass	16	(wood)	32
43.	Open Diapason (ex. No. 1)	16	(metal)	—
44.	Violon	16	(metal)	32
45.	Bourdon	16	(std. wood)	32
46.	Quintaten (from Choir No. 28)	16	(std. wood and metal)	—
47.	Octave Bass (ex. No. 42)	8	(wood)	12
48.	Flute (ex. No. 45)	8	(std. wood)	12
49.	Octave Flute (ex. No. 45)	4	(std. wood)	12
50.	Cornet (12, 15, 17)	3 ranks	(std. and open metal)	96
51.	Tromba (from No. 11)	16	(metal)	—
52.	Dulzian (from Swell No. 22)	16	(metal)	—
*53.	Contra Trombone (ex. No. 54)	32	(metal)	12
*54.	Trombone H.P.	16	(metal)	32
*55.	Tuba (from No. 40)	8	(metal)	—

* Enclosed in Choir Swell Box

(xiii) Swell to Pedal
(xiv) Great to Pedal
(xv) Choir to Pedal
(xvi) Great and Pedal Combinations Coupled

Accessories

6 Pistons to Great Organ
6 Pistons to Swell Organ
6 Pistons to Choir Organ
6 Toe Pistons to Pedal Organ
6 "General Pistons"

} All instantly adjustable by single locking piston on the "Willis" capture system.

*1 Reversible Piston to Great to Pedal Coupler
*1 Reversible Piston to Swell to Great Coupler
*1 Reversible Piston to Choir to Great Coupler
1 Reversible Piston to Swell to Pedal Coupler
1 Reversible Piston to Choir to Pedal Coupler
1 Reversible Piston to Swell to Choir Coupler
1 Reversible Piston to Swell Tremolo
1 Reversible Piston to Choir Tremolo
1 Reversible Piston to Tuba
*1 Reversible Piston to Pedal Trombone
*1 Reversible Piston to Great and Pedal Combinations Coupled
1 Reversible Toe Piston to Pedal Sub-bass 32 ft.
1 Reversible Toe Piston to Pedal Trombone 32 ft.

* Duplicated by Toe Pistons

1 Cancel Piston to each department—Great, Swell, Choir, Pedal and Couplers.
1 "General Cancel" Piston.
1 Piston "Octave Couplers Cancel".
1 switch "Bass toe pistons exchange—from 'Generals' to 'Swell'".
Tablet "Doubles Off"—Tablet "Pedal stops Off."
General Register Crescendo by Balanced Pedal *pp* to *ff* with indicator.
"Full Organ" by reversible Toe Piston with indicator.
Electro-pneumatic Balanced Swell Pedals—to Swell and Choir—"Willis" Infinite Gradation type with indicator.
Electro-pneumatic action.
Detached all-electric Console at east end—"Willis" drawstop type. Jambs, keys, fittings etc. all ebonised in contrast to the solid ivory drawstop knobs and keys. Pedal board "Willis" pattern with ebony topped sharps. Toe pistons of phosphor-bronze. The console can be swung to any desired angle, being pivoted.
Electric Rotary Blower. Transformer-rectifier unit to provide the low-voltage action current.

There are 45 complete speaking stops, 5 manual stops derived to the pedal and 5 pedal stops by extension, making a total of 55 registers.

There is no manual extension of any sort.

69

The Cathedral, Liverpool (1925 and later).

The instrument consists of 5 manuals, CC to C, 61 notes, and a "Willis" pedal board, CCC to G, 32 notes. There are 168 speaking stops, and 49 couplers, etc., together with 5 spares, making a total of 222 drawstop knobs.

Pedal Organ

(35 stops)

(partially enclosed)

			feet	*Wind pressure (inches)*
1.	Resultant Bass (20 from No. 2)	(wood)	64	10
2.	Double Open Bass (20 from 6)	(wood)	32	10
3.	Double Open Diapason (20 from 9)	(metal)	32	10
4.	Contra Violone (from 59 great)	(metal)	32	6
5.	Double Quint (20 from 15)	(stp. wood)	$21\frac{1}{3}$	6
6.	Open Bass No. 1	(wood)	16	10
7.	Open Bass No. 2	(wood)	16	6
8.	Tibia (from 61 great)	(wood)	16	5
9.	Open Diapason	(metal)	16	6
10.	Contra Basso	(metal)	16	10
11.*	Geigen	(metal)	16	6

12.*	Violin	(metal)	16	6
13.	Dolce	(metal)	16	6
14.	Bourdon	(stp. wood)	16	6
15.	Quint	(stp. wood)	$10\frac{2}{3}$	6
16.	Octave (20 from 6)	(wood)	8	10
17.	Principal (20 from 9)	(metal)	8	10
18.*	Violoncello	(metal)	8	6
19.	Stopped Flute (20 from 14)	(stp. wood)	8	6
20.*	Open Flute	(wood)	8	6
21.	Twelfth (20 from 15)	(stp. wood)	$5\frac{1}{3}$	6
22.	Fifteen (20 from 9 and 17)	(metal)	4	10
23.*	Flûte Triangulaire	(wood)	4	6
24.	Mixture (17, 19, 22)	(metal)	3 ranks	6
25.	Fourniture (15, 19, 22, 26, 29)	(metal)	5 ranks	6
26.*	Fagotto	(metal)	16	6
27.*	Octave Bassoon	(metal)	8	6
28.*	Contra Trombone	(metal)	32	20
29.*	Trombone	(metal)	16	20
30.	Ophicleide	(metal)	16	20
31.	Clarion	(metal)	8	20
32.	Contre Bombarde (20 from 33)	(metal)	32	30
33.	Bombarde	(metal)	16	30
34.	Bombarde (20 from 33)	(metal)	8	30
35.	Bombarde (20 from 34)	(metal)	4	30

Stops Nos. 11, 12, 18, 20, 23, 26, 27, 28, 29 (marked *) are enclosed in a separate swell box.

Choir Organ
(23 stops)
(partially enclosed)

Unenclosed Section

36.	Contra Dulciana	(metal)	16	4
37.	Open Diapason	(metal)	8	4
38.	Rohr Flöte	(stp. metal)	8	4
39.	Dulciana	(metal)	8	4
40.	Flûte Ouverte	(metal)	4	4
41.	Dulcet	(metal)	4	4
42.	Dulcina	(metal)	2	4

Enclosed Section

43.	Contra Viola	(metal)	16	4
44.	Violin Diapason	(metal)	8	4
45.	Viola	(metal)	8	4
46.	Claribel Flute	(wood)	8	4
47.	Unda Maris (FF)	(wood)	8	4
48.	Octave Viola	(metal)	4	4
49.	Suabe Flöte	(wood)	4	4

50.	Lieblich Piccolo	(stp. metal)	2	4
51.	Dulciana Mixture (10, 12, 17, 19, 22)	(metal)	5 ranks	4
52.	Bass Clarinet	(metal)	16	4
53.	Baryton	(metal)	16	4
54.	Corno-di-bassetto	(metal)	8	4
55.	Cor Anglais	(metal)	8	4
56.	Vox Humana	(metal)	8	4
57.	Trumpet } harmonic	(metal)	8	7
58.	Clarion } trebles	(metal)	4	7

Great Organ
(29 stops)

			feet	Wind pressure (inches)
59.	Contra Violone	(metal)	32	6
60.	Double Open Diapason	(metal)	16	10
61.	Contra Tibia	(wood)	16	5
62.	Bourdon	(stp. wood)	16	5
63.	Double Quint	(stp. wood)	$10\frac{2}{3}$	5
64.	Open Diapason No. 1	(metal)	8	10
65.	Open Diapason No. 2	(metal)	8	10
66.	Open Diapason No. 3	(metal)	8	5
67.	Open Diapason No. 4	(metal)	8	5
68.	Open Diapason No. 5	(metal)	8	5
69.	Tibia	(wood)	8	5
70.	Doppel Flöte	(wood)	8	5
71.	Stopped Diapason	(stp. wood)	8	5
72.	Quint	(metal)	$5\frac{1}{3}$	5
73.	Octave No. 1	(metal)	4	10
74.	Octave No. 2	(metal)	4	5
75.	Principal	(metal)	4	5
76.	Flûte Harmonique	(metal)	4	5
77.	Flûte Couverte	(stp. wood)	4	5
78.	Tenth	(metal)	3	5
79.	Twelfth	(metal)	$2\frac{2}{3}$	5
80.	Super Octave	(metal)	2	10
81.	Fifteenth	(metal)	2	5
82.	Mixture (12, 17, 19, ♭21, 22)	(metal)	5 ranks	5
83.	Fourniture (19, 22, 24, 26, 29)	(metal)	5 ranks	5
84.	Double Trumpet (harmonic trebles)	(metal)	16	15
85.	Trompette Harmonique	(metal)	8	15
86.	Trumpet } harmonic	(metal)	8	15
87.	Clarion } trebles	(metal)	4	15

Swell Organ

(31 stops)

88.	Contra Geigen	(metal)	16	5
89.	Contra Salicional	(metal)	16	5
90.	Lieblich Bourdon	(stp. wood and metal)	16	5
91.	Open Diapason	(metal)	8	5
92.	Geigen	(metal)	8	5
93.	Tibia	(wood)	8	7
94.	Flauto Traverso (harmonic)	(metal)	8	5
95.	Wald Flöte	(wood)	8	5
96.	Lieblich Gedackt	(stp. metal)	8	5
97.	Echo Viola	(metal)	8	5
98.	Salicional	(metal)	8	5
99.	Vox Angelica (FF)	(metal)	8	5
100.	Octave	(metal)	4	5
101.	Octave Geigen	(metal)	4	5
102.	Salicet	(metal)	4	5
103.	Lieblich Flöte	(stp. metal)	4	5
104.	Nazard	(stp. metal)	$2\frac{2}{3}$	5
105.	Fifteenth	(metal)	2	5
106.	Seventeenth	(stp. metal)	$1\frac{3}{5}$	5
107.	Sesquialtera (10, 12, 17, 19, 22)	(metal)	5 ranks	5
108.	Mixture (15, 19, 22, 26, 29)	(metal)	5 ranks	5
109.	Contra Hautboy	(metal)	16	7
110.	Hautboy	(metal)	8	7
111.	Krummhorn	(metal)	8	7
112.	Waldhorn } harmonic	(metal)	16	10
113.	Cornopean } harmonic	(metal)	8	10
114.	Clarion } harmonic	(metal)	4	10
115.	Double Trumpet (harmonic trebles)	(metal)	16	15
116.	Trompette Harmonique	(metal)	8	15
117.	Trumpet } harmonic trebles	(metal)	8	15
118.	Octave trumpet } harmonic trebles	(metal)	4	15

Solo Organ

(22 stops, 1 *coupler*)
(partially enclosed)

	Unenclosed Section			
119.	Contra Hohl Flöte	(wood)	16	10
120.	Hohl Flöte	(wood)	8	10
121.	Octave Hohl Flöte	(wood)	4	10
	Enclosed Section			
122.	Contra Viole	(tin) (metal)	16	10
123.	Viole-de-Gambe	(tin) (metal)	8	10

124.	Viole d'Orchestre	(tin) (metal)	8	10
125.	Violes Célestes (FF)	(tin) (metal)	8	10
126.	Flûte Harmonique	(metal)	8	10
127.	Octave Viole	(tin) (metal)	4	10
128.	Concert Flute (harmonic)	(metal)	4	10
129.	Violette	(tin) (metal)	2	10
130.	Piccolo Harmonique	(metal)	2	10
131.	Cornet de Violes (10, 12, 15)	(tin) (metal)	3 ranks	10
132.	Cor Anglais	(metal)	16	10
133.	Clarinet (orchestral)	(metal)	8	10
134.	Oboe (orchestral)	(metal)	8	10
135.	Bassoon (orchestral)	(metal)	8	10
136.	French Horn	(metal)	8	10
137.	Contra Tromba } harmonic	(metal)	16	20
138.	Tromba Réal } harmonic	(metal)	8	20
139.	Tromba } harmonic	(metal)	8	20
140.	Tromba Clarion } harmonic	(metal)	4	20
141.	*Solo Trombas on Great*			

Bombarde Organ
(5 stops, 1 *coupler*)
(unenclosed)

			feet	*Wind pressure (inches)*
142.	Grand Chorus: *Sub-unison; unison* (5, 8, 12, 15, 19, 22, 26, 29)	(metal)	10 ranks	10
143.	Contra Tuba } harmonic	(metal)	16	30
144.	Tuba } harmonic	(metal)	8	30
145.	Tuba Clarion } harmonic	(metal)	4	30
146.	Tuba Magna } harmonic	(metal)	8	50
147.	*Grand Chorus on Great*			

Played from the fifth keyboard, the action being controlled by drawstop knob "Bombarde On".

Echo Organ (prepared for only)
(4 pedal and 19 manual stops)
(enclosed)

	Echo Pedal			
148.	Salicional	(wood)	16	$3\frac{1}{2}$
149.	Echo Bass	(stp. wood)	16	$3\frac{1}{2}$
150.	Fugara	(metal)	8	$3\frac{1}{2}$
151.	Dulzian (reed)	(metal)	16	7
	Echo Manual			
152.	Quintaton	(stp. metal)	16	$3\frac{1}{2}$
153.	Echo Diapason	(metal)	8	$3\frac{1}{2}$

154.	Cor-de-Nuit	(stp. metal)	8	3½
155.	Carillon (gongs. Tenor C)	(metal)	8	
156.	Flauto Amabile	(wood)	8	3½
157.	Muted Viole	(metal)	8	3½
158.	Æoline Céleste (FF)	(metal)	8	3½
159.	Célestina	(wood)	4	3½
160.	Fern Flöte	(stp. metal)	4	3½
161.	Rohr Nasat	(stp. metal)	2⅔	3½
162.	Flautina	(metal)	2	3½
163.	Harmonica Ætheria (10, 12, 15)	(metal)	3 ranks	3½
164.	Chalumeau	(metal)	16	7
165.	Trompette	(metal)	8	7
166.	Cor Harmonique	(metal)	8	7
167.	Musette	(metal)	8	3½
168.	Hautbois d'Amour	(metal)	8	3½
169.	Voix Humaine	(metal)	8	3½
170.	Hautbois Octaviante	(metal)	4	3½

Manual stops played from fifth keyboard, the action being controlled by drawstop knob "Echo On".[1]

Couplers, etc.

171. Choir to Pedal
172. Great to Pedal
173. Swell to Pedal
174. Solo to Pedal
175. Solo, Tenor Solo to Pedal
176. Bombarde and Echo to Pedal
177. Swell to Choir
178. Solo to Choir
179. Echo to Choir
180. Bombarde to Choir
181. Choir to Great
182. Swell to Great
183. Solo to Great
184. Bombarde to Great
185. Echo to Great
186. Solo to Swell
187. Echo to Swell
188. Echo to Solo
189. Choir Octave
190. Choir Unison Off
191. Choir Sub-octave
192. Swell Octave
193. Swell Unison Off
194. Swell Sub-octave
195. Solo Octave
196. Solo Unison Off
197. Solo Sub-octave
198. Echo-octave
199. Echo Unison Off
200. Echo Sub-octave
201. Great Pistons to Pedal Pistons
202. Pedal Box on Swell Pedal
203. Pedal Box on Solo Pedal
204. Pedal Box on Choir Pedal
205. Echo "On"
206. Bombarde "On"
207. Tremulant to Choir
208. Tremulant to Swell (5-in. Wind)
209. Tremulant to Swell (7-in. Wind) (wood-wind)
210. Tremulant to Solo
211. Tremulant to Echo
212. Great Adjustable Piston Lock
213. Swell Adjustable Piston Lock
214. Choir Adjustable Piston Lock
215. Solo Adjustable Piston Lock
216. Echo Adjustable Piston Lock
217. Pedal Adjustable Piston Lock

Five Spare Knobs

[1] It does not seem possible that this section will be installed.

Accessories: Manual

Great (*in key slip*)

9 Pistons to Great Organ (adjustable at switchboard).
*1 Adjustable Piston (with locking knob).
6 Reversible Pistons to Great to Pedal, Swell to Great, Choir to Great, Solo to Great, Bombarde to Great and Solo Trombas on Great.

* These Great Pistons also control the four Solo Trombas together with the Coupler Solo Trombas on Great and also the Bombarde Grand Chorus and the Coupler Grand Chorus on Great.

Swell (*in key slip*)

9 Pistons to Swell Organ (adjustable at switchboard).
1 Adjustable Piston (with locking knob).
3 Reversible Pistons to Swell to Pedal, Echo to Swell, Solo to Swell.

Choir (*in key slip*)

9 Pistons to Choir Organ (adjustable at switchboard).
1 Adjustable Piston (with locking knob).
5 Reversible Pistons to Choir to Pedal, Bombarde to Choir, Echo to Choir, Solo to Choir and Swell to Choir.

Solo (*in key slip*)

9 Pistons to Solo Organ (adjustable at switchboard).
1 Adjustable Piston (with locking knob).
2 Reversible Pistons to Solo to Pedal and Echo to Solo.

Bombarde and Echo (*in key slip*)

4 Pistons to Bombarde Organ.
9 Pistons to Echo Organ (adjustable at switchboard).
1 Adjustable Piston to Echo (with locking knob).
1 Reversible Piston to Bombarde and Echo to Pedal.
9 Pistons (3 each in tops of Choir, Great and Swell Bass key-frames), giving Great and Pedal combinations, 1 to 9. These Pistons are duplicated in the treble frames.
5 Adjustable Pistons in fronts of Treble key-frames (and duplicated also in the Bass key-frames), giving special combinations on manuals, pedals and couplers.

Accessories: Pedal

9 Pedal Pistons to Pedal Organ (adjustable at switchboard).
1 Adjustable Piston (with locking knob).
10 Pedal Pistons duplicating Swell Pistons.

These Pedal Pistons in addition to duplicating the Swell Pistons actuate suitable Pedal combinations which are separately adjustable at a special switchboard and entirely independent of the normal Pedal combinations.

3 Reversible Pedals, duplicating Reversible Pistons to Great to Pedal, Bombarde to Pedal and Bombarde to Great.
4 Reversible Pedals to Solo, Swell, Choir and Echo Tremulants.
1 Reversible Pedal to Great and Pedal combinations coupled.
2 Pedals (Crescendo and Decrescendo respectively), actuating Great and Pedal Organs simultaneously.
Balanced Crescendo Pedals to Swell, Choir, Solo, Echo, and Pedal Boxes.

Analysis of Contents

	speaking stops	*pipes*		*speaking stops*	*pipes*
Pedal Organ	35	996	Solo Organ	22	1,459
Choir Organ	23	1,642	Bombarde Organ	5	854
Great Organ	29	2,257	Echo Organ	23	1,343
Swell Organ	31	2,374			

Total: Speaking Stops, 168; Pipes, 10,925.
Couplers, etc., 49. Gongs, 49. Spares, 5. Total number of drawstop knobs, 222.

Alterations Since 1926

"*Doubles Off*" device introduced in 1927 cutting off all manual stops of 16 ft., pitch and below, pedal stops of 32 ft. pitch and below.
Gemshorn, 4 ft. *Great* replaced Flûte Harmonique, 4 ft., in 1931.
Blowing Apparatus.—Converted to A.C. 3-phase current in 1935, the total horse-power now being 50.

In 1940 a new console was placed at the north-east side of the central space —an admirable position, not only for the accompaniment of services held in the central space, but also for the reason that at this console the player hears his giant instrument in almost perfect balance, as opposed to audition from the original console which is with the sections of the organ on the north side of the chancel.

This great all-electric drawstop knob console has its own generator (the dynamo to provide the low-voltage current for its mechanism giving 100 ampères), which, together with the remote-control adjustable piston mechanism, is sited in the basement below the console. At the same time the old 32 station swell engines were replaced by the Willis "Infinite Speed and Gradation" type, with indicators at the console.

The 1940 console provides for three additional sections:

(1) *Corona Section.* To be placed in the corona or tower for aetherial and antiphonal effects.
(2) *West End Section.* To be placed at the west end of the central space for the accompaniment of large congregations.
(3) *Central Space Accompanimental Section.* For the accompaniment of the choir when services are held in the central space.

The specifications of these sections are given below.

Corona and West Sections. These were under construction in September 1939, but the outbreak of war caused the suspension of work on the West Section. The Corona Section was completed in the works in 1940, but the violent enemy air action over the Liverpool area caused suspension of its installation in the cathedral. The entire section was destroyed at the London works in 1941 and circumstances have not yet permitted its reconstruction and installation.

With the opening of the central space the instrument can now be heard as it was planned and voiced by Mr. Henry Willis; and previously somewhat overwhelming, it is now found to be in perfect tonal proportion to the requirements of this our greatest modern cathedral.

Specifications of the Three New Sections Prepared for at the 1940 Console

All drawstop knobs are situated on the bass jamb

WEST END SECTION

Great Organ

1.	Lieblich Bourdon	(wood and metal)	16
2.	Major Diapason	(metal)	8
3.	Minor Diapason	(metal)	8
4.	Flûte Ouverte	(wood and metal)	8
5.	Pianissimo	(metal)	8
6.	Octave	(metal)	4
7.	Principal	(metal)	4
8.	Quartane (12, 15)	(metal)	2 rks.
9.	Mixture (17, 19, 22)	(metal)	3 rks.

Swell Organ
(enclosed)

10.	Open Diapason	(metal)	8
11.	Flûte à Cheminée	(wood and metal)	8
12.	Æeoline	(metal)	8
13.	Voix Celestes (bass, No. 12)	(metal)	8
14.	Gemshorn	(metal)	4
15.	Cornet (12,15,17)	(metal)	3 rks.
16.	Ripieno (12, 15, 19, 22)	(metal)	4 rks.
17.	Double Horn	(metal)	16
18.	Trumpet	(metal)	8
19.	Flugel Horn	(metal)	8
20.	Clarion	(metal)	4

Bombarde Organ

21.	Trompette Militaire	(metal)	8

Pedal Organ

22.	Sub-bass (Resultant)		32
23.	Open Diapason	(metal)	16
24.	Major Bourdon	(wood and metal)	16
25.	Lieblich Bourdon (Great)	(wood and metal)	16
26.	Octave Diapason (ex. No. 23)	(metal)	8
27.	Bass Flute (ex. No. 24)	(metal)	8
28.	Cornet (12, 15, 17)	(metal)	3 rks.
29.	Trombone	(metal)	16
30.	Horn (Swell)	(metal)	16

CENTRAL SPACE SECTION

Choir Organ

1.	Principal	(metal)	8
2.	Koppel Flöte	(metal)	8
3.	Sylvestrina	(metal)	8
4.	Spitz Flöte	(metal)	4
5.	Flageolet	(metal)	2
6.	Sesquialtera (12, 17)	(metal)	2 rks.

Swell Organ
(enclosed)

7.	Fugara	(metal)	8
8.	Cor-de-Nuit	(metal)	8
9.	Æolian	(metal)	8
10.	Ottava	(metal)	4
11.	Vienna Flute	(wood)	4
12.	Mixture (15, 19, 22)	(metal)	3 rks.
13.	Posaune	(metal)	8

Pedal Organ

14.	Gedackt-Pommer	(wood)	16
15.	Flute (ex. No. 14)	(wood)	8
16.	Posaune (ex. of Swell)	(metal)	16

CORONA SECTION

Corona Organ
(enclosed)

1.	Quintaten	(metal)	16
2.	Flauto Amabile	(wood)	8
3.	Muted Viole	(metal)	8
4.	Vox Ætheria (undulating)	(metal)	8
5.	Celestina	(metal)	4
6.	Rohr Nasat	(metal)	$2\frac{2}{3}$
7.	Flautino	(metal)	2
8.	Tierce	(metal)	$1\frac{3}{5}$
9.	Sifflöte	(metal)	1

Pedal

10. Quintaten (from No. 1) (metal) 16
11. Dulzian (Reed) (metal) 16

Swell Pedal Switches

Choir Acc. Swell
West Swell
Central Corona

Pistons

Corona Organ (Bombarde keyboard) Treble End 0, 1, 2, 3, 4
Central Swell (Swell keyboard) Treble End 0, 1, 2, 3, 4
Central Choir and Pedal (Choir keyboard) Treble End 0, 1, 2, 3, 4

Details of 1940 All-Electric Console

Couplers operated by luminous "light touches" in a row on music desk (bass to treble)

1. Choir Sub-octave
2. Choir Octave
3. Choir Unison Off

4. Swell Sub-octave
5. Swell Octave
6. Swell Unison Off

7. Solo Sub-octave
8. Solo Octave
9. Solo Unison Off

10. Choir to Pedal
11. Great to Pedal
12. Swell to Pedal
13. Solo to Pedal
14. Solo Tenor Solo to Pedal
15. Bombarde to Pedal

16. Swell to Choir
17. Solo to Choir
18. Bombarde to Choir

19. Choir to Great
20. Swell to Great
21. Solo to Great
22. Bombarde to Great

23. Solo to Swell
24. Great to Bombarde

25. Choir Acc. Sub-octave
26. Choir Acc. Octave
27. Choir Acc. On

28. West On
29. Corona On Choir
30. Corona On Bombarde
31. Pedal Stops Off
32. All Doubles Off

33. Great and Pedal Combinations Coupled

Operated by stop knobs

34. Solo Trombas On Great
35. Grand Chorus On Great

Adjustable Pistons (*M* represents manual cancel)

M. 1, 2, 3, 4, 5, 6, 7, 8, 9, 10 Toe Pistons to Pedal Organ
M. 1, 2, 3, 4, 5, 6, 7, 8, 9, 10 Thumb Pistons to Choir Organ

M. 1, 2, 3, 4, 5, 6, 7, 8, 9, 10 Thumb Pistons to Great Organ
M. *1, 2, 3, 4, 5, 6, 7, 8, 9, 10 Thumb Pistons to Swell Organ
M. 1, 2, 3, 4, 5, 6, 7, 8, 9, 10 Thumb Pistons to Solo Organ
M. 1, 2, 3, 4 Thumb Pistons to Bombarde Organ
M. 1, 2, 3 Thumb Pistons to Central Space Organ
(Treble end of Choir key slip)
1, 2 Thumb Pistons to Couplers
(Treble end of Great key slip)
M. 1, 2, 3 Thumb Pistons to Central Space Swell Organ
(Treble end of Swell key slip)
M. 1, 2, 3, 4 Thumb Pistons to Corona Organ
(Treble end of Bombarde key slip)
1, 2, 3, 4, 5 General Pistons
(Bass and Treble key checks, duplicated)
1 Locking Piston and Yale lock
* Duplicated by Toe Pistons

REVERSIBLES

(In Choir key slip)
1. Bombarde to Choir
2. Solo to Choir
3. Swell to Choir
4. Choir to Pedal

(In Great key slip)
5. Bombarde to Great
6. Solo to Great
7. On to Great
8. Swell to Great
9. Great to Pedal
10. Solo Trombas on Great (Stop Knobs)
11. Grand Chorus on Great (Stop Knobs)

(In Swell key slip)
12. Pedal Stops Off
13. All Doubles Off
14. Solo to Swell
15. Swell to Pedal

(In Solo key slip)
16. Solo to Pedal

(In Bombarde key slip)
17. Great to Bombarde
18. Bombarde to Pedal

(Toe Pistons)
19. Great to Pedal
20. Bombarde to Pedal
21. Bombarde to Great
22. Full Organ

Cancels

(Great key slip)
1. All Couplers Off
2. Octave Coupler Cancel

(In Choir key slip)
3. Other Console Cancel
4. General Cancel

The seven Swell Boxes are controlled by means of three Balanced Swell Pedals and a Multi-switch Plate.

Grand Solo
Grand Swell
Grand Choir

Grand	Pedal
Choir Acc.	Swell
West	Swell
Central	Corona

(Switch positions for each of the three pedals)
0 1 2 3

There is also a Balanced Pedal for the register crescendo and diminuendo operating Great, Swell and Pedal stops of the main organ pp to ff with illuminated indicator.

70

St. Sulpice, Paris. Rebuilt by A. Cavaillé-Coll, 1857–1862. (This is the largest organ in France.)

Grand Chœur
(C–g³)

1.	Octave	4
2.	Doublette	2
3.	Cornet	
4.	Grosse fourniture	4 ranks
5.	Plein jeu	4 ranks
6.	Grosse cymbale	6 ranks
7.	Bombarde	16
8.	Basson	16
9.	1re Trompette	8
10.	2de Trompette	8
11.	Basson	8
12.	Clairon	4
13.	Clairon-doublette	2

Grand Orgue
(C–g³)

1.	Principal harmonique	16
2.	Montre	16
3.	Bourdon	16
4.	Flûte conique	16
5.	Montre	8
6.	Diapason	8
7.	Bourdon	8
8.	Flûte harmonique	8
9.	Flûte à pavillon	8
10.	Flûte traversière	8
11.	Salicional	8
12.	Grosse quinte	$5\frac{1}{3}$
13.	Prestant	4

Positif
(C–g³)

Jeux de fond

1.	Violonbasse	16
2.	Quintaton	16
3.	Quintaton	8
4.	Flûte traversière	8
5.	Gambe	8
6.	Salicional	8
7.	Unda maris	8
8.	Flûte octaviante	4
9.	Flûte douce	4

Pédale

Jeux de fond

1.	Principalbasse	32
2.	Contrebasse	16
3.	Soubasse	16
4.	Diapason (added 1934)	16
5.	Flûte	8
6.	Violoncelle	8
7.	Octave (added 1934)	8
8.	Flûte	4

10.	Dulciana	4
11.	Quinte	$2\frac{2}{3}$
12.	Doublette	2

Jeux de combinaison

13.	Tierce	$1\frac{3}{5}$
14.	Larigot	$1\frac{1}{3}$
15.	Piccolo	1
16.	Plein jeu harm.	3–6 ranks
17.	Basson	16
18.	Trompette	8
19.	Baryton	8
20.	Clairon	4

Récit Expressif
(C–g³)

Jeux de fond

1.	Quintaton	16
2.	Diapason	8
3.	Bourdon	8
4.	Flûte harmonique	8
5.	Violoncelle	8
6.	Voix céleste	8
7.	Prestant	4
8.	Flûte octaviante	4
9.	Doublette	2
10.	Basson hautbois	8
11.	Cromorne	8
12.	Voix humaine	8

Jeux de combinaison

13.	Dulciana	4
14.	Nazard	$2\frac{2}{3}$
15.	Octavin	2
16.	Cornet	5 ranks
17.	Fourniture	4 ranks
18.	Cymbale	5 ranks
19.	Bombarde	16
20.	Trompette	8
21.	Clairon	4
	Trémolo	

Jeux de combinaison

9.	Contre bombarde	32
10.	Bombarde	16
11.	Basson	16
12.	Trompette	8
13.	Ophicléide	8
14.	Clairon	4

Solo (*Bombardes*)
(C–g³)

Jeux de fond

1.	Bourdon	16
2.	Flûte conique	16
3.	Principal	8
4.	Bourdon	8
5.	Flûte	8
6.	Violoncelle	8
7.	Kéraulophone	8
8.	Viole di gamba	8
9.	Prestant	4
10.	Flûte octaviante	4

Jeux de combinaison

11.	Grosse quinte	$5\frac{1}{3}$
12.	Octave	4
13.	Grosse tierce	$3\frac{1}{5}$
14.	Quinte	$2\frac{2}{3}$
15.	Septième	$2\frac{2}{7}$
16.	Octavin	2
17.	Cornet	5 ranks
18.	Bombarde	16
19.	Trompette harmonique	8
20.	Trompette	8
21.	Clairon	4

There are also stops for the combination action.
The chief couplers are controlled by hitch-down pedals.

71

Prague [Prag] Cathedral and Castle Church. Friedrich Pfannmüller, Hirsau, 1556–60; Joachim and Albrecht Rudner, Budweis, 1563–88.

Hauptwerk		*Oberwerk*		*Brustwerk*	
Principal	16	Principal	8	Octav	2
Octav	8	Octav	4	Quint rep.	1½
Octav	4	Superoctav	2	Sedecima	1
Quint	3	Rauschquint	3 ranks	Scharfe zimbel	3 ranks
Superoctav	2	Coppel	1½ and 1	Gedackt	8
Sexta	2	Mixtur	6 ranks	Kleingedackt	4
Superquint	1½	Quintade	16	Quintade	4
Mixtur	10 ranks	Gemshorn	8	Regal	16
Zimbel	4 ranks	Hohlflöte	8	Jungfernregal	8
Grossgedackt	16	Nachthorn	4		
Gedackt	8	Sordun	16		
Offenflöte	4	Krummhorn	8		
Spitzflöte	2				
Kützialflöte	1				

Rückpositiv		*Pedal*	
Principal	12	Principal	32
Principal	8	Principal	16
Octav	4	Octav	16
Quint	3	Octav	8
Superoctav	2	Grossquint	6
Sexta	2	Superoktav	4
Mixtur	5 ranks	Coppel	4
Salicional	16	Quint	3
Quintade	8	Octav	2
Rohrflöte	8	Sexta	2
Blockflöte	4	Mixtur	8 ranks
Querflöte	4	Salicional	16
Gemshorn	2	Nachthorn	4
Waldflöte	2	Spitzflöte	2
Sifflöte	1	Bauernflöte	1
Dulcian Holz	16	Grossposaune	32
Trompete	8	Posaune	16
Cornet	4	Trompete	16
		Trompete	8
		Schalmey	4
		Cornet	2

(This was an extraordinary organ at the time of its completion.)

72

The Old Church, Amsterdam, 1539. Organ Henrick Niehoff, brother Harman and H. van Coelen (or Covelen).

Hauptwerk		*Oberwerk*		*Rückpositiv*		*Pedal*	
Prestant	16	Prestant	8	Prestant	8	Trompete	8
Prestant	8	Rohrflöte	8	Quintatön	8	Nachthorn	
Mixtur		Flöte	4	Oktave	4		
Scharf (1618)		Gemshorn	2	Rohrflöte	4		
Trompete	8	Nasard		Sifflöte			
		Sifflöte		Mixtur			
		Zimbel		Scharf			
		Trompete	8	Krummhorn	8		
		Zink		Schalmei	4		

The stop names have been translated to modern equivalents. This was one of the organs played by J. P. Sweelinck.

73

Salzburg. Hornwerk at Hohensalzburg. Unknown builder 1502. Restored by Rochus Egedacher, Salzburg, 1754.

Sub bass	16
Principal	8
Octav	4
Quint	3
Superoctav	2

[This organ, actuated by a pinned barrel, still plays, three times daily, tunes by Salzburg composers.]

74

St. John Lateran, Rome. San Giovanni in Laterano. Built by Luca Blasi of Perugia in 1599.

I Manual (59 notes)		*II Manual* (59 notes)	
1. Principale	16	13. Principale	16
2. Principale spezzato	16	14. Principale spezzato	16
3. Principale	8	15. Principal	8
4. L'Ottava	4	16. Ottava	4
5. Quinta	$2\frac{2}{3}$	17. Quinta dezima	2
6. Quinta dezima	2	18. Vigesima nona	1
7. Quinta	$1\frac{1}{3}$	19. Flauto	4
8. Vigesima nona	1	20. Flauto in quinta	$2\frac{2}{3}$

9. Trigesima terz	$\frac{2}{3}$	21. Cornetto (mixture)	
10. Vigesima seconda	$\frac{1}{2}$	22. Quinta	$2\frac{2}{3}$
11. Flauto	8	23. Vigesima sesta	$1\frac{1}{3}$
12. Flauto in ottava	4		

Pedal "pull-downs" of 20 notes. This organ was played by Frescobaldi.

75

Merseburg Cathedral. Organ by F. Ladegast, 1853.

Hauptwerk
(20 stops)

1. Sub-bourdon to tenor C		32
2. Principal	(in front English tin)	16
3. Bourdon	(wood)	16
4. Principal	(in front English tin)	8
5. Doppel gedact	(wood)	8
6. Gamba	(tin)	8
7. Hohlflöte	(wood)	8
8. Gemshorn	(tin)	8
9. Quint gedact	(tin)	$5\frac{1}{3}$
10. Octave	(tin)	4
11. Gedact	(metal)	4
12. Gemshorn	(metal)	4
13. Quint	(metal)	$2\frac{2}{3}$
14. Octave	(metal)	2
15. Doublette	2 ranks	4 and 2
16. Mixture		4 ranks
17. Scharf		4 ranks
18. Cornet		3–5 ranks
19. Fagotto		16
20. Trompette		8

Oberwerk
(16 stops)

21. Quintaton	(metal)	16
22. Principal	(tin)	16
23. Rohrflöte	(tin)	8
24. Gamba	(tin)	8
25. Gedact	(tin)	8
26. Flauto amabile	(wood)	8
27. Octave		4
28. Rohrflöte		4
29. Spitzflöte		4
30. Quint		$2\frac{2}{3}$

31. Waldflöte		2
32. Terz		$1\frac{3}{5}$
33. Sifflöte		1
34. Mixture		4 ranks
35. Schalmey	(metal)	8
36. Stahlspiel		

Rückpositiv
(11 stops)

37. Bourdon	(wood)	16
38. Principal	(English tin)	8
39. Flauto traverso		8
40. Quintaton		8
41. Fugara		8
42. Octava		4
43. Gedact		4
44. Octave		2
45. Mixture		4 ranks
46. Cornet		2 to 5 ranks
47. Oboe		8

Brustwerk
(14 stops)

48. Lieblich gedact	(wood)		16
49. Geigen principal	(tin)		8
50. Lieblich gedact	(wood)		8
51. Salicional	(tin)		8
52. Flauto dolce	(wood)		8
53. Unda maris	(tin)	2 ranks	8
54. Octave	(tin)		4
55. Zartflöte	(wood)		4
56. Salicional	(metal)		4
57. Nasat	(metal)		$2\frac{2}{3}$
58. Octave	(metal)		2
59. Cymbale			3 ranks
60. Progressiv harmonica			2 to 4 ranks
61. Aeoline			16

Pedal
(20 stops)

62. Untersatz		32
63. Principal	(English tin in front)	16
64. Sub-bass		16 tone
65. Violin-bass		16
66. Salicet-bass		16
67. Grossnasat		$10\frac{2}{3}$
68. Principal		8

69. Bass-flöte		8
70. Violoncello		8
71. Terz	(metal)	$6\frac{2}{5}$
72. Rohr quint	(metal)	$5\frac{1}{3}$
73. Octave	(metal)	4
74. Flöte	(wood)	4
75. Scharf-flöte	(metal)	4
76. Mixture		4 ranks
77. Cornett		4 ranks
78. Posaune		32
79. Posaune		16
80. Dulzian		16
81. Trompette		8

Accessories

82–84. Inter-manual couplers.
85–87. Pedal couplers.
88–91. Four ventils to manuals } for preparing registration.
92–94. Four ventils to pedals } for preparing registration.
95. Tremulant.
96. Collectivzug to pedal (for supplying appropriate basses).
97. Calcenten (signal to blowers).
98. Cymbelstern (revolving star with bells in the organ front).
99. Echozug (reducing organ to pp).
100. Vacant.

[This was a remarkable organ and contained Ladegast's improvements in pneumatic action and aids to registration. This instrument made possible the performance of Liszt's major works. Liszt always championed the organ-builder Ladegast.]

76

Frankfurt-on-the-Main, St. Paul's Church, designed in 1833: organ by Walcker.

Great Organ

1. Principal		16
2. Viola di gamba		16
3. Flauto major		16
4. Untersatz		32
5. Octave		8
6. Viola di gamba		8
7. Gemshorn		8
8. Flute	(open)	8
9. Quint	(open)	$5\frac{1}{3}$
10. Octave		4
11. Hohlpfeife	(open)	4

Choir Organ

1. Principal		8
2. Quintatoen		16
3. Harmonica		8
4. Bifra	(tin)	8
5. Hohlflute		8
6. Spitzflute		4
7. Lieblich gedeckt		4

First Pedal

8. Principal		16
9. Sub bass	(open)	32

12. Fugara 4
13. Terce $3\frac{1}{5}$
14. Quint $2\frac{2}{3}$
15. Octave (repeating) 2
16. Waldflute 2
17. Terce discant $1\frac{3}{5}$
18. Octave 1
19. Cornet (quintuple) $10\frac{2}{3}$
20. Mixture (quintuple) 2
21. Sharp (quadruple) 1
22. Tuba (tin) 16
23. Trumpet (tin) 8

Swell Organ

24. Principal (English tin) 8
25. Bourdon (wood) 16
26. Salicional 8
27. Dolce 8
28. Flute traversiere 4
29. Gedeckt 8
30. Quint flute (open) $5\frac{1}{3}$
31. Octave 4
32. Quintatoen 8
33. Quint $2\frac{2}{3}$
34. Rohrflute (tin) 4
35. Octave 2
36. Mixture (quintuple) 2
37. Posaune 8
38. Vox humana 8

10. Contra bass (open) 32
11. Octave bass (open) 16
12. Violon (open) 16
13. Octave 8
14. Violoncell 8
15. Terce (open) $6\frac{2}{5}$
16. Quint (open) $5\frac{1}{3}$
17. Octave 4
18. Posaune 16
19. Trumpet 8
20. Clarine 4
21. Clarinetto 2
22. Dolcissimo 8
23. Lieblich gedeckt 8
24. Flute d'amour 4
25. Flautino 2
26. Nasard $2\frac{2}{3}$
27. Hautbois 8
28. Physharmonica 8

Second Pedal

29. Gedeckt 16
30. Violon 16
31. Principal 8
32. Flute 4
33. Waldflute 2
34. Fagott 16

[This large organ established the fame of the firm of Walcker. This firm built more than 40 organs in Frankfurt alone, some of which were known to the composer Felix Mendelssohn.]

77

Doetinchem, Ned. Herv. Kerk. D. A. Flentrop, 1952.

Hoofdwerk

Quintadeen 16
Prestant 8
Roerfluit 8
Octaaf 4
Ged. fluit 4
Nasard $2\frac{2}{3}$
Octaaf 2
Mixtuur (5–6 ranks) $1\frac{1}{3}$
Trompet 8

Rugwerk

Holpijp 8
Quintadeen 8
Prestant 4
Roerfluit 4
Octaaf 2
Quint $1\frac{1}{3}$
Scherp (4 ranks) 1
Sesquialter (2 ranks)
Dulciaan 8

Borstwerk		*Pedal*	
Eikenfluit	8	Prestant	16
Fluit	4	Octaaf	8
Prestant	2	Octaaf	4
Gemshoorn	2	Nachthoorn	2
Octaaf	1	Mixtuur (4 ranks)	2
Cymbel (2 ranks)	$1\frac{1}{3}$	Bazuin	16
Regaal	4	Schalmai	4

2 Pedal couplers.
2 Manual couplers.

78

The Parish Church, Oakham, Rutland, Roger Yates (1940). The organ incorporates the best portions of the old organ and consists of three manuals and pedals, with 45 speaking stops, 17 couplers, etc., two tremolos and a Glockenspiel, making a total of 65 registers.

Great Organ
(12 stops, 6 *couplers*)
(unenclosed)

1. Violone (partly from No. 35)	(metal)	16
2. Principal	(metal)	8
3. Viola	(metal)	8
4. Hohl flöte	(wood)	8
5. Quint	(metal)	$5\frac{1}{3}$
6. Octave	(metal)	4
7. Flöte	(metal)	4
8. Quint	(metal)	$2\frac{2}{3}$
9. Super octave	(metal)	2
10. Sesquialtera	(metal)	2 ranks
11. Cymbale	(metal)	4 ranks
12. Posaune	(metal)	8

(i) Swell sub octave to great
(ii) Swell to great
(iii) Swell octave to great
(iv) Choir sub octave to great
(v) Choir to great
(vi) Choir octave to great

Swell Organ
(11 stops, 2 *couplers and tremolo*)
(enclosed)

13. Principal	(metal)	8
14. Gedeckt	(wood)	8

15. Salcional	(metal)	8
16. Unda maris (Tenor C)	(metal)	8
17. Octave	(metal)	4
18. Gedeckt flöte	(metal)	4
19. Cornet	(metal)	3 ranks
20. Fagott	(metal)	16
21. Trompet	(metal)	8
22. Oboe	(metal)	8
23. Clarion	(metal)	4

(vii) Sub octave
(viii) Octave
(ix) Tremolo

Choir Organ
(9 stops, 5 *couplers and tremolo*)
(enclosed)

24. Viola da gamba	(metal)	8
25. Gross gedeckt	(metal)	8
26. Dulciana	(metal)	8
27. Waldflöte	(wood)	4
28. Nasat	(metal)	$2\frac{2}{3}$
29. Octavin	(metal)	2
30. Terz	(metal)	$1\frac{3}{5}$
31. Krummhorn	(metal)	8
32. Posaune (from No. 12)	(metal)	8
33. Glockenspiel	(metal)	8

(x) Sub octave
(xi) Octave
(xii) Tremolo
(xiii) Swell sub octave to choir
(xiv) Swell to choir
(xv) Swell octave to choir

Pedal Organ
(13 stops, 4 *couplers*)
(partly enclosed)

34. Principal bass	(wood)	16
35. Violone	(metal)	16
36. Sub bass	(wood)	16
37. Gross quint (partly from No. 35)	(metal)	$10\frac{2}{3}$
38. Principal	(metal)	8
39. Flöten bass (partly from No. 36)	(wood)	8
40. Nachthorn	(metal)	4

41. Blockflöte	(metal)	2
42. Cornet	(metal)	3 ranks
43. Posaune bass (partly from No. 12)	(metal)	16
44. Fagott (from No. 20)	(metal)	16
45. Posaune (from No. 12)	(metal)	8
46. Krummhorn (from No. 31)	(metal)	4

(xvi) Great to pedal
(xvii) Swell to pedal
(xviii) Choir to pedal
(xix) Great and pedal combinations coupled

Accessories

5 combination pistons to the great organ.
5 combination pistons to the swell organ.
5 combination pistons to the choir organ.
5 combination pedal pistons to the pedal organ.
5 combination pedal pistons to the swell organ.
1 reversible piston acting on the great to pedal coupler.
1 reversible piston acting on the swell to pedal coupler.
1 reversible piston acting on the choir to pedal coupler.
1 reversible piston acting on the swell to great coupler.
1 reversible piston acting on the full organ, with indicator.
The combination pedal pistons duplicate either the swell or reversible pistons, by switch "bass pedal pistons exchange".
1 general cancel piston
2 balanced swell pedals.
"Discus" blower with automatic push-button starter.

79

St. Paul's Cathedral, Order of the British Empire Chapel. Organ by Henry Willis, 1960.

Manual compass CC to C, 61 notes. Pedal compass CCC to G, 32 notes.

Great Organ

1. Open diapason	8
2. Rohrflöte	8
3. Sylvestrina	8
4. Gemshorn	4
5. Flautina	2

(i) Swell to great
(ii) Swell to great octave

Swell Organ

6. Nason	8
7. Gedeckt	8
8. Coppel	4
9. Quartane (12, 15)	
10. Trompette	8

(iii) Swell octave
(iv) Tremolo

Pedal Organ

11.	Sub bass (derived)	32
12.	Open diapason	16
13.	Bordun	16
14.	Octave	8
15.	Choral bass	4

(v) Swell to pedal
(vi) Swell to pedal octave
(vii) Great to pedal
(viii) Great and pedal combinations coupled.

Accessories

4 pistons to each of great, swell and pedal.
2 pistons to great to pedal reversible.
Reversible pistons to swell to great and great to pedal
Octave coupler cancel.
General cancel piston, etc.

Detached and mobile console. Pitch A.440. C523.3.

80

St. Peter's Italian Church, Clerkenwell, London. Organ by Walker, 1959.

Compass of Manuals, CC to C, 61 notes. Compass of pedals, CCC to G 32 notes.

Great Organ

		feet	pipes
1.	Quintaton	16	61
2.	Principal	8	61
3.	Rohr flute	8	61
4.	Octave	4	61
5.	Flute octave	4	61
6.	Quint	$2\frac{2}{3}$	61
7.	Super octave	2	61
8.	Tertian (19, 24)	2 ranks	122
9.	Mixture (19, 22, 26, 29)	4 ranks	244
10.	Trumpet	8	61

Swell Organ

1.	Open diapason	8	61
2.	Gedeckt	8	61
3.	Viola	8	61
4.	Celeste T. C.	8	49
5.	Gemshorn	4	61
6.	Melophone	4	61
7.	Nazard	$2\frac{2}{3}$	61
8.	Fifteenth	2	61
9.	Scharf (22, 26, 29, 33)	4 ranks	244
10.	Bassoon	16	73
11.	Trumpet	8	61
12.	Hautboy (from No. 10 swell)	8	61 notes
	Tremulant		

Choir Organ
(unenclosed)

	feet	pipes
1. Bourdon	8	61
2. Fugara	4	61
3. Harmonic flute	4	61
4. Octave	2	61
5. Blockflute	2	61
6. Larigot	$1\frac{1}{3}$	61
7. Sesquialtera (26, 31)	2 ranks	122
8. Mixture (29, 33, 36)	3 ranks	183
9. Crumhorn	8	61
Tremulant		

Pedal Organ

1. Double open diapason	32	32 pipes
2. Open diapason	16	32 ,,
3. Violone	16	51 ,,
4. Sub bass	16	44 ,,
5. Principal	8	44 ,,
6. Violoncello (from No. 3 pedal)	8	32 notes
7. Bass flute (from No. 4 pedal)	8	32 ,,
8. Twelfth (from No. 3 pedal)	$5\frac{1}{3}$	32 ,,
9. Rohr flute	4	32 pipes
10. Fifteenth (from No. 5 pedal)	4	32 notes
11. Mixture (19, 22, 26, 29)	4 ranks	128 pipes
12. Trombone	16	44 ,,
13. Bassoon (from No. 10 swell)	16	32 notes
14. Trumpet (from No. 12 pedal)	8	32 ,,
15. Clarion	4	32 pipes

Couplers

1. Choir to pedal
2. Great to pedal
3. Swell to pedal
4. Swell to great
5. Swell to choir
6. Choir to great
7. Great and pedal combinations coupled

Accessories

5 thumb pistons to choir.
5 thumb pistons to great.
5 thumb pistons to swell.
5 toe pistons to pedal.

5 toe pistons to swell (duplicating).
1 reversible thumb piston for great to pedal.
1 reversible toe piston for great to pedal.
1 reversible thumb piston for swell to great.
1 reversible thumb piston for choir to great.
3 general thumb pistons.
3 general toe pistons (duplicating).
1 general cancel thumb piston.
Balanced swell pedal.
Attached drawstop console.
Electro-pneumatic action.

81

The Minster, Basle, Switzerland. Organ by Th. Kuhn of Männedorf, Switzerland, 1956.

Hauptwerk
(II Manual—56 töne)

1. Prinzipal	16
2. Quintaden	16
3. Prinzipal	8
4. Offenflöte	8
5. Bordun	8
6. Oktave	4
7. Hohlflöte	4
8. Gemshorn	4
9. Superoktave	2
10. Mixtur maj. (5–6 ranks)	2
11. Mixtur min. (5–6 ranks)	1
12. Kornett (5 ranks)	8
13. Bombarde	16
14. Trompete	8
15. Clairon	4

Rückpositiv
(I Manual—56 töne)

16. Prinzipal	8
17. Gedackt	8
18. Quintaden	8
19. Praestant	4
20. Rohrflöte	4
21. Superoktave	2
22. Flöte	2
23. Sesquialter	$2\frac{2}{3}$ ft. and $1\frac{3}{5}$
24. Mixtur (4 ranks)	1
25. Zimbel (3–4 ranks)	$\frac{1}{2}$
26. Dulzian	16
27. Cromorne	8
28. Musette	4

Oberwerk, schwellbar
(III Manual—56 töne)

29. Gedackt	16
30. Prinzipal	8
31. Rohrflöte	8
32. Salizional	8
33. Unda maris	8
34. Oktave	4
35. Nachthorn	4
36. Superoktave	2
37. Waldflöte	2

Brustwerk, schwellbar
(IV Manuel—56 töne)

46. Suavial	8
47. Gedackt	8
48. Oktave	4
49. Gedacktflöte	4
50. Flageolet	2
51. Quintflöte	$2\frac{2}{3}$
52. Larigot	$1\frac{1}{3}$
53. Sifflöte	1
54. Scharf (3–4 ranks)	1

38. Quinte	$2\frac{2}{3}$	55. Terzzimbel (3 ranks)	$\frac{1}{5}$
39. Terz	$1\frac{3}{5}$	56. Regal	8
40. Mixtur (4–5 ranks)	2	57. Schalmei	4
41. Scharf (4 ranks)	1		
42. Basson	16		
43. Trompette harm.	8		
44. Oboe	8		
45. Clairon	4		

Pedal

(30 töne)

58. Prinzipalbass	32	67. Nachthorn	2
59. Prinzipalbass	16	68. Rauschpfeifen (5 ranks)	4
60. Subbass	16	69. Acuta (5 ranks)	2
61. Gedacktbass	16	70. Posaune	16
62. Prinzipal	8	71. Sordun	16
63. Gedackt	8	72. Zink	8
64. Spitzflöte	8	73. Dulzian	8
65. Oktave	4	74. Klarine	4
66. Flöte	4		

Tracker action to manuals and pedal. Electric stop action to sliders.

Couplers

P + HW	HW + OW
P + RP	HW + RP
P + OW	OW + BW
P + BW	

82

Newark, New Jersey, U.S.A., Cathedral of the Sacred Heart. Built by Schantz, Orrville, Ohio, 1954.

Great

(unenclosed) $4\frac{1}{2}$ in. pressure

	feet	pipes
1. Open diapason (1–32 in case)	16	61
2. Open diapason I	8	61
3. Open diapason II	8	61
4. Melodia	8	61
5. Bourdon	8	61
6. Gemshorn	8	61
7. Viola da gamba	8	61
8. Octave I	4	61
9. Octave II	4	61

10. Harmonic flute	4	61
11. Octave quint	$2\frac{2}{3}$	61
12. Super octave	2	61
13. Tierce	$1\frac{3}{5}$	61
14. Fourniture (19, 22, 26, 29)	IV	244
15. Scharf (26, 29, 33)	III	183
16. Trompette	8	61
17. Clarion	4	61
18. Chimes (from Solo)		

Swell

(flues $4\frac{1}{2}$ in., reeds 8 in.)

19. Flute conique	16	73
20. Open diapason	8	73
21. Gedeckt	8	73
22. Spitzfloete	8	73
23. Flute celeste	8	73
24. Salicional	8	73
25. Voix celeste	8	66
26. Geigen octave	4	73
27. Hohlfloete	4	73
28. Fugara	4	73
29. Twelfth	$2\frac{2}{3}$	61
30. Flautino	2	61
31. Plein jeu (19, 22, 26, 29)	IV	244
32. Cornet (12, 15, 17)	III	183
33. Contra fagotto	16	73
34. Trompette	8	73
35. Oboe	8	73
36. Clarion	4	73
37. Tremulant		

Choir

($4\frac{1}{2}$ in. pressure)

	feet	pipes
38. Quintaton	16	73
39. Geigen principal	8	73
40. Rohrfloete	8	73
41. Dulciana	8	73
42. Unda maris	8	61
43. Viola	8	73
44. Viola celeste	8	66
45. Principal	4	73
46. Flute d'amour	4	73
47. Nachthorn	4	73

48. Nazard	$2\frac{2}{3}$	61
49. Piccolo	2	61
50. Tierce	$1\frac{3}{5}$	61
51. Cymbel (29, 33, 36)	III	183
52. Cromorne	8	73
53. Tremulant		

Solo
(All 10 in. pressure except as marked *)

54. Contra gamba	16	73
55. Principal	8	73
56. Doppelfloete	8	73
57. Gross gamba	8	73
*58. Gamba celeste	8	66
*59. Octave	4	73
*60. Flute Ouverte	4	73
*61. Doublette	2	61
*62. Grand cornet (15, 19, 22, 26, 29)	V	305
63. Tuba major	16	73
64. Tuba mirabilis	8	73
65. Tuba clarion	4	73
66. Cor anglais	8	73
67. French horn	8	73
68. Chimes (Deagan "A")		25
69. Tremulant		

Pedal
(independent flues 6 in., reeds 10 in. pressure)

70. Contra bourdon (8 x 10 at 16 ft.; 12 x 14 at 32 ft.)	32	12
71. Principal (1–32 in case) $4\frac{1}{2}$ in. pressure	16	32
72. Open diapason	16	32
73. Bourdon	16	56
74. Flute conique	16	
75. Quintaton	16	
76. Echo lieblich	16	44
77. Contra gamba	16	
78. Gemshorn	16	12
79. Dulciana (1–12 in case)	16	44
80. Quint	$10\frac{2}{3}$	44
81. Octave	8	32
82. Cello	8	32
83. Gemshorn	8	
84. Bourdon	8	
85. Gedeckt	8	
86. Dulciana	8	
87. Octave quint	$5\frac{1}{3}$	
88. Super octave	4	32

89. Flute	4	
90. Flute conique	4	
91. Blockfloete	2	32
92. Mixture (4–$2\frac{2}{3}$–2)	III	96
93. Sesquialtera ($5\frac{1}{3}$–$3\frac{1}{5}$)	II	64
94. Contra fagotto	32	12
95. Posaune	16	56
96. Fagotto	16	
97. Tromba	8	
98. Fagotto	8	
99. Clarion	4	

Couplers

Great 4
Swell 16–4 unison
Choir 16–4 unison
Solo 16–4 unison
Swell to great 16–8–4
Swell to choir 16–8–4
Swell to Solo 8–4
Choir to great 16–8–4
Choir to solo 8
Solo to great 16–8–4
Solo to choir 8
Great to solo 8

Great to pedal 8–4
Swell to pedal 8–4
Choir to pedal 8–4
Solo to pedal 8–4

Two tilting tablets:
"Main organ on"
"Chancel organ on".

"Master expression".

Combinations (*Manual*) (*Remote Control*)

Great 1 2 3 4 5 6 7 8
Swell 1 2 3 4 5 6 7 8
Choir 1 2 3 4 5 6 7 8
Solo 1 2 3 4 5 6
General 1 2 3 4 5 6 7 8 9 10 11 12
Sforzando I (right, under great).
Sforzando II (right, under great).
General cancel (right, under choir).
Great to pedal
Swell to pedal
Choir to pedal
Solo to pedal
} "Off" motion to take off both 8 and 4. Left of manual pistons.
Coupler cancel (right, under solo).
3 pistons at right, under great: "Main organ"; "Both", "Chancel organ".
5 cancel tabs: one for each stop jamb at top.

Combinations (*pedal*)

Pedal 1 2 3 4 5 6 7 8 (right side).
General 1 2 3 4 5 6 7 8 9 10 11 12 (left side, duplicating manuals).

Sforzando I (right side) } duplicating manuals.
Sforzando II (right side) }
Great to pedal (duplicating).
Swell to pedal (duplicating).
Choir to pedal (duplicating).
Solo to pedal (duplicating).
"32-ft. stops" reversible.
"Master expression".
"Tremulants off".
"Main organ"; "Both"; "Chancel organ" (duplicating manuals).

Pedals

Swell
Choir
Solo
Crescendo

Mixture Compositions

Great IV

19	15	12	5
22	19	15	8
26	22	19	12
29	26	22	15
12	18	18	13

Swell IV

19	15	12	8
22	19	15	12
26	22	19	15
29	26	22	15
18	12	16	15

Great III

26	22	15	8
29	26	19	12
33	29	22	15
18	18	12	13

Swell III

12 (rohrfloete pipes)
15 (open cylindrical)
17 (open tapered)
61 (top octave of tierce repeats)

Solo V

15	12	8	5
19	15	12	8
22	17	15	10
26	19	17	12
29	22	19	15
24	12	12	13

Choir III

29	22	19	15	8
33	26	22	19	12
36	29	26	22	15
12	12	12	12	13

83

Brooks School, U.S.A. Built by the Aeolian-Skinner Organ Company, 1938, under the direction of G. Donald Harrison and Edward Flint.

Great Organ

Spitzflöte	8
Bourdon	8
Principal	4
Octave	2
Fourniture	IV

Swell Organ

Viola	8
Chimney flute	8
Gemshorn	4
Cymbel	III
Trompette	8
Tremolo	

Positiv Organ		*Pedal Organ*	
Koppelflöte	8	Bourdon	16
Nachthorn	4	Gedacht	8
Nazard	$2\frac{2}{3}$	Principal	4
Blockflöte	2	Mixture	III
Tierce	$1\frac{3}{5}$	Bombarde	16

Couplers

Great to pedal	8
Swell to pedal	8–4–2
Positiv to pedal	8
Swell to great	16–8–4
Positiv to great	16–8
Swell to positiv	16–8–4
Swell to swell	16–4

Mechanicals

4 pistons to each division and 4 general pistons, all duplicated by toe studs. Reversibles to all unison couplers.
Swell pedal.
Crescendo pedal.
Sforzando.

[An enlightened small three-manual design.]

84

Massachusetts Institute of Technology. Designed and built by Walter Holtkamp of Cleveland, Ohio, the auditorium organ was given to M.I.T. by Alvan T. Fuller, former Governor of Massachusetts.

Swell	feet	pipes	*Great*	feet	pipes
Rohrflöte	8	61	Quintadena	16	61
Gambe	8	61	Principal	8	61
Gambe celeste	8	56	Flute	8	61
Dulciane	8	61	Gedackt	8	61
Octave geigen	4	61	Octave	4	61
Bourdon	4	61	Spitzflöte	4	61
Flautino	2	61	Doublette	2	61
Piccolo	1	61	Octave quinte	$1\frac{1}{3}$	61
Cymbal	3R	183	Plein jeu	4R	244
Fagott	8	61	Dulzian	16	61
Clarion	4	61	Trumpet	8	61
Voix humaine	8	61			

Pedal			*Positiv*		
Principal	16	32	Copula	6	56
Sub bass	16	51	Praestant	4	56
Quintadena	16	Great	Rohrflöte	4	56
Octave	8	32	Nazard	$2\frac{2}{3}$	56
Gedackt	8	32	Flute	2	56

Choralbass	4	32	Octava	2	56
Nachthorn	4	32	Tierce	$1\frac{3}{5}$	56
Mixture	3R	96	Fourniture	3R	168
Cornet	32	160	Cromorne	8	56
Posaune	16	32			
Dulzian	16	Great			
Trumpet	8	32			
Schalmey	4	32			

Couplers

Great to pedal	Swell to great
Swell to pedal	Positiv to great
Positive to pedal	Swell to positiv

85

Immanuel Lutheran Church, Des Plaines, Illinois. Built by the Schlicker Organ Company, Buffalo, New York.

Great Organ

	feet	pipes
Quintadena	16	61
Principal	8	61
Rohrfloete	8	61
Octave	4	61
Waldfloete	2	61
Larigot	$1\frac{1}{3}$	61
Mixture	V	293
Trumpet	8	61

Swell Organ

	feet	pipes
Gedeckt	8	61
Salicional	8	61
Voix céleste	8	49
Rohrfloete	4	61
Weitprincipal	2	61
Nasat	$2\frac{2}{3}$	61
Tierce (Tenor C)	$1\frac{3}{5}$	49
Scharfzimbel	III	183
Krummhorn	8	61
Tremolo		

Pedal Organ

Sub bass	16	32
Quintadena (from great)	16	
Principal	8	32
Quintadena (from great)	8	
Choralbass	4	32
Rauschpfeife	II	64
Fagott	16	32
Schalmai	4	32
Tremolo		

Couplers

Great to pedal	8
Swell to pedal	8
Swell to great	16
Swell to great	8
Swell to swell	16
Swell to swell	4
Swell to great	4

Wind pressures: Manual $2\frac{1}{2}$ in.—$2\frac{3}{4}$ in. Pedal 3 in.

86

First Presbyterian Church, Kirkwood, Missouri, U.S.A. Built by Wicks Organ Co., Highland, Ill., 1959.

Great Organ

	feet	pipes
1. Quintaten	16	61
2. Diapason	8	61
3. Bourdon	8	61
4. Gemshorn	8	61
5. Octave	4	61
6. Quinte	$2\frac{2}{3}$	61
7. Super octave	2	61
8. Fourniture	III	183 notes
9. Bombarde	8	61 tubes
10. Chimes		21
11. Tremolo		

Swell Organ

	feet	pipes
12. Flute conique	16	61
13. Geigen diapason	8	61
14. Rohrflöte	8	61
15. Flauto dolce	8	12
16. Flute celeste T. C.	8	49
17. Viole de gambe	8	61
18. Gamba celesta T. C.	8	49
19. Prestant	4	61
20. Harmonic flute	4	61
21. Flautino	2	61
22. Plein jeu	III	183
23. Fagot	16	61
24. Trompette	8	61
25. Oboe	8	61
26. Rohrschalmei	4	61
27. Tremolo		

Choir Organ

	feet	pipes
28. Viola	8	61
29. Gedeckt	8	61
30. Dolcan	8	61
31. Dolcan celeste T. C.	8	49
32. Nachthorn	4	61
33. Nazard	$2\frac{2}{3}$	61
34. Blockflöte	2	61
35. Tierce	$1\frac{3}{5}$	61
36. Clarinet	8	61
37. English horn	8	61
38. Bombarde	8	61
39. Tremolo		

Antiphonal Organ

	feet	pipes
40. Viola	8	61
41. Gedeckt	8	61
42. Principal	4	61
43. Spitzflöte	4	61 notes
44. Bombarde	8	61
45. Tremolo		

Pedal Organ

	feet	
46. Contre bass	16	32 pipes
47. Bourdon	16	56 ,,
48. Violone	16	12 ,,
49. Quintaten	16	32 notes
50. Flute conique	16	32 ,,
51. Octave	8	44 pipes

52. Bourdon	8	32 notes
53. Flute conique	8	32 „
54. Quintaten	8	32 „
55. Octave quinte	$5\frac{1}{3}$	32 pipes
56. Octave	4	32 notes
57. Bourdon	4	32 „
58. Flute conique	4	32 „
59. Bombarde	16	12 pipes
60. Fagot	16	32 notes
61. Bombarde	8	32 „
62. Fagot	8	32 „
63. Oboe	8	32 „
64. Bombarde	4	32 „
65. Chimes		

Standard couplers.

87

Trinity Church, Staunton, Virginia, U.S.A. Organ built by Austin, Hartford, Connecticut, U.S.A. 1957.

Great Organ

Quintaten	16
Principal	8
Bourdon	8
Spitzflöte	8
Octave	4
Nachthorn	4
Twelfth	$2\frac{2}{3}$
Fifteenth	2
Fourniture (15, 19, 22, 26)	4 ranks

Swell Organ

Geigen	8
Rohrflöte	8
Gambe	8
Voix celeste	8
Flauto dolce	8
Flute celeste	8
Principal	4
Waldflöte	4
Octavin	2
Sesquialtera (12, 17)	2 ranks
Plein jeu (19, 22, 26, 29)	4 ranks
Contra fagotto	16
Trompette	8
Fagotto	8
Clairon	4
Tremulant	

Choir Organ

Spitzprincipal	8
Gedeckt	8
Dulciana	8
Unda maris	8
Spitzflöte	4

Rückpositiv

Nason flute	8
Koppelflöte	4
Oktav	2
Larigot	$1\frac{1}{3}$
Sifflots	1

Nasard	$2\frac{2}{3}$
Blockflöte	2
Tierce	$1\frac{3}{5}$
Krummhorn	8
Bombarde	8
Tremulant	

Cymbal (29, 33, 36)	3 ranks

Pedal Organ

Contra bass	16
Bourdon	16
Quintaten (great)	16
Gedeckt	16
Principal	8
Bourdon	8
Quintaten (great)	8
Gedeckt (choir)	8

Fifteenth	4
Nachthorn	4
Flute	2
Mixture (17, 19, 22)	3 ranks
Bombarde	16
Fagotto (from swell)	16
Trompette	8
Krummhorn (choir)	4

88

St. Elisabeth, Stuttgart. Organ by Rieger, Schwarzach-VIbg, Austria, 1959.

Hauptwerk

1.	Pommer	16
2.	Prinzipal	8
3.	Oktav	4
4.	Mixtur (7 ranks)	2
5.	Spitzflöte	8
6.	Rohrflöte	4
7.	Nachthorn	2
8.	Trompete	16
9.	Trompete	8
10.	Kornett (5 ranks)	

Rückpositiv

11.	Quintade	8
12.	Prinzipal	4
13.	Oktav	2
14.	Scharf (4 ranks)	1
15.	Rohrflöte	8
16.	Koppelflöte	4
17.	Terz	$1\frac{3}{5}$
18.	Quintlein	$1\frac{1}{3}$
19.	Krummhorn	8
20.	Schalmey	4
21.	Terzzimbel (3 ranks)	$\frac{1}{4}$, $\frac{1}{5}$, $\frac{1}{6}$
	Tremulant	

Brustwerk

36.	Holzgedackt	8
37.	Holzprinzipalflöte	4
38.	Prinzipal	2
39.	Holzzimbelflöte (2 ranks)	$\frac{2}{3}$ and $\frac{1}{2}$
40.	Cembaloregal	16
41.	Vox humana	8
42.	Mollzimbel (4 ranks)	$\frac{2}{7}$, $\frac{1}{3}$, $\frac{1}{4}$, $\frac{4}{19}$
	Tremulant	

Italienisches werk

22.	Principale	16
23.	Ottava	8
24.	Decima quinta	4
25.	Vigesima seconda	2
26.	Vigesima sesta	$1\frac{1}{3}$
27.	Vigesima nona	1
28.	Trigesima iii e vi	$\frac{2}{3}$ and 1
29.	Quadragesima e iii	$\frac{1}{3}$ and $\frac{1}{4}$
30.	Flauto in xv	4
31.	Flauto in xix	$2\frac{2}{3}$

Pedal

43.	Prinzipal	16
44.	Prinzipal	8
45.	Hintersatz (5 ranks)	4
46.	Rauschpfeife (3 ranks)	2, $1\frac{1}{3}$, 1
47.	Sub bass	16
48.	Spillflöte	8
49.	Sesquialter (2 ranks) ($5\frac{1}{3}$ ft. stopped, $3\frac{1}{5}$ ft. open)	
50.	Rohrpfeife	4
51.	Hohlpfeife	2

32. Flauto in xxiv	$1\frac{3}{5}$	52. Fagott	32
33. Flauto in xxviii	$1\frac{1}{7}$	53. Posaune	16
34. Flauto in xxx	$\frac{8}{9}$	54. Trompete	8
35. Flauto in xxxii	$\frac{8}{11}$	55. Trompete	4
Tremulant		Kleinpedal: Tremulant	

89

Nürnberg, U.L. Frau (Our Lady's Church). Organ by Johannes Klais, Bonn, 1959.

I. Hauptwerk C—a³		*II. Positiv C—a³*		*Pedal C—g¹*	
1. Gedackt	16	9. Holzgedackt	8	18. Principal	16
2. Principal	8	10. Quintadena	8	19. Gedackt	16
3. Rohrflöte	8	11. Principal	4	20. Octavbass	8
4. Spitzflöte	4	12. Salicional	4	21. Rohrgedackt	8
5. Nasard	$2\frac{2}{3}$	13. Blockflöte	2	22. Octav	4
6. Octav	2	14. Terz	$1\frac{3}{5}$	23. Nachthorn	2
7. Mixtur	4–6 ranks	15. Sifflöte	$1\frac{1}{3}$	24. Hintersatz	4 ranks
8. Trompete	8	16. Scharff	4 ranks	25. Posaune	16
		17. Vox humana	8	26. Basstrompete	8

90

Organ in the Festsaal, Deutsches Museum, Munich. Built by Steinmeyer, 1938 (op. 1660).

I. Manual C—a³ Hauptwerk		*II. Manual C—a³ Positiv*	
1. Prinzipal	16	16. Quintade	8
2. Prinzipal I	8	17. Koppel	8
3. Prinzipal II	8	18. Salizional	8
4. Gedackt	8	19. Prinzipal	4
5. Gemshorn	8	20. Gemshorn	4
6. Oktave	4	21. Nasat	$2\frac{2}{3}$
7. Offen nachthorn	4	22. Geigenprinzipal	2
8. Quint	$2\frac{2}{3}$	23. Spillflöte	2
9. Oktave	2	24. Terzian	$1\frac{3}{5}$
10. Koppelflöte	2	25. Hintersatz (5 fach)	1
11. Oktave	1	26. Quintzimbel (2 fach)	$\frac{1}{6}$
12. Mixtur (6 fach)	$1\frac{1}{3}$	27. Rankett	16
13. Trompete	16	Tremulant	
14. Trompete	8		
15. Trompete	4		

III. Manual C—a^3
Oberwerk (schwellbar)

28.	Gedackt	16
29.	Prinzipal	8
30.	Zartgamba	8
31.	Vox coelestis	8
32.	Holzflöte	8
33.	Metallflöte	8
34.	Oktav	4
35.	Nachthorn	4
36.	Salizet	4
37.	Quintflöte	$2\frac{2}{3}$
38.	Terzflöte	$1\frac{3}{5}$
39.	Oktav	2
40.	Waldflöte	2
41.	Scharf (4 fach)	1
42.	Bombarde	16
43.	Trompette harm.	8
44.	Clairon	4
	Tremulant	

Pedal C—g^1

58.	Prinzipalbass	16
59.	Metallprinzipal	16
60.	Subbass	16
61.	Ital. prinzipal	8
62.	Quintbass	$10\frac{2}{3}$
63.	Cornettbass (6 fach)	4
64.	Posaune	16
65.	Trompete	8
66.	Clarine	4

Transmissionen:

67.	Gedecktbass (aus Nr. 28)	16
68.	Quintade (aus Nr. 16)	8
69.	Koppel (aus Nr. 17)	8
70.	Prinzipal (aus Nr. 19)	4
71.	Geigenprinzipal (aus Nr. 22)	2
72.	Bombarde (C–H selbständig c–g^1 aus Nr. 64)	32
73.	Rankett (aus Nr. 27)	16
74.	Krummhorn (aus Nr. 55)	8
75.	Glocken (aus Nr. 57)	

IV. Manual C—a^3
Brustwerk (schwellbar)

45.	Quintade	16
46.	Harfenprinzipal	8
47.	Pommer	8
48.	Geigenprinzipal	4
49.	Rohrflöte	4
50.	Ital. prinzipal	2
51.	Quint	$1\frac{1}{3}$
52.	Sedez	1
53.	Plein jeu (4 fach)	2
54.	Terzzimbel (2 fach)	$\frac{1}{8}$
55.	Krummhorn	8
56.	Vox humana	4
57.	Glocken	
	Tremulant	

Nebenzüge und Spielhilfen

1–10. 10 Manual- u. pedalkoppeln (normalkoppeln).
11–14. 3 freie generalkombinationen nebst auslöser.
15–19. Einzelkombinationen für jedes manual u. das pedal.
20–21. 2 pedalkombinationen.
22–24. Handregister zu den 3 generalkombinationen.
25. Generalcrescendo als walze.
26. Koppeln aus walze.
27–28. Absteller für handregister und zungen.
29–30. Absteller für walze und pedalregister.
31. Tutti.
32. Generalkoppel.
34–35. Schwelltritte 3. u. 4. manual.
36–38. Zeiger für schwellwerke und walze.
39. Voltmeter.

Betätigung:

Knopf u. Kugeltritt (wechselwirkung): Nr. 1–14.

Kugeltritt: Nr. 15–21 und 29–32.

Knopf: Nr. 22–24 und 26–28.

91

The Cathedral Cologne (*Dom zu Köln*). Organ by J. Klais of Bonn, 1957.

I. Positiv C—c⁴
Rückpositiv

4.	Lieblich gedackt	8
6.	Blockflöte	4
8.	Superoctav	2
10.	Sesquialter	2 ranks
12.	Scharff	4–6 ranks
15.	Krummhorn	8

Brustwerk

1.	Principal	8
2.	Metallflöte	8
3.	Rohrflöte	8
5.	Octav	4
7.	Nasard	$2\frac{2}{3}$
9.	Waldflöte	2
11.	Mixtur	4–5 ranks
13.	Dulcian	16
14.	Trompete	8
16.	Vox humana	8

II. Hauptwerk C—c⁴

17.	Principal	16
18.	Bordun	16
19.	Principal	8
20.	Octav	8
21.	Offenflöte	8
22.	Quintadena	8
23.	Gemshorn	8
24.	Quinte	$5\frac{1}{3}$
25.	Octav	4
26.	Rohrflöte	4
27.	Spitzflöte	4
28.	Terz	$3\frac{1}{5}$
29.	Superoctav	2
30.	Weitflöte	2
31.	Rauschpfeife	3 ranks
32.	Mixtur	6–8 ranks
33.	Terzcymbel	5–6 ranks
34.	Trompete	16
35.	Trompete	8
36.	Kopftrompete	4

III. Oberwerk C—c⁴

37.	Quintade	16
38.	Principal	8
39.	Grobgedackt	8
40.	Viol di gamba	8
41.	Spitzgedackt	8
42.	Octav	4
43.	Koppelflöte	4
44.	Hohlflöte	2
45.	Octävchen	1
46.	None	8–9
47.	Septime	4–7
48.	Tertian	2 ranks
49.	Mixtur	5–6 ranks
50.	Quintcymbel	3 ranks
51.	Bombarde	16
52.	Trompett harm.	8
53.	Rohrschalmey	8

IV. Schwellwerk C—c⁴

54.	Gedacktpommer	16
55.	Principal	8
56.	Holzflöte	8
57.	Spitzgamba	8
58.	Octav	4
59.	Querflöte	4
60.	Quinte	$2\frac{2}{3}$
61.	Schwegel	2
62.	Sifflöte	$1\frac{1}{3}$
63.	Nachthorn	1
64.	Nonenkornett	4 ranks
65.	Mixtur	4–6 ranks
66.	Septimcymbel	3 ranks
67.	Fagott	16
68.	Trompete	8
69.	Schalmey	8
70.	Trompete	4

Pedal C—g¹		*Koppeln*	
71. Untersatz	32	89. Manualkoppel	III—I
72. Principalbass	16	90. Manualkoppel	IV—I
73. Kontrabass	16	91. Manualkoppel	I—II
74. Subbass	16	92. Manualkoppel	III—II
75. Zartbass	16	93. Manualkoppel	IV—II
76. Octavbass	8	94. Manualkoppel	IV—III
77. Flötenbass	8	95. Pedalkoppel	I—P
78. Gedacktbass	8	96. Pedalkoppel	II—P
79. Choralbass	4	97. Pedalkoppel	III—P
80. Bassflöte	4	98. Pedalkoppel	IV—P
81. Octav	2		
82. Hintersatz	6 ranks		
83. Mixtur	4 ranks		
84. Contraposaune	32		
85. Posaune	16		
86. Fagott (derived)	16		
87. Basstrompete	8		
88. Clarine	4		

92

St. John's Hospital in Bonn, Germany. Organ by J. Klais, 1958.

I. Hauptwerk C—g³		*II. Schwellwerk C—g³*		*Pedal C—f¹*	
1. Rohrflöte	8	7. Gedackt	8	13. Untersatz	16
2. Salicional	8	8. Holzflöte	4	14. Pommer	8
3. Principal	4	9. Principal	2	15. Choralflöte	4
4. Quintade	4	10. Larigot	$1\frac{1}{3}$		
5. Blockflöte	2	11. Sifflöte	1		
6. Mixtur	3–4 ranks	12. Holz-krummhorn	8		

93

St. Paul's Abbey, Oosterhout, Holland. Organ by Pels & Son (Alkmaar and Lier), 1956.

Hoofdwerk C—g³		*Hoofdorgel Positief C—g³*		*Bovenwerk C—g³*	
1. Prestant	16	11. Gemshoorn	8	19. Prestant	8
2. Prestant	8	12. Quintadena	8	20. Roerfluit	8
3. Holpijp	8	13. Prestant	4	21. Prestant	4
4. Octaaf	4	14. Fluit	4	22. Fluit	4
5. Fluit (Nr. 3)	4	15. Nachthoorn	2	23. Nasard	$2\frac{2}{3}$
6. Octaaf	2	16. Sesquialtera (2 st.)		24. Zwegel	2

7. Mixtuur (5–8 st.) $2\frac{2}{3}$
8. Mixtuur (3–4 st.) 1
9. Cornet (2–5 st.)
10. Trompet 8

17. Mixtuur (3 st.) $1\frac{1}{3}$
18. Kromhoorn 8

25. Terts $1\frac{3}{5}$
26. Larigot $1\frac{1}{3}$
27. Cornet (5 st.) (Nr. 20, 22, 23, 24, 25)
28. Trompet 8
29. Regal 4

Pedaal C—f^1

30.	Prestant (Nr. 1)	16
31.	Subbas	16
32.	Octaaf	8
33.	Gemshoorn (Nr. 11)	8
34.	Ital. prestant	4
35.	Trompet	8

Koppelingen

1. P + I
2. P + II
3. P + III
4. P + III[4]
5. I + II
6. I + III
7. II + III

Koororgel

Grondregisters: Gedekt 8ft.; Spitsfluit 8 ft.

Koor I

36.	Fluit	8
37.	Fluit	4
38.	Nasard	$2\frac{2}{3}$
39.	Fluit	2

Koor II

40.	Spitsfluit	8
41.	Spitsfluit	4
42.	Spitsfluit	2
43.	Larigot	$1\frac{1}{3}$

Pedaal

44.	Bas	16
45.	Fluit	8
46.	Spitsfluit	4
47.	Spitsfluit	2

Speelhulpen
Drukknoppen

1. 3 vrije combinaties I
2. 3 vrije combinaties II
3. 3 vrije combinaties III
4. 3 vrije combinaties ped.
5. 3 vrije combinaties echowerk
6. vrije combinaties gehele orgel
7. Nulknop
8. Zetknop
9. Koortoon
10. Koororgel
11. Begeleiding
12. Echowerk
13. Oplosser voor Nrs. 9–12
14. Aut. pedaal omschakelaar, vrij instellbaar
15. Oplosser voor Nr. 14

Voetpistons

Tutti
Tongwerken Af.
7 pistons voor de koppelingen in wisselwerking met de handregisters

Diversion

5 labels tongwerken Af.
Tremolo bovenwerk
Voltmeter
drukknoppen motor hoofdorgel
drukknoppen motor koororgel

94

Church of St. Mary, Helsingør, Denmark. Organ by Th. Frobenius & Co. of Kongens Lyngby, Denmark, with entirely mechanical action and slider chests, inside the original casework, carefully restored.

Hovedverk (9)		*Rygpositiv* (7)		*Brystverk* (5)		*Pedal* (8)	
Principal	8	Gedakt	8	Gedakt	8	Subbas	16
Rorflojte	8	Principal	4	Gedaktflojte	4	Principal	8
Oktav	4	Rorflojte	4	Principal	2	Gedakt	8
Spidsflojte	4	Gemshorn	2	Sivflojte	1	Oktav	4
Nasat	$2\frac{2}{3}$	Quint	$1\frac{1}{3}$	Sesquialtera	–	Mixtur	—
Oktav	2	Scharf	—			Fagot	16
Mixtur	—	Dulcian	8			Trompet	8
Cymbel	—					Cornet	2
Trompet	8						

Couplers

Rygpositiv—Pedal; Hovedverk—Pedal; Brystverk—Hovedverk; Rygpositiv—Hovedverk.

[Buxtehude was organist of this church from 1660 to 1668.]

95

Some Positive organs made by Walcker of Ludwigsburg, Germany.

Model A

Manual C—f^3 divided at B/c^1

A 1		*A* 2		*A* 3	
Stopped flute	4	Stopped	8	Stopped	8
Principal	2	Flute	4	Flute	4
Regal	8	Principal	2	Principal	2
				Cymbal	1 rank

Slider chest with mechanical action; equipped with electric fan suitable for connection to domestic 230–250 V supply; readily movable.

96

Model E

Manual I C—g^3		*Manual II C—g^3*		*Pedal C—f^1*	
Stopped	8	Nachthorn	4	Sub-bass	16
Principal	2	Quint	$1\frac{1}{3}$		
		Cymbal	2 ranks		

Couplers: II/I; I/P; II/P; each coupler acting independently.

Slider chests with mechanical action; equipped with electric fan suitable for connection to the domestic 230–250 V supply.

97

Model F

Manual I C—g³		*Manual II C—g³*		*Pedal C—f¹*	
Stopped	8	Quintadena	8	Sub-bass	16
Principal	4	Nachthorn	4		
Mixture	2–3 ranks	Schwiegel	2		

Couplers: II/I; I/P; II/P; each coupler acting independently.

98

Model H

Manual I C—g³		*Manual II C—g³*		*Pedal C—f¹*	
Stopped	8	Quintadena	8	Sub-bass	16
Principal	4	Nachthorn	4	Gedacktpommer	4
Mixture	3–4 ranks	Schwiegel	2		
		Cymbal	2 ranks		

Couplers: II/I; I/P; II/P; each coupler acting independently.

Slider chests; mechanical action; equipped with an electric fan suitable for connection to the domestic 230–250 V supply.

99

Kufstein, Tirol, Austria, Heroes' "Open Air" Organ in Fortress Tower. Organ by Walcker, 1926–7.

Manual I c—g³		*Manual II c—g⁴*		*Pedal c—f¹*	
1. Bordun	16	1. Principal	8	1. Kontrabasz	16
2. Principal major	8	2. Gamba—vox coelestis 2 ranks	8	2. Subbasz	16
3. Doppelflöte	8	3. Oktave	4	3. Violon	8
4. Fugara	4	4. Quinte	$2\frac{2}{3}$	4. Oktave	4
5. Kornett	6–10 ranks	5. Oktave	2	5. Mixtur	5–6 ranks
6. Cymbel	3–4 ranks	6. Mixtur	4–6 ranks	6. Tuba	16
7. Trompete	8	7. Tromba	16	7. Tromba	16
Thirteen tubular bells		8. Helltrompete	8	8. Helltrompete	8
		9. Clairon	4	9. Clairon	4
		(An extra octave of pipes for use with coupler.)		Seventeen "steel plate" bells.	

The organ has 1,831 pipes and 30 bells, the tower is 250 ft. high, above the top of the cliff and the cable connecting the console and organ is 330 ft. long. There is upwards of a $\frac{1}{4}$-second delay between pressing a key and hearing the sound. The wind pressure for both flue and reed work is 250 mm. (10 inches) and the tone near the instrument is very powerful and fierce.

100

House Organ in Munich. Built, including pipe-work, by Karl Bormann, 1956–9 in 3,200 hours.

I. Hauptwerk

Gedackt	8
Prinzipal	4
Koppelflöte	4
Waldflöte	2
Mixtur (3–4 ranks)	1
Terzsept	$\frac{8}{5}$ and $\frac{8}{7}$
Quint	$2\frac{2}{3}$
Harfenregal	16

II. Koppelmanual

III. Oberwerk
(in a swell box)

Pommer	8
Rohrflöte	4
Prinzipal	2
Kleingedackt	2
Blockflöte	1
Zimbel (2 ranks)	$\frac{1}{2}$
Terz	$\frac{8}{5}$
Quinte	$\frac{4}{3}$

Pedal

Subbass	16
Oktavbass	8
Spitzflöte	4
Gedacktflöte	4
Locatio (3 ranks)	2
Fagott	8

Koppeln I/P & II/P
Tremulanten

APPENDIX II

THE COMPASSES OF BACH'S ORGANS

	Number of Stops	*Manual*	*Pedal*	*Keyboard Compass*	
				Manual	*Pedal*
1. Arnstadt, St. Boniface	23	2	1	C,D,E-d^3	C,D,E-d^1
2. Muhlhausen, Divi Blasii (after rebuild)	37	3	1	C,D-d^3	C,D-d^1
3. Weimar, Castle church (*a*) Compenius Organ	21	2	1	C,D,D♯,E,F-c^3	C,D,D♯,E,F-e^1 (without d♯^{1})
(*b*) Rebuilt Organ	24	2	1	C-c^3	C-d^1
4. Weissenfels, Augustusburg	30	2	1	C,D-c^3	C,D-f^1
5. Kothen, Agnuskirche	28	2	1	C,D-d^3(e^3,f^3)	C,D-d,e^1,f^1
6. Kothen, Castle chapel	13	2	1	C-e^3	C-e^1
7. Hamburg, St. Katharine	58	4	1	C,D,E,F,G,A-c^3	C,D,E,F,F,G, A-d^1
8. Leipzig Organs				C,D-c^3	C,D-d^1
Thomaskirche	35	3	1		
Nikolaikirche	36	3	1		
Paulinerkirche	53	3	1		

APPENDIX III

ANALYSES OF COMPOUND STOPS

5 rank Mixture (*G. Silbermann*)

C	2′	$1\frac{1}{3}'$	1′	$\frac{2}{3}'$	$\frac{1}{2}'$
c	$2\frac{2}{3}'$	2′	$1\frac{1}{3}'$	1′	$\frac{2}{3}'$
c^1	4′	$2\frac{2}{3}'$	2′	$1\frac{1}{3}'$	1′
c^2	8′	4′	$2\frac{2}{3}'$	2′	$1\frac{1}{3}'$
c^3	8′	8′	4′	$2\frac{2}{3}'$	2′

5 rank Fourniture (*Dom Bédos*)

C	2′	$1\frac{1}{3}'$	1′	$\frac{2}{3}'$	$\frac{1}{2}'$
f	4′	$2\frac{2}{3}'$	2′	$1\frac{1}{3}'$	1′
f^1	8′	$5\frac{1}{3}'$	4′	$2\frac{2}{3}'$	2′
f^2	16′	$10\frac{2}{3}'$	8′	$5\frac{1}{3}'$	4′

3–5 *rank Cornet* (*G. Silbermann*)

C	$2\frac{2}{3}'$	2′	$1\frac{3}{5}'$		
c	4′	$2\frac{2}{3}'$	2′	$1\frac{3}{5}'$	
c^1	8′	4′	$2\frac{2}{3}'$	2′	$1\frac{3}{5}'$
c^2	8′	4′	$2\frac{2}{3}'$	2′	$1\frac{3}{5}'$
c^3	8′	4′	$2\frac{2}{3}'$	2′	$1\frac{3}{5}'$

4–6 *rank Mixture* (*Arp Schnitger*)

C	1′	$\frac{2}{3}'$	$\frac{1}{2}'$	$\frac{1}{3}'$		
c	$1\frac{1}{3}'$	1′	$1\frac{1}{3}'$	$\frac{1}{2}'$		
c^1	2′	$1\frac{1}{3}'$	1′	$\frac{2}{3}'$		
c^2	2′	$1\frac{1}{3}'$	1′	$\frac{2}{3}'$	$\frac{2}{3}'$	
c^3	4′	$2\frac{2}{3}'$	2′	2′	$1\frac{1}{3}'$	$1\frac{1}{3}'$

Pedal Mixture, 5 *ranks* (*Silbermann*)

Throughout	$2\frac{2}{3}'$	2′	$1\frac{1}{3}'$	1′	$\frac{2}{3}'$

Campanella (*Bell Tone*), 3–4 *ranks* (*Walcker*)

C	$1\frac{1}{3}'$	$1\frac{1}{7}'$	1′	$\frac{1}{2}'$
c	$1\frac{1}{3}'$	$1\frac{1}{7}'$	1′	$\frac{1}{2}'$
c^1	$1\frac{1}{3}'$	$1\frac{1}{7}'$	1′	$\frac{1}{2}'$
c^2	$1\frac{1}{3}'$	$1\frac{1}{7}'$	1′	
c^3	$2\frac{2}{3}'$	$2\frac{2}{7}'$	2′	
c^4	$2\frac{2}{3}'$	$2\frac{2}{7}'$	2′	

4–6 *rank Mixture* (*K. Riepp, Ottobeuren*)

C—B	22	26	26	29		
c—e	19	22	26	26	29	
f—b	19	22	22	26	29	
c^1—e^1	12	15	19	22	22	
f^1—b^1	12	15	15	19	22	
c^2—e^2	5	8	12	15	19	19
f^2—c^3	5	8	12	12	15	15

3 *rank Cymbel* (*K. Riepp, Ottobeuren*)

C—B	26	29	33
c—b	22	26	29
c^1—e^1	19	22	26
f^1—b^1	15	19	22
c^2—e^2	12	15	19
f^2—c^3	8	12	15

Xylophone: $\frac{2}{11}$ ft., $\frac{1}{7}$ ft., $\frac{1}{9}$ ft. (*C. Elis*). $1\frac{1}{7}$ ft., $\frac{8}{9}$ ft., $\frac{4}{5}$ ft. (*Rieger*).

Schreipfeife: $2\frac{2}{3}$ ft., $1\frac{3}{5}$ ft., $1\frac{1}{7}$ ft. (*C. Elis*).

Glöckleinton: 2 ft. and 1 ft.

APPENDIX IV

THE CHIEF COMPOSERS OF ORGAN MUSIC

Conrad Paumann (1410–1473). Germany. Fundamentum organisandi.

Arnold Schlick (1455–1527). Germany. Tabulaturen etlicher Lobgesäng. 1512.

Paul Hofhaimer (1459–1537). Austria. Pieces in various styles.

Hans Buchner (1483–1538). Germany. Fundamentum.

Marcantonio Cavazzoni (*c.* 1490–*c.* 1560). Italy. Recherchari, motetti, canzoni.

Feliz Antonio de Cabezón (1510–1566). Spain. Obras de musica para tecla. 1578.

Andrea Gabrieli (*c.* 1510–1586). Italy. Canzoni and Richerchari.

Jan Pieterszoon Sweelinck (1562–1621). Holland. Variations, canzoni, etc.

Jehan Titelouze (1563–1633). France. Organ hymns, magnificat, etc.

Michael Praetorius (1571–1621). Germany. Organ chorales and works in many styles.

Giralamo Frescobaldi (1583–1643). Italy. Toccatas, fugues, chorales, organ, masses.

Samuel Scheidt (1587–1654). Germany. Tabulatura Nova 1624. Organ masses and chorales, variations, etc.

François Roberday (*c.* 1610–*c.* 1685). France. Fugues and caprices.

Johann Jakob Froberger (1610–1667). Germany and Austria. Works in many styles.

Matthias Weckmann (1621–1674). Germany. Preludes, fugues, toccatas.

Nicolas Gigault (1624–1707). France. Organ masses.

Dietrich Buxtehude (1637–1707). Denmark, Germany. Preludes, fugues, chorale-preludes, canzonas, etc.

Georg Muffat (1645–1704). Germany, Alsace. Apparatus musico-organisticus 1690.

Johann Kaspar Ferdinand Fischer (1650–1746). Germany. Ariadne musica 1702. Pieces in various forms.

Johann Pachelbel (1653–1706). Germany, Austria. A large output of pieces in various organ forms, many magnificat fugues.

Vincent Lübeck (1654–1706). Germany. Preludes and fugues and other pieces.

Georg Böhm (1661–1733). Germany. Chorale-preludes, preludes and fugues, etc.

Nikolaus Bruhns (1665–1697). Germany. Pieces in various organ forms.

François Couperin (1668–1733). France. Organ masses, magnificat suite, etc.

Nicolas de Grigny (1671–1703). France. Organ masses, vesper hymns and toccata.

Louis Nicolaus Clérambault (1676–1738). France. Livre d'Orgue. Pieces in various styles.

Jean François d'Andrieu (1682–1738). France. Pieces d'orgue, 1739.

Johann Gottfried Walther (1684–1748). Germany. A large output in various organ forms.

George Friedrich Handel (1685–1759). Germany, England. Organ concerti and fugues.

John Sebastian Bach (1685–1750). Germany. Both in the quantity and the quality of his works the most notable of all organ composers.

Johann Ludwig Krebs (1713–1780). Germany. Preludes and fugues and other works mostly in the style of J. S. Bach.

Joseph Seeger (1716–1782). Germany. Toccatas and fugues.

Wolfgang Amadeus Mozart (1756–1791). Austria. Three outstanding pieces for mechanical organ.

Felix Mendelssohn-Bartholdy (1809–1847). Germany. Three preludes and fugues, six sonatas and a few trifles.

Robert Schumann (1810–1856). Germany. Fugues and sketches for pedal piano.

Franz Liszt (1811–1886). Hungary. Four major works and some smaller pieces.

Julius Reubke (1834–1858). Germany. Sonata on 94th Psalm.

Camille Saint-Saëns (1835–1921). France. Preludes, fugues, fantasias.

César Franck (1822–1890). Belgium, France. Three chorales and pieces in other forms.

Johannes Brahms (1833–1897). Germany. Eleven chorale-preludes, fugues.

Charles-Marie Widor (1845–1937). France. Symphonies, masses and other forms.

Alexandre Guilmant (1837–1911). France. Organ sonatas and many pieces in a variety of forms.

Josef Gabriel Rheinberger (1840–1901). Liechtenstein, Bavaria. Twenty organ sonatas and a hundred shorter pieces.

Gustav Merkel (1827–1885). Germany. Organ sonatas and shorter pieces in many forms.

Max Reger (1873–1916). Bavaria. A great output of large-scale works mostly in classical style. Many easier works, mostly chorale-preludes.

Sigfrid Karg-Elert (1877–1935). Germany. A large output of chorale-preludes, fantasias, fugues, variations and highly-coloured descriptive pieces.

Louis Vierne (1870–1937). France. Organ symphonies and many excellent shorter pieces.

Léon Boellmann (1862–1897)
Joseph Bonnet (1884–1944)
Eugene Gigout (1844–1925)
Theodore Dubois (1837–1924)
Theodore Salomé (1834–1896)
Henri Mulet (1878–1947)
} France. Many original works, some light in character.

Marcel Dupré (1886). France. Preludes and fugues, variations, chorales, suites of descriptive pieces.

Maurice Duruflé (1903). France. Miscellaneous compositions.

Jean Langlais (1907). France. Miscellaneous pieces, modern and original.

Charles Tournemire (1870–1940). France. L'Orgue mystique. Fifty-one organ masses.

Paul de Maleingreau (1887). Belgium. Passion symphony.

Joseph Jongen (1873). Belgium. Miscellaneous pieces.

Max Drischner (1891). Scandinavia. Many chorale preludes and other pieces.

Johann Nepomuk David (1895). Germany. Large-scale works in classical organ forms.

Paul Hindemith (1895). Germany, Austria. Three sonatas, etc.

Otto Sandberg Nielsen (1900–1941). Scandinavia. Classical organ forms.

Ernst Pepping (1901). Germany. Many works in large and small forms.

Josef Ahrens (1901). Germany. Choral partiti, toccata, organ mass, etc.

Flor Peeters (1903). Belgium. Large output of chorale preludes, symphonies, suites, etc.

Günter Raphael (1903). Germany. Many large-scale works.

Finn Viderö (1904). Denmark. Passacaglia.

Hugo Distler (1908–1942). Germany. Organ sonata and organ choral preludes, etc.

Olivier Messiaen (1908). France. Many descriptive pieces in original idiom.

Valdemar Söderholm (1909). Scandinavia. Germany. Improvisations, toccatas and sonatinas.

Jehan Alain (1911–1940). France. Chorals, variations, descriptive and other pieces in original style.

Franz Schmitt (1887). Austria. Toccata, etc.

Arnold Schönberg (1874–1956). Austria, America. Variations on a recitative.

CHRONOLOGICAL LIST OF COMPOSERS UNTIL THE END OF THE EIGHTEENTH CENTURY

Period	*England*	*Netherlands and Northern Germany*	*Central Germany*	*Southern Germany and Vienna*	*Italy*	*France*
1600 to 1640	W. Byrd (1543–1623) J. Bull (1563–1628)	J. P. Sweelinck (1562–1621) S. Scheidt (1587–1654)			G. Frescobaldi (1583–1643)	J. Titelouze (1563–1633)
1640 to 1680	M. Locke (1632–1677)	M. Weckmann (1621–1674)		W. Ebner (1610–1665) J. Froberger (1616–1667) J. K. Kerll (1627–1693) A. Poglietti (*d.* 1683)		J. Chambonnières (1600–1670)
1680 to 1720	J. Blow (1649–1708) H. Purcell (1658–1695) W. Croft (1678–1727) M. Greene (1695–1755)	J. A. Reinken (1623–1722) D. Buxtehude (1637–1707) G. Böhm (1661–1733)	J. Pachelbel (1653–1706) J. Krieger (1651–1735) J. Kuhnau (1660–1722)	J. K. F. Fischer (1650–1746)	B. Pasquini (1637–1707) D. Zipoli (*b.* 1675)	J. d'Anglebert (*e.* 1690) F. Couperin (1668–1733)
1720 to 1760	G. F. Handel (1685–1759) W. Boyce (1710–1779) C. J. Stanley (1713–1786) W. Walond (1725–1770) T. S. Dupuis (1733–1796)	G. Ph. Telemann (1681–1767) J. Mattheson (1681–1764)	J. S. Bach (1685–1750)	Chr. Graupner (1683–1760) G. Muffat (1645–1704)	F. Durante (1684–1753) D. Scarlatti (1685–1757) B. Marcello (1686–1739)	L. Marchand (1669–1732) J. Ph. Rameau (1683–1764) J. Ph. Dandrieu (1684–1740)

THE CHIEF COMPOSERS OF CHORALE-PRELUDES UNTIL 1750

The chorale treatments of these masters fall into the following four groups: The organ chorale, the chorale fantasia, the chorale fughetta, the chorale partita.

Period	*South German*	*Middle German*	*North German*
17th cent. (1st half)	J. U. Steigleder J. E. Kindermann	M. Praetorius	S. Scheidt H. Scheidemann M. Schildt
17th cent. (2nd half)	J. Pachelbel	J. Pachelbel J. R. Ahle J. Chr. Bach J. M. Bach J. H. Buttstedt A. Armsdorf Joh. Krieger J. F. Alberti N. Vetter F. W. Zachau	M. Weckmann J. A. Reinken D. Buxtehude N. Brahms N. Hanff F. Tunder D. Strungk
18th cent. (1st half)	J. K. F. Fischer	G. F. Kaufmann J. G. Walther J. Seb. Bach J. L. Krebs	G. Boehm V. Luebeck G. Ph. Telemann

In recent years an original school of organ-composers has arisen in America. The chief figures are Richard Arnell, Edward Barnes, R. R. Bennett, R. K. Biggs, Seth Bingham, F. Campbell-Watson, F. Candlyn, Robert Crandell, J. Clokey, Eric Delamarter, Clarence Dickinson, Richard Donovan, Garth Edmundson, Cecil Effinger, Robert Elmore, Lynwood Farnum, W. A. Goldsworthy, E. Haines, F. Jacobi, Phillip James, Harry B. Jepson, Gail Kubik, Walter Piston, Clarence Mader, Richard Purvis, Gardner Read, Myron Roberts, Roger Sessions, Bruce Simonds, Leo Sowerby, Everette Titcomb, Virgil Thomson, Camil Van Hulse, Searle Wright, E. Zechiel, Alec Wyton, William Carl, William Hawk, P. Yon, Vincent Persichetti, W. Middelschulte, Healey Willan (Canada), most of whom are still living and composing. There are remarkable pedagogic works by Harold Gleason, William Carl, Leslie Spelman, Seth Bingham, Clarence Dickinson, E. S. Barnes, etc.

There is no definite school of organ composition in Britain, but the following is a selection of names of those who have composed for the instrument in the nineteenth and twentieth centuries:

Thomas Adams (1785–1858), Samuel Sebastian Wesley (1810–1876), John Stainer (1840–1901), Henry Smart (1813–1879), William Thomas Best (1826–1899), Charles Villiers Stanford (1852–1924), Charles Hubert H. Parry (1848–1918), Basil Harwood (1859–1949), Charles Wood (1866–1926), Edward Elgar (1857–1934), Ralph Vaughan Williams (1872–1959), John Ireland, Alfred Hollins, William Wolstenholme, Edwin Lemare, F. W. Holloway, William Faulkes, Alan Gray, Harold Darke, Percy Buck, Walter G. Alcock, R. Goss-Custard, E. Bryson, Robin Milford, Purcell J. Mansfield, H. Walford Davies, Frank Bridge, Gordon Slater, E. Bullock, Benjamin Britten, Harvey Grace, Norman Cocker, Henry Ley, Edward C. Bairstow, William H. Harris, Alec Rowley, Herbert Howells, Charles F. Waters, Lloyd Webber, Percy Whitlock, Heathcote D. Statham, C. S. Lang, Francis Jackson, Gordon Phillips. Peter R. Fricker, G. Thalben Ball, Cyril S. Christopher, Robert Ashfield, Robin Orr, Ivan Langstroth, Reginald Dixon, A. L. Flay, Arthur Milner, Malcolm Williamson, John T. Brydson, Michael Tippett.

In the present century, in addition to the composers mentioned already, the following may be mentioned:

Holland

Hendrik Andriessen, Jacob Bijester, Albert de Klerk, Jan Nieland.

Italy

Enrico Bossi, Gennaro d'Onofrio, Alessandro Esposito, Giocondo M. Fino, Fernando Germani, Ulisse Matthey, Oreste Ravanello.

Norway

Conrad Baden, Fartein Valen.

Denmark

Carl Nielsen.

Switzerland

Frank Martin, Otto Barblan.

These lists of composers are representative rather than exhaustive.

Since practically every major publisher of music in the world has an organ catalogue there is available to the player an enormous amount of music composed during the last five centuries for the instrument. Moreover, the output at present is considerable. See also:

Geschichte des Orgelspiels (2 vols), G. Frotscher; *The Development of Organ Music*, C. F. Waters; *Netherlands Organ Music* (pub.) Hinrichsen; *Musique de l'Orgue Française*, N. Dufourcq; *The Complete Organ Recitalist*, H. Westerby; *The Organist's Repertoire Guide*, H. Westerby; *Music Book*, Vol. viii, Hinrichsen; *Organ and Choral Aspects and Prospects*, Hinrichsen.

APPENDIX V

A FEW OBSERVATIONS ON THE REBUILDING OF OLD ORGANS

1. An organ is not necessarily useless or obsolete because its pipes are choked with dirt, its action uncertain and noisy and its wind supply inadequate and leaky. Some of the finest organs in Europe are two or three centuries old.

2. Because of the very high cost of tin and naturally-seasoned, straight-grained wood, the value of an organ, even when it is used as a quarry for materials, is considerable. Unscrupulous organ-builders should not be permitted to purchase a good, old instrument for a mere trifle, or even "to do the church a kindness" by removing it.

3. A smaller organ, properly designed, standing in the open in a church or on a gallery, is far more effective than a large instrument, crammed into an inadequate chamber. The utmost follies in organ placement may be seen in thousands of English churches.

4. Much old pipe-work may be used with more efficiency than was possible in old "romantic" designs. Some of the 8-ft. stops may be used in higher mutational pitches, or used to augment the pedal organ. It might be possible to add a 16-ft. bass to a swell oboe and so on. Open metal pipes, except in the highest and lowest pitches, should be fitted with tuning-slides (cylinders).

5. If a proper tonal balance has been worked out for each manual, the extension upwards of manual compasses for use with octave couplers is not necessary. Octave couplers spoil tonal balance and their use should be reserved for special effects.

6. Mechanical action to the manuals is by no means obsolete. In small or moderate-sized organs it is ideal. Organ builders, who have standardised to electro-pneumatic actions (miscalled electric actions) may be unwilling to produce or refurbish mechanical actions. If possible, swell-pedal actions should be mechanical, but pedal organ, stop actions and combination mechanism may be electro-pneumatic or pneumatic.

7. Generally speaking, it is folly to rebuild an organ so that too large a proportion of the money is spent on elaborate console equipment. An organ is a machine up to its pipe feet. Only the pipe work of the organ is (or should be) heard.

8. Organs built with slider-chests cannot be converted to "extension" organs, nor would this be desirable. Separate chests may be provided for such stops as "extended" dulcianas, if it is desired to add these.

9. Steps should be taken to improve the tonal resources of pedal organs, both in the ranges of pitch and tone, and in the musical qualities of the ranks of pipes.

10. An organ should be pleasing to eye as well as ear. There are many hypertrophied organs in England, where, with advantage, a few heavy, unison stops might have been sacrificed to provide money for the adequate clothing of the instrument.[1] The House of God is not beautified by rows of zinc chimney cans!

[1] Sidney Smith, the witty Canon of St. Paul's Cathedral, said to John Goss, the organist, "You organists are like a broken-winded cab-horse, always longing for another stop."

BIBLIOGRAPHY

ADLUNG, Jakob, *Anleitung zu der musikalischen Gelahrheit* (Erfurt, 1758).

ADLUNG, Jakob, *Musica mechanica organoedi* (Berlin, 1768).

AGRICOLA, Martin, *Musica instrumentalis deudsch* (Wittenberg, 1528; 4th ed., 1545. A facsimile was published in Leipzig, 1896.)

ALLIHN, Max, *Die Theorie und Praxis des Orgelbaues* (Leipzig, 1888).

ANDERSON, Paul-Gerh, *Orgelbogen* (Copenhagen, 1955).

ANONYM, *De mensura fistularum in organis und Tractatus de mensura fistularum* (Gerbert. Scr. eccl. et. mus.) (See under Gerbert.)

ANTEGNATI, Costanzo, *L'Arte Organica* (Brescia, 1608. A facsimile, Mainz, 1935).

AUDSLEY, George Ashdown, *The Art of Organ-Building* (New York, 1905).

AUDSLEY, George Ashdown, *The Organ of the Twentieth Century* (New York, 1919).

AUDSLEY, George Ashdown, *Organ-Stops and Their Artistic Registration* (New York, 1921).

BANCHIERI, A., *L'Organo Suonarino* (Venice, 1611).

BARNES, W. H., *The Contemporary American Organ* (New York, 1925; 4th ed., 1950).

BARON, John, *Scudamore Organs* (London, 1858).

BÉDOS DE CELLES, François, *L'Art du Facteur d'Orgues* (Paris, 1766–78. Facsimile, Kassel, 1934).

BEDBROOK, G. S., *Keyboard music from the Middle Ages* (London, 1949).

BERMUDO, J., *Libro primo de la declaración de instrumentos musicales* (Ossuna, 1549).

BISHOP, Charles K. K., *Notes on Church Organs, Their Position and the Materials Used in Their Construction* (London, 1873).

BLANTON, J. E., *The Organ in Church Design* (Albany, Texas, 1958).

BONAVIA-HUNT, N. A., *Modern Organ Stops* (London, 1923).

BONAVIA-HUNT, N. A., *Modern Studies in Organ Tone* (London, 1933).

BONAVIA-HUNT, N. A., *The Modern British Organ* (London, 1948).

BONAVIA-HUNT, N. A., *The Organ Reed* (New York, 1950).

BORNEFELD, H., *Das Positiv* (Kassel, 1942).

BOUMAN, A., *Orgels in Nederland* (Amsterdam, 1943).

BOXBERG, C. L., *Ausführliche Beschreibung der grossen neuen Orgel in der Kirchen zu St. Petri und Pauli zu Görlitz* (Görlitz, 1704).

BRISAY, A. C. Delacour de, *The Organ and its Music* (London, 1934).

BURNEY, Charles, *The Present State of Music in France and Italy* (London, 1771).

BURNEY, Charles, *The Present State of Music in Germany, the Netherlands, and United Provinces* (London, 1773).

BURNEY, Charles, *A General History of Music, from the Earliest Ages to the Present Period* (London, 1776–89).

CASSON, Thomas, *The Modern Organ* (Denbigh, 1883).

CASSON, Thomas, *Reform in Organ-Building* (London, 1888).

CASSON, Thomas, *The Pedal Organ* (London, 1905).

CAVAILLÉ-COLL, Aristide, *De la Détermination du Ton normal ou du Diapason pour l'Accord des Instruments de Musique* (Paris, 1859).

CAVAILLÉ-COLL, Aristide, *Grand Orgue de l'Eglise métropolitaine Notre-Dame de Paris* (Paris, 1868).

CAVAILLÉ-COLL, Aristide, *De l'Orgue et de son Architecture* (Paris, 1872).

CAVAILLÉ-COLL, C. et E., *Aristide Cavaillé-Coll: ses origines, sa vie, ses oeuvres* (Paris, 1929).

CELLIER, Alexandre, *L'Orgue moderne* (Paris, 1913).

CLUTTON, C., and DIXON, G., *The Organ: Its Tonal Structure and Registration* (London, 1950).

COUWENBERGH, H. V., *L'Orgue Ancien et Moderne* (Lierre, 1888).

CUMMING, A., *A Sketch of the Properties of the Machine Organ Invented for the Earl of Bute* (London, 1812).

DÄHNERT, V., *Die Orgeln Gottfried Silbermanns in Mitteldeutschland* (Leipzig, 1953).

DEGERING, H., *Die Orgel, ihre Erfindung und ihre Geschichte bis zur Karolingerzeit* (Munster, 1905).

DICKSON, W. E., *Practical Organ-Building* (London, 1881; 2nd ed., 1882).

DIRUTA, G., *Il transilvano* (Venice, 1595; Chioggia, 1609).

DUFOURCQ, N., *Esquisse d'une Histoire de l'Orgue en France* (Paris, 1935).

DUFOURCQ, N., *Documents Inédits sur l'Orgue en France* (Paris, 1931).

DUFOURCQ, N., *L'Orgue* (Paris, 1948).

EDWARDS, C. A., *Organs and Organ-Building* (London, 1881).

ELLERHORST, W., *Handbuch der Orgelkunde* (Weingarten, 1926).

ELLIS, Alex J., *The History of Musical Pitch* (London, 1881).

ELLISTON, Thomas, *Organs and Tuning* (London, 1898).

FARMER, H. G., *The Organs of the Ancients from Eastern Sources* (London, 1931).

FARMER, H. G., *History of Music in Scotland* (London, 1947).

FÉTIS, F. J., *L'Orgue et les Improvisateurs* (Paris, 1856).

FLADE, E., *Der Orgelbauer Gottfried Silbermann* (Leipzig, 1926).

FORKEL, Johann N., *Allgemeine Geschichte der Musik* (Leipzig, 1788–1801).

FÖRNER, Christian, *Vollkommener Bericht, wie eine Orgel aus wahrem Grunde der Natur in allen ihren Stücken nach Anweisung der mathematischen Wissenschaften soll gemacht, probiert und gebraucht werden, und wie man Glocken nach dem Monochordo mensurieren und giessen soll* (Berlin, 1684).

FREEMAN, A., *English Organ Cases* (London, 1921).

FREEMAN, A., *Father Smith* (London, 1932).

FREEMAN, A., *Church Organs and Cases* (London, 1946).

GERBER, E. L., *Historisch-biographisches Lexicon der Tonkunstler* (Leipzig, 1790–2).

GERBERT, Martin, *De Cantu et Musica Sacra, a prima Ecclesiae aetate usque ad praesens tempus* (St. Blaise, 1774).

GERBERT, Martin, *Scriptores ecclesiastici de Musica Sacra potissimum* (St. Blaise, 1784).

GOODRICH, (John) Wallace, *The Organ in France* (Boston, U.S.A., 1917).

GROVE, Sir George, *A Dictionary of Music and Musicians* (London, 1879–90; eds. 1922, 1926).

HAMEL, Marie Pierre, *Nouveau Manuel Complet du Facteur d'Orgues* (Paris, 1849).

HAMILTON, David, *Remarks on Organ-Building, and the Causes of Defective Instruments* (Edinburgh, 1851).

HAMILTON, David, *Remarks on the State of Organ-Building Past and Present* (London, 1863).

HAMILTON, James Alex., *Catechism of the Organ* (London, 1842).

HARDMEYER, W., *Einführung in die schweizerische orgelbaukunst* (Zurich, 1947).

HARTMANN, Ludwig, *Die Orgel. Gëmeinverständliche Darstellung des Orgelbaues und Orgelspiels* (Leipzig, 1904).

HAWKINS, Sir John, *A General History of the Science and Practice of Music* (London, 1776).

HAYNE, L. G., *Hints on the Purchase of an Organ* (London, 1867).

HELMHOLTZ, Hermann L. F. Von, *Die Lehre von den Tonempfindungen als physiologische Grundlage fur die Theorie der Musik* (Brunswick, 1865. Eng. Trans. by Ellis, 1872: *On the Sensations of tone*).

HEMSTOCK, A., *On Tuning the Organ* (Weekes, 1876).

HICKMANN, H., *Das Portativ* (Kassel, 1930).

HILL, A. G., *The Organs and Organ Cases of the Middle Ages and Renaissance* (London, 1883).

HINTON, John William, *Facts about Organs* (London, 1882).

HINTON, John William, *Organ Construction* (London, 1900).

HINTON, John William, *Story of the Electric Organ* (London, 1909).

HOPKINS, EDWARD JOHN and RIMBAULT, E. F., *The Organ: Its History and Construction* (London, 1855; 3rd ed. 1877).

HOPE-JONES, R., *Recent Developments in Organ Building* (New York, 1904).

HULL, A. Eaglefield, *Organ Playing: Its Technique and Expression* (London, 1911).

HURÉ, J., *L'Esthetique de l'Orgue* (Paris, 1925).

KAUFMANN, W., *Der Orgelprospekt* (Mainz, 1938; 2nd ed., 1949).

KELLER, H., *Die Kunst des Orgelspiels* (Leipzig, 1941).

KIRCHER, Athanasius, *Musurgia universalis: sive ars magna consoni et dissoni in X libros digesta* (Rome, 1650).

KIRCHER, Athanasius, *Phonurgia nova: sive Conjugium mechanico-physicum artis et naturae* (Kempten, 1673).

KLOTZ, H, *Uber die Orgelkunst, der Gotik, der Renaissance und des Barock*, (Kassel, 1934).

KLOTZ, H., *Das Buch von der Orgel* (Kassel und Basel, 1955).

KNAPP, W. H. C., *Het Orgel* (Amsterdam, 1952).

JAHNN, H. H., *Die Orgel* (*Melos. Jahrgang* 14) (Berlin, 1925).

KRAFT, W., *Das Lübecker Orgelbuch* (Lübeck, 1930; 2nd ed., 1949).

LAFAGE, J. A. de, *Orgue de l'Eglise Royale de St. Denis* (Paris, 1845).

LAHEE, Henry C., *The Organ and its Masters* (London, 1909).

LAUKHUFF, Aug., *Katalog der Orgelregister* (Weikersheim, 1956).

LEWIS, T. C., *Organ Building and Bell Founding* (London, 1871), 6th ed. 1883.

LEWIS. Walter and Thomas, *Modern Organ Building* (London, 1911).

LOCHER, Carl, *An Explanation of the Organ Stops with Hints for Effective Combinations* (London, 1888).

LOOTENS, C., *Aanmerking over de oudate Orgelen* (*c.* 1760).

MACE, Thomas, *Musick's Monument* (London and Cambridge, 1676; facsimile, Paris, 1958).

MACRORY, Edmund, *A Few Notes on the Temple Organ* (London, 1861).

MAHRENHOLZ, C., *Die Orgelregister: ihre Geschichte und ihr Bau* (Kassel, 1930).

MAHRENHOLZ, C., *Die Berechnung der Orgelpfeifen Mensuren* (Kassel, 1938).

MATTHESON, Johann, *Der vollkommene Kapellmeister* (Hamburg, 1739).

MAYES, Stanley, *An Organ for the Sultan* (London, 1954).

MERCER, D. M. A., "The Voicing of Organ Flue Pipes", *J. Acoust. S. America*, vol. xxiii, no. 1.

MERKLIN, A., *Organologia* (Madrid, 1924).

MERSENNE, M., *L'Harmonie Universelle*, vol. ii (Paris, 1637).

MUEREN (van der), *Het orgel in der Nederlanden* (Leuven, 1931).

MILLER, George Laing, *The Recent Revolution in Organ Building* (New York, 1909).

MOSER, L., *Gottfried Silbermann, der Orgelbauer* (Langensalza, 1857).

MOSER, L., *Das Brüderpaar, die Orgelbaumeister Andreas und Gottfried Silbermann* (Freiberg, 1861).

NIEDT, Friedrich E., *Musikalische Handleitung* (Hamburg, 1721).

NORBURY, John, *The Box of Whistles* (London, 1877).

PEARCE, Charles W., *Notes on English Organs of the Period 1800–1810, Cathedral, Collegiate, Parochial and Otherwise, Taken Chiefly from the MS. of Henry Leffler* (London, 1911).

PEARCE, Charles W., *Notes on Old London City Churches, Their Organs, Organists, and Musical Associations* (London, 1911).

PESCHARD, A., *Application de l'électricité aux grandes orgues* (Caen, 1865).

PESCHARD, A., *Les premières applications de l'électricité aux grandes orgues* (Paris, 1890).

PFATTEICHER, C., *John Redford* (Kassel, 1935).

PIRRO, A., *L'Orgue de J. S. Bach* (Paris, 1895).

POLE, William, *Musical Instruments in the Great Industrial Exhibition of 1851* (London, 1851).

PRAETORIUS, Michael, *Syntagma musicum* (Wolfenbüttel, 1619).

RAUGEL, Félix, *Les Grandes Orgues des Eglises de Paris et du Département de la Seine* (Paris, 1927).

ROBERTSON, Frederick E., *A Practical Treatise on Organ Building* (London, 1897).

RUBARDT, P., *Alte Orgeln Erklingen Wieder* (Kassel, 1937).

SCHLICK, Arnold, *Spiegel der Orgelmacher und Organisten allen Stifften und Kirche so Orgel halte oder machenlassen hochnutzlich* (Mainz, 1511. Reprints, Mainz, 1936, 1938).

SCHLICK, Arnold, *Tabulaturen etlicher Lobgesang und Liedlein uff die Orgeln und Lauten* (Heidelberg, 1512).

SCHNEIDER, THEKLA, *Die Orgelbauerfamilie Compenius in Archiv für Musik forschung*, vol. ii (Berlin 1937).

SCHOLES, P., *The Puritans and Music* (Oxford, 1937).

SCHWEITZER, Albert, *Deutsche und Französische Orgelbaukunst und Orgelkunst* (Leipzig, 1906).

SEIDEL, Johann Julius, *Die Orgel und ihr Bau* (Breslau, 1843, 4th ed. 1887).

SERVIÈRES, G., *La Décoration Artistique du Buffet de l'orgue* (Paris, 1928).

SKINNER, Ernest M., *The Modern Organ* (New York, 1917).

SMETS, P., *Neuzeitlicher Orgelbau* (Mainz, 1947).

SMETS, P., *Die Orgelregister* (2nd ed., Mainz, 1946).

SPONSEL, Johann U., *Orgelhistorie* (Nuremburg, 1771).

STATHAM, Heathcote, *The Organ and Its Position in Musical Art* (London, 1909).

SUMNER, W. L., *The Organs of St. Paul's Cathedral* (London, 1930).

SUMNER, W. L., *Henry Willis* (London, 1957).

SUMNER, W. L., *The Organs of Bach* (in *Music Book* VIII, London, 1954).

SUTTON, Frederick Heathcote, *Church Organs* (London, 1872).

SUTTON, Sir John, *A Short Account of Organs Built in England from the Reign of King Charles the Second to the Present Time* (London, 1847).

THEOBALD, WILHELM, *Technik des Kunsthandwerks im zehnten Jahrhundert: Des Theophilus Presbyter Diversarum Artium Schedula in Auswahl* (Berlin, 1933).

TÖPFER, Johann Gottlob, *Lehrbuch der Orgelbaukunst nach den besten Methoden älterer und neueren in ihrem Fache ausgezeichneter Orgelbaumeiste und begründet auf mathematische und physikalische Gesetzen* (Weimar, 1855; New Edition, Mainz, 1945).

TRUETTE, Everett E., *Organ Registration* (Boston, U.S.A., 1919).

VIRDUNG, S., *Musica getutscht und ausgezogen* (Strasburg, 1511).

WARMAN, John W., *The Organ: Its Compass, Tablature, and Short and Incomplete Octaves* (London, 1884).

WARMAN, John W., *The Organ: Writings and Other Utterances on Its Structure, History, Procural, Capabilities, etc.* (London, 1901–4).

WEDGWOOD, James Ingall, *A Comprehensive Dictionary of Organ Stops, English and Foreign, Ancient and Modern* (London, 1905).

WEDGWOOD, James Ingall, *Continental Organs and Their Makers* (London, 1910).

WERCKMEISTER, Andreas, *Orgelprobe* (Frankfort, 1681 and 1698; Eng. trans. Sumner, Andover, 1953).

WERCKMEISTER, Andreas, *Musikalische Temperatur* (Frankfort, 1691).

WERCKMEISTER, Andreas, *Organum Groningense redivivum* (Quedlinburg, 1704).

WHITWORTH, R., *The Electric Organ* (3rd. ed., London, 1948).

WHITWORTH, R., *The Cinema and Theatre Organ* (London, 1934).

WICKS, Mark, *Organ Building for Amateurs* (London, 1887).

WILLIAMS, C. F. Abdy, *The Story of the Organ* (London, 1903).

SUPPLEMENTARY LIST

ADELUNG, Wolfgang, *Einführing in der Orgelbau* (Leipzig, 1955).

ADELUNG, Wolfgang, *Elektronen instrument und Pfeifenorgel* (Berlin, 1956).

ALBERTI, L., *L'organo nelle sue attinenze colla musica sacra, appunti di storia organaria* (Milano, 1889).

ALBRECHT, Felix, *Die Orgel. Ein Alt-deutsches Spiel* (Berlin, 1937).

AMEZUA, Aquilino, *La Catedral de Sevilla y sus organos* (Barcelona, 1899).

ANDERSEN, Paul Gerh., *Orglet* (Copenhagen, 1929).

ANDERSEN, Paul Gerh., *Orgelbogen* (Copenhagen, 1955).

ANTONY, Joseph, *Geschichtliche Darstellung der Enstehung und Vervollkommnung der Orgel* (Münster, 1832).

APEL, Willi, *Early history of the organ in "Speculum"* (Cambridge, 1948).

ARRIGONI, Luigi, *Organografia ossia descrizione degli instrumenti musicali antichi* (Milan, 1881).

BAUMANN, O., *Die Orgel, ihre Geschichte und ihr Bau* (Leipzig, 1887).

BEDWELL, G. G., *The Evolution of the Organ* (London, 1907).

BENDELER, Joh. Philipp., *Organopoeia, oder Unterweisung wie eine Orgel nach ihren Hauptstücken aus wahren mathem. Gründen zu erbauen sei* (Frankfurt und Leipzig, 1690 and 1739).

BIE, Oskar, *Klavier, Orgel und Harmonium* (Leipzig, 1910 and 1921).

BIEDERMANN, Hans, *Aktuelle Orgelbaufragen* (Kassel, 1927–29).

BIERMANN, J. H., *Organographia Hildesiensis specialis* (Hildesheim, 1738).

BIOVIA, Giambattista, *Pel nuovo Organs, opera di Signori Serassi Sanctuario del Conciliso* (Como, 1808).

BLEW, W. C. A., *Organs and Organists in Parish Churches* (London, 1878).

BLUME, Friedrich, *Michael Praetorius und Eseias Compenius Orgeln Verdingnis* (Wolfenbüttel, 1934).

BONDT, L. and LYR, R., *Histoire de l'Orgue* (Brussels, 1924).

BONITZ, Eberhard, *Das Positiv und die Orgel der Zukunft* (Dresden, 1944; Ellwangen, 1951).

BONUZZI, Antonia, *Alcunni Scritti sopra la Questione della Riforma dell' Organo in Italia* (Verona, 1885).

BONUZZI, Antonia, *Saggio di una storia dell'arte organaria in Italia nei tempi moderni* (Milano, 1889).

BONY, Louis, *Une excursion dans l'orgue* (Paris, 1892).

BÖSKEN, F., *Die orgelbaufamilie Stumm* (Mainz, 1960).

BOUMAN, A., *Kort begrip van den orgelbouw* (Organum I) (Amsterdam, 1939, 1941, 1953).

BOURDON, G., *Orgue et acoustique* (Paris, 1932).

BOYLE, W. H., *The Art of Pipe Organ Tuning* (Syracuse).

BREE, Petrus de, *Moderne orgelbouwkunst in Nederland* (Tilburg, 1935).

BROADHOUSE, J., *The Organ Viewed from Within* (New York, 1914 and London, 1926).

BROOKSBANK, J., *The Organ's Echo* (London, 1641).

BROOKSBANK, J., *The Organ's Funeral* (London, 1642).

BROOKSBANK, J., *The Holy Harmony* (London, 1643).

BROOKSBANK, J., *The Well-tuned Organ* (London, 1660).

BROSSET, Jules, *J. B. Isnard, facteur de grandes orgues au* 18*e siècle, 1726–1800* (Blois, 1921).

BRUGGER, Columban, *Ein Beitrag zur Geschichte des Orgel-baues im 19. Jahrhundert* (Wijl, 1894).

BRUNOLD, Paul, *Le grand orgue de St. Gervais à Paris* (Paris, 1934).

BRUSONI, E., *Il moderno organo italiano* (Milano, 1887).

BUCK, Dudley, *The Influence of the Organ in History* (London, 1882 and 1911).

BÜHLER, Franz G., *Etwas über Musik, die Orgel und ihre Erfindung* (Augsburg, 1811).

BULYOVSKY DE DULIOZ, M., *De emendatione Organorum, order kurze Vorstellung von Verbesserung des Orgelwerkes* (Strassburg, 1680).

BUNK, Gerard, *Liebe zur Orgel* (Dortmund, 1958).

BURGEMEISTER, L., *Der Orgeban in Schlesien* (Strassburg, 1925).

CALLA, M., *Rapport sur la construction et facture de grandes orgues de Cavaillé-Coll* (Paris, 1854).

CAUS, Sal. de, *Les Raisons des Forces mouvantes, avec diverses Machines* (Part III on Organ-building) (Frankfurt, 1615).

CARUSTIUS, C. E., *Examen Organi Pneumatici* (Cüstrin, 1683).

CERF, G. le and LABANDE, R., *Les traités d'Henri Arnaut de Zwolle et de divers anonymes* (Paris, 1932).

CHRIST, Friedrich, *Die Einrichtung der Kirchenorgel* (Nördlingen, 1882).

CHRYSANDER, W. C. J., *Historische Untersuchungen von der Kirchenorgel* (Rinteln, 1755).

CLARKE, William Horatio, *An Outline of the Structure of the Pipe Organ* (Boston, 1877).

CLARKE, William Horatio, *Concerning Organ Mixtures* (Boston, 1899).

CLARKE, William Horatio, *Standard Organ Building* (Boston, 1913).

CLERK, Adrian le, *Recueil de Proces-Verbal de Reception et d'Inauguration d'Orgues et notice sur les travaux executes dans les ateliers de Société Anonyme Etablissements Merklin-Schütze* (Paris, 1863).

CONGRESS REPORTS

Internationales Regulativ für Orgelbau (Wien 25–29 Mai 1909) (Leipzig, 1909).

Réglement géneral international pour la facture d'orgues (Leipzig und Wien, 1909).

Beiträge zur Organistentagung Hamburg–Lübeck, 6–8 Juli, 1925 (Klecken, 1925).

Bericht über die Freiburger Tagung für Deutsche Orgelkunst, W. Gurlitt (Augsburg, 1926).

Bericht über die 3e Tagung für Deutsche Orgelkunst in Freiberg i. Sa 2–7 Oktober, 1927. C. Mahrenholz (Kassel, 1928).

Die Tagung für Orgelbau in Berlin vom 27–29 September, 1928. J. Biehle (Kassel, 1929).

(Reports were also printed of congresses in Amsterdam, September 1931, Strasbourg, May 1932, Freiburg 1938 (Kassel 1939), Ochsenhausen 1951. The Gesellschaft der Orgelfreunde (G.D.O. W. Supper) publish from time to time accounts of their congresses on organ design, organ history, etc.)

CONWAY, M. P., *Playing a Church Organ* (London, 1949).

CORTUM, Th., *Die Orgelwerke der Ev. Luth. Kirche im Hamburgischen Staate* Kassel, 1928).

DAVID, Werner, *Gestaltungsformen des modernen Orgelprospektes* (Berlin, 1951).

DAVID, Werner, *Joh. Seb. Bach's Orgeln* (Berlin, 1951).

DUFOURCQ, Norbert, *Les Cliquot, facteurs d'orgues du Roy* (Paris, 1942).

DUFOURCQ, Norbert, *Jean de Joyeuse* (Paris, 1957).

EBERSTALLER, Oskar, *Orgeln und Orgelbauer in Oesterreich* (Graz, 1955).

EICHLER, C., *Die Orgel, ihre Beschreibung, Behandlung und Geschichte* (Stuttgart, 1858).

ELIS, Carl, *Neuere Orgeldispositionen* (Kassel, 1930).

ELIS, Carl, *Orgelwörterbuch* (Kassel, 1933).

ENGEL, D. H., *Beitrag zur Geschichte des Orgelbauwesens. Denkschrift zur Einweihung der durch Fr. Ladegast erbauten Dom-Orgel zu Merseburg, nebst Dispositionen ders* (Erfurt, 1855).

FAGE, J. A. de la, *Orgue de l'église Royale de St. Denis* (Paris, 1845).

FAUST, Oliver C., *A Treatise on the Construction, Repairing and Tuning the Organ* (Boston, 1949).

FINK, Friedrich, *Die elektrische Orgeltraktur* (Stuttgart, 1909).

FLEURY, Paul de, *Dictionnaire biographique des facteurs d'orgues nés ou ayant travaillé en France* (Paris, 1926).

FLIGHT, Benjamin, *Practical Theory and Instruction to Tune the Organ o Pianoforte* (London, 1818).

FRENZEL, Robert, *Die Orgel und ihre Meister* (Dresden, 1894).

FRIIS, Neils, *Orgelbygning i Danmark* (København, 1949).

FRITZ, Barthold, *Anweisung, wie man Klaviere, Clavecins und Orgeln nach einer mechanischen Art in allen 12 Tonen gleich rein stimmen könne, dass auch solchen allen sowohl dur und moll wohlklingend zu spielen sei* (Leipzig, 1756).

FROTSCHER, Gotthold, *Die Orgel* (Leipzig, 1927).

FROTSCHER, Gotthold, *Geschichte des Orgelspiels* (Berlin, 1934 and 1959).

FROTSCHER, Gotthold, *Deutsche Orgeldispositionen aus 5 Jahrhunderte* (Wolfenbüttel, 1939).

GÄRTNER, Rudolf, *Gottfried Silbermann, der Orgelbauer* (Dresden, 1938).

GEER, E. H., *Organ Registration in Theory and Practice* (New York, 1959).

GESSNER, A., *Zur elsässich-neudeutschen Orgelreform* (Strassburg, 1912).

GIROD, P. L., *Connaissance pratique de la facture des grandes orgues* (Namur, 1875).

GRAAF, G. A. C. de, *Literatuur over het orgel* (*Literature on the organ*) (Amsterdam, 1958).

GRABNER, Franz, *Die moderne Orgel* (Graz, 1912).

GRABNER, Hermann, *Die Kunst der Orgelbaues* (Berlin, 1958).

GRAY, Alan, *The Modern Organ* (London, 1913).

GUERICKE, Walrad, *Die Orgel und ihre Meister* (Braunschweig, 1923).

HAACKE, Walter, *Orgeln* (pub. Langewiesche, 1959).

HARDOUIN, Pierre, *Le grand orgue de St. Gervais à Paris* (Paris, 1949).

HAUPT, Rudolf, *Zur Situation der Orgel in Deutschland* (Northeim, 1953).

HAUPT, Rudolf, *Die Orgel im evangelischen Kultraum in Geschichte und Gegenwart* (Northeim, 1954).

HILES, J., *Catechism of the Organ* (London, 1876).

HOPKINS, Edw. John, *The English Mediaeval Church Organ* (Exeter, 1888).

HUYGENS, Constantijn, *Gebruyck of ongebruyck van 't orgel in de kerchen der Vereenighde Nederlanden* (Leiden, 1641).

INGERSLEV, Fritz and FROBENIUS, Walther, *Some Measurements of the end-corrections and Acoustic Spectra of Cylindrical Open Flue Organ Pipes* (København, 1947).

JAHN, Hans Henny, *Die Orgel und die Mixtur ihres Klanges* (Klecken, 1922).

JAHN, Hans Henny, *Der Einflusz der Schleifenwindlade auf die Tonbildung der Orgel* (Hamburg, 1931).

KOTHE, B., *Kleine Orgelbaulehre* (Leobschütz, 1874).

KOTHE, B. and Th. FARCHHAMMER, *Führer durch die Orgel-Literatur* (Leipzig, 1890).

KRAUSS, Samuel, *Zur Orgelfrage* (Wien, 1919).

KREPS, Jozef, *De Belgische orgelmakers* ("*Musica Sacra*" 1932).

KWASNIK, Walter, *Die Orgel der Neuzeit* (Krefeld, 1948).

LABAT, J. B., *Histoire de l'orgue* (Montauban, 1864).

LAMAZOU, Abbé, *Etude sur l'orgue monumental de St. Sulpice et de la facture d'orgue moderne* (Paris, 1863).

LAMAZOU, Abbé, *Grand orgue de l'eglise metropolitaine Notre Dame de Paris, reconstruit par M. A. Cavaillé-Coll* (Paris, 1868).

LANGE, Martin, *Kleine Orgelkunde* (Kassel, 1954).

LEHMAN, J. T., *Anleitung die Orgel rein und richtig stimmen zu lernen und in guter Stimmung zu erhalten, nebst eine Beschreibung über den Bau der Orgel* (Leipzig, 1830).

LEWIS, Thomas C., *A Protest against the Modern Development of Unmusical Tone* (London, 1897).

LOTTERMOSER, Werner, *Klanganalytische Untersuchungen an Zungenpfeifen*, (*Diss. Berlin, 1936*) (Berlin, 1936).

LUNELLI, Renato, *L'organo di S. Maria Maggiore in Trento e l'arte organica italiana del secolo XVI* (Trento, 1925).

LUNELLI, Renato, *Der Orgelbau in Italien* (Mainz, 1956).

MATTHEWS, John, *A Handbook of the Organ* (London, 1897).

MATTHEWS, John, *The Restoration of Organs* (London, 1918).

MEHL, Joh. G., *Die Denkmalpflege auf dem Gebiete der Orgelbaukunst* (Kassel, 1939).

MEHRKENS, Karl, *Die Schnitger Orgel in der Hauptkirche St. Jakobi zu Hamburg* (Kassel, 1930).

MILNER, Herbert Frank, *How to Build a Small Two-manual Chamber Pipe-organ; A Practical Guide for Amateurs* (London, 1925).

MOSER, H. J., *Ueber deutsche Orgelkunst*, 1450 *bis* 1500 (Kassel).

MOSER, H. J., *Orgelromantik* (Ludwigsburg, 1961).

MUEREN, Floris v. d., *Het orgel in de Nederlanden* (Amsterdam-Brussel, 1931).

MULET, Henri, *Les Tendances néfastes et antireligieuses de l'orgue moderne, suivi d'une étude sur les mutations et les mécanismes rationnels de cet instrument* (Paris, 1922).

MUND, Hermann, *Joachim Wagner* (Kassel).

NAGY, Lajos, *Az aquincumi organo* (Budapest, 1934).

PERRIER DE LE BATHIE, Ernest, *Les insectes des orgues* (Ugine, 1922).

PERRIER DE LA BATHIE, Ernest, *La faune des orgues* (Anneçy, 1925).

PERRIER DE LA BATHIE, Ernest, *La flore des orgues* (Anneçy, 1927).

PESCHARD, Albert, *Perfectionnements au système électro-pneumatique* (Paris, 1896).

PESCHARD, Albert, *Etudes sur l'orgue électrique* (Paris, 1896).

PESCHARD, Albert, *Notice biographique sur A. Cavaillé-Coll et orgues électriques* (Paris, 1899).

PRICK VAN WELY, M., *Het orgel en zijn meesters* (Den Haag, 1931).

QUOIKA, Rudolf, *Die altösterreichische Orgel der späten Gotik, der Renaissance und des Barock* (Kassel, 1953).

QUOIKA, Rudolf, *Altösterreichische Hornwerke* (Berlin, 1959).

RAUGEL, Felix, *Deux chefs-d'oeuvre de la facture d'orgues française* (*Basilique de Saint-Denis et Notre Dame de Paris*) (Paris, 1914).

RAUGEL, Felix, *Les orgues et les organistes de la cathédrale de Strasbourg* (Strasbourg, 1948).

REGNIER, Joseph, *L'orgue, sa connaissance, son administration et son jeu* (Nancy, 1850).

REITER, Moritz, *Die Orgel unserer Zeit* (Berlin, 1880).

RIEMANN, Hugo, *Katechismus der Orgel* (Leipzig, 1888).

RIHSÉ, V. und S. and SEGGERMANN, G., *Klingendes Friesland* (Cuxhaven, 1959, G.D.O.16).

RIHSÉ, V. und S. and SEGGERMANN, G., *Klingende Schätze* (Cuxhaven, 1957, G.D.O.10).

RITTER, A. G., *Die Orgel und das Orgelspiel* (Leipzig).

RITTER, A. G., *Die Erhaltung und Stimmung der Orgel durch den Organisten* (Erfurt und Leipzig, 1861).

RÖSSLER, E. K., *Klangfunktion und Registrierung* (Kassel, 1952).

RUPP, Emile, *Die Entwicklungsgeschichte der Orgelbaukunst* (Einsiedeln, 1929).

RUPP, J. F. Emil, *Die Elässisch-neudeutsche Orgelreform* (Bremen, 1910).

SATTLER, Heinrich, *Die Orgel, nach den Grundsätzen der neuesten Orgelbaukunst dargestellt* (Langensalza, 1857).

SCHAIK, J. A. S. van, *Het Orgel* (Utrecht, 1915).

SCHMIDT, H., *Die Orgel unserer Zeit in Wort und Bild* (Munchen, 1904).

SCHNEIDER, Thekla, *Die Namen der Orgelregister* (Kassel, 1958).

SCHOLZE, Ant., *Orgellehre* (Wien, 1898).

SCHOUTEN, Hennie, *Nederlandse orgels en organisten* (Leiden, 1944).

SCHUBERT, F. L., *Die Orgel, ihr Bau, ihre Geschichte und Behandlung* (Leipzig, 1867).

SCHUBERT, F. L., *Het Orgel* (*Vert. Joh. Bastiaans*) (Haarlem, 1868).

SMETS, Paul, *Orgeldispositionen. Eine Handschrift aus dem XVII Jahrhundert, im Besitz der Sächsischen Landesbibliothek Dresden* (Kassel, 1931).

SPENGEL, P. R., *Handwerk und Kunst der Orgelbau* (Berlin, 1795).

SPIES, Hermann, *Abt Vogler und die von ihm* 1805 *simplificierte Orgel von St. Peter in Salzburg* (Mainz, 1932).

SUMNER, W. L., *The Parish Church Organ* (London, 1961).

SUPPER, Walter, *Architekt und Orgelbaumeister* (*Diss. Stuttgart*) (Würzburg, 1934).

SUPPER, Walter, *Wege zu neuem Orgelgestalten durch die Orgelbewegung* (Würzburg, 1934).

SUPPER, Walter, *Architekt und Orgelbau* (Kassel, 1940).

SUPPER, Walter, *Der Kleinorgelbrief an alle, die sich eine Hausorgel bauen* (Kassel, 1940).

SUPPER, Walter, *Die Orgeldisposition* (Kassel, 1950).

SUPPER, Walter, *Lesebuch für Orgelleute* (Kassel, 1951).

SUPPER, Walter, *Kleines orgelbrevier für Architekten* (München, 1959).

THORNSBY, Frederick W., *Dictionary of Organs and Organists* (contains a useful organ bibliography by J. H. Burn) (Bournemouth, 1912 and 1922).

UTZ, Kurt, *Die Orgel in unserer Zeit* (Marburg, 1950).

VENTE, M. A., *Nederlandse orgel in de 16e eeuw* (Amsterdam, 1942).

VENTE, M. A., *Proeve van een repertorium van de archivalia betrekking hebbende op het Nederlandse Orgel en zijn makers tot omstreeks 1630* (Brussels, 1956).

VENTE, M. A., *Die Brabanter Orgel* (Amsterdam, 1958).

VOGLER, Georg Joseph, *Vergleichungsplan der nach seinem Simplifikations-system umgeschaffenen Neu-Münster-Orgel* (Würzburg, 1812).

WALCKER, Oscar, *Erinnerungen eines Orgelbauers* (Kassel, 1948).

WEBER, Rob., *Die Orgeln von Joseph Gabler und Johannes Nepomuk Holzhay* (*Diss. Tübingen* 1931) (Weilheim-Teck, 1931; Mainz, 1936).

WEIPPERT, J., *Die Orgel* (Regensburg, 1834).

WIDOR, Charles Marie, *Die moderne Orgel und der Verfall im zeitgenössischen Orgelbau* (Göttingen, 1931).

WOERSCHING, Joseph, *Der Orgelbauer Karl Riepp* (Mainz, 1940).

WOERSCHING, Joseph, *Der Orgelbauer Joseph Gabler* (Mainz, 1959).

WOERSCHING, Joseph, *Die Orgelbauerfamilie Silbermann in Strassburg im E. Lieferung I und II* (Mainz).

ZANG, Joh. Heinrich, *Der volkommene Orgelmacher, oder Lehre von der Orgel und Windprobe, der Reparatur und Stimmung der Orgel und anderer Tasteninstrumente* (Nurnberg, 1804).

ZIMMER, Fr., *Die Orgel* (Quedlinburg, 1884).

ZSCHALER, G., *Gottfried Silbermann* (Dresden, 1858).

Since practically every organ of note in the world has been the subject of at least one book or booklet, it has not been possible to list all of them here. The reader is referred to the *Dictionary of Organs and Organists* (London, 1922), G. A. C. de Graaf, *Literatuur over the orgel* (Amsterdam, 1957) and the organ literature catalogue of Rheingold Verlag (Mainz).

There is also a considerable periodical literature of the organ. In Britain: *The Organ*, *The Organ Club Journal* and occasional handbooks, *Musical Opinion*, *Musical Times*, *The Choir*, *The Organists' Quarterly Journal*, *The Journal of the Incorporated Society of Organ-Builders*, and the magazines of the local organ societies. In America: *The Diapason*, *The American Organist*, *The Tracker*, *The Organ Institute Quarterly*. In France: *L'Orgue*. In Switzerland: *Le Tribune de l'Orgue* and *Musica* (*International*). The Netherlands: *Praestant*. Germany: *Musik und Kirche*, the publications of G.D.O., (*Gesellschaft der Orgelfreunde*), etc. In Italy: *L'Organo* (*International*).

INDEX

Generally, organ-stops have not been given because an alphabetical list commences on p. 297. The abbreviation o.b. means organ-builder or -builders.

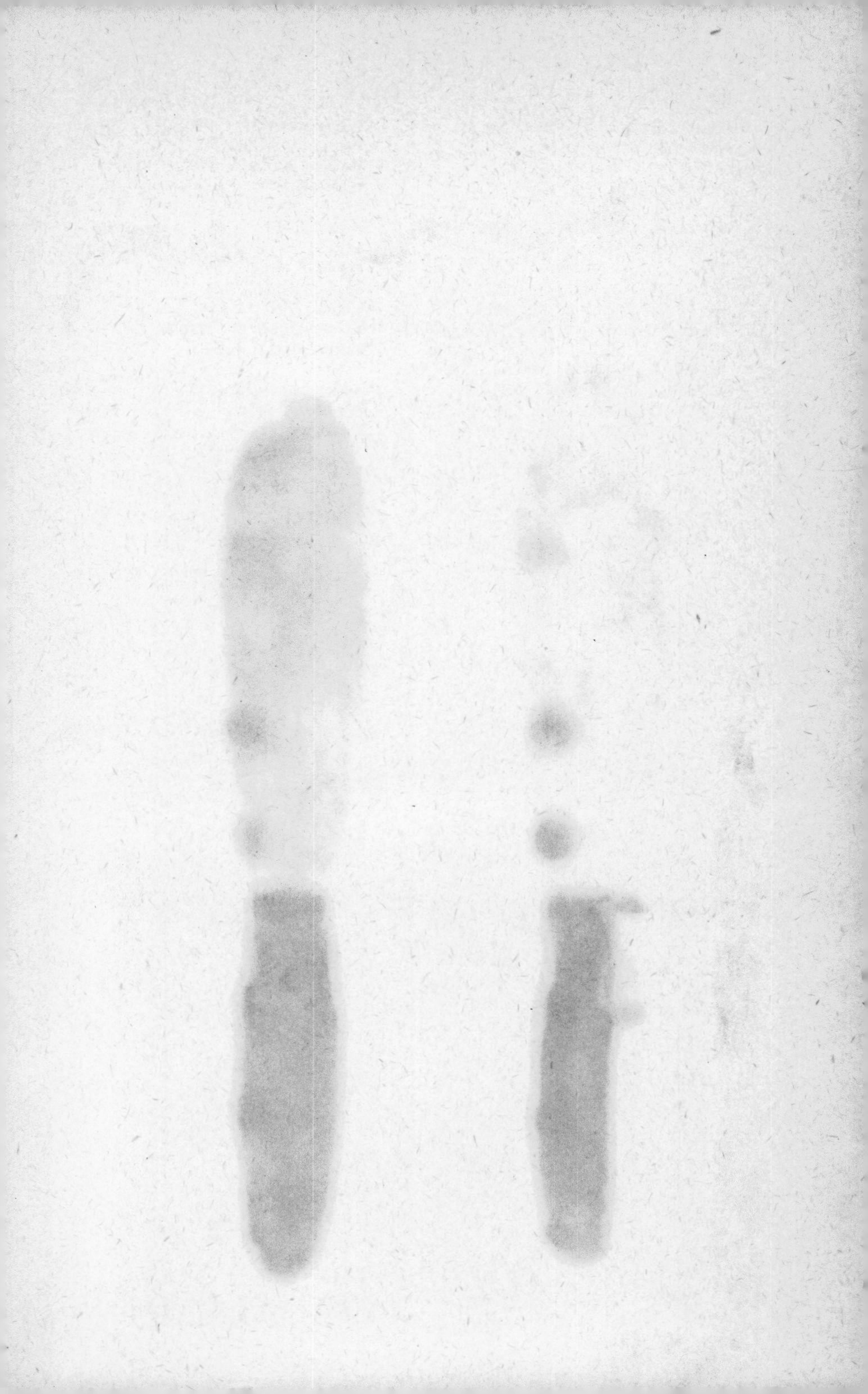